GOVERNORS STATE UNIVERSITY
MAT-CTR.LC1099.C84X1994   C001 V001

CULTURGRAMS GARRETT PARK MD   MAX

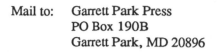
P9-BYH-278

3 1611 00004 9149

ORDER FORM

Mail to: Garrett Park Press
            PO Box 190B
            Garrett Park, MD 20896

Please send me _____ copies of *Culturgrams: The Nations Around Us, Volume I: The Americas and Europe.*

Please send me _____ copies of *Culturgrams: The Nations Around Us, Volume II: Africa, Asia, and Oceania*

➁ Check for $30.00 enclosed for each book ordered. ($45.00 retail for profit-making organizations).

➁ Please bill our organization at $_____ per copy.

Ship to: Bill to (if different):

_____   _____

_____   _____

_____   _____

_____   _____

- -

ORDER FORM

Mail to: Garrett Park Press
            PO Box 190B
            Garrett Park, MD 20896

Please send me _____ copies of *Culturgrams: The Nations Around Us, Volume I: The Americas and Europe.*

Please send me _____ copies of *Culturgrams: The Nations Around Us, Volume II: Africa, Asia, and Oceania*

➁ Check for $30.00 enclosed for each book ordered. ($45.00 retail for profit-making organizations).

➁ Please bill our organization at $_____ per copy.

Ship to: Bill to (if different):

_____   _____

_____   _____

_____   _____

_____   _____

WITHDRAWN

CULTURGRAMS:
The Nations Around Us

developed by the
David M. Kennedy Center
for International Studies

Brigham Young University

Volume I
The Americas and Europe

GOVERNORS STATE UNIVERSITY
UNIVERSITY
IL 60466

About the Culturgram Series...

This book (Volume I) includes *Culturgrams* for the Americas and Europe.

A related volume (Volume II) includes *Culturgrams* for Africa, Asia and Oceania.

These bound volumes of *Culturgrams* should be ordered from the Garrett Park Press, PO Box 190B, Garrett Park, MD 20896; phone (301) 946-2553 at $30.00 per volume for nonprofit groups and $45.00 retail per volume for profit-making organizations.

Because the reproduction of the *Culturgrams* in this volume is strictly prohibited, copies should be ordered from the David M. Kennedy Center for International Studies. All *Culturgrams* currently available are sold individually or in batches. To order individual or multiple copies of *Culturgrams*, contact Brigham Young University, Kennedy Center Publications, P.O. Box 24538, Provo, UT 84602; phone (800) 528-6279 or (801) 378-6528.

Library of Congress Cataloging-in-Publication Data

Culturgrams : the nations around us / developed by the David M.
   Kennedy Center for International Studies, Brigham Young University.
      2 v. : maps ; 28 cm.
      Contents: v. 1. The Americas and Europe -- v. 2. Africa, Asia, and
Oceania.
      ISBN 0-912048-86-7 (set)

      1. Manners and customs.   2. Intercultural communication.
I. David M. Kennedy Center for International Studies.
   GT150.C85   1993
   390--dc20   93-29643

MAT-CTR. LC 1099 .C84x 1994
v. 1

Culturgrams
     316981   v.1

Copyright © 1994 Brigham Young University, David M. Kennedy Center for International Studies.
Grant P. Skabelund, Managing Editor; Susan M. Sims, Associate Editor; Lisa Ralph, Assistant Editor

ISBN 0-912048-86-7

Library of Congress Card 94-29643 (for set)

Contents

Foreword

Introduction

Glossary

Countries in order of their appearance

Foreword

As one who has continually tried to search out useful materials in the relatively new field of intercultural and cross-cultural affairs, I have long been impressed by the Brigham Young University *Culturgram* series. When they were first produced little else was available. Now with more resources on the market, I still find that when I try to answer a wide range of questions about what to study and what to read about a particular country, *Culturgrams* are still among the first good resources to be mentioned. And I am constantly amazed to learn that more people already know of *Culturgrams* than of any other single country-specific material on the market.

I like Lynn Tyler's term "people maps" to describe *Culturgrams*. Few other materials present a country's people — with their unique values, customs, and cultural assumptions — as well as *Culturgrams* do. Simple, direct, and brief, they pack a lot of valuable information into an amazingly small package.

The thing that first attracted me to *Culturgrams* was their obvious and unabashed modesty. They clearly had a very specific goal. They do not claim to present the definitive or final work on any culture. Yet, in a brief reading, they can increase almost anyone's knowledge of a country and its people many-fold.

The care with which *Culturgrams* are developed and field tested before they are released to the general public is unique. Dozens of country experts have checked them for accuracy and suggested changes, and they have gone through countless editings for precision in language and sensitivity to total impact. Such thoroughness should be the standard for all publications.

The people behind the conceptualization and creation of *Culturgrams* have always made it very clear that they consider their work to represent only a minor contribution to the most basic and initial stage of the ever-changing intercultural field. The field itself is still in its initial stage — measured by their standards and mine. The *Culturgram* series has played and will continue to play a major part in its development.

L. Robert Kohls
Institute for Intercultural Leadership
San Francisco

Introduction

In 1974, President Spencer W. Kimball of the Church of Jesus Christ of Latter-day Saints issued a challenge to Mormons to build more effective bridges of understanding and friendship with people all over the world. Brigham Young University contributed to the effort by inviting people from about 50 countries to share what they thought was the essential information about their country and its people. These interviews laid the foundation for the *Culturgrams*, which were first published by BYU's Language and Intercultural Research Center and were transferred in 1981 to the David M. Kennedy Center for International Studies.

There are 128 *Culturgrams* in the 1994-95 edition. Included for the first time in this edition is a glossary for some of the concepts used throughout the *Culturgrams*. Each four-page *Culturgram* introduces the reader to the daily customs and lifestyle of a society, as well as to its political and economic structure. Each text represents the efforts of individuals from all over the world who have had experience living and working in each particular country. Kennedy Center Publications requests and receives input from scholars within each target culture, academics in the United States and Europe, volunteers from such organizations as the Peace Corps and the International Red Cross, expatriate diplomats and business people, educators, and many others.

This approach allows the Center to take advantage of a wide variety of perspectives and professional backgrounds to bring our readers a unique look at daily culture around the globe. It also means that *Culturgrams* contain information that is based as much on opinion as on fact, although a wide variety of perspectives are consulted. *Culturgrams* do not focus on statistical data. Other resources present statistics for each country, but none tell a reader about people on a personal level. Our goal is to bring the people of a culture into the reader's view, thus encouraging understanding and appreciation between people of different nationalities.

Each new *Culturgram* is written by someone who meets certain residence, educational, and professional criteria. Each draft is reviewed by a panel of individuals with similar qualifications, but usually different backgrounds. This panel is asked to correct errors, comment on accuracy, and generally help us know whether the expressed opinions and facts form a fair and broad description of the culture. A *Culturgram* cannot contain everything about a culture or about each ethnic group in a particular country, but it does endeavor to paint a broad picture about life for the majority of people in a country. All project participants are asked to be as fair and current as possible. Once a new *Culturgram* has been published (after six to twelve months of work), it is reviewed annually by our professional staff of editors trained in international studies. When necessary, information is updated and the text revised to keep abreast of current events. This helps ensure that each *Culturgram* text is an up-to-date source of information about people's lives, their society, and their culture.

The list of contributors to and supporters of *Culturgrams* is long and irretrievable. We thank the hundreds of individuals who have contributed their valuable expertise to make the *Culturgrams* a beneficial intercultural learning tool. We also acknowledge the support of the current university leadership.

Culturgrams meet the needs of a wide variety of individuals. Students, teachers, resource librarians, international student advisors, business travelers, health care workers, government and military personnel, tourists, missionaries, international development workers, and many others benefit from *Culturgrams*. With your purchase of *Culturgrams*, you join the millions who have come to count on the accurate, up-to-date information that continues to build bridges of understanding between Earth's peoples. Enjoy.

Grant P. Skabelund
Managing Editor

CULTURGRAM ™ '95

Aa Glossary Zz

The following is a list of some common concepts found in the Culturgrams. *These are not definitions; they are explanations of how the terms are used in the series, of what significance they hold in regard to understanding the culture, and often of how they are calculated. For explanations of international organizations (United Nations, European Union, and so forth), please refer to reference sources in a library.*

Cash Crops

A cash crop is an agricultural product that is grown not for the farmer's consumption but for sale. It is often a crop (coffee, cotton, sugar cane, rice and other grains) that cannot be or is not usually consumed upon harvesting; it generally requires manufacturing or processing. It may also be a crop (oranges, potatoes, bananas) that can be consumed upon harvest, but is cultivated for the primary purpose of being sold. Cash crops are most effectively produced on a large scale, but they can also be grown on small plots of land. When grown on a large scale, the crops are more likely to be exported than consumed locally, but small growers in developing countries often sell to a local buyer who then sells larger quantities domestically and abroad. The economics of many countries are heavily dependent on the sale of cash crops.

Diversified Economy

An economy is considered diversified if its stability relies on a broad base of different kinds of industries rather than on one or two commodities. For example, oil-rich countries that rely almost solely on the petroleum industry for their income are vulnerable to changes in the price of oil on the world market. When the price drops significantly, the countries are suddenly unable to pay debts or finance social development projects. The same is true for countries that rely on agricultural products such as coffee or on minerals such as copper for their income. Countries in which the economy is based not only on agricultural products, but also on manufacturing, services, technology, and so forth, are better able to withstand global price changes. Thus, the more diversified a country's economic base, the better.

Extended Family

As used in the *Culturgram*, this term refers to a family unit that includes parents, their children, and one or more relatives. The relatives most often include grandparents, and sometimes cousins, aunts, and uncles. Some extended family units are organized with older parents, their married sons

What is a *Culturgram*?

Each four-page *Culturgram* is designed to introduce the reader to the daily customs and lifestyle of a society, as well as to its political and economic structure. Each text represents the efforts of individuals from all over the world who have had experience living and working in each particular country. Brigham Young University's David M. Kennedy Center for International Studies requests and receives input from scholars within each target culture, academics in the United States and Europe, volunteers from such organizations as the Peace Corps and the International Red Cross, expatriate diplomats or business people, educators, and many others.

This approach allows us to take advantage of a wide variety of perspectives and professional backgrounds to bring our readers a unique look at daily culture around the globe. It also means that *Culturgrams* contain information that is based as much on opinion as on fact, although a wide variety of perspectives are consulted. *Culturgrams* do not focus on statistical data. Other resources present statistics for each country, but none really tell a reader about people on a personal level. Our goal is to bring the people of a culture into the reader's view, thus encouraging understanding and appreciation between people of different nationalities.

Each new *Culturgram* is written by someone who meets certain residency, educational, and professional criteria. Each draft is reviewed by a panel of individuals with similar qualifications, but usually different backgrounds. This panel is asked to correct errors, comment on accuracy, and generally help us know whether the expressed opinions and facts form a fair and broad description of the culture. A *Culturgram* cannot contain everything about a culture or about each ethnic group in a particular country, but it does endeavor to paint a broad picture about life for the majority of people in a country. All project participants are asked to be as fair and current as possible. Once a new *Culturgram* has been published (after six to twelve months of work), it is reviewed annually by our professional staff of editors trained in international studies. When necessary, information is updated and the text is revised to keep abreast of current events. This helps ensure that each *Culturgram* text is an up-to-date source of information about people's lives, their society, and their culture.

Copyright © 1994. Brigham Young University. Printed in the USA. All rights reserved. It is against the law to copy, reprint, store in a retrieval system, or transmit any part of this publication in any form by any means for any purpose without written permission from the Publications Division of the David M. Kennedy Center for International Studies, Brigham Young University, PO Box 24538, Provo, UT 84602–4538. *Culturgrams* are available for more than 125 areas of the world. To place an order, to receive a free catalog, or to obtain information on traveling abroad, call toll free (800) 528–6279.

(occasionally daughters) and their families, and all unmarried sons and daughters. Extended families may share a single household or may live in a compound that includes living structures for each nuclear unit, in which case families share work and other responsibilities. When a *Culturgram* states the extended family is the basic unit of society, it means the average household is comprised of the extended family.

Foreign Language Phrases

Most *Culturgrams* contain phrases and words in the target culture's official or common language. In general, the *Culturgram* does not provide a pronunciation guide for these phrases due to the limited amount of space. Also, including pronunciation and a translation tends to interrupt the flow of the text rather than contribute to it. A *Culturgram* is not designed to teach foreign languages. Rather, the phrases contained in a *Culturgram* are there to facilitate the description of how people interact with one another. Their translation often provides insights about the culture, but pronunciation is not necessary to gain that insight. In the few cases where pronunciation hints are provided, they are necessary for English-speakers to properly pronounce a word not otherwise expressed in English. For instance, the country Lesotho is not pronounced as it would seem. Instead of saying "le-SEW-tho," one should say "le-SUE-too." It is important to make the proper pronunciation to be correct in English.

Free and Compulsory Education

Most countries provide free education to their citizens, meaning there is a public school system operated by the government that is open to all children who fall into certain age groups. It does not necessarily mean there are no costs involved in attending school. Students may be required to wear uniforms (which must be purchased), they might live far away from the nearest school (and parents must pay for transportation), or they may need to supply their own paper and pencils and other basic items. In addition, having a child in school can cost a rural family one laborer on the family farm. This can become such a burden to poorer families that free education is still not accessible to them.

Compulsory education refers to the fact that the law requires children to attend school for a certain number of years. In many countries this rule is seldom enforced. It may therefore reflect the government's target for how long a child should remain in school to obtain a basic education, rather than how long children are actually required to attend. Compulsory education usually encompasses six to nine years, and optional schooling usually continues for three or more years.

Gross Domestic Product (GDP) Per Capita

This economic statistic refers to the value of all goods and services produced in an economy in a year per person. Naturally, not every person produces goods and services, but the total is averaged for the entire population. If the term is expressed as "gross national product," it is essentially the same statistic except for the addition of income earned abroad, minus the income earned in the country by non-citizens. This is significant when part of the population works in other countries and sends back money to their families. It is also significant for countries that have substantial investments abroad. But for most countries, the statistic is almost interchangeable. The "value" of goods as averaged for the entire population can be taken almost as the "average income" for each person, since the gross value of the economy can be assumed to consist of the gross income of the economy. While this is not entirely true (some money goes abroad, and some "values" do not translate into actual income), it is still a standard measurement for how much money a person has for meeting his or her needs.

In the past, gross domestic product was calculated in terms of the U.S. dollar after conversion from the local currency at official exchange rates. This caused accuracy problems because of artificially set exchange rates and by the fact that what a dollar buys in the United States may not be what it will buy in another country. Researchers have more recently developed the concept of Purchasing Power Parity (PPP), a measurement that tries to account for the inconsistencies of the past. When gross domestic product is figured in terms of PPP, an international dollar that is not affected by exchange rates is used. Likewise, PPP attempts to express the relative ability of a person to purchase goods with the local currency. Therefore, $500 will buy essentially the same things in the United States as it will in Brazil or Japan. For many countries, PPP data does not yet exist and only estimates are available for others. Most *Culturgrams* use the PPP with GDP, as expressed with the phrase "real gross domestic product." When the word "real" is absent, only the GDP has been calculated. The real GDPs in the *Culturgrams* are usually taken from the *Human Development Report 1993* (New York: Oxford University Press for the United Nations Development Program, 1993). In cases when the real GDP is low (below $1,000, for example), one can assume that people have very little disposable income. But one should also remember that rural families may grow their own food and therefore need less disposable income to meet basic needs. In other cases, such a low figure indicates people may indeed be without food, shelter, clothing, or other necessities.

Human Development Index

Originating with the United Nations Development Program, the Human Development Index (HDI) attempts to address the inability of income or GDP indicators to accurately describe living conditions for the average person. For example, if a country has a gross domestic product of US$10,000, it may really mean that a few wealthy individuals earn far more than that and most other people earn far less. Also, the statistic does not reflect the value of those dollars in the local economy. In addition, a low income might not necessarily mean a socially poor existence, since governments can often initially provide a better or more promising life through social programs. HDI combines a number of different data that, together, more accurately reflect whether the average person enjoys access to the basic elements of life that can allow one to enjoy it. For example, one's access to schooling, health care, and purchasing power (income) are all considered for this index, since such access has proven vital to a person's ability to participate fully in the community and take advantage of economic opportunities. People who are sick (and cannot get well), illiterate, or living on limited funds are often locked into an existence that provides little hope for the future. But in countries where health and education are adequately available, people have a greater chance of improving their purchasing power and ultimately their lives. The *Culturgrams* have adopted the Human Development Index as a way to gauge whether the average person has access to the many benefits of a modern, prosperous global community.

Income Distribution

This phrase is generally used in connection with the gap between what the poorest people in a country earn and what the richest earn. If income distribution is highly unequal, a small wealthy class generally controls the economy (and often the government) and owns most property. The much larger poor class is often landless, which is significant since the people are probably farmers who must then rent property and receive only a small share of the benefits from their own labor. When income distribution is unequal, but not highly so, then it is often because a middle class is beginning to grow. When the distribution is fairly equal (in a minority of countries), it is due mostly to a large and prosperous middle class. However, it can also be due to a broad poor class and the absence of a wealthy elite. Generally, having a highly unequal income distribution means the economy is unhealthy, whereas the existence of a strong middle (consumer) class is good for an economy.

Infant Mortality Rate

This statistic is expressed as the number of children per 1,000 live births who die before their first birthday. It is an important indicator for the overall health of a population, since infants who die at this age are usually subject to preventable diseases or birth defects related to the mother's health. Those who die at birth often do so because of a lack of prenatal care and medical attention at birth. When the people of a country have access to health care, clean water, nutritious food, and education, they are more likely to have a low infant mortality rate than in countries where people lack such access. Industrialized countries generally have a low rate (below 10 per 1,000), while developing countries usually have a higher rate (averaging more than 30). The poorest countries may have rates higher than 100.

Life Expectancy

This measurement refers to how long a person can expect to live from birth if mortality patterns remain unchanged. Someone born today may be expected to live 80 years if living in some European countries, but only 58 years if living in parts of Africa. However, since mortality patterns do change throughout a person's lifetime, the statistic is really a better reflection of how long an adult who is currently living can

expect to live. So, a person who is 50 today can expect to live until 80 in some countries, or only a few more years in other countries. Women live longer than men in most countries, and people in industrialized countries live longer than those in developing countries. People in countries with high pollution have lower rates of life expectancy. The *Culturgram* usually expresses this statistic as a range between the low and the high, which most often corresponds to an average for women at the high end and men at the low end. This statistic, like infant mortality, helps the reader understand the overall healthiness of a population and whether the people have access to nutritious food, clean water, health care, and proper sanitation.

Literacy Rate

Most countries and international organizations define literacy in terms of those who are older than 15 years of age who can read and write. Sometimes that only means they can read and write their names or perform other basic tasks. In a few cases, literacy is defined as having attended school, even if it was only for a short time. Most educational experts agree that current definitions fall short of actually measuring whether the population is literate, since being able to write one's name does not mean the person can read a newspaper or understand such things as a bus schedule or work instructions. Literacy may also be defined in terms of an official language not spoken on a daily basis by a majority of the population, which can make the definition even more irrelevant. However, since world organizations cannot agree on exactly how to measure functional (or actual) literacy, and since collecting such data is very difficult, the current definitions remain in force. Researchers try to add to the statistic by also looking at such things as how many years of schooling the average person completes, whether the labor force is skilled or unskilled, and so forth. In the *Culturgrams*, we usually list the official literacy rate or an expert estimate, and we often add other information as appropriate.

Nuclear Family

As used in the *Culturgrams*, this term refers to a family unit that includes one or two parents and their children. The nuclear family usually lives in a single-family dwelling. When a *Culturgram* states the nuclear family is the basic social unit, it means the average household is composed of the nuclear family.

Population and Population Growth Rate

The population listed for each country in the *Culturgram* series is an estimate for the year previous to publication (i.e., 1993 population for text published in 1994). The estimate is based on the actual population at the last census multiplied by an annual growth rate. The estimate may seem to conflict with other sources, since other sources often only print the population as of the latest census (whenever it may have been taken) or an estimate made in a base year (i.e., 1990).

Culturgram estimates are in keeping with figures in U.S. government publications, but they are sometimes modified by information from the government of the target culture. Each population estimate is revised on an annual basis; it is rounded to the nearest 100,000 or 10,000 depending on the size of the population.

The population growth rate is an estimate, rounded to the nearest 10th of a percent, based on the previous year's difference between births and deaths and the net number of migrants leaving or entering the country. The growth rate may change substantially in a single year if there is a large influx of immigrants, a massive emigration, a natural disaster, or an epidemic. Growth rates tend to be low in industrialized countries because people live long and families are small (averaging one or two children). Growth rates tend to be high in developing countries, especially in areas where subsistence farming is the primary economic activity. These cultures require large families to help farm the land, and they are often cultures in which the infant mortality rate is high; many children are born to ensure that enough will survive into adulthood. In small nations, the growth rate may be low due to emigration, as people must go elsewhere to find work.

Staple Food

Staple foods are those foods that supply the majority of the average person's calories and nutrition. A culture's primary staple food is usually a starchy food, such as rice, wheat, millet, cassava (manioc), or corn. In addition, staple foods include the meats, fruits, and vegetables eaten in the largest quantities or on a frequent basis.

Subsistence Farming

Subsistence farming refers to farming as the main source of a family's livelihood. That is, a family will grow its own food, raise its own livestock, build its own home, and often make its own clothing. Members of such a family usually do not earn a wage by working at a job, but they are not usually entirely without a cash income. Family members might sell surplus produce or livestock, or make crafts or other items (blankets, baskets, etc.), in order to buy items they cannot provide for themselves. These usually include such things as sugar, cooking oil, clothing, rice or another staple food, and so forth. Subsistence farmers may also set aside part of their land to grow cash crops in order to earn money. Subsistence farmers usually do not grow an abundance of anything. They often live on small, owned or rented plots of land, and they seldom enjoy the luxuries of running water or electricity.

Underemployment

Underemployment refers to the case when workers are not officially unemployed but are not able to either find enough work in their profession or are working in jobs below their skill level. For example, if a country's universities graduate many people in engineering or other professional fields, but the economy is not diversified or well developed, those professionals may find themselves unemployed, working in jobs that do not take advantage of their skills, or only working part-time as engineers. In the latter case, they may return to farming or local retailing. In too many cases, the most educated people simply emigrate to another country to find work. Government unemployment figures do not usually include underemployment, which must be estimated. However, when unemployment is high (more than 10 percent), one can usually assume that underemployment affects at least as many or more workers. This condition reflects an economy that is not dynamic or growing, and it can lead to social unrest. High underemployment (more than 40 percent) often leads to political turmoil and violence. Employing and paying people according to their skill level is an important way to secure social stability and encourage economic growth.

Western/Western-style

This term usually refers to dress habits, culture, eating customs, and other traditions as found in Western Europe, the United States, and Canada. Their culture is often referred to as Western culture because of their common ancient (primarily Greek and Roman) philosophical, legal, political, and social heritage. It also usually refers to cultures that have a Judeo-Christian value system and are primarily Christian in religious orientation.

Metric Conversions

Celsius	Fahrenheit	Kilometers	Miles	Meters	Inches/Feet
0°	32°	1	.62	1mm	.039"
4°	39°	10	6.2	50mm	1.95"
8°	46°	50	31	100mm	3.9"
12°	54°	100	62	1m	39.37"
16°	61°	250	155	50m	164'
20°	68°	500	311	100m	328'
24°	75°	750	465	500m	1,640'
28°	82°	1,000	621	1,000m	3,280'
32°	90°	2,000	1,242	1,609m	5,280'
36°	97°	3,000	1,860	5,000m	16,400'
40°	104°	5,000	3,100	10,000m	22,960'

A *Culturgram* is a product of native commentary and original, expert analysis. Statistics are estimates and information is presented as a matter of opinion. While the editors strive for accuracy and detail, this document should not be considered strictly factual. It is a general introduction to culture, an initial step in building bridges of understanding between peoples. It may not apply to all peoples of the nation. You should therefore consult other sources for more information.

CULTURGRAM™ '95

Antigua and Barbuda

BARBUDA

Codrington

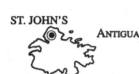

ST. JOHN'S

ANTIGUA

USA

Atlantic
Ocean

Bahamas

Dominican
Republic

Cuba

Puerto   St. Kitts
Rico

Haiti   Guadeloupe

Jamaica   **Antigua and**   Dominica
                               Barbuda   St. Lucia

Nicaragua   Caribbean   Barbados
             Sea   Grenada
Costa Rica   Tobago
          Panama   Trinidad

                              Venezuela

Pacific   Guyana
Ocean   Suri-
             Colombia   name

Boundary representations not necessarily authoritative.

THE AMERICAS

BACKGROUND

Land and Climate

Located 250 miles (400 kilometers) southeast of Puerto Rico, Antigua is relatively low and flat, and has a dry, sunny, desert-like climate most months of the year. Boggy Peak (1,319 feet—402 meters), the island's highest elevation, is located near a small tropical rain forest.

Barbuda, located across shallow water 30 miles north of Antigua, is even flatter, with its highest elevation being only 207 feet (63 meters). Sparsely populated, with most people living in Codrington, it is covered by shrubs and brush. It features soft pink sand beaches, a frigate bird sanctuary, abundant wild deer, and lobster. Including small uninhabited islands, the country covers 170 square miles (440 square kilometers).

History

Called *Wadadli* by the Amerindians who maintained a lively culture through the 17th century, the island was renamed by Christopher Columbus in 1493 for the Santa Maria de la Antigua cathedral in Spain. Antigua is pronounced without the "u." A lack of water and a thriving indigenous population discouraged European settlement for many years, but English settlers crossed over from St. Kitts in 1632. Despite attempts to dislodge them, the settlers persisted, cultivating tobacco, indigo and ginger. The two islands eventually became part of the British Leeward Islands colony in 1666.

In 1674, Christopher Codrington came from Barbados and established the first large sugar plantation, called "Betty's Hope." His success prompted other settlers to turn to sugar, and during the next 100 years the landscape was cleared of all vegetation to grow this high-demand cash crop. More than 150 wind-powered sugar mills (the ruins of many are still standing) soon dotted the island. Antigua was divided into parishes, the boundaries of which remain.

The plantation economy thrived on slave labor, the British having imported thousands of Africans to Antigua. Colonists even used Barbuda as a slave-breeding center. When emancipation finally came in 1834, many of the newly-freed African people began new lives in villages that bear such names as Freetown, Liberta, and Freeman's Village. But land owners continued exploitation by charging former slaves for hoe rentals and other services; this kept them working for minimal compensation into the 1930s. Reduced profitability of sugar and growing labor unrest led to the demise in the 1940s of the island's sugar industry, and by 1970 the last sugar refinery on the island had closed. Most light industries were replaced by the steadily growing tourism industry.

When Britain began granting greater autonomy to its colonies following World War II, Antigua's Vere Cornwall Bird was named chief minister. Antigua joined the West Indies Federation in 1958, but that body dissolved in 1962. In 1967 Antigua and Barbuda became a West Indies Associated State. This status granted internal autonomy, with V. C. Bird as premier. In 1981, Antigua, with Barbuda as a dependency, achieved full independence under the leadership of Bird's Antigua Labour Party (ALP). Barbuda attempted to remain a British colony, but the request was denied. The ALP consistently won elections, and Bird remained prime minister

Copyright © 1994. Brigham Young University. Printed in the USA. All rights reserved. It is against the law to copy, reprint, store in a retrieval system, or transmit any part of this publication in any form by any means for any purpose without written permission from the Publications Division of the David M. Kennedy Center for International Studies, Brigham Young University, PO Box 24538, Provo, UT 84602–4538. *Culturgrams* are available for more than 125 areas of the world. To place an order, to receive a free catalog, or to obtain information on traveling abroad, call toll free (800) 528–6279.

until he retired in 1994. His son, Lester Bird, became prime minister when the ALP won elections in March 1994.

THE PEOPLE
Population
The country's population is about 65,700 (1,600 living on Barbuda). Nearly half of all Antiguans live in the area surrounding the capital, St. John's. Despite its size, Antigua's various regions are identified with distinct population groups. For example, Old Road prides itself on connections to certain family and West African lines that Freetown may not share.

Barbuda's population consists almost entirely of African descendants. Most Barbudans go to Antigua to shop, work, or live, but many Antiguans have never been to Barbuda. Antigua's population is 96 percent Black African and 3 percent white. One percent is a mixture of Syrian, Lebanese, Asians, and other immigrants. Most whites are foreigners engaged in business and tourism.

A crossroads in the Caribbean, Antigua has historically attracted seafaring peoples, so there are both Spanish and French elements mixed with the African people. The island is also home to more recent immigrants from countries in the region. Although racial disputes are virtually unheard of, the different racial groups do not mix socially. Likewise, while tourism brings thousands of people to the island (especially in winter), contact between tourists and locals is mostly limited to professional services.

Language
Most Antiguans speak English. But they also speak a dialect similar to others in the region; it is a mixture of English, various African tongues, and some European languages. Commonly used words such as *nyam* (to eat) have African origins. Forms of speech vary between areas and classes. Barbudans have their own accent. Many upper class Antiguans look down on those who speak the dialect, but most people appreciate it for its color and expressiveness. Traditional sayings are still popular, such as *No tro way you belly and tek trash tuff um* (Don't lose the substance for the shadow) and *Wah eye no see heart no grieve* (What you don't know won't hurt you). The dialect is used in casual, friendly situations. *T'all* means "not at all," and *How!* means "But of course!" *You lie* can mean "you're kidding."

Religion
Antiguans are religious people. Women and children attend church regularly, with men going less frequently. Most people belong to various Protestant groups. The Anglican church, with the island's largest cathedral (St. John's), is the nation's state religion. The Methodist church also has a long tradition in the country. A significant Catholic population (mostly non-Africans) also exists. Various other Christian groups also have facilities and churches on the island, and there are some followers of Islam, Bahai, and Rastafarianism.

General Attitudes
The people of Antigua and Barbuda are relaxed, friendly, and warm. They take a casual approach to life, sometimes expressed in the phrase *Soon come*. This is related to the general feeling that life presents or takes care of itself, that it is in God's hands and not necessarily in mankind's. Time is also viewed on a more casual basis. People are more important than schedules. They may have things to do along the way to an event or appointment, so it is rarely a problem for them to be late.

Antiguans have a great deal of pride in their families, their homes, and their nation. This is manifest by the community spirit that surrounds school and church events and displays of local talent. People are especially proud of their international cricket reputation. A number of star players for championship West Indies teams are from Antigua. National pride also emerges during the annual Carnival arts festival, when performers compete in various events.

Personal Appearance
Public dress is neat, sharply-pressed, and stylish. Funerals, weddings, and other special events bring out the most elegant and formal clothes in one's wardrobe. Sunday is particularly a day for dressing up. At parties or recreational events, Antiguans combine vivid Caribbean colors with international fashions.

On a daily basis, men do not wear shorts. Lightweight trousers and pressed shirts with colorful designs are popular. Some men wear ties and a few wear suits. The combination *shirt-jacket* (formal embroidered, cotton shirt cut square and worn like a jacket) is common in offices. Laborers wear work pants or uniforms.

Women wear stylish dresses, high-heeled shoes, and jewelry in offices; for some occupations, they wear dress uniforms. Around the home, men and women dress in shorts, T-shirts, and athletic shoes or sandals. Women also wear comfortable dresses. In this modest society, bathing suits are worn at the beach, not in town.

CUSTOMS AND COURTESIES
Greetings
Antiguans and Barbudans are generally informal in greeting one another. "How are you?" or "Hi" is common, but friends also use variations like "What's up?" or "How you do?" or "Alright?" The response to "Alright?" is "Okay, Okay." The general "Good morning," "Good day," "Good evening," and "Good night" are spoken at specific times of the day, with "Good evening" being inappropriate, for example, after dark.

Most Antiguans address friends by first names, but a boss is addressed by a title (Mr., Mrs., Miss), and professional exchanges between people (such as between a customer and a shop-keeper) are kept on this level. Children and young people address their elders and relatives with "aunt," "uncle" or an appropriate familial title.

Male friends use various hand-slapping, fist-touching, and thumb-locking handshakes as well as long handshakes. An entire brief conversation might be conducted with hands together. A man waits for a woman to extend her hand before shaking it.

Gestures
Although modest and reserved in appropriate circumstances, Antiguans are generally lively and expressive among friends. A conversation can include a person "acting out" or "demonstrating" something with body gestures. Pointing is usually done with the index finger, but some situations call for the use of hands, arms, even the head, eyes, or shoulders.

Hand and facial gestures punctuate conversation and often express something better than words. Raising the hand, palm out, and wagging an extended index finger from side to side indicates disagreement. It is usually accompanied with "no, no, no." A hearty "thumb's up" means things are going well. Sucking teeth (called *chups* or *choops*), expresses exasperation or annoyance (such as at a flat tire or the store being out of bread). Often, a mild "chups" provokes laughter and is a good release of tension. However, when directed at an individual, the noise is very rude.

People do not like to hear their names called out in public, so a discreet "psssst" is often used to get someone's attention. A quick "hey" or "yo" is also common between friends.

Visiting

Antiguans enjoy socializing with relatives, neighbors, and friends. They use the term *lime* or *liming* for the time spent relaxing and chatting with each other. Most visits occur on weekends or after work. Appointments or plans are rarely made; people sitting in the yard or on the porch are usually willing to chat. Friendly encounters elsewhere can turn into a social visit. For example, much socializing occurs in public, whether among men meeting to repair a fishing net or among women who are washing or shopping in public areas. Neighbors socialize while preparing meals.

When visiting someone who is inside a home, a person often approaches the gate and shouts *Inside*. The occupant then comes out to greet the person and the two may spend the entire visit on the porch. Friends or relatives will often be invited inside. It is polite to offer light refreshments, such as fruit juice or herbal tea. Visitors often *walk with* (carry) fresh fruit from trees in their yards to share with hosts. Visits can be of any length, and hosts rarely ask guests to leave. Whole families may visit, especially among relatives. Conversation is seasonal, with cricket or calypso dominating, but people might also sit for extended periods without talking. At more formal, invitation events (birthdays, graduations, holidays), hosts provide food and drink, while guests bring appropriate gifts.

Eating

During the work week people start the day with a simple breakfast of fruit, porridge or eggs. Most workers stop for a full meal at midday, either in the workplace, at restaurants, or at home. Boys and girls usually help with cooking at home. Clay ovens (*coal pots*) are often used to cook food; they are placed outside the kitchen. Saturday is a busy day for chores and errands, so people might buy barbecued chicken or fried fish at the market for the main meal. Evening meals are light if the main meal is eaten at midday.

On Sundays the family has a large breakfast. Later, grand preparations precede an extended family evening meal featuring roast pork, leg of lamb, or beef. So much food is usually served that plates are sent home with relatives for those who could not come. When fishermen bring in a good catch, there is usually a pot of *fish water* (fish stew) cooked up and shared. Church picnics or celebrations bring many cooks out cooperating on a large scale, serving such dishes as *goat water*, a spicy stew made with goat meat.

LIFESTYLE
Family

The extended family forms the heart of Antiguan society. Grandparents, aunts and uncles often raise children for parents who live out of the country for economic reasons. Families are large and living space is often shared between nuclear units. No matter what the living arrangements, family ties are strong and there are frequent gatherings. In Antigua, people like to joke that everybody is really related to each other if one traces the line back far enough.

Children are highly prized and bearing or fathering them is valued by all. The traditional two-parent family is the norm, but it is not uncommon for young unmarried women to have children and live with her parents. In such cases the baby's father provides financial support and is encouraged by both families to be involved in the child's life. Half-siblings live with their mother and women are not uncommon as heads of households. Men may have children with different women and never marry, and some women choose to remain single parents.

Dating and Marriage

There are many opportunities for girls and boys to socialize and interact, including school parties and dances, church functions, and holiday events. Couples are affectionate, but not in public. At some point in a courtship the young man is brought home for the approval of the young woman's family. Parents and churches encourage marriage over other types of relationships. Weddings are lavish, with a decorated church service, formal attire, and plenty of food and dance music.

Diet

Small gardens are kept in people's yards, but most food is imported. Antigua is subject to drought and supports very little agriculture or livestock raising. Tropical fruits (coconuts, mangoes) and vegetables (pumpkins, yams, potatoes) grow well. There is some fishing, but hotels are increasingly expanding into spawning areas of the mangrove wetlands, threatening future catches.

The basic diet revolves around rice, beans (*peas*, usually red beans or white pigeon peas) and meat (chicken, pork, beef, goat) and fish, plus fruits and vegetables as they come in season. During mango season, when mangoes literally pour off trees by the thousands, it is not uncommon for people to *turn their pots down* (cook less) and eat large amounts of the fruit. At Christmas time, the bright red sorrel fruit is mixed with sugar and spices in a delicious tea. Antiguans boast that their local pineapple (Antigua Black) is the sweetest in the world.

Popular dishes include seasoned rice (rice, peas, vegetables, and meat chunks with seasonings). *Fungee* is a spoon bread made with corn meal and okra. *Doucana* is coconut, sweet potatoes, flour, sugar and spices, served with spicy *saltfish* (dried cod). *Pepperpot*, a spicy vegetable stew, is different from home to home. Specialties include *Johnny Cakes* (sweet fried dumplings), *souse* (pickled pigs' feet), and blood sausage (called "rice" or "black" pudding). Fast food is making its way into the national diet, and sidewalk vendors sell roasted corn or peanuts as snacks.

Recreation

Antiguans have a passion for sports. Cricket is most popular, with formal and casual games played during the November to May season. Soccer dominates the rest of the year, and basketball is almost as popular. Girls are less involved with athletics than boys, but they compete in *netball* (similar to basketball) leagues. Water sports remain the domain of tourists and some upper class, and most Antiguans do not swim. At beach parties, they *sea bathe* in shallow water.

Antiguans also love music and dancing; anyone with the right speaker system can get a party going at a restaurant or picnic. Church choirs (with mostly women as members) are numerous and they practice regularly. Other social activities for women usually center around household duties or their children's activities.

Dominoes and *draughts* (a form of checkers) are also popular with men and boys, who play on tables set up under trees or on porches. A direct link to the nation's African heritage is the strategy game *Warri*. Complicated stratagems are required to capture the opponent's 24 seeds (four each in six cups) and win.

Holidays

Old Year's Night (31 December) and New Year's Day (1 January) cap off the important Christmas season that is marked by religious and secular celebrations. Easter (Friday–Monday) is as significant as Christmas. Labour Day (1 May, marked the first Monday in May) is important because of the role labor unions had in gaining independence. Pentecost (50 days after Easter) is a time of spiritual renewal and also coincides with Barbuda's *Caribana* (Carnival). CARICOM Day (4 July) celebrates Caribbean unity.

During Antigua's Carnival and the national arts festival, emancipation from slavery (1 August) is celebrated. This is an important time for Antiguans and Barbudans living abroad to return home. Parades, dancing, and music fill the streets for a week. Calypso music competitions are especially prominent. Aspiring "Calypsonians" perform all-new original songs. Calypsos can be comical, political, or whatever, and the event is long anticipated. The climax of Carnival is the Calypso King show, when a winner is crowned. Street dancing at dawn the next morning celebrates the first morning of freedom from slavery.

Christmas is celebrated on 25 and 26 December, the 26th being Boxing Day, a day to relax and visit. Boxing Day comes from the old British tradition of giving servants a holiday and boxed gifts. The prime minister can also call for holidays, such as the case in 1994 during an important cricket match in Antigua between the West Indies and England.

Commerce

Major shops and businesses are located in St. John's. Most are open between 8:00 A.M. and 5:00 P.M. St. John's also has a large open air market featuring fresh produce. Large supermarkets offer a full variety of food.

SOCIETY

Government

As part of the Commonwealth, Antigua continues to recognize Britain's Queen Elizabeth II as nominal head of state. She is represented by a governor general, who serves as ceremonial head of government after elections before a prime minister is named. Parliament has two houses, a Senate and a House of Representatives. The voting age is 18.

Economy

Tourism is the primary industry. St. John's is also home to a commercial deep-water harbor. While most revenues from tourism belong to foreign developers, Antiguans benefit from jobs and taxes on the industry. The country's Human Development Index (0.785) ranks it 60 out of 173 countries. Real gross domestic product per capita is $4,000.

The government employs one-third of the labor force, but tourism employs most of the rest. Some manufacturing exists, most often to supply the tourist industry (beds, towels, etc.). A member of the Caribbean Community (CARICOM) and the Organization of Eastern Caribbean States (OECS), Antigua uses the stable Eastern Caribbean dollar (EC$) as its currency.

Transportation and Communication

Plentiful buses serve the island, although private cars are common and a fleet of taxis caters to tourists. Following the British tradition, traffic moves on the left. Buses leave the station when full and do not follow written schedules; they stop on request. Locations in St. John's are accessible by foot, but long walks are avoided in the hot afternoon. Telecommunication systems are modern and extensive. One broadcast television station is supplemented by satellite and cable services. There are two radio stations.

Education

Literacy is 89 percent, and most Antiguans have had some secondary schooling. The system is modeled after Britain's. Public schools are free; more expensive private schools exist and are often church-affiliated. Children are required to wear uniforms; parents purchase their textbooks. Mandatory schooling lasts to age 16. Antigua State College provides post-secondary vocational training and college preparatory classes. Qualified students attend universities in other countries. Many of these never return home due to the lack of advanced career opportunities.

Health

The one hospital is adequate for minor treatment and surgeries, but serious cases may be flown to Puerto Rico. Most people have health insurance, and the government provides a Medical Benefits program. Most parishes are served by a clinic and doctor, with basic care provided free of charge. Nurse practitioners and nurse midwifes play an important role. The infant mortality rate is 19 per 1,000; life expectancy is 72 years.

FOR THE TRAVELER

Proof of citizenship (a passport is best) and a return ticket are required for U.S. citizens to visit Antigua and Barbuda. There is a $10 departure tax. More than 350 beaches, old British forts, and a variety of sights await the visitor. Facilities are well developed. For more information, contact the Embassy of Antigua and Barbuda, 3400 International Drive NW, Suite 4M, Washington, DC 20008.

A *Culturgram* is a product of native commentary and original, expert analysis. Statistics are estimates and information is presented as a matter of opinion. While the editors strive for accuracy and detail, this document should not be considered strictly factual. It is a general introduction to culture, an initial step in building bridges of understanding between peoples. It may not apply to all peoples of the nation. You should therefore consult other sources for more information.

CULTURGRAM '95

Argentina

(Argentine Republic)

Boundary representations not necessarily authoritative.

BACKGROUND

Land and Climate

With an area of 1,068,296 square miles (2,766,890 square kilometers), Argentina (literally "silver") is the eighth largest country in the world; it is one-third the size of the United States. Laced with rivers, Argentina is a large plain rising from the Atlantic in the east to the towering Andes Mountains in the west, along the Chilean border. The Chaco region in the northeast is dry except during the summer rainy season. The *Pampa*, the central plains, is famous for wheat and cattle production. Patagonia, to the south, consists of flat to rolling hills that are known for sheep raising. Approximately 60 percent of the land is used for agriculture; another 22 percent is covered by forests.

The nation's landscape varies, containing such wonders as the Iguazú Falls (1.5 times higher than the Niagara Falls) in the north and the Perito Moreno Glacier of Santa Cruz to the south. The Moreno Glacier is one of the few glaciers in the world that is still advancing. Argentina's climate is generally temperate, though hot in the subtropical north and cold in the subantarctic region of southern Patagonia. Cool ocean breezes help keep Buenos Aires relatively smog free. The seasons are opposite of those in the northern hemisphere: the warmest month is January, the coolest is July.

History

Before the Spanish began to colonize Argentina in the 1500s, the area was populated by various indigenous groups, some of whom (in the north) belonged to the Incan empire. Most groups were, however, nomadic or autonomous. Colonization got off to a slow start, but it increased in the 1700s as more indigenous peoples became marginalized and the Spanish established more cities. The British tried to capture Buenos Aires in 1806, but they were defeated. This, and friction with Spain, led to calls for independence. At the time, the colony included not only Argentina, but Paraguay and Uruguay as well.

A revolution erupted in 1810 and lasted six years before independence was finally declared. *Porteños* (coastal inhabitants favoring a centrist government based in Buenos Aires) then fought with those who favored a federal form of government. The actual fighting did not last long, but tensions remained and Argentina (Paraguay and Uruguay had long since become independent) finally became a unified nation in 1862. Civilian rule was generally peaceful and stable until a military coup of 1930. Another coup occurred in 1943, after which Juan Domingo Perón (a key figure in the coup) emerged as the country's leader. He was elected president in 1946 and ruled until 1955, when he was overthrown. After a series of

Copyright © 1994. Brigham Young University. Printed in the USA. All rights reserved. It is against the law to copy, reprint, store in a retrieval system, or transmit any part of this publication in any form by any means for any purpose without written permission from the Publications Division of the David M. Kennedy Center for International Studies, Brigham Young University, PO Box 24538, Provo, UT 84602–4538. *Culturgrams* are available for more than 125 areas of the world. To place an order, to receive a free catalog, or to obtain information on traveling abroad, call toll free (800) 528–6279.

military governments, Perón returned to power in 1973 but died in 1974, leaving his wife, Isabel, as the first woman to head a national government in the Western Hemisphere. She was ousted in 1976 by the military, which then waged a "Dirty War" against civilians to maintain power; thousands died or disappeared.

In 1982, Argentina went to war with Great Britain over the Malvinas (Falkland Islands). The military's defeat in the war led to 1983 elections that broke military rule and brought Raúl Alfonsín to power. In May 1989, he became the first leader in nearly half a century to be replaced through peaceful elections, when Carlos Saúl Menem, the son of Syrian immigrants, was elected president. Menem promised to improve the economy by introducing free-market principles. Although his policies were initially unpopular and there were even rumors of a potential coup, Menem's economic policies lowered inflation, produced growth, and opened the market to freer trade. By 1993, the economy was stable and Menem's popularity had risen significantly.

Menem had also stabilized democratic institutions in the country, paving the way for a future of peaceful transfers of power. Congressional elections in 1993 gave a strong victory to Menem's party (*Partido Justicialista*, also known as the Perónist Party) over the other major party, the Radical Civic Union. The strong victory enabled Menem and his supporters to call for a constitutional assembly to rewrite the constitution allowing a sitting president to run for re-election. The assembly was elected in 1994, but a third party, the Broad Front, made a strong showing and became an important part of the process. When the new constitution is unveiled before the 1995 national elections, it is expected to lift the ban on re-elections, reduce the presidential term to four years, change how senators are elected, and make changes to the executive branch of government. Menem plans to run for re-election, but he will face a strong challenge from the Broad Front and the Radicals.

THE PEOPLE

Population

The population of Argentina is about 33.5 million (the second largest in South America) and is growing yearly by 1.1 percent. More than 85 percent of the people live in urban areas. With more than 12 million people, the Buenos Aires metropolitan area is one of the most populated areas in the world. Approximately 85 percent of the people are descendants of European immigrants (Italian, Spanish, German, Welsh, English, French, and Russian). *Mestizos* (Spanish and Indian mix), Indians, and others make up the remaining 15 percent. More than 45 percent of the population is under age 15.

Language

While Spanish is the official language of Argentina, many people speak some English. German, French, and Italian are also widely spoken, as are several indigenous languages. Argentine Spanish also contains many distinct phrases and terms not used in other Spanish-speaking countries.

Religion

Roughly 90 percent of the people belong to the Roman Catholic church, which exercises great influence over many social customs and celebrations. Most weddings and funerals follow traditional Catholic norms. Despite this, a majority of Catholics are not actively involved with their church. Other Christian churches are gaining popularity. Approximately 2 percent of the people are members of various Protestant churches, another 2 percent are Jewish, and the remaining 6 percent belong to other religious organizations. Religious freedom is guaranteed, as church and state are officially separate.

General Attitudes

Argentines are proud of their nation, which has risen above difficult times to become a modern, thriving, democratic, and economically sound state. Political problems are solved through democratic institutions rather than coups, and the days of the Dirty War are past. People now look forward to improving their economic and social status, providing a better future for their children, and improving the country's image in the world. Prosperity, family, education, and personal relationships are important values to Argentines.

Urban Argentines tend to be cosmopolitan, progressive, and outgoing. Those who live in rural areas are more conservative and traditional. Throughout the country, it is important to show respect to the elderly and to honor friendships.

Personal Appearance

While dress may differ considerably from region to region, it is generally conservative. In Buenos Aires, European fashions are popular and readily available. In other areas, dress may reflect regional culture, such as among the *gauchos* (cowboys) of the Pampa region, who wear traditional clothing. Older women seldom wear pants but the younger generation prefers dressing more casually.

CUSTOMS AND COURTESIES

Greetings

It is customary to address people by a title (*Señor, Señora, Doctor*, among others) when being introduced. A handshake and a slight nod show respect. In some places such as Buenos Aires, a brief embrace with a kiss on the cheek is also common. Women are most likely to kiss each other, but a man and women may greet in this manner if well acquainted. A person might wave and smile at an acquaintance who is too distant to greet verbally; it is not polite to call out a greeting. The Spanish *¡Buenos días!* (Good morning—*¡Buen día!* in Buenos Aires) or *¡Buenas tardes!* (Good afternoon) are appropriate terms when passing on the street or greeting friends and acquaintances. When approaching someone such as a policeman or customs official for information, one should always greet the official before asking any questions.

Gestures

It is improper for a man and woman to show affection in public. During conversation, personal space tends to be smaller, and conversants might touch each other or stand close when speaking. Yawning without covering the mouth, as well as placing one's hands on the hips, is impolite. Eye contact is considered important in conversation. Hats are removed in buildings, houses, elevators, and in the presence of women.

Visiting

Argentines often visit friends and relatives without prior arrangement. People enjoy having guests in the home, and usually offer them refreshments. Espresso-style coffee is typical. Invited guests are not expected to arrive on time, as punctuality is not as important as the individual person. Guests will not offend hosts by arriving up to 30 minutes or more late. Visitors greet each person of the group individually; a group greeting is inappropriate. Dinner guests often bring a small gift such as flowers, candy, or pastries to their hosts. Guests are not seated until the host directs them to do so. Compliments about the home, meal, or hosts' family are appreciated. When leaving, a guest again addresses every person present, using such common phrases for good-bye as ¡Cíao! or hasta luego. The host usually opens the door for guests when they leave.

Eating

Three meals are eaten each day. The main meal is traditionally served at midday, although urban work schedules have affected many families. The evening meal is often served after 9:00 P.M. Argentines use the continental style of eating, with the knife in the right hand and the fork in the left. Hands (but not elbows) should always be above the table, not in the lap. Using a toothpick in public is considered bad manners, as is blowing one's nose or clearing one's throat at the table. Restaurant waiters may be summoned by raising the hand with the index finger extended. Tipping is not required, but it is becoming customary in many restaurants. Porters and other individuals providing personal services are tipped about 10 percent. Eating in the street or on public transportation is inappropriate.

LIFESTYLE

Family

Families tend to be rather small, averaging two children. The responsibility of raising children and managing household finances falls heavily on the mother, and she, in turn, exerts great influence in family decisions. More women are working outside the home, but they presently comprise less than 30 percent of the work force. Men tend to be more occupied with their work, often not coming home before 9:00 P.M. Children are central to the family and receive a great deal of attention. Families will sacrifice much to give their children a good education. Until 1987, divorce was illegal in Argentina, but it is now increasing.

Dating and Marriage

Group activities between boys and girls begin at about age 15, when girls have their most important birthday (*cumpleaños de quince*) that ends their childhood. Young couples' favorite activity is dancing. Serious relationships develop slowly over several years; most couples marry between 23 and 27 years of age. Weddings are very elaborate, containing three different events: the civil ceremony, the church wedding (no brides-maids or groomsmen; instead, the parents stand with the couple), and a large reception (dinner and dancing). Gifts are not brought to the reception but are purchased at and delivered by a gift shop where the couple has registered.

Diet

Beef is the staple of the Argentine diet; in fact, Argentines eat more beef per capita than any other people in the world, including citizens of the United States. Because Argentina is a major beef producer, domestic prices are low enough for most people to eat beef every day. Road and construction companies are known to provide workers access to portable grills for use at lunchtime. A favorite way to entertain is the *asado* (barbecue) on weekends. Other foods include baked stuffed beef and *empanadas* (meat or vegetable pies). A preferred winter stew is *locro* (made of meat, corn, and potatoes). The government and health officials are encouraging lower beef consumption for health and economic reasons. *Maté* is a popular hot tea. Italian and French foods are widely available.

Recreation

Soccer is the national sport and is enjoyed by children and adults alike. Argentina's national soccer team competed in the 1994 World Cup. Other popular sports include horse racing, rugby, field hockey, tennis, polo, and basketball. A fine opera house (the *Colón*) is located in Buenos Aires, as are many excellent movie theaters that are regularly attended. In Buenos Aires, there are many late-night theaters, restaurants, and clubs. The popular tango dance originated in Argentina.

Holidays

Holidays are generally opportunities for family gatherings; Christmas and New Year are celebrated with fireworks. Other holidays include Good Friday and Easter; Labor Day (1 May); Anniversary of the May Revolution (25 May); Malvinas Day (10 June); Flag Day (20 June); Independence Day (9 July); Death of General José de San Martín, who is known as the "Liberator" of Peru, Chile, and Argentina for his defeat of the Spanish in 1812 (17 August); Student Day (21 September); and Columbus Day (12 October).

Commerce

In Buenos Aires, stores generally open at 9:00 A.M. and close at 8:00 P.M. In other cities, they open at 8:00 A.M., close for lunch between noon and 3:00 or 4:00 P.M., and remain open until 8:00 P.M., Monday through Friday. On Saturday, stores close around 1:00 P.M. for the day. Professional and government offices have variable hours depending on their function, but most government offices are open weekdays between 9:00 A.M. and 5:00 P.M. Any shopping items, including groceries, are wrapped or placed in shopping bags before being taken from the store. Workers in Argentina enjoy an *aguinaldo* (13th-month bonus) equal to one month's pay; it is often paid in two semiannual installments.

SOCIETY

Government

The executive branch consists of a president, a vice president, and a cabinet. The National Congress has two houses, a Senate and a Chamber of Deputies. Members of the independent Supreme Court are appointed by the president. The president is both chief of state and head of government. The voting age is 18. Argentina is comprised of 23 provinces and one federal district.

Economy

Agriculture, which currently employs about 12 percent of the people, has always been the mainstay of the Argentine economy, although industry is also vital. Argentina is famous for its livestock and is a major exporter of beef, hides, and wool. The country also exports large amounts of wheat, corn, and flaxseed, as well as soybean and cotton. Important industries include food processing, meat packing, motor vehicles, consumer goods, textiles, chemicals, printing, and metallurgy.

Argentina's Human Development Index (0.832) ranks it 46 out of 173 countries. Real gross domestic product per capita is $4,295, which has improved steadily in the last generation. These figures indicate a growing number of Argentines are able to earn a decent income and that economic opportunities are available to a majority of the people. Since 1991, economic growth has averaged above 6 percent annually. Inflation has been brought under control, and is less than 10 percent. Foreign investment has increased substantially, further stimulating growth. The currency is the *peso*.

Transportation and Communication

Transportation and communication systems are well developed. Buses, trains, subways, taxis, and a large number of private automobiles are the main means of travel. Airlines link major cities in Argentina and neighboring countries. Buenos Aires is the most important seaport. The Plata River system is vital to Argentina and neighboring countries. Televisions and telephones are increasingly common and service is likewise improving. Postal service is extensive but not always reliable. The U.S. news station CNN broadcasts 24 hours a day in Argentina. Newspapers are widely available; Buenos Aires also has an English-speaking daily paper, the *Buenos Aires Herald*.

Education

The literacy rate in Argentina is 95 percent, the highest in Latin America. School is compulsory and free from ages six through fourteen. Secondary and higher education are also free but must be entered by examination. Nearly three-fourths of all eligible students are enrolled in secondary schools. There are 26 national universities and 24 private ones.

Health

Argentines enjoy relatively good health and have access to both public and private health care facilities. Public hospitals provide care free of charge to Argentines. It is also often the responsibility of trade unions to provide health services to their members. The most modern facilities are found in Buenos Aires. Care is less reliable and less available in rural areas. The average life expectancy is 67 to 74 years. The infant mortality rate is 30 per 1,000.

FOR THE TRAVELER

If staying for less than three months, a visa is not required of U.S. citizens traveling to Argentina. However, a valid passport is necessary. A passport is often required to register at a hotel and should be carried at all times. There are no immunizations required for the country, although yellow fever vaccinations may be recommended for those visiting the northeastern forests. Protections against malaria are sometimes advisable when traveling to outlying rural areas. A doctor should be consulted before traveling for extended periods. Water is generally safe to drink. Good medical facilities are available in Buenos Aires.

Argentina offers a great deal to the traveler, from the European-style city of Buenos Aires and large beach resorts to virgin forests and breathtaking waterfalls (such as Iguazú Falls). Dual-voltage small appliances and plug adaptor kits are necessary to use electrical outlets. For more information, contact the Argentina Tourist Information Office, 12 West 56th Street, New York, NY 10019. You may also wish to contact the Embassy of Argentina, 1600 New Hampshire Avenue NW, Washington, DC 20009. Consulates, which provide the same services as embassies, are located in several major U.S. cities.

A *Culturgram* is a product of native commentary and original, expert analysis. Statistics are estimates and information is presented as a matter of opinion. While the editors strive for accuracy and detail, this document should not be considered strictly factual. It is a general introduction to culture, an initial step in building bridges of understanding between peoples. It may not apply to all peoples of the nation. You should therefore consult other sources for more information.

Republic of
Austria

Boundary representations not necessarily authoritative.

BACKGROUND

Land and Climate

A landlocked country in central Europe, Austria covers 32,375 square miles (83,850 square kilometers) and is slightly smaller than Maine. Spectacular mountains, clear lakes, beautiful scenery, and green valleys all comprise Austria's grandeur. The famous Alps cover much of the west and south, while flatlands dominate in the east and northeast. The country generally enjoys a mild climate. Spring and summer are temperate. However, winters in some mountain areas can be very cold. In Vienna, the average winter temperature is 32°F (0°C) and in summer it is 67°F (20°C).

History

Despite its present size, Austria has had a significant impact on European history and world culture. Present-day Austria was once part of both the Roman and Charlemagne's empires. Otto I, who later became emperor of the Holy Roman Empire, began his rule in 955. He is often considered the real founder of Austria because of the borders he established. "Austria" is the Latin equivalent of the German *Österreich* (realm of the east).

In 1156 and with Vienna as its capital, Austria became an autonomous duchy under the Babenburgs. The Habsburg dynasty came to power in 1273. For 600 years, the Habsburgs gradually spread their Austro-Hungarian empire over central Europe through marriages and other strategies. They helped push the Ottoman Turks out of Europe after the 18th century. Their power was greatest in the early 19th century after they helped defeat Napoleon.

By 1914, the empire covered present-day Austria, Hungary, the Czech Republic, Slovakia, Slovenia, Croatia, and Bosnia-Herzegovina, and parts of Poland and Romania. Still, it was in decline due to growing nationalism among its various peoples. In 1914, when the Archduke Franz Ferdinand, heir to the Habsburg throne, was assassinated in Sarajevo (Bosnia), what should have been a local civil conflict quickly mushroomed into World War I, as most nations of Europe became involved. "The Great War," as it was called, led to the empire's destruction. Yugoslavia and Czechoslovakia were new countries created from parts of the old empire. Both of those countries have since become divided.

The first Austrian republic (1918–38) struggled to survive and was swallowed up by Hitler's Germany before the start of World War II. After 1945, Austria was divided into four zones, each governed by one of the four Allied powers (Great Britain, France, the United States, and the Soviet Union). Ten years later, Austria was reborn as an independent and permanently neutral democratic republic, with strong ties to Western Europe. The republic has since been a model of political, economic, and social stability.

Because of Austria's political neutrality, Vienna has become a key United Nations city where nations meet to discuss problems or negotiate treaties. Austria's trade ties with Hungary prompted the Hungarian government to tear down the barbed-wire fence along the Austrian-Hungarian border in 1989. This action is recognized as a significant event that encouraged the 1990 political reforms in Eastern Europe. In a June 1994 ballot, Austrians voted by almost a two-to-one

EUROPE

Copyright © 1994. Brigham Young University. Printed in the USA. All rights reserved. It is against the law to copy, reprint, store in a retrieval system, or transmit any part of this publication in any form by any means for any purpose without written permission from the Publications Division of the David M. Kennedy Center for International Studies, Brigham Young University, PO Box 24538, Provo, UT 84602–4538. *Culturgrams* are available for more than 125 areas of the world. To place an order, to receive a free catalog, or to obtain information on traveling abroad, call toll free (800) 528–6279.

margin in favor of Austria joining the European Union (EU) on 1 January 1995. Entering the EU will allow Austria to take advantage of economic integration.

PEOPLE

Population

Austria's population is 7.91 million, which is growing at 0.5 percent. At least 99 percent of the people are Germanic, while minorities include Croatians, Slovenes, and various other groups. In addition, approximately 200,000 foreign workers—mainly from Turkey and the former Yugoslavia—live and work in Austria, but they are not counted as part of the population. About 58 percent of the people live in urban areas.

Language

The official language is High German, but each area has its own dialect. Dialects are more pronounced in rural areas. A minority in southern Austria speaks Croatian. English is a required language in high schools and is spoken by many people.

Religion

Some 85 percent of all Austrians are Roman Catholic, while 6 percent are Protestant. The other 9 percent belong either to various other Christian churches, some non-Christian religions, or no denomination. Younger people are generally less devout than the older generation, with many having withdrawn their membership in the Catholic church. At the same time, Austrians are generally more religious than people in many other Western European countries, and Catholic traditions, shrines, and churches are still treasured. The Jewish community has about 10,000 members, down from 200,000 before World War II.

General Attitudes

Austrians are known for their *Gemütlichkeit*, a relaxed and happy approach to life. A good-natured sense of frustration and bittersweet attitude toward reality are considered unique national traits. Although a relaxed people, Austrians are hardworking. They value cleanliness, neatness, and order. Litter is rare. People love to learn and engage in conversation. There is a deep regard for the environment, and Austrians take pride in their country's beautiful landscape. Austrian society values its professionals, academics, and artists. Cultural arts are important to all segments of society, as Austrians are extremely proud of their culture's contributions to Western civilization.

Austrians are not Germans and should not be referred to as such; it can be considered an insult. While the two peoples speak the same basic language (with important differences in dialect), Austrians and Germans have a different historical and political heritage; they also differ in some customs, values, and attitudes.

Personal Appearance

Austrians generally wear European clothing fashions, but they often add a distinctive Austrian touch to their wardrobes. They take pride in dressing well, even if they are only going grocery shopping. It is important to dress properly for all events. While older people might mix traditional Austrian clothing with conservative European fashions, young people prefer modern European attire. Folk costumes (*Trachten*) are often worn on formal occasions and for celebrations. Each area has its own particular costume. This traditional clothing includes *Lederhosen* (leather knee pants) and *Trachtenjacken* (woolen jackets) for men and a *Dirndl* (dress with an apron) or *Trachtenanzug* (suit) for women. Both may have intricate designs and are usually prized items in a person's wardrobe. Those who have more than one outfit will have an especially nice one reserved for special occasions.

CUSTOMS AND COURTESIES

Greetings

Austrians shake hands when greeting and parting. Even children shake hands with adults when greeting, as this is an important social courtesy. In Vienna, a man may still kiss the hand of a woman when introduced to her. Common greetings in Austria include *Grüß Gott* (May God greet you), *Guten Morgen* (Good morning), *Guten Tag* (Good Day), and *Guten Abend* (Good evening). Popular casual greetings include *Servus* (used as "Hi") and *Grüß Dich!* (Greetings to you). Austrians do not ask, "How are you?" (*Wie geht es Ihnen?*) unless they wish to hear a detailed account.

Professional titles are important among the adult population and are used whenever known. Otherwise, titles such as *Herr* (Mr.), *Fräulein* (Miss), and *Frau* (Mrs. or Ms.), are combined with family names when addressing acquaintances and strangers. Close friends and the youth use first names.

Gestures

Hand gestures are used conservatively in polite company, as verbal communication is preferred. It is impolite for adults to chew gum in public. Motioning with the entire hand is more polite than using the index finger. Touching the index finger to one's forehead or temple is an insult. Yawns and coughs are covered when they cannot be avoided.

Visiting

Austrians enjoy entertaining in their home and having guests. It is impolite to drop by unannounced. It is better to make arrangements in advance or telephone ahead of an impromptu visit. Invited guests should arrive on time. Punctuality is important to Austrians. Customarily, guests remove their shoes when entering a home. This tradition is not practiced in many homes today, however, and guests who reach for their shoes might be told by the hostess that it is all right to leave them on. In homes where the hosts expect guests to remove shoes, guest slippers are usually visible near the door. Guests remain standing until invited to sit down; they often remain standing until told just where to sit. Hosts customarily offer the best seats to their guests. If the host must leave the room for a moment, the guest is offered something to read or occupy the time until the host returns. Men stand when a woman enters the room or when talking to a woman who is standing.

While a drink (tea, coffee, mineral water, juice, or soda) is usually offered to guests, further refreshments depend on the hosts. Invited guests bring flowers, candy, or a small gift (such as a handcrafted item or something appropriate for the occasion). Even married children often bring such a gift when visiting their parents. Gifts are given to the wife, or perhaps the children, but not the husband—even if the gift is for the family. Flowers are given only in odd numbers (even numbers are bad luck) and they are unwrapped in the presence of the hostess. Red roses are only given as a sign of romantic love. Giving purchased flowers is more polite than flowers from one's own garden.

To show courtesy to the hosts, guests do not ask to use the telephone (all calls are billed, even local ones, and the cost is high), nor do they offer to help make any preparations if they are not well acquainted with the hosts or if the hostess seems to not have everything under control. When guests leave, they are accompanied outside to the gate. Hosts remain until the guests are out of sight. It is polite and generally expected for guests on foot to turn once or twice while walking away and wave to the hosts.

While most Austrians prefer to entertain in the home, they also socialize in restaurants and other public places. For many people, especially in small villages, it is a custom on Sunday after church (usually Catholic) services for the women to go home and fix dinner and the men to go to a *Gasthaus* (pub) to do business, exchange ideas, and drink. This socializing is less about drinking and much more about networking and socializing with male friends.

Eating

Eating habits are changing in Austria. For example, where the midday meal was once at midday, it is now becoming more common in the evening. This is necessary for families where both the husband and wife work outside of the home. Likewise, afternoon "tea" is now less common among working Austrians. At the same time, certain traditions remain strong, such as keeping hands above the table during the meal, not gesturing with utensils, and not placing elbows on the table while eating. It is impolite to begin eating until all persons at the table are served. Austrians eat in the continental style, with the fork in the left hand and the knife remaining in the right. When guests are present, the hostess will nearly always offer second helpings, but a polite *Danke, nein.* (Thank you, no) is gracefully accepted.

In restaurants, tap water is not served but mineral water is available. Tap water is generally only drunk in the home. The bill is paid at the table to the server, and a service charge is usually included. Most people round the bill up to the nearest *Schilling* as a tip.

LIFESTYLE

Family

Austrian families are usually small, having one or two children. However, rural families are often a bit larger. Most Austrians expect to marry and have a family. Both parents generally work outside the home, with women comprising nearly 40 percent of the labor force. In such cases, married couples tend to share duties related to the household and children. Some homes, especially in rural areas, maintain a more strict patriarchal family structure. The government gives families financial allowances for each child. Children who are not in school and whose parents both work are cared for privately or in day care centers. Most urban Austrians live in apartments; sometimes extended families will share one large house that contains several apartments. About one-fifth of all housing is publicly owned. Rural families generally live in single-family homes.

Dating and Marriage

Austrian youth begin associating in groups. When they start getting together as couples, they usually only date one person at a time and the relationship is generally considered serious. Actual dates are rather casual affairs, as people often just agree to meet somewhere. Boys and girls pay their own expenses, with one or the other offering to pay for both only on special occasions. Eating out, going to movies, and dancing are favorite activities.

Couples often decide to live together before or instead of marriage. The typical age for marriage is between 25 and 28 years. A civil ceremony must be performed for the marriage to be legal; church weddings are optional.

Diet

Austrians love good food and have a rich and varied cuisine drawn from the various cultures that once comprised the Austro-Hungarian Empire. Specialties vary by region but include such favorites as *Wienerschnitzel* (breaded veal cutlet), *Sachertorte* (a rich chocolate cake with apricot jam and chocolate icing), *Knödel* (moist potato dumplings), and goulash.

A typical day begins early with a light breakfast of coffee or hot chocolate, rolls, bread, and jam or marmalade. Later in the morning, some eat a second, heartier breakfast, including goulash or hot sausages. The main meal, whether at midday or in the evening, may include soup, meat (often pork) with potatoes or pasta, vegetables, a salad, and often dessert (such as a homemade pastry). Afternoon tea (*Jause*) may include sandwiches, pastries, and coffee. If the main meal is eaten at midday, families have *Abendbrot* (evening bread) in the evening. It generally includes cold cuts, eggs, cheese, rye bread and other breads, and a salad. After a visit to the theater or other evening activity, a light supper might end the day. Austrians enjoy beer, wine, herbal teas, apple juice with sparkling mineral water, fruit juices, and soft drinks.

Recreation

Austrians love the outdoors. Talking a walk (*ein Spaziergang*) is a national pastime. Hiking, skiing, boating, and swimming are all popular activities. Soccer is a favorite sport, but Austrians are most known for their excellence in winter sports. They are consistent medalists in Winter Olympic events. Gardening is popular, even when space is limited. Window boxes full of flowers are favorites throughout the country.

Cultural arts play a key role in Austrian society. People enjoy modern art and music, but they also treasure more traditional music. Even large numbers of the youth attend opera performances and orchestral concerts. The names Haydn, Mozart, Schubert, Strauss, Beethoven, and Brahms (who all worked in Vienna), as well as Wolf, Mahler, Bruckner, and others attest to Austria's traditional musical splendor. The Vienna State Opera, the Vienna Philharmonic, the Vienna Boys Choir, and the Salzburg Festival are four of many music institutions that enjoy worldwide fame. Austria is also noted for its writers (Franz Kafka, Hofmansthal, Karl Kraus). Painters and architects have also flourished in Austria in the 20th century, especially since World War II. With Vienna as its center, Austria continues to give strong support to the development and performance of cultural arts.

Folk music is important in Austria. Common folk instruments include the *hackbrett* (hammered dulcimer) and *zither* (a stringed instrument). Guitars and harps are also prevalent in folk music. In addition, nearly every village has a band (usually brass), any town of size has a professional orchestra, and there are many local theaters.

Holidays

Austrians celebrate New Year's Day, *Heilige Drei Könige* (Three Kings, 6 January), Easter (Saturday–Monday), Labor Day (1 May), Flag Day (26 October; this is the national holiday), All Saints Day (1 November), and Christmas (25–26 December), as well as various religious holidays throughout the year. Christmas Eve (*Heiliger Abend* or Holy Evening) is the most important part of Christmas. Families gather for a meal and to sing Christmas carols. Children receive their presents, which are customarily put under the tree by the Christ child when they are out of the room. There is little tradition of Santa Claus, although it is making its way into the commercial aspect of Christmas. Christmas Day is reserved for visiting family. In the summer, most family vacations are taken in August. Small, family-owned shops might be closed the entire month while the family is away.

Commerce

Large stores are open from 8:00 A.M. until 6:00 P.M. on weekdays and from 8:00 P.M. until noon on Saturdays. Large chain stores remain open on Saturday until evening. Small open-air markets often open at 6:00 A.M. Banks close at 4:30 P.M. An increasing number of stores are open on Sunday. Small, private shops might still close for the traditional *Mittagspause* (midday break), which was once universal as the two or three-hour break for the main meal.

SOCIETY

Government

Austria has nine states. The executive branch consists of a federal president, a federal chancellor, and the chancellor's cabinet. The president, Thomas Klestil, was elected in 1992. The Federal Assembly (*Bundesversammlung*) has an upper house, called a Federal Council (*Bundesrat*), and a lower house, called a National Council (*Nationalrat*). Austria's various political parties have a tradition of cooperation, which has promoted political stability. The voting age is 19. For presidential elections, voting is mandatory. There are three types of high courts, each one having jurisdiction over either justice, administration, or the constitution.

Economy

Austria is an industrialized nation with a mixed free-market/social-welfare economy. Social-welfare programs are fairly extensive and provide support for the unemployed. Agriculture plays only a minor role in the economy, although the country is mostly self-sufficient in food. Important resources include iron ore, timber, tungsten, coal, and other minerals. Austria exports machinery, lumber, textiles, iron, steel, chemicals, and paper products. Tourism is also an important industry.

The economy is generally strong and stable, a result of a unique system of social partnerships in which unions and owners or employers cooperate to exercise restraint on prices and wages. They also try to reach a consensus on managing the national economy. Austria's Human Development Index (0.952) ranks it 15 out of 173 nations. Real gross domestic product per capita is $16,504, nearly four times higher than it was in 1960. These figures reflect the economy's expansion in the last generation and that most people earn a decent income or have access to economic opportunities. The currency is the Austrian *Schilling* (S).

Transportation and Communication

Most families own at least one car, and private cars are important for daily transportation. The public system of trains, buses, and streetcars is also heavily used, especially in large urban areas. Buses reach even the remotest areas and a good system of trains crisscross the country. On the expressway, there is a speed limit of 80 miles per hour (120 km per hour); seat belt laws are strictly enforced. Children under age 12 must ride in the back seat.

The communication system is efficient and extensive. Most homes have televisions and phones. Daily newspapers are available throughout the country.

Education

Each state is responsible for public schooling, which is free and compulsory between the ages of 6 and 15. Most Austrians complete this amount of schooling and also gain other training or higher education. Education has traditionally been important in Austria, which is home to many Nobel prize winners and noted scholars. Sigmund Freud was Austrian. Austrian universities offer a high quality education; they attract many students from abroad. The literacy rate is 99 percent.

Health

Health care is provided for retired persons and those in need. Working persons have private health insurance. Austrians enjoy good health and have access to adequate care. The infant mortality rate is 7 per 1,000. Adults can generally expect to live an average of between 73 to 80 years.

FOR THE TRAVELER

No visa is required of U.S. travelers for up to three months, although a passport is necessary. Most hotels reserve the right to bill those who do not keep their reservations. There are countless things to do in Austria, from shopping to eating, visiting the many folk museums, attending concerts, hiking around a lake or in the mountains, or just taking in the scenic beauty. For more information, contact the Austrian National Tourist Office at 500 Fifth Avenue, Suite 2009–22, New York, NY 10110. You may also wish to contact the Embassy of Austria, 3524 International Court NW, Washington, DC 20008–3035.

A *Culturgram* is a product of native commentary and original, expert analysis. Statistics are estimates and information is presented as a matter of opinion. While the editors strive for accuracy and detail, this document should not be considered strictly factual. It is a general introduction to culture, an initial step in building bridges of understanding between peoples. It may not apply to all peoples of the nation. You should therefore consult other sources for more information.

Printed on recycled paper

Barbados

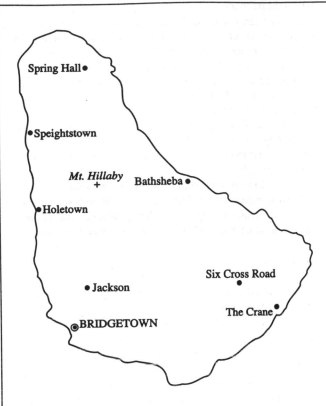

Boundary representations not necessarily authoritative.

THE AMERICAS

BACKGROUND

Land and Climate

Barbados lies farthest east in the Caribbean archipelago. The island is 166 square miles (430 square kilometers) in size—just smaller than 2.5 times the size of Washington, D.C.—and is mostly flat. The tropical climate provides an average temperature of 85°F (29°C). The rainy season is from June to October. From 43 to 80 inches of rain falls each year. A thin layer of topsoil covers the thick layer of coral that forms the island. The soil is very fertile, making the island lush with flowering trees, shrubs, and tropical flowers. Three-fourths of the island is suitable for cultivation. Natural resources include crude oil, fish, and natural gas.

History

The original inhabitants of Barbados were Arawak and Carib Indians. However, they disappeared before British settlers arrived—maybe even by 1536—but the reason is uncertain. The British came to the island in 1625, when Captain John Powell claimed it in the name of King James I. In 1627, Powell brought the first colonists (80 of them) and settled Holetown. As the population grew, sugarcane was introduced, and slave labor was brought in from Africa. Independence-minded colonists were forced to surrender to England's forces in 1652 by signing the Articles of Capitulation, which became the Charter of Barbados.

Later, Barbados moved toward independence by emancipating its slaves between 1834 and 1838, enfranchising women in 1944, and providing universal suffrage in 1951. A leader of the independence movement, Sir Grantley Adams, became the first premier under home rule in 1954. Barbados became part of the West Indies Federation in 1958, but it dissolved in 1962. Barbados thereafter sought full independence from Great Britain, which was granted on 30 November 1966. The first prime minister of an independent Barbados was Errol Barrow. The country remains a member of the British Commonwealth. Since independence, it has enjoyed a high degree of political stability. The island capitalized on its natural strengths and, by the 1980s, had developed a successful tourist industry. With economic and political stability, the nation was able to establish a high standard of living for its inhabitants.

Copyright © 1994. Brigham Young University. Printed in the USA. All rights reserved. It is against the law to copy, reprint, store in a retrieval system, or transmit any part of this publication in any form by any means for any purpose without written permission from the Publications Division of the David M. Kennedy Center for International Studies, Brigham Young University, PO Box 24538, Provo, UT 84602–4538. *Culturgrams* are available for more than 125 areas of the world. To place an order, to receive a free catalog, or to obtain information on traveling abroad, call toll free (800) 528–6279.

THE PEOPLE

Population

The population of Barbados is approximately 255,000 and is growing at 0.1 percent annually. The island has a high population density: 1,533 persons per square mile (592 per square kilometer). About 60 percent of the population lives in urban centers stretching along the western side of the island, which is more sheltered from storms. The capital city of Bridgetown is the largest urban area. Actually, the island is almost a city-country, with Bridgetown serving as "downtown" for the whole island. Only 4 percent of the people have a European heritage, while 16 percent are of mixed descent, and 80 percent have African origins. The people of Barbados are called Barbadians, but they are often referred to as Bajans.

Language

The official language is English. Bajans also speak a dialect that can be understood by foreign English speakers if they listen carefully. German, Spanish, French, and Italian are taught in the schools and in classes offered by the Board of Tourism.

Religion

The majority (67 percent) of Barbadians are Protestant Christians, with about 40 percent belonging to the Anglican Church and 7 percent to the Methodist Church. A number of Christian organizations are active on the island, including the Roman Catholic church (4 percent). Nearly 30 percent of all people either belong to no church at all or smaller Christian and non-Christian organizations. There is a small Jewish community. A Jewish synagogue was first built on the island in 1654. Regardless of one's religious affiliation, funeral attendance is considered important. Bajans make a special effort to go to the services and offer condolences to the family.

General Attitudes

Bajans are warm, happy, and friendly, although they may act reserved around strangers. They are hospitable to visitors and will welcome them to their homes. They take pride in their nation, their cultural heritage, and their people's accomplishments. A generally peaceful atmosphere allows the police to patrol unarmed. Social unity is important to Barbadians. Their view of life is evident in the carefully kept homes, beautiful pastels used to paint houses, and lively festivals that represent past and present culture. They love music and dancing.

Personal Appearance

Women usually wear tailored dresses or blouses and skirts to work, but they get very dressed up for parties and other social events. They wear their finest dresses and hats to church meetings. For casual events, women usually dress in colorful, long skirts with open-type sandals. Sometimes they wear their hair in small braids with colorful beads at the ends. Men usually wear lightweight pants with a casual shirt of white, pastel, or flowered fabric (usually locally made). The "shirt-jac" suit is generally accepted everywhere (parties, offices, churches), but a more formal suit is normally required for certain party functions and formal events. Swim wear is limited to the beach and is not worn in the city or other public places.

CUSTOMS AND COURTESIES

Greetings

Bajans generally they greet each other with a handshake and a smile. Acquaintances often embrace upon meeting. A common greeting is "How do you do?" An answer such as "Not bad" does not carry any negative feeling but is a friendly response. An evening telephone call begins with "Hello, good night. . . ."

Gestures

Taxis and buses are called by waving the hand. Barbadians often use their hands when conversing. A wave of the hand is also used to say hello in passing. People often express disgust by making a sound with puckered lips (sounding something like "chupse") and show defiance by placing their hands on their hips (akimbo) while arguing a point. Bajans will frequently fold their arms as a sign that they are paying complete attention to what is going on.

Visiting

Bajans usually visit one another on weekends, but an especially favorite time for men to get together is Sunday morning when topics of conversation range from politics to cricket. Drinks are usually served to guests in the home. Other significant visiting occurs at cricket and other sporting events when old friends see each other. Shops in the country districts and barber salons in the city are important places for lively discussion, especially around election time. As in English households, guests are often invited to afternoon tea.

Eating

Barbadians eat in the continental style, with the fork in the left hand and the knife remaining in the right. Bajan food is unique, a combination of African and English traditions, and can be found in most restaurants. Fast food is also becoming popular, as is pizza. A 5 percent tax is applied to all meals, and a 10 percent service charge is added to the bill or included in the menu prices. International cuisine is available in resort areas.

LIFESTYLE

Family

The extended family is important in Barbados, and parents, children, grandparents, and cousins enjoy substantial interaction. This pattern is changing somewhat with modernization, but it is still important. Extended families may live together or near one another. Single-parent (usually a mother) families are common. In homes where the father is present, he is the leader. Economic circumstances have caused many women to seek employment outside the home, leaving the care of children to grandparents. Nearly half of the work force is female. Some people have emigrated to the United States, Canada, or the United Kingdom for work, but they still maintain extended family ties through monetary support and visits.

Many families live in traditional *chattel houses*. These look like mobile wooden homes, set on coral stone three or four feet above ground for better air circulation. *Chattel houses* are designed for easy assembly and disassembly, as plantation workers in the past were often required to move from one working area to another. They are so well built that they may be passed from one generation to the next. Other permanent homes exist, of course. They are made from cement and painted with pastel colors.

Dating and Marriage

Dating usually begins in the early teens. Many young people marry after they have established themselves financially or have begun their careers. Marriage is an important event in the life of a Bajan. Weddings are traditionally held in churches, followed by a gala reception in a local hall, hotel, or restaurant. Bajan steel bands perform local or English music. Bridal dresses are similar to those in North America, and brides wear long veils. Elaborate wedding cakes are provided by the family or are purchased.

Diet

Barbados offers a wide variety of foods in plentiful supply. The national dish is the flying fish and *cou cou* (made of okras and cornmeal). Also popular are lobster, shrimp, dorado, red snapper, turtle, tuna, kingfish, and the Crane Chubb fish. White sea urchin eggs are a delicacy. The tropical soil yields mangoes, papayas, bananas, cucumbers, guavas, avocados, and coconuts, as well as squash, tomatoes, eggplant, breadfruit, and numerous other vegetables. Popular local dishes include *jug-jug* (Guinea corn and green peas), *Pepperpot* (a spicy stew), and *conkies* (cornmeal, coconut, pumpkin, raisins, sweet potatoes, and spice steamed in a banana leaf). Black-bellied sheep and goats provide meat. Both cow and goat milk are popular.

Recreation

Cricket is the national sport. With excellent wind and water conditions, windsurfing and surfing are favorites, as are yachting, waterskiing, sailing, scuba diving, and skin diving. Diving is popular because of the extensive coral reefs and three sunken ships. Swimming is enjoyed on the south and west coast beaches. Other sporting activities include polo, horse racing, golf, squash, and tennis. The national table game is dominoes. Bajans also enjoy soccer, bridge, chess, cycling, basketball, rugby, and volleyball. Sunday and holiday picnics at the beach are popular. When vacationing, Barbadians may visit another part of the island, another English-speaking island, or relatives in the United States, Canada, or England. The people often relax with Bajan folk songs, calypso songs, and dancing. Many of these date back to slave songs brought by West Africans to the West Indies in the 1600s.

Holidays

Four annual festivals celebrate important events in Barbados. The Holestown Festival (three days in February) celebrates the arrival of the first settlers; the Oistins Fish Festival is held on Easter weekend as a tribute to the fishing industry; the Crop Over Festival (mid-July to early August) celebrates the end of the sugarcane harvest; and, the National Independence Festival of the Creative Arts (November) allows people to display talents in various fields. Other holidays include New Year's Day, Errol Barrow Day (21 January), Good Friday, Easter Monday, May Day (1 May), Whit Monday, Kadooment Day (first Monday in July), United Nations Day (first Monday in October), Independence Day (30 November), Christmas, and Boxing Day (26 December). Boxing Day, a British tradition of giving small boxed gifts to servants and tradesmen the day after Christmas, is now a day to visit friends and family.

Commerce

Most businesses are open from 8:00 A.M. to 4:00 P.M., Monday through Friday, and until NOON on Saturday. Grocery stores are open somewhat later, closing either at 6:00 or 7:00 P.M. on weekdays and at 1:00 P.M. on Saturdays. Some convenience stores are open until 9:00 P.M. Most businesses close on Sunday, although large stores remain open on Sunday when cruise ships are in port. Banking hours are generally shorter. Banks are open from 9:00 A.M. until 3:00 P.M., Monday through Thursday, and from 9:00 A.M. to 1:00 P.M. and 3:00 to 5:00 P.M. on Friday. The average workweek is 40 hours.

SOCIETY

Government

As a sovereign member of the Commonwealth of Nations, Barbados recognizes Queen Elizabeth II as the head of state. She is represented by a governor general, currently Dame Nita Barrow. The prime minister is the leader of the majority party in the National Assembly which has 28 seats. Parliament also has a Senate, whose members are appointed. Barbados is divided into 11 parishes. National elections are held every five years; the last one was in 1991. Lloyd Sandiford was reelected prime minister. All citizens may vote at age 18.

Economy

Barbados has one of the highest standards of living in the Caribbean. Its Human Develoment Index (HDI) rating is 0.928, meaning that most people have a good income, a useful education, and access to adequate health care. Tourism, light manufacturing, and the sugar industry are primary sources of foreign exchange. Tourism has expanded in importance in recent years, and it provides much of the country's employment. Barbados exports sugar, rum, electrical equipment, and textiles. It trades with the United States, other Caribbean nations, the United Kingdom, and Canada. One of the greatest problems in Barbados is a high unemployment rate above 20 percent. The economy grows at an annual rate of 3.5 percent. A diversified agriculture provides the people with an adequate food supply. The currency is the Barbadian dollar (Bds$).

Transportation and Communication

Barbados has one international airport. Exports and imports are served by the Bridgetown Harbor or the Air Freight Terminal airport. A central paved highway serves Barbadians, and the island is covered by an adequate network of roads. Following the British tradition, cars travel on the left side of the road. Public transportation consists of buses and taxis, which are readily available. Barbados has one government-owned television station and a satellite subscription television service; there are many radio stations. In addition to two daily newspapers, foreign-language papers are also available. Telecommunication links to other nations are well established.

Education

With a literacy rate of 99 percent, the public education system in Barbados is one of the finest in the Caribbean. Actual literacy may be somewhat lower because that figure is based on a person having ever attended school, rather than demonstrating literacy skills. Still, more than 85 percent of all pupils complete primary schooling and attend secondary school. Attendance is compulsory to age 16. Private schools have less than 5 percent of the total enrollment. The government sponsors qualified students to study at the University of the West Indies in Jamaica and Trinidad, but the university also has a campus in Barbados that offers a college-level education. Technical training schools are also available in Barbados. Schools for physically and mentally handicapped children are also provided. Primary and secondary schools generally require school uniforms.

Health

The Bajans are a relatively healthy people. The infant mortality rate has improved to the level of an industrial nation. It is currently 11 per 1,000. Barbadian water is some of the purest in the world. Tap water is safe to drink and most homes have running water. Medical care, including maternity and dental care, is provided free to all Barbadians at local *polyclinics*. Care is also offered in private offices and in the Queen Elizabeth Hospital. Preschool immunization is mandatory, and fluoride mouth-rinse programs are improving dental health. Health inspectors monitor meat and poultry production, and garbage collection is well organized. Life expectancy ranges from 70 to 76 years.

FOR THE TRAVELER

Although U.S. citizens do not need a visa for visits of up to three months, a passport is necessary. Light clothing is best for the tropical climate. Barbados is known for its good food and excellent beaches, which provide a variety of activities. Also of interest is a wide variety of animal and plant life. No immunizations are required. Electric outlets use the same plugs and voltage as in the United States. Contact the Barbados Board of Tourism (800 Second Avenue, 17th Floor, New York, NY 10017) for information regarding travel opportunities. You may also wish to contact the Embassy of Barbados, 2144 Wyoming Avenue NW, Washington, DC 20008.

A *Culturgram* is a product of native commentary and original, expert analysis. Statistics are estimates and information is presented as a matter of opinion. While the editors strive for accuracy and detail, this document should not be considered strictly factual. It is a general introduction to culture, an initial step in building bridges of understanding between peoples. It may not apply to all peoples of the nation. You should therefore consult other sources for more information.

Kingdom of
Belgium

Boundary representations not necessarily authoritative.

BACKGROUND

Land and Climate

With an area of 11,780 square miles (30,510 square kilometers), Belgium is slightly larger than Maryland. It is generally flat, with increasingly hilly terrain near the southeast Ardennes forests. The highest elevation is only 2,275 feet (693 meters). Like the Netherlands, Belgium has a system of dikes and seawalls along the coast to prevent tidal flooding. The climate is mild, damp, and temperate. Summer temperatures range from 54°F to 72°F (12–22°C); winter temperatures generally do not go below 32°F (0°C). Belgium's maritime climate is heavily influenced by the sea. Hence, fog and rain are common and there is little snow in winter. June through September are the most pleasant months.

History

The history of Belgium is one of great achievement in art and commerce, as well as heavy conflict. Before the area was known as Belgium, dukes and counts ruled four basic regions. As the 15th century approached, the French dukes of Burgundy began to consolidate territory and eventually gained all of what is now Belgium, reigning over several decades of prosperity and progress. Belgians were the first to land on the island of Manhattan in 1623 and later founded New York at Albany, calling it *Novum Belgii*. A Belgian named Minuit purchased Manhattan Island from the local Indians for goods worth only 24 dollars.

From the 1600s to 1830, Belgium was a battleground for France, the Netherlands, Austria, Germany, the Protestant-Catholic wars, Napoleon (Waterloo is south of Brussels), and Spain. The territories of Belgium gained independence in 1830 from the Netherlands and became a constitutional monarchy. Although united by the monarchy, divisions existed based on linguistic patterns. Celtic tribes had settled in the south and spoke what later became French. Germanic Franks, speaking low German (basically Dutch), settled in the north. The two groups developed separate cultural and linguistic traditions, but continued to remain together politically.

Because of Belgium's location and topography, it was often subject to battle, as evident in the period preceding independence and again in the 20th century. Despite its claims to neutrality during both World Wars, Belgium was overrun by conquering German armies in 1914 and again in 1940. Some of World War I's fiercest battles were fought in Flanders (northern Belgium). In World War II, the famous "Battle of the Bulge" was fought in Bastogne, where the American 101st Airborne division held off a massive assault by German troops that were attempting to reach the Allied port at Antwerp. This pivotal battle helped secure an Allied victory in the war.

As a consequence of its vulnerability and size, Belgium has had a strong inclination toward European cooperation and integration since the 1940s. It was a founding member of NATO (North Atlantic Treaty Organization) and is that

Copyright © 1994. Brigham Young University. Printed in the USA. All rights reserved. It is against the law to copy, reprint, store in a retrieval system, or transmit any part of this publication in any form by any means for any purpose without written permission from the Publications Division of the David M. Kennedy Center for International Studies, Brigham Young University, PO Box 24538, Provo, UT 84602–4538. *Culturgrams* are available for more than 125 areas of the world. To place an order, to receive a free catalog, or to obtain information on traveling abroad, call toll free (800) 528–6279.

alliance's headquarters. Brussels is also home to the European Union headquarters, making it an important city for business and diplomacy. Domestically, Belgium has also devoted attention to internal cultural conflicts, creating a system to meet the needs of both major linguistic groups and various minorities. In 1960, Belgium granted independence to its African colony called the Belgian Congo (now Zaire).

After World War II, Belgium remained a constitutional monarchy. From 1951 to 1993, King Baudouin I ruled as head of state. Upon his death he was succeeded by King Albert II.

THE PEOPLE

Population

The population of Belgium is more than 10 million and is growing at 0.2 percent. Nearly 95 percent of the people live in cities or towns. Walloons occupy the south (Wallonia) and comprise 33 percent of Belgium's population. The Flemish (55 percent) live in the northern half (Flanders), and the remaining 12 percent are of various mixed groups. The German-speaking minority (1 percent) lives east of Wallonia. Many Italians, Spaniards, and North Africans (mainly Moroccans) work in Belgian industry. Due to Brussels's international importance, nearly 25 percent of its inhabitants are foreigners. In all, almost 10 percent of Belgium's population is non-Belgian.

Language

French and Dutch (Flemish) are the primary official languages of Belgium. French dominates in southern areas and the capital, and Dutch is more prominent in the north. Most Belgians also speak English. Although bilingual Brussels is in Flanders, visitors should speak French or English, as 85 percent of its people speak French. Some towns in Wallonia have retained Latin dialects for festivals and folklore. Eleven percent of the Belgian population is officially bilingual and 1 percent speaks German (also an official language). Because of the two distinct languages, French and Dutch names for the same city are often quite different. For example, the Wallonian city of Mons is referred to in Flanders as Bergen (both names mean "mountains"). Road signs are generally not bilingual but carry only the language of the region in which they stand.

Religion

Belgium is traditionally Roman Catholic, with 75 percent of the population belonging to the church. In fact, most cultural festivals have their origin in, or have been strongly influenced by, Catholicism. The Walloons have a history of being less devoted to the Catholic faith than the Flemish. Most other major world religions can also be found in Belgium. All Catholic, Protestant, Jewish, and Islamic clergy that have official recognition from the government receive their salaries from the state. Private religious schools are also subsidized with government funding.

General Attitudes

A strong work ethic and an appreciation of culture are important to Belgians. The people tend to have tight regional and family ties, holding to the traditions of both. Nevertheless, Belgium's geographical position in Europe also makes the people very cosmopolitan and open to outside interaction. Both the Walloons and the Flemish have a love for life and live it to the fullest, working and playing hard. If one thing distinguishes the Walloons from the Flemish, it is their views on personal relations. The Flemish tend to be more reserved, while the Walloons exhibit greater warmth.

Similar to the situation in other European countries, Belgians are struggling with their feelings toward immigrants. Most people accept them and would like to see their living conditions improved. Yet, very little is done to integrate some immigrant groups into mainstream society. This tends to alienate immigrants, especially their children born in Belgium. Therefore, violence sometimes erupts in immigrant sections of large cities. Adding to the tensions is a small but vocal segment of the population that would like to end immigration from certain countries.

Personal Appearance

Belgians follow European fashions and tend to dress well in public. Tattered or extremely casual attire is reserved for the privacy of the home. Men who wear hats remove them in the building. Suits and dresses are standard in offices.

CUSTOMS AND COURTESIES

Greetings

Belgians greet each other with a handshake, which is often quick with light pressure. However, firmer handshakes are given in some areas. The phrases used for greeting depend on the region. English and German greetings would not be out of place in Brussels and some other cities. Close friends, even younger people, greet each other with three light kisses on the cheek. These are actually more like "kissing the air" while touching cheeks. Only friends and relatives are greeted by first names; otherwise, last names are used. When leaving a group, Belgians usually shake hands with and bid farewell to each person in the group.

Gestures

As in most of Europe, Belgians do not talk with something in their mouths (gum, a toothpick, or food). It is rude to talk with one's hands in one's pant pockets. Good posture is important, and people do not put their feet on tables or chairs. Pointing with the index finger, scratching, yawning, or using a toothpick in public are all avoided. Handkerchiefs are used discreetly.

Visiting

A Belgian host or hostess appreciates a small gift or some flowers from an invited visitor. Chrysanthemums are avoided because they are associated with funerals. Punctuality is important; arriving more than 30 minutes late is considered rude. In rural communities, it may be appropriate to remove one's shoes, if dirty, before entering the home. Personal privacy is important; discussions on personal matters or the linguistic divisions in Belgium should be avoided. Although Belgians tend to be somewhat cautious toward new people, proven friends may become like part of the family.

Eating

Meals are a social and cultural event in Belgium, and they are not to be finished quickly. The continental style of eating, with the knife in the right hand and the fork in the left, is most common. Belgians are thrifty and do not like waste; finishing one's food is expected. In restaurants, one pays at the table and the tip is included in the bill. Still, one may also leave extra change if desired.

LIFESTYLE

Family

Even though the youth are becoming more independent, the family is still a strong and vital part of Belgian society. The average family has one or two children. Married children in Flanders seldom live with their parents, except in rural areas where families share farmland. Holidays and Sundays are often spent taking family excursions. In the past, Wallonian extended families shared a large single house, but today they live separately. Still, they often remain in the same town or city as the rest of their family. In fact, throughout Belgium mobility tends to be low and people settle in or near the towns in which they were raised. This illustrates how important family and community roots are to Belgians. The elderly are generally well respected.

Dating and Marriage

Group dating usually begins by age 16, but it may vary according to regional traditions. Public transportation and bikes are used at first, but when the youth reach driving age (18), private cars are preferred for dating. Young people go to movies, dances, and cafés. Long engagements are common. Living together before or instead of marriage is common. Only civil marriages are accepted by the government. Many families also have a religious ceremony.

Diet

Belgians eat a rich variety of foods, including pork, game birds, fish, cheeses, fruits, vegetables, breads, and soups. Wine, beer, or mineral water is often served with meals. Belgium is famous for mussels, chocolates, 300 varieties of beer, waffles, and french fries—which Belgians claim to have invented. French fries are served with mayonnaise rather than ketchup. Breakfast consists of a hot drink along with rolls or bread with jam or jelly. At midday, a larger meal is eaten. Dinner is usually at 7:00 or 8:00 P.M. Belgians take great pride in the quality of their food and the variety of cuisine—from domestically developed dishes to those adapted from other cultures. Restaurants offer a wide variety of international dishes.

Recreation

Participation in sporting activities is nearly universal; cycling and football (soccer) are most prominent. Belgium's national soccer team competed in the 1994 World Cup. The beach is a popular attraction, as are the beautiful forests in the south. Hunting, fishing, and pigeon racing have large followings in some rural areas. In pigeon racing, male pigeons are released far away from the females and owners bet on which will be the quickest to fly back to its mate. Families enjoy picnics, the theater, and movies. Festivals, local and national, such as *Carnaval*, are popular. Most families take a one-month vacation each year.

All Belgians are intensely proud of their rich cultural heritage, especially in art and architecture. World-renowned masters such as Brueghel, Van Eyck, and Rubens came from Belgian cities. Van Gogh lived 20 years in the small city of Stavelot. While Flemish architecture displays a clear Germanic influence, Wallonian architecture maintains a definite French flavor.

Holidays

Fairs, festivals, parades, and religious holidays are an integral part of the Belgian way of life. Legal holidays include New Year's Day, Easter Monday, Labor Day (1 May), Ascension Day, Whit Monday, Independence Day (21 July), Assumption (15 August), All Saints Day (1 November), Veteran's Day (11 November), and Christmas. *Carnaval* is celebrated in February or March, depending on the city. This festival is characterized by parades, parties, colorful costumes, and traditional ceremonies. It has both medieval and ancient roots: the Catholic church claims it to be the final celebration before the somber period of Lent, but pre-Christian tradition also claims it as a celebration to drive away the evil spirits of winter. Local spring and fall cultural and folklore festivals, such as the annual Cat Festival in Ieper, can be found throughout the country.

Commerce

Because it is still customary to shop daily for fresh food, many open-air markets do business in the larger cities. Butcher shops are plentiful and well maintained. Supermarkets are available, although Belgium still has many small specialty shops. Businesses are open from 9:00 A.M. to 6:00 P.M., with a one or two-hour break for lunch. Once a week (usually Friday), they remain open until 9:00 P.M. The average workweek is 35.8 hours.

SOCIETY

Government

Belgium is a constitutional monarchy under King Albert II, who holds executive power with the prime minister. Day-to-day affairs are handled by the prime minister and his cabinet.

All governments have been coalitions, meaning no single political party has ever had a majority in parliament. Parliament has two chambers: a senate and a more powerful chamber of representatives. The cabinet contains an equal number of French and Dutch-speaking ministers. Elections for parliament are held every five years. The last elections were held in 1991, when Jean-Luc Dehaene became prime minister. All citizens over 17 years old are required to vote. The major political parties are split along linguistic lines.

Under the revised constitutions of 1981, 1988, and 1993, new government bodies were created to give greater decision-making authority to regions and communities in such areas as education, investment, welfare, and public works—allowing different linguistic areas to develop their own policies. The German-speaking minority is also protected.

Economy

Belgium's economy is one of the strongest in the world, although the global recession of the early 1990s caused its annual growth to slip below 2 percent. Belgium's Human Development Index (0.952) ranks it 16 out of 173 countries. Real gross domestic product per capita is $16,381. These figures indicate economic prosperity is available to the majority of the population. The poorest 40 percent of the population earns more than 20 percent of the nation's income.

While less than 3 percent of the labor force is involved in agriculture, Belgium is a major world exporter of wool, beer, and meats, and a key producer of automobiles for major foreign companies. Belgian steel, the principal export, is world famous. However, due to steel and textile market fluctuations in the 1980s, other industries such as engineering, chemicals, food processing, and biotechnology were able to grow. Exports now include items from each of these industries. Diamonds, crystal, and glass are well-established industries. Belgium is strong in foreign trade, partly because the third largest seaport in the world is located at Antwerp and because of its central location among European Union (EU) countries. Most Belgian trade (74 percent) is conducted with EU members. Unemployment is currently under 10 percent. The currency is the Belgian *franc* (BF).

Transportation and Communication

Belgium claims the most complete transportation system in the world, with the fourth most tracks per mile and the fifth most roads per mile (all freeways are lit at night). Coupled with a high population density, this system makes Belgium visible at night to orbiting spacecraft. Trains are the fastest and most practical form of public transportation between cities. Buses and streetcars are widely available, but most people also own cars. Bicycles are still popular for personal transportation. The efficiency of Belgium's postal system is recognized worldwide. Television and radio stations are government owned, although there is an increasing number of private stations. Cable television is available in all parts of the country.

Education

Public education is free and compulsory through age 18. Classes are often very demanding. Many Flemish families send their children to schools operated by the Catholic church and subsidized by the state. A large portion of the federal budget is allotted to education and 20 percent of the population is enrolled in school at any given time. All students learn at least one foreign language. Beginning at age 14, students have opportunities to choose between different career and educational paths; comprehensive examinations are used to determine one's entrance to higher education. Those who do not go on to a university are trained in vocational and technical schools for their chosen careers. Schools for the arts are also popular. Belgium's literacy rate is 99 percent.

Health

Socialized medicine provides for the health care of all citizens. Health concerns are similar to those in the United States, as is the quality of care. There are many English-speaking doctors and dentists. Life expectancy ranges from 73 to 80 years and the infant mortality rate is 7 per 1,000. Although the water is generally safe, Belgians do not drink from the tap. Bottled water is preferred.

FOR THE TRAVELER

U.S. and Canadian citizens do not need a visa for visits of less than three months, but a passport is required. English is widely understood. Art museums are excellent and recommended, as are the Ardennes forests, the castles throughout Belgium, and the beaches in the north. Dual-voltage small appliances and plug adaptors are necessary to use electrical outlets. If flying out of Brussels, hand carry all film, as it will otherwise be damaged by X rays. The Belgium Tourist Information Office in Brussels (Grasmarkt 61, Rue du Marché aux Herbes, Brussels) offers free help in arranging lodging, and provides maps and cultural information. The Belgian Tourist Office in the United States (745 Fifth Avenue, Room 714, New York, NY 10151) also has information. Belgium's embassy is located at 3330 Garfield Street NW, Washington, DC 20008. Consulates, which can provide the same services as the embassy, are located in Atlanta, Chicago, Houston, Los Angeles, and New York.

A *Culturgram* is a product of native commentary and original, expert analysis. Statistics are estimates and information is presented as a matter of opinion. While the editors strive for accuracy and detail, this document should not be considered strictly factual. It is a general introduction to culture, an initial step in building bridges of understanding between peoples. It may not apply to all peoples of the nation. You should therefore consult other sources for more information.

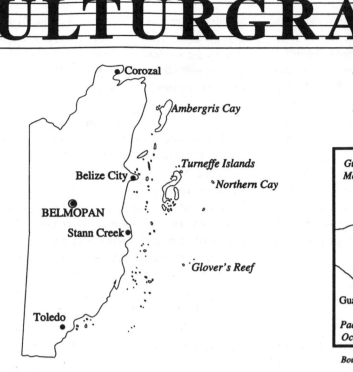

Belize

Boundary representations not necessarily authoritative.

BACKGROUND

Land and Climate

Covering 8,866 square miles (22,963 square kilometers), Belize is about the size of Massachusetts. It is bordered by Mexico, Guatemala, and the Caribbean sea. For such a small area, the landscape is very diverse. The northern half of Belize is flat with marshes and lagoons, while coastal areas are covered by mangrove swamps. The land rises to the south and west, reaching an elevation of about 3,000 feet (915 meters) in the Maya Mountains. Over 60 percent of the country is forested. Beautiful rivers, greenery, the reef, and the *cayes* add to the nation's diversity.

There are two seasons: wet and dry. Humidity is high year-round. The south receives the most rain. Temperatures average between 80°F and 85°F (26–29°C), although they are cooler in the mountains. In Belmopan, the capital, days are hot and nights are cool. Belize is subject to hurricanes between June and October.

History

The Maya thrived in the area between the third and ninth centuries A.D. as part of an empire that included Guatemala, Honduras, Mexico, and El Salvador. Mayan ruins are still evident all over the country. Little is known of the period after the decline of the Mayan empire until the arrival of the first Europeans in the 16th century. The Spanish came in search of gold and found none. British pirates arrived during the 17th century and took advantage of the islands and reef to lure ships onto the rocks for looting. British woodcutters soon followed and brought slaves to help in logging the huge forests. The pirates also turned to woodcutting. The mahogany trade later became very lucrative for these British, who were known as the Baymen. The Spanish (and later Guatemala) continued to lay claim to the region, even though they had never settled it. At the decisive Battle of St. George's Caye in 1798, the Baymen and their slaves fought back Spanish invaders. With the Spanish empire all around them, the Baymen asked Britain for protection. Belize became a crown colony in 1862 and was called British Honduras until 1973.

The British granted Belize self-government in 1964. In 1981, with support from the United Nations and a strong independence movement, Belize became a sovereign country within the Commonwealth of Nations. British troops remained to protect the borders, but after a 1991 agreement in which Guatemala relinquished its claim to Belize, Britain decided (in 1993) to withdraw its troops.

THE PEOPLE

Population

The population of Belize is about 200,000 and it is growing at 2.5 percent. Nearly one-third of all people live in Belize City. Each of the country's six districts has a main town where the bulk of that district's population lives. Many Belizeans live and work abroad.

Belize has a diverse blend of peoples. Creoles account for about 40 percent of the total population, and Mestizos (mixed Spanish and Indian) 33 percent. Creoles, who dominate in Belize City, are persons with some degree of African ancestry. Many are descendants of early European (mostly English or Scottish) settlers and African slaves. The Mestizos are descendants of 19th century immigrants from Mexico.

Copyright © 1994. Brigham Young University. Printed in the USA. All rights reserved. It is against the law to copy, reprint, store in a retrieval system, or transmit any part of this publication in any form by any means for any purpose without written permission from the Publications Division of the David M. Kennedy Center for International Studies, Brigham Young University, PO Box 24538, Provo, UT 84602–4538. *Culturgrams* are available for more than 125 areas of the world. To place an order, to receive a free catalog, or to obtain information on traveling abroad, call toll free (800) 528–6279.

Most rural villages are comprised of Mestizos and Mayas (Kek'chi, Mopan, and Yucatan). The Mayas make up 9.5 percent of the population, while the Garinagu (Caribbean and African mix), who live in the south, comprise 8 percent. East Indians (2.1 percent) have been in Belize for generations and are joined by other minorities, including Mennonites, Arabs, Chinese, North Americans, and others. Refugees from neighboring countries (mainly El Salvador and Guatemala) make up over 5 percent of the total population.

Language

English is the country's official language, and with the exception of people in remote areas, everyone speaks it. Most people also speak Creole, and everyday speech is often a combination of Creole and English. Creole is based in English, but is distinct from it. It is a melodic dialect of English with roots in the days of slavery. It does not have a written tradition, but it does have a definite grammatical structure. Spanish is spoken by Mestizos in the Cayo, Corozal, and Orange Walk districts, but not at all by some other Mestizos. While English must be used in school, Creole or Spanish may be used in the first few years to clarify certain things to children who do not speak English. Mayan groups speak their native languages, and the Garinagu speak Garífuna.

Religion

Freedom of religion is valued and respected in Belize. Most major Western Christian denominations are represented, but the Roman Catholic (60 percent) and Anglican (12 percent) churches dominate. Most Mestizos and Mayas are Catholic. Creoles generally belong to Protestant churches, but many are also Catholic. A number of other Christian faiths are practiced. Schools are generally run by churches, so most people are affiliated with a religion. The only distinct indigeneous religious practices are found among the Maya and Garinagu.

General Attitudes

Belizean society is nonconfrontational. Belizeans are fun-loving, happy, and generally "laid-back." The pace of life is not regulated by a clock so much as it is by events or people. Punctuality may be admired, but it is not generally practiced. For a small nation of so many different ethnic groups and cultures, Belize is relatively free of racial tension. Equality and coexistence are important concepts. Prejudices exist, but not on the level of hatred. A neighborhood in Belize City might consist of every possible ethnic group and have few racial problems. One reason is that the people don't mix; they coexist. But another more powerful reason is that most ethnic groups subscribe in some degree to Creole cultural practices, and Belizean Creoles have adopted aspects of the cultures around them. Most people can speak Belizean Creole, which further enhances harmony.

Although Belize is located in Central America, it claims itself as a Caribbean country and its culture is more closely linked to the Caribbean than to Central America. One attitude it does share with its neighbors is *machismo*, the general habit of men to demonstrate or claim their manliness through macho acts or sexually oriented language. Women generally ignore it and accept it as part of life.

Personal Appearance

Belizeans are concerned about how they look, and U.S. fashions are the most popular in Belize City and other cities. The way a person is dressed is considered a mark of taste and status. Many offices, banks, hotels, and schools have uniforms for their employees. Many men, especially professionals, wear *guayaberas*, which are untucked cotton shirts that sometimes have embroidery.

The Maya often wear traditional clothing. This might include long, brightly colored, heavy skirts with embroidered, white blouses for women, and work clothes and straw hats for men. Garinagu women also tend to retain traditional dress, which might include a simple, colorful blouse, a matching knee-length skirt, and a head scarf. The Mennonites, a group originally from Germany, maintain conservative, simple clothing and do not follow modern fashions.

CUSTOMS AND COURTESIES

Greetings

Belizeans are informal and friendly in greeting (hailing) one another. It is rude to not hail even a slight acquaintance or to not return a hail. When entering a place of business, one also greets the clerk or receptionist. While passing on the street, a simple nod of the head or a wave is acceptable for strangers, and it might be accompanied with "Hey, how?" or "Y' aright?" for acquaintances.

When greetings precede conversation, a handshake is common. Among friends, one might shake by clasping the palms and locking thumbs, or by locking all fingers, or just pressing fists together. Men might pat each other on the back when they shake hands. Mestizos might say ¡Buenos días! (Good morning), ¡Buenas tardes! (Good afternoon), ¡Buenas noches! (Good evening), or just ¡Buenas! any time of day. In Creole, one might use Wa di gwan? (What's happening?) or a number of other phrases.

In formal settings, people address others with proper titles, but first names are used in informal situations. Children usually address their elders by adding Miss or Mister before the name, and they often answer questions by saying, "Yes, ma'am," or "No, sir."

Gestures

Belizeans, especially Creoles and Mestizos, are very animated. Nonverbal communication plays a vital role in all situations. Hand and facial gestures are varied and often complicated. Belizeans might indicate direction with the head or lips. Staring or pointing at someone is rude. Sucking air through the teeth can mean "Give me a break." People might hiss to get one's attention, but this is offensive to many (especially women). To hail a taxi or bus, people move the hand up and down before the vehicle passes.

Visiting

Belizeans are very hospitable. Unannounced visitors are welcomed and made to feel at home, sometimes even if they are strangers. Arranged visits most often occur on weekends.

Before television was introduced in 1980, visiting was an integral part of everyday life. It has since diminished in cities, but it is still important in villages. When visiting a home, it is polite to hail the occupants from the gate or street until they come out. A lengthy conversation might take place over the fence before one is invited into the yard or home. It is considered good manners to offer a guest refreshments, usually at least a drink. Fresh coconut might be offered in areas without refrigeration. Though not expected, it is also polite for the guest to bring the host something.

Eating

Families generally spend mealtime together, although in some Mayan and Mestizo families, women eat after or separate from the men. Conversation is usually limited and mainly carried out between adults. An urban breakfast may include fruit, bread, cheese, beans, eggs, or cereal. Rural breakfasts usually consist of beans. For most, the main meal of the day is dinner, eaten at midday. Schools let out and businesses close so people can eat at home. In cities, people also often go to restaurants. The evening meal, called supper or tea, is lighter than dinner. For some groups (such as the Kek'chi Maya), the main meal is in the evening.

Rural meals are usually less varied than in cities; rice, beans, tortillas, and chicken are often the only available foods. In addition, urban people might eat burgers, *tamales*, fish, and a variety of other dishes.

LIFESTYLE

Family

Families tend to be large and often include the extended family. It is common for grandparents to raise grandchildren after their own children have left Belize for economic or other reasons. Leaving children behind has actually created quite a problem in Belize, as minors have become a majority of the population in Belize City. Adult children usually remain at home until they get married or have a child. Single-parent families are abundant among the Creole population, and women have become the leading family figure in that group. In a Creole village, it is common to have a female head of household and several generations with no adult men.

In most other homes, the father takes the leading role. Younger mothers are more inclined to work outside the home than older women, but women are generally expected to take care of the home and family.

Apartment living is not popular. Most families have their own homes. In rural areas, this may be a simple thatched hut. In coastal towns and villages, houses are built of wood or cement and rest on stilts because of the threat of hurricane flooding. In the interior, house designs are similar, but stilts become less common as elevation increases. Because of the small population, the government can allot land to Belizeans who apply for it, making land and home ownership easier.

Dating and Marriage

Urban dating (courting) tends to follow the same basic pattern as in North America. Schools may prohibit their students from attending popular dating destinations, such as discos, so private parties and school dances are the primary way for young people to meet. Village dating revolves around church activities or dances. Among the Maya and some Mestizos, boys are often only allowed to meet with a girl in her home.

Many Belizean young women become single mothers early and never marry. Likewise, many young men father a number of children by several women and never formally marry. Or they may enter into common-law marriage relationships. For those who do marry formally, a church ceremony is usually followed by a colorful reception that includes food, music, and dancing.

Diet

The most common staple is white rice and kidney beans. That dish may be accompanied by stewed chicken, beef, or fish. A staple among the Mayas is corn, which is usually present in some form (such as *tortillas*) at every meal. Fish and seafood are common on the coast. Other popular foods include *tamales*, *panades* (fried corn shells with beans or fish), meat pies, *escabeche* (onion soup), *chirmole* (soup), and *garnaches* (fried *tortillas* with beans, cheese, and sauce). Fruits (bananas, oranges, mangoes, papayas, limes, and so forth) are abundant and part of the daily diet. Vegetables are more limited and often imported.

Recreation

The most popular sports are football (soccer) and basketball. Organized leagues receive great local support, including fledgling semiprofessional leagues. Women often have softball teams. Volleyball, track and field, and boxing are enjoyed in many areas. Cycling is very popular; the largest athletic event is the annual "cross-country" race held Easter weekend. It is a source of pride and a national tradition that attracts an international group of cyclists.

Belizeans enjoy going to concerts, school fairs, and sometimes movies. There is only one movie theater in Belize City, so most people watch the latest films at home on cable and video. Belizeans appreciate reggae, calypso, *soca*, and various types of American music. A local favorite is called *punta-rock*, which has its roots in the Garífuna culture.

Belize has the world's second largest barrier reef with hundreds of small islands called *cayes* (pronounced "keys"). Urban people like to go to the *cayes* for recreation, although this is not common for rural people.

Holidays

The largest and most celebrated national holidays occur in September. *Carnival* is a large street parade/party that takes place the Saturday before St. George's Caye Day (10 September). Independence Day is 21 September. Various "September Celebrations" are held between these two holidays. Also important is Baron Bliss Day (9 March), in honor of a Portuguese noble who left his wealth to the country and its people. Garífuna Settlement Day (19 November) marks the arrival of the Garinagu to Belize. They originally came from St. Vincent and had settled in Honduras and Guatemala before migrating to Belize.

Christmas is a time for family, religion, and community; it is a quiet holiday for most. Easter weekend is popular for vacations; religious ceremonies are limited. Belize also celebrates Labor Day (1 May) and a number of other Western holidays.

Commerce

Weekday business hours are 8:00 A.M. to 5:00 P.M. Stores generally open again in the evening for two hours. Most businesses close for lunch. Banks close at 1:00 P.M. On Friday, they open again from 3:00 to 6:00 P.M. Larger grocery stores are open all day Saturday and on Sunday morning. Small shops have varying hours and are usually part of someone's home.

SOCIETY

Government

Belize is a three-party democracy with a bicameral legislature. Britain's Queen Elizabeth II is officially the head of state and is represented in Belize by a governor general. The head of government is the prime minister, who is the leader of parliament's dominant party. General elections are held at least every five years, but they can be called sooner if politically necessary. The last elections were in 1993 and Manuel Esquivel was elected prime minister. His term lasts until 1998. The voting age is 18.

Economy

Belize's economy has been expanding since independence and maintains a growth rate of about 5 percent. Large amounts of foreign aid have greatly contributed to this success. About half of the labor force is employed in agricultural production. The country's main exports are sugar, molasses, citrus fruits, bananas, wood and wood products, and clothing. Sugar is the primary cash crop. Many staple foods must be imported. Tourism is the fastest growing source of income, with many people capitalizing on the natural beauty of the country. Environmental tourism and adventure tours are popular. Unemployment tends to run above 10 percent, and even higher for the youth. The currency is the Belizean dollar (Bz$). Belize's Human Development Index (0.689) ranks it 82 out of 173 countries. Real gross domestic product per capita is estimated at $3,000. These figures indicate economic prosperity is lacking for a majority of people.

Transportation and Communication

The Northern, Western, and Hummingbird highways are paved and link most cities. Getting to remote areas is more difficult, as roads are rough. The national bus system is inexpensive and widely used. In the cities and towns, most people get around by walking or riding bikes. The number of private cars is growing. Several small, private domestic airlines provide commuter and tourist travel.

In major towns, most people have telephones; villages usually have at least one phone. Radio and television broadcasts together reach nearly all Belizeans, who remain informed not only on local matters but on regional and international news as well.

Education

The vast majority of primary and secondary schools are church operated, even though they receive large subsidies from the government. Students pay fees, buy their own books and supplies, and must usually wear uniforms. Because some families cannot afford these costs, a few government schools exist to provide their children an education, but there are usually not enough spaces to accommodate all. Children are required to attend school until standard six (equivalent to the eighth grade in the U.S.), but secondary schooling is not required. Many students are not able to complete their primary education due to cost, family obligation, or a number of other factors. The official literacy rate is above 90 percent, but the actual figure is closer to 50 or 60 percent.

Space in secondary schools is limited and dependent on passing the Belize National Selection Exam. Those who complete a secondary education can attend junior college, teacher's college, or the University College of Belize. The government is focusing reform efforts on standardizing curriculum in all schools and providing more vocational education in each district.

Health

Health care is accessible to all citizens, although many preventable diseases still afflict the country. Each district has a small hospital and there is a large hospital in Belize City. A health worker is assigned to each village, but might not always be present. Clinics and private doctors serve those who can afford to pay. Water is generally clean; water safety is only a problem in some rural areas. The infant mortality rate is 23 per 1,000. Life expectancy averages between 67 and 73 years.

FOR THE TRAVELER

U.S. citizens need a valid passport to enter Belize, but a visa is not necessary for stays of up to 30 days. Belize has a great deal to offer tourists, from snorkeling, fishing, and relaxing in the spectacular cayes to beautiful scenery, Mayan ruins, and various wildlife inland. Avoid wearing expensive jewelry in public or going out alone after dark. For more information, contact the Belize Tourist Bureau, 15 Penn Plaza, 415 7th Avenue, New York, NY 10001. You may also wish to contact the Embassy of Belize, 2535 Massachusetts Avenue NW, Washington, DC 20008.

A *Culturgram* is a product of native commentary and original, expert analysis. Statistics are estimates and information is presented as a matter of opinion. While the editors strive for accuracy and detail, this document should not be considered strictly factual. It is a general introduction to culture, an initial step in building bridges of understanding between peoples. It may not apply to all peoples of the nation. You should therefore consult other sources for more information.

Republic of
Bolivia

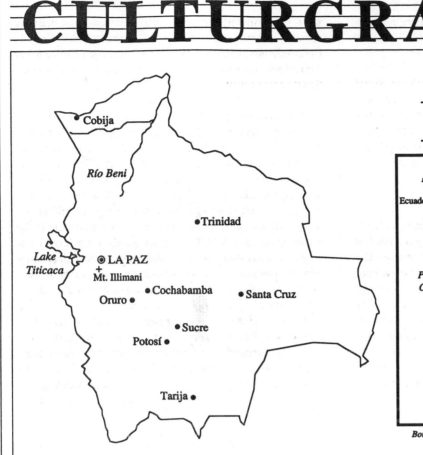

Boundary representations not necessarily authoritative.

THE AMERICAS

BACKGROUND

Land and Climate

Located in the heart of South America, Bolivia is a land-locked country. With 424,165 square miles (1,098,581 square kilometers), it is almost three times the size of Montana. There are three distinct geographical areas: the high, cold, and dry mountain-rimmed Altiplano to the west; the medium-elevation valleys in the middle; and the low, wet, hot, forested plains of the east and northeast. Grasslands are common on these plains, which makes the area good for cattle ranching. Forests cover about half of Bolivia. The famous Lake Titicaca, the highest navigable body of water in the world (12,500 feet—3,749 meters), lies on the north end of the Altiplano. Only a short distance from La Paz, the lake is shared equally by Bolivia and Peru.

Surrounding the Altiplano are the mineral-rich Andes mountains, which climb to over 21,000 feet (6,400 meters) and are permanently covered with snow above 16,000 feet (4,877 meters). These mountains are known for their beauty, especially Mount Illimani near La Paz. The eastern foothills are home to a surprisingly diverse variety of plants and animals. For example, scientists have found over 700 bird species there. Although Bolivia experiences four seasons, they are not all perceptible in some areas because elevation plays a more important role in climate than seasons do. Summer, which lasts from December to March, is the rainy season. Winter is from June to September. In La Paz, the average annual temperature is 65°F (18°C).

History

Aymara and other Indians were conquered in the 1400s by Incan armies, bringing the area into the Inca empire. The Incas introduced the Quechua language and a new social system. The Spanish began their conquest in 1532, and by 1538 all of present-day Bolivia was under Spanish control. Known as Upper Peru during Spanish rule, Bolivia was one of the first colonies to rebel. Political uprisings occurred frequently in the 1700s, but they were always crushed. It wasn't until the independence movement of 1809 that Upper Peru began to see success. After a 16-year War of Independence, the area gained independence on 6 August 1825 and was named after its liberator, Simón Bolívar.

Bolivia's first president was overthrown in 1828 and the country experienced decades of factional strife, revolutions, and military dictatorships. Much of its original territory was lost between 1879–1935 in wars with Chile, Brazil, and Paraguay. The War of the Pacific (1879–84) was most significant because Bolivia lost its access to the sea. This event basically doomed the economy, and Bolivians regularly appeal to Chile for the return of the territory. With a seaport, Bolivia could increase international trade and improve its economy.

The government attempted to improve conditions and stabilize the country during the 1950s, but a military coup

Copyright © 1994. Brigham Young University. Printed in the USA. All rights reserved. It is against the law to copy, reprint, store in a retrieval system, or transmit any part of this publication in any form by any means for any purpose without written permission from the Publications Division of the David M. Kennedy Center for International Studies, Brigham Young University, PO Box 24538, Provo, UT 84602–4538. *Culturgrams* are available for more than 125 areas of the world. To place an order, to receive a free catalog, or to obtain information on traveling abroad, call toll free (800) 528–6279.

ended the reforms in 1964. A series of coups brought various dictatorships to power, each of them oppressive to the majority Indian populations. In elections held in late 1979, none of the candidates received a majority vote. Congress gave the presidency to Walter Guevara Arze, but he was overthrown by a military coup that same year. The military government changed hands once again and a national election was finally held in 1980. Hernán Siles Zuazo won the race, but he was overthrown less than a month later by General Luis García Meza Tejada. His regime instituted a wave of terror, and he was replaced a year later. Under terrible economic conditions, characterized by spiraling inflation that peaked at 11,700 percent, it became clear that military governments could not effectively lead the country.

A representative democracy was finally established in August 1985 with the election of President Víctor Paz Estenssoro. He reduced inflation to below 20 percent and stabilized the economy. His term ended peacefully in 1989, when Jaime Paz Zamora was elected. This peaceful transition of power signified Bolivia's commitment to civilian rule. National elections in 1993 marked another peaceful transfer of power, when Gonzalo Sánchez de Lozada was elected president. Significantly, his vice president, Victor Hugo Cárdenas, is Aymara. He is the first indigenous person to rise to such a high office in Latin America. He, along with a variety of native groups, seeks social change that will allow native peoples to fully participate in the economy, the government, and other social institutions without discrimination.

THE PEOPLE
Population
The population of Bolivia is 7.5 million and is growing at 2.3 percent annually. About half of the population lives in urban areas. Nearly 70 percent of the total population is composed of native Americans, including Quechua (30 percent), Aymara (25 percent), Guaraní, Mojeño, Chimane, and other smaller groups. About 25 percent of the people are *mestizo* (or *criollo*), who are of mixed indigenous and European heritage, and another 5 percent are of European descent.

Language
Spanish, Quechua, and Aymara are all official languages. Spanish is used in government, schooling, and business and is spoken as the mother tongue by about 40 percent of the population. The Indians speak their own languages, but they also often speak Spanish.

Religion
Approximately 95 percent of the people are Roman Catholic, although there is an active Protestant minority and various other religions, including some indigenous to the Indians. Bolivians also mix Aymaran, Quechuan, and other religious traditions with Catholic beliefs. *Pachamama,* or goddess Mother Earth, is very popular. People often toast to her or bless things in her name. For instance, a *ch'alla* consists of blessing any material possession or event by offering symbolic articles and alcohol to *Pachamama* and *Achachila*, god of the mountains.

General Attitudes
Time is generally not as important in Bolivia as in other countries. People enjoy getting as much pleasure out of an experience as possible, with less regard to how much time they spend. Kindness, gentleness, and concern for another's welfare are the keys to friendship in Bolivia. The people like to remind others that they are also "Americans" because they live in South America. Visitors from the United States should avoid saying, "In America . . ." but should use, "In the United States. . . ."

Tensions exist in society between the ruling class—those of European or mixed heritage—and the Indian groups. The latter have often been barred from participating in society because of their race. Those who have wanted to assimilate into society have had to change their way of dress and speak Spanish. Many also adopt Spanish names. The indigenous movement would like to extend all the benefits of a democratic society to all of the peoples in the country without forcing them to abandon their traditions. The ruling class feels that other groups should assimilate into society by leaving tradition behind and adopting a more Westernized culture.

Personal Appearance
Bolivians wear different clothing depending on where they live and their social class. Generally, people in urban areas wear Western-style clothing. Some women wear a *pollera* (very full colorful skirt). Women from rural areas wear a *pollera* with a shawl *(manta)*. They may also wear hats (bowler derbies) that differ from area to area; one can tell where a person comes from by looking at their hat. Women often wear their hair in braids. Some Indians make their own clothing out of wool. Common colors include red, black, and off-white. Indian men might wear shin-length pants, a shirt, and a thick leather belt. They often wear a *poncho* and a hat. Indian women wear a long, dark-colored dress tied at the waste with a colorful belt. A small shoulder cape and oval hat may also be worn.

CUSTOMS AND COURTESIES
Greetings
Spanish-speaking Bolivians greet friends and acquaintances with a cheerful *¡Buenos días!* (Good morning), *¡Buenas tardes!* (Good afternoon), or *¡Buenas noches!* (Good evening). *Hola* (Hi) or *¿Cómo estás?* (How are you?) are also common. The title *Señor* (Mr.), *Señora* (Mrs.), or *Señorita* (Miss) is added for first-time introductions or in greeting strangers (such as a store owner). *Señorita* is used for any woman, unless she is older or the speaker knows she is married. Greetings are usually accompanied by a handshake. However, if a person's hand is wet or dirty, an arm or elbow may be offered to shake.

Bolivians maintain little personal space and stand close to another person during conversation. The *abrazo* is a greeting used frequently by close friends and relatives. It consists of a hug, a handshake, two or three pats on the shoulder, and another handshake. Women friends often embrace and kiss each other on the cheek. They commonly walk arm in arm. Teenage girls may also hold hands. First names are not used between strangers. Common Spanish farewells are *Hasta luego* (Until soon) or *Hasta mañana* (Until tomorrow). Friends use the casual *Chau* or *Chau, chau*. *Adiós* usually implies a good-bye for a long period of time; it might be used in seeing someone off on a trip.

Gestures

Bolivians often use hands, eyes, and facial expressions to communicate. To beckon children, the fingers are waved with the palm down. Patting someone on the shoulder is a sign of friendship. A raised hand, palm outward and fingers extended, twisting quickly from side to side, is a way of saying "no"—a gesture often used by taxi and bus drivers when their vehicles are full. Waving the index finger is another way to say "no." The mouth should be covered when yawning or coughing. Eye contact in conversation is essential. Avoiding another's eyes shows suspicion or lack of trust; it may also be interpreted as shyness.

Visiting

Bolivians enjoy visiting one another. It is customary to drop by unannounced as a way of showing someone you are thinking of them. Arranged visits are also common. Hosts try to make their guests as comfortable as possible. Flowers and small gifts are generally given to the host upon arrival. Visitors might also be presented with gifts. They are not opened in the presence of the giver. When invited to dinner, a guest is expected to try all types of food offered. Compliments on the food are appreciated. Compliments given during the meal instead of after will bring a second helping. Guests address their hosts by first name, preceded by *Don* (for men) or *Doña* (for women). This allows a guest to show respect for, and familiarity with, the hosts.

Upon arrival, visitors are invited inside the home and offered a drink or light refreshments; it is impolite to refuse them. It is also impolite to start a conversation on the doorstep. Visitors staying a few days are welcomed with a hug and kiss on the cheek. A special meal is provided as a welcoming gesture and, if possible, all family members are present to greet the guest. Guests are not asked how long they will stay, as this is interpreted as a desire to have them leave soon.

Eating

Generally, one is not excused from the table until all are finished eating. It is proper to remain at the table to enjoy the company of the others. Everyone (including guests) is expected to eat everything on the plate. It is not polite to eat meat with the hands; utensils are used. In restaurants, the waiter may be summoned by raising the hand, clapping two or three times, or snapping the fingers softly. The host usually insists on paying for the meal. A tip is generally included in the bill (10 percent), but leaving a little extra (up to 5 percent) is polite. Eating on the streets is in poor taste.

LIFESTYLE

Family

Among the middle and upper classes, parents generally limit families to one or two children. Poorer families are traditionally much larger, but many children die in infancy. The family is the central unit in the social system. Although many rural couples live together in common-law arrangements, marriage relationships are still more common in cities. Children almost always live with their parents until they are married and sometimes even after marriage.

Most women work in the home. Because many are without modern conveniences, the work is difficult and requires more time. This can prevent women from pursuing work in the labor force. Maids are commonly employed by the upper and middle classes. While the father makes most family decisions, the mother exerts a lot of influence on household affairs. Although children are taught the importance of education, illiteracy is still high among the poor. Children are generally well disciplined and share in family responsibilities. The elderly live with their children's families.

Dating and Marriage

Chaperoned dating begins at about age 15. Dating is preceded by boys flirting with girls. They may even flirt with strangers on the street. The process of getting acquainted, dating seriously, and being engaged can take up to three years. Men marry between the ages of 20 and 25, while women marry from 19 to 23. People usually do not marry until they have acquired some sort of financial security or property. For a marriage to be legal, a civil ceremony must be performed. However, most also have a religious ceremony; a dance and reception generally follow the wedding. Because weddings are expensive, many rural people cannot afford them and choose common-law marriages instead. Bolivians wear their wedding rings on the right hand.

Diet

Potatoes, rice, soups, and fruits are common staples in the Bolivian diet. Many Bolivian foods are fried and very spicy. Milk and cheese are commonly eaten by most of the people. Breakfast usually consists of tea or coffee, bread, and sometimes cheese. Lunch is the main meal, with soup and a main course being served. In the cities, people enjoy *salteñas* (meat or chicken pies with potatoes, olives, and raisins) at about 10:00 A.M. Potatoes are the main Bolivian staple and there are hundreds of varieties prepared in many different ways. Fine restaurants serving European cuisine can be found in major cities, such as the capital, La Paz.

Recreation

Fútbol (soccer) is a popular sport enjoyed through the country. Bolivia's national soccer team competed in the 1994 World Cup. Other popular sports vary with the region. Leisure activities include watching television (in urban areas), visiting (more so in rural areas), and attending festivals. Dancing and singing are popular at various events.

Music is an integral part of the Bolivian culture. Played and promoted throughout the world, Bolivian music can be divided into three types: fast, happy rhythms from the east and northeast; slow, romantic, and melancholic rhythms from the Andes Mountains; and happy, romantic rhythms from the central valleys. A common instrument is the *charango*, a twelve-string, convex, guitar-like instrument made from armadillo shells. A *zampona* is many different flutes joined together to make a variety of notes.

Holidays

Holidays include New Year's Day, *Carnival* (the Saturday before Ash Wednesday), *Día del Mar* (Sea Day, 23 March), Holy Week before Easter (March or April), Father's Day (19 March), Labor Day (1 May), Mother's Day (27 May), Independence Day (6 August), All Saints Day (1 November), and Christmas. On Christmas Eve, children place their old shoes in a window for Santa Claus to take them in exchange for new gifts.

Dancing, costumes, and pouring water on people are common during *Carnival*; a favorite treat at this festival is *confite* (candy stuffed with nuts or fruit). On Labor Day, citizens donate their labor to help improve their communities. Each of the nine provinces also celebrates regional holidays rich in folklore. In fact, Bolivia has been called "The Capital of Folklore." These local events are noted for their wonderful music and colorful costumes. Almost every *pueblo* (village) has its fascinating and unique *fiestas* in honor of its patron saint or the Virgin Mary. Some, especially in small hamlets far from the capital, are quite exotic.

Commerce

Business is generally conducted Monday through Friday from 9:00 A.M. to noon and 3:00 to 7:00 P.M. The break allows people to have lunch and relax.

SOCIETY

Government

A president, vice president, and cabinet form the executive branch. The national congress (*Congreso Nacional*) consists of a chamber of Senators and Chamber of Deputies. The Supreme Court forms the independent judicial branch. Elections are held every four years. Voting is mandatory beginning at age 18 for married individuals and 21 for singles.

Economy

Bolivia's Human Development Index (0.398) ranks it 122 out of 173 countries. Real gross domestic product per capita is $1,572. These figures indicate that a majority of the people do not have access to a sufficient income. The lack of a seaport and past political instability have contributed to Bolivia's economic troubles. Current economic growth is, however, encouraging. In 1992 it was 4 percent. Hoping to stimulate growth, the government is promoting foreign investment through its Investment Guarantee Law. Unemployment is about 10 percent.

Government policies encourage the development of small business and exports. With natural resources such as tin, natural gas, crude oil, zinc, silver, gold, lead, and tungsten, mining is one of the major industries. Unfortunately, with 50 percent of the labor force engaged in agriculture, coca (used in making cocaine) has become the impoverished nation's largest cash crop. In fact, Peru and Bolivia together produce 90 percent of the world's coca. The government, however, works closely with the United States to fight drug trafficking. This is not only difficult because of the money earned from the drug trade, but because the coca leaf has been a traditional crop for centuries. It has many legitimate uses in society, including medicinal and dietary, and is a basic part of the culture. Other industries include petroleum, coffee and food production, textiles, and timber. The standard monetary unit is the *boliviano* ($Bs).

Transportation and Communication

Throughout its modern history, Bolivia has been handicapped by its isolated inland location and lack of internal transportation and communication. The difficulties of overland transportation have been alleviated by the development of air transport and railways. Buses, taxis, and trains are the most common forms of transportation. Buses are often crowded, so men offer their seats to women. More expensive minivans are faster and less crowded. Taxis will often stop to pick up other passengers going the same way. Only a few major highways are paved. Airlines connect major cities and allow one to avoid travel over rugged terrain. Several radio and television stations are in operation.

Education

For four centuries, a rigid social structure reserved education for only the elite. However, the educational system has expanded greatly since the 1930s and many schools have been built in rural areas. Schooling is free and compulsory for ages six to fourteen. Yet, while illiteracy is declining, problems still exist. Less than half of all children complete their primary education, and only about one third go on to secondary school. Many indigenous children cannot receive instruction in their own languages, as Spanish is used to teach in all schools. The literacy rate is about 78 percent; it is higher for urban areas and men. Since 1985, six universities have been built, bringing the total to fifteen. Two entrance exams must be passed to be admitted to a university.

Health

Because of disease and widespread poverty, the infant mortality rate in Bolivia is 77 per 1,000. The average life expectancy ranges from 60 to 65 years. Sanitation facilities are poor and tap water is not potable. There have been recent efforts by local nurses and doctors to train community health care workers (*Responsables Populares de Salud*) in basic skills. These trainees help serve the needs of the rural population. Still, traditional medicine is used in many rural areas to cure illness. Only about half of the population has adequate access to medical care.

FOR THE TRAVELER

U.S. visitors must have a passport, but a visa is only required if a tourist is staying longer than 30 days. Bolivia is in the yellow fever endemic zone; vaccinations are recommended. Visitors entering from other infected areas must have proof of vaccination. Malaria is also a problem that should be guarded against. Travel groups have rated La Paz as one of the best travel bargains because it is inexpensive and the Andes mountains are breathtakingly beautiful. However, one should take caution: the extremely high altitude of La Paz (11,910 feet—3,360 meters) means there is less oxygen than most people are used to, and travelers may be weak and short of breath. Plenty of rest is recommended. The Bolivian remedy for altitude sickness is to drink a lot of water and coca tea. It is also a good idea to avoid a big evening meal, since digestion is also affected. Eat a main meal at lunch. Dual-voltage small appliances or an adaptor and plug adaptor kits are necessary to use electrical outlets. For more information, you may want to contact the Embassy of Bolivia, 3014 Massachusetts Avenue NW, Washington, DC 20008. The embassy's phone number for travel information is (202) 232–4828.

A *Culturgram* is a product of native commentary and original, expert analysis. Statistics are estimates and information is presented as a matter of opinion. While the editors strive for accuracy and detail, this document should not be considered strictly factual. It is a general introduction to culture, an initial step in building bridges of understanding between peoples. It may not apply to all peoples of the nation. You should therefore consult other sources for more information.

CULTURGRAM '95™

Federative Republic of
Brazil

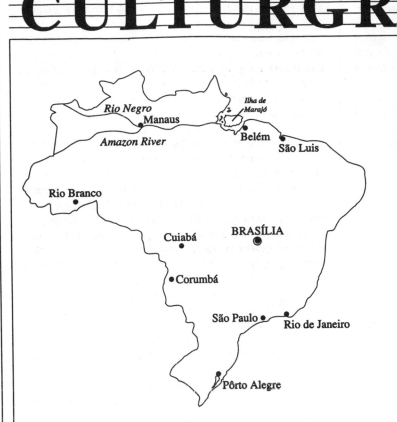

Boundary representations not necessarily authoritative.

BACKGROUND

Land and Climate

Brazil is the fifth largest country in the world and the sixth most populous. At 3,286,470 square miles (8,511,965 square kilometers), it is larger than the continental United States and makes up half of South America. Forests cover 65 percent of its territory and include the world's largest tropical rain forest in the Amazon River Basin. The Amazon is the world's largest river. Recent concerns over the destruction of this region for development have prompted a global effort to save the rain forests. Less than 5 percent of Brazil lies above three thousand feet. The country is south of the equator and has a mostly tropical climate. Humidity is high in coastal and forest regions, but the highlands (such as around São Paulo) have a more moderate climate. The south is more temperate than the north. The warmest month is January; the coolest is July. Freezing temperatures are possible in the southernmost areas.

History

Brazil does not have a written history prior to the arrival of Europeans, but various groups did inhabit the area when Pedro Álvarez Cabral arrived in 1500 and claimed the region for Portugal. Brazil was colonized by Portugal. The French and Dutch both attempted to establish colonies but were eventually driven out. Spain actually controlled Brazil from 1580 to 1640 because Spain had conquered Portugal. Colonization took several decades and expansion did not really begin until after 1650.

When Napoleon captured Lisbon, Portugal, in 1808, the royal family fled to Brazil and established Rio de Janeiro as the seat of the Portuguese Empire. At this time, Brazil ceased to be a colony but was part of the Kingdom of Portugal and Brazil. The royal family returned to Portugal in 1821, leaving Dom Pedro I to govern Brazil. He declared Brazil's independence in 1822 after people in Portugal demanded that Brazil be returned to colonial status. He was followed by his son, Dom Pedro II, who was deposed in 1889 by a military coup.

Since that time, the military has seized control five times, although with little violence. The dictator Getúlio Vargas ruled from 1930 to 1945, after which elected presidents governed. Another coup in 1964 gave the military control again. After the return to civilian rule, a president was appointed by an electoral college in 1985, but Tancredo Neves died before assuming office. His vice president, José Sarney took office. A new constitution was ratified in 1988. Elections in 1989 brought conservative Fernando Collor de Mello to office as the first directly elected president in 29 years; he took office in March 1990. Collor began an austerity campaign to revive the economy. Unfortunately for Brazil, the "shock"

Copyright © 1994, Brigham Young University. Printed in the USA. All rights reserved. It is against the law to copy, reprint, store in a retrieval system, or transmit any part of this publication in any form by any means for any purpose without written permission from the Publications Division of the David M. Kennedy Center for International Studies, Brigham Young University, PO Box 24538, Provo, UT 84602–4538. *Culturgrams* are available for more than 125 areas of the world. To place an order, to receive a free catalog, or to obtain information on traveling abroad, call toll free (800) 528–6279.

therapy crippled the economy, and many measures only covered Collor's corrupt activities. Upon discovering this in 1992, legislative leaders called for Collor's impeachment. Collor resigned in December 1992 before full impeachment proceedings could be carried out. The entire process was an historic test of democracy since it marked the first time a leader was removed from office by legal, constitutional means. Itamar Franco, Collor's vice president, assumed the presidency until elections in October 1994. The man defeated by Collor in 1990, Luiz Inácio Lula da Silva, is expected to win the presidential election. A socialist and peasant's son, Lula (as he is known in Brazil) has promised to end corruption and achieve economic stability.

THE PEOPLE
Population
The population of Brazil is approximately 156.6 million and is growing at a rate of 1.3 percent annually. Ninety percent of the people live on 10 percent of the land—mostly in the 200-mile-wide (322 kilometers) east coast region. In fact, the two largest cities of the southeast, São Paulo and Rio de Janeiro, together hold more than 16 million people. Nearly 50 percent of the people are younger than age 20. Brazilians of European (mostly Portuguese) descent make up 55 percent of the population, while 32 percent are of mixed heritage, and 11 percent have Black African ancestry.

There are only about 150,000 native Indians in Brazil, many of whom inhabit the Amazon region (including some that have never been contacted by modern society). But many of the mixed peoples have some Indian heritage through intermarriage. Groups of German, Italian, and Japanese immigrants settled in the southern half of the country and still maintain ethnic communities. In fact, Brazil is home to the largest cohesive community of Japanese outside of Japan. The black population descended from African slaves brought to Brazil before the 1880s; they live mostly in northeastern provinces such as Bahia. All groups have had an influence on Brazilian culture through religion, food, festivals, music, and dances.

Language
Portuguese is Brazil's official language. English, German, and French are popular second languages. Although Spanish is also generally understood by Portuguese speakers, some Brazilians may be offended when deliberately spoken to in Spanish. A visitor should try to speak some Portuguese. The Indians speak a variety of more than 100 Amerindian languages.

Religion
Brazil is traditionally a strong Roman Catholic country, at one time claiming membership of nearly 95 percent of the large population. Data from 1993 indicates membership to be dropping, now standing at about 73 percent. Other Christian churches are growing rapidly, and some 20 percent of Brazilians belong to various groups, mostly Protestant. Under Portuguese rule, the Catholic church had great influence over politics. Since the founding of the Republic in 1889, however, there has been a separation of church and state, and religious freedom is guaranteed. Although Brazilians consider themselves quite religious, most attend church only on special occasions. In the northeast, many practice Afro-Brazilian religions (such as *Candomblé*) that combine tribal beliefs with Catholicism.

General Attitudes
Brazilians are friendly, warm, and free-spirited. They are also outgoing and enjoy being around others. Men tend to stare at and make comments about women passing by. This is not considered rude and is generally ignored by the women. Brazilians are often opinionated and will argue for their conviction with a vigor that may seem like anger, but is not. Brazilians tend to view time more as a sequence of events rather than hours and minutes (except in São Paulo). For this reason they appear to have an extremely casual attitude about time in most regions of the nation. People are polite in crowds and shoving is considered discourteous. A pessimism about the economy affects people's outlook on life—evident in current literature and plays, street riots, and increasing emigration. Still, Brazilians have overcome difficult circumstances in the past, and they can do so again.

Personal Appearance
Brazilians prefer to wear European fashions, specifically Italian and French, in the cities. The people are very fashion conscious, especially women, and wear the latest styles—sometimes even a season before the Europeans because of the opposite seasons south of the equator. Shoes are well kept and polished. Manicures and pedicures are popular. In rural regions, more traditional clothing is common, especially among the native Indians.

CUSTOMS AND COURTESIES
Greetings
Brazilians greet each other with a handshake; good friends often embrace. Women often kiss each other on alternating cheeks, although they may actually touch cheeks and "kiss the air." Common terms are *Tudo bem?* (Is everything fine?) or *Como vai?* (How are you?). Young friends greet each other with a simple *Oi* (Hi). When joining or leaving a small group, it is polite to shake hands with all who are present. A common term for parting is *Tcháu* (Good-bye); also common is *Até logo* (See you soon).

Gestures
The American "OK" sign, with the thumb and index finger forming a circle, is an offensive gesture. The "thumbs up" sign is used to show approval. To beckon, all fingers of the hand wave with the palm facing down. To get someone's attention from a distance, people say "pssssst." Whistling at people is considered rude. Using a toothpick in public is rude if not done with discretion—by covering the hand holding the toothpick with the other hand.

Visiting

Brazilians enjoy visiting with one another. Their tropical climate allows for much time outdoors, including chatting outside late into the evening. When invited to a home, guests generally arrive several minutes late, except perhaps in São Paulo. If invited to dinner, a gift of candy, wine, or a small figurine is appropriate. One is generally expected to stay at least two hours. All visitors will be offered coffee or some other refreshment, or may even be invited to share in a meal, if in progress. While conversation is enjoyed by Brazilians, controversial subjects (politics, religion) should be avoided in social gatherings. It is rude to ask personal questions, such as about age or salary.

Eating

Brazilians eat in the continental style, with the knife held in the right hand and the fork remaining in the left. People wash their hands before eating and refrain from touching food while eating. One's mouth is wiped each time before drinking. After-meal conversation often takes place over a cup of strong black coffee (*cafezinho*). In restaurants, the waiter is called by holding up the index finger or by softly saying *garçon*. The check is requested with the phrase *A conta, por favor*. While the tip is usually included in the bill, extra change may be left, and if the tip is not in the bill, 10 to 15 percent is customary.

LIFESTYLE

Family

Families are traditionally large and may include the extended family. The elderly who cannot care for themselves live with their children because it is improper to send them to a nursing home. The family is strong and is led by the father. The mother does have an influence in decisions, however, especially those affecting the home. Children usually only leave the home when they marry and rarely before. Men may leave early for employment reasons, but it is not uncommon for them to live at home until they are 30 if unmarried. Family members rely on each other for assistance and enjoy being together. Among the youth, however, some of these values are becoming less important. While middle income families live in modest homes or apartments, the poor often lack the basic necessities of life, including food, sanitation, and shelter. Women and youth often work to help support families.

Dating and Marriage

Group dating starts at about age 14. Couples gradually emerge from the group. Serious dating and engagements may last as long as two or three years. Traditional families expect the young man to ask the girl's father for permission to be her boyfriend. Weddings may include two ceremonies: a legal civil ceremony and an optional religious ceremony. Wedding parties are lavish and elegant, with much food, drink, and music.

Diet

Breakfast usually consists of *café com leite* (coffee with milk), bread, cheese or marmalade, and butter. Lunch and dinner are the main meals and may include beans, rice, meat, salad, fruit (some varieties unknown in North America, such as *imbu*), potatoes, and bread. Local favorites vary with the region. Brazilian food is tasty. In Bahia and other provinces, foods are often spiced with *dendê* oil (palm oil) and, for North American visitors, may be difficult to eat. In Rio de Janeiro, the favorite is *feijoada* (black beans with beef, pork, sausage, tongue, and even sometimes a pig's ears, nose, and tail). Areas in the south enjoy *churrasco*, a barbecue with a variety of meats. Popular in many areas is *bife à cavalo come fritas* (meat with egg and french fries). The people drink plenty of coffee and *mate*, an herbal tea.

Recreation

The national sport is soccer (*futebol*); Brazil's soccer teams are among the finest in the world. In fact, the people have such a passion for soccer that they have been known to close businesses and schools during the World Cup or important national competitions. Brazil's team competed in the 1994 World Cup. The legendary soccer player Pelé is from Brazil. Basketball and volleyball are also popular. Because the nation has many fine beaches, boating, fishing, and swimming are enjoyed by Brazilians and tourists alike. Brazilians are avid fans of auto racing. Brazilians in major cities often join athletic clubs for recreation. Family vacations are often taken the week before Easter or during school breaks. Traditional dances and festivals are popular and vary with the region.

Holidays

New Year's Eve is a time for large parties, but *Candomblé* tradition also honors the sea goddess at this time. People dress in white and blue to honor *Iemanjá* and to get energy for the new year. Flowers and candles are placed on beaches as part of the celebration. *Carnival*, a five-day festival preceding Ash Wednesday, is the most famous holiday in Brazil. It is marked by street parades, *Samba* and *Bloco* dancing, parties, drinking, costumes, conga drums, and music. Some spend months preparing and saving for *Carnival*. Tiradentes Day (21 April) celebrates the death of Joaquim José da Silva Xavier, a dentist and nationalist who was known as Tiradentes and died in the struggle for independence.

The *Festas Junina* (June festivals) coincide with the feasts of St. John and St. Peter, and are celebrated with local fair-type activities. During the Christmas celebration, Christmas Eve is the day when the big meal (turkey or ham) is eaten and gifts are exchanged. Gifts from Santa Claus are found on Christmas, but all other gifts are given the day before. Other holidays include Easter, Labor Day (1 May), Independence Day (7 September), Memorial Day (2 November), and Republic Day (15 November).

Commerce

A *padaria* is like a bar because it serves alcoholic drinks, but it is also comparable to a neighborhood store where milk, bread, sandwiches, sweets, and soft drinks can be purchased. These bars are open as early as 5:00 A.M. Most other stores are open from 8:00 A.M. to 6:00 P.M. weekdays, and until noon on

Saturday, while some larger stores remain open until 9:00 P.M. on Fridays. Supermarkets are open every day of the week. Some business offices and stores close from noon to 2:00 P.M. for the afternoon meal. The 24-hour clock is used to schedule events (3:00 P.M.=15.00).

SOCIETY

Government

Brazil is a federal republic consisting of 26 states and one federal district (Brasília, the capital). Each state is technically autonomous, with a legislative body and elected governor, but all rights not delegated to the state are reserved by the federal government. The president is head of state and government. The National Congress has a Federal Senate and a Chamber of Deputies. In April 1993, citizens were asked by referendum to determine whether the country should switch to a parliamentary system, with a prime minister as head of government. Voters elected to retain the current presidential system. Voting is universal and compulsory for ages 18 to 70. Voluntary voting is allowed for 16 and 17-year-olds and for those older than 70.

Economy

Brazil has the largest economy in South America, but the benefits of its overall prosperity do not reach a significant portion of the population. The country's Human Development Index (0.730) ranks it 70 out of 173 countries. Real gross domestic product per capita is $4,718, which has tripled in the last generation. However, income distribution is highly unequal: the poorest 40 percent of households earns less than 10 percent of the nation's income. Poverty is a serious problem in both rural and urban areas. Due to the "shock" therapy and subsequent corruption of the early 1990s, as well as policy directions of previous years, Brazil's economy is poorly managed and inefficient. Inflation is more than 2,000 percent and the unemployment rate is equally disturbing.

Despite its troubles, Brazil's economy has great potential for prosperity. Agriculture employs about 30 percent of the population. The nation is the world's largest producer of coffee, oranges, and bananas. It is second in soybean and cocoa production, third in corn and beef, fourth in pork, and eighth in rice. Much of Brazil's sugarcane is used to produce ethyl alcohol, a fuel used in more than 1.5 million Brazilian cars. Brazil's industrial sector exports automobiles and parts, textiles, minerals, iron ore, steel, and metals; other industries include cement and chemicals. Natural resources include gold, nickel, tin, oil, timber, and several minerals. Most electric power is generated by hydroelectric dams. Brazil is largely self-sufficient in food and consumer goods. The currency is the *cruzeiro* (Cr$).

Transportation and Communication

While domestic air travel is well developed between hundreds of local airports, flights can be expensive. Travel by intercity bus is more common, although buses tend to be crowded. São Paulo and Rio de Janeiro have rapid transit systems. City buses do not stop automatically but are hailed by the wave of a hand. Readily available in large cities, taxis with red license plates have fixed meter rates. Brazil has a highly developed media, with one of the world's largest television networks. Urban telephone service is good. Pay phones are operated by tokens, not coins. A media-oriented society, Brazil enjoys a large film and music industry. The most popular television programs include soap operas (*telenovelas*). Televisions are found in even the poorest urban and rural areas.

Education

A national adult literacy program has raised the literacy rate from 66 to 81 percent. Education consists of eight years of compulsory elementary education (to age 14) and three years of secondary education. About 40 percent of those who enter school proceed to the secondary level. Entrance into one of Brazil's top universities is difficult and is preceded by a special college preparation course and entrance exams. About half of the secondary-school graduates go on to trade schools. Brazil has many fine libraries and research centers. There are hundreds of higher education institutions.

Health

Excellent medical care is available in the cities to those who can afford it. Other areas are, however, rarely equipped with adequate facilities. Water is often not potable. Sanitation in some areas is insufficient. Yellow fever and malaria are found in rural areas. The infant mortality rate is 61 per 1,000. Life expectancy ranges from 62 to 68 years. A grass roots effort is providing mobile health care workers to rural areas to fight infant mortality through education and basic care.

FOR THE TRAVELER

U.S. citizens need a passport and visa to travel to Brazil. Although not required, yellow fever, typhoid, polio, and gamma globulin immunizations are recommended. Travelers coming from yellow fever endemic zones are required to show proof of vaccination. Do not eat uncooked or unpeeled fruits and vegetables. A tourist visa may restrict travel to certain rural areas where disease is a problem. Brazil offers visitors spectacular scenery, food, and festivals. One can visit modern cities as well as simple rural villages. Recent increases in robbery and violent crime in major cities, especially Rio de Janeiro, have prompted the government to warn visitors against wearing expensive jewelry in public or carrying large amounts of cash. The Brazilian Vacation Center (16 West 46th Street, Second Floor, New York, NY 10036) offers further information regarding travel and accommodations. You may also wish to contact the Embassy of Brazil, 3006 Massachusetts Avenue NW, Washington, DC 20008.

A *Culturgram* is a product of native commentary and original, expert analysis. Statistics are estimates and information is presented as a matter of opinion. While the editors strive for accuracy and detail, this document should not be considered strictly factual. It is a general introduction to culture, an initial step in building bridges of understanding between peoples. It may not apply to all peoples of the nation. You should therefore consult other sources for more information.

CULTURGRAM '95

Republic of
Bulgaria

Boundary representations not necessarily authoritative.

BACKGROUND

Land and Climate

Slightly larger than Tennessee, Bulgaria covers 42,823 square miles (110,910 square kilometers). Much of the terrain is mountainous; the Rila Mountains in the south are the highest on the Balkan peninsula. The north and central regions are dominated by plains. To the east lies the Black Sea. The northern border is the Danube River, which separates Bulgaria from Romania. The climate is similar to that of the U.S. corn belt, with cold, damp winters and hot, dry summers. Northern regions tend to be colder than southern areas.

History

Thracians are the oldest known inhabitants of the area now called Bulgaria. They founded the Odrisaw kingdom in the fifth century B.C. Slavic tribes began migrating to the area several hundred years later. In the seventh century, Bulgars (a central Asian people) migrated to the area and mixed with the Slavs and Thracians. A Bulgarian state was recognized by the Byzantine empire in 681. Three Bulgarian kingdoms existed before Bulgaria was conquered by the Ottoman Turks in 1396. The period that followed is known in Bulgaria as the "Turkish yoke." The struggle for political and religious independence gave rise to a cultural renaissance at the end of the 18th century. The Ottomans ruled until 1878, when Bulgaria became independent as a result of the Russian-Turkish War. It was briefly divided into the Kingdom of Bulgaria (to the north) and Eastern Romelia (to the south). Eastern Romelia remained part of the Ottoman empire until it was reunited with Bulgaria in 1886.

Allied with Germany in World Wars I and II, Bulgaria was twice defeated. Communists seized control in 1944 and consolidated power when Soviet troops marched into the country later that year. The prominent Bulgarian Communist leader, Georgi Dimitrov, who had been a nationalist hero against the Nazis in World War II, died in 1949. The 1947 constitution was named after him.

From 1954 to 1989, Todor Zhivkov held power. His authority remained unquestioned until a 1989 palace coup removed him as reforms swept through Eastern Europe. Petar Mladenov was named the new leader of the Communist party and head of state by the National Assembly, which also began considering constitutional reform. The Communists renamed their party the Socialists prior to free elections in 1990. They were victorious, but they had trouble forming a stable government. Mladenov and his prime minister soon resigned under pressure. A coalition government was formed under the leadership of Dimitar Popov (prime minister) and Zhelyu Zhelev (president). A new constitution was approved in 1991 and subsequent elections established a nonsocialist, multiparty parliament. Zhelev, a popular former dissident, was reelected president in 1992. His government has worked to privatize industry, liquidate collective farms, and return property that was confiscated in 1948 to its owners or heirs.

PEOPLE

Population

The population of Bulgaria is slightly more than 8.8 million and is not growing. The majority of people are ethnic

Copyright © 1994. Brigham Young University. Printed in the USA. All rights reserved. It is against the law to copy, reprint, store in a retrieval system, or transmit any part of this publication in any form by any means for any purpose without written permission from the Publications Division of the David M. Kennedy Center for International Studies, Brigham Young University, PO Box 24538, Provo, UT 84602–4538. Culturgrams are available for more than 125 areas of the world. To place an order, to receive a free catalog, or to obtain information on traveling abroad, call toll free (800) 528–6279.

EUROPE

Bulgarians (85.3 percent). Of the rest of the population, 8.5 percent are Turks, 2.6 percent are Romas (Gypsies), and 2.5 percent are Macedonians. Armenians, Russians, and other smaller groups also inhabit Bulgaria. Sofia, the capital, has more than one million residents and is the largest city. The majority (68 percent) of people live in urban areas.

Language

The official language is Bulgarian, and nearly all inhabitants speak it. About half of the Turkish population speaks Turkish as its mother tongue, but most also speak Bulgarian. Bulgarian is a Slavic language that uses an alphabet first developed in the ninth century by Cyril and Methodius. The Cyrillic alphabet preceded, and is similar to, the Russian alphabet. Russian was previously a required subject in school, so many people can speak it. English is now the most popular language for children to study, followed by German and French.

Religion

The Bulgarian Orthodox Church claims a membership of more than 85 percent of all Bulgarians. Muslims make up about 13 percent of the population. Orthodox monasteries are held in high regard for their religious and artistic significance. Many monasteries and churches contain frescoes and icons of significant historical value.

While religious worship was discouraged during the Communist era, it is unrestricted today. Rural people and the older generation are more devout in attending services, but the urban youth are showing an interest in religion Once banned, religious holidays are now openly celebrated throughout the country. Numerous Christian and non-Christian organizations from other countries have sent missionaries to Bulgaria. Because some groups have questionable practices, Bulgarians have developed some animosity toward outside groups.

General Attitudes

Bulgarians face many challenges relating to their country's continuing transition from communism to democracy. They have faced economic hardship, difficult constitutional questions, and ethnic tensions, but they are generally optimistic about the future. The youth are particularly interested in Western pop culture. They admire the United States as a wealthy and fortunate country, and they also look to Western Europe as a model for their own development. An entrepreneurial spirit is being fostered; a person who owns a business is considered wealthy. The hardworking Bulgarians are also strengthening a work ethic that had been weakened during the years of guaranteed employment under communism. Careers are becoming more important, and jobs in private business are generally pursued.

Bulgarians generally respect those who are open, strong, capable, gregarious, good humored, loyal to family and friends, and forthright. Families and group concerns are very important and play a role in individual decisions.

Bulgarians take pride in their heritage and culture, which have been preserved despite centuries of foreign domination. They are particularly sensitive about Ottoman rule. Democracy has always been important to Bulgarians. In fact, the 1879 constitution was one of the most progressive in Europe at the time. People are interested in politics, both domestic and international, and try to be well informed. Political discussions are popular. Art and science are appreciated.

Personal Appearance

European and American fashions are popular, but clothing is expensive. Many women knit sweaters for themselves and their families, and most people include sweaters in their wardrobe. Women are more concerned with their appearance than men, always making an effort to be well dressed and well groomed in public. They may wear something more casual at home to keep nicer clothing in good condition. Professional women usually wear a skirt and blouse or sweater and high heels to work. Clothing is neatly pressed; wrinkled items are rarely seen in public. Sneakers are not worn with dresses, only with jogging suits. Young women wear blue jeans and either a sweater or a shirt with buttons. Flannel is a popular fabric. Older rural women often wear a house dress, sweater, and scarf with conservative shoes.

Professional men wear suits and ties to work, although older men prefer trousers and sweaters. Young men wear baggy jeans or other blue jeans, denim or sports jackets, flannel shirts, and sneakers or loafers. Young children are considered the best dressed people in the country, wearing imported clothing and newly hand-knit items. Hats, boots, scarves, gloves, and winter jackets or fur coats are worn during the cold winters.

CUSTOMS AND COURTESIES

Greetings

When meeting someone, Bulgarians usually shake hands. The handshake might be accompanied in formal situations by *Kak ste?* (How are you?) or *Zdraveite* (Hello). The informal terms for these greetings, *Kak si?* and *Zdrasti* or *Zdrave*, are used among friends, relatives, and colleagues. Close female friends might kiss each other on the cheek. Handshakes are not used when saying *Dobro utro* (Good morning), *Dober den* (Good day), *Dober vetcher* (Good evening), or *Leka nosht* (Good night). First names are used in informal settings. Otherwise, titles and family names are used to address people. *Gospodin* (Mr.), *Gospozha* (Mrs.), or *Gospozhitsa* (Miss) are common titles, but professional titles are also used. When joining a small gathering, it is polite to greet each person individually, beginning with the elderly.

When parting, it is common to say *Dovishdane* (Till I see you again). Friends might also say *Vsichko hubavo* (All the best) or *Ciao* (Good-bye). It is not common for urban people to greet strangers while passing on the street, but this is considered polite in rural areas.

Gestures

"Yes" is indicated by shaking the head from side to side, and "no" is expressed with one or two nods of the head. One might shake the index finger back and forth to emphasize the "no" and even add a "tsk" sound to express displeasure. Hands are not generally used to replace or emphasize verbal communication. It is impolite to point with the index finger. It is impolite for men to cross an ankle over the knee. In a line or crowd it is not impolite or uncommon for one to touch or press against another person. Bulgarians often touch while conversing, and female friends might walk arm in arm down the street.

Visiting

Socializing is an important part of Bulgarian life. Friends and neighbors commonly drop by for a short visit without prior arrangement, but it is more typical for an invitation to be extended. Hosting friends for afternoon coffee and cake is popular, as is inviting them over for dinner. People often socialize at a café. Outdoor cafés provide opportunities to spend warm summer evenings visiting.

Guests in the home are usually offered refreshments and a drink, even if not invited for a meal. Invited guests often bring flowers for the hostess, a bottle of alcohol for the host, and candy for the children. An odd number of flowers are appropriate, as even numbers are reserved for funerals. Women usually enter the home before men. In rural areas, guests remove their shoes upon entering the home; this courtesy is also practiced in many urban homes. Slippers might be offered to guests, or they wear their stockings.

Evening visits usually start after 8:00 P.M. and may last until after midnight (until 3:00 A.M. for special occasions). Bulgarians enjoy showing hospitality to guests and having long conversations, so it is rude to leave early. Eating and dancing are typical parts of an evening visit in urban areas. Rural families might get together to enjoy a meal made of produce from the family garden.

Eating

In addition to three meals a day, Bulgarians might have a mid-morning snack and afternoon coffee. Breakfast is usually light, consisting of coffee and a cheese-filled pastry or some other bread product (sweet roll, toast, etc.). Traditionally, the main meal of the day is eaten at midday. It consists of a soup and/or salad, a main course, and dessert. Alcohol is usually served with this meal. When family schedules conflict with the traditional mealtime, people eat a lighter lunch—perhaps at one of the many new fast food establishments, a kiosk, or café, if not at home—and eat their main family meal after 7:00 P.M. If dinner is not the main meal, it is light and consists of some of the same foods as lunch, but not soup or dessert.

The continental style of eating is most common, with the fork in the left hand and the knife in the right. When guests are present, it is polite for them to accept second helpings. An empty plate and glass will usually be refilled. A small amount of food left on the plate (usually after second helpings) indicates one is full. Conversation is expected and everyone waits for all to finish before leaving the table. Napkins are placed on the table, not in the lap. Meals for special occasions can include several courses and last for many hours.

Although Bulgarians generally eat at home, they are eating out more often because so many new restaurants are opening. Bills are paid at the table. Diners round the bill up to the next *lev* as a tip. A traditional eating establishment common in rural areas is called a *mehana*; it features traditional food, folk music, and dancing.

LIFESTYLE
Family

The family unit is strong and supportive of its members. The elderly are often cared for by their adult children. Unmarried adults live with their parents until they get married. Young couples often live with one set of parents until they are able to get housing for themselves. Most urban families live in apartments, which are in short supply. Rural families usually have their own homes. Many village homes are owned by urban families, who use them for summer retreats, for retired parents, and to keep family gardens. Bulgarians still feel tied to their agricultural heritage.

Most urban families do not have more than two children, while rural families are slightly larger. Women receive three years of maternity leave, two of which are paid. Because urban women usually work outside the home, grandmothers play an important role in child care. Men traditionally do not help with household duties, but the younger generation is assuming greater responsibilities.

Dating and Marriage

The youth associate in groups at first. One-on-one dating does not usually occur until people are in their twenties. Favorite activities involve getting together at a café to drink and talk, going to a movie, dancing at discos, or relaxing in the park. In rural towns the youth enjoy socializing in the town square. Most Bulgarians expect to marry and have children. The average age for women to marry is between 18 and 25. Rural men marry in their twenties and urban men in their thirties.

Weddings involve big celebrations. A legal civil ceremony is often followed by a church wedding. A big reception is held in the evening. Folk music, dancing, and eating are common at the reception. Many traditions are kept by families, including pinning money on the bride's dress to represent future prosperity, the groom serenading the bride at her home, and pulling on opposite ends of a loaf of bread (whoever gets the largest piece will be the boss of the family). Couples are only now beginning to go on a honeymoon.

Diet

Bulgarians eat pork, fish, or lamb with most main dishes. Dairy products such as yogurt and cheese are common ingredients in many dishes. Popular main meals include *moussaka* (a casserole with pork or lamb, potatoes, tomatoes, and yogurt) and *nadenitsa* (stuffed pork sausage). *Kufteta* is a fried meat patty mixed with bread crumbs. *Sarmi* is a pepper or cabbage stuffed with pork and rice. Grilled meat (*skara*), such as *shishcheta* (a lamb shish kebab), is popular, especially in restaurants. *Shopska* is a salad made with Bulgarian cheese (called *cerene*), cucumbers, and tomatoes. A favorite cold soup is *tarator*, which includes cucumbers, yogurt, garlic, dill, walnuts, and oil. Cheese *banitsa* (a layered pastry) is eaten as a snack or for breakfast, while pumpkin *banitsa* is a popular dessert. Various cakes and *baklava* (a thin, leafy pastry with a syrup and nut filling) are also enjoyed for dessert. Coffee is usually either espresso or Turkish style. Meals are usually accompanied by a soft drink, alcohol, or coffee.

Recreation

Skiing is extremely popular in Bulgaria. People also generally enjoy being out in nature, hiking, walking, or touring in the countryside. Soccer and basketball are popular sports. Bulgari's national soccer team competed in the 1994 World Cup. August is the favorite time to go to the beach on the Black Sea. Summer vacations also typically include a trip to the mountains. Many professional organizations, schools, and local governments own lodges in the mountains where their members can stay for minimal cost.

Folk dancing and music are very much alive in Bulgaria. Festivals held throughout the year highlight various aspects of traditional Bulgarian culture. Urban dwellers enjoy the performing arts (ballet, opera, classical music), and even small towns have a local theater. Movie attendance is high, and American movies are quite popular. The youth enjoy rock, pop, disco, and folk music. The urban youth have access to recreation centers.

Holidays

Public holidays include New Year's Day, National Day of Freedom and Independence (3 March), Labor Day (1–2 May), the Day of Bulgarian Culture and Science (24 May), and Christmas Day (25 December). On 24 May, St. Cyril and Methodius are honored for developing the Cyrillic alphabet, but the country's accomplishments in science and culture are also celebrated. Religious holidays such as Easter are popular, but they are not public holidays. Name days are important and are celebrated with a family meal.

The most celebrated holiday season stretches from Christmas Eve to New Year's Day. On Christmas Eve, no meat is traditionally served. Rather, products of the soil are eaten to represent a successful past harvest and wish for a future good harvest. On New Year's Day, a large meal is eaten and presents are exchanged. People often decorate a tree. Children go door-to-door wishing good fortune to friends and relatives, carrying with them a small decorated stick (*survachka*), with which they touch people they visit in exchange for candy and money.

At the beginning of March, Bulgarians celebrate spring with *Martenitsa*. People exchange red and white yarn designs to symbolize luck and happiness. They are worn on the clothing until one sees a swallow. The person then either puts the *martenitsa* on a tree branch to bring on spring or hides it under a rock to represent the wish that the evil spirits in nature (and man) will go to sleep.

Commerce

Offices are open from 9:00 A.M. to 6:00 P.M. in most cases, but private shops often have additional hours. Some businesses close for the midday meal. Many close by noon on Saturday, and most are closed on Sunday. A strong capitalist spirit exists in the country and entrepreneurs are turning their garages or vacant buildings into shops or other small enterprises. Each town has an open-air market that is open every day. Selection is best on a designated weekly market day. Bulgarians shop daily for bread and other fresh foods. They purchase dairy, meat, and shelf products from small stores, and fresh produce at the open-air market.

SOCIETY

Government

Bulgaria is a multiparty democracy. The president is head of state and the prime minister is head of government. Members of the National Assembly (*Narodno Sobranyie*) are directly elected by the people. All citizens are eligible and required to vote at age 18.

Economy

Bulgaria's transition to a market economy has been painful for people whose salaries cannot keep up with inflation (50–80 percent) or who are among the unemployed (10–12 percent). The growth of the private sector is expected to improve conditions. Unfortunately, foreign investment is most critical to success, and it is lacking in most industries. In addition, the blockade of the Danube, due to conflicts in the former Yugoslavia, has severely hindered trade for Bulgaria. And the country's main trading partner before 1990, the Soviet Union, no longer exists as a market. Thus, many challenges face the Bulgarian economy.

Despite economic hardships, the country's Human Development Index (0.854) ranks it 40 out of 173 countries. Real gross domestic product per capita is estimated to be $4,700. These figures indicate most Bulgarians do not have access to the economic prosperity of their Western European counterparts.

Bulgaria exports agricultural products (grains, tobacco, wine, dairy foods) and some machinery. It imports consumer goods, food, and heavy machinery. Tourism is an important source of foreign capital. The currency is the *lev*.

Transportation and Communication

Most people use the reliable public transportation system, which consists of buses, trams, trolleys, and trains. Many families own cars, but the price of gasoline is so high that they use them only for special occasions. Taxis are plentiful in urban areas.

There are two national newspapers associated with the major political parties and several private papers that are increasing their circulation. Television broadcasts are changing rapidly, as American and European programming is becoming more popular. Telephone service is available, but it is expensive and not fully developed.

Education

Education is free and compulsory to age 15. It is also free at higher levels. Science and technical training are stressed in school, but the lack of modern equipment hampers advanced training. Entrance to secondary schools is determined by competitive exam, and urban students can often choose from one of five types of school, each offering a different focus (such as math and science or foreign languages). A number of universities and three-year training institutions offer higher education. The literacy rate is 93 percent.

Health

A national health care system provides free medical care to all citizens, but facilities are often not well equipped. Private doctors offer better care to those who can pay for it. The infant mortality rate is 13 per 1,000; life expectancy averages 69 to 76 years.

FOR THE TRAVELER

U.S. visitors need a valid passport to enter Bulgaria, but no visa is required for stays of up to 30 days. Rental cars are available. Interesting sites include Plovdiv's old town and Roman ruins, Black Sea resorts, ski resorts near Blageovgrad, Sofia's museums, and small towns throughout the country. Be aware that toilet paper is not always available in public restrooms. For information on travel to Bulgaria, contact: Balkan Holidays, 41 East 42d Street, Suite 508, New York, NY 10017. You may also wish to contact the Embassy of Bulgaria, 1621 22d Street NW, Washington, DC 20008.

A *Culturgram* is a product of native commentary and original, expert analysis. Statistics are estimates and information is presented as a matter of opinion. While the editors strive for accuracy and detail, this document should not be considered strictly factual. It is a general introduction to culture, an initial step in building bridges of understanding between peoples. It may not apply to all peoples of the nation. You should therefore consult other sources for more information.

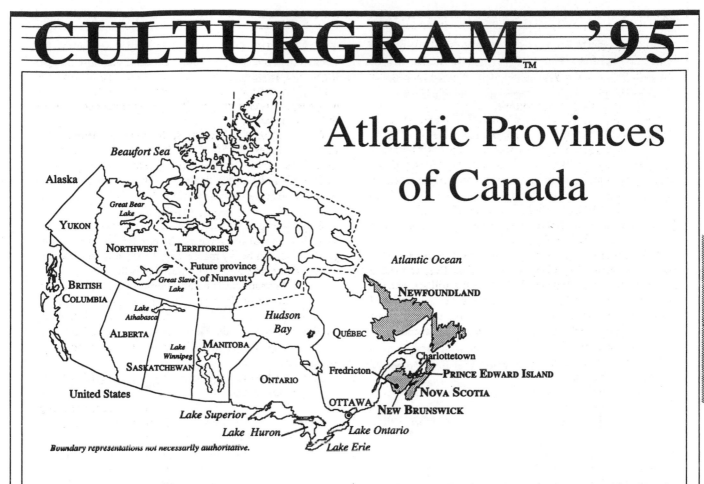

Atlantic Provinces of Canada

THE AMERICAS

BACKGROUND

Land and Climate

Canada is the second largest country in the world, after Russia. It covers 3,851,788 square miles (9,976,140 square kilometers). However, much of the north is sparsely inhabited because of the arctic climate and permanently frozen ground. Therefore, most of the people live within 100 miles (160 kilometers) of the U.S. border. The combined Atlantic provinces are a bit smaller than Texas and cover only 5 percent of Canada's total land area. This area is generally subject to a humid continental climate, although the coast of Newfoundland experiences a subarctic effect from the Labrador current. Winters are cold; summers are warm and humid. Fog is common in the spring. During the warmest month (July), temperatures average between 60°F and 65°F (15–18°C). Although the four provinces are referred to as Atlantic Canada, three of them—New Brunswick, Prince Edward Island, and Nova Scotia—are called the Maritime Provinces. Newfoundland includes the mainland area of Labrador. The Appalachian mountains cover much of the lower Atlantic Provinces, but the region also offers plateaus, valleys, and rocky coasts.

History

In 1604, the French began to settle in an area they called *Acadia*. However, in 1713 the English began to gain control over the region. Because the Acadians were not trusted by the English, many were forced to leave the region in the 1750s for other parts of North America. Indeed, Acadians were among the first people to settle in Louisiana, and the term *Cajun* is derived from the word *Acadian*. Not too many years after their expulsion, many Acadians returned to the Maritimes and settled throughout the region. At about the same time, English "Loyalists," who left the 13 colonies after the American Revolution, also began settling in the region.

In 1867, the British North America Act created the Dominion of Canada out of Nova Scotia, New Brunswick, and a colony called Canada (present-day Québec and Ontario). Prince Edward Island did not join until 1873 and Newfoundland remained a separate colony until 1949.

With the Statute of Westminster in 1931, Great Britain relinquished its formal authority over Canadian affairs, retaining only the right to have the last word on constitutional matters. In 1982, Britain agreed to give up that right and Canada's constitution was altered to reflect its full formal sovereignty. A Charter of Rights and Freedoms was also ratified in 1982. The nation still acknowledges Britain's Queen Elizabeth II as the official head of state, but Canada operates independently from the British government. The Queen is represented in Canada by Governor General Ramon Hnatyshyn.

Copyright © 1994. Brigham Young University. Printed in the USA. All rights reserved. It is against the law to copy, reprint, store in a retrieval system, or transmit any part of this publication in any form by any means for any purpose without written permission from the Publications Division of the David M. Kennedy Center for International Studies, Brigham Young University, PO Box 24538, Provo, UT 84602–4538. *Culturgrams* are available for more than 125 areas of the world. To place an order, to receive a free catalog, or to obtain information on traveling abroad, call toll free (800) 528–6279.

In 1984, Pierre Trudeau retired after 15 years as prime minister. His Liberal Party had governed Canada for 42 of the previous 50 years. Trudeau was succeeded by Brian Mulroney, head of the Progressive Conservative Party. Mulroney was reelected in 1988 but resigned in 1993 ahead of new parliamentary elections. The Liberal Party returned to power through the 1993 elections, and Jean Chrétien became prime minister.

Canada is an active member in the United Nations. It frequently contributes troops to UN peacekeeping missions and relief operations.

THE PEOPLE

Population

Canada's population is 27.7 million people. The combined population of the four provinces of Atlantic Canada comprises about 9 percent of that total, or about 2.5 million. However, because these provinces are small, population density is much higher than the national average. The ethnic origins of the people are basically French and English, with some German, Dutch, Scottish, and Irish. But there are also native peoples (Abnaki, Micmac, etc.) and African-Canadian descendants of black slaves who fled the United States. The French are concentrated in New Brunswick, while more than 95 percent of the people of Newfoundland are of British descent.

Language

English and French are both official languages in Canada. French is a key language in New Brunswick and is spoken as the first language by about 34 percent of that province's citizens. Most others in Atlantic Canada speak English as their first language, even those of non-British descent.

Religion

Religious beliefs in Canada follow traditional lines. The French are generally Roman Catholic while those of British descent are mostly Protestant. Of course, many other Christian faiths are represented in Atlantic Canada, as well as non-Christian organizations. Canada, overall, has 47 percent Roman Catholics, 41 percent Protestants, and 12 percent other groups. Although there is an official separation of church and state in Canada, religion is publicly recognized and some private religious schools are subsidized by the state.

General Attitudes

Most of the people are friendly and open to one another. The people are proud of their cultural heritage, which includes French, British, and other European influences. Atlantic Canadians are considered conservative and traditional, in part due to their rural heritage. They are very patriotic, as their area was one of the first to be part of Canada. Despite close ties and many similarities between their nation and the United States, Canadians emphasize they are not U.S. citizens and not U.S.-type people just living in Canada. Canadians often see Americans as more aggressive and materialistic than themselves. They also feel they are more tolerant and community oriented than Americans and less condescending to foreigners. The preservation of Canadian culture, especially against influence from the United States, is important.

Atlantic Canadians see themselves as hard-working, unpretentious people who value nature, community involvement, and education. They feel their unique sense of humor and rural values set them apart from other Canadians in many ways. Due to economic difficulties in the region, they approach Atlantic Canada's future with cautious optimism and a will to preserve their way of life.

Personal Appearance

Although dress habits are very similar to those in the United States, the people are somewhat more conservative in their attire. It is polite to remove sunglasses when speaking to someone and to remove hats in buildings.

CUSTOMS AND COURTESIES

Greetings

Because the people of the Atlantic Provinces have various cultural backgrounds, greetings vary from place to place. A handshake is the most common greeting. Nodding the head often replaces handshaking in informal situations. Some French speakers might use a light kiss to the cheek to greet friends. French-speaking people are often more outgoing and open than those of British descent. French speakers might use *Bonjour* (Good day) or *Tu vas bien?* (How are you doing?) to greet others. Common for English speakers are "Hi," "Good morning," or "How are you?" Smiles are always appreciated.

When passing strangers on the street, a smile and a nod are appropriate. Rural people also often greet the person verbally, but this is less common in large cities. When addressing others, first names are used in informal situations or when the more senior person requests it. Titles are used with new acquaintances and on formal occasions.

Gestures

Most gestures, positive and negative, are the same in Canada as in the United States. Between cultural groups, however, there may be some gestures common in the United States that would be offensive in a specific area. A visitor should use gestures conservatively. Pointing at someone with the index finger is rude; using the entire hand to motion to someone is more polite. Eye contact is important when talking to another person. French speakers use hand gestures somewhat more often than others during conversation.

Visiting

Atlantic Canadians enjoy visiting with one another. Close friends might drop by unannounced, but most visits are otherwise arranged in advance—especially in urban areas. It is impolite to drop by during regular mealtimes. Guests are nearly always offered refreshments, usually including at least a drink and often a small snack. It would be rude of the hosts not to offer something. Refreshments are considered an unspoken invitation to stay a while. Invited dinner guests often receive appetizers and a drink before the meal. It is appropriate for them to take a gift, such as wine or chocolate and sometimes flowers, to the hosts. This is especially true if the guests are not related to the hosts. Etiquette is important to most people but will depend on the situation and the hosts. For example, it is appropriate in some homes to remove street shoes upon entering, but that is not important in other homes—unless one's shoes are muddy or wet.

Eating

The standard three meals a day are often complemented by afternoon tea (especially among those of English heritage) or snacks at work. It is important for the family to eat dinner (supper) together when possible. In some rural areas, the main family meal is at midday. When eating as a guest, especially in a formal situation, it is often impolite to rest one's hands in the lap during the meal. Taking second helpings is a way to compliment the hosts on the food. It is considered polite to offer another table guest a dish before serving oneself.

Adults dress well when dining at fine restaurants. Although younger people dress more casually, they are still well dressed when dining formally. There are, of course, a number of casual and fast food restaurants where nicer clothing is not necessary. Tipping is generally the same as in the United States: 10 to 15 percent.

LIFESTYLE

Family

While the family unit is the center of society, it is common to have both parents working outside the home. Traditional norms have changed somewhat over the last decade, as in other industrialized countries. However, rural values continue to be important to most people. The average size of the family is comparable to that in the United States, but the divorce rate is lower in Canada. Family homes are generally wood-frame structures with various exteriors. Outside of large cities where many live in rented apartments, the majority of homes (62 percent) are single-family dwellings owned by the occupant. In Newfoundland, this figure rises above 75 percent.

Dating and Marriage

Dating and marriage customs are similar to those in the United States. Dating usually begins around age 13. The youth enjoy going to movies, eating out, going to the beach, and attending sporting events like hockey games. People generally marry in their twenties. Wedding traditions depend on a couple's religious affiliation. In some areas, a three-day celebration is popular.

Diet

Since Atlantic Canada is so closely associated with the ocean, fish and seafood are important to the diet. For instance, lobster is a favorite and inexpensive food. Dulse, an edible seaweed, is popular in some areas. Despite a short growing season, fresh fruits are common, including apples and a variety of berries. Fruit pies are popular in season. Dairy products are consumed in fairly large quantities. *Donair*, popular throughout the region, is pita bread stuffed with meat and sauce. Commonly eaten meats include chicken, beef, and pork. A main meal might consist of meat or fish, a vegetable, potatoes, dessert, and a drink. Prince Edward Island is famous for growing 70 different types of potatoes.

Recreation

Both spectator and participant sports are popular. Favorites include swimming, hockey, speed and figure skating, football, baseball, soccer, rugby, curling, skiing, tennis, golf, track and field, and gymnastics. Since the Atlantic Ocean surrounds many of these provinces, lobster cookouts and beach parties are common social events. In their leisure time, people enjoy gardening, hiking, fishing, and other outdoor activities. Spending weekends at summer cottages is very popular. People also like to visit, shop, watch television, and read.

Art galleries and museums are numerous. Many old churches are popular centers of attraction, as they symbolize the heritage of the people. Atlantic Canadians are a people of the sea, so the ocean has great influence on songs, art, poetry, and prose. It also influences folk festivals and other leisure activities. Dance and music festivals with a Scottish flavor are common in Nova Scotia ("New Scotland"), and there are Irish and Acadian events in other areas. Prince Edward Island, birthplace of Lucy Maud Montgomery (author of *Anne of Green Gables*), is a popular recreation spot for those interested in seeing places associated with her books.

Holidays

Official Canadian holidays include New Year's Day, Easter, Victoria Day (third Monday in May), Canada Day (1 July), Labor Day (first Monday in September), Thanksgiving Day (second Monday in October), Remembrance Day (11 November), Christmas, and Boxing Day (26 December). Boxing Day is a day to visit friends and relatives. It comes from an old British tradition of presenting small boxed gifts to tradesmen (postal carriers, delivery persons, and, in the past, servants). In addition to public holidays, local festivals are held throughout the region each year to commemorate everything from the shrimp harvest to military battles to cultural heritage.

Commerce

Many people in the Atlantic Provinces work in agriculture or fishing; both occupations require long hours of hard work. The service sector employs the most people. Business hours are similar to those in the United States. Offices are generally open weekdays between 8:00 or 9:00 A.M. and 5:00 P.M. Most stores close on Sunday, except for convenience stores or shops in tourist areas. Canadians usually begin full-time work between the ages of 16 and 25.

SOCIETY

Government

Canada's parliamentary system is patterned partly after Great Britain's, but it also has a federal system like that in the United States. The federal government holds considerable power in areas of national concern, such as health insurance, trade, the military, and development. Still, individual provinces have great control over their regions. Relations between the provincial and federal governments have not always been easy. For example, residents of the Atlantic region have felt in the past that the federal government has not done enough to stimulate economic development in their area—many young people leave the area to find jobs. The provinces each have one-chamber legislatures, and the leader of the dominant political party is the province's premier. Parliamentary elections may be called at any time but must be held at least every five years.

Economy

Canada has one of the strongest economies in the world, even though it has suffered from the global recession of the early 1990s. Canada ranks second in the world in gold and uranium production, third in silver, and fourth in copper. It is a world leader in the supply of wood pulp and other timber-related products. It has also been a leading exporter of wheat for many years. Other resources include nickel, zinc, lead, potash, oil, and natural gas. Barley, oats, and other agricultural products are also important exports.

In the Atlantic Provinces, people are generally employed in manufacturing, construction, fishing, mining, and the pulp and paper industries. Tourism is also important. Some Atlantic Provinces have developed offshore petroleum resources. In addition, Newfoundland is heavily involved in hydroelectric development, which provides energy to the area. The local economy was dealt a serious blow when cod fishing, a traditional occupation, was banned due to dwindling resources. This and other factors have driven regional unemployment to levels of more than 30 percent.

For Canada, inflation and unemployment rates vary according to region. Unemployment in 1993 was above 10 percent. Inflation is around 5 percent. The currency is the Canadian dollar (C$). Canada's Human Development Index (0.982) ranks it second out of 173 countries. Real gross domestic product per capita is $19,232. These figures indicate economic prosperity is available to the majority of the population. The poorest 40 percent of all households earn only 17 percent of the nation's income.

Canada has a free-trade agreement with the United States. In 1993, it also signed the North American Free Trade Agreement (NAFTA) with Mexico and the United States. That agreement provides for the freer movement of capital and goods, more cross-national investment, and a large market for many goods from each country.

Transportation and Communication

In the Atlantic Provinces, the use of ferries between islands is common. On secondary roads, cars must often be driven with caution because of farm equipment traveling on the road. Major cities have bus systems. As in the United States, personal cars are important modes of transportation. Communication systems are well developed: 98 percent of the people have telephones, 95 percent have televisions. Numerous cable-television systems provide service to all segments of the population. Radio broadcasts and newspapers reach millions of Canadians each week.

Education

Each province is responsible for its own educational system. In all provinces, education is compulsory for eight years beginning at age six or seven. Primary and secondary education is free. Newfoundland has a public-denominational system; every school uses similar curricula, but the schools themselves are operated by different religious groups. All provinces have their own public universities. College attendance has risen from 16 percent (of college-age people) in 1960 to nearly 40 percent today. About 10 percent of the total population holds university degrees. The literacy rate is 99 percent.

Health

In general, Canadians enjoy very good health. Their infant mortality rate is 7 per 1,000 and life expectancy ranges between 74 and 81 years. Hospitals and quality of care are excellent. Canada has a universal, compulsory national health insurance that covers doctors' fees and most hospital costs for all Canadians. It is funded by taxes and premiums collected by the federal and provincial governments.

FOR THE TRAVELER

Visas are not required of U.S. citizens staying up to 180 days; only proof of citizenship and a photo ID are necessary. U.S. travelers entering Canada from a country other than the U.S. must have a valid passport. Drivers should be aware that the use of seatbelts is required, radar detectors are illegal, and speed limit signs are in metrics. Contact the Canadian Consulate General, 1251 Avenue of the Americas, New York, NY 10020, for more specific information on the areas you plan to visit. Or you may wish to call (800) 565–2627 for travel guides and other free information. Canada's embassy is located at 501 Pennsylvania Avenue NW, Washington, DC 20001.

A *Culturgram* is a product of native commentary and original, expert analysis. Statistics are estimates and information is presented as a matter of opinion. While the editors strive for accuracy and detail, this document should not be considered strictly factual. It is a general introduction to culture, an initial step in building bridges of understanding between peoples. It may not apply to all peoples of the nation. You should therefore consult other sources for more information.

Ontario and the Western Provinces of Canada

Boundary representations not necessarily authoritative.

THE AMERICAS

BACKGROUND

Land and Climate

Canada is the second largest country in the world, after Russia. It covers 3,851,788 square miles (9,976,140 square kilometers). However, much of the north is uninhabitable because of the arctic climate and permanently frozen ground. Most of the population lives within 100 miles (160 kilometers) of the U.S. border. Ontario's climate is generally mild. Summers are warm and humid, while winters can be very cold, due to the Great Lakes. The prairies, which consist of Manitoba, Saskatchewan, and Alberta, are flat and vast; they have a very dry climate, with cold winters and short, hot summers. British Columbia, a very mountainous region, enjoys a wet, mild climate. Beautiful scenery can be found in every region, from lakes and the Niagara Falls in Ontario to national parks and the towering Rocky Mountains in Alberta to British Columbia's coastline.

History

Although Britain's John Cabot first landed in Canada in 1497, the French were mostly responsible for its early colonization. France established settlements in the 1600s at Québec and Montréal. The area was called New France. Britain fought often with France for control of the territory throughout the 1600s. In 1759, Britain captured Québec and then Montréal in 1760. In 1763, the Treaty of Paris gave Britain control over all of New France, which was renamed Québec.

Québec was divided in 1791 but united in 1840 as Canada. In 1867, Canada was divided into Québec and Ontario. In that year, the British North America Act created a federal union, called the Dominion of Canada, from the provinces of Québec, Ontario, Nova Scotia, and New Brunswick. This new federal government was based on the parliamentary system. Only three years later, much of the west (known as Rupert's Land) was purchased by Canada, out of which the provinces of the prairies were carved. British Columbia joined as a full province in 1871.

Although Canada still retains formal ties with Britain and Queen Elizabeth II is the official head of state, Britain has no control over Canadian affairs. These were deeded to Canada first through the 1931 Statute of Westminster and then through constitutional changes in 1982. A Charter of Rights and Freedoms was also established in 1982, guaranteeing many traditional personal freedoms. Ontario has generally supported more liberal political parties, one reason why Pierre

Copyright © 1994, Brigham Young University. Printed in the USA. All rights reserved. It is against the law to copy, reprint, store in a retrieval system, or transmit any part of this publication in any form by any means for any purpose without written permission from the Publications Division of the David M. Kennedy Center for International Studies, Brigham Young University, PO Box 24538, Provo, UT 84602–4538. *Culturgrams* are available for more than 125 areas of the world. To place an order, to receive a free catalog, or to obtain information on traveling abroad, call toll free (800) 528–6279.

Trudeau was prime minister for 15 years. The prairie provinces and British Columbia have traditionally been more conservative, giving strong support to governments such as the one led by Brian Mulroney and the Progressive Conservative party. Mulroney, who took office in 1984, was reelected in 1988 but resigned in 1993 near the end of his term. Elections in that same year brought the Liberal Party to power. Its leader, Jean Chrétien, became prime minister.

In 1991, the government announced plans to grant the native Inuit control of 772,000 square miles (1,999,500 square kilometers) in the north. The measure was approved by Northwest Territory voters in 1992, officially splitting that territory into the west and east (now called *Nanavut*, which is Inuit for "our land"). The Inuit have limited control over mineral rights but have extensive political and hunting rights. Nanavut has long been considered the "true north" in Canada, a place where Canadian character was built through facing a tough climate and difficult challenges. What is left of the Northwest Territories will be renamed, and both areas will receive separate territorial governments. This will occur when parliament can agree on a variety of constitutional changes.

THE PEOPLE

Population

The total population of Canada is 27.7 million. Of this, approximately 37 percent (10.25 million) lives in Ontario, making it the most heavily populated province in the country. Twenty-eight percent (7.8 million) lives in the combined region of the prairie provinces, British Columbia, Yukon, and Northwest Territories. Canada is made up of a mosaic of nationalities that have, for the most part, remained distinct. Ontario is not only populated by those of British and French descent but also by sizable German, Italian, Ukrainian, Chinese, and Japanese communities. Immigration from Asia has increased over the last few years. In fact, Vancouver's population of 1.5 million is 15 percent Chinese (mostly from Hong Kong). Most European nations are represented. Native peoples live mainly in the northern territories. British Columbia was settled primarily by British, Chinese, and Japanese groups, while the prairies attracted many European nationalities in the 1800s and have a rather diverse ethnic population.

Language

Both English and French are official languages in Canada. French is spoken by about 5 percent of the people in Ontario and Manitoba, but English dominates in these and all other western provinces. In fact, in western provinces, less than 3 percent of the people are fluent in French, and many speak a language other than English or French as their mother tongue. Among native groups, there are over 50 different languages. Canada's English differs slightly from American English. Canadians use British spelling (*centre* instead of center), and they have some phrases and idioms not used in the United States. For instance, *Eh!* is used much like "Ya know" or "Isn't it?" is used in the United States.

Religion

Most Canadians are Christians, but the beliefs and doctrines of the different Christian churches are diverse, and society is highly secularized. The United church is the most prevalent in western provinces, followed by Catholics, Anglicans, Lutherans, and Presbyterians. In Ontario, 29 percent belong to the United Church, 25 percent to the Roman Catholic church, and 21 percent to the Anglican church. A number of other Christian churches are present, as well as various non-Christian denominations.

General Attitudes

The people of Ontario are fairly reserved and formal, while those in the prairie provinces and British Columbia are more open and friendly. As Ontario contains large urban areas, life is faster paced—similar to New York City—whereas the pace of life in the west is more relaxed. The people have great pride in their individual provinces, as well as in being Canadian. Despite many similarities between their nation and the United States, the people emphasize they are not Americans and not American-type people just living in Canada. They note the differences. They have their own heritage and culture, as well as lower crime rates, less violence, and cleaner cities.

Personal Appearance

Although dress habits are similar to those in the United States, the people are generally more conservative and somewhat more formal in dress. Tattered or very casual clothing may not be acceptable in many areas, except in some parts of Ontario. Men who wear hats remove them in buildings.

CUSTOMS AND COURTESIES

Greetings

As in the United States, a firm handshake and sincere "Hello" are the most common greetings when meeting new people. Otherwise, a wave of the hand or nod of the head are acceptable gestures when saying "Hello." The majority of people in Ontario, the prairie provinces, British Columbia, Yukon, and Northwest Territories speak English. Still, in cities near Québec with large French communities, French greetings are common. In Vancouver, British Columbia, Chinese greetings are common among the ethnic Chinese minority.

Gestures

Most gestures, positive and negative, are the same in Canada as in the United States. Between cultural groups, however, there may be some gestures common in America that would be offensive in a specific area. A visitor should act conservatively. Eye contact is important during conversation and smiles are always welcome.

Visiting

While Canadians are generally more reserved than Americans, they are very friendly and kind to guests. Although Canadians enjoy getting together often, unannounced visits are not very common. It is considered polite to only visit when invited. In most areas, guests customarily remove their shoes when entering a home to avoid tracking in dirt. Guests follow the cue of the host or hostess. That is, if the host is fairly relaxed, guests will be the same. More often, hosts will offer a seat to the guests, who then sit more formally. Refreshments are usually offered, but it is not necessarily impolite to refuse them. Guests invited for a casual dinner often offer to help with preparations and/or bring part of the meal. It is polite to compliment the hostess on the meal. It is impolite to reach for things on the table. Houseguests staying for more than a day usually write a letter of thanks, and either send or leave a thank-you gift. Promptness in showing gratitude is important.

Eating

Adults are expected to dress well when dining at fine restaurants. Dresses or nice pants are appropriate for women. Although younger people dress more casually, they are still well dressed when dining out. There are, of course, a number of casual and fast-food restaurants that don't require nicer clothing. Tipping is generally the same as in the United States—about 10 to 15 percent. When one finishes a meal, utensils should be placed together on the plate.

LIFESTYLE

Family

While the family unit is the center of society, it is common to have both parents working outside the home. Traditional norms have changed somewhat during the last decade; however, the father in a family usually takes the lead, while the mother exercises influence on all decisions. The average size of the family is comparable to that in the United States. Families are close, and the divorce rate is lower in Canada than in the United States. Outside large cities, most people (62 percent) own their own home. Homes are of wood-frame construction.

Dating and Marriage

Dating usually begins between the ages of 14 and 16. Favorite activities include dancing and going to the movies. Marriage customs are similar to those in the United States.

Diet

Because Canada has a multicultural heritage, a variety of foods and dietary habits are represented, especially in Toronto and Ottawa, Ontario's two largest cities. Throughout the prairies, one can find wild rice, smoked fish, beef, ethnic dishes, Pacific salmon, and a variety of foods similar to those in the United States. A particular region's diet is a reflection of location and the largest ethnic group of the area. For example, grains are more common inland because they are grown there; seafood is most popular on the coast; and various immigrant groups eat foods common to the countries from which they came.

Recreation

Ice hockey is the most popular sport, but Canadians are certainly not limited in their interests or opportunities. They engage in such activities as boating, fishing, swimming, baseball, football, basketball, skiing, hunting, horseback riding, lacrosse, soccer, rugby, and curling. In curling, two four-person teams slide a large "stone" (with a gooseneck handle) over ice toward a target. Movies, local festivals and fairs, parks, and museums also offer recreational opportunities. From the Calgary Stampede in Alberta to the Vancouver Sea Festival to the Toronto Film Festival, there are many celebrations in which to participate.

Holidays

Official holidays include New Year's Day, Family Day (third Monday in February), Easter, Victoria Day (third Monday in May), Canada Day (1 July), Labor Day (first Monday in September), Thanksgiving Day (second Monday in October), Remembrance Day (11 November), Christmas, and Boxing Day (26 December). Boxing Day is a day to visit friends and relatives. It comes from an old British tradition of giving small boxed gifts to service employees or the poor. In addition to official holidays, local festivals are held throughout the region to commemorate various events. Each province also has its own official holidays.

Commerce

A normal business day is from 8:00 A.M. to 5:00 P.M., Monday through Friday. Canadians usually begin full-time work between the ages of 16 and 25. Business habits are similar to those in the United States. Stores are open at least until 6:00 P.M., and many remain open until 9:00 P.M. on at least some weeknights. Some businesses also operate on Saturday and Sunday.

SOCIETY

Government

Provincial governments have administrative and legislative authority over issues of education, property laws, and medical facilities. The federal parliament includes an appointed Senate and an elected House of Commons. The prime minister is the leader of the dominant political party in the House. Each provincial premier is the leader of the provincial assembly's dominant party. Queen Elizabeth II is represented by a governor general, currently Ramon Hnatyshyn.

Economy

Canada has one of the strongest economies in the world, but growth slowed in the early 1990s due to global recession. Canada's Human Development Index (0.982) ranks it second out of 173 countries. Real gross domestic product per capita is $19,232. These figures indicate economic prosperity is available to the majority of the population, with regional variations. The poorest 40 percent of all households earn only 17 percent of the nation's income.

Canada ranks second in the world in gold and uranium production, third in silver, and fourth in copper. It is a world leader in the supply of wood pulp and other timber-related products, the most important of which is newsprint. Many newspapers in the United States are printed on Canadian paper.

Canada has a free-trade agreement with the United States. In 1993, it also signed the North American Free Trade Agreement (NAFTA) with Mexico and the United States. That agreement provides for freer movement of capital and goods, more cross-national investment, and a large market for many goods from each country.

As the industrial heart of the nation, Ontario leads Canada's economy. As the financial and political center of Canada, it plays a role much like both New York and California in the United States. Copper, nickel, and other minerals are mined in Ontario's Sudbury Basin. The western provinces serve as the hinterland to Ontario, providing raw materials, agricultural goods, and other products for export and manufacturing. The prairies are the breadbasket of the nation and also have important potash, oil, and natural gas reserves. Major products of British Columbia include timber, coal, oil, and minerals. British Columbia also serves as Canada's gateway to Pacific Rim markets. The north is rich in minerals and other natural resources. Economies in many provinces have expanded in recent years to include manufacturing, chemicals, and food processing. The currency is the Canadian dollar (C$).

Transportation and Communication

There are more cars per capita in the west than elsewhere in Canada because public transportation systems cannot serve the wide expanses of the prairies and north. Domestic air transportation provides an important link to isolated regions in the north. The national railway ships freight from the west to the east and vice versa. Communication systems are highly developed, including satellite systems, cable television, and excellent broadcast networks. Television is often dominated by American-made programs, but the federal government actively supports the development of Canadian films and television shows.

Education

Each province is responsible for its own educational system. In all provinces, education is compulsory and free for at least eight years, beginning at age six or seven. Each province also administers its own colleges and universities. While colleges are subsidized by the federal and provincial governments, students must pay tuition. Many students choose to complete a two-year technical training program and enter the work force; about 40 percent enter a university. While only about 10 percent have college degrees, an additional 20 percent have completed at least partial post-secondary training. Literacy is 99 percent.

Health

Canadians enjoy very good health in general. Their infant mortality rate is 7 per 1,000. Life expectancy ranges between 74 and 81 years. Hospitals and quality of care are excellent. Facilities and personnel are less available in the rural and isolated regions. Canada has a universal, compulsory national health insurance that covers doctors' fees and most hospital costs for all Canadians. It is funded by taxes and premiums collected by the federal and provincial governments.

FOR THE TRAVELER

Visas are not required of U.S. citizens for stays of up to 180 days, only proof of citizenship and a photo ID. U.S. citizens entering from another country need a valid passport. Travelers driving to Canada should be aware that radar detectors are illegal and could be confiscated if discovered. It is illegal to take a firearm from the United States into Canada.

All provinces discussed in this *Culturgram* offer many attractions, even beyond the standard tourist points such as Niagara Falls. More specific information may be obtained through the Canadian Consulate General, 1251 Avenue of the Americas, New York, NY 10020–1175. Or you may wish to call for information on Ontario (800) 668–2746, Manitoba (800) 665–1040, Saskatchewan (800) 667–7191, Alberta (800) 661–8888, British Columbia (800) 663–6000, or the Northern Territories (800) 661–0788. You may also wish to contact the Embassy of Canada, 501 Pennsylvania Avenue NW, Washington, DC 20001.

A *Culturgram* is a product of native commentary and original, expert analysis. Statistics are estimates and information is presented as a matter of opinion. While the editors strive for accuracy and detail, this document should not be considered strictly factual. It is a general introduction to culture, an initial step in building bridges of understanding between peoples. It may not apply to all peoples of the nation. You should therefore consult other sources for more information.

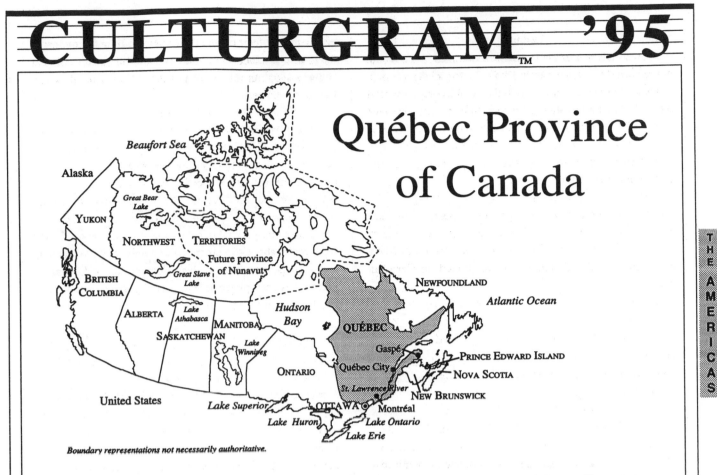

Québec Province of Canada

Boundary representations not necessarily authoritative.

BACKGROUND

Land and Climate

Canada is the second largest country in the world, after Russia. It covers 3,851,788 square miles (9,976,140 square kilometers). However, much of the north is uninhabitable because of the arctic climate and permanently frozen ground. Therefore, most of the people live within 100 miles of the U.S. border. Québec is the largest province and is one-sixth the size of the United States. The Canadian Shield—a vast, U-shaped, rocky expanse surrounding the Hudson Bay—covers most of the province and includes 470,000 square miles (1,217,300 square kilometers) of rocky, coniferous forest. The bulk of the population lives in the St. Lawrence Valley to the south. Winters are very cold and snowy; summers are humid and warm.

History

In 1534, Jacques Cartier landed in Gaspé and announced French sovereignty over the territory. The following year, he traveled up the St. Lawrence River to the present site of Québec and Montréal, but real colonization did not begin until the 1600s. Québec City was founded in 1608. More settlements were eventually established and the number of French settlers gradually increased. By 1663, the area was under the firm control of Paris and was called New France. But the British also had settlements, and the two European powers fought for control of the land. In 1713, a war ended with France ceding most of its Atlantic coast holdings.

War also ensued from 1744–48. But major fighting and conquest did not take place until the 1750s. In 1756, France and England declared what became the Seven Years War (French and Indian War). In 1759, the British conquered Québec City and, in the following year, Montréal. Peace was declared in 1763 with the signing of the Treaty of Paris, through which Britain gained control of all of New France. The area was then renamed Québec. At the time of the British takeover, the 70,000 French-speaking people in Québec were outnumbered by English speakers. However, the French culture was firmly established and has continued to dominate the region. In 1791, Québec was divided into Upper and Lower Canada, but the two were joined again in 1840 as the province of Canada.

In 1867, Canada was divided into Québec and Ontario, as the British North America Act created the Dominion of Canada. The new federal union included Québec, Ontario, Nova Scotia, and New Brunswick. Much of western Canada (then known as Rupert's Land) was added a few years later, and British Columbia joined the Dominion in 1871. Canada eventually gained self-governing status within the Commonwealth.

Copyright © 1994. Brigham Young University. Printed in the USA. All rights reserved. It is against the law to copy, reprint, store in a retrieval system, or transmit any part of this publication in any form by any means for any purpose without written permission from the Publications Division of the David M. Kennedy Center for International Studies, Brigham Young University, PO Box 24538, Provo, UT 84602–4538. *Culturgrams* are available for more than 125 areas of the world. To place an order, to receive a free catalog, or to obtain information on traveling abroad, call toll free (800) 528–6279.

Throughout its history as part of Canada, Québec's inhabitants have debated the issue of their status within the federation. Various independence and "special status" drives were launched in the 20th century. The movement gained momentum after the 1960s and seemed to peak by the 1980s under the political leadership of the *Parti Québécois* (PQ).

Although a public vote on the question of independence was defeated in 1980, Québec opposed a new Canadian Constitution in 1982. It then became necessary to seek compromise, which was embodied in the 1987 Meech Lake Agreement. The agreement would have recognized Québec as a distinct society within Canada and accorded them certain rights that other provinces would not have. A crisis developed in 1990 when several provinces balked at signing the agreement and Québec threatened to secede. An emergency meeting between Prime Minister Brian Mulroney and opposing provincial premiers failed to pass the agreement and it was defeated.

Demands again in 1991 for secession led the federal government to seek an acceptable compromise between Québec and other provinces. By early 1992, many Canadians had determined secession would harm the economy. So, an increasing number came to favor recognizing Québec's distinct status. However, a referendum on the issue failed to pass in October 1992. Still, Québec decided not to leave the union, opting to take advantage of other proposed constitutional changes and remain part of Canada's strong economy. Faced with increasing opposition to his policies and his support of the referendum, Mulroney resigned in 1993. Subsequent elections brought Jean Chrétien to power as the new prime minister. He heads the Liberal Party.

THE PEOPLE

Population

Québec's 6.93 million people account for 25 percent of Canada's total population (27.7 million). Because Québec is more urbanized than other provinces in Canada, its population density is more than twice the national average of seven persons per square mile. About 83 percent of the people are of French origin, while 10 percent have a British heritage. Native Inuits live in the north. Various other ethnic groups are represented in the larger cities.

Language

Although both French and English are official languages in Canada, French is used almost exclusively in some parts of Québec. According to provincial law, all public signs must be in French. Bilingual (French and English) signs are allowed inside buildings, but all street signs and external signs must be in French. Various groups have challenged this law and revisions are expected that will allow bilingual signs on storefronts, and perhaps in other cases.

Less than one million people in Québec claim English as their first or primary language. Most of the rest have French as their mother tongue. Many people are bilingual, of course, and French and English are sometimes mixed during conversation—especially in large urban areas.

While a separate English-language school system exists, most children go to schools where French is used to teach all subjects. Visitors who attempt to use French are appreciated by the French-speaking citizens of Québec. The Inuit speak Inuktitut, a complex and ancient language.

Religion

Religious beliefs in Canada follow traditional lines. The French are generally Roman Catholic; those of British descent are mostly Protestant. Of course, other religious groups are found in Québec, but the majority of the people are Catholic. In fact, before Québec was controlled by Great Britain, it was largely ruled by the Catholic Church through French civil law. Although there is an official separation of church and state in Canada, religion is publicly recognized and private religious schools are often subsidized by the state. Religious organizations have played a greater role in politics in Canada than in the United States.

General Attitudes

Both French- and English-speaking Canadians are friendly and hospitable. Etiquette and politeness are important. For example, a man will give his seat to a woman on a bus or will open a door for her. The French Canadians, or *Québécois*, are proud of their language and French cultural heritage. This is evident in their preservation of the French culture in Québec. Even today, there is a strong nationalist movement in Québec. And while Québec is a vital part of Canada, opinions are strong about French-English relations in certain circumstances. Over the past few years, feelings that Québec should be a separate country have run high in Québec, causing tensions with other provinces. The *Québécois* insist their province is distinctly different than the others and should be so recognized by the rest of Canada.

Personal Appearance

Although dress habits are very similar to those in the United States, the people are more conservative and somewhat more formal in the clothes they wear. European fashions are popular. Tattered or very casual clothing may not be acceptable in Québec. It is polite to remove sunglasses when speaking to someone.

CUSTOMS AND COURTESIES

Greetings

Due to past cultural and linguistic ties to France, Switzerland, and Normandy, Québec has experienced the most European influence of any Canadian region. Therefore, traditional European greetings are used in Québec, which include a firm handshake in most cases. *Bonjour* (Good day) is the common French greeting. Women who are close friends may embrace, and both men and women often exchange kisses on both cheeks as a greeting. Of course, not all of Québec is French, and greetings in predominantly English areas will be similar to those in other parts of Canada. Throughout Québec, first names and informal language forms are not used by adults except with close friends or relatives. Conversation is direct and polite. The term in French for "Good-bye" is *Au revoir*.

Gestures

Many gestures are the same in Québec as throughout the rest of Canada. However, some differences do occur. For instance, even if one excuses oneself, it is offensive to burp in public. The U.S. sign of thumbs-down (meaning "no" or that something is bad) is an offensive gesture in Québec and should be avoided

Visiting

Guests invited to a person's home often bring a small gift to the lady of the house, including either flowers, candy, or wine. Houseguests who stay overnight leave a thank-you letter and either leave or promptly send a thank-you gift to their host or hostess. Etiquette is important in Québec, and is adhered to on formal occasions. However, the atmosphere is much more relaxed for informal visits. A quick call in advance is all that is needed before dropping by a friend's home. When French Canadians invite guests to their home, they usually provide a meal. It is polite to remove shoes, hats, and coats at the door.

Eating

In French-speaking areas, one should keep both hands above the table during a meal. Women rest their wrists on the table, men their forearms. Elbows may only be placed on the table after the meal is finished. Supper time is generally at 6:00 P.M. This time is so important to families that a telephone call between 6:00 and 7:30 P.M. is considered impolite. Québec City and Montréal are well-known for their fine French cuisine. Tipping rates are the same as in the United States—about 10 to 15 percent. It is improper to eat on the streets unless one is sitting down at an outdoor café or standing outside a food stand. During a meal, it is polite to wipe one's mouth before drinking from a glass.

LIFESTYLE

Family

While the family is the center of society, it is common to have both parents working outside the home. Although traditional norms have changed somewhat over the last decade, the father is usually head of the family, but the mother exercises influence on all decisions. The average family size is comparable to that in the United States. The divorce rate is lower in Canada than in the United States. In urban areas, nearly half of the people live in rented apartments. But outside large cities, home ownership is 62 percent. To encourage growth, the government gives a parent approximately US$500 at the birth of a child and adds a small monthly stipend. This amount increases over time and with the addition of each child.

Dating and Marriage

Dating and marriage customs are similar to those in the United States. Dating usually begins before age 16. Favorite activities include dancing and going to the movies. Many couples enjoy sporting activities together. Going out to eat is one of the most common dates in Québec. In the summer, picnics and outdoor dance festivals are popular. In Québec, it is now common for couples to live together for years before officially getting married. After two years, even without an official ceremony, the government recognizes the union as a common-law marriage.

Diet

Food in Québec displays a definite French influence. Some foods associated with Québec include pea soup, meat pies, French pastries and breads, special cheeses, lamb, and veal. Potatoes and red meats are common with evening suppers. A favorite fast food is *poutine*, fries covered with spicy gravy and cheese curds. Maple syrup is produced in Québec and is a favorite in desserts. Food connoisseurs consider Québec's cuisine to be among the best in North America.

Recreation

Both spectator and participant sports are popular in Canada. The favorites are swimming, hockey, baseball, curling, rugby, skiing, tennis, golf, and lacrosse (Canada's official national sport). Québec offers a variety of outdoor recreational opportunities, such as fishing, hunting, and hiking. In cities such as Montréal, activities involving the fine arts are also enjoyed. Montréal's annual film and jazz festivals are popular attractions.

Holidays

There are at least two holidays unique to Québec: the two-week-long *Carnaval de Québec* (usually in February) and St. Jean-Baptiste Day (24 June), which is celebrated as Québec's national holiday (quite distinct from Canada Day). Other holidays celebrated throughout Canada include New Year's Day, Easter, Victoria Day (for the English, the third Monday in May), *Dollard Des Ormeaux* (for the French, same as Victoria Day), Canada Day (1 July), Labor Day (first Monday in September), Thanksgiving Day (second Monday in October), All Saints Day (1 November), Remembrance Day (11 November), Christmas, and Boxing Day (26 December). Boxing Day comes from the British tradition of presenting small boxed gifts to service workers, tradesmen, and in the past, servants. It is now primarily a day for visiting family and friends. Almost every town has a winter carnival with parades and sports. Since Québec is "maple syrup country," the people often have parties centered on syrup making. These are called sugaring-off parties. Dancing at these celebrations is similar to square dancing.

Commerce

A normal business day is from 8:00 A.M. to 5:00 P.M., Monday through Friday. People usually begin full-time work between the ages of 16 and 25. Stores are open at least until

6:00 P.M., and many remain open until 9:00 P.M. on a few nights. Some businesses also operate on Saturday and Sunday.

SOCIETY

Government

The current Canadian parliamentary system provides for a two-chamber parliament at the federal level and a one-chamber national assembly at the provincial level. The Queen of England is head of state and is represented in Canada by Governor General Ramon Hnatyshyn. Québec's National Assembly is located in Québec City. As with the federal government, the leader of the largest party in the assembly is the provincial premier. Unless otherwise scheduled, elections are held at least every five years. Voting is universal for those ages 18 and older.

Economy

Canada has one of the strongest economies in the world, but growth slowed in the the early 1990s due to the global recession. Canada ranks second in the world in gold and uranium production, third in silver, and fourth in copper. In fact, mining is a major primary industry in Québec. Forestry is also important in the province, as are manufacturing industries. Tourism has become an increasing source of revenue in the past several years. One-third of all U.S. international travel is to Canada. The St. Lawrence Seaway makes Montréal Canada's most important port city. Hydroelectric power is generated through the James Bay project, acting as the second main source of power for the province.

Canada's national unemployment average is 8 percent. The recession caused unemployment to rise above 10 percent in 1993, but economic recovery in 1994 is encouraging job creation. The currency is the Canadian dollar (C$). Canada's Human Development Index (0.982) ranks it second out of 173 countries. Real gross domestic product per capita is $19,232. These figures indicate economic prosperity is available to the majority of the population, with regional variations. The poorest 40 percent of all households earn only 17 percent of the nation's income.

Canada has a free-trade agreement with the United States. In 1993, it also signed the North American Free Trade Agreement (NAFTA) with Mexico and the United States. That agreement provides for freer movement of capital and goods, more cross-national investment, and a large market for many goods from each country.

Transportation and Communication

Transportation systems are excellent, especially in Montréal and Québec City, where bus systems are well developed. Montréal has one of the best subway systems in the world. Personal cars are used for transport in other areas. The national railroad system carries passengers as well as freight and the airways are an increasingly popular way to travel. Communication systems are highly developed, as most people have telephones and televisions. Radio networks and newspapers service the entire populace. All systems are highly modern, and Canada has several satellites in orbit to aid communication.

Education

Québec, as with all provinces, is responsible for its own educational system. Local Catholic and Protestant school boards are supported by the government to direct school curricula. School is free and compulsory for children ages six to sixteen. While students may get permission to leave school at sixteen, high school continues another two years, and the government actively encourages students to finish. After graduation, students may enter a two-year, technical-training program similar to a trade school or community college in the United States, or they may attend a two-year college preparatory program (similar to filling general education requirements in the United States). Those who opt for technical training then enter the labor force, while the others attend a three-year university. Although university education is subsidized by the provincial government, students pay tuition costs. College attendance has risen from 16 percent (of college-age students) in 1960 to nearly 40 percent today. About 10 percent of the total population holds university degrees. The literacy rate is 99 percent.

Health

Canadians enjoy very good health in general. Their infant mortality rate is 7 per 1,000 and life expectancy ranges from 74 to 81 years. Hospitals and quality of care are excellent. Canada has a universal, compulsory national health insurance that covers doctors' fees and most hospital costs for all Canadians. It is funded by taxes and premiums collected by the federal and provincial governments. While patients must often wait months for elective surgery and certain expensive procedures, all citizens have access to the system and basic health needs receive prompt attention.

FOR THE TRAVELER

Visas are not required of U.S. citizens for stays of up to 180 days, only proof of citizenship and a photo ID. U.S. citizens entering from another country need a valid passport. Travelers to Québec should make an attempt to speak French. Travelers driving to Canada should note that radar detectors are illegal in some provinces and may be confiscated. For more detailed information, contact the Canadian Consulate General, 1251 Avenue of the Americas, New York, NY 10020–1175 or call (800) 363–7777. You may also wish to contact the Embassy of Canada, 501 Pennsylvania Avenue NW, Washington, DC 20001.

A *Culturgram* is a product of native commentary and original, expert analysis. Statistics are estimates and information is presented as a matter of opinion. While the editors strive for accuracy and detail, this document should not be considered strictly factual. It is a general introduction to culture, an initial step in building bridges of understanding between peoples. It may not apply to all peoples of the nation. You should therefore consult other sources for more information.

Republic of
Chile

Arica

La Serena

Valparaíso ⦿ SANTIAGO

Concepción

Punta Arenas

Venezuela
Colombia
Ecuador
Peru
Pacific Ocean
Brazil
Bolivia
Paraguay
Chile Argentina
Uruguay
Atlantic Ocean
Falkland Islands
(Islas Malvinas)

Boundary representations not necessarily authoritative.

THE AMERICAS

BACKGROUND

Land and Climate

While Chile is larger than Texas, it is stretched out along 3,996 miles (6,250 km) of South America's western coast. Its average width is only about 100 miles (160 kilometers). Because of the north to south distance, Chile has many different climates and landscapes. Being in the Southern Hemisphere, Chile's seasons are opposite those in North America; summer is between December and March. The climate ranges from subtropical in the north to moderate in the central region and subarctic in the south. One can find deserts, swamps, forests, the Andes Mountains, beautiful lakes, rich agricultural regions, volcanoes, and a wide variety of plants and animals. Chile has been called the Switzerland of South America for its natural beauty. The country is subject to earthquakes.

History

Ferdinand Magellan became the first European to sight Chilean shores in 1520, after successfully navigating around the southern tip of the American continent. Diego de Almagro claimed Chile as part of the Spanish Empire for Pizarro in 1536, and Pedro de Valdivia commenced the Spanish conquest in 1541 against very strong Indian resistance. Many early Indian warriors, such as Caupolican, are now revered as national heroes.

Chile began to fight for independence from Spain in 1810. Although initial revolts were suppressed, Chilean patriots eventually joined with the armies of José de San Martín in Argentina. In 1817, San Martín's forces invaded Chile by crossing the Andes mountains. The Spanish were quickly defeated and one of the revolution's heroes, Bernardo O'Higgins, became the new country's leader. Unable to establish a stable government, O'Higgins left the country in 1823 and Chilean politics remained unstable for several years. After 1830, however, stability and periodic reform allowed Chile to make progress. From 1879 to 1884, Chile fought a war, the War of the Pacific, against Peru and Bolivia. Victorious, Chile annexed the provinces of Arica and Antofagasta in the north.

A civil war in the latter 1880s was followed by less stable governments and military interventions until elections in 1932. During most of the 20th century, Chile concentrated on economic growth and addressing social problems. By 1970, many people had become convinced that socialism could solve some of those problems without hindering growth. That feeling allowed Salvador Allende to become the first freely elected, Marxist president in South America. Allende's policies were too radical and the country faced economic disaster by the end of 1972. Because of the chaos, General Augusto

Copyright © 1994. Brigham Young University. Printed in the USA. All rights reserved. It is against the law to copy, reprint, store in a retrieval system, or transmit any part of this publication in any form by any means for any purpose without written permission from the Publications Division of the David M. Kennedy Center for International Studies, Brigham Young University, PO Box 24538, Provo, UT 84602–4538. *Culturgrams* are available for more than 125 areas of the world. To place an order, to receive a free catalog, or to obtain information on traveling abroad, call toll free (800) 528–6279.

Pinochet Ugarte led a military coup in 1973 that ended Allende's socialist government.

Backed by the military, Pinochet ruled by decree. He determined that authoritarianism was better than liberal democracy. In 1980, a new constitution gave him the right to rule until 1988. In 1988, Pinochet subjected himself to a plebiscite to determine if he should continue in power or allow free elections. Upon losing the plebiscite, he called for elections in December 1989. Pinochet's choice for president was defeated by the centrist-left candidate, Patricio Aylwin Azocar. Aylwin took office in 1990 as the first elected president since 1970. Pinochet continues to wield significant power as head of the armed forces, a post from which he cannot legally be removed. Despite his reputation for years of human rights abuses and a dictatorial style, Pinochet is credited for building a successful and productive economy. Aylwin built upon that strong base with innovative programs, allowing Chile to be among the most prosperous of Latin American countries. Aylwin is especially credited with lifting 25 percent of Chile's poor out of poverty with progressive social programs. He also maintained a careful balance between opposing political forces.

Aylwin did not run for reelection in 1993, but supported Eduardo Frei Ruiz-Tagle. Frei won the December elections and took office in March 1994. The son of a former president, Frei is very popular in Chile. He plans to continue Aylwin's anti-poverty measures and seek closer economic ties with the United States.

THE PEOPLE

Population

The population of Chile is about 13.74 million and is growing at 1.5 percent annually, one of the lowest rates among all South American countries. Only about 15 percent of the population lives in rural areas. More than four million people live in the Santiago region. About 95 percent of the people have either a European heritage or are *mestizo* (mixed European-Native American descent). Only 3 percent are pure Native Americans (Indians) and 2 percent have other ethnic origins. The people enjoy one of the highest standards of living in Latin America.

Language

Spanish, called *Castellano*, is the official language. However, as in all South American countries, some terms common to Chile will not have the same meaning elsewhere. English is taught in the schools and understood by many in the larger cities. Small minorities also speak German (southern Chile), Italian, and Mapuche, an Indian language.

Religion

Most Chileans profess a Christian faith. It is estimated that more than 80 percent of the population belongs to the Roman Catholic church. Most other people belong to various Protestant groups or other Christian churches. There is a small Jewish minority, and many Indians follow traditional beliefs. Church and state are separated, and religious freedom is guaranteed.

General Attitudes

The Chilean people are friendly, both among themselves and with strangers. The people are known for their sharp and witty sense of humor. This and their cultural and educational refinements have earned them the distinction of the "British of South America." They take pride in their literacy, their nation, and their heritage. Confidence and optimism are commonly expressed by people when asked how they view Chile and its future. There is a strong middle class in Chile, and education enables many of the poorer people to excel and build a better life. Chileans respect the elderly. They are a law-abiding, pragmatic people who believe in progress.

Personal Appearance

Fashions follow European styles and are quite sophisticated in urban areas. Appearance is quite important to individuals and much care is given to it. Even in rural areas, where people are not as wealthy, it is important to be neatly and cleanly dressed. Sloppy or tattered clothing is considered in poor taste to many Chileans.

CUSTOMS AND COURTESIES

Greetings

Greetings in Chile are very important because they stress an individual is welcome and recognized. The *abrazo* is the most common greeting among friends and relatives. It consists of a handshake and hug, sometimes supplemented with a kiss to the right cheek for women or family members. A handshake is appropriate when meeting someone for the first time. Eye contact is very important when greeting someone. Traditional verbal greetings include *¿Qui'ubo?* (What's up?), *¿Cómo está?* (How are you?), and *¡Gusto de verte!* (Nice to see you). Men stand to greet a woman entering the room. The Chilean people show significant outward affection to friends and relatives. The *abrazo* is repeated with each individual when one leaves a small social gathering of friends or family.

Titles are important when addressing people. The title used depends on the situation. *Señor* (Mr.), *Señora* (Mrs.), and *Señorita* (Miss) are common for strangers and acquaintances, as are professional titles (*Doctor, Director, Profesor*). *Don* and *Doña* are used with the person's first name for men and women, respectively, to show special respect and familiarity.

Gestures

Eye contact and correct posture are important during conversation, while excessive hand gestures are avoided. Yawns are suppressed or politely concealed with the hand.

One does not beckon other people with hand gestures, except for a waiter in a restaurant. Items, including money, are handed, not tossed, to other people. Respect and courtesy are important to the Chileans.

Visiting

Contrary to some areas in South America, guests wait outside the door of a home until invited inside. Dinner guests often bring flowers, wine, or bread for the host family. Guests invited to lunch often offer to bring a dessert, such as cookies or ice cream. It is appropriate to greet the head of the family first. Chileans appreciate guests who show genuine interest in their family, especially their children. Light, casual conversation usually precedes any business discussion; political topics are avoided unless initiated by the host. Guests are usually offered something to eat.

Eating

Chileans converse freely at the table. The hostess is complimented on the meal. The continental style of eating is used, with the fork in the left hand and the knife remaining in the right. Both hands are kept above the table at all times. It is impolite to ask for second helpings. Even if second helpings are offered, the guest is expected to decline. Only if the host insists should the guest take more food. It is impolite to leave directly after eating; guests should stay for conversation.

In a restaurant, a waiter can be summoned with a raised finger. It is usually considered bad manners to eat food, except for ice cream, while walking in public. As fast food increases in popularity, however, this habit is changing.

LIFESTYLE

Family

The family is important in Chile, including the extended family. While men have tended to dominate private and public life in the past, recent years have seen a change in the attitudes about women in the home and professional world. Nearly 30 percent of the labor force is female. There are many women in important political and business positions in the country. And, while the father takes the lead in the family, the mother has considerable influence in decisions. The relationship between the husband and wife is characterized by reciprocity, with the man performing courtesies for the woman and vice versa. It is customary for a child to bear two family names; the last name is the mother's family name and the second-to-last name is the father's family name. People use either their full name or go by their father's family name, which is the official surname. Therefore, a person named José Felipe Correa Peres could be addressed as Señor Correa or Don José.

Dating and Marriage

Young people begin dating by the time they are 16. Group dating is emphasized early on. Men begin to marry at about age 22 and women marry between 18 and 23. Couples often date from one to three years before getting engaged. Getting an education before marriage is often important. Traditional Christian wedding ceremonies are common. Divorce is not recognized by the Catholic church, but legal means of canceling or nullifying a marriage are available.

Diet

Many national dishes are prepared with fish, seafood, chicken, beef, beans, eggs, and corn. The main meal is eaten at midday, between 12:30 and 2:30 P.M. A lighter meal is eaten between 8:00 and 10:00 P.M. During the afternoon it is customary to have teatime. At teatime, a beverage, small sandwiches, and cookies or cakes are served.

There are large supermarkets in major cities. Traveling markets (ferias) provide fresh fruits, vegetables, meat, fish, and flowers to smaller cities and towns. What is eaten depends on the region, but some favorites include empanadas de horno (meat turnovers with beef, hard-boiled eggs, onions, olives, and raisins), pastel de choclo (a baked meal of beef, chicken, onions, corn, eggs, and spices), cazuela de ave (chicken soup), and seafood casseroles and stews. On rainy days, children enjoy eating sopaipillas, which are made from a pumpkin dough, deep fried, and, sprinkled with sugar. Manjar, made by boiling an unopened can of sweetened condensed milk for hours, is a favorite bread spread or baking ingredient.

Recreation

Popular activities include sports, theater, music, and movies. Fútbol (soccer) is the most popular sport. Swimming and going to parks are also enjoyed. During the summer, vacations to the coast or the countryside are common. In a nation with a very long coastline, Chileans enjoy fishing as well. Weekend or holiday barbecues are frequent social gatherings. In areas where cattle have been important, rodeo is very popular. Rodeo in Chile is very different from U.S. rodeo. Cowboys (huasos) wear handwoven capes and straw hats. The main event consists of a pair of huasos skillfully guiding their horses to trap a steer against a padded arena wall. Points are earned for the portion of the steer that is pinned.

Holidays

Chile's important holidays include New Year's Day, Easter, Labor Day (1 May), Naval Battle of Iquique (21 May), Independence Day (18 September), Armed Forces Day (19 September), Columbus Day (12 October), All Saints Day (1 November), and Christmas. The independence holiday is celebrated at parks where people eat empanadas, drink chicha (sweet drink made with fermented grapes), and dance the cueca (the national dance) to guitar music. Christmas is celebrated much the same way as it is in the United States, but it takes place in summer rather than winter, making some activities different than those in the Northern Hemisphere.

Commerce

In Santiago, Chile's capital, and other large cities, people usually work from 9:00 A.M. to 6:00 P.M., five or six days a week. Depending on the location, however, siesta hours (midday meal break) are still observed, and shops and offices may close. Chile has an active and modern business climate; its exports and investments link it to world markets.

SOCIETY

Government

The republic of Chile is a multiparty democracy. President Frei is chief of state and head of government. His term expires in the year 2000. The National Congress has two houses: the Senate (46 members) and the Chamber of Deputies (120 members). There are several political parties officially represented in the government. The legislature sits at Valparaíso in a newly constructed Congress building. The voting age is 18. All eligible citizens are required by law to vote.

Economy

Chile's economy is prosperous and growing. Growth has averaged 5 percent annually, and was above 7 percent in 1993. Chilean foreign debt has decreased steadily, and the country enjoys considerable foreign investment. Unemployment and inflation have both dropped to manageable levels.

Chile's Human Development Index (0.864) ranks it 36 out of 173 countries. Real gross domestic product per capita is $5,099, which has improved significantly in the last generation. These figures indicate Chileans generally have greater access to economic prosperity than they did 30 years ago and the average person can earn an income sufficient to meet basic needs.

President Aylwin instituted a program aimed at helping the poor by extending special small business loans and other credits to them, investing more in the poorest schools, building permanent homes for low-income families, and sponsoring work-study programs for the youth. The income of the poorest Chileans has subsequently risen by 20 percent and more than one million people have been lifted above the poverty line. While much progress is still needed, the program's success has encouraged greater productivity and prosperity in Chile.

Copper accounts for about 50 percent of all exports. Fresh fruit is fast becoming one of Chile's main exports, with over 40 countries importing the country's grapes, apples, nectarines, peaches, and other fruits. Mining of other minerals, agriculture, and light manufacturing are all important to the economy. The currency is the Chilean *peso* (Ch$).

Transportation and Communication

Public transportation in Chile is good. Santiago has a subway, and elsewhere the bus systems are efficient and inexpensive. Several airports also serve domestic and international travelers. A satellite communications system, cable television, and other technological advances have helped Chile increase telephone access, have global communication links, and improve radio and television service to the country.

Education

Chileans are among the best-educated people in Latin America with a literacy rate of 93 percent. Schooling is free and compulsory between ages five and seventeen. In addition to public schools, there are many private, commercial, and industrial educational institutions. The people value education as the way to a better life. There are eight universities in Santiago alone; others are located throughout the country. The Nobel Prize for literature was awarded in 1945 to a Chilean, Gabriela Mistral, for her verse and prose, and in 1971 to another Chilean, Pablo Neruda, for poetry.

Health

Currently, health care is nationalized. However, the system is being decentralized somewhat and private insurance institutions are taking over some portions of care payment (over 10 percent). Citizens have a choice as to whether they use the private or public health care system. Chileans have enjoyed increasingly good health over the past few years, with infant mortality rates dropping from above 60 per 1,000 in the 1970s to 16 per 1,000 today. Life expectancy has also increased to between 71 and 77 years. Water is potable in most areas.

FOR THE TRAVELER

A U.S. citizen does not need a visa for a visit of less than 90 days. A valid passport is necessary. No vaccinations are required. Remember that the seasons are reversed from North America. Chile has a wide variety of attractions in every part of the country because of its natural beauty. A visitor can enjoy beaches, skiing, hiking, and other opportunities. The tourist industry is well developed. Santiago is subject to severe smog, particularly in the winter; care should be taken by those with respiratory problems. Dual-voltage small appliances or an adaptor and a plug adaptor kit are necessary to use electrical outlets. The Chile National Tourism Board (866 United Nations Plaza, Suite 302, New York, NY 10017) has more information. You may also wish to contact the Embassy of Chile, 1732 Massachusetts Avenue NW, Washington, DC 20036.

A *Culturgram* is a product of native commentary and original, expert analysis. Statistics are estimates and information is presented as a matter of opinion. While the editors strive for accuracy and detail, this document should not be considered strictly factual. It is a general introduction to culture, an initial step in building bridges of understanding between peoples. It may not apply to all peoples of the nation. You should therefore consult other sources for more information.

Republic of
Colombia

Boundary representations not necessarily authoritative.

THE AMERICAS

BACKGROUND

Land and Climate

With 439,733 square miles (1,138,910 square kilometers), Colombia is the fourth largest country in Latin America and is about the size of California and Texas combined. It is located at the juncture between Central and South America. Colombia has snowcapped mountains as well as tropical jungles. Divided by three branches of the Andes mountains, Colombia has low coastal plains on the Caribbean Sea and the Pacific Ocean; cool mountain plateaus, valleys, and active volcanoes in the center; and an eastern region with plains in the north and jungle in the south.

There are no distinct seasons in Colombia, but differing elevations offer a great variety of temperatures. Medellín, at 5,000 feet (1,524 meters) above sea level, averages 70°F (21°C), while Bogotá, the capital, averages 55°F (13°C) at 8,000 feet (2,438 meters) above sea level. The coast is hot and humid. With such diversity in temperature, altitude, and rainfall, Colombia produces an incredible variety and abundance of vegetation and animal life. When Middle Eastern coffee seeds were brought to Colombia by Spanish missionaries, they found a perfect climate in Colombia. Coffee has flourished ever since, becoming the country's most important export crop.

History

The history of Colombia before the arrival of Europeans is uncertain, but many peoples thrived in the area and were present when the Spanish began to settle the region in the 1500s. The area was soon part of New Granada, which encompassed present-day Venezuela, Ecuador, and Panama in addition to Colombia. Resentment against Spanish rule grew in the late 1700s until 1810, when nationalists claimed independence. This was not really achieved until after several years of struggle, when Simón Bolívar assembled an army to defeat Spanish troops at the Battle of Boyacá in 1819. He established a new Greater Colombia (Gran Colombia) republic, from which Venezuela and Ecuador withdrew in 1830.

Known first as the State of New Granada, Colombia's name was changed several times before it became the Republic of Colombia. Panama declared itself independent in 1903 to make way for U.S. construction of the Panama Canal. Civil war between conservatives and liberals from 1948 to 1957 led to a constitutional amendment requiring the presidency to alternate between the Liberal and Conservative political parties until 1974. Elections have been held regularly since that time.

The M–19 guerrilla movement and the Medellín and Cali drug cartels caused unrest and violence in the 1980s. M–19

Copyright © 1994. Brigham Young University. Printed in the USA. All rights reserved. It is against the law to copy, reprint, store in a retrieval system, or transmit any part of this publication in any form by any means for any purpose without written permission from the Publications Division of the David M. Kennedy Center for International Studies, Brigham Young University, PO Box 24538, Provo, UT 84602–4538. Culturgrams are available for more than 125 areas of the world. To place an order, to receive a free catalog, or to obtain information on traveling abroad, call toll free (800) 528–6279.

renounced terrorism and joined the democratic process in the 1990 presidential elections. Drug traffickers, often called narcoterrorists, killed several presidential candidates and committed violent acts to dissuade Colombians from voting. Despite the violence, elections were successfully held. César Gaviria Trujillo was elected president.

Gaviria took a solid stand against violence and drug trafficking. However, to encourage peace in the country, he offered terrorist groups the right to participate in the 1991 constitutional convention if they would disarm and renounce violence. While most groups accepted the offer and began participating in the political process, two rejected it. Gaviria also offered drug traffickers leniency and certain rights if they would quit dealing in narcotics and confess their crimes. Many traffickers began accepting the offer in late 1990 and drug-related violence diminished for a time.

In December 1990, a national assembly was formed to rewrite the 1886 constitution. For the first time, nearly all segments of the population—including former terrorists, Indians, and nontraditional political parties—were represented in the process. The convention was given the right to make whatever changes it chose to. The new constitution took effect in July 1991, and it enjoys wide support throughout the country. It encourages political pluralism, the rule of law, and special rights for the long-ignored Indians. Colombia's black population also eventually (1994) received special rights, such as reserved seats in Congress and a recognition of basic civil rights. Elitism is discouraged through a provision that prohibits two people of the same family from being members of Congress at the same time.

Drug-related violence increased in 1992 and 1993 as opposing factions battled for control over segments of the drug industry. In addition, some guerrilla groups continued their campaign against the government by sabotaging oil fields and other economic sites. Violence subsided considerably by the end of 1993, partly due to the death of noted drug baron, Pablo Escobar. National presidential elections held in 1994 were peaceful and democratic. Ernesto Samper Pizano of the Liberal party was elected president to serve a four-year term.

THE PEOPLE

Population

Colombia's population of 34.9 million is growing at 1.8 percent annually. The majority of Colombians live in the western half of the country; much of the southeast is covered by jungle. A mixed Spanish-Indian ethnic group *(mestizo)* composes 58 percent of the population. Whites account for 20 percent. Others include 14 percent black-caucasian mix, 4 percent black, 3 percent Indian-black mix, and 1 percent Indian. Blacks are descendants of slaves imported during the Spanish colonial era. Many mixed with other peoples, especially when slavery was abolished in 1851. Blacks generally live along the Pacific and Caribbean coasts, comprising the majority of some large cities; Quibdó has 300,000 people, mostly of black or mixed black groups. The largest cities are Bogotá (4.35 million), Medellín (2.1 million), and Cali (1.4 million). About 70 percent of the population lives in urban areas, and more than 40 percent is younger than age 20.

Language

The official language is Spanish. English is spoken by some in large cities and is a required course in school. Most Indian ethnic groups have their own languages; among 80 groups, there are 40 different languages. Dialects spoken by some blacks reflect their African roots.

Religion

While Colombians are guaranteed freedom of religion, the Roman Catholic church is the state religion, to which nearly 95 percent of the people belong. Through the courts, the church has jurisdiction over marriages and divorce. While religion remains an important influence on culture, society is nevertheless becoming more secularized. Many people of the indigenous or black ethnic groups retain beliefs from non-Christian traditional worship systems.

General Attitudes

Colombians value courtesy and smiles. The individual is important in society. For this reason, timetables and punctuality are not stressed. It is not impolite to be late for an appointment, especially in rural areas. Colombians are proud of their history of democracy and independence. They do not appreciate outside interference and are confident they can meet challenges on their own. This is evident in the success of attempts to end violence that gripped many of their cities in the late 1980s and early 1990s. Colombians are hardworking and peace loving, and are experiencing a new appreciation for cultural and political pluralism. The historical class structure and closed political system are slowly dying, but society faces many challenges to creating a truly egalitarian society.

Personal Appearance

An individual's appearance is important. Clothing is conservative, clean, and well kept. The proper clothing for each occasion is essential. Men wear suits, white shirts, and ties in urban areas. Comfortable dresses are worn by women and urban youth dress casually. Dress in rural areas is less fashionable, but the people wear neat, clean clothing. Indians often wear traditional clothing, which can include wraparound dresses, bowler hats, and *ponchos*.

CUSTOMS AND COURTESIES

Greetings

The most common greeting is a handshake, although it is not too vigorous. Men often shake hands with everyone when entering a home, greeting a group, or leaving. Women kiss each other on the cheek if they are acquainted, but offer a verbal greeting otherwise. Young people will also kiss each other on the cheek if they are good friends. It is customary to address people by a title (*Señor, Señora, Doctor*, among others) when being introduced. First names are not used between strangers. The *abrazo* (hug) is common between close friends or relatives. Common terms include *¡Buenos días!* (Good day), *¿Cómo está?* (How are you?), and *¡Adiós!* (Good-bye).

Gestures

Yawning in the presence of strangers or in a group is impolite because it is a sign of hunger. People beckon others with the palm down, waving the fingers or the whole hand. Toothpicks are used discreetly. Smiling is an important gesture of goodwill.

Visiting

Visiting is an important part of Colombian culture. Friends and relatives may visit unannounced, especially in rural areas where telephones are not widely available, but it is otherwise polite to call ahead or make arrangements in advance. Colombians are gracious hosts. Guests are usually offered refreshments and made to feel comfortable. In return, hosts are treated with courtesy and respect.

When invited for dinner, guests usually arrive at least a few minutes and often 30 or more minutes late. They may bring a small gift to the hosts, but this is not expected. On more formal visits, guests wait to sit until the hosts have directed them to a seat. Customs vary with ethnic group and region. Upon departing, the guests are often accompanied out the door or even down the street by the hosts. Politeness and proper etiquette are emphasized in Colombia. It is improper to put one's feet on furniture when visiting.

Eating

Good manners and courtesy when eating are important to Colombians. Pleasant conversation is welcome at the table, as it stimulates a feeling of goodwill. Overeating is impolite; a host may offer more helpings, but these should be politely refused. For many, it is important to keep hands above the table during the meal. In a group, it is impolite to take anything to eat without first offering it to others. Eating on the streets is not proper. In restaurants, a 10 percent service charge is usually included in the bill; if not, a tip should be left at the table.

LIFESTYLE

Family

The family is important in Colombian society and family members share their good fortunes with one another. Traditional values still maintain a very strong influence on family relations. The father feels the obligation to provide for his family. The mother is responsible for most of the affairs of the home. An increasing number of women work outside the home. More than 20 percent of the labor force is female. It is the custom for a child to bear two family names; the last name is the mother's family name and the second-to-last name is the father's family name. People use either their full name or go by their father's family

name, which is the official surname. Therefore, a person named José Muñoz Gómez would be called Señor Muñoz.

Upper-class families enjoy many modern conveniences and can hire household help. However, most Colombians lead simpler lives. About one-third live in absolute poverty.

Dating and Marriage

Depending on family custom, dating begins around age 14 or 15. In large cities, the age is somewhat lower. Couples date and decide on marriage much as in the United States. Marriage ceremonies generally follow Catholic traditions.

Diet

Breakfast often consists of juice, coffee or hot chocolate, fruit, eggs, and bread; or a smaller "continental" breakfast is eaten. Lunch, usually between noon and 2:00 P.M., is the main meal of the day. When possible, the family gathers at this time (many schools and businesses close) for the meal. However, in urban areas there is a trend to have the main meal in the evening. Soup, rice, meat, potatoes, salad, and beans are the staple foods. *Arroz con pollo* (chicken with rice) is a popular national dish. *Arepa* is a cornmeal pancake. *Sancocho* is a meat and vegetable stew. Supper is usually at 7:00 or 8:00 P.M. Coffee, the chief agricultural product in Colombia, is the favorite drink of many.

Recreation

Fútbol (soccer) is the most popular sport in Colombia. World Cup action is carefully followed by most people, especially men. Colombia's national team competed in the 1994 World Cup. Other favorite activities include cycle racing, swimming, track and field, volleyball, basketball, and baseball. Attending bullfights is also popular. Wealthy individuals belong to sport clubs offering golf and tennis. Aside from playing or watching sports, people enjoy dancing, especially at folk festivals, and music.

Holidays

Holidays in Colombia include New Year's Day, Epiphany (6 January), St. Joseph's Day (19 March), Easter, Labor Day (1 May), Feast of Saints Peter and Paul (29 June), Independence Day (20 July), Battle of Boyacá (7 August), Assumption Day (15 August), *Día de la Raza* (12 October), All Saints Day (1 November), Independence of Cartagena (11 November), and Christmas.

Commerce

The Colombian workweek is basically Monday through Friday, from 8:00 A.M. to 6:00 P.M., with lunch between noon and 2:00 P.M. Shops, however, are open from 9:00 A.M. to 6:30 P.M., Monday through Saturday, with some closing Saturday afternoon. Banks close at 3:00 P.M.

SOCIETY

Government

Colombia has a bicameral Congress, with a Senate and Chamber of Representatives. Senators are elected in a national vote, while Representatives are elected regionally. The president is head of state and head of government. He and a cabinet run the government. The judicial branch is independent. All citizens may vote at age 18. Colombia has 23 states, called departments.

Economy

Colombia has a fairly strong, vibrant economy. It benefits from very high rates of foreign investment and solid growth, which is possible because of its free-market policies. Colombians are proud of the fact that they are current on all foreign debt payments and have never defaulted. The country has a reputation for managing the economy according to sound principles. Colombia's Human Development Index (0.770) ranks it 61 out of 173 countries. Real gross domestic product per capita is $4,237, which has more than doubled in the last generation. With rural poverty and an unequal distribution of income, these figures suggest that economic opportunities are more accessible to the ruling class in urban areas. Blacks and Indians are generally marginalized, but new laws recognizing their rights and providing for greater political integration are expected to lead to better economic conditions for these lower socioeconomic groups.

Agriculture plays a key role in Colombia's economy. Coffee is the most important export, accounting for 30 percent of all export earnings; freshly cut flowers and bananas also provide export earnings for the nation. Other agricultural products are sugar, cotton, rice, and corn.

The mining of Colombia's many natural resources as well as manufacturing are also key elements in the economy. More than 90 percent of the world's emeralds are mined in Colombia. Crude oil, natural gas, iron ore, nickel, gold, copper, textiles, chemicals, and other products all contribute to the economy. The production and export of illicit drugs (such as cocaine) also generates revenue for the economy—revenue that must be replaced through legitimate activity before the drug industry's significance decreases. With half of the country covered by forests and woodlands, the timber industry is becoming important. The currency is the Colombian *peso* ($ or P).

Transportation and Communication

Domestic bus service is the most common link between the cities of Colombia, but air-passenger travel is on the rise. Although a minority of the people own cars, travel on highways has increased, and with it so has road construction and repair. Still, only about 10 percent of the roads are paved. With coasts on two oceans, port cities provide the country with shipping access to North American, European, and Asian markets. Communication systems have improved with various projects. There are more than 1.8 million telephones in the nation and a fiber-optic system is scheduled to link the country with the United States. The country has a free press that has been active in resisting violence from terrorists.

Education

Primary education is free and compulsory, although many schools are private. Boys and girls often attend separate schools. Rural schools have increased in number in recent years, helping the literacy rate to rise to about 87 percent. Unfortunately the literacy rate is only 40 percent for the Indian and black populations. Overall, just fewer than 60 percent of all students actually complete their primary education and move on to the secondary level. Secondary and vocational schools are found in major cities, and several universities are now in operation; Bogotá has eight, the largest being the National University. Scholarly achievement has been important throughout Colombia's history.

Health

Hospital and personal health care are available in the cities but are lacking in rural areas. Private clinics and public or charity hospitals are available. As many tropical diseases have been eradicated, life expectancy has risen to between 69 and 74 years. However, malaria and yellow fever are still dangerous in rural and tropical regions, and tap water is often not safe for drinking. The infant mortality rate is 30 per 1,000. Infant mortality is significantly higher and life expectancy lower among blacks and Indians.

FOR THE TRAVELER

A tourist visa (from a consulate) or tourist card (obtained at the airport) is required of U.S. citizens for stays of as long as 90 days. A valid passport and proof of onward passage are also required. Minors (younger than 18) traveling alone or without one of their parents or guardian must carry a notarized authorization (authenticated by the embassy or consulate) from the absent parent or guardian. Tourists leaving the country by air are charged an airport tax that must be paid in U.S. dollars or *pesos*. There are some restrictions on what one can bring into the country. The U.S. government has issued travel advisories in the past because of violence. For the latest updates, call (202) 647–5225. One should take precautions against pickpockets operating in some cities. Also, officials recommend that only taxis with green and off-white paint be used, as those vehicles are registered and considered trustworthy. Electrical outlets use either flat blade or round pin plugs and have different voltages; an adaptor may be necessary. For additional information, you may wish to contact the Embassy of Colombia, 1825 Connecticut Avenue NW, Washington, DC 20009.

A *Culturgram* is a product of native commentary and original, expert analysis. Statistics are estimates and information is presented as a matter of opinion. While the editors strive for accuracy and detail, this document should not be considered strictly factual. It is a general introduction to culture, an initial step in building bridges of understanding between peoples. It may not apply to all peoples of the nation. You should therefore consult other sources for more information.

Republic of
Costa Rica

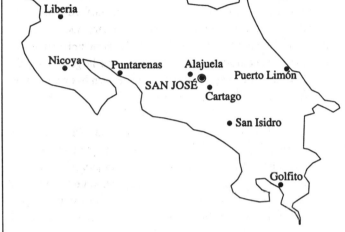

Boundary representations not necessarily authoritative.

BACKGROUND

Land and Climate

Costa Rica covers 19,730 square miles (51,100 square kilometers) and is just smaller than West Virginia. It shares its northern border with Nicaragua and its southern neighbor is Panama. About 60 percent of Costa Rica is covered by different types of forests. More than 11 percent of the total territory is reserved as national parks. This small nation has a diverse landscape of tropical rain forest, mountain cloud forest, volcanoes, green countryside, and beautiful rivers. Although the country lies entirely in the tropical climate zone, elevation changes allow for cooler temperatures in the central highlands. The coastal lowlands are hot and humid. Most people live at elevations where the climate is generally mild the entire year. Rainfall varies between the dry season (December–April) and the wet season (May–November). The land is subject to earthquakes, hurricanes, and volcanic eruptions.

History

A variety of native peoples lived in present-day Costa Rica before Columbus arrived in 1502. In the north, the indigenous cultures were influenced by Mayan civilization. Southern groups were more related to the indigenous peoples of South America. Today's museums offer a glimpse of pre-Columbian life. Spain eventually colonized the Costa Rican area along with most of Central America. Because minerals were scarce, it was ignored by the Spanish crown and remained isolated. In 1821, Costa Rica joined other Central American nations in declaring independence from Spain during a nonviolent revolution. In 1824, it became a state of the Federal Republic of Central America. After the Republic collapsed in 1838, Costa Rica became a sovereign nation.

Costa Rica has a long tradition of changes in government via democratic means. Its democratic tradition has been interrupted by military coups only three times in 150 years. Consequently, Costa Rica has one of the most stable democratic governments in Central America, a rare occurrence in Latin America. Civil war erupted for six weeks in 1948 after a dispute over elections. José Figueres Ferrer led an interim government until 1949 when the election dispute was settled. Figueres (who was elected president in 1953 and again in 1970) abolished the army in 1948, and a new constitution was introduced in 1949. Costa Rica has enjoyed peace and democracy ever since.

The nation practices a philosophy of nonintervention in the affairs of foreign governments. Former president Oscar Arias Sánchez (who left office in 1990) was an avid supporter of the Central American Peace Plan. Arias won the Nobel Peace Prize for his efforts to bring peace to the region. The award is a great source of pride for all Costa Ricans, as they feel it emphasizes their distinct heritage.

Rafael Calderón Fournier was elected president in 1990. When his successor, José Maria Figueres Olsen, was elected in 1994, it marked the 11th peaceful transfer of power since 1948. Figueres is the son of the former three-term president.

Copyright © 1994. Brigham Young University. Printed in the USA. All rights reserved. It is against the law to copy, reprint, store in a retrieval system, or transmit any part of this publication in any form by any means for any purpose without written permission from the Publications Division of the David M. Kennedy Center for International Studies, Brigham Young University, PO Box 24538, Provo, UT 84602–4538. *Culturgrams* are available for more than 125 areas of the world. To place an order, to receive a free catalog, or to obtain information on traveling abroad, call toll free (800) 528–6279.

THE PEOPLE

Population

The population of Costa Rica is 3.2 million and is growing at 2.3 percent a year. The population is relatively young, with over 45 percent under age 20. Most people live in the Central Valley highlands. The majority of people (87 percent) have a European heritage. About 7 percent are of mixed heritage (European and Indian), although many of these are immigrants from other Latin American countries. Two percent of the population is black and lives mostly on the Atlantic Coast. These people are descendants of laborers brought from the Caribbean to build a railroad. One percent are native American Indians, some of whom still live in the Talamanca mountain region. Another 1 percent are ethnic Chinese.

Language

Spanish is the official language of Costa Rica. English is widely understood. Patua (Creole English) is spoken by the black population. Bribri, an indigenous language spoken by the Bribri people, is the most common native language. There are ten other native groups, some of which speak Spanish and some a native tongue.

The Costa Rican people are called *Ticos* by other Central Americans and by themselves as well. The nickname comes from the habit of rural people ending words or phrases with the suffix *tico* (instead of the more common Spanish diminutive *tito*). So, instead of saying *un momento* or *un momentito* (one moment), they say *un momentico*. Individually, men are called *ticos* and women *ticas*, but the mixed company reference is *ticos*.

Religion

The Roman Catholic church claims membership of about 95 percent of the population. Until the mid 1980s, the Catholic church was the nation's official church, but it lost that status when the government decreed a democratic nation should support no particular religion. The constitution guarantees religious freedom to the people. As is the trend elsewhere, secularization in Costa Rica is leading some people away from organized religion. At the same time, a growing number of religious people are joining other Christian churches—and religion continues to play an important role in society.

General Attitudes

Costa Rica is a land of courtesy, domestic enterprise, honesty, and gentleness. Militarism is despised by nearly all. Children are taught in school that armies are created to oppress people rather than to protect them. *Ticos* say they are lovers of dialogue, peace, and conciliation. They also value privacy and quiet behavior. However, personal honor is vigorously defended.

Individuality is an important characteristic, expressed in Costa Rica's relations with other nations and, to a lesser extent, on a personal level. This is partly due to Costa Rican isolation during the colonial period: with little contact to the colonial rulers, *Ticos* developed greater independence. Still, group conformity in values, interests, and thought is important in society. Individuals are recognized as such and all people are given respect, regardless of their social class. There is little resentment between the classes, due to this traditional respect and a belief that some things are determined by God. A feeling that Deity controls some aspects of life, such as one's health or success at a given venture, is evident in daily speech. People often attribute their achievements to and place hope in God. This tradition is changing with greater education and people's desire for material progress.

Personal Appearance

Western dress is common throughout the country. Women generally pay more attention to their appearance than men, and always try to be fashionably dressed. Clothing is neat and clean and generally modest.

CUSTOMS AND COURTESIES

Greetings

Women friends or relatives greet each other with a light kiss on the cheek. If women are not yet acquainted, they often pat each other on the arm. Men shake hands. It is an insult to not shake every man's hand in a small group. Common terms for greeting include *¡Buenos días!* (Good day), *¡Buenas tardes!* (Good afternoon), and *¡Buenas noches!* (Good evening) or *¿Cómo está?* (How are you?). *¡Hola!* (Hi) is a casual greeting popular among the youth. Older people find it disrespectful if it is used to greet them. In rural areas, people greet each other while passing on the street, regardless of whether they are acquainted. One might simply say *¡Adios!* or *¡Buenas!* or be more formal and say *¡Adios, Señora!* or *¡Buenos días!* This tradition is less common in urban areas. Rural people often bow their heads slightly and touch their hats in greeting. Greetings between strangers or acquaintances are brief, but people who know each other usually take a few minutes to talk about family, work, or health.

When addressing others, professional titles are used either with or without a surname, depending on the situation. *Señor* (Mr.) and *Señora* (Mrs.) are also used, especially for people with whom one is not well acquainted. First names are used to address friends, children, coworkers, and subordinates. The titles *Don* and *Doña* are used with the first name for older men and women, respectively, to show special respect for and familiarity with the person. For example, a child might call the mother of his best friend, *Doña Maria*.

Gestures

Hand gestures are common and important to everyday conversation. In fact, Costa Ricans use their hands a lot to express an idea, either with or without verbal communication. To say no, the index finger (palm out, finger up) is waved vigorously. To express shock or when faced with a serious situation, *ticos* will shake the hand vigorously enough to snap (slap) the fingers together three or four times. There are many different hand greetings in addition to the handshake or wave. For instance, young people slap hands together in a greeting similar to a "high five." Eye contact is very important, especially when discussing a serious issue or talking to a superior. It is traditionally understood that the lack of eye contact means the person cannot be trusted. Chewing gum while speaking is impolite.

Visiting

Costa Ricans generally prefer that visits are arranged in advance. Only close friends or relatives drop by unannounced, and then mostly in the afternoon after most housework has been done. Otherwise, uninvited visitors may not be asked into the home. Costa Ricans enjoy socializing, but do not visit as often as people in other Latin American or Caribbean countries. Invited guests are generally expected to arrive within a few minutes of being on time. Punctuality is not required, but being very late is also not appreciated. Guests invited for dinner usually bring a small gift to their hosts, such as flowers, wine, a plant, or something to share or mark the occasion. Close friends often bring more personal gifts. Gifts are also exchanged on special occasions.

Dinner guests are usually first given refreshments and drinks while they socialize with their hosts for an hour or so before the meal is served. After dinner, coffee and dessert accompany more conversation. Guests generally leave shortly thereafter.

If a Costa Rican invites someone to come and spend a few days at his home, the potential guest must determine whether the invitation is sincere or whether the host is just trying to be polite. Such an invitation does not always carry the expectation that the guest will show up.

Eating

At the table, Costa Ricans enjoy active conversation on a variety of subjects. Mealtime is to be enjoyed and is extended by conversation. Costa Ricans eat rice and beans in various combinations for nearly every meal. Typical at breakfast is *gallo pinto* (mixture of rice and black beans). *Casado* (rice, beans, eggs, meat, and plantain) is a common lunchtime meal. Bread is eaten with most meals, although *tortillas* are also common. Table manners vary from family to family, but one general rule is that both hands should be kept above the table, rather than in the lap. In restaurants, a tip of 10 percent is customarily included in the bill. Further tipping is not expected.

Most people eat three meals a day, with mid-morning and afternoon coffee breaks or snacks. Breakfast and dinner are the most important meals, as lunch is becoming more rushed and is more often eaten away from home. Business professionals make lunch dates, but dinner is otherwise the meal for entertaining guests.

LIFESTYLE

Family

Costa Ricans value family tradition and heritage. The immediate family has an average of three to five children. Rural families are usually larger. Women retain their maiden names when they marry. Children carry the surnames of both parents. The second-to-last name in a full name is the family surname. While the husband makes most final decisions in the home, he shares many responsibilities with his wife. Most women do not work outside the home, but a growing number are entering the labor force. Nearly 30 percent of the work force is female. Many families, even many of the poor, own their own homes, which are wood-frame houses.

Dating and Marriage

Girls are generally more restricted in dating than boys. They are seldom visited past 10:00 P.M., unless courtship is close to marriage. Early dating is usually done in groups, except for rural areas where there are fewer people. Movies, dances, picnics, and a yearly civic carnival are favorite activities for dates. The December bullfights are also popular. A boy usually asks permission of a girl's parents to date her, but this custom is slowly disappearing, especially in urban areas.

Marriage is still a valued institution; Costa Rica has one of the highest marriage rates in Latin America. Families visit each other to show formal agreement on their children's marriage. Women generally marry in their early 20s, men somewhat later.

Diet

Many varieties of food are enjoyed in Costa Rica. Popular in some areas is *olla de carne*, a beef stew with potatoes, onions, and many vegetables. *Tamales* (meat, vegetables, and flour wrapped in plantain leaves and boiled) is served for Easter and Christmas. Along with rice and beans, bread, tortillas, and fruits are staple items eaten with main meals. Also common are *lengua en salsa* (tongue in sauce), *mondongo* (intestine soup), *empanadas* (turnovers), *arroz con pollo* (rice with chicken), and *gallos* (*tortillas* with meat and vegetable fillings). Coffee is popular for *ticos* of all ages.

Recreation

Fútbol (soccer) is the most popular sport, both for spectators and participants. Basketball, baseball, volleyball, surfing, auto racing, swimming, and tennis are also popular. Fishing is good in many parts of the country. Golf and polo are enjoyed by the wealthy. The beautiful beaches are crowded between January and April. Local carnivals, festivals, and bullfights are popular attractions at various times throughout the year.

Costa Ricans enjoy music that is popular in the Caribbean and Brazil, as well as music common throughout Central America. There is really no type of music that is unique to Costa Rica. Cultural arts are popular, and people enjoy stories and poetry. Media broadcasts from the United States are popular and have a significant impact on urban trends.

Holidays

Costa Rican holidays include New Year's Day; Feast of St. Joseph (19 March); Anniversary of the Battle of Rivas against Walker (11 April), in which the national hero, Juan Santamaría, the drummer boy, lost his life; *Semana Santa* (Holy Week) and Easter; Labor Day (1 May); Annexation of Guanacaste to Costa Rica (25 July); Feast of St. Peter and St. Paul (29 June); Feast of Our Lady of the Angels (2 August); Central American Independence Day (15 September); Columbus Day (12 October); Feast of Immaculate Conception (8 December); and Christmas. Christmas is celebrated with family, but New Year's is a time for friends, parties, drinking, and dancing.

Commerce

Most businesses are open weekdays from 8:00 A.M. to noon and 2:00 to 6:00 P.M. Many shops are open on Saturday, but most are closed on Sunday. Government offices close weekdays at 4:00 P.M. Few business meetings are strictly formal, and socializing is an important part of a business relationship.

SOCIETY

Government

The country has an elected president and two vice presidents in the executive branch. There is a unicameral National Assembly, whose 57 legislators are elected to four-year terms. The judicial branch is separate. Costa Rica has seven provinces. All citizens age 18 and over are required to vote in national elections. Election day is always declared a national holiday and people travel to their town of birth to vote.

Economy

Despite a relative lack of minerals and other traditional natural resources, Costa Rica has a relatively prosperous economy. The country's Human Development Index (0.852) ranks it 42 out of 173 nations. Real gross domestic product per capita is $4,542, a figure that has doubled in the last generation. The economy is growing at above 2 percent annually. These figures reflect Costa Rica's stability, successful tourism, timber, and agricultural industries, and generally egalitarian society. Most people earn enough to meet basic needs and can take advantage of a variety of economic opportunities. Unemployment is low, although inflation is above 15 percent. Costa Rica has been a major recipient of foreign aid, and foreign investment in the country is increasing.

Agricultural products comprise the bulk (70 percent) of Costa Rica's exports; 27 percent of the people are employed in agriculture. Exports include coffee, bananas, beef, sugar, cocoa, and fertilizer. Ornamental flowers are becoming an increasingly important export. Cattle raising is centered in the Guanacaste province, but is expanding to other areas. Other industries include food processing, textiles, and construction materials. Costa Rica has excellent potential for hydroelectric power, and nearly all of its electricity comes from hydroelectric power plants. Tourism facilities are well-developed, so the industry is prosperous and important to the economy. Ecotourism is currently especially popular. The monetary unit is the Costa Rican *colón* (¢, plural=*colones*).

Transportation and Communication

While personal automobiles are becoming more affordable, the most common form of transportation within and between cities is the bus. Fares are inexpensive and the system is efficient. About half of the roads are paved. Taxis are commonly available; legal taxis are red. There are 26 airports with paved runways. The domestic phone system is very good, and telephones are located throughout the country. The telephone system was expanded between 1989 and 1994, although remote rural areas still lack service. Satellite systems are used for international communication. Many AM radio stations transmit throughout the country. There are also a number of television stations in Costa Rica. Several national newspapers receive wide circulation. The postal system is very efficient.

Education

Costa Rica has one of the finest urban public education systems in the Americas. Primary education is compulsory and free for six years, beginning with age seven. Where facilities exist, children may also attend kindergarten at age five and a preparatory year at age six. Enrollment in secondary schools is not mandatory, but more than 40 percent of all pupils do advance to that level. Secondary schooling is also free. The literacy rate is 93 percent. Four public universities serve the population. There are a number of private universities as well. Evening schools operate to educate the older generations. Costa Rica is home to four international education centers.

Health

Medical care is considered very good and a national health care system serves all citizens. The life expectancy has risen in recent years to between 75 and 79 years, and the infant mortality rate has fallen to 12 per 1,000. Infant malnutrition and inadequate prenatal care remain problems in rural areas. Malaria is common along the Nicaraguan border and at lower elevations. Dysentery and typhoid are found in areas outside the capital.

FOR THE TRAVELER

U.S. travelers need a passport to visit Costa Rica, but a visa is not required for stays of fewer than 90 days. Those who stay longer must have an AIDS test performed in Costa Rica and must apply for permission to stay. Short-term U.S. travelers are sometimes allowed to enter Costa Rica without a passport if they present their original birth certificate and a photo ID. But because a passport is safer and more convenient to use, travelers are advised to carry one. Various plug types are used for electrical outlets, but the voltage/currency is similar to that in the United States. Major credit cards are accepted in most areas. The Costa Rican Tourist Bureau (Plaza de La Cultura Fifth Street, Central and Second Avenue, San José, Costa Rica) has more specific information regarding lodging and travel. You may also wish to contact the Embassy of Costa Rica, 2114 S Street NW, Washington, DC 20008.

A *Culturgram* is a product of native commentary and original, expert analysis. Statistics are estimates and information is presented as a matter of opinion. While the editors strive for accuracy and detail, this document should not be considered strictly factual. It is a general introduction to culture, an initial step in building bridges of understanding between peoples. It may not apply to all peoples of the nation. You should therefore consult other sources for more information.

CULTURGRAM '95 ™

Republic of
Croatia

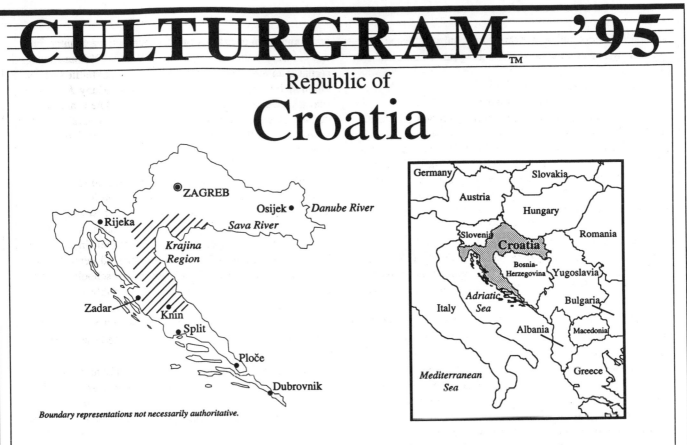

ZAGREB

Osijek • — Danube River

Rijeka

Sava River

Krajina
Region

Zadar

Knin

Split

Ploče

Dubrovnik

Boundary representations not necessarily authoritative.

Germany / Slovakia
Austria / Hungary
Slovenia / Croatia / Romania
Bosnia-Herzegovina / Yugoslavia
Adriatic / Bulgaria
Italy / Sea / Albania / Macedonia
Mediterranean / Greece
Sea

E
U
R
O
P
E

BACKGROUND

Land and Climate

Croatia is situated along the eastern coast of the Adriatic Sea, and its hinterland stretches close to the slopes of the Julian Alps in Slovenia, and into the Pannonian Valley to the banks of the Drava and Danube rivers. Covering 21,829 square miles (56,538 square kilometers), Croatia is about the size of West Virginia. Along the Adriatic are hundreds of islands that hug the highly indented coastline. The coast enjoys a Mediterranean climate with hot, sunny summers and pleasant winters. Many famous cities, including the medieval port of Dubrovnik, lie along the long coast. In mountainous regions, winters are cold and snowy, while summers are cool. In the Pannonian area, winters are cold and dry; summers are hot. The capital, Zagreb, lies on the Sava River.

History

Slavs began settling the Balkan peninsula as early as the sixth century A.D. Croatians were first united into a single state by King Tomislav in 925. Following Catholicism's Great Schism in the 11th century, Croats accepted Roman Catholicism and became associated with the West. In 1102, the Croatian and Hungarian monarchies came together in a personal union. In the 1500s, Croatia and Hungary became part of the Austro-Hungarian (Hapsburg) Empire.

The entire Balkans were embroiled in World War I, which was sparked by Serbia's move for greater unification and the assassination (in 1914) of Austria's crown prince in Sarajevo

(Bosnia). At the end of the war (1918), the Croatian Diet (legislature) broke ties with Hungary and Austria and proclaimed the State of the Slovenes, Croats, and Serbs. The state unified with the Kingdom of Serbia, and the new state was called the Kingdom of Serbs, Croats, and Slovenes, but relations between ethnic groups were hostile. When the kingdom's constitution was abolished in 1929, it became the Kingdom of Yugoslavia. Croats opposed the resulting dictatorship until the king stepped down in 1941 in the wake of internal conflicts and World War II. An independent State of Croatia was declared, but it soon joined Germany and Italy in the war.

While Croatians were involved in fascist activities that persecuted Jews, Serbs, and other groups, a great many also joined the antifascist (partisan) movement that opposed union with Germany. This struggle led to civil war for control of Yugoslavia; Communist forces (antifascists) were victorious over the *Chetniks* (royalists) in 1943. When Germany was defeated, Croatia became part of the Socialist Republic of Yugoslavia that was subsequently created under partisan leader Josip Broz Tito. The Yugoslav federation was quickly consolidated and Tito became its president in 1953. To keep opposing groups together, Tito's Communist party carefully controlled nationalist sentiments among all ethnic groups and promoted the federalism concept. Attempts in Croatia to revive Croat nationalism and culture were suppressed. When Tito died in 1980, his authority was transferred into a collective

Copyright © 1994. Brigham Young University. Printed in the USA. All rights reserved. It is against the law to copy, reprint, store in a retrieval system, or transmit any part of this publication in any form by any means for any purpose without written permission from the Publications Division of the David M. Kennedy Center for International Studies, Brigham Young University, PO Box 24538, Provo, UT 84602–4538. *Culturgrams* are available for more than 125 areas of the world. To place an order, to receive a free catalog, or to obtain information on traveling abroad, call toll free (800) 528–6279.

state presidency, which had a rotating chairman. That body was not able to effectively rule for many years before simmering ethnic tensions erupted. By the end of the 1980s, the federation was on the verge of breaking up under such pressure.

With the fall of communism elsewhere in Europe and the weakening of Yugoslavia's federation, Croatia held elections in 1990 and seated a government that desired autonomy. In June 1991, based on a popular referendum, Croatia declared its independence. Croatia was recognized by the international community in January 1992, but it faced heavy military intervention from the Yugoslav Army and Serbian government, which strongly opposed independence. Entire cities were nearly destroyed in fierce fighting between these forces, as well as between local Serbs and Croats.

The United Nations helped broker a cease-fire in 1992. Many people had been killed; thousands had been forced to leave their homes, creating a serious refugee problem; and ethnic hatred rooted in historical conflicts ran deep. Local Serbs had gained control of Krajina, or roughly one-third of Croatia's territory. They declared their own independence in 1992, but this has not been recognized outside of Yugoslavia (Serbia). The uneasy peace did not last long, as fighting between Croats, Serbs, and Muslims broke out again in 1993. Serbs launched attacks on Croatian cities to retaliate against Croatian military advances in Krajina. Croatia considers it essential to retake Knin, now held by Serbs, because its south (Dalmatia region) is otherwise isolated from the rest of the country. Serbs in Knin prefer war to any settlement that would restore Knin and the Krajina to full Croatian control. The tensions created by the Krajina issue, as well as Croatia's involvement in the war in Bosnia-Herzegovina, have fueled fears that civil war may again shatter the 1992 cease fire.

THE PEOPLE

Population

Croatia has a population of 4.78 million, which is presently not growing. Croats form the majority (78 percent); Serbs account for 12 percent. About 2.2 percent of the people claim to be Yugoslavs, although such an ethnic group does not really exist. It was promoted under Communist rule to suppress nationalism and provide an optional ethnic distinction for children of mixed marriages. Muslims of Slavic origin account for 1 percent of the population, and another 1 percent are Hungarian. Slovenes and other small groups make up the rest of the population. Serbs are more greatly concentrated in the Krajina region, although they and other minorities live throughout Croatia. A large number of Croatians live and work in other European countries as guest workers.

Language

Croatian is the country's official language. It is a Slavic language that adopted a Latin alphabet in the 14th century. Because the Cyrillic alphabet is used in some neighboring countries, it can be used by Serbs and other ethnic groups to write their own languages or Croatian. Although one would not see the Cyrillic alphabet on signs or public documents, recent laws guarantee the right to teach and use it. Serbian, Hungarian, Czech, Slovakian, Italian, Albanian, and Slovenian are all spoken by their respective groups in Croatia. English, French, German, and Italian may be studied in the schools beginning at age 10.

Religion

With the collapse of communism and Yugoslav socialism, religion is once again playing an important role in Croatian society. Most Croats are Roman Catholic; some are Protestant or Jewish. Serbs are mostly Orthodox Christian. There are also many Muslims. Freedom of worship is guaranteed. Religion has traditionally been very important to Croats. With the demise of communism, the Catholic church has regained much of its former prominence. This allows it to play an active role in political and social affairs.

General Attitudes

The people of Croatia are sociable, optimistic, proud of their heritage, and hospitable to strangers. They value their families, education, and good careers. For centuries, Croats did not have their own independent state, and for decades, Croatia was part of Yugoslavia. Croats now have an internationally recognized sovereign country, which they share with other ethnic groups. Croats are extremely proud of their new nation and are anxious for other countries to accept them and learn of Croatian history and culture. Most people in Croatia are loyal citizens of the new country, although tensions and disagreements clearly exist. People hope that the establishment of democratic principles and rights on the entire territory will ease some of these tensions and bring peace and prosperity to all citizens of Croatia. This will be difficult to do in light of wider regional conflicts and Serbian claims to Croatia's Krajina region. Mutual tolerance and respect must precede any lasting establishment of peace.

Personal Appearance

It is important for clothing to be neat and clean. Adults do not wear shorts in public, except for recreation or on the coast. Women wear skirts and dresses more often than pants. In the workplace, it is customary for women to wear dresses. Urban men wear suits and ties for special occasions and in some business or professional circles. The European tradition of wearing a tie (*kravata*) comes from the 18th century Croatian soldier's uniform. For informal situations, men prefer more practical daily clothing, such as jeans, knit shirts or sweatshirts, and casual shoes or sneakers. Natural fiber fabrics (cotton, wool) are generally preferred over synthetics. Rural women often wear scarves on their heads.

CUSTOMS AND COURTESIES

Greetings

A handshake is the most common greeting in Croatia, along with a phrase such as *Dobro jutro* (Good morning), *Dobar dan* (Good day), or *Dobra večer* (Good evening). The most common phrases used among friends and neighbors for saying hello are *Zdravo* (Health) and *Bok* (literally "God," it means "Hi"). Good-bye can either be *Zbogom* (With God) or *Do vidjenja* (Until we meet again). When friends and relatives greet, they may embrace and appear to kiss cheeks. Croats kiss twice—once to each cheek—while Serbs generally add a third kiss. Actually, most people brush cheeks and "kiss the air." In formal situations, a man waits for a woman to extend her hand. In formal greetings, the family name is preceded by *gospodine* (Mr.), *gospodjo* (Mrs.), *gospodjice* (Miss), or a professional title. The younger person greets first. Among close friends and relatives, first names are used. Kinship is important and terms used when addressing family depend on that relationship. For example, the word for "aunt" can be either *teto* (mother's sister) or *ujna* (father's sister or mother's brother's wife).

Gestures

Hand movement is common during conversation and includes gestures popular throughout Europe. Money is indicated by rubbing the thumb and index finger of the right hand. Beckoning is done with the index finger, or by waving all fingers inward with the palm up. It is impolite to yawn in public. On public transportation, it is polite to offer one's seat to pregnant women or the elderly. While public approval is displayed by applause, disapproval is shown by whistling or shouting "ouuuu."

Visiting

Croats enjoy visiting one another to socialize. Most visits are arranged in advance, but unexpected guests are also welcomed. When invited to a home, guests bring a gift to the hosts. It is usually a bottle of wine, sweets, or an odd number of flowers. Gifts are unwrapped in the presence of the giver, whom the hosts thank. Flowers are given to the hostess, other types of gifts to the host. Flowers, if wrapped, are unwrapped before the hosts open the door. The hostess puts them in a vase and places them in the room where the guests are seated. The host offers something to drink or a snack and the hostess makes coffee (usually Turkish) and offers biscuits or cookies. It is impolite not to accept refreshments. At small gatherings, newly arrived guests greet each person separately. Evening visits usually end before 11:00 P.M., except on special occasions. The host accompanies departing guests out the door if living in an apartment, or a little way down the street if living in a house.

Eating

Breakfast is light and usually accompanied by black coffee. Lunch is the main meal of the day and consists of soup, meat, salad, bread or potatoes, and a dessert. In urban areas, dinner usually consists of cold cuts, bread, cheeses, and eggs. Rural people might have this or a cooked meal. People eat in the continental style with the fork in the left hand and the knife remaining in the right. Hands are kept above the table. Conversation at the table is often lively. Regional cuisine varies, with northern food being somewhat heavier and spicier than southern food. In coastal areas, people might break at midmorning for *marenda*, a light meal of fish, cheese, and bread. A light midday snack is common in other areas, too.

At restaurants, the bill is paid at the table. A 5 to 10 percent tip is customary; it is given to the waiter with the bill and not left on the table. Among friends or colleagues, it is often customary for one person to pay for the entire meal. Care is taken that the burden is shared over time by all group members.

LIFESTYLE

Family

Rural families traditionally include grandparents, parents, and two or more children. The father or grandfather has a dominant role in the family. Urban families usually have two children. Both husband and wife work and share in decision making. Grandparents may also be included, but less often than in rural areas. Children of working mothers may go to day care centers or may be cared for by family members (usually grandparents). Parents often feel obligated, especially in rural areas, to support grown or married children by giving them money or housing. In turn, children are expected to care for their elderly parents. Adult children often live with their parents until they marry or are able to be on their own.

Dating and Marriage

The youth begin dating around age 15, beginning with small groups. They like to gather downtown in cities or at the town square in rural areas. Small cafés and disco clubs are popular dating destinations. Rural people get married in their early twenties and urban dwellers in their late twenties to early thirties. To be legally married, one must have a civil ceremony. Having a church wedding before the civil one has become popular since 1991. After the ceremony, the wedding party is usually held at a restaurant or home. Weddings in rural areas are a particular cause for celebration, and the festivities may last for days.

Diet

A variety of foods are found in Croatia due to its varied climate and landscape, as well as influences from neighboring countries. Seafood and vegetables are most popular in coastal areas. Dishes made from chicken, beef, fish, pork, and lamb are common throughout Croatia. An inland specialty is *štrukli* (boiled or casseroled salt cottage cheese strudel). Meals in the countryside are large and made with seasonal ingredients. The main meal of the day usually consists of some sort of meat or fish, potatoes, and rice or corn. Urban families have less time to cook than their rural counterparts, and therefore eat foods more convenient to prepare. Wine is the most popular drink with a meal. Also popular are beer, mineral water, and fruit drinks.

Recreation

People are sociable and enjoy getting together for historical, religious, cultural and sporting events, or on family occasions. Folk festivals and cultural arts are well developed and enjoyed. The most popular sport is soccer, followed by basketball, handball, water polo, and sailing. Other sports such as tennis, chess, volleyball, archery, hockey, boxing, skiing, swimming, bowling, rowing, fishing, and hunting are also enjoyed.

People enjoy going on walks and having picnics. Families usually have summer vacations of one to four weeks. Urban people enjoy outings in the countryside, vacationing on the Adriatic Coast, and traveling abroad. In many northern villages, people enjoy painting on glass. Television is watched in the evening and on weekends. Movie theaters and museums are popular.

Holidays

Official public holidays include the New Year (1–2 January), May Day (1 May), Day of Croatian Statehood (30 May), Day of the Anti-Fascist Struggle (22 June), Ascension (15 August), All Saints Day (1 November), and Christmas (25–26 December). Orthodox Christians celebrate Christmas on 7 January, and they receive a paid holiday for it. Muslims may take paid leave to celebrate *Ramasan Bairam* (the feast at the end of the month of fasting) and *Kurban Bairam* (Feast of the Sacrifice). Jews may also have paid leave for *Yom Kippur* and *Rosh Hashanah*.

Commerce

Weekday business and work hours begin at 8:00 A.M. and end at 4:00 P.M. Stores are open until 8:00 P.M. On Saturday, stores close at 1:00 P.M., except in tourist areas where they stay open later. Socializing, especially after meetings, is important among business associates.

SOCIETY

Government

The Republic of Croatia's parliament (*Sabor*) consists of a Chamber of Deputies and a Chamber of Counties. The president is Franjo Tudjman, who was elected in 1990 and re-elected in 1992 to a five-year term. He is the head of state. He appoints the prime minister (currently Hrvoje Sarinić) as head of government. The constitution was enacted in December 1990 and is called the "Christmas Constitution." Croatia's voting age is 18.

Economy

Central planning and state domination were ineffective in developing Croatia's economy when it was part of Yugoslavia, even though it was among the most prosperous of the federation's republics. In 1991, the Croatian government began to institute market-oriented reforms by encouraging privatization and entrepreneurship. Progress was interrupted by the war, and continues to be hindered by the large number (over 700,000) of Bosnian refugees that fled their civil war.

Croatia has a developed industrial sector, and it exports ships, equipment, chemicals, textiles, and furniture. Many factories are currently idle due to the region's conflicts. Tourism is a vital source of revenue and jobs, but it has declined sharply because travelers are avoiding the area. This has crippled the economies of some cities. Remittances from expatriate workers living in other European countries continue to be a key source of income for the country. Monthly inflation is about 30 percent and unemployment is about 20 percent. The currency is the Croatian *Kuna* (HK), which replaced the Croatian *dinar* in May 1994.

Transportation and Communication

Although many people own private cars, they often use public streetcars and buses for urban transportation because they are inexpensive and convenient. In small cities and rural areas, bicycles are popular for getting around. Air and waterway links connect Croatian cities together and with other countries. The communications system functions well, but lags behind Western European standards. The government expects to update it within the next few years. The number of private newspapers is increasing.

Education

Eight years of basic education are required, beginning at age seven. There are a number of secondary schools and four universities. Secondary schooling lasts for four years, but is not mandatory. Education is free to citizens at all levels. Those who gain entrance to a university may attend free. Those who can or will pay tuition are also allowed to enroll above the normal entrance quotas. Ethnic minorities may run their own schools. The literacy rate is about 95 percent.

Health

Health care is provided by the government, but people can visit private doctors, too. Income taxes pay for the national health care system. Facilities are most modern in large cities. The infant mortality rate is 9 per 1,000. Life expectancy averages 69 to 76 years.

FOR THE TRAVELER

U.S. citizens need a valid passport and visa to visit Croatia. The tourist industry is well developed. Many scenic areas untouched by fighting may be safe to visit. To obtain current travel warnings from the U.S. State Department, call (202) 647–5225. Questions regarding travel opportunities may be answered by your travel representative, the Croatian embassy, the Ministry of Tourism (Gunduliceva 3, 41000 Zagreb, Croatia), or Pan Adriatic (34–08 Broadway, Second Floor, Astoria, NY 11106). Croatia's embassy is located at 2343 Massachusetts Avenue NW, Washington, DC 20008.

A *Culturgram* is a product of native commentary and original, expert analysis. Statistics are estimates and information is presented as a matter of opinion. While the editors strive for accuracy and detail, this document should not be considered strictly factual. It is a general introduction to culture, an initial step in building bridges of understanding between peoples. It may not apply to all peoples of the nation. You should therefore consult other sources for more information.

Czech Republic

Boundary representations not necessarily authoritative.

BACKGROUND

Land and Climate

Covering 30,387 square miles (78,703 square kilometers), the Czech Republic is just smaller than South Carolina. It is roughly divided between Bohemia in the west and Moravia in the east. Bohemia's rivers flow north to the *Labe* (Elbe) River, while Moravia's rivers flow south to the Danube. The *Vltava* (Moldau) River flows through Prague. Bohemia is slightly more industrialized, while Moravia is known for its agriculture. Rolling hills typify both regions. Agricultural products include wheat, rye, hops, corn, potatoes, and some vineyard grapes. Mountains run along the western and northern borders, as well as in the south. The Bohemian forest is located on the southwest border.

A continental climate prevails. Summers are warm and sunny; fall and spring tend to run long, with high temperatures ranging between 40°F and 55°F (4–13°C). Winters can be cold and snowy, with temperatures often below freezing.

History

In the fifth century, Slavic tribes began settling the area, and by the middle of the ninth century they lived in a loose confederation known as the Great Moravian Empire. Its brief history ended in 907 with the invasion by the nomadic Magyars (ancestors of today's Hungarians). The Slovak region became subject to Hungarian rule, while Czechs developed the Bohemian Empire, centered in Prague. In the 14th century, under the leadership of Charles IV, Prague became a cultural and political capital that rivaled Paris. In the 15th century, Bohemia was a center of the Protestant Reformation led by Jan Hus, who became a martyr and national hero when he was burned at the stake in 1415 as a heretic. Civil war in Bohemia and events elsewhere in Europe led the Czechs (as well as Hungary and Slovakia) to become part of the Austrian Habsburg Empire in 1526.

When the Habsburg (Austro-Hungarian) Empire collapsed upon defeat in World War I (1918), Czech and Slovak lands were united to form a new Czecho-Slovak state (the hyphen was dropped in 1920). Tomas Masaryk became the first president. Democracy flourished and affluence began to spread, but the country was not able to withstand German aggression. Hitler first annexed the Sudetenland, a region of German-speaking people, in 1938. By 1939 all Czech lands had fallen into German possession. The Czechoslovak people then suffered through World War II, in which more than 350,000 citizens (250,000 Jews) lost their lives. After the war, three million Germans were forced out of the country.

Liberated in 1945 by Allied forces, Czechoslovakia held elections in 1946 under Soviet auspices. Left-wing parties performed well and by 1948 the Communists had seized total control of the government. The Soviet-style state promoted rapid industrialization in the 1950s. Social and economic policies began to liberalize in the 1960s in response to a deteriorating quality of life. This led to discussions about easing political restrictions. In 1968, reform-minded Alexander Dubček, a Slovak, assumed leadership of the country and put into motion a series of reforms known as "socialism with a human face." Leaders in other East-bloc countries and the Soviet Union, as well as top Communists in Czechoslovakia, activated Warsaw Pact troops to crush the movement later

Copyright © 1994. Brigham Young University. Printed in the USA. All rights reserved. It is against the law to copy, reprint, store in a retrieval system, or transmit any part of this publication in any form by any means for any purpose without written permission from the Publications Division of the David M. Kennedy Center for International Studies, Brigham Young University, PO Box 24538, Provo, UT 84602–4538. *Culturgrams* are available for more than 125 areas of the world. To place an order, to receive a free catalog, or to obtain information on traveling abroad, call toll free (800) 528–6279.

EUROPE

that summer. The Communist party was purged of liberals and reforms were abolished.

In the 1970s many dissident groups organized against the regime. Many of these groups' members joined with workers, university students, and others in peaceful demonstrations in 1989 in what was called the "Velvet Revolution." A crackdown on a student protest in November 1989 prompted a general strike that led General Secretary Milos Jakes to resign. Dubček returned to prominence and was elected leader of Parliament. Vaćlav Havel, dissident playwright and leader of Civic Forum, became president in 1990.

Full multiparty elections under a new constitution were held in 1992. Havel remained president of the federal union, while Vaćlav Klaus became prime minister of the Czech national government. Vladimír Mečiar became prime minister of the Slovak national government. Differences between Slovak and Czech leaders regarding such things as the distribution of resources, infrastructure investment, and the course of economic reform led the two national governments to agree to split the country into two sovereign states. Havel resigned, refusing to oversee the dissolution of the country, but he was reelected president of the Czech Republic after the two countries split on 1 January 1993. The breakup was peaceful and ties between the countries remain strong. Klaus soon launched an impressive program of economic reform that made the Czech Republic the envy of Europe.

THE PEOPLE
Population
The Czech Republic has 10.4 million people. About 81 percent are ethnic Czechs (Bohemians), and 13 percent are Moravians. Ethnic Slovaks (3 percent) also live in the republic. The rest (2.5 percent) of the population is comprised of several groups: Poles and Silesians in northern Bohemia; Germans in the west (Sudetenland); and Romanians, Bulgarians, Ukrainians, Russians, and Greeks in the south and east. The Romany ethnic group (Gypsies) is nomadic and difficult to count, but they officially form 0.7 percent of the total population. The Romany are subject to intense discrimination throughout Europe and have not integrated into mainstream society.

Language
Czech is a Slavic language; it is similar to Slovak but also related to others (such as Polish, Croatian, or Russian). Czech uses a Latin alphabet with several distinct accent marks and letters. The most common accents include ˇ, ´, and °. These appear over consonants or vowels to soften or lengthen the sound. Minority groups speak their own tongues, but Czechs also often speak German, Russian, or English depending on their generation.

Religion
Although 80 percent of Czechs consider themselves Christians, many people were influenced by 40 years of official (Communist) atheism. Therefore, their link to religion may involve more of the country's historical heritage than belief. In addition, Czechs tend to think of worship as a private matter. While they believe in a Universal Being, they may not necessarily be devoted to a religious institution. Still, more than 40 percent belong to the Catholic church, and many are

Protestant. The Czech Brethren (a Lutheran/Calvinist group) claims 2 percent of the population as members. Many younger people are joining churches, some of which have been imported or established since 1990.

General Attitudes
Czechs value education, cleverness, social standing, modesty, and humor. Czech humor is dry and ironic, rather than slapstick, and jokes and rustic parables are commonly used in conversation. Irony also colors Czech realism, making it seem more like pessimism. Professionals (doctors, engineers, etc.) are admired, but so are skilled manual workers. While Czechs are individualistic to the degree that they may be stubborn in stating opinions or wishes, society's emphasis is on conformity and cooperation. For instance, community leaders (those who organize others) are held in high esteem. Young people are encouraged to belong to organizations such as the Boy Scouts or sports teams.

Moravians and Slovaks are known to be more lighthearted and jovial than Czechs. Moravians tend to preserve the traditional culture through costumes and folk music more than Czechs. Still, Czechs pride themselves on their support of the cultural arts. Theater performances, concerts, and exhibits are held throughout the year. In the summer, small towns often sponsor informal, outdoor "forest theaters."

Personal Appearance
European fashions are commonly worn in the republic, and the youth wear the latest styles. Jeans and T-shirts are popular. Work attire for men is generally more casual (e.g., sports jackets instead of suits, or blue overalls or jogging suits instead of shirts and ties) than in some Western European nations. Older women generally do not wear slacks as does the younger generation, and they wear hats more often. Adults wear shorts in parks or for recreation, but not on city streets. In Moravia, traditional national costumes are still worn on festival days or for weddings and other special events.

CUSTOMS AND COURTESIES
Greetings
When strangers meet or when a young person greets an older person, they shake hands firmly and say their last names, followed by a verbal greeting, such as *Teši mne* (Pleased to meet you) or *Dobrý deň* (Good day). A man usually waits for a woman to extend her hand before shaking. To show respect, one addresses both men and women by their professional titles (engineer, doctor, professor) and last names. It is common to preface the title with *Pán* (sir) or *Pani* (madam) when greeting the person: *Dobr den, Pani Doktorko Cekan*. One also uses *Pán* and *Pani* for persons without professional titles. First names are not used until people are well acquainted, but relatives generally hug upon meeting and address each other by first names, as do young people of the same age.

To say good-bye, the formal *Na chledanou* or the informal *Čiao* are used. *Ahoj* is used as an informal "Hi" and "Bye." *Dekuji* (Thank you) is responded to with *Prosím* (Please), meaning "You're welcome."

Gestures
People maintain eye contact while conversing. It is common for Czechs to look at or even stare at other people in public, but usually with no ill intentions. People often em-

phasize conversation by gesturing with their hands. People beckon and point with their index finger. When one counts on the fingers, the thumb (not index finger) is number one. Speaking loudly is impolite.

Visiting

Czechs consider the home to be private. They do not visit one another unannounced and even spontaneous visitors (only relatives and very close friends) call ahead. Other people are not invited to a Czech's home for more than a drink or coffee. Most guests invited to dinner are taken to a restaurant; it is an honor to be invited to a home for a meal. Friends often socialize in pubs, coffee houses, and wine bars.

Czechs remove their shoes when entering a home and leave them in the entryway. Visiting etiquette is fairly formal, but the atmosphere is warm. Guests are offered something to drink or, prior to a meal, hors d'oeuvres. Women guests may offer to help prepare the meal in the kitchen or to clear dishes, but the offer will be politely declined. Invited guests usually bring an odd number of flowers to the hostess. Any type of flower is acceptable, except chrysanthemums (used mostly in funeral arrangements). Small gifts for the children are appreciated. Guests might also bring wine or chocolates for the hosts. Flowers are given to students at graduation.

Eating

Czechs eat three meals a day and often a mid-morning snack. For most families, lunch is the main meal. Dinner and breakfast are light. Meals are prepared by the women, and men might help with cleanup. Few Czech men cook. Plates are usually prepared in the kitchen and carried to the table. The head of the household is served first. People eat in the continental style, with the fork in the left hand and the knife remaining in the right. Hands, but not elbows, are kept above the table. Depending on the family, there is little dinner conversation unless the head of the household begins to speak first or unless special guests are present. The hostess generally offers seconds to guests, but it is not impolite to decline them after commenting on how good the food is.

Most Czechs do not eat out often. In restaurants, mineral water and bread and butter can be ordered, but they do not come with the meal. In pubs, there may be two waiters, one for the drinks and the other for the food, and the head waiter adds up the bill at the table. Toasting is common for both formal and informal events.

LIFESTYLE

Family

Urban families are usually small, with rarely more than two children. Rural families tend to be larger. Both parents generally work outside the home, but women are also responsible for the household and children. Urban housing is in short supply, so many families live in large apartment complexes on the outskirts of the city. Mothers receive several months of paid maternity leave, a subsidy for each birth, and child-care services for when they return to work. Grandparents often help with child care, especially when a young couple is just starting out. Parents feel responsible for their adult children until they are financially independent. At the same time, adult children expect to take care of aging parents. Parents and children tend to share more expensive things like cars or

chatas (vacation homes) for many years. Pets, especially dogs, are cherished members of many families.

Dating and Marriage

Young people tend to date in groups; they enjoy going to movies or the theater, hiking or camping, attending music festivals, or dancing at discos. Most men are married by the age of 30; women marry a few years earlier. Young urban couples tend to live with their parents after marriage because of a housing shortage, but they strive to become independent as soon as possible. Most urban weddings are held at city hall, with only the immediate family and closest friends present. A family luncheon or dinner will be held afterward at a nearby hotel. Suit jackets and short dresses have been the standard wedding attire, but more formal gowns and tuxedos are being worn today. A church wedding after the civil ceremony is becoming increasingly common. Honeymoons are also gaining in popularity. Rural weddings tend to incorporate more people, such as village members. Traditional costumes might be worn and celebrations can last all day.

Diet

Traditional Czech food is heavy and arduous to prepare. In the last decade, a healthier diet (fewer heavy sauces, leaner meat, more vegetables) that is easier to prepare has become more popular. Lunch usually begins with a hearty soup, followed by a main dish of meat and potato or bread dumplings. A common dish is *vepro-knedlo-zelo* (pork roast, dumplings, and sauerkraut). Ham on bread and sausages in buns are popular snack foods that can be purchased from sidewalk vendors.

A wide variety of breads and bakery items are available. Breakfast usually consists of rolls, coffee cake, butter, jam, and coffee. Many desserts are made from fruit. Beer, soda, and juice are common drinks.

Recreation

Czechs are known for their love of nature, and hardly a weekend goes by without forests, fields, mountains, and lakes being filled with Czechs (especially urban residents). A surprising number of families own vacation homes. Urban families often tend garden plots of flowers, fruit trees, and vegetables that are either near their vacation home or in communal garden areas on city outskirts. Camping, hiking, swimming in lakes, gathering mushrooms and berries, and snow skiing are all favorite outdoor activities.

The most popular sports are soccer, tennis, and ice hockey. Leisure pursuits include watching television, going to movies or concerts, dancing, taking walks, or getting together with friends. Gardening and home improvement projects are also widely enjoyed in leisure time. In the evening, men often gather in pubs to drink beer and talk, while women visit close friends at home. In smaller towns, people socialize while doing errands.

Czechs enjoy touring in a car or taking bus tours. Forty years of travel restrictions have led to a pent-up desire for travel outside of the republic. However, because the currency is not yet convertible, there is an annual limit on how much one can exchange for other currencies. This limits vacations to short weekend trips or requires vacationers to go where the bill can be paid (usually in advance) with the Czech *koruna*.

Holidays

Public holidays include New Year's Day, Easter Monday, End of World War II (8 May), Cyril and Methodej's Day (5 July), Jan Hus Day (6 July), Founding of the First Republic in 1918 (28 October), and Christmas (25–26 December). Cyril and Methodej are honored for introducing Christianity and creating the Cyrillic alphabet (used before the current Latin alphabet). Christmas Eve is the most important part of Christmas, and people eat carp for dinner in honor of their Catholic heritage. *Vanocka*, a fruit bread, is eaten in the days leading to Christmas and during Lent, and small marzipan candies or paper cards in the shape of pigs are given in the New Year for good luck.

All Saints Day (1 November), Velvet Revolution Day (17 November), and St. Nicholas Day (6 December) are celebrated but are not days off from work. Each village or town also celebrates a day for its patron saint with fairs, dancing, feasting, and Mass.

Commerce

The workday usually begins between 7:00 and 8:00 A.M. and ends between 3:00 and 4:00 P.M. It is not unusual for businesses and offices to close for lunch. Women might shop for fresh foods during this time. Government offices are usually open until 6:00 P.M., but people often leave for home by 4:00 P.M. Since 1989, more stores in town centers have been staying open later in the evening. Czechs shop weekly for groceries and other items, but they rely on small shops and market stalls for daily purchases of bread, fruit, and vegetables.

SOCIETY

Government

The 1993 constitution provides for a president as head of state who has mostly ceremonial duties. A prime minister is head of government and is the leader of Parliament's majority party or a coalition of parties. Parliament is composed of a Senate (81 seats) and a Chamber of Deputies (200 seats). The voting age is 18.

Economy

Making the transition from a planned economy to a free market has been painful in most former East-bloc nations, often causing political instability. But the Czech Republic has so far enjoyed great success with Václav Klaus's measured approach. Although low salaries have made it hard for people to earn a living, most at least have jobs. Unemployment is 3.5 percent (0 percent in Prague) and inflation is relatively low. Those who get laid off by sagging industries are absorbed by private enterprise. Exports of manufactured goods are booming due to low labor costs and high quality. Agriculture is important to the domestic economy, and the country is nearly self-sufficient in food. Tourism is especially important; 70 million people visited the country in 1993 alone.

Czechs form a cohesive, well-educated, and hardworking labor force that has attracted substantial foreign investment. At the same time, the country's privatization program concentrates on selling stock to individual citizens rather than outside interests or large firms. This means everyone has a stake in economic performance.

The country's Human Development Index (0.892) ranks it 26 out of 173 nations. Real gross domestic product per capita is around $7,300. The currency is the Czech *koruna* (Kc).

Transportation and Communication

Public transportation is extensive and reliable in most urban areas and between towns and cities. The fleet of trams, buses, and trains is aging, and the industry is being pressed to privatize and modernize. This will increase prices and decrease service along unprofitable routes. More and more people are buying cars and the Czech-manufactured *Skoda* is popular.

Daily newspapers are widely read, as are an abundance of other printed media. Many homes have cable television and have access to international programming in addition to local broadcasts. Prepaid calling cards are used for most public phones. Post offices sell transit tickets, accept utility payments, and provide many other services; postal delivery is efficient.

Education

The literacy rate is 99 percent. Young children go to nursery school or kindergarten, but compulsory education begins at age six. Public education is free. Primary education had been for eight years, followed by four years in secondary school. In 1994, the structure changed so grade school lasts five years. At age 11, children begin 8 years of secondary school in one of three basic tracks: academic (leading to university studies), technical (for learning an occupation such as electrician, mason, etc.), or teaching.

Higher education had been free to those who gain entrance based on difficult exams. Beginning in 1994, university students were required to pay one-fourth of their education costs. There are 23 institutions of higher learning, the oldest of which is Charles University, founded in 1348.

Health

Health care is universal and the government covers most costs. People pay a minimal insurance premium and pay for some prescriptions. Employers assist in covering these costs. Pollution is the most serious threat to health. The infant mortality rate is 10 per 1,000; life expectancy ranges from 69 to 77 years.

FOR THE TRAVELER

U.S. travelers do not need a visa for stays of up to 30 days, but a passport is required. Advance hotel and bed-and-breakfast reservations are often necessary during peak travel times. Money exchange booths charge higher rates than banks. Settle on a taxi fare in advance of an airport-to-Prague trip to avoid being overcharged. For more information about travel to the Czech Republic, check with your travel agency or contact the Czech Embassy, 3900 Spring of Freedom Street NW, Washington, DC 20008.

A *Culturgram* is a product of native commentary and original, expert analysis. Statistics are estimates and information is presented as a matter of opinion. While the editors strive for accuracy and detail, this document should not be considered strictly factual. It is a general introduction to culture, an initial step in building bridges of understanding between peoples. It may not apply to all peoples of the nation. You should therefore consult other sources for more information.

CULTURGRAM '95

Kingdom of
Denmark

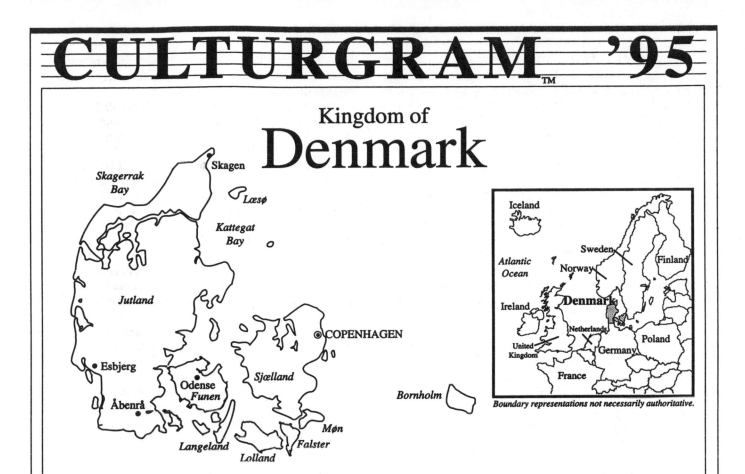

Boundary representations not necessarily authoritative.

EUROPE

BACKGROUND

Land and Climate

Denmark is about the size of Switzerland and is made up of several small islands in the North and Baltic Seas. The largest islands include Jutland (which connects to the European continent), Sjælland (commonly called Zealand), Funen, Lolland, Falster, and Bornholm. Actually, there are over 400 islands, but only about 90 are inhabited. The islands are relatively flat, with some hills but no mountains. Moors, lakes, fertile agricultural land, and woodlands are all part of the landscape. The climate can be unpredictable and skies are often overcast. Despite the warming influence of the Gulf Stream, it is often windy and winters can be quite cold. January averages about 30°F (–1°C) and July warms to about 65°F (18°C).

History

The Kingdom of Denmark (*Kongeriget Danmark*) has been a monarchy as long as it has existed. During the rule of the Vikings (c. 750–1035), Denmark was a great power, but it is not known exactly when it was controlled and by whom in the first decades of that time period. The first known king was Gorm the Old, who ruled in the early 900s. His son, Harald Bluetooth united the country under Christianity and ruled in the latter half of the 900s. Gorm's grandson, Canute the Great, commanded a vast empire that included England until 1035. Queen Margrethe I united Denmark, Norway, and Sweden in the Union of Kalmar in 1397. Sweden left the union in 1523 and Norway in 1814. King Frederik VII signed a liberal constitution in 1849, making the country a constitutional monarchy rather than an autocracy. Some territory was lost to Prussia (Germany) in 1864, but the country remained stable.

Denmark was neutral during World War I, but Nazi Germany occupied it during World War II. Denmark joined the North Atlantic Treaty Organization (NATO) in 1949 and the European Union (EU) in 1973. During the 1970s and 1980s, Denmark concentrated on maintaining its social welfare system, broadening opportunities, and increasing the standard of living. During the mid-1980s, Denmark became interested in environmental protection and has passed some of the world's toughest environmental legislation. In the 1990s, Denmark looks forward to greater economic integration with its EU partners. After first rejecting the Maastricht treaty in 1992 that would have prepared the way for a common European currency and greater political union, Danish voters accepted a modified treaty in 1993. It exempts Denmark from participating in certain

Copyright © 1994. Brigham Young University. Printed in the USA. All rights reserved. It is against the law to copy, reprint, store in a retrieval system, or transmit any part of this publication in any form by any means for any purpose without written permission from the Publications Division of the David M. Kennedy Center for International Studies, Brigham Young University, PO Box 24538, Provo, UT 84602–4538. *Culturgrams* are available for more than 125 areas of the world. To place an order, to receive a free catalog, or to obtain information on traveling abroad, call toll free (800) 528–6279.

aspects of the union and allows the country some flexibility in how it interacts with other EU nations. Many provisions of the treaty will not be enacted until later in the decade.

THE PEOPLE

Population

The population of Denmark is 5.17 million. The country is growing at just over 0.2 percent annually. Fears that the population will someday decline seem to be influencing the Danes, as a slight increase in births has occurred over the past few years. The majority of the population lives in urban areas. In Denmark, most people (99 percent) are Danish. Part of the Danish Kingdom, but autonomous nations, are Greenland and the Faroe Islands. These areas have small populations: 56,500 and 48,000, respectively. The Faroese belong to the old Nordic, and mostly Danish, ethnic background. The Greenlanders are Eskimos or are of mixed Eskimo and European origin. Because these groups are autonomous, with their own languages and cultural heritages, they are only mentioned here as part of Denmark's kingdom, but they will not be discussed culturally in the text.

Language

Danish is the official language of the country. As a Scandinavian language, its written form can be understood by Swedes and Norwegians. But spoken Danish is more difficult for other Scandinavians to understand because of differences in pronunciation and intonation. Vocabulary also differs. There is a very small German-speaking minority along the border with Germany. These people also speak Danish. English is widely understood and spoken; in fact, it is part of the school curriculum after the fifth grade. German is also a popular language to study in school.

Religion

The national church is the Evangelical Lutheran Church, in which most Danes are automatically enrolled. This has resulted in 91 percent of the people being Evangelical Lutheran, but it does not mean they attend church services on a regular basis. Except for Christmas and Easter, when attendance is high, less than 5 percent go to Sunday meetings. Although most Danes are not active churchgoers, most participate in religious ceremonies such as baptism and confirmation. Tolerance is extended to most other religious groups, whose numbers are increasing.

General Attitudes

Denmark's high standard of living reflects the progressive attitude of the people. Danes are well educated and respected for their accomplishments in science, art, literature, and architecture. Danes are also known for their tolerance of other people and diverse points of view. They are proud to take responsibility for their nation's social welfare, despite heavy taxes imposed on the individual as a result. This attitude has encouraged their contributions to the development of Third World countries.

Personal Appearance

Because of the cool, rainy climate and constant, brisk winds, coats and woolens are important to the Danish wardrobe. Danes follow general European fashion trends, which change frequently with the year or season. While casual dress is generally appropriate and fashionable, sloppy dress is not. As throughout Europe, business and formal situations call for suits and dresses.

CUSTOMS AND COURTESIES

Greetings

A handshake is the most common form of greeting among adults. Young people and close acquaintances usually nod or wave and say *Dav* or *Davs* (pronounced DOWSE), which is like saying hello. The youth also say *Hej* (pronounced HEY) or even "Hi" when greeting or parting. Danish people are informal and friendly. While traditionally only close friends and family members addressed one another by the first name, the current trend in many areas is for most people to use first names. In formal situations, however, using a person's surname is still most common. The term for "Good day" is *Goddag*.

Gestures

Danes appreciate courtesy in all interactions. Yawning without covering the mouth is impolite. Eye contact is important during conversation. Danes generally do not use hand gestures in conversation.

Visiting

Proper etiquette is important when visiting in Denmark. One does not enter a home until invited to do so. The host suggests where one should sit, and one does not follow a host into other rooms unless invited. Leaving directly after a meal is impolite, and conversing about one's personal life is avoided. Those visiting a home for the first time often bring a gift to the hostess, such as a bouquet of flowers. The Danes enjoy having visitors in their homes and do their best to make guests feel welcome. Guests are nearly always offered refreshments.

Eating

Danes eat in the continental style, with the fork in the left hand and the knife remaining in the right. At family meals, the father and mother sit at opposite ends of the table. Everyone is seated and served before anyone begins to eat. A parent will often say *Vær så god* (Please, eat well) to begin the meal, especially if guests are present. On formal occasions, guests of honor are served first and sit at the head with the host. When passing and receiving food, one might say *Vær så god* and *Tak* (Thank you). One does not leave the table until the hostess rises. Then, upon leaving, the guest thanks the hostess for the meal by saying *Tak for mad!* (Thanks for the meal!). In restaurants, a service charge is included in the bill, but some people also leave a small tip.

LIFESTYLE

Family

Families in Denmark are generally close-knit and stable. As in most other industrialized nations, both father and mother usually work away from home. Increasingly, the father is expected to share household duties, as the mother also shares the burden of earning an income. More than 60 percent of all families with children are single-family homes. Because the individual is important in the Danish culture, children are not usually punished for their mistakes. Parents basically feel children have the right to make decisions for themselves. Being ethnically homogeneous, about 65 percent of the people have surnames that end in "sen" (Hansen, Christensen, Andersen, and so forth). With one of the highest standards of living in the world, Denmark also has one of the highest tax rates. For example, taxes and duties on a new car cause its price to triple.

Dating and Marriage

Dating begins by the age of 15. Youth enjoy dancing, sporting activities, and going to movies. Many couples are engaged for a long time, often living together for a while before deciding whether to get married. In many cases the traditions of rice-throwing and dancing the bridal waltz are important to wedding celebrations. About half of all couples are recognized under common-law marriage, where living together is considered marriage, especially if children are born. Those who do marry have their weddings either in a church or a town hall. There are twice as many weddings as divorces in Denmark.

Diet

Breakfast consists of coffee or tea, pastries or rolls, cheese, eggs or cereal, and milk. For lunch, many enjoy traditional open-faced sandwiches and a drink. Pumpernickel and rye are common types of bread for sandwiches. On weekdays the main meal is dinner, where a main course (meat or fish), potatoes and gravy, and perhaps a salad are served. On weekends or special occasions, dinner often consists of soup, a main course (meat or fish), potatoes and gravy, and a vegetable. Desserts are often part of the meal. The many staple foods include pork roast (a favorite), fish, beans, brussels sprouts, potatoes, various fresh vegetables, and breads such as wheat and rye. Pork roast or goose is served at Christmas and a lamb roast is served at Easter. The *frokostbord*, a cold buffet of many different foods, is very popular in Denmark. Favorite drinks include coffee, tea, milk, beer, soft drinks, and mineral water.

Recreation

Soccer (called "football" by most soccer nations) was brought to Denmark in the mid-1800s by British experts sent to help build a railroad. It caught on rapidly and has become the country's favorite sport. Soccer is not the only recreation in Denmark, however, as people also enjoy handball, badminton, swimming, sailing, rowing, and jogging. Families also spend a great deal of time watching television. Attending cultural events is also popular, and reading is a favorite pastime.

Holidays

Danes enjoy great holiday traditions. On New Year's Eve, for instance, people enjoy parties, listen to the Queen's and the prime minister's annual speeches, wait for Copenhagen's City Hall bells to mark midnight, and then light fireworks to welcome the new year. Other traditions follow throughout the year. Danes light the Christmas tree for the last time on Twelfth Night (5 January); participate in Mardi Gras-type activities during *Shrovetide* (February or March); and take a long Easter holiday (Thursday through Monday) to eat, drink a special potent Easter beer, and have family gatherings. Constitution Day (5 June) is a half holiday; Queen Margrethe's birthday (16 April) is a school holiday; and Christmas is celebrated over three days, with 24 December being the most important day. On Christmas Eve, the tree is lit, songs are sung while dancing in a circle around the tree, gifts are exchanged, and a special meal is eaten. Since 1909, Danish-Americans and their guests have commemorated the U.S. Fourth of July with festivities at Rebild Park in Jutland. While this is a private initiative, Danish officials often attend because of good relations between the two countries.

Commerce

The Danish workweek is one of the shortest in the European Union (EU) with an average of 37 hours. Businesses are usually open from 8:00 A.M. to 4:00 or 5:00 P.M., Monday through Friday. Shops open at 9:00 or 10:00 A.M. and close around 5:30 P.M., except on Thursday or Friday when they stay open until 7:00 P.M. and Saturday when they close at 2:00 P.M. Wages and working conditions are determined jointly by employer and employee organizations for two-year periods. Each worker receives five weeks paid vacation each year.

SOCIETY

Government

The 1849 Constitution (revised in 1953) gave the monarchy and parliament joint legislative authority. The monarchy must sign all legislation passed by parliament, but executive power rests with the prime minister. Queen Margrethe II presides over the Council of State and performs numerous other duties as well. She came to the throne in 1972 as the first female monarch to rule since Margrethe I. Between 1513 and 1972, all kings were either named Christian or Frederik. The crown prince's name is Frederik. Parliament is called the *Folketing*. Elections are held at least every four years and all over age 18 may vote. Both Greenland and the Faroes Islands have representatives in parliament. Elected in 1990 as the current prime minister was Nyrup Rasmussen. The next parliamentary elections are scheduled for December 1994.

Economy

Denmark has a shortage of natural resources, but it has been able to rely on its high-quality agricultural produce for revenue. About 60 percent of the land is arable, employing 6 percent of the population in agricultural pursuits and producing 15 percent of the nation's exports. Economic diversification has allowed manufacturing to become the most important exporting sector. Small and medium-sized companies are most prominent, producing furniture, medical goods, and machinery. *Lego* building blocks originated in Denmark and are known worldwide. Besides the meat, beer, and dairy products exported from Denmark, fresh and processed fish is also shipped around the world.

Traditionally strong economic growth of 3 to 4 percent slowed during the 1991–92 global recession but is growing stronger in 1994. Inflation is about 3 percent and unemployment is 10 percent. The currency is the Danish *Krone* (DKK). Denmark's Human Develoment Index (0.955) ranks it 13 out of 173 countries. Real gross domestic product per capita is $16,781. These figures indicate the majority of Danes earn a decent income and have access to economic prosperity.

Transportation and Communication

While personal automobiles are important, rail traffic, bus lines, and ferry services continue to meet the transportation needs of the country. Copenhagen has a rapid-transit system for daily commuters. Work on a bridge over the Great Belt (between Funen and Sjælland) is due to be completed between 1993 and 1996. This will allow cars and trains to travel between the islands, a connection otherwise made by ferries. Another bridge between Copenhagen and Southern Sweden is being planned for the late 1990s, while tentative plans are being discussed for a link across the Baltic between the island of Lolland and northern Germany. All communications systems are modern and efficient. Until 1988, only one state-owned television channel existed, but another now exists that uses commercials. Most Danes can view stations from neighboring countries. The majority of households receive at least one daily newspaper.

Education

Primary education is free and compulsory for nine years at the *Folkeskole* (People's School). Among other required courses, students must study a foreign language. About two-thirds then choose practical training schools for job training and the rest choose a secondary school to prepare for a college education. Entrance to universities is determined by a highly competitive examination, but the education is free. Denmark was a pioneer in the community college (*Folkeshøjskole*) concept. Today, this type of school instructs resident students in literature and history to encourage personal development; no exams are given. The literacy rate is 99 percent. Denmark ranks among the highest in the world in per capita expenditures on education.

Health

Health care in Denmark is provided through a comprehensive socialized medicine system. Each citizen may choose a family doctor to coordinate services, nearly all of which are provided free of charge (paid for by taxes). Danes boast a life expectancy of between 72 and 78 years. The infant mortality rate is 7 per 1,000. Medicine is either low cost or free of charge, depending on the medicine and patient. Paid maternity leave is required and may last up to six months; the father may also receive some of this time.

FOR THE TRAVELER

While passports are required, U.S. citizens do not need visas for visits of up to three months total time in Scandinavia—Denmark, Iceland, Finland, Norway, and Sweden. Travelers should take warm clothing for the cool climate. Denmark offers a variety of interesting sights, from *Legoland* (a theme park with giant *Lego* statues and structures), to castles, to clean beaches. Adaptors or converters are necessary to use North American small appliances with electrical outlets. Write to the Danish Tourist Board (655 Third Avenue, New York, NY 10017) for more information. Or you may wish to contact the Royal Danish Embassy, 3200 Whitehaven Street NW, Washington, DC 20008.

A *Culturgram* is a product of native commentary and original, expert analysis. Statistics are estimates and information is presented as a matter of opinion. While the editors strive for accuracy and detail, this document should not be considered strictly factual. It is a general introduction to culture, an initial step in building bridges of understanding between peoples. It may not apply to all peoples of the nation. You should therefore consult other sources for more information.

Dominican Republic

Boundary representations not necessarily authoritative.

THE AMERICAS

BACKGROUND

Land and Climate

The Dominican Republic occupies the eastern two-thirds of the island of Hispaniola, which it shares with Haiti. Covering 18,815 square miles (48,730 square kilometers), it is about twice the size of New Hampshire. The central mountain range, *Corillera Central*, boasts the highest point in the Caribbean, *Pico Duarte*, at just higher than 10,000 feet (3,048 meters). The Cibao Valley lies in the heart of the country and is the major agricultural area.

This land of contrasts provides a wide variety of landscapes, from deserts in the southwest to alpine forests in the central mountains. Sugarcane fields spread over vast coastal plains in the north and east, and banana plantations cover most of the tropical peninsula of Samaná. Pebble beaches under rocky cliffs afford spectacular views on the southern coast. Elsewhere, white sand beaches and warm waters attract tourists to popular resort areas.

Weather is generally tropical, warm and humid, especially in summer months and along southern and eastern coasts. A dry, desert-like climate, due to little rainfall and deforestation, prevails in the western and southwestern regions. Rainy seasons may vary in different parts of the country, but they are generally in the late spring and early fall.

History

In pre-Columbian times, Arawaks and Tainos occupied the island. The arrival of Columbus in 1492 brought Christianity, colonization, slavery, and disease, decimating the native population within decades. With the vanishing indigenous workforce came the increased importation of West Africans to provide cheap labor for the mines, sugar plantations, and cattle farms.

The first permanent European settlement in the New World was established in 1496 as Santo Domingo, the city from which Spain set out to conquer the Americas. Here stands the first New World university and Catholic church, the latter claiming Columbus's remains. Santo Domingo's Colonial Zone is one of the great treasures of Spanish America today, with many original buildings intact and restored.

In 1697, the western portion (now Haiti) of Hispaniola was given to France. In 1795, the entire island was ceded. Rebellious slaves seized Santo Domingo in 1801 and established Haiti as the first independent country in Latin America. The resulting Haitian domination of the Dominicans (1822 to 1844) left a legacy of mistrust and strained relations that still endures. The Dominicans declared independence in 1844. Spain returned intermittently between local attempts at government. After an occupation by U.S. Marines (1918–24), a constitutional government was established.

The Trujillo era followed, bringing the country under a military dictatorship. Rafael Leonidas Trujillo gained the presidency in 1930 and ruled for three decades until he was assassinated in 1961. His merciless persecution of Haitians in the late 1930s further added to the list of grievances between the two countries. His death brought a division of the army, civilian unrest, and political revolt. U.S. Marines and

Copyright © 1994. Brigham Young University. Printed in the USA. All rights reserved. It is against the law to copy, reprint, store in a retrieval system, or transmit any part of this publication in any form by any means for any purpose without written permission from the Publications Division of the David M. Kennedy Center for International Studies, Brigham Young University, PO Box 24538, Provo, UT 84602–4538. *Culturgrams* are available for more than 125 areas of the world. To place an order, to receive a free catalog, or to obtain information on traveling abroad, call toll free (800) 528–6279.

an Inter-American peacekeeping force stepped in (1965). With stability restored, elections were held and in 1966 the constitutional government was reestablished. Continuing under this system, today's Dominican Republic is the largest and most populous democracy in the Caribbean region.

An ally of Trujillo, Joaquín Balaguer, was appointed president in 1960. For much of the next three decades, power rested either in his hands or that of his rival, Juan Bosch. Only in the 1994 elections did the two face a strong challenge from another candidate. Balaguer, however, narrowly won the election for a seventh term.

THE PEOPLE
Population
The population is about 7.6 million. More than one million of these people live full or part-time in New York City, and are called "Dominican Yorks." Nearly 40 percent of the population is younger than age 16. The rural population is steadily decreasing through migration to cities. Mixed-race people account for 73 percent of the total population, while 16 percent is Caucasian and 11 percent black. The mixed-race group is a combination of Europeans, Spaniards, West African slave descendants, and descendants of natives. A minority of Haitians is included in the black population.

Language
The official language is Spanish, but Caribbean phrases, accents, and regional expressions give it a distinct personality. For example, when eating, people request *un chin* instead of the Spanish *un poquito* (a little bit) of something. Many people drop the "s" on the end of words, turning *dos* (two) into *do'*. Cibao Valley residents, or *Cibaeños* may pronounce the "r," "l," and "i" differently. The formal Spanish form of address for "you" (*usted*) is used, but urban people prefer the more familiar *tú*. Some Creole is spoken near the Haitian border and in the *bateys* (sugarcane villages) where many Haitian workers live.

Religion
Dominicans are 95 percent Catholic by record, but a much smaller number regularly attends church or follows a strict doctrine. Rural residents might combine Catholic traditions with local practices and beliefs. Although Dominicans are fairly secular, Catholic traditions are evident in daily life. Some children are taught to "ask blessings" of their parents and other relatives upon seeing them. They might say, *Bendición, tía* (Bless me, aunt), and the response is *Dios te bendiga* (May God bless you).

Evangelical Christians, Seventh-Day Adventists, Latter-day Saints, and other denominations also exist throughout the country. A Jewish colony in Sosua dates from World War II immigration policies that welcomed refugees.

General Attitudes
Dominicans are warm, friendly, outgoing, and gregarious. They are curious about others and forthright in asking personal questions. Children are rarely shy. Machismo permeates society, especially among rural and low-income groups, with males enjoying privileges not accorded to females. A proud and aggressive attitude is admired in sports, games, or business, and many people have a sharp entrepreneurial sense. That does not mean, however, that business etiquette is aggressive.

By the common expression *Si Dios quiere* (If God wishes), Dominicans seem fatalistic or indifferent to goals. However, it more fully expresses the attitude that personal power is intertwined with one's place in the family, community, and grand design of Deity. Friends and relationships are more important than schedules, so being late for appointments and spending time socializing instead of working are socially acceptable.

Confianza (trust) is highly valued and not quickly or easily gained by outsiders. Borrowing is common, and although an item may be forgotten and never returned, everyone is generous and helpful. Class divisions, most evident in larger cities, are economic, social, and political, favoring historically prominent families. Light skin and smooth hair are preferred over strong African features, but most social relationships are not openly affected by race.

Personal Appearance
Dominicans are clean and well-groomed. They take pride in their personal appearance and place importance on dressing well. Dominicans draw upon New York fashions, wearing the latest in dresses, jeans, or athletic shoes. Clothes tend to be dressy, always clean and well pressed, with bright colors, shiny fabrics, and, for some people, lots of jewelry. Jeans and short skirts are acceptable for women in urban areas, but dresses or skirts and blouses are more common in the countryside. A special event, such as a town meeting, always requires dressing up. Men wear long pants and stylish shirts, except at the beaches or if doing manual labor. Professional men wear business suits or the traditional *chacabana*, a white shirt worn over dark trousers. Children are also dressed up, especially for church or visiting.

CUSTOMS AND COURTESIES
Greetings
Men shake hands firmly when they greet. A wrist or elbow is offered if one's hand is dirty. Friends may also embrace. Most women kiss each other on both cheeks. A man with the *confianza* of a woman will also kiss her. A handshake and ¿*Cómo está usted?* (How are you?) is a common formal greeting. The *usted* is dropped for more casual situations. It is polite to ask about one's family. ¡*Hola!* is an informal "hi," as is ¡*Saludos!* Adults, particularly in the *campo* (countryside), often address each other as *compadre* (for men) or *comadre* (for women). One might not greet a stranger on the street, but one would never enter a room without greeting everyone present. Nor would a person leave without saying good-bye to everyone.

Formal introductions are rare, but professional titles are used to address respected persons. Older and more prominent people may be addressed as *Don* or *Doña* with or without their first names. The use of *Doña* for older women is especially common.

Gestures
Dominicans are animated in conversation and have many gestures. Pointing is done with puckered lips instead of a finger. Wrinkling the nose indicates one does not understand, rubbing fingers and the thumb together refers to money, and an upright wagging forefinger means "no." To express disapproval, one points (with lips) at the object and rolls the eyes. "Come here" is indicated with the palm down and fingers

together waving inward. One also says "psssst" to get another's attention. To hail a taxi or bus, one wags a finger or fingers (depending on the number of passengers needing a ride) in the direction one is going. Numbers are often expressed by one's fingers instead of verbally. Hands may be clapped to request a check in a restaurant.

It is unladylike to sit with legs apart and most women ride "sidesaddle" on the backs of motorcycles. Personal space is limited, touching is normal, crowding is common.

Visiting

Visiting is an important form of social recreation, especially in rural areas and poor *barrios* (neighborhoods). Visits in the home are common, but much socializing also takes place in public (while shopping, washing, and so forth). Women often get together in the kitchen. A visit may be long or short and may occur at any time, usually without prior notice. Urbanites with telephones may call ahead, but whether expected or not, company is always genuinely welcomed. In rural areas, doors are kept open and it is considered strange to close them and not accept visitors. Privacy is unimportant and the desire for solitude is perceived as sadness; Dominicans equate being alone with being lonely. Sitting in *mecadoras* (rocking chairs) talking or just sharing time is common. Nearly all homes have *mecadoras*. Visitors are offered something to drink (coffee or juice) and are invited to eat if mealtime is near. It is not impolite to refuse such offers.

If guests interrupt (or passersby happen upon) someone eating, the person will immediately and sincerely invite them to share what is left by saying *A buen tiempo* (You've come at a good time). Guests may decline by saying *Buen provecho* (Enjoy), or they may sit down and eat.

Eating

The main meal is the *comida,* which is served at midday and often lasts two hours. Families prefer eating together at home. Urban workers unable to return home may eat at inexpensive cafés or buy from vendors. *Desayuno* (breakfast) is usually light: sweetened coffee and bread, and a bit more in urban areas. The *cena* (evening meal) is also light, often not more than a snack or leftovers from *comida*. Guests are served first, and sometimes separately and more elaborately. Table conversation is often lively. Dining out is only popular among those who can afford it. Service is included in the bill.

LIFESTYLE

Family

Dominican family ties are important. Extended families are common, especially in rural areas and poor *barrios*. Many households are headed by women—widowed, divorced, those with husbands who work elsewhere, or older women with adult children and grandchildren. Women, men, and often boys all work outside the home. The boys shine shoes or sell snacks on the streets. Large families are normal, and many rural villages are composed of interrelated families. Within the extended family, informal adoption is common, with other family members taking in and raising children whose parents need help. Likewise, siblings raised by one mother may have different fathers, but all children are cared for equally. Cousins are often as close as siblings. Some men have more than one

wife and family. Smaller, nuclear families are more common among the educated urban population.

Most families live in small houses, either rented or self-built. They may be constructed of cement, wood, or palm bark. They are brightly painted, have cement or dirt floors, and are covered with a zinc roof. Electricity and running water are luxuries. Affluent urban houses are larger and often have walled and landscaped grounds. Urban apartments are becoming more popular, as are newly constructed condominiums.

Dating and Marriage

Movies, discos, dances, baseball games, and sitting on park benches are all social activities for couples. Dating is relatively open and increasingly free of parental control. Girls are more closely supervised than boys and they often go out in groups. Rural couples might have a sibling tagging along as chaperone. Marriages are often common-law (*por la ventana*), but many couples also marry in a church or civil ceremony. Elaborate urban weddings are major social events.

Diet

If Dominicans do not eat rice and beans at midday, they feel they have not eaten. Rice is served at most meals in large quantities, along with such favorites as *habichuelas* (beans) and *yuca* (cassava). *Yuca* is usually boiled or prepared as fritters and also baked into rounds of crisp cracker bread called *casabe*. *Plátanos* (plantains) and bananas are plentiful. Mangos, papayas, pineapples, guavas, avocados, and other tropical fruits (passion fruit, coconuts, and star fruit) are grown locally and eaten in season. Small quantities of chicken, beef, pork, or goat may be eaten with a meal. *Bacalau* (dried fish, usually cod) is eaten in some areas, and fresh fish is only eaten along the coast. Food is usually not spicy.

The popular national dish is *sancocho*, a rich stew made with vegetables and meats and served on special occasions. *Habichuelas con dulce* (a sweetened drink made from beans) is eaten at Easter. Dominican coffee is usually served sweet and strong. National beers and rums are highly regarded and widely consumed, as are bottled soft drinks and sweetened fruit juices.

Recreation

Dominicans love music and dancing. The country is alive with *merengue*, a fast-paced, rhythmic music. *Salsa* and other Latino styles are popular, as are North American pop and jazz. Discos are found in rural communities.

The game of dominos is a national pastime. Outdoor tables in front of homes, bars, and rural *colmados* (neighborhood markets) are surrounded by men who play for hours, especially on Sundays. Outdoor players are almost exclusively men, but everyone may play at home. Even young children become adept. Cockfighting is another national pastime. Cockfight gambling stakes can be high. The lottery has high participation.

Baseball is the most popular sport. Competition is keen, and many Dominicans have become famous major league players in the United States and Canada. Strolling in parks, visiting friends, and watching television are popular activities. A variety of cultural activities (theater, concerts, etc.) are available in large urban areas.

Holidays

National holidays include New Year's Day (1 January), *Día de los Reyes* (Day of Kings, 6 January), *Nuestra Señora de la Alta Gracia* (Our Lady of High Gratitude, 21 January), Duarte's Day (26 January), Independence Day (27 February), Easter, Labor Day (1 May), Corpus Christi, Restoration of Independence (16 August), *Nuestra Señora de las Mercedes* (Our Lady of Mercies, 24 September), Columbus Day (12 October), and Christmas. *Semana Santa* (Holy Week before Easter) is a favorite vacation time, with many urban families spending time at the beaches or mountains. Mother's Day in May is popular. *Carnaval* is celebrated for several weeks in the early spring. Costume parades, complete with masked participants hitting spectators with pig bladders, and other festivities are held. Gifts are not exchanged at Christmas, but they may be given to children on 6 January. Special holidays may be called by the government to celebrate an event or project completion.

Commerce

Business hours vary, but most establishments are open from around 8:00 or 9:00 A.M., closed between 12:00 and 2:00 P.M., and open again until 5:00 or 6:00 P.M. Banks close by 3:00 P.M. Telephone offices do not close at midday and remain open until 10:00 P.M. Most shops are closed on Sunday. Small *colmados* have their own hours. Street vendors are most busy at midday. Bargaining is common in open-air markets, in some owner-operated stores, and on the streets. Prices in supermarkets and elsewhere are fixed.

Family ties and social relationships are important in obtaining employment or doing business. Business arrangements are seldom made between strangers.

SOCIETY

Government

The president and vice president are elected by the people. A bicameral Congress of Senators and Deputies is also directly elected, as are local officials. National and local elections are held simultaneously every four years. The voting age is 18. There are 29 provinces. A nine-member Supreme Court is appointed by the Senate.

Economy

The economy is based on agriculture. Coffee, sugar, pineapple, cocoa, tobacco, and rice are key crops, both for export and domestic use. Fluctuating world prices impact earnings and contribute to a volatile domestic market. Inflation is usually high. Earnings from Dominican Yorks are often sent back to families in the Republic; the money constitutes an important source of revenue. Tourism is another vital source of income. The currency is the *peso* (RD$).

Industrial activity includes sugar refining, cement, and pharmaceuticals. Assembly plants for various products are located in duty-free zones. The environment has suffered from the exploitation of mineral and natural resources, but efforts at conservation are being made.

The country's Human Development Index (0.586) ranks it 97 out of 173 countries. Real gross domestic product per capita is $2,404, which has doubled in the last generation.

Poverty continues to affect more than 40 percent of people, and there is a wide gap between rich and poor.

Transportation and Communication

Main roads are paved and heavily traveled. Rural roads are often not paved and may not be passable during rainy seasons. Public transportation varies between a ride on the back of a motorcycle, local and long-distance trips in *guaguas* (economical vans or buses), or traveling on larger buses. Travel to and from rural villages is often by pickup trucks or small vans that carry passengers, animals, and cargo together. Local urban travel is also done by *carros públicos* (public cars), taxis that follow certain routes. Private cars are expensive but by no means rare. More people have motorcycles.

Telephone service is available throughout the country; middle and upper-class families have phones at home. Daily newspapers are widely read. Postal service is slow and unreliable. Most businesses use private messenger services. Private radio and television stations broadcast regionally and nationally.

Education

Free public education is provided through the high school level. Attendance is mandatory to sixth grade, but many children cannot attend or do not complete school for various reasons (work, lack of transport, lack of money to buy required uniforms), especially in the *campos*. Whereas three-fourths of Dominicans begin schools, only one-third finish.

Scarce funding results in limited resources and understaffed facilities. Parents and teachers must provide basic supplies like pencils and paper. Textbooks and other materials are scarce. Many urban families send their children to private schools called *colegios*. University education is available, and trade schools provide technical training. The adult literacy rate is estimated to be about 75 percent.

Health

Public hospitals and clinics provide free care, but private doctors are preferred when affordable. Public institutions tend to be poorly equipped and understaffed. Village health-care workers have enough training to administer basic services, but rural areas often have no doctors and people must travel elsewhere for care. Many people still consult *curanderos* (native healers). Lack of early treatment and preventive care are genuine concerns. Vaccination campaigns are helping fight disease, but such things as intestinal parasites and malaria pose serious challenges. The infant mortality rate is 53 per 1,000; life expectancy is 66 to 70 years.

FOR THE TRAVELER

U.S. citizens require proof of citizenship (a passport is the best form) and a tourist card (available through the airlines) to visit the Dominican Republic. The departure tax is $20. Food and water are generally safe in tourist areas, but it is best to drink bottled water. Cook vegetables and peel fruits. Information on travel opportunities can be obtained through the Dominican Tourist Information Center, 485 Madison Avenue, New York, NY 10022. For more information, contact the Embassy of the Dominican Republic, 1715 22d Street NW, Washington, DC 20008.

A *Culturgram* is a product of native commentary and original, expert analysis. Statistics are estimates and information is presented as a matter of opinion. While the editors strive for accuracy and detail, this document should not be considered strictly factual. It is a general introduction to culture, an initial step in building bridges of understanding between peoples. It may not apply to all peoples of the nation. You should therefore consult other sources for more information.

CULTURGRAM '95 ™

Republic of
Ecuador

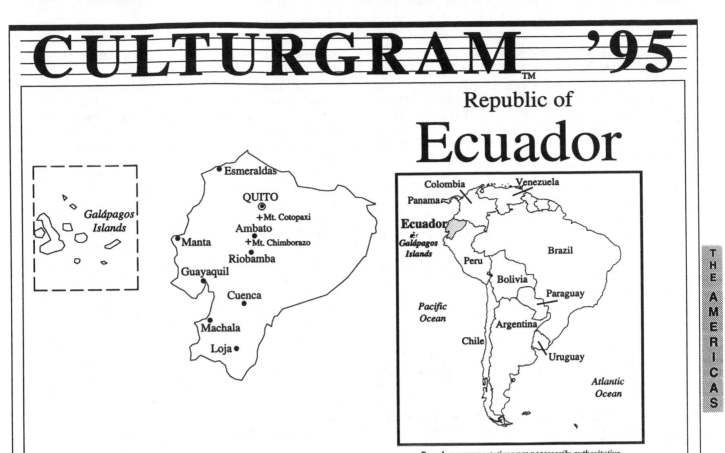

Esmeraldas
QUITO
+Mt. Cotopaxi
Ambato
+Mt. Chimborazo
Manta
Riobamba
Guayaquil
Cuenca
Machala
Loja

Galápagos Islands

Colombia
Venezuela
Panama
Ecuador
Galápagos Islands
Peru
Brazil
Bolivia
Paraguay
Pacific Ocean
Argentina
Chile
Uruguay
Atlantic Ocean

Boundary representations not necessarily authoritative.

THE AMERICAS

BACKGROUND

Land and Climate

Ecuador was named after the equator and is located on it. The country is just smaller than Nevada, covering 109,483 square miles (283,560 square kilometers). Ecuador has four major geographical regions: the *Costa* (coastal plain), which contains rich agricultural land; the *Sierra* (highlands), with snow-capped volcanoes; *La Amazonia* (the Amazon), mostly tropical rain forest; and the *Archipiélago de Colón* (or Galápagos Islands), a group of islands in the Pacific about 600 miles (960 kilometers) off the coast. Charles Darwin did the majority of his evolution studies on those islands. Ecuador is subject to earthquakes, volcanoes, and landslides. In the central highlands, the Avenue of the Volcanoes consists of eleven peaks south of Quito.

The climate varies with elevation more than with season, but the rainy season is generally from November to May. The driest months are June to September. The coastal lowlands are hot and humid, while the highlands include everything from subtropical valleys to frigid mountains. Quito's temperature averages 71°F (22°C) year-round. The Amazon has a tropical climate, while the Galápagos Islands are rather cool. Among Ecuador's many volcanos are its two highest: Chimborazo at 20,561 feet (6,267 meters) and Cotopaxi at 19,347 feet (5,897 meters).

History

Small tribes of Indians whose ancestors first inhabited Ecuador were conquered in the latter 1400s by Incas from the south. The Inca empire ruled the area until, during an internal power struggle, the Spanish conquered it in 1534. The Spanish era was characterized by Spaniards taking ownership of large tracts of land and large numbers of Indians. In the early 1800s, Antonio José de Sucre, a compatriot of Simón Bolívar, led a successful military campaign against the Spaniards. The country, along with Colombia and Venezuela, gained its independence in 1822 and became part of Gran Colombia, a federation led by Bolívar that was dissolved a few years later. Ecuador declared itself a republic in 1830.

In 1941, Peru invaded Ecuador in the southern Amazon region. Global politics and World War II forced Ecuador to sign a treaty that gave Peru half of its territory, nearly all of it Amazon jungle. Ecuador still claims the territory, and the issue has caused violence to erupt between the two nations. International maps show the territory as part of Peru, while maps sold in Ecuador reflect pre-1941 boundaries. Negotiations to resolve the dispute and restore friendly relations between the two countries have been unsuccessful.

Between 1830 and 1948, Ecuador had 62 presidents, dictators, and military juntas. In 1948, President Galo Plaza Lasso became the first freely elected president to serve a full term. His presidency was followed by two other peaceful administrations, but military rule followed again in 1963. The military alternated with civilian governments until 1979 when a new constitution allowed for the first freely elected president in a decade. That president, Jaime Roldos, died in a 1981 plane

Copyright © 1994. Brigham Young University. Printed in the USA. All rights reserved. It is against the law to copy, reprint, store in a retrieval system, or transmit any part of this publication in any form by any means for any purpose without written permission from the Publications Division of the David M. Kennedy Center for International Studies, Brigham Young University, PO Box 24538, Provo, UT 84602–4538. *Culturgrams* are available for more than 125 areas of the world. To place an order, to receive a free catalog, or to obtain information on traveling abroad, call toll free (800) 528–6279.

crash, but he was succeeded by his vice president. Ecuador has thus had a stable political system since 1979. Elections in 1992 marked the fourth consecutive peaceful transition of power and emphasized Ecuador's commitment to democracy and civilian rule. Sixto Durán Bellén was elected president.

THE PEOPLE
Population
There are approximately 10.4 million people in Ecuador, a population that is growing at 2 percent annually. The majority (55 percent) are *mestizo* (Spanish-Indian mix). About 25 percent are native Indian (descendants of various ancient tribes). Another 10 percent are of Spanish descent, and 10 percent are black. Quito, the capital, is one of the oldest continuously inhabited cities in the Western Hemisphere and has 1.2 million people. The largest city is Guayaquil, with 1.7 million inhabitants. About 56 percent of all Ecuadorians live in urban areas.

Language
Spanish is Ecuador's official language, although the Indian language Quechua is spoken in highland rural areas by about 7 percent of the population. Quechua—recognized by the constitution as an important part of Ecuadorian culture—is a combination of many different dialects. While Quechua is not an official language, many of its words have been adopted into the colloquial language to replace Spanish words or describe something for which there is no Spanish term. Indeed, many Ecuadorian interjections come from Quechua and not Spanish. English is understood by many people in business. Spanish tends to be spoken quicker on the coast, and slower in the Sierra highlands. Some consonants are pronounced differently between the two regions.

Religion
As a country settled by the Spanish, Ecuador is predominantly Catholic. In fact, 95 percent of the people belong to the Catholic church, and many official holidays center around the Catholic faith. However, religious freedom is also guaranteed by the constitution. Many other Christian churches are growing in popularity, and people are generally tolerant of other beliefs.

General Attitudes
General attitudes vary throughout Ecuador, as there is a great diversity of cultures living in the country. However, most Ecuadorians are proud of their country and history. Although Ecuador is considered a developing country, the people do not appreciate being thought of as inferior, inefficient, or backward; they remind others that their nation is civilized and progressive. No matter the living conditions, it is important to keep one's home clean and presentable.

Overlaying Ecuador's ethnic diversity are regional differences that tend to influence politics and internal relations. The *Serranos* (people from mountainous areas, including Quito) are more formal, conservative, and reserved than their countrymen in the coastal regions, the *Costeños*. *Costeños* are considered cosmopolitan, open, and liberal; they are generally the business people of Ecuador. *Serranos* are associated with government and banks. The two groups, political rivals, distrust each other in many respects, but are still united in others. One common trait for all Ecuadorians is that once a family opens its doors to a guest, the door is always open.

Indigenous peoples (Indian groups from the Sierra, Coastal, and Amazon areas) tend to not assimilate into mainstream society. They prefer to retain their own proud traditions and remain in their home regions. Some who move to urban areas adopt parts of the *mestizo* culture, but others remain culturally distinct.

Personal Appearance
Clothing habits differ between rural and urban areas. In urban areas, standard Western-style clothing is found. While younger women wear pants, older women tend to prefer skirts. However, every rural region has its own traditional clothing, colors, and fabrics. Generally, people from coastal areas wear bright, clear colors (white, yellow, red), while those from the highlands prefer blues, browns, and blacks. Rural women seldom wear pants and often wear hats—made of straw in coastal areas and wool or leather in the highlands. Families often dress up in new clothing for special celebrations. These items might be purchased at a store, but are more often made by local tailors.

CUSTOMS AND COURTESIES
Greetings
A handshake is usually used when meeting someone for the first time. It is then used in subsequent greetings, along with the exchange of good wishes. Close friends appear to kiss each other on the cheek. Actually, they "kiss the air" while brushing or touching cheeks. Men often embrace if well acquainted. It is customary to address people by a title (*Señor, Señora, Doctor, Doctora*, etc.) when being introduced. First names are generally not used between strangers. Among friends, the title *Don* or *Doña*, followed by the first name, is a common greeting because it indicates both respect and friendship. Common terms for greeting include: *¡Buenos días!* (Good day) or *¿Cómo está?* (How are you?). Friends commonly greet each other with *¡Hola!* (Hello). After a long absence, one might greet another with *¿Como has pasado. A los tiempos que nos vemos?* (How have you been? It has been a long time.) or *¿Que viento te trajo por acá?* (What wind blew you this way?).

Gestures
Yawning in public, whistling to get someone's attention, or pointing with the index finger are considered impolite in Ecuador, as they show a lack of respect for others. Ecuadorians might point by puckering or pursing the lips. One can also indicate "up the road" by lifting the chin, and "down the road" by lowering the chin. Hands are often used to emphasize or replace verbal communication. Drawing a circle or two in the air with the index finger means "I'll be back." To indicate, "Sorry, the bus is full," or "Sorry, we're out of tomatoes," or anything along that line, a person sticks out the hand, as if to shake hands, and twists it almost like he is waving. During conversation, a person might touch another person of the same sex to show friendly concern.

Visiting

When Ecuadorians (both families and friends) visit, it is usually for a meal and conversation. However, unannounced visits are common and welcomed. Even if unexpected guests arrive during mealtime, they will be offered a full meal. It would be impolite to refuse. When guests leave the home, they are often given a small gift (*regalito*) of something the family has on hand (fruit, candy, etc.). Guests are typically offered something to drink, and it is generally impolite to refuse the offer. When inviting a guest to visit, the host will state the starting time, but it is considered bad taste to specify an ending time. Instead, an ending time is generally understood depending on the nature of the visit. Guests are not expected to arrive on time, and can be anywhere from 10 minutes to an hour late, depending on the event. Guests invited specifically to dinner do not leave right after the meal, but stay for conversation.

Evening socials (for birthdays, reunions, parties) might extend past midnight, especially on the coast. They usually involve eating, dancing, and drinking. Furniture is placed near the wall so there is room in the middle of the main room for everyone, including children, to dance. Refreshments are served by the hosts on serving trays; guests do not serve themselves from a central location. A meal is then usually served late in the evening, after which many guests will leave and others will stay for more socializing.

At small gatherings, arriving guests greet each person individually. The host introduces the guests to people with whom they are not yet acquainted. Guests who fail to say hello to those they know are not placing enough worth on their relationship. When leaving, a person should also say good-bye to each individual. Among the youth, more formal customs are being replaced by informal ones. For instance, young people often use group greetings rather than personal ones.

Eating

Food and eating habits play an important part in Ecuadorian culture. Every holiday is associated with a special kind of food and every town has a specialty dish. Mealtime is considered a good time for conversation—catching up, conducting business, or socializing. When inviting a guest to a restaurant, the host is expected to pay for the meal. Youth, however, will often split a bill. In fact, what people in the United States call "going Dutch," the Ecuadorians call "doing as the North Americans."

LIFESTYLE

Family

Families are important in society and generally close-knit. The elderly are respected and treated well. Several generations may live under the same roof. Many families lead a simple life in small homes or rented apartments. While traditional roles are followed in most families, urban families are changing as more women work outside the home and more men share household duties. Other traditions are changing as well. Children used to live with their parents until they got married. Now, they often leave to get an education or to experience life. A young woman would traditionally go directly from her parent's home to her husband's, but more are experiencing independence before marriage. Families are also getting smaller. Urban families average two children, while rural families average three or four. Only about 5 percent of the population lives in wealthy conditions. About 12 percent lives in absolute poverty, without modern sanitation and other conveniences.

Dating and Marriage

Dating usually begins in groups, when the youth get together for dances or other activities. In couples dating, a girl must ask for the parents' approval when invited out. Girls often do not begin dating until after their *quincinera* (coming out party) at age 15. A Catholic ceremony officially presents the girl to society. If the family can afford it, a party with food, drinks, and dancing will follow. Women usually marry by age 23 (by 14 in some rural areas) and men around age 25. Families often emphasize that young people should complete their education before marrying. Many urban couples do not live together before their church wedding, even if they have already been married by law. Common-law marriage (referred to as *Estilo Manabita*) is common in rural, costal areas. It is accepted as a legal marriage, even though no ceremony has been performed. For most of these unions, the ceremony is only lacking because of the expense of a wedding.

Diet

Of the three daily meals, the midday meal is most important. *Serranos* favor corn and potatoes, while *Costeños* favor rice, beans, and bananas, of which there are several varieties. Fresh fruits are abundant and fish is a staple item. Soup is almost always served at both the midday and evening meals. Hot bread is a popular afternoon snack. Some favorite dishes include *arroz con pollo* (fried chicken with rice), *locro* (a soup made with potatoes, cheese, meat, and avocados), *llapingachos* (cheese and potato cakes), *ceviche* (raw seafood marinated in lime and served with onions, tomatoes, and various spices), *fritada* (fried pork), *empanadas* (pastries filled with meat or cheese), *arroz con menestra* (rice with spicy beans, barbecued beef, and refried plantains), and *caldo de bola* (plantain-based soup with meat and vegetables).

Recreation

Fútbol (soccer) is the favorite sport in Ecuador, followed by volleyball and track. Others include tennis, basketball, and boxing. Ecuadorian volleyball (*Ecuavolley*) is played with a heavy ball by three players on each side. Most sports are played by men and boys, with only a few girls involved in each. Various museums, cultural sites, and outdoor activities offer other forms of recreation to many people. Quito offers an active cultural life for the wealthy.

Holidays

Ecuadorians celebrate the new year by burning effigies of the Old Year in the streets on New Year's Eve. *Carnival* (in February or March), Easter, Labor Day (1 May), and The Battle of Pichincha (24 May), which marks Ecuador's liberation, are all national holidays. But the most important national holiday is Independence Day (10 August), the day in 1809 when efforts were first made to become independent from Spain. When a new president is elected, he takes the oath of office on 10 August. The independence of Guayaquil is celebrated 9 October. All Souls Day (2 November) is observed by visits to cemeteries; many people place bread-dough dolls on gravestones to honor the dead. The independence of Quito (6 December) is celebrated by large festivals, bullfights, and sporting events. Of course, Christmas is an important holiday. Several local festivals and fairs are held throughout the year in various regions. Each city and province celebrates the anniversary of its own founding.

Commerce

Stores are generally open weekdays between 8:00 A.M. and 12:30 P.M., when they close for lunch. They open again between 2:30 and 6:00 P.M. Stores remain closed after 12:30 P.M. on Saturday and do not open on Sunday. Banks close at 1:30 P.M. each weekday. Most local businesses are family owned and operated.

Urban families often shop at large supermarkets and department stores, but they also enjoy frequenting open air markets. Rural Ecuadorians usually shop at the open air markets and small local businesses. The open air markets operate a few days a week, but not every day. The particular days depend on the region. These markets offer everything from food to clothing to household items. They are often the only source of certain locally grown fruits and vegetables.

SOCIETY

Government

Ecuador has a president, a unicameral legislature, and an independent judiciary. Elections are held every four years. All those over 18 have the right to vote, but those who are literate are required by law to vote.

Economy

Despite relative poverty and various setbacks, including a devastating 1987 earthquake, the economy enjoyed steady growth in 1993. New government policies that encourage foreign investment, trade, and free market mechanisms have led to expanded opportunities. Ecuador's Human Development Index (0.646) ranks it 89 out of 173 countries. Real gross domestic product per capita is $3,074, which has doubled in the last generation. These figures indicate a growing number of people have the opportunity to earn a decent income. Still, more than half of the population lives in poverty.

At least 35 percent of the population is employed in agriculture, producing bananas, coffee, sugarcane, fruits, corn, potatoes, rice, and other foods. Petroleum accounts for 47 percent of the nation's exports, followed by coffee, bananas, cocoa, shrimp, and fish. Other industries important to the economy include food processing, textiles, chemicals, fishing, and timber. Inflation is above 50 percent, and 10 percent of the labor force is unemployed. The currency is the *sucre* (S), named for the national hero Antonio José de Sucre.

Transportation and Communication

In cities, transportation is provided by buses, taxis, and *colectivos* (small minibuses that are more comfortable and faster than buses). In rural areas, *busetas* replace the *colectivos*. Roads connecting cities have been improved and about half are fully paved. There are about 650 miles of railroad in Ecuador, providing some train transportation within the country. Communication systems function fairly well, with telephone services as well as radio, television, and newspaper organizations. Seaports provide shipping to other nations. Air travel to and within Ecuador is increasing.

Education

Both public and private educational institutions are controlled by the government. The school system is comprised of nursery schools, kindergartens, rural and urban elementary schools, secondary and vocational schools, night schools, and special-education schools. There are 21 autonomous universities. The largest university is located in Quito and has 45,000 students.

In recent years the literacy rate has increased to 86 percent. Children attend school daily either from 7:00 A.M. to 12:30 P.M. or from 1:00 to 6:00 P.M., eating lunch at home. They are usually required to wear uniforms.

Health

The government provides medical care to all citizens at low (sometimes no) cost to the patient. Yet, rural clinics are not always well-equipped. Those who can afford it might go to a private clinic or doctor. The country still battles such diseases as typhoid, cholera, polio, malaria, and yellow fever. Medical care has improved over the years and the infant mortality rate dropped from 60 per 1,000 in 1988 to 40 per 1,000 in 1993. Life expectancy has risen to between 67 and 72 years. Tap water is generally not potable. Poverty tends to intensify health problems.

FOR THE TRAVELER

With a valid passport, U.S. visitors need to show proof of onward transportation (such as a return ticket) and adequate finances. They may stay up to 90 days with a migratory control card issued upon such proof. One should bring adequate film for the trip, as it may be hard to find outside of major tourists areas. It is also advisable to save film for developing back home. If departing by plane, a tax must be paid upon leaving. While no vaccinations are required for entry, one may want to take precautions against typhoid, cholera, polio, tetanus, hepatitis, malaria, and yellow fever. Consult your physician. Altitude sickness is common in Quito, which has an elevation of 9,300 feet (2,835 meters). Contact Ecuador's National Tourist Office (*Feprotur*) at 7270 Northwest Twelfth Street, Suite 400, Miami, FL 33126, or the Embassy of Ecuador, 2535 15th Street NW, Washington, DC 20009 for more information.

A *Culturgram* is a product of native commentary and original, expert analysis. Statistics are estimates and information is presented as a matter of opinion. While the editors strive for accuracy and detail, this document should not be considered strictly factual. It is a general introduction to culture, an initial step in building bridges of understanding between peoples. It may not apply to all peoples of the nation. You should therefore consult other sources for more information.

Republic of
El Salvador

Boundary representations not necessarily authoritative.

THE AMERICAS

BACKGROUND

Land and Climate

With 8,124 square miles (21,040 square kilometers), El Salvador is just smaller than Massachusetts. It is located south of Guatemala and west of Honduras in Central America. The land is characterized by mountain ranges, extinct volcanoes (nearly 200 of them), coastal lowlands, and a central plateau. The soil has been enriched by lava from the volcanoes. Earthquakes are frequent in most areas. The climate is tropical in the lowlands, semitropical on the plateau, and more temperate on the mountain slopes. The average yearly temperature is about 75°F (24°C) and temperatures rarely fluctuate more than five degrees. The rainy season is between May and October, but most rain falls in relatively short evening storms. San Salvador, the capital, lies at the foot of the San Salvador Volcano.

History

Various native civilizations inhabited the area long before the Spanish conquest. Mayans, Lencas, and Nahuats all lived in the region at some time. The Pipil Indians were those encountered by the Spanish when they arrived in 1524. In that year, Pedro de Alvarado conquered the area in the name of Spain, which then ruled for almost 300 years. The indigenous peoples were nearly wiped out under harsh colonial rule. For most of its early history, El Salvador (literally, "The Savior") was part of Guatemala, as ruled by Spain. Attempts led by Father José Matias Delgado to gain independence from Spain in 1811 and 1814 were unsuccessful but earned Matias a hero's recognition.

A wider regional attempt to gain independence was successful in 1821, but El Salvador simply ended up as part of another kingdom because it was annexed by Mexico's Emperor Agustín Iturbide. When that empire collapsed two years later, El Salvador, with its neighbors, formed the United Provinces of Central America. Political strains between the union's members led to its collapse in 1838. Dominated by Guatemala for several more years, a nominally independent El Salvador did not achieve full sovereignty until 1856.

For more than a century after that, El Salvador was plagued with internal strife and military dictatorships. Following a

Copyright © 1994. Brigham Young University. Printed in the USA. All rights reserved. It is against the law to copy, reprint, store in a retrieval system, or transmit any part of this publication in any form by any means for any purpose without written permission from the Publications Division of the David M. Kennedy Center for International Studies, Brigham Young University, PO Box 24538, Provo, UT 84602–4538. *Culturgrams* are available for more than 125 areas of the world. To place an order, to receive a free catalog, or to obtain information on traveling abroad, call toll free (800) 528–6279.

1979 coup that overthrew President Carlos Humberto Romero, a military-civilian junta took control of the government. For years, the government of José Napoleón Duarte was accused of human rights violations, corruption, and other abuses. The Farabundo Martí National Liberation Front (FMLN) waged a civil war to change the country's leadership. Violence marked 12 years of struggle between the leftist FMLN and the right-wing government. As many as 75,000 people died on both sides of the conflict.

Elections were held in 1989 and Alfredo Cristiani became president. The elections were marred by violence and the war intensified. Peace talks that had begun earlier broke off and rebel forces mounted large offensives around the capital. Cristiani reopened discussions with FMLN leaders in 1990, and the United Nations was accepted by both sides as a mediator. Fighting continued into 1991 and peace talks faltered several times. Key concessions were finally made by both sides, which then signed a UN-sponsored peace agreement in January 1992.

The subsequent cease-fire held, as huge celebrations marked the historic event. Formal peace was declared in December 1992. The peace agreement called for rebel forces to disarm and join the political process; they later joined a coalition of parties called the Democratic Convergence. A new constitution was drafted and a new police force was established that is to be autonomous from the military. During the war, right-wing death squads associated with the military and police reportedly killed citizens who opposed the government; hence, the importance of a new security force. The transition to full reconciliation and democracy was shaky throughout 1992 and 1993, but elections were held on schedule in March 1994. Although irregularities at various polling stations cast a shadow on the voting, the event still marked an important step forward for the entire nation. Armando Calderon Sol, leader of the National Republican Alliance (ARENA), was elected president.

THE PEOPLE

Population

The population of El Salvador is about 5.6 million. Rapid growth rates have decreased in recent years and the current annual rate is 2 percent. The average population density is 686 persons per square mile (265 per square kilometer), a high rate compared to most nations in the Americas. The majority of the people (89 percent) are *mestizos* (mixed Spanish and Native American), while about 10 percent are Native Americans and only 1 percent are white (mostly of Spanish descent).

Language

Spanish is the official language, although Nahua and other Native American languages are spoken by many. English is often spoken among the educated.

Religion

El Salvador is largely a Catholic nation, with close to 75 percent of the people belonging to the Roman Catholic church. About 20 percent practice a variety of other Christian faiths, including an assortment of Protestant religions.

General Attitudes

Salvadorans are known for their hospitality to visitors. The people love their country and are proud of its accomplishments. Salvadorans are hardworking individuals who care for others. Having endured a 12-year civil war, Salvadorans now look to their future in a peaceful democracy. Past feelings of hatred and revenge are being replaced with hope, optimism, and cooperation. Groups that used to fight each other are pledging to establish a democratic society that will represent all viewpoints. They will succeed if disagreements over the progress of the transition to full democracy and peace are settled. These disagreements include how to handle human rights violations that occurred during the war. Despite continued difficulties, people are relieved that their children's future is now more promising.

Personal Appearance

Because of the warm climate, summer clothing is suitable all year. Business representatives wear suits. During winter months, light jackets are sometimes necessary at night. Although poor people do not have large wardrobes, they try to keep their appearance neat and clean.

CUSTOMS AND COURTESIES

Greetings

A handshake is the customary greeting, but sometimes a slight nod of the head is also used. Children also appreciate having adults shake their hands. The use of titles shows respect, which is particularly important when greeting the elderly. The first name or family name alone is used only among close acquaintances. Placing an arm around the shoulders of another is a common way to show friendship, and friends often stand very close when conversing. Women who have not seen each other in a while will exchange hugs. Common greetings include *¡Buenos días!* (Good day or Good morning), *¡Buenas tardes!* (Good afternoon), and *¡Buenas noches!* (Good evening).

Gestures

It is poor manners to use extensive hand or head gestures in conversation or to express feelings. Yawns should be avoided or covered with the hand. It is not appropriate to point feet or fingers at anyone. Only close friends are beckoned with a hand wave.

Visiting

Visitors are expected to show dignity, courtesy, warmth, and friendship. It is appropriate to stand when a woman enters the room and when meeting other people. Salvadorans appreciate sincere compliments about their homes, children, gardens, or country. Small gifts may be exchanged with first-time visitors.

Eating

It is polite for guests to try some of every dish that is served. Leaving a little food on the plate is considered good manners. Men stand when a woman leaves the table. Guests compliment the host or hostess on the meal, something which assures the hosts that the guests feel welcome.

LIFESTYLE

Family

Salvadorans have close family ties, which include caring for the elderly. The father is the head of the family, which has an average of five members. However, single-parent families are also common, with a large number of children being born to unwed mothers. The majority of families belong to the peasant class (*campesinos* who work on the land but do not own it) and the "blue-collar" working class. While most of these families have electricity, many do not have telephones, cars, or televisions. Only a small percentage of the people have access to luxury items.

Dating and Marriage

Group dating begins around age 15. Traditionally, it was not proper for couples to be seen in public unless engaged or married, but this has changed significantly in urban areas, with trends more closely matching those in industrialized nations. In most cases, wedding ceremonies follow Catholic traditions.

Diet

Salvadoran food is less spicy than that of many other Latin American countries. Most people eat black beans (*frijoles*), refried beans, thick tortillas, rice, eggs, and fruit. Meat is also important, but it is not always available to poorer people.

Recreation

Salvadorans love sports, especially soccer, the national sport. Some consider El Salvador the sports capital of Central America, as Salvadorans have excelled in many sports and most towns have a gym and athletic field. Basketball is also popular.

Holidays

The Salvadoran love for beauty and gaiety finds expression in the many colorful festivals held throughout the country during the year. National holidays include New Year's Day; Easter Week; Labor Day (1 May); Mother's Day (10 May); Father's Day (17 June); August religious festivities (1–5 August); Independence Day, which commemorates the day Father José Matias Delgado declared the country independent (15 September); Columbus Day (12 October); and Christmas.

Commerce

Salvadorans work hard and farmers often work ten or more hours a day. Businesses are open from 8:00 A.M. to noon and from 2:00 to 6:00 P.M., Monday through Friday. They close at noon on Saturday. Government offices open at 7:30 A.M. and close at 3:30 P.M. on weekdays. While fixed prices prevail in the stores, bargaining is common in open markets.

SOCIETY

Government

El Salvador's executive branch is led by a president and vice president. They govern for a five-year term and are ineligible for immediate reelection. The National Assembly has 84 members, all of whom are elected. The voting age is 18. The country is divided into 14 departments and 262 municipalities.

Economy

Mostly due to war, El Salvador has one of the weakest economies in Latin America. The country's Human Development Index (0.503) ranks it 110 out of 173 countries. Real gross domestic product per capita is $1,950. These figures reflect the fact that more than one-fourth of all people live in poverty and many more do not earn an income sufficient for their needs. However, basic infrastructure exists to allow for ecnomic prosperity once political stability is well established.

About 40 percent of the labor force is employed in agriculture. The war forced many from their farms and villages to work for subsistence wages or to live in Honduran refugee camps, but these refugees are returning to again work the land. Coffee accounts for 60 percent of the country's export earnings. El Salvador also exports sugar, cotton, and shrimp. Although training programs have been established to teach new skills, there is a shortage of skilled labor in the country. Unemployment is around 30 percent. Inflation is about 20 percent. Important industries focus on food processing, cement, textiles, and petroleum products. The currency is the Salvadoran *colón* (¢).

Transportation and Communication

Because few people own cars, public travel is mostly done by bus. Taxis are available in San Salvador. Roads are good and many are either paved or gravel. However, others are not paved and are impassable during the rainy season. Fighting damaged some roads and inhibited repairs on others. An effort is being made to improve communications, which are not well developed. There are currently fewer than 125,000 telephones in the country.

Education

While the overall literacy rate for the country is 73 percent, only about 35 percent of the rural population is literate. The government is engaged in a vigorous campaign to increase literacy in the country, including the establishment of new kindergartens, primary schools, and secondary schools. Local residents have also built schools in areas where war had interrupted regular educational opportunities. It may take some time before these are replaced by public facilities. Public schooling is free to all and there are many private schools. The school year begins in mid-January. The National University of El Salvador includes schools of law, medicine, engineering, dentistry, and economics.

Health

El Salvador's health care system, like many institutions, was damaged during the war. Facilities in rural areas are lacking, but urban clinics and hospitals offer better care. The government is improving conditions with free immunization clinics, education in sanitation and hygiene, development of water and sewage systems, and more modern hospital administration. The infant mortality rate is estimated to be 42 per 1,000; life expectancy ranges from 64 to 70 years. Malaria, measles, and other diseases continue to afflict people, especially in rural areas.

FOR THE TRAVELER

A standard tourist visa and passport are required for U.S. citizens to travel to El Salvador. U.S. citizens arriving in El Salvador must have at least US$300. No vaccinations are required unless one is coming from a yellow fever endemic zone. Malaria suppressants are recommended for rural visits. Water is considered safe in some areas. While electrical outlets use the same basic voltage as is found in the United States, plug types vary and an adaptor may be necessary.

Some Salvadorans are offended when a person from the United States introduces himself as an "American" because Salvadorans also consider themselves Americans, as they live in Central America. It is best to identify oneself as a U.S. citizen and to avoid terms such as "In America, we . . . ." To apply for a visa, contact the Consulate General of El Salvador, 1010 16th Street NW, Third Floor, Washington, DC 20036. You may also wish to contact the Embassy of El Salvador, 2308 California Street NW, Washington, DC 20008 for more information.

A *Culturgram* is a product of native commentary and original, expert analysis. Statistics are estimates and information is presented as a matter of opinion. While the editors strive for accuracy and detail, this document should not be considered strictly factual. It is a general introduction to culture, an initial step in building bridges of understanding between peoples. It may not apply to all peoples of the nation. You should therefore consult other sources for more information.

England
(United Kingdom)

Boundary representations not necessarily authoritative.

BACKGROUND

Land and Climate

While the United Kingdom is about the same size as Oregon, England's share is about 50,363 square miles (130,357 square kilometers), or about the size of the state of New York. England is one of three nations that make up the island of Great Britain. The other two are Scotland and Wales. The United Kingdom is composed of Great Britain and Northern Ireland. But the British Isles include the islands of Britain, Ireland, the Isle of Man, and the Channel Islands (in the English Channel).

Low mountains and rugged hills in the north contrast with flat countryside in the east and level and rolling plains in the southeast and southwest, the direction from which the prevailing wind blows. Nearly 30 percent of the land is cultivated. Almost half is meadows or pasture. The climate is temperate, but skies are overcast more often than not. The north is wetter and slightly cooler than the south. Winter temperatures rarely drop below 25°F (–4°C) and summer averages seldom rise above 75°F (24°C). Humidity levels ranging from medium to high can make it seem colder or warmer than temperatures indicate.

History

Julius Caesar's expeditionary forces reached Britain in 55 B.C. but it was not until 43 A.D. in the reign of Tiberius that the Romans invaded. They incorporated the area into the Roman Empire and stayed until 426, when Rome was in decline and raiding Angles and Saxons (two Germanic tribes) drove them out of Britain. Vikings began raiding the islands in the late eighth century. In 865, Danish-led forces invaded and ushered in two centuries of Viking domination. Other groups also invaded, included the Norsemen. The last invasion was in 1066, when William the Conqueror (or William of Normandy) won the Battle of Hastings. This Norman conquest ushered in a new chapter in English history that saw great political and social change take place. The signing of the Magna Carta in 1215 was one such change; it established important principles of human rights and limits on the monarchy.

A long period of dynastic struggle ended in the 15th century with the War of the Roses. Henry Tudor emerged with the crown. Henry VIII was his son and the king who established the crown as head of the Church of England. His daughter, Elizabeth I, reigned in an age when the empire began to span the globe, leading to the saying that "the sun never sets on the British empire." Through acts of union, Wales (1535) and Scotland (1707) joined England, and the empire was known as the United Kingdom of Great Britain. An act of union in 1801 brought Ireland to the empire, which was then called the United Kingdom of Great Britain and Ireland. When most of Ireland became independent in 1921, the name changed to the United Kingdom of Great Britain and Northern Ireland.

Britain established itself as a great naval power by defeating the mighty Spanish Armada in 1588. It became the world's most powerful economy during the Industrial Revolution. With these strengths and by acquiring colonies around the globe, Britain was firmly established as an international force and one of the Great Powers of Europe. Although its American colonies were lost in 1776 (Canada was a colony until 1867, and then became an autonomous part of the Commonwealth), new lands were acquired in the Mediterranean, the Caribbean, Africa, and Asia.

EUROPE

Copyright © 1994. Brigham Young University. Printed in the USA. All rights reserved. It is against the law to copy, reprint, store in a retrieval system, or transmit any part of this publication in any form by any means for any purpose without written permission from the Publications Division of the David M. Kennedy Center for International Studies, Brigham Young University, PO Box 24538, Provo, UT 84602–4538. Culturgrams are available for more than 125 areas of the world. To place an order, to receive a free catalog, or to obtain information on traveling abroad, call toll free (800) 528–6279.

After World War I, expansion halted and the empire began to shrink (some colonies had already claimed independence well before the war). During World War II, under the leadership of Winston Churchill, the British withstood intense Nazi bombings, which nearly destroyed many areas. After the war, most British colonies (more than 50) were given independence. The majority remained voluntarily in the Commonwealth and some even retain Queen Elizabeth II as their nominal head of state. Britain was a founding member of the North Atlantic Treaty Organization (NATO) in 1949. It joined the European Union (EU) in 1973.

Winston Churchill's Labour party established the country's modern welfare state. All governments since have retained these policies, even though the Conservative party governments of Margaret Thatcher and John Major placed more emphasis on the private sector. Despite strong opposition over Tory (Conservative) policies regarding the sluggish economy, Major was reelected in 1992.

THE PEOPLE

Population

England is the largest nation of the United Kingdom, which has an overall population of 57.8 million and is growing at only 0.3 percent annually. The English comprise about 81 percent (about 46.8 million) of that total. The nation is highly urbanized, with nearly 90 percent of the people living in cities. Although most people living in England are Caucasian, Britain's past colonial heritage has brought many cultures together. Therefore, various ethnic groups from India, Africa, and Asia also reside in England (up to 2.8 percent of the total population).

Language

English is the official language of the United Kingdom. Dialects do exist throughout England, as do the foreign languages of minority groups. But nearly everyone speaks British English, also known as BBC or Oxford English.

Religion

During the reign of King Henry VIII, England split from the Roman Catholic church to form the Anglican church of England, and it became the country's established religion. The Church of England exercised great influence over the country throughout history, but it no longer has political power. Still, the queen is the head of the church. There are at least 27 million Anglicans in the United Kingdom. Throughout the country, there are also large Catholic (more than five million), Presbyterian (two million), Methodist (0.7 million), and Jewish (0.4 million) populations. Other Christian and non-Christian religious organizations are also active in England. Society is generally secular, despite the presence of an established church. That is, the English generally do not get actively involved with religion. The Anglican church, for example, as representative of its English heritage, is high on ceremony but is not as involved in evangelical activity. Only about one-tenth of all adults regularly attend Sunday church services; of that number, only about one-third attend the Church of England. The English consider religion a very private matter. It is impolite to ask about one's religious beliefs.

General Attitudes

Having a long and rich history, the English enjoy tradition and custom more so than Americans. They often find Americans to be too casual, especially with the English language. In fact, they do not consider the language spoken in the United States (American English) the same language as that spoken in Great Britain (British English). This point should be appreciated by visitors. In general, the English are suspicious of extremes and may be embarrassed by displays of emotion or excessive enthusiasm. Rather, they value moderate behavior and emotional reserve. Britons are known for a wry sense of humor that allows them to be self critical, but this does not give the same freedom to visitors. Britons appreciate visitors who have some knowledge of their history and system. A fairly dominant feature of society is the class system. It is not strictly related to wealth or education, and it is not discussed. But it is carefully observed and impacts daily life. Accents, educational backgrounds, clothing, tastes in furnishings, and leisure activities are all indicative of one's position in the class structure.

Personal Appearance

The English dress much the same way as people in the United States, except that fashion trends are more closely tied to Europe. Older women tend to wear dresses more often than women in the United States. Business attire is conservative.

CUSTOMS AND COURTESIES

Greetings

A handshake is the most common form of greeting among the English, whether for formal occasions, visits, or introductions. Handshakes are generally firm but not aggressive. When people are already acquainted, verbal greetings are often used instead. Among friends, women are often kissed (by men and women) lightly on both cheeks. When passing a stranger on the street, it is appropriate to smile and say "Good morning," "Hello," "Good afternoon," or "Good evening," if eye contact is established with that person. Such an exchange occurs less frequently in large cities than elsewhere. Young people and friends are called by their first name, but titles (Mr., Mrs., Doctor, etc.) are used in formal situations or to show respect.

Gestures

The English are in general a reserved people. They do not approve of loud or demonstrative behavior (except in very informal gatherings). Personal space is respected, and people feel uncomfortable when someone stands too close to them during conversation. Touching is generally avoided. Manners are important, although standards are not as high among the youth, which comprise nearly one-fifth of the population.

Visiting

It is a common courtesy to telephone ahead before visiting someone. In fact, just showing up is considered impolite, even among friends. Refreshments are not always served to visitors. While not customarily required, it is not uncommon for guests to bring gifts. In informal situations, a friend might ask to bring something to the meal (such as a bottle of wine), or a guest might bring chocolates, flowers, or wine as a gift to the host. In formal settings, gifts are less likely, but a thank-you note will likely be sent afterward. The English admire good manners, which are expected of visitors. Traditionally, men hold doors open for women and stand when a woman enters the room. The English enjoy discussing a wide variety of topics during *tea*. This is a 4:00 P.M. snack of tea, buns (cupcakes), or biscuits (cookies). The food is often substantial enough to act as a meal. When using someone's phone, it is courteous to offer to pay, as even local calls are billed separately. However, hosts rarely accept the offer.

Eating

The English eat in the continental style, with the fork in the left hand and the knife in the right. Proper manners are a must at the table; loud behavior is avoided. The English generally eat three meals a day. What each meal (except breakfast) is called depends on family background and local tradition. The majority call the noon meal *lunch* and the evening meal *dinner*. Some, however, call the noon meal *dinner* and the evening meal *tea*. Others call the evening meal *supper*, while still others use *supper* to refer to a snack before bedtime. At a restaurant, a waiter is summoned by raising the hand. The waiter brings the bill on a plate, on which a 10 to 15 percent tip should be left.

LIFESTYLE

Family

English families are small and tightly knit. The traditional standard has been two children in a family. This pattern is changing, however. Fewer people are getting married and those that do, get married later. Women are having fewer children and having them later. More women work outside the home, and there are more single-parent families.

Most families enjoy a comfortable standard of living. The middle class represents Britain's majority. The English ideal is to have a house and garden. Two out of three families have their own homes. Apartment (*flat*) living is not popular, and is only common in the large cities. There is a current trend away from urbanization. People are moving to the countryside to develop an attachment to the land and to avoid big-city problems.

Dating and Marriage

Dating activities are similar in England to those in the United States, but dating patterns are different. While U.S. teenagers enjoy casual dating, British youth generally have only one boyfriend or girlfriend at a time and do not date other people during that time. Marriage becomes legal at age 16, but usually occurs in the mid- to late twenties. Marriage customs are much the same as in the United States.

Diet

The traditional cooked breakfast consists of any or even all of the following: bacon, sausages, grilled or fried tomatoes, mushrooms, eggs, and bread fried in fat or oil. Fewer people now eat this heavy meal on a regular basis, preferring to stick with various combinations of cereal, toast, juice or fruit, and tea or coffee. The British eat a wide variety of European and ethnic foods. Many traditional foods such as beef and potatoes have given way to poultry and pasta dishes. Fast food has also become more prevalent, and hamburger restaurants now rival the traditional fish and chip (french fries) shops in popularity. Numerous Chinese and Indian restaurants and pizza houses provide take-away service, and many pubs serve anything from snacks to full meals. Traditional English dishes include roast beef and Yorkshire pudding (a baked batter usually served in muffin form) and steak and kidney pie.

Recreation

A variety of activities are enjoyed in England, which developed many of the world's favorite sports. For example, football (soccer) was first codified in England. It and rugby are the most popular sports. There are two types of rugby, Union and League, the latter of which is played in the north). One of the most popular spectator sports is horse racing (over jumps in the winter and on a flat track in the summer). Cricket is enjoyed in the summer. Modern lawn tennis was first played in England, and modern boxing rules came from the country. Other favorite forms of recreation include badminton, sailing, swimming, snooker (a billiards game), darts, and squash.

The English like to walk and golf, and many participate in *angling* (fishing). Gardening represents a favorite way to relax and is a huge industry (gardening books can become best-sellers). Flowers, shrubs, and other decorative plants are most common, but some vegetables are also planted. Pubs offer a place to meet, socialize, and relax with friends and neighbors. Relaxing in the home, however, is more popular. The English watch more television than any other people except the Americans. The English claim it is because of the quality of their programming. Videos are also popular, but many people equally enjoy the cinema. The English also support the performing and cultural arts.

Holidays

The English have the fewest public holidays in Europe. They include New Year's Day, Good Friday and Easter Monday, May Day (1 May), Spring and Summer Bank holidays, Christmas, and Boxing Day (26 December). For New Year's Day and May Day, a day off of work is given on the holiday's closest Monday. Virtually everything closes for Christmas, including shops and restaurants. There is a trend for many offices to shut down between Christmas and New Year's because it is a slow business period. Boxing Day is named for the tradition of giving small, boxed gifts to servants and tradesman. It is now just considered a second day for Christmas, a day for visiting friends and family.

Holidays that are celebrated but not treated as days off from work include the Queen's Birthday (second Saturday in June), Remembrance Day (closest Sunday to 11 November), and Guy Fawkes Day (5 November). Guy Fawkes Day, or Bonfire Night, commemorates the capture of Guy Fawkes, who plotted to destroy the houses of parliament in 1605. In some areas huge bonfires are lit and firework displays are put on for the public. Most people receive four or five weeks of personal vacation from work. July and August are popular months for taking trips, and many people also vacation in the winter.

Commerce

Businesses are open generally from 9:00 A.M. to 5:00 P.M., Monday through Friday. An increasing number of shops are lengthening business hours and staying open on weekends. Government offices and some rural shops close for lunch between 1:00 and 2:00 P.M. and stay open until 5:30 P.M. Most stores and businesses are closed on Sunday.

SOCIETY

Government

Britain has no written constitution. The constitutional arrangements are the result of acts of Parliament, common law, and precedent. The importance of a parliament was established following the 1649 civil war and execution of King Charles I. Upon the death of Oliver Cromwell, who had led the violent revolution, the monarchy was reestablished but parliamentary sovereignty remained prominent. The monarch, Queen Elizabeth II, is head of state, but elected officials govern through parliament.

The House of Commons is the main legislative body. It has 650 members. The party with the most members of parliament (MPs) forms the government, and that party's leader becomes the prime minister (officially appointed by the Queen). The prime minister and cabinet govern as the executive body. The voting age is 18, and elections are held at least every five years. In practice, they are held more often, as they can be called for by the prime minister at any time.

Parliament's upper chamber is the House of Lords, which has 1,184 members. About two-thirds are hereditary members, and the other third are appointed members for life, including those who sit on Britain's highest court of appeals. Anglican archbishops and bishops also sit in the House of Lords. The chamber's chief legislative role is to veto legislation, which in practice simply delays it. Since the House of Lords is not an elected body, it rarely chooses to completely block legislation.

Economy

The Industrial Revolution made England one of the strongest industrial powers in the world. Political trends after World War II led to the nationalization of many sectors of the economy, including electricity, coal, railroads, and steel. In the 1980s, political trends led to increased privatization of some sectors and the encouragement of less-regulated industry, which helped England ease some economic pressures, but it also increased long-term unemployment and other problems. The United Kingdom's Human Development Index (0.964) ranks it 10 out of 173 nations. Real gross domestic product per capita is $15,804, a figure that is generally lower than in other European nations. This is indicative of England's competitive status in the European Union (EU).

Britain does the bulk of its trading within the EU. Natural resources include oil, coal, natural gas, tin, iron ore, and salt. Important exports include crude oil (from the North Sea), manufactured goods, and consumer items. The service sector is more important than manufacturing, and London is one of the world's most important financial centers. Britain's farmers supply the country with about 60 percent of its needs. The currency is the pound sterling (£).

Transportation and Communication

Travel by road has become the favored method of transportation for both people and freight since the railway system that was created in the 19th century began to cut back service in the 1960s. The British drive on the left side of the road and a car's steering wheel is on the right side of the car. Taxis are common in the cities. Public transportation is well developed in most urban areas, with a subway in London called the *Tubes* or the *Underground* and subways in such cities as Manchester and Newcastle. Buses and trains service major cities, but public transport in rural areas is not as extensive. Domestic and international air travel is well developed. London's Heathrow airport is the busiest in the world.

In 1994, years of planning and work were celebrated in the official opening of the Channel Tunnel, which connects England and France by rail under the English Channel. People normally cross the channel by ferry or air. With full service available in 1995, the tunnel offers a three-hour ride between London and Paris (about 35 minutes in the actual tunnel) for passengers, freight, and private cars. High-speed trains operate on the French side and will be in place on the English side by 2002.

Telecommunications are well advanced, with fiber optic cable links and satellite systems. Most British homes have telephones and televisions. Several daily newspapers are available throughout the nation.

Education

England's education system has produced a 99 percent literacy rate. A large portion of tax revenues is spent on education needs. Schooling is free and compulsory between ages five and sixteen. Many begin earlier with nursery school and some stay beyond age 16 to prepare for entrance to college. A grade is called a "form," Public schools are called "state" schools and private ones are called "public" schools. At age 16 students take an exam to earn the General Certificate of Secondary Education. At 18 they may take the General Certificate of Education, which is used basically as an entrance exam by England's universities and colleges. In addition to more than 40 universities and various professional schools, England has an Open University, which offers correspondence and broadcast courses to anyone interested. England's quality of higher education is evident in many important scientific and technological contributions, as well as British achievement in the arts and other areas.

Health

Britain's National Health Service (NHS) provides, on the basis of taxation, free medical treatment and many other social services to the people. Only prescriptions and some dental services must be paid for by the individual. The quality of care and facilities is high, but the country struggles under the increasing cost of financing the NHS. Private care is also available, and many people now have private insurance programs to avoid long waits for surgical treatment covered by the NHS. Life expectancy averages 76 years; the infant mortality rate is 8 per 1,000.

FOR THE TRAVELER

While a valid passport is necessary, no visa is required of U.S. citizens for stays in the United Kingdom lasting as long as six months. No vaccinations are required. Tap water is safe to drink. Dual-voltage small appliances or a converter and plug adaptor are necessary to use electrical outlets. There is much to see and do in England. For suggestions and lodging information, one should contact the British Tourist Authority (551 Fifth Avenue, Seventh Floor, New York, NY 10176). You may also wish to contact the Embassy of the United Kingdom, 3100 Massachusetts Avenue NW, Washington, DC 20008, or the British Information Service, 845 Third Avenue, New York, NY 10022.

A *Culturgram* is a product of native commentary and original, expert analysis. Statistics are estimates and information is presented as a matter of opinion. While the editors strive for accuracy and detail, this document should not be considered strictly factual. It is a general introduction to culture, an initial step in building bridges of understanding between peoples. It may not apply to all peoples of the nation. You should therefore consult other sources for more information.

CULTURGRAM ™ '95

Republic of Estonia

Boundary representations not necessarily authoritative.

BACKGROUND

Land and Climate

Estonia is a small European country, similar in size to Switzerland or the combined states of New Hampshire and Vermont. It is one of the three countries known as the Baltic States (Estonia, Latvia, and Lithuania). While Russia lies to the east and Latvia to the south, Estonia is otherwise bordered by the waters of the Baltic Sea and the Gulf of Finland. More than 1,500 islands in the Baltic Sea make up nearly 10 percent of Estonia's total 17,400 square miles (45,100 square kilometers). The two largest islands are Saaremaa and Hiiumaa, each of which is populated.

Estonia is mostly flat, with hills in the south. The highest hill is *Suur Munamägi* (Great Egghill) at 318 meters. Historically an agrarian country, Estonia is also endowed with oil shale deposits and phosphorite, particularly in the northeast. The country's major rivers include the Emajõgi (Mother River), Pärnu, Narva, and Pirita. Lake Peipus dominates the eastern border. A number of smaller lakes and rivers, many rich in fish, dot Estonia's landscape. Forests, wetlands, and meadows harbor wildlife, berries, and mushrooms.

The climate is usually wet with many cloudy days. Winters are cold and snowy with temperatures often below freezing. Summers are cool; temperatures average around 65°F (18°C). Estonia is warmed by the Gulf Stream, which also brings rain at the end of summer.

History

The Estonian people belong to the ancient Finno-Ugric tribe that has inhabited the region for thousands of years. Before the 13th century, Estonians generally lived in free association, without an aristocracy of any kind. This changed with the invasion and domination of German and Danish crusaders in the 1200s. Baltic Germans remained the ruling class into the 20th century. Estonia came under Swedish control in 1561 but became linked to Russia beginning in 1710.

Estonia took advantage of the chaotic conditions of Russia's Bolshevik Revolution in 1917 to declare its independence. The Red Army invaded but was defeated in the Battle of Võnnu. Estonia maintained its independence for 22 years. However, under the secret Molotov-Ribbentrop pact between Germany's Adolf Hitler and Russia's Josef Stalin, Estonia was invaded in 1940 by the Soviet Union. Until it was defeated in World War II, Germany occupied the territory from 1941 to 1944 . The Soviets then reestablished their power and incorporated Estonia into the Soviet Union.

With the relaxed political climate under Soviet leader Mikhail Gorbachev, Estonia's quest for independence became visible outside the USSR. At large demonstrations and nighttime festivals, people sang outlawed nationalistic songs to show their determination. As the Soviet Union weakened and finally collapsed in 1991, Russian president Boris Yeltsin accepted Estonia's declaration of restored independence. Es-

Copyright © 1994. Brigham Young University. Printed in the USA. All rights reserved. It is against the law to copy, reprint, store in a retrieval system, or transmit any part of this publication in any form by any means for any purpose without written permission from the Publications Division of the David M. Kennedy Center for International Studies, Brigham Young University, PO Box 24538, Provo, UT 84602–4538. *Culturgrams* are available for more than 125 areas of the world. To place an order, to receive a free catalog, or to obtain information on traveling abroad, call toll free (800) 528–6279.

tonia has since moved steadily toward reestablishing its sovereign and democratic government.

THE PEOPLE

Population

The population of Estonia is about 1.6 million and is growing at 0.7 percent per year. The majority (61 percent) are ethnic Estonians. Russians (33 percent), Ukrainians (3 percent), Belarusians (1.8 percent), and Finns (1 percent), among others, make up the rest of the population. Most non-Estonians migrated to the area during the Soviet era. They are eligible for Estonian citizenship if they meet residency, language, and other requirements. For instance, they must take language classes to learn Estonian. Citizenship is vital for property ownership, social benefits, and other privileges of living in Estonia. Many ethnic Russians, heartened by Estonia's economic and social development, are choosing to seek formal citizenship.

During World War II, thousands of Estonians fled their homeland and settled all over the world. The largest expatriate communities are located in Toronto, Canada, and New York City. Groups are found throughout the United States, in Australia, and in Sweden. These communities retain their roots through festivals, church worship, and newspapers.

Tallinn, the capital, is the largest city with about 485,000 inhabitants. Tartu (116,000) and Narva (83,000) are the next largest cities. Nearly three-fourths of all people live in urban areas.

Language

Estonian uses a Latin alphabet and is similar to Finnish. Many Estonians can speak Finnish. Most learned Russian during the Soviet era, but they prefer to speak Estonian. Most of the Russian population speaks Russian and many cannot yet speak Estonian. English is popular, particularly with the youth, and it is taught in school.

Religion

Estonia was one of the last nations in Europe to convert to Christianity. Before the 13th century, Estonians followed a religion that was closely tied to nature and included the worship of a god called Taara. The adoption of Christianity came through foreign invasions and missionary work. Following the Reformation, the Lutheran Church became dominant in Estonia.

Because religious worship was suppressed during the Soviet era, the country today is quite secular. Indeed, less than one-fourth of the population is religious. Most of those still attend the Lutheran Church, although other Christian denominations are also active. Religious freedom is guaranteed. Although the government is not tied to a particular religion, prayers are sometimes offered at official functions.

General Attitudes

Estonians view themselves as industrious and efficient people who maintained these values even during the Soviet era. They are patriotic and they are proud of their ancient heritage. Although they are not part of Scandinavia, Estonians tend to identify with the Scandinavian value system and way of life. Estonians cherish freedom and their traditional culture. Despite occupation by other nations, particularly since 1940, Estonians are proud that they have retained their traditions and language.

Estonians place a high value on family, education, and work. They value a good personal reputation for themselves and others. People desire future opportunities to travel and to obtain a higher standard of living.

Personal Appearance

Estonians tend to have fair-colored hair and blue eyes so they appear to be Scandinavian or Nordic. They like to dress well in public. People always dress more formally when going out to eat, going to theater, or visiting friends. Women generally wear dresses more than slacks, although the youth are adopting a more varied approach. Young people prefer European fashions. People dress warm during the winter, preferring coats to jackets. Clothing styles in rural areas are more relaxed than in cities. Each of Estonia's 11 counties has its own traditional costume that is worn for special occasions, such as festivals, holidays or weddings.

CUSTOMS AND COURTESIES

Greetings

Estonians usually greet with a simple *Tere* (Hello) and a handshake. The younger person initiates the greeting, and men greet women first. In a group, the elderly are first to be greeted. People often begin a conversation with *Kuidas käsi käib?* (How are you?) or *Kuidas läheb?* (How is it going?). Other greetings include *Tere hommikust* (Good morning), *Tere päivast* (Good day), and *Tere Õhtust* (Good evening).

When approached, it is polite to stand and acknowledge the other person's presence, maintaining eye contact during the greeting. It is a courtesy to use the formal pronoun *Teie* (you) when meeting someone for the first time, with older people, and with those in authority. The informal *Sina* (you) is used with friends and relatives.

Gestures

When passing someone on the street, it is polite to offer a greeting. Chewing gum in public is impolite, especially when talking to someone. Estonians use the "thumbs-up" gesture to indicate things are going well. Pointing with the index finger is impolite, as is talking with one's hands in the pockets. Hand gestures are kept to a minimum during conversation.

Visiting

An important aspect of social life is visiting or receiving friends. Punctuality is expected. When visiting friends or when visiting someone for the first time, it is common to bring flowers to the hosts. Tea or coffee is usually offered to guests. People enjoy inviting friends over for dinner. Estonians appreciate conversation during the meal.

Hosts often give departing guests a bouquet of flowers as a token of friendship. Guests staying in the home generally give a gift to thank the hosts for their hospitality.

Eating

Dark rye bread, eggs, cheese, pastries, sandwiches, and porridge are common breakfast foods, accompanied by milk or coffee. The main meal is at midday. It consists of three courses: soup, a main dish of meat or fish and potatoes, and dessert. Common soups include bouillon, cabbage, or pea. Dessert is often cake, ice cream, fruit, or fruit preserves.

Dinner is a lighter meal and is eaten after 6:00 P.M. It might include potatoes, stew, pasta, or soup.

Hands are generally kept above the table during a meal. One waits for all to be finished before leaving the table. Requesting second helpings pleases the cook.

LIFESTYLE

Family

Families tend to be small, with one to three children being common. Ties with extended family members are important. Grandparents often care for their grandchildren while both parents work. In many cases, newlywed couples live with their parents until they are more financially established. Parents try to assist their adult children financially, if possible. Adult children take direct responsibility (financial and physical) for their aging parents. Nursing homes are used only for those who have no close relations.

Urban families tend to live in apartments or small, single-family homes that have a fence and garden. Rural families often live on farms and usually live in larger homes.

Dating and Marriage

Common dating activities include attending cultural events, going to the theater, dancing, participating in sporting events, and eating and drinking. Estonians usually marry after they have finished their education, which is usually in their early twenties. Couples often live together before or instead of marriage. Weddings are generally secular, but church weddings are becoming more popular. Parents from both sides help to organize the celebration, to which plenty of friends and relatives are invited. Estonians often have their first child early in their marriage.

Diet

Dark rye bread and fish (salmon, cod, herring, sole, pike, perch, whitefish) are commonly eaten. Potatoes, cabbage, carrots, and beans are the prevalent vegetables. The more popular fruits are apples, cherries, pears, and a number of wild berries (raspberries, strawberries, cranberries, cloudberries, and blueberries). Pork, beef, lamb, veal, and chicken are common meats. Dairy products such as milk, butter, yogurt, sour cream, and cottage cheese are staples of the diet. Most people drink tea and coffee each day. *Pirukad* (a pastry with meat and vegetables) is a popular dish. A favorite national dish is *rosolje*, pink potato salad made with beets and herring. Sauerkraut soup is served with sour cream. At Christmas, people eat *verivorst* (blood sausage), jellied meats, *sült* (head cheese), roast pork or goose, sauerkraut, potatoes, rye bread, and homemade ale.

Recreation

Music is highly appreciated and attending concerts of all types is a frequent form of recreation. Nearly all age groups and professions have their own choirs. These choirs, and the more famous *Hortus Musicus* professional group, often play and sing folk music. Estonia is one of the few countries in the world that has a national epic poem (*Kalevipoeg* or "Son of Kalev") that tells the mythical story of Estonia's early development. Every city has a theater or community playhouse, and their performances are enjoyed by many. This has been true throughout history. Estonians have always been quick to perform popular Western plays along with works from their own playwrights.

A national song festival has been held roughly every four years since 1869. At each one a combined choir with as many as 30,000 voices sings a variety of traditional folk songs. The first weekend in July is usually the date of the festival. It begins with a parade through Tallinn. Dance festivals and colorful costumes add to this celebration of both history and culture. The festival's international and local audience has been as large as 500,000 people.

Estonians love sports. The country has produced a number of Olympic champions, and it has a strong national basketball team. In addition to basketball, volleyball, sailing, ice boating, ice skating, swimming, and cycling are all popular.

In their leisure time, Estonians enjoy working in their gardens. This is true even in urban areas, as the people feel tied to the land and their agricultural heritage. A favorite summer pastime is picking wild berries and mushrooms in the forest.

Holidays

New Year's Day (1 January) is followed by a number of holidays throughout the year. For *Vastlapäev* (15 February), people go sledding and eat special foods; a long sledding ride indicates good luck with the fall harvest. Independence Day (24 February) celebrates freedom in 1918. Even though 20 August marks Estonia's reestablishment of freedom in 1991, the 24 February holiday remains the primary focus of independence celebrations. Easter is celebrated Friday through Sunday and includes the tradition of painting eggs and eating special foods. On Fool's Day (1 April), people play tricks on each other. Two days in June commemorate historical events: 14 June honors those who were deported to Siberia by Stalin in 1949; and 23 June remembers the Day of Victory at Võnnu.

Jaanipäer (Midsummer's Day) is 24 June. This marks the beginning of the summer's "white nights," during which the sun sets for only a few hours. People light huge bonfires or place fires on small rafts. Parties, dancing, and concerts are held. People also traditionally search for a fern blossom on this night because it will bring happiness to them (but ferns do not have blossoms). Girls pick seven types of flowers to put under their pillows in hopes of dreaming about their future husband.

The Day of the Souls (2 November) remembers the dead. *Kadri* Day (25 October) and *Mardi* Day (10 November) are days for girls and boys, respectively, to paint their faces, dress up in old clothes, and go to their neighbors' houses. They knock, sing special national songs, and sometimes dance, asking to be let in out of the cold. They are given candy and fruit. Christmas is celebrated over three days (24–26 December), with a special meal eaten on Christmas Eve.

Commerce

Businesses are usually open between 8:00 or 9:00 A.M. and 5:00 P.M. Offices often close for lunch, but shops and restaurants do not. Goods are sold in stores, open-air markets, and kiosks. Food stores are usually open until 9:00 P.M. on weekdays and are open on weekends. Other stores that are open on Saturday close by noon. They are closed on Sunday.

SOCIETY

Government

Estonia is governed by a combined parliamentary and presidential system. The first democratic elections since the 1991 independence were in 1992. Elected as president was Lennart Meri. His term extends to 1996. The current prime minister is Mart Laar, who is the leader of parliament's majority party. He faces elections in March 1995. Members of parliament are elected by region. There are a number of different parties represented. The 1937 Constitution is currently in effect, but it is being amended and updated.

Economy

A free-market economy is successfully being reestablished in Estonia. The process has been difficult, causing many to lose their jobs and initially leading to a lower standard of living. However, Estonia's skilled, industrious work force and highly efficient agricultural sector give the country great potential for future development. By 1994, signs of progress were clearly evident. Privatization of state enterprises is proceeding quickly. Consumption per capita is high, and the economy is growing by 5 percent annually. Production is up, unemployment is dropping, and inflation is among the lowest in the region. The country's Human Development Index (0.872) ranks it 34 out of 173 countries. Real gross domestic product per capita is $6,438. These figures indicate that the necessary infrastructure exists in Estonia for the average person to take advantage of increasing economic opportunities.

The original Estonian currency (*kroon*) was reintroduced in 1992, replacing the Russian *ruble*. Estonia also restored trade links with Finland, Germany, Sweden, and several other countries. Russia is still an important market for Estonian goods, but Estonians are actively pursuing markets in the West. This is a great challenge and Estonian businesses are learning how to operate in a capitalist, democratic environment.

Estonia's main industries include textiles, agriculture, tourism, and chemicals. Lumber, meat products, and textiles are exported. The country is generally self-sufficient in food production.

Transportation and Communication

In cities, both public transportation (buses, streetcars) and private cars are used. Many families own a car. Tallinn has both trams, which run on tracks, and trolleys, which run without tracks. Electric trains are used in suburban areas. People older than 75 years of age do not have to pay for public transportation. Trains and buses are used for transport between cities. Train service is also available to neighboring countries. Ferries travel between Estonia and Finland, Sweden, and Germany.

Not every family has a telephone, but the system is expanding. Several commercial radio and television stations now broadcast in Estonia, replacing only one of each during the Soviet era. Broadcasts from other European countries are also received.

Education

Estonia's literacy rate is above 96 percent. Tallinn is home to several universities and technical colleges. Tartu University, located in Tartu, was built in 1632 by Swedish King Gustav Adolphus and is one of Europe's oldest academic institutions. Its library holds more than three million scientific dissertations.

Day-care centers and kindergartens provide preschool education before age six, when primary schooling begins. Students are required to attend school until age 14, at which time a student can choose to attend a technical school to learn such trades as carpentry or mechanics. Most students, however, go on to four years of high school. Many then continue on to a university or technical school.

Estonia's education system is currently under reform, which involves the time-consuming process of rewriting textbooks and curricula to more accurately reflect Estonia's history, culture, and values.

Health

Public and private health-care facilities exist in Estonia, and more than 93 percent of the population has access to health care. Most hospitals are run by the government and care is free. Care provided by private doctors and visits to the dentist must be paid for. The health-care system is under reform. Improvements are being researched and developed, including a new insurance system. One challenge is the modernization of hospitals, clinics, and other facilities that have outdated equipment. Estonian physicians are also making contacts with Western counterparts to improve their expertise and understanding of new technology.

The infant mortality rate is 15.3 per 1,000; life expectancy averages between 64 and 75 years. The leading causes of death in Estonia are cardiovascular disease, cancer, and accidents (mainly traffic).

FOR THE TRAVELER

U.S. citizens do not need visas to enter Estonia, but a valid passport is required. The weather is most pleasant in May and June, and these are the months for many popular festivals. Tallinn's Old Town is one of Europe's best preserved medieval villages, complete with cobblestone streets, Gothic buildings, and defense towers. Other interesting sites include the ruins of St. Birgita's convent (where outdoor concerts are often held) and Rocca-al-Mare, an open-air museum that features early farmhouses and traditional folk dancing. Travelers should take an umbrella, as unexpected rain showers can develop quickly. For further information, contact the Consulate General of Estonia, 630 Fifth Avenue, Suite 2415, New York, NY 10111.

A *Culturgram* is a product of native commentary and original, expert analysis. Statistics are estimates and information is presented as a matter of opinion. While the editors strive for accuracy and detail, this document should not be considered strictly factual. It is a general introduction to culture, an initial step in building bridges of understanding between peoples. It may not apply to all peoples of the nation. You should therefore consult other sources for more information.

Republic of
Finland

Boundary representations not necessarily authoritative.

BACKGROUND

Land and Climate

Finland is a Scandinavian country that borders Russia. It is just smaller than the state of Montana and covers 130,127 square miles (337,030 square kilometers). Forests, lakes, and rivers dominate the Finnish landscape; more than 70 percent of the land is covered by forests and lakes. Only 8 percent is arable. Known as the *Land of 10,000 Lakes*, there are actually more than 187,800 lakes in the country. The terrain is low and flat in the south, but gives way to rolling plains farther north and low hills in the far north. A few minor mountains are found in the far north of Lapland and in Saariselkä.

Finland is located at about the same latitude as Alaska, Siberia, and southern Greenland, but the climate is not as harsh because of the warming North Atlantic current, the Baltic Sea, and Finland's lakes. Still, winters are long and cold, averaging temperatures below freezing. Summers are short and cool, averaging from 63°F to 68°F (17–20°C). North of the Arctic Circle, the sun remains above the horizon day and night in the summer and below the horizon day and night in the winter. The aurora borealis lights up the northern night in winter. South of the Arctic Circle, where most of the population lives, the summer day lasts 19 hours and the nights are only partly dark. By contrast, midwinter daylight lasts only six hours. To protect its environment, Finland has banned the use of chlorofluorocarbons (CFCs), has signed an agreement with Russia to limit cross-border pollution, and has implemented other protective initiatives.

History

Finnish people have lived in the area known as Finland since about 3000 B.C. Germanic peoples and other tribes also inhabited the area thousands of years ago, including the Tavasts, Same (Lapps), and Karelians. Over time, the Finno-Ugric tribe became dominant. In 1155, a crusade from Sweden to Finland brought Catholicism and Swedish rule to the region. Finland was part of the Swedish kingdom for the next several hundred years, although Catholicism was replaced by Protestantism during the Reformation. Upon losing a war to Russia in 1809, Sweden ceded Finland to Russia.

The Russian czar, Alexander I, had promised to grant Finland extensive autonomy, and he did so. Finland thus became a Grand Duchy of the Russian empire, with Alexander as the Grand Duke. Under Sweden, Finland did not exist as a unified entity, but was only a group of provinces. Finnish historians consider the years under Alexander one of the best periods in Finnish history. A Finnish national movement led to the switch from Swedish to Finnish as the official language (in 1863) and the Finns had a semi-autonomous legislature to administer local affairs. This autonomy was eventually resented in Russia, and in 1899 attempts were made to integrate Finland more fully into Russia. These "Russification" policies were resisted in Finland and would have eventually led to armed rebellion. Before that could happen, however, the Bolshevik revolution gripped Russia. On 6 December 1917, Finland declared its independence, which was recognized by the Bolsheviks.

EUROPE

Copyright © 1994. Brigham Young University. Printed in the USA. All rights reserved. It is against the law to copy, reprint, store in a retrieval system, or transmit any part of this publication in any form by any means for any purpose without written permission from the Publications Division of the David M. Kennedy Center for International Studies, Brigham Young University, PO Box 24538, Provo, UT 84602–4538. *Culturgrams* are available for more than 125 areas of the world. To place an order, to receive a free catalog, or to obtain information on traveling abroad, call toll free (800) 528–6279.

After a brief civil war, the Finns adopted a republican constitution in 1919. During World War II, Finland twice fought the Soviet Union—in the 1939–40 Winter War and then in the Continuation War until 1944. As a result, Finland was forced to cede one-tenth of its territory (roughly Karelia) to the Soviets. Finland avoided Soviet occupation, however, and preserved its independence.

In 1948, the Finns signed a friendship treaty with the Soviet Union that bound Finland to repel any attack on the Soviet Union that involved Finnish territory. The treaty still allowed trade and good relations with the West, but it created a situation where the Soviet Union could influence Finnish foreign policy. In 1989, Soviet President Mikhail Gorbachev officially recognized Finland's neutrality for the first time. In 1992, Russian President Boris Yeltsin signed a treaty with Finland's president to void the 1948 agreement. The new treaty recognizes Russia's and Finland's equality, sovereignty, and positive economic relations. Also in 1992, Finland decided to more fully integrate with Europe by applying for membership in the European Union (EU).

THE PEOPLE

Population

The population of Finland is just over five million, growing only at a rate of 0.3 percent annually. The majority of the people are Finns, although there is a significant Swedish-speaking minority. Finland also has very small minorities of native Same and Russians. The overall population density is only six persons per square mile, but most people live in the southern part of the country. More than 60 percent of Finns live in towns or cities, with nearly 40 percent residing in rural areas. Urbanization is a relatively new trend, so most people still have roots in the countryside and their home villages.

Language

More than 93 percent of the population speaks Finnish. Still, it is not the only official language, as Swedish is also officially recognized and is spoken by about 6 percent of the people. While Same is spoken only by the Same minority, it is still recognized in Finland (although not officially). English is a popular second language, especially among the youth and the educated. Those who speak Finnish as a native language must study Swedish for three years in school. Likewise, Swedish speakers learn Finnish. Finnish is a language that has very few consonants, but many vowels. With 15 different cases, it is often difficult for foreigners to learn. As part of the Finno-Ugric language family, it is most closely related to Estonian.

Religion

Although almost 90 percent of the population belongs to the Evangelical Lutheran Church of Finland, the government has an official policy of religious neutrality. In fact, since 1923, freedom of religion has been guaranteed. The Evangelical Lutheran Church still performs important functions as a state church, however, including population registration and cemetery maintenance, and it is supported by state taxes. The Finnish Orthodox Church, which is also supported by the state, claims the next largest following in Finland (1 percent). Several other Christian groups and other religions are also active in Finland, with membership totaling 3 percent of the population. Growing secularization has caused a decline in church attendance and membership, as in many European nations.

General Attitudes

The Finns maintain high ideals of loyalty and reliability, taking promises and agreements seriously. The people are generally reserved, and they appreciate etiquette and punctuality. They are, of course, proud of their Finnish heritage, as their language, culture, and national identity survived centuries of domination by other powers. Finns are especially proud of their small nation's status in the world. Finland has been a leading nation in peace conferences and initiatives. The Finns are proud to have one of the cleanest environments in the world, and they stress values that maintain this. Enjoying nature (such as berry picking in the forests) is an important part of their lives. Finland is also a leader in the area of women's rights. Indeed, there is little talk of "feminism" because women expect to be involved in careers, politics, social issues, and motherhood all as a matter of course. In addition, an increasing number of men expect to share household responsibilities with their wives.

Personal Appearance

Finnish fashion standards are very high and internationally recognized. Finnish designs follow European lines. Formal wear is popular on festive occasions. Hats are worn during the winter. Men remove their hats when entering a building or elevator, or when speaking to another person. Colorful native Finnish costumes can be seen during festival times, at weddings, or at some graduation balls. They vary from region to region, but usually involve a layered dress (including apron) and bonnet or cap for women and trousers, shirt, and waist-length jacket or vest for men. Young women wear ribbons like a headband instead of a cap. Men also usually wear a peaked cap, a felt hat, or woolen cap. These costumes have their origins in the 18th and 19th centuries. Stripes are popular for the dresses and jackets, but there are literally hundreds of variations.

CUSTOMS AND COURTESIES

Greetings

It is customary to shake hands with men and women when greeting. People may sometimes use both hands, but further physical contact is usually avoided. When introduced, people mention their full names or a title and last name. Although it was traditionally not appropriate to use first names until invited to do so, it is now quite common, especially among the youth, to use first names on first meeting. Men may raise hats (if worn) to greet people at a distance; otherwise, a nod is acceptable. The term for a general greeting is *Hyvää päivää.* (Good morning/afternoon), or even just *Päivää.* Another expression for "Good morning" is *Hyvää huomenta.*

Gestures

It is considered bad manners to talk with one's hands in one's pockets. Eye contact is important, but folding one's arms while speaking can be a sign of arrogance and pride. While it is proper to cross the legs with one knee over the other, it is inappropriate to sit with one ankle over the other knee. When yawns cannot be suppressed, one covers the mouth.

Visiting

Punctuality is expected when visiting. Finns usually take cut flowers as a gift, or they may send them afterwards to thank the hosts. Visits are nearly always an occasion for coffee and cakes or biscuits. Guests wait until the host has taken a first sip before they drink. Most visits are more informal and involve relaxing and socializing. On special occasions, guests may be invited to sit in a sauna with the hosts. Spending time in the sauna is a national pastime.

Eating

When invited to dinner, visitors sit where the host asks them to and they do not begin eating until the hostess or host begins. Table conversation is generally light, but topics such as religion or politics are not avoided. Guests do not ask personal questions of their hosts. The Finns eat in the continental style, with the fork in the left hand and the knife remaining in the right. Dress is conservative in restaurants, but it may vary between casual and formal depending on the restaurant. The check is presented on request and is paid at the table. While some people leave small change on the table, a 15 percent tip is usually included in the bill and therefore not otherwise expected. However, porters, doormen, and coat checkers receive tips.

LIFESTYLE

Family

The average size of a Finnish family is three. The population has been growing so slowly that the Finnish government is trying to increase the birthrate because the number of working people is declining compared to the number of people receiving retirement benefits. Women are offered paid maternity leave of up to 11 months, and their husbands can share a portion of that leave. In addition, women receive a small monthly allowance for each child until the child is 17. Day-care facilities are provided by the government free of charge. Both parents usually work outside the home. In fact, half of all Finnish wage earners are women. Women hold 77 of parliament's 200 seats, and many women hold important government and business positions.

Most families own their own homes. Traditionally, houses were made of Finland's plentiful wood. Over time, however, brick has become more common—it lasts longer, requires less care, and is less flammable than wood. Taxes are high and housing is expensive, but the Finns enjoy a high standard of living. Most families have access to summer cottages for vacations.

Dating and Marriage

Dating begins at about age 15, first in groups, then in couples. Movies and dances are popular activities. Many young couples choose to live together rather than get married or before getting married. The youth are moving away from many traditions and accepting more secular views of personal relationships. When a couple marries, the two have the right to keep their original surnames or take that of their spouse. Their children may also bear either surname.

Diet

Finnish cuisine has been influenced by many cultures, from French to Russian, but it includes a wide variety of Finnish specialties using fish and seafood, wild game, and vegetables. Reindeer steak is a traditional specialty, as is salmon. Wild berries (blueberries, cloudberries, strawberries, and raspberries) are popular in desserts and liqueurs. Potatoes, cheeses, and a Finnish buffet (such as the *smörgåsbord*) are also very popular. Rye bread is common and open-faced sandwiches are eaten for snacks and at breakfast. Milk and coffee are the most common beverages for everyday drinking. Traditional Christmas foods include salmon, ham, herring, and various casseroles. Ginger cookies and other sweets are also common for Christmas.

Recreation

Recreation and general fitness are important to the Finns, whose favorite hobbies include fishing, hunting, camping, and other sporting activities. Ice fishing is popular on weekends in the winter. Favorite sports include skiing, track and field, basketball, Finnish baseball (*Pesäpallo*), ice hockey, cycling, and boating activities. Golf is gaining popularity; some even play on the ice in the winter. The sauna is a traditional way to relax for people of all ages. During retreats to summer cottages, people like to run from their hot saunas for a swim in the cold, clear lakes that are nearby. *Sauna* is a Finnish word that has been adopted by English and other languages. Because Finns traditionally relate to the forest, many of their most favorite recreational activities revolve around the forest, from picking wild berries and mushrooms to hiking and taking vacations. Lakes likewise play an integral role in recreation.

Holidays

The most important holidays include New Year's Day (1 January), Easter (two days), *Vappu* or May Day (1 May), Whitsunday (Pentecost), Midsummer (summer solstice), Independence Day (6 December), and Christmas (24–26 December). The Finland Festivals (16 of them) are held between June and September around the country and include art, music, dance, opera, theater, and other festivities.

At Easter, families decorate Easter eggs and grow grass on plates in the home. On Palm Sunday of the previous week, children dress up as Easter witches to go door to door and recite charms. They receive sweets or money for their verses. For *Vappu*, people enjoy street carnivals and other celebrations in honor of both springtime and laborers. Midsummer is celebrated with huge bonfires by the lake; people usually leave cities and towns to go to the countryside for this day. The blue and white Finnish flag is also prominent on this day. Christmas is a time of peace, family, and gifts. A main meal is eaten Christmas Eve after a visit to family graves. Later, Father Christmas (who looks like Santa Claus) arrives with gifts for the children. Rural families enjoy time in the sauna on Christmas Eve as well. Christmas Day and 26 December are days for visiting and relaxing.

Commerce

Stores are usually open from 9:00 A.M. to 6:00 P.M., Monday through Friday, and Saturdays from 9:00 A.M. to 2:00 P.M. Some shops and department stores are open until 8:00 P.M. on weekdays and 5:00 P.M. on Saturdays. Shops in Helsinki's subway stay open even later. Banks close at 4:15 P.M. on weekdays and do not open on weekends. The Finnish worker enjoys a workweek averaging 37.5 hours.

SOCIETY
Government

Elections in 1991 brought Finland its first nonsocialist government in several years, sending the once-ruling Social Democrats into the Parliament's opposition. The current coalition government is headed by the Centre Party, with Esko Aho as prime minister. Finland also has an elected president who serves as head of state for a six-year term. Martti Ahtisaari was elected president in 1994. Members of parliament and the prime minister serve four-year terms. All men are expected to serve at least 18 months in the military. The voting age is 18.

Economy

The Finnish economy is based on the free market and relies heavily on imports for many raw materials and important goods. Finland's most important exports are timber and timber-related products. Also important are shipbuilding, chemicals, and textiles. Natural resources include timber, silver, iron ore, and copper. High-technology industries are growing in importance. Finland's economy usually grows at above 3 percent annually, but growth was lower during the early 1990s due to global recession. Finland is self-sufficient in grains, dairy products, and some meats. Other foods are imported. The currency is the *markka* or *Finmark* (FIM).

Finns enjoy a high standard of living. The country's Human Development Index (0.954) ranks it 14 out of 173 countries. Real gross domestic product per capita is $16,446. These figures indicate most people have access to economic prosperity in spite of the high cost of living in Finland.

Transportation and Communication

Although fuel is expensive, most Finnish families own at least one car. Overall, the roads in Finland are in good condition. The railway system is an excellent form of transportation. There are buses, a good domestic air service, and ferries (for transport on lakes and across rivers). Helsinki has a subway. Taxis are also available. Finland has modern communications systems, with numerous television and radio stations, an efficient phone system, and over 250 newspapers.

Education

Education is a major priority for the Finnish government. Beginning at age seven, every child is required to attend a free comprehensive school for at least nine years, after which he or she may attend a vocational school or complete three years of senior secondary school. Finland has a high rate of enrollment in secondary schools, and literacy is nearly 100 percent. Many students go on to further studies at one of Finland's several university level institutions. The University of Helsinki was founded in 1640. Although students do not pay tuition, they do pay small annual fees (for health insurance and student services) while at a university. Finns are also well-read, and public libraries have high attendance.

Health

Finland takes great pride in its health programs. Health care is socialized, reliable, and modern. Citizens receive free basic health care from municipal health centers, but they can also pay to visit a private doctor if they choose. Specialized care is provided at public and private hospitals. The health care system is funded by national and local taxes. Finland has one of the lowest infant mortality rates in the world at 6 per 1,000. This is due, in part, to an extensive network of maternity clinics. Life expectancy ranges from 71 to 80 years. Finland ranks among the world's best in doctor-patient and nurse-patient ratios.

FOR THE TRAVELER

While passports are required, U.S. citizens do not need visas for visits of up to three months total time in Scandinavia—Denmark, Iceland, Finland, Norway, and Sweden. No vaccinations are required, and the water is safe to drink. Dual-voltage small appliances or a voltage converter and a plug adapter are necessary to use electrical outlets. There are numerous travel packages and different types of vacations available in Finland, from skiing on the ice pack to camping by lakes. The Finnish Tourist Board (655 Third Avenue, New York, NY 10017) can offer more complete information on travel possibilities. Call them at (800) 346–4636. You may also wish to contact the Embassy of Finland, 3216 New Mexico Avenue NW, Washington, DC 20016.

A *Culturgram* is a product of native commentary and original, expert analysis. Statistics are estimates and information is presented as a matter of opinion. While the editors strive for accuracy and detail, this document should not be considered strictly factual. It is a general introduction to culture, an initial step in building bridges of understanding between peoples. It may not apply to all peoples of the nation. You should therefore consult other sources for more information.

CULTURGRAM™ '95

France
(French Republic)

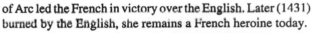

Boundary representations not necessarily authoritative.

E
U
R
O
P
E

BACKGROUND

Land and Climate

Slightly smaller than Texas, France covers 211,208 square miles (547,030 square kilometers). The terrain is varied, from plains to mountains and forests to farmland. The north coast lies along the English Channel and the west coast along the Atlantic Ocean. The southeast coast is on the Mediterranean Sea. Mountains stretch along the borders with Spain, Italy, and Switzerland. France boasts Europe's highest peak, Mt. Blanc (15,771 feet or 4,807 meters). The Rhine River forms part of the border with Germany; the northern border with Belgium is a flat plain with rolling hills. The southern climate is Mediterranean, with warm, moist winters and hot, dry summers. The north is temperate and prone to rain. The west is also rainy and is influenced by the Atlantic, which moderates winter temperatures. The central east and upland areas have a continental climate, with fluctuating temperatures; in the mountains, thunderstorms are prevalent in summer. French sovereignty extends to the island of Corsica as well as 10 overseas *départements* and territories.

History

By 51 B.C., the Romans had conquered the Celtic inhabitants of France, the Gauls, beginning nearly five centuries of Roman domination. The Gauls adopted the Roman's customs, language, and laws. Clovis I, king of the Franks, defeated the last Roman governor in 486. In the late eighth century, France was just one part of the vast empire ruled by Charlemagne. In 987, France emerged as one of the empire's successor kingdoms. The following centuries brought intermittent conflict, particularly with the English, including the Hundred Years War from 1337 to 1453. In 1429, after 80 years of war, Joan of Arc led the French in victory over the English. Later (1431) burned by the English, she remains a French heroine today.

By the late 1600s, France dominated Europe. Under Louis XIV (the Sun King), the movement toward centralized government reached its peak. His palace at Versailles was the envy of the continent. But by 1789, royal extravagance and defeats in foreign wars resulted in the French Revolution. The monarchy of Louis XVI was toppled and the country entered the "reign of terror." Despite the conflict, the French Revolution marks a milestone in world history: the general movement towards democratic government. After a decade of instability, Napoleon Bonaparte took power, declaring himself Emperor in 1804. Napoleon conquered most of Europe before embarking on a disastrous campaign in Russia in 1812. In 1814, Austrian and Prussian forces seized Paris and Napoleon was exiled. He returned in 1815 for the Hundred Days War, which ended in his defeat to the English at Waterloo.

The monarchy was restored but was followed by the Second Republic (1848–52) and then the Second Empire (1852–70) under Napoleon III. Defeat at the hands of Germany led to the Third Republic in 1871. France was a major battle ground during both world wars. It was occupied by the Germans between 1940 and 1944 and is famous for the D-Day invasion that turned the tide of World War II in favor of the Allies. In 1946, the Fourth Republic was declared, and after a referendum in 1958, a new constitution for a Fifth Republic was approved. Charles de Gaulle became president. France was a founding member of the European Union (EU) and is a central force in EU politics today.

In 1968, students and workers protested over poor working conditions and a rigid educational system, resulting in lasting

Copyright © 1994. Brigham Young University. Printed in the USA. All rights reserved. It is against the law to copy, reprint, store in a retrieval system, or transmit any part of this publication in any form by any means for any purpose without written permission from the Publications Division of the David M. Kennedy Center for International Studies, Brigham Young University, PO Box 24538, Provo, UT 84602–4538. *Culturgrams* are available for more than 125 areas of the world. To place an order, to receive a free catalog, or to obtain information on traveling abroad, call toll free (800) 528–6279.

social change. The 1968 events were still fresh in the public mind when students in the early 1990s took to the streets, protesting conditions in public schools and proposed changes in wage laws. The social unrest and economic difficulties led the prime minister to resign in 1991 and two successors to also step down. In 1993, Eduoard Balladur, a conservative, was named prime minister. He shares power with the president, François Mitterrand, who has been in office since 1981.

THE PEOPLE
Population
France has a population of nearly 57.5 million people and is growing at 0.5 percent annually. Three-fourths of the population lives in urban areas. Greater Paris claims eight million inhabitants, and Marseilles one million. Ethnically, the French have a Celtic heritage that has mixed with various other European groups (Latin, Nordic, Teutonic, Slavic, and others) over the centuries. Immigrants and descendents of immigrants from France's old colonial possessions also inhabit France. These include North Africans (Algerians, Tunisians, Moroccans), West Africans, Caribbean peoples, and Asians from the former Indochina region. Although they have integrated into French society, the various ethnic groups generally do not mix with one another. North Africans remain the most separate because of their religion.

Language
French is an important international language. It is an official language of the United Nations and is second only to English in use between nations for communication, business, and diplomacy. The French government has stressed the language so much that almost everyone in France speaks French, despite the different nationalities represented. Even regional dialects have lost their importance in recent years.

Despite French's prominence, France has recognized its citizens' need to learn other languages. In 1992, it announced that traditional language learning in school would start earlier (age nine) and that all students will be required to learn a second foreign language beginning at age 13. In addition, past emphasis on grammar and theory will be replaced by a focus on communication skills. English is the most common foreign language. Even before 1992, parents were having their children learn English outside of school. Despite this move toward other languages, the French government resists the inclusion of foreign words and phrases in the French language.

Religion
The majority of the French (nearly 90 percent) are Roman Catholic and practice their faith by celebrating the various religious holidays and attending mass once or twice a year. While regular attendance at Mass is increasingly rare, many people visit places of special devotion, such as shrines, to worship. A small percentage of the people belong to other Christian churches (2 percent), the Jewish faith (1 percent), and Islam (1 percent). About 6 percent claim no religion. Those belonging to Islam are generally from North Africa.

General Attitudes
The French believe success is judged by educational level, family reputation, and financial status. They are extremely proud of their culture, heritage, and way of life. They are among the most patriotic people in the world, which is illustrated by their attempts to limit the influence of other cultures in France. This includes a general expectation that visitors have some knowledge of French and show appreciation for French culture. While French attitudes have traditionally been dominated by Paris, there seems to be a growing decentralization in administration as well as attitudes. The French are reserved and private, and people tend to be more hospitable outside Paris. Politeness is valued in human interaction, and *s'il vous plaît* (please) is a valued phrase.

Political and social trends have caused the French to reexamine their national identity. Society seems divided over issues related to the central government's structure, education, immigration, economics, and even language. This introspection has led some to predict that French society will experience fundamental change during the next generation.

Personal Appearance
The French in general take great care to dress well and fashionably, whether they are wearing formal or casual attire, and they feel more at ease with visitors who show the same degree of attention to appearance. Paris is the home of many of the world's leading fashion designers. Professional attire, depending on the business and location, tends to be formal. Parisians dress more formally than people in other cities. In the southern sunbelt, dress is more casual but not less stylish.

CUSTOMS AND COURTESIES
Greetings
Shaking hands upon greeting and parting is customary in France. An aggressive handshake is considered impolite. The French handshake is a light grip and a single quick shake. Generally, a woman does not offer her hand to a man but waits for him to initiate the greeting. If their hands are dirty or wet, some Frenchmen will offer their elbow or arm to shake. Among friends it is normal for women to be kissed (by both men and women) on both cheeks. Actually, they touch cheeks and kiss the air. The standard phrases for greeting include *Bonjour* (Good day) and *Comment allez-vous?* or the more informal *Ça va?* (both meaning "How are you?"). Greetings are usually combined with the person's name or a title and always precede any conversation or request. Good-bye is *Au revoir* (Until we meet again) or the less formal *A bientôt!* (See you soon). A favorite among young people is *Salut!* for both greeting and parting. First names are used between friends and close colleagues; otherwise titles are important and customary. Besides professional titles, *Monsieur* (Mr.), *Madame* (Mrs.), or *Mademoiselle* (Miss) are commonly used.

Gestures
The American "okay" sign (rounded index finger and rounded thumb touching at the point) means "zero" to the French. The French gesture for "okay" is the "thumbs up" sign. Slapping the open palm over a closed fist is vulgar and should be avoided. It is impolite to sit with legs spread apart. One should sit straight with knees together or with legs crossed at the knee. Feet are not placed on tables or chairs. Toothpicks, nail clippers, and combs should never be used in public. It is improper to speak with hands in the pockets or to chew gum in public. The French are discreet when they sneeze or blow their noses, and they always use a handkerchief or tissue. They avoid yawning and scratching in public.

Visiting

The French are formal in their visiting customs, and people do not often visit unannounced. Guests usually arrive on time because punctuality is a sign of courtesy. However, for some social events it is also polite to arrive a few minutes late—to allow the hosts extra time for final preparations. Guests do not enter a home until invited inside. They generally sit where the host directs. It is a polite gesture to bring candy, wine, or flowers to the hostess, except red roses (which express love) and chrysanthemums (used in cemeteries). When ending a visit, a guest waits for a polite silence before rising. At the door, small talk, expressions of thanks, and repeated good-byes continue; it is impolite to be in a hurry to leave. A thank-you note is often sent the day after one has been a dinner guest. At mealtime, pleasant conversation is appreciated as much as fine food. However, because the French are private people, it is best to avoid personal questions and sensitive topics such as politics and money. The hosts should be complimented on the meal; good cooking is a matter of pride in French homes.

Eating

Etiquette is important. Both hands remain above the table at all times. A man may rest his wrists, and a woman her forearms, on the table edge. Elbows are not placed on the table. It is impolite to speak with food in the mouth. It is improper to help oneself twice to cheese. The French eat in the continental style, with the fork in the left hand and the knife remaining in the right. Lettuce is folded into small pieces with the fork but never cut. Fruit is peeled with a knife and eaten with a fork. Bread is broken with the fingers and used to wipe the plate. One places the knife and fork parallel across the plate when finished. Formal lunches and dinners may last more than two hours, with as many as eight to twelve courses (although a typical family meal has two to four courses). Social meals are served in separate courses, beginning with an appetizer in the living room, then hors d'oeuvres, a course of fish or pasta or something cooked in a crust or sauce, the main course accompanied by vegetables, then salad, then cheese, then fruit, and then a dessert. Coffee finishes the evening. When eating out, the person who invites or makes the suggestion is the one who pays.

Wine is consumed with most meals (except breakfast) and there are dozens of varieties. The French know the difference between fine wine and poorer varieties. Unless certain of its high quality, foreign guests should not give wine as a gift.

LIFESTYLE

Family

While the nuclear family is still the most important unit of society, many people are now moving away from their extended families to work or study. Still, many children remain at home until they finish their education, and families enjoy getting together when possible. Most families enjoy a comfortable standard of living, although class distinctions are still fairly visible. In the cities, most people live in apartments. The average family has fewer than two children. Pets outnumber children in France and receive special attention.

Dating and Marriage

The average youth starts dating around age 15. Favorite activities are dances and going to movies. The French cinema is well developed, and American films are also popular.

Because French teenagers do not normally have jobs, their finances for social activities are limited. In France, social class, wealth, and level of education are important in the choice of a mate. Civil ceremonies are required by law. Religious ceremonies are optional but common. Many couples choose to live together before getting married or as an alternative to formal marriage. Many couples choose not to have children.

Diet

The French consider cooking an art, and French cuisine is famous and popular around the world. French cookbooks date back to the Middle Ages, and French standards were the early gauge of fine cooking. Regional traditions are strong. There are several types of cooking, ranging from hearty, inexpensive fare to sophisticated dishes with costly ingredients and rich, complex sauces. *Nouvelle cuisine*, which emerged in the 1960s, was a reaction to the heaviness of this style of cooking. While still using expensive ingredients, it is much lighter, the portions smaller, and the presentation more artistic.

Most French eat a light continental breakfast (croissants or bread and coffee). Lunch was once the main meal of the day, but urban society has changed and many people now have a light lunch and eat their main meal in the evening. In Paris, lunch (*déjeuner*) is usually eaten at around noon or 1:00 P.M. and dinner is frequently not before 9:00 P.M. In other parts of the country, particularly rural areas, people eat earlier.

Fast food has been resisted by the French. In its most traditional form there are filled croissants and sandwiches that can be purchased in vending machines, shops, and cafés. Cafés also offer toasted ham and cheese (*croque-monsieur*) and a plate of salad-type vegetables for a light meal. Patisseries sell cakes and some places sell crêpes. The resistance to foreign fast food has not been entirely successful, as many hamburger restaurants operate across the country.

Recreation

The French are enthusiastic spectators, but actual participation in team sports is less than might be expected. Soccer and rugby are popular spectator sports. Participation is highest in individual sports: fishing, cycling, tennis, hiking, skiing, and sailing. Others enjoy hunting, horse riding, and golf. *Pétanque*, a form of bowling originating in southern France, is enjoyed by people of all ages. Leisure activities include watching television, visiting museums, or attending plays and concerts. The annual *Tour de France* cycling race is a popular national event. Most people take five weeks of vacation each year, four weeks in the summer and one week at Christmas. Camping is popular in the summer. During August, when many people travel, some shops and factories close. Summer music festivals occur throughout France. Recent years have seen increased support for concerts, theater, and the opera.

Holidays

The French celebrate several holidays each year. For New Year's (*Etrennes*), gifts might be exchanged and flowers are often presented to older members of the family. People celebrate New Year's Eve with parties and fireworks. In February, Mardi Gras (Shrove Tuesday) is celebrated with parades and parties. Easter Sunday and Monday are legal holidays. Labor Day (1 May) is marked by parades and celebrates the coming of spring. The French Armistice Day (*Le Huit Mai*) is 8 May and Bastille Day (*La Fete Nationale*) is 14 July. Bastille Day commemorates the storming of Bastille prison in Paris during the French Revolution. At Christmas (Noël), the tree is decorated on Christmas Eve, followed by a big meal and midnight Mass. Shoes are left by the fireplace for Santa Claus to fill. Other holidays include Ascension, Pentecost, Assumption (15 August), All Saints Day (1 November), and World War I Armistice Day (11 November).

Commerce

Businesses and non-food shops open from 9:00 or 9:30 A.M. to 6:00 or 6:30 P.M., Monday through Saturday. Some large stores stay open until 9:00 P.M. one or two evenings a week. Small shops, especially in rural towns, may close for lunch and on Mondays. Many food shops open as early as 7:00 A.M. and on Sunday mornings. Banks close at 4:30 P.M. Many businesses close on holidays. The average workweek is 39 hours.

SOCIETY

Government

France's constitution provides for a strong president who is both head of state and executive head of government, and who serves a seven-year term. The president also appoints the prime minister, who must always come from the party with the most representatives in the National Assembly and has the right to dissolve the Assembly to call for new elections. The president does not have veto power, but does have extensive rights to rule by emergency decree in a crisis. President Mitterrand, reelected in 1988, faces elections in 1995. The National Assembly has 575 members who are elected for five-year terms. The voting age is 18. The Senate has 319 members who serve nine-year terms and are elected by thirds every three years by about 130,000 local councilors. There is a separate judicial branch. France has 22 regions, divided into 96 departments, not including the overseas departments.

Economy

France enjoys a high standard of living. The country's Human Development Index (0.971) ranks it eighth out of 173 countries. Real gross domestic product per capita is $17,405, which has tripled in a generation. These figures reflect France's success within the European Union and indicate most people enjoy access to the benefits of economic prosperity. France is one of Europe's leading agricultural producers, allowing self-sufficiency in most foods. The agricultural sector employs about 7 percent of the workforce and is a world leader in the production of wine, milk, butter, cheese, barley, and wheat. Major industries include steel, motor vehicles, aircraft, textiles, chemicals, and food processing. Exports include machinery and transport equipment, iron and steel products, and agricultural products. The services sector employs two-thirds of the labor force. More than half of France's power is generated by nuclear power plants. France has approved the Maastricht Treaty of the European Union that deals with greater economic integration. With most other industrialized nations, France suffered in the recession of the early 1990s, but it is now regaining growth momentum. Privatization of state-owned industry is also improving economic conditions. France's currency is the French *franc* (F).

Transportation and Communication

The public transportation system is well developed. Buses serve most cities and train service extends to even the smallest towns. Trains are best for long distance travel. The TGV (*train à grande vitesse*) is one of the world's fastest passenger trains with a top speed of 300 MPH (480 KPH). Most people own private cars, which are generally small French brands, such as Renault or Peugeot. Taxis in urban areas are expensive. Paris has a subway. The French domestic air system is efficient, and car ferries link France with Corsica and Great Britain. In 1994, a new rail link to England opened. A trip from Paris to London, crossing under the English Channel, takes three hours. The actual time in the tunnel is 35 minutes.

The communications system is modern. Pay phones generally use phone cards (*telecarte*) purchased at a post office. They are based on time used and can be used more than once—until the time paid for runs out. The post office is the center for various forms of communication and transactions.

Education

Schooling is free and compulsory from ages six to sixteen. The literacy rate is almost 99 percent. Nearly 20 percent of all children attend Catholic schools that are partly subsidized by the state. Secondary education, lasting seven years (11–18), is offered by the *lycées* and *collèges*. *Lycée* students gain the equivalent of a U.S. junior college education with an additional emphasis on philosophy. After secondary education, students take an exam to determine if they may go on to higher education.

There are 60 universities (where education is practically free) in France, the *Sorbonne* in Paris among them. However, the best students take further preparatory classes in order to attend the *Grandes Ecoles*, where they study for careers in government, the military, education, and industry (engineering, marketing, and management). Students of the *Ecoles Polytechnique* and the *Ecoles Normale Superieure* are paid during their studies, while the marketing schools require tuition.

Health

Medical care is generally good and is available to all citizens through a socialized system. Prices and fees are fixed by the government. Many French also carry private insurance to pay fees not covered by the government. In addition to public hospitals, private clinics are available. The French enjoy good health, with an infant mortality rate of 7 per 1,000 and life expectancy rates ranging from 74 to 82 years.

FOR THE TRAVELER

U.S. citizens can travel in France for up to three months without a visa, but a valid passport is required. Visas for longer stays can be obtained through an embassy or consulate. No vaccinations are required. Dual-voltage small appliances or a voltage converter and a plug adaptor are necessary to use electrical outlets. Try to learn some French before going, as the people not only appreciate the attempt but may expect visitors to use French when possible. For more information, contact the French Tourist Office (610 Fifth Avenue, New York, NY 10020–2452), or the Embassy of France (4101 Reservoir Road NW, Washington, DC 20007–2185).

A *Culturgram* is a product of native commentary and original, expert analysis. Statistics are estimates and information is presented as a matter of opinion. While the editors strive for accuracy and detail, this document should not be considered strictly factual. It is a general introduction to culture, an initial step in building bridges of understanding between peoples. It may not apply to all peoples of the nation. You should therefore consult other sources for more information.

Germany

(Federal Republic of Germany)

Boundary representations not necessarily authoritative.

BACKGROUND

Land and Climate

Covering 137,803 square miles (356,910 square kilometers), Germany is just smaller than Montana. There are four main geographical zones: the broad lowlands in the north; the central uplands, including various small mountain ranges; the wide valley and gorge of the Rhine River in the southwest; and the forested mountains and plateaus of the south. About 40 percent of Germany is forested. The Rhine, Danube, and Elbe rivers flow through Germany. The climate is generally temperate and mild, with warm summers and wet winters. Pollution is a problem throughout Germany, but more so in eastern states, where the Communist regime neglected the health of rivers, forests, and entire communities.

History

Before becoming a nation-state (1871), Germany was divided into a patchwork of small separate principalities and was once part of the Holy Roman Empire. Through three wars (1864–70), Prussian leader Otto von Bismarck united Germany into a powerful, industrialized nation. In World War I (1914–18), Germany allied with Austria and Turkey. The United States joined (in 1917) Britain, France, Russia, Italy, and Japan to defeat the German empire. Germany was made to pay huge reparations, admit guilt for the war, and cede about one-tenth of its territory. A democratic government, known as the Weimar Republic, was established in 1918.

The country's humiliation was made worse by the economic depression of the 1930s and a general lack of support for the Weimar leaders. Germany's distress gave rise to Austrian-born Adolf Hitler and his National Socialist (Nazi) party. In 1933, President von Hindenburg named Hitler chancellor, after the Nazis had emerged as the dominant party in elections. In 1934, the day after von Hindenburg died, the posts of president and chancellor were combined, and Hitler declared himself *Führer* (leader) of the Third Reich. He soon embroiled Germany and the world in World War II. The Nazis occupied much of the continent, killing many, including six million Jews. Allied nations turned the tide against German forces in 1944, and Germany was defeated in 1945.

Germany was split into occupation zones to facilitate disarmament and to organize a democracy. When the Soviet Union did not comply with the agreement, the zones occupied by the Western Allies became the Federal Republic of Germany (FRG), a democratic nation. The Soviets in turn created out of the five eastern states the German Democratic Republic (GDR), which followed the Soviet model of development. When thousands of people fled the east, the GDR built the Berlin Wall (1961) to shut off access to West Berlin. The Wall remained a symbol of the Cold War until late 1989 when it was opened to traffic on both sides. The Wall was eventually torn down and the two nations became the Federal Republic of Germany on 3 October 1990. Berlin was named the capital of Germany, a fulfillment of decades of commitment from FRG leaders. The cost of the change, as well as resistance by Bonn, delayed the move for several years. In 1993, a timetable was established to complete the move by the year 2000.

Germany was a founding member of the European Union (EU). It joined the North Atlantic Treaty Organization (NATO) in 1955, but German troops were restricted by constitution to German soil. In 1993, policy changes allowed troops to participate in the United Nations relief operations in Somalia. Disillusionment over the cost of German unification, low economic growth, immigration, and right-wing violence were all key issues in the 1994 elections.

Copyright © 1994. Brigham Young University. Printed in the USA. All rights reserved. It is against the law to copy, reprint, store in a retrieval system, or transmit any part of this publication in any form by any means for any purpose without written permission from the Publications Division of the David M. Kennedy Center for International Studies, Brigham Young University, PO Box 24538, Provo, UT 84602–4538. *Culturgrams* are available for more than 125 areas of the world. To place an order, to receive a free catalog, or to obtain information on traveling abroad, call toll free (800) 528–6279.

THE PEOPLE
Population

The population of Germany is about 80.7 million and is growing at 0.4 percent annually. At least two-thirds of all Germans live in urban areas. In eastern states, this figure is closer to 80 percent. The population is primarily ethnic German, especially in eastern states. Noncitizen minorities from Turkey, the former Yugoslavia, Italy, Greece, and other nations live in Germany as guest workers (*Gastarbeiter*). They comprise up to 20 percent of some metropolitan populations. In western states, there are groups of political refugees from the Middle East, India, Africa, and Asia. They are asylum seekers who do not have work permits; rather, the government provides them with room and board until their applications are processed. There is a small Slavic (Serbian) minority in the east, and many peoples from various eastern European nations have emigrated to Germany to find work. The much-publicized violence against immigrant groups reflects the feelings of only a small minority of Germans. Most Germans do not support such activity but do support stemming the flow of "economic" refugees. New laws restrict the definition of a valid asylum seeker and limit other forms of immigration.

Language

German is the official language. However, the German taught in school and used in the media is often not the German spoken daily. Various dialects have a strong influence in most areas. In fact, a German from Bonn or Hannover may have trouble understanding a person from München (where Bavarian is spoken) or Halle (Saxon). While the dialects are mostly verbal languages, they are part of folk literature and music, and are written. English, widely understood, is a required school subject. Many in the eastern states know Russian. Visitors who attempt to learn German are appreciated.

Religion

Germany is essentially a Christian, but secular, society. About 37 percent of the population belongs to the Roman Catholic church and 45 percent is Protestant (mostly Lutheran). A number of Christian denominations are active throughout the country. About 15 percent of the people have no official religious affiliation. Historically, entire towns and regions belonged to one faith, according to the local ruler's choice. These lines are still visible today, as Catholics reside mostly in the south and west, and Protestants in the north and east.

General Attitudes

Germans are industrious, thrifty, and orderly. They appreciate punctuality, privacy, and skill. They have a strong sense of regional pride, a fact that the federal system of government recognizes and accommodates. World War II broke down class distinctions because most people lost their possessions and had to start over again. Germany has emerged as a land of freedom and opportunity. Germans appreciate intelligent conversation but are often wary of unfamiliar or different ideas. Many are also prone to pessimism. Most Germans have a strong classical education because of the nation's rich heritage in music, history, and art, and they expect others to appreciate that background. Former East Germans share this approach to culture and are proud of how they have nurtured their cultural heritage through the performing arts and museums. After four decades of life under communism, however, it is not surprising that those in the east have somewhat different attitudes toward daily life and work.

Tensions exist between people in the west and east over matters relating to unification. Easterners feel they are treated as second-class citizens, receiving lower salaries, getting blamed for tax hikes, and being ridiculed by their western counterparts. Westerners resent the economic burden of rebuilding the east; they feel the easterners are less capable and unrefined. Such tensions will continue to exist until living standards in the east more nearly equal those in the west. Despite the emotional divisions, reconstruction and revitalization are building a truly united Germany.

Personal Appearance

Clothing styles are similar to those in the United States, but with a distinct European flavor. In southern Germany (mostly southern Bavaria), traditional clothing such as *Lederhosen* (leather pants, either short or knee-length), *Dirndlkleider* (dresses with gathered waists and full skirts, worn with an apron), Bavarian suits, and alpine hats may be part of a more modern wardrobe. Traditional costumes of other regions are worn during festivals and celebrations. Shorts and sandals are commonly worn in summer. Cosmetics are worn sparingly. Sloppy or overly casual attire is inappropriate in public.

CUSTOMS AND COURTESIES
Greetings

A handshake is the most common form of greeting. If a one's hand is dirty, the person may offer an elbow or forearm to be shaken. A man waits for a woman to extend her hand before shaking it; in mixed company he shakes a woman's hand before a man's. In groups, several people do not shake hands at once; crossing someone else's handshake is inappropriate. Germans do not generally greet strangers on the street; although sincere smiles are appreciated. The most common term for greeting is *Guten Tag!* (Good day!). A simple *Hallo* (Hello) is also used. Many people in southern Germany use *Grüß Gott!* By tradition, only family members and close friends address each other by their first names. Others use titles and surnames. However, this is changing among the youth. When addressing strangers, acquaintances or colleagues, one combines a person's professional title with *Herr* (Mr.), *Frau* (Mrs.), *Fräulein* (Miss), or other titles and the last name. The titles can also be used without the name. For example, a male professor with a doctorate degree is addressed as *Herr Professor Doktor*; a female head of a department in business or government could be addressed as *Frau Direktorin*.

Gestures

Chewing gum in public is not appropriate, nor is cleaning one's fingernails. Talking with one's hands in the pockets is disrespectful. Legs are crossed with one knee over the other and not placed on furniture. Pointing the index finger to one's own head is an insult to another person. Instead of crossing one's fingers for luck, Germans "squeeze the thumb" between the index and middle fingers. Only the thumb tip is between the fingers; allowing it to protrude is an offensive gesture. In some areas, public displays of affection are not appropriate.

Visiting

Punctuality is appreciated, but it is not an insult for guests to arrive a few minutes late. Dinner guests often bring an odd number of flowers to the hostess, but not roses (symbols of love) or carnations (for mourning). Flowers are unwrapped before they are given. Guests usually stand when the host enters the room and remain standing until offered a seat again. It is also courteous to stand when a woman enters the room. Not everyone adheres to these rules of etiquette, but it is polite to do so. Refreshments are almost always served to guests, even during short visits. Spontaneous visits, even between neighbors, are not very common. Arrangements are generally made in advance. Germans enjoy gathering for conversation and social events. While dinner parties may last well into the night, daytime visits are usually short, except afternoon *Kaffeetrinken*, where tea or coffee and snacks are served.

Eating

The continental style of eating is used, with the fork in the left hand and the knife remaining in the right. Hands are kept above the table with wrists resting on the edge. Potatoes and fish are not cut with a knife because this indicates they are not fully cooked. It is considered wasteful to leave food on the plate. Most Germans prefer beer, wine, or mineral water with meals; they rarely drink tap water. Soft drinks and fruit juices are also popular. Germans prefer their drinks without ice, as cold drinks are not considered healthy. Germany does not have drinking fountains because of the tradition of bottled water. In restaurants, the bill usually includes a service charge and is paid at the table. Customers often round up the total due to the next *Mark*, giving the waiter the difference as an extra tip (*Trinkgeld*). This is more common in western states. If served by the restaurant owner, it is inappropriate to leave a tip.

LIFESTYLE

Family

The father is generally the head of the family. Both parents often work, more so in the east than in the west. Large families are not common, even in rural areas. The average family has only one or two children. While order, responsibility, and achievement are still traditional family values, a greater variety of lifestyles exists today, especially among those in the west. Most young adults prefer to live away from home once they become wage earners or go on to a university. Most families live in apartments. Single family homes are by no means rare, just very expensive. About 40 percent of all western homes (whether houses or apartments) are owned by the occupants. The rate is lower in the east. In urban areas, people often own or rent small garden plots in or near the city.

Dating and Marriage

Dating is different in Germany than in the United States. There isn't even a word in the German language for it. Boys and girls socialize on a casual basis. If one wants to go out with another, either sex can suggest a *Verabredung* (appointment). They each pay for their own food and entertainment (unless one offers to pay for a special occasion). Young people usually marry in their twenties, but they often wait until they have some financial security. It is common for young people to live together before or instead of marriage. Legal marriages are performed at city hall; religious ceremonies are optional.

Diet

While regional dishes vary among Germans, potatoes, noodles, dumplings, sauces, vegetables, cakes, and pastries are common. Pork is a popular meat, along with beef and, to a lesser extent, chicken. Pork is prepared according to regional tradition; it may be boiled with cabbage in Frankfurt, roasted with dumplings in München, or prepared as ham in Westphalia. Lamb is widely available in the north. Fish is popular in North Sea areas such as Hamburg, but also in Bavaria where trout is plentiful. Every region has its own type of *Wurst* (sausage).

Breakfast consists of rolls, marmalade, and coffee or another hot drink. The main meal, traditionally served at midday, includes soup, a main dish, and dessert. For the lighter evening meal (*Abendbrot*), open-faced sandwiches (cheese, meats, spreads) are common, unless people eat in a restaurant, where full meals are served. Two-income families rarely have a big midday meal, but they eat the main meal in the evening and they may or may not have *Abendbrot*. Germans buy groceries often and prefer fresh foods for cooking. Ethnic foods (especially Italian and Greek) and fast foods are popular. Germans are known for their beer making and drinking. They also enjoy domestic and other wines. However, soft drinks are increasingly popular among the youth, who consume less alcohol overall than the older generation.

Recreation

Germans enjoy hiking, skiing, swimming, cycling, touring in cars, or playing tennis, among other things. Garden plots with small gazebos offer relaxation on summer evenings. People also enjoy watching television or visiting with friends. Soccer (*Fußball*) is the most popular sport and millions belong to soccer clubs. Germany's team competed in the 1994 World Cup. Organized sports participation is changing because of reunification. A uniform club system is being organized. Germans in the west have long relished travel, something those in the east are also beginning to enjoy. Carnival is important in some regions, where dances, parades, and other celebrations take place before the Catholic Lent. Of the performing arts, music and theater are most popular. Generous government subsidies allow even the smallest cities to have professional orchestras and opera companies. Summer arts and music festivals are held throughout the country.

Holidays

New Year's celebrations begin on *Sylvester* (31 December) with midnight fireworks and parties, followed by a public holiday on 1 January. Easter Sunday and Monday are celebrated, with Sunday worship services and Monday family gatherings. Labor Day (1 May) is characterized by labor union parades. Various religious holidays (Catholic and Protestant) are celebrated, such as Pentecost, Ascension, and All Saints Day (1 November). The Day of German Unity is celebrated on 3 October. At Christmas, gifts are given on Christmas eve (*Heiliger Abend*); the family relaxes on Christmas day. People enjoy visiting on 26 December, also a legal holiday. Musical and arts festivals are popular in the summer.

Commerce

Before unification, business hours were different, and not all differences have been resolved. Shops in the east were open late to accommodate working spouses, while stores in the west closed by 6:30 P.M. It may be some time before a uniform system is developed. Business hours range from 8:00 A.M. to 5:00 P.M. weekdays. In western states, shops close at 2:00 P.M. on Saturdays, except one Saturday each month when they remain open into the evening. Banks close for lunch and then at 4:00 P.M., but they remain open a bit later on Thursdays.

SOCIETY

Government

Germany has a president, Richard von Weizäcker, who is head of state and has mostly ceremonial and statesman duties. He is elected by members of the federal and state legislatures for up to two five-year terms; Weizäcker has been in office since 1984. A chancellor is head of government. Helmut Kohl was elected to the post in 1982 and served as a powerful figure through unification. Kohl faces reelection in October 1994. Germany's legislature has two houses, an upper chamber called the *Bundesrat* and a lower house called the *Bundestag*. The country has 16 states (*Länder*), each of which has its own legislature and autonomy over schools and other matters. The state governments elect the 68 members of the *Bundesrat*, while the 622 members of the *Bundestag* are elected by popular vote. The voting age is 18.

Economy

Germany is one of the top five economic powers in the world. The country's Human Development Index (0.957) ranks it 12 out of 173 countries. Real gross domestic product per capita is $18,213, but this figure represents data from western states. Conditions in eastern states are not as advanced. Eastern prices are as high as in the west, but salaries and rents remain lower. Germany's prosperity generally reaches all levels of society through the social network, but to varying degrees according to region and socioeconomic status.

The shift to a market economy in the east cost more than one million jobs. Money from economically powerful western states is being used to revive the eastern economy, and some areas are beginning to do well. Western companies are buying the east's factories and shops; the government is rebuilding roads, railways, and public transportation facilities; and workers are being retrained. Germany exports cars, steel, aluminum, televisions, and other manufactured goods. Germany's construction and service industries are strong components of the domestic economy. The German currency, the *Deutsche Mark* (DM), is one of the strongest in the world.

Unfortunately, reunification costs and a global recession have hurt the German economy. Unemployment in the west is above 7 percent; in the east it is more than twice that. The government faces opposition from both regions. In the east, strikes in 1993 demonstrated workers' frustrations when promised pay increases were not delivered. People in the west are resisting higher taxes and the reforms necessary to revitalize the economy. Economic growth for 1992 was only 1 percent.

Transportation and Communication

Most families own cars and the car is more important to Germans than to many other Europeans. They especially favor cars for touring or traveling long distances. Public transportation is more efficient for daily travel in major cities because of heavy traffic and limited parking. Subways, buses, streetcars, and trains form the main transportation network. Trains travel to nearly every town and city. Traffic rules are carefully obeyed by drivers and cyclists. One must attend expensive and rigorous driver training schools to qualify for a driver's license. While there is no speed limit on sections of the *Autobahn* (freeway) in western states, there are strict limits on all other roads. The communications system is fully developed. Telephone and postal services are centrally controlled.

Education

Education is a source of pride, especially in the areas of technology and craftsmanship. The states administer public education. Preschool begins around age four. Full-time schooling is mandatory between the ages of six and fifteen, and part or full-time schooling continues on a chosen track until age 18. Students may enter a job training program, train for specific professional careers, or study to enter a university. Nearly every occupation, from mechanic to waiter to accountant, has a school or program designed specifically for it. For example, waiters and waitresses might be in school for up to four years before being certified as servers. Because of this training, their salaries are much higher than their American counterparts. In all schools, considerable attention is given to equipping students with real-life skills.

German literacy is 99 percent. Education is free at all levels, but entrance to universities is difficult and can only be accomplished through success on the *Abitur* exam, taken at the end of the *Gymnasium*, or college preparation school. Adults can continue their education through evening classes.

Health

Medical care is provided free or at minimal cost to all citizens. Private doctors also practice, but most people have access to care in hospitals and clinics. Fees are controlled by the government and some co-payments are required. In addition to government health insurance, private insurance is available. When workers become ill, they receive up to six weeks of full pay while they recover. People in eastern states suffer more often from pollution-related illnesses. Germany's infant mortality rate is 7 per 1,000. Life expectancy ranges from 73 to 79 years.

FOR THE TRAVELER

U.S. visitors do not need a visa to travel for as long as three months in Germany, but a valid passport is required and should be carried at all times for identification. No vaccinations are necessary. Tap water is safe, but people drink bottled water. Dual-voltage small appliances or voltage converters and plug adaptors are necessary to use electrical outlets. When traveling on any public transit system, retain your ticket until your ride is over, as conductors may check them anytime. On subways and buses, travelers validate their own tickets in machines on board. Germany offers beautiful scenery, historical sites, and many recreational activities. Travel in the east offers a unique look at German culture. For complete information on travel opportunities, contact the German National Tourist Office (122 East 42d Street, 52d Floor, New York, NY 10168). You may also wish to contact the Embassy of the Federal Republic of Germany, 4645 Reservoir Road NW, Washington, DC 20007–1998.

A *Culturgram* is a product of native commentary and original, expert analysis. Statistics are estimates and information is presented as a matter of opinion. While the editors strive for accuracy and detail, this document should not be considered strictly factual. It is a general introduction to culture, an initial step in building bridges of understanding between peoples. It may not apply to all peoples of the nation. You should therefore consult other sources for more information.

CULTURGRAM ™ '95

Greece

(Hellenic Republic)

Boundary representations not necessarily authoritative.

BACKGROUND

Land and Climate

Covering 50,942 square miles (131,940 square kilometers), Greece is just smaller than Alabama. It is situated south of Macedonia and Bulgaria and also shares a short border with Albania. Although it lies farther east than most of Western Europe, it is generally considered part of the West because of its heritage and its membership in the North Atlantic Treaty Organization (NATO) and the European Union (EU). Sparsely populated mountain areas cover much of the land. Earthquakes are possible in these regions. Nearly 25 percent of Greece is arable. The fertile valleys, plains, and coastal areas are more densely populated. An archipelago of more than 2,000 islands is part of the country, but only 166 of the islands are suitable for habitation. A warm, temperate Mediterranean climate prevails in the south, while the north is wet and cool. In general, winters are mild but wet; summers are hot and dry.

History

Although the history of ancient Greece stretches back to 3000 B.C., Athens had its beginnings in 1300 B.C. and city-states began forming around 1000 B.C. From this point, Greek culture began to thrive. The first Olympics were held in 776 B.C., and literature, philosophy, and art began to flourish. By 400 B.C., the glory of ancient Greek civilization reached its peak. Athens was the center of a vast overseas empire. Much of the West's first studies of government, law, and the concepts of justice and liberty began in Greece. Its rich heritage of architecture, sculpture, science, drama, poetry, and government established a foundation for Western civilization.

Philip of Macedonia conquered Greece in 338 B.C., but he was assassinated. His son, Alexander the Great, led the Greeks to an empire that covered much of what is now the Middle East. After his death in 323 B.C., the empire began to decline, and by 146 B.C. it had become part of the Roman Empire.

Centuries later, along with Constantinople (now Istanbul, Turkey), Greece was the center of the Byzantine Empire, which fell in 1453. In 1460, Greece became a Turkish province. After four centuries of Turkish rule (the Ottoman Empire), the Greeks began a war of independence, supported by Britain, France, and Russia. In 1832, Prince Otto of Bavaria was made king of Greece. In World War II, Greece was occupied by German and Italian forces and lost one-eighth of its population to fighting and starvation. After liberation in 1944, a civil war between the government and Communist guerrillas cost another 120,000 lives. The government, with aid from the United States, was victorious in 1949.

In 1965, a political crisis developed between Prime Minister George Papandreou and King Constantine II, which resulted in Papandreou's dismissal. A group of army colonels staged a coup in 1967, and the royal family fled. From 1967

EUROPE

Copyright © 1994. Brigham Young University. Printed in the USA. All rights reserved. It is against the law to copy, reprint, store in a retrieval system, or transmit any part of this publication in any form by any means for any purpose without written permission from the Publications Division of the David M. Kennedy Center for International Studies, Brigham Young University, PO Box 24538, Provo, UT 84602–4538. *Culturgrams* are available for more than 125 areas of the world. To place an order, to receive a free catalog, or to obtain information on traveling abroad, call toll free (800) 528–6279.

to 1974, the colonels ruled as a repressive dictatorship. Their eventual fall allowed for general elections, through which a republic was established when voters rejected a return to a monarchy. In 1981, Andreas Papandreou's Socialist party won a majority in parliament and he became prime minister. He was reelected in 1985, but lost the majority in 1989 in the face of various financial and political scandals.

Elections had to be held three times before Konstantinos Mitsotakis and his New Democracy party received enough votes to form a government in 1990. Mitsotakis worked to privatize state enterprises, cut government spending, and prepare Greece for greater economic integration within Europe. Austerity measures that were necessary to accomplish those goals led to voter discontent. Hence, in the 1993 elections, the Socialist Party regained parliamentary leadership and Andreas Papandreou was returned to office as prime minister. He immediately began to reverse various privatization efforts and other economic policies.

THE PEOPLE

Population

The population is about 10.4 million and is growing annually at 0.9 percent. The majority live in urban areas. Nearly 98 percent are ethnic Greeks, but there is a small Turkish minority. Much smaller minorities include Albanians, Pomachs, and Slavs.

Language

Greek is the official language of Greece. Turkish is spoken by 1 percent of the population. English and French are widely understood, and English is a popular subject in the schools.

Religion

About 98 percent of the people belong to the Eastern (Greek) Orthodox church, which is the official religion in Greece and quite powerful. Although freedom of religion is guaranteed, the state supports the Eastern Orthodox church through taxes, and other religions are not allowed to proselyte. The Orthodox church is a Christian church directed by an archbishop (independent of the Roman Catholic church) and the Holy Synod. Eastern Orthodox principles are taught in the schools. About 1 percent of the people (mostly of Turkish origin) are Muslim; there are also members of other Christian churches and some of the Jewish faith in Greece. Jewish communities are located in Thessaloníki and Athens.

General Attitudes

While women have gained greater prominence and rights in the last generation, Greek society is still male dominated. Men consider it a matter of personal honor to fulfill obligations to their families and others. They may attribute their failures to external circumstances rather than to personal inadequacies. Also, a man may praise the food served in his home as especially good, or be the hero of his own tales. Such self-praise is not, however, considered bragging. While Greece's older generations value family, religion, tradition, and education, the younger generation tends to view status and friends as also very important. Greeks like to "pass" time, not "use" it. That is, they may not be prompt in keeping appointments, and they consider it foolish to set a specific length of time for a meeting. Greeks are very proud of their cultural heritage, which they view as being central to Western civilization. Greeks see themselves as being individualists, brave, and hardworking.

Personal Appearance

Greeks generally wear clothing influenced by European fashions. Conservative dress is preferred. Traditional costumes are worn at folk festivals and on special occasions. Women wear dresses more often than in North America.

CUSTOMS AND COURTESIES

Greetings

Greeks are often expressive in their greetings. Friends and relatives hug and kiss when they greet each other. Otherwise, people shake hands. Young men often slap each other's back or arm at shoulder level instead of shaking hands. There are many different verbal greetings; their usage depends on the situation. One term for "Good morning" is *Kaliméra sas*. "Good evening" is *Kalispéra sas*.

Close friends and family members are called by their first names, but acquaintances and strangers are addressed by their title (Doctor, Professor, Mrs., etc.) and surname. In urban areas, people do not greet strangers while passing in the street. When getting on an elevator, one usually nods at the others present and might give a short general greeting. Villagers briefly greet passing strangers in rural areas.

Gestures

To indicate "no," one can either tilt the head backward or side to side. To indicate "yes," one nods the head slightly forward. A Greek may smile not only when happy but sometimes when angry or upset. A puff of breath through pursed lips may be a sign to ward off the jealousy of the "evil eye" after a compliment has been given or received. Hands are used a great deal in conversation, both to accompany and replace verbal expressions.

Visiting

Ancient Greeks believed a stranger might be a god in disguise and were therefore kind to all strangers. This tradition of hospitality continues to the present. It is very common for friends and relatives to drop by unannounced in small towns. This happens less often in large cities, but only because schedules are more hectic. Greeks enjoy inviting friends to their homes for dinner or for special occasions—such as name days or New Year's Day. Christmas and Easter present opportunities for family gatherings.

Invited guests usually take a gift to the hosts, including flowers, a bottle of wine, or cookies. All guests, invited or unannounced, are offered refreshments. A cup of coffee is most common, but other drinks, a homemade fruit preserve, or cookies are also popular. If Greek hosts insist several times about anything (that a guest stay longer or eat more, for example), they usually mean it, and guests try to accommodate them so as not to hurt their feelings.

Eating

Traditionally, the main meal of the day is lunch, served in the early afternoon (between noon and 2:00 P.M.). Due to changing work schedules, however, lunch is becoming less important. The urban family, for example, can rarely gather to eat lunch. Only where practical does it remain the main meal. Otherwise dinner is the largest meal. It may be eaten as late as 8:00 or 9:00 P.M. It is impolite to leave the table before everyone is finished eating. It is also impolite to not finish everything on one's plate. Leaving food insults the cook; taking second helpings is the best way to show appreciation for the meal and to compliment the hostess.

At restaurants, a group will often order a number of different dishes that everyone shares. It is not unusual for guests to go into the restaurant kitchen and choose their dinner by looking into the different pots of food. A tip is not only left for the server but for the busboy as well.

LIFESTYLE

Family

The family unit is strong in Greece. It is vital that no member bring shame or dishonor to the family. If one's parents die, the family's oldest sibling usually helps younger children finish their education and get out on their own. The elderly are respected, addressed by courteous titles, served first, and have much authority. Greeks care for their elderly parents at home when possible. If the parents must live in a home for the elderly, their children take care of all arrangements and make frequent visits. Children are treated with firm discipline, but their parents (even the poorest) spend a large portion of their income to clothe, feed, and educate them. In fact, parents believe it is their duty to provide for a good education. And they will always help their children, married or not, if they can. Some newlywed couples live with their parents or inlaws until they can afford a home of their own.

Dating and Marriage

Traditionally, the man asks the woman's parents for permission to marry her. If the parents approve, the two date and become better acquainted during a formal engagement. Such formalities are now quite rare, except among rural people.

Young people socialize as they do throughout Europe, and it is common for a couple to live together before or instead of getting married. In rural areas, the youth often gather Sunday afternoon in the village square to socialize. The average age for getting married is between 20 and 26 for women and between 25 and 35 for men.

Diet

While tastes vary between urban and rural dwellers, certain foods are common to all Greeks. These include lamb, seafood, olives, and cheese. The people also eat potatoes, rice, beans, breads, chicken, fruit, and vegetables. Olive oil is used in cooking. Garlic, onions, and spices are also popular. Salads are often eaten with the main meal. *Souvlaki* is a shish kebab with cubes of meat (pork or lamb), mushrooms, and vegetables. A common everyday dish is bean soup. Eggplant, zucchini, stuffed tomatoes, and pasta are all favorites. For Easter, Greeks enjoy roast lamb and *kokoretsi* (lamb liver, lungs, and spleen wrapped in intestines and roasted on a spit).

Recreation

Coffee houses were once the focal point of leisure activity for men. Now rare in urban areas, they still provide a place to play cards and discuss politics for rural men. Rural women stay at home with other women to do crafts and enjoy conversation. Movies (both Greek and foreign) and the theater are also popular. Many festivals throughout the year highlight ancient Greek theater and literature, and are enjoyed by many. With an Olympic tradition, the Greeks love sports, especially soccer, basketball, swimming, and sailing. Greece's national soccer team competed in the 1994 World Cup. On weekends, urban dwellers like to go to the beach, or go skiing or fishing. Folk dancing is common, and foreign visitors may be invited to join in.

Holidays

Almost every city and village has a patron saint who is honored with a yearly festival. Easter is by far the most important holiday, celebrated with special feasts, processions, and gatherings. January 1st is celebrated as St. Basil's Day and is traditionally a day of gift giving, although many people now prefer to exchange gifts on Christmas (25 December). For many holidays, a traditional greeting is *Chronia polla* (Many years). At midnight on New Year's Eve, a special cake *(vasilopitta)* with a coin in it is cut into various pieces. Whoever gets the coin is supposed to have good luck during the new year. Other holidays include Independence Day (25 March), St. Constantine and Helen Celebration (21 May), Assumption (15 August), and Ochi Day (28 October). Ochi Day commemorates the day that Joannis Metaxas, then prime minister, said *Ochi* (No) to Hitler, and Greece entered into World War II on the side of the Allies. It is considered a heroic decision because of the size of the German and Italian armies.

Commerce

Work and business hours vary, depending on the season and type of business. In general, most Greeks work from 8:00 A.M. to 1:30 P.M. and from 5:00 to 8:00 P.M., Monday through Friday. Offices are generally open between 8:00 A.M. and 3:00 P.M. Shops may open and close when they want. During the hot summer months, many close between 2:00 and 5:00 P.M. Larger department stores have longer business hours.

SOCIETY

Government

Greece's president is head of state, but the prime minister is head of government. Konstantinos Karamanlis is the current president. The parliament (Vouli) has three hundred members. Elections are held at least every four years. The judiciary is independent. All citizens are eligible and required to vote at age 18.

Economy

Greece is traditionally an agricultural nation; over 25 percent of the labor force works in agriculture. Greece produces wine, wheat, wool, cotton, olives, raisins, and tobacco. The industrial sector has made important advances in recent years, and it accounts for 50 percent of export earnings. In addition to manufactured goods, food, fuels, and raw materials are exported.

Greece's Human Development Index (0.902) ranks it 25 out of 173 countries. Real gross domestic product per capita is estimated at $7,366, which has doubled in the last generation. These figures indicate most people are able to earn enough to meet their needs and a growing number have access to economic prosperity. Greece's currency is the drachma (Dr).

Transportation and Communication

Principal highways connect Athens with Thessaloníki and Petrai, but roads are poor in mountain areas. Some villages can only be reached by rough trails. Buses and trains are the most common forms of public transportation. There are 20 commercial airports. In Athens, people commute by car and bus. Young people often drive motorbikes. Athens has one short subway line that cannot accommodate many travelers, so the government began building the Athens metro subway in 1992. It is scheduled for completion by 1996. Because traffic congestion is so bad in Athens, cars with license plates ending in an even number are only allowed to drive in the center of town on even days of the month (with odd numbers driving on odd-numbered days). There are over 100 daily newspapers in Greece and at least 30 are published in Athens. The government owns and administrates the telephone, radio, and television systems.

Education

Education is free and mandatory, beginning with kindergarten for children over age five. Elementary schooling begins two years later and lasts six years. Three years of gymnasia are also compulsory. Lyceums are also available in three or four-year courses and generally prepare a student for higher education. Universities, technical colleges, and schools of higher education are free to those who achieve enrollment through entrance exams. The literacy rate is 93 percent.

Health

A portion of one's salary must be paid to the Institute of Social Insurance (IKA) in return for state-supported health care. While this system provides all citizens with health benefits, it is not as efficient as people would like. Hospitals, for example, are generally understaffed and overcrowded. Doctors who work in public hospitals are not allowed to have private patients. A few private clinics do exist, but their services are not covered by state insurance. Many people feel they would obtain better care through a private system. Still, Greeks enjoy good health, with a life expectancy of 75 to 81 years. The infant mortality rate is 9 per 1,000.

FOR THE TRAVELER

While no visa is necessary for U.S. citizens to enter Greece, a valid passport is required. Visas are necessary for stays lasting longer than three months. Standard European electrical outlets are used, so plug adaptors and voltage converters are necessary. Water outside of Athens and major resorts may not be safe for drinking. Greece offers beach resorts, historical sites, and both modern and ancient cultural events. For information on travel opportunities, contact the Greek National Tourist Office (645 Fifth Avenue, New York, NY 10022). There are also offices in Los Angeles and Chicago. You may also wish to contact the Embassy of Greece, 2221 Massachusetts Avenue NW, Washington, DC 20008.

A Culturgram is a product of native commentary and original, expert analysis. Statistics are estimates and information is presented as a matter of opinion. While the editors strive for accuracy and detail, this document should not be considered strictly factual. It is a general introduction to culture, an initial step in building bridges of understanding between peoples. It may not apply to all peoples of the nation. You should therefore consult other sources for more information.

CULTURGRAM '95

Republic of
Guatemala

Boundary representations not necessarily authoritative.

BACKGROUND

Land and Climate

Covering 42,043 square miles (108,890 square kilometers), Guatemala is just smaller than Tennessee. Mexico is to the north, while El Salvador and Honduras border the south. About two-thirds of Guatemala is mountainous and volcanic. Some of the volcanoes are active and tremors are frequent; the last major earthquake was in 1976. Rich forests cover 40 percent of Guatemala. These forests are particularly dense in the Petén region of the northwest. Most people live on the slopes of the highlands or in the fertile, well-watered lowlands along the Pacific Coast. In the coastal lowlands, hot, humid weather prevails. In the highlands, days are warm and nights are usually cool. The people call Guatemala "The Land of the Eternal Spring" because 75°F (24°C) is the average annual temperature in the capital, which is on a plateau 4,800 feet (1,460 meters) above sea level. November to May is the dry season; from May to October there is abundant rainfall. The Caribbean Coast is wet year-round.

History

The Mayan empire flourished in what is now Guatemala for more than 1,000 years until it began to decline in the 1100s. As one of the chief centers of the Mayan culture, Guatemala abounds in archaeological ruins, notably the majestic ceremonial city of Tikal in the Petén region. From 1524 to 1821, the Spanish ruled Central America. After winning its independence in 1821, Guatemala was briefly annexed by Mexico and then became a member of the Central American Federation until the federation was dissolved in 1838.

Until a 1944 revolution, Guatemala was controlled by military dictatorships. From 1945 to 1982, leaders tried to cure some of Guatemala's social ills, but democracy was still absent. Violence was common, and rebels began a civil war in 1954 after an elected president (Jacobo Arbenz Guzmán) was overthrown by a U.S.-backed military coup. Coups and civil war made political stability seem impossible until 1984 when a constituent assembly was elected to write a new constitution.

In 1986, Guatemala returned to civilian rule under Marco Vinicio Cerezo Arévalo. Cerezo withstood two military coups, but the military has strong ties to the country's principal landowners and therefore wields much power. In fact, the military has more control over some regions than civilian authorities. Because the military is primarily responsible for human rights abuses, such control presents enormous problems for political and economic progress.

Elections in 1990 brought the first transfer of power from one elected official to another. President Jorge Serrano Elías began peace talks with the rebels in 1991. The end of decades of civil war seemed possible early in 1993. Unfortunately, talks were interrupted by a May 1993 political crisis when Serrano dissolved Congress and the Supreme Court, and suspended the constitution. Backed by the army, he announced emergency rule, which touched off civilian street protests. As pressure mounted, the military withdrew its

Copyright © 1994. Brigham Young University. Printed in the USA. All rights reserved. It is against the law to copy, reprint, store in a retrieval system, or transmit any part of this publication in any form by any means for any purpose without written permission from the Publications Division of the David M. Kennedy Center for International Studies, Brigham Young University, PO Box 24538, Provo, UT 84602–4538. *Culturgrams* are available for more than 125 areas of the world. To place an order, to receive a free catalog, or to obtain information on traveling abroad, call toll free (800) 528–6279.

support, forcing Serrano to flee to Panama. Military leaders recalled Congress, which chose a popular human rights crusader, Ramiro de León Carpio, to finish Serrano's term in office. This move encouraged Guatemalans that peace and democracy are yet possible. Talks with rebels opened again in 1994 and the two sides agreed to allow a broad-based assembly to recommend solutions to the country's social ills. Negotiations are expected to lead to a peace treaty by 1995.

THE PEOPLE
Population
Guatemala's population is 10.4 million and is growing at 2.6 percent annually. While 56 percent is *ladino* (*mestizo*), 44 percent is composed of some 28 indigenous groups descended from the Maya. The largest of these are the Quiché, Cakchiquel, Kekchí, Mam, and Ixil. They live throughout the country, but significant numbers are in the western highlands. Collectively they refer to themselves as Maya or Indigenous. The *ladinos* descend from the Spanish and Maya, but they relate more to their Spanish heritage. Some of the largest are Quiché, Cakchiquel, Kekchí, Ixil, and Mam (Pocomam).

Language
Spanish is Guatemala's official language, but each indigenous group speaks its own language. Male indigenous Guatemalans are generally bilingual, speaking their own language and Spanish. Indigenous women have less contact with the Spanish-speaking *mestizos* than the men and thus have fewer opportunities to learn Spanish. English is understood in tourist centers.

Religion
Roman Catholicism is the dominant religion in Guatemala, although many indigenous groups have combined it with their Mayan beliefs. Some indigenous groups have not accepted Catholicism. Other Christian groups are active in Guatemala, where freedom of religion is guaranteed. While Catholicism influences most Guatemalans' celebrations and habits, regardless of religious preference, devotion to the Catholic church is declining. Many are converting to Protestant and other Christian churches. Protestants are usually referred to as *evangélicos* (evangelicals). About 45 percent of the people are now *evangélicos*. The increased religious devotion is credited with decreasing alcoholism and other social problems. However, because of their differing approaches to practicing Christianity, tension between Catholics and *evangélicos* is rising.

General Attitudes
Guatemalans are polite and humble. They value honesty, family unity, personal honor, work, and education. Optimism is less common than the acceptance of misfortune. People often feel they are not able to change their condition, either for lack of empowerment or because some things are accepted as God's will. Personal criticism is taken seriously and should be avoided. Punctuality is admired but not strictly observed because people are considered more important than schedules.

Family status and wealth are important to *ladinos*. Being treated as an equal is highly desired by the Maya. Tension exists between *ladinos* and the Indigenous. The *ladinos* consider the Maya to be inferior and uncivilized. They avoid contact with the Indigenous who do not adopt *ladino* ways. Those Maya who wear Western clothing and assimilate into *ladino* culture are treated somewhat better. The Maya have

been subjected to discrimination and human rights abuses for centuries. There is hope their condition may improve, especially considering that a Quiché Maya, Rigoberta Menchú, won the 1992 Nobel Peace Prize for her fight to have the plight of the indigenous population heard.

Personal Appearance
In cities, people generally wear Western-style clothing. However, the rural Maya have retained traditional dress. Each group's clothing has unique qualities, but basic features include a *faja* (woven belt worn by both sexes), wraparound skirts for women, and knee or calf-length trousers for men. Women often wear ribbons or woolen fabric in their hair. Men generally wear hats, usually made from straw or blocked felt. Skirts, pants, and blouses are often colorful. Women treasure their *guipil* (blouse); its design identifies her status and hometown. Woolen jackets and shawls are also common.

CUSTOMS AND COURTESIES
Greetings
When meeting for the first time, people greet with a handshake and *¡Mucho gusto!* (Pleased to meet you). Among general acquaintances, the most common greetings are *¡Buenos días¡* (Good day), *¡Buenas tardes!* (Good afternoon), and *¡Buenas noches!* (Good evening). Among friends, a casual *¡Buenas!* or *¡Hola!* (Hi) might be used. After an initial greeting, one might ask *¿Como esta?* (How are you?). Shaking hands heartily is common in most areas. Among friends, men usually shake hands and sometimes embrace, and women kiss each other on the cheek. A younger woman will kiss a male friend, but older women only kiss relatives. Some older women greet by grasping the person just below each elbow.

In small groups, it is important to greet each individual. In larger groups, it is acceptable to offer a group greeting or to simply greet as many persons as possible. Guests greet hosts individually, regardless of the size of the group. When addressing others, using a title (*Señor, Señora, Señorita, Doctor*, etc.) shows respect. Special respect for older individuals is shown by using *Don* and *Doña* with the first name. Common phrases for parting include *Que le vaya bien* (May you go well), *Nos vemos* (See you later), and *Mas tarde* (later).

Gestures
Guatemalans beckon by waving the hand downward and in. A taxi or bus is hailed by sticking the hand out horizontally, palm facing down. Getting someone's attention in public is commonly done by making a "tssst tssst" sound. Pointing with the finger or the hand can be misinterpreted because many finger and hand gestures are vulgar. To point, people most often purse (pucker) their lips in the direction of whatever they are indicating. To emphasize something, express surprise, or indicate "hurry," one shakes the hand quickly so that the index and middle fingers slap together and make a snapping sound.

Urban couples tend to be more affectionate in public than rural ones. Rural people hold hands, but rarely kiss or show other affection. Personal space during conversation is relatively close, although touching is not common.

Visiting
Visiting friends and relatives is important to building strong relationships. Not visiting frequently can be an insult, as it reflects the relationship's value. People who live close,

especially in rural areas, drop by unannounced (or send a child to announce the adults are coming later); nearly any time of day is acceptable. Those who visit frequently may establish a pattern of visiting at certain times so they can be expected. Socializing also takes place outside the home; friends and relatives may meet at the market, community meetings, church, or water well. While important, it is also proper to visit the home to show that one's hospitality is valued. For formal events, longer stays, or if people do not live close, visits are often prearranged. When extended, invitations may be for dinner or for a special event or celebration.

Frequent visitors do not usually bring gifts to the hosts, but anyone staying more than a day will give flowers, chocolates, or something for the home. The longer the stay, the nicer the gift. Gifts are also given for birthdays and weddings. Hosts often send food or something from the garden home with their dinner guests. Nearly all guests are offered coffee, tea, water, or another drink and sweet bread or other snack. It is impolite to refuse. When leaving a home, guests graciously thank the hosts and often invite them to visit.

Eating

Most people eat three meals a day; poorer families might eat only one meal and then snack on *tortillas* the rest of the day. A rural breakfast may consist of *tortillas* and leftover beans. The main meal is eaten at midday; anyone in the family not working eats this meal. Usually eaten after 7:00 P.M., dinner is lighter than lunch. The entire family gathers for the main meal on weekends; these meals are important for socializing. In some cases, women serve the meal and eat later. Many people have coffee and sweet breads around 4:00 P.M., and men working in the fields might have a snack at midmorning. School children are served hot cereal at 10:00 A.M.

Tortillas are often used as a scoop for some foods. Other foods are eaten with the hands, but utensils are otherwise used at most meals. Hands are kept above the table, not placed in the lap. Upon finishing the meal, each person at the table (even the cook) often thanks all others at the table with *Muchas gracias*, to which all reply *Buen provecho* (Good appetite).

When guests eat, they finish everything on their plates and wait for the host to offer more food. Asking for more might embarrass a host who is out of food, but eating more compliments the cook. If additional food is offered, it is first politely declined, but then always accepted and eaten completely.

LIFESTYLE

Family

The extended family forms the basis of society and exerts significant influence on an individual's life and decisions. The father is the head of the family, but the wife controls the household; she is considered the heart of the family. Rural extended families often share a single home or live next to each other in a family compound. This includes parents, their married sons and their families, unmarried children, and often grandparents. Urban families generally live in nuclear family settings, although grandparents are often present. Unmarried adults live with their parents unless they must go elsewhere for work. Family members are expected to share responsibilities and to be devoted to the unit. Adult children are responsible for the care of their elderly parents.

Ladino women often work as secretaries, teachers, nurses, and in other professions. One-fourth of the labor force is female. Mayan women also work, but less often in professional capacities. They may sell produce at markets, embroider or weave products for sale, or work in community groups. Within the home, women are responsible for the food, household, children, education, and religion. Men work professionally or do field work and other physically demanding labor.

Ladino families generally live in urban areas or towns in small, single-family homes. Although apartment living is often necessary, people prefer the privacy of homes. Housing for indigenous groups follows their various traditions, such as a modest adobe or bamboo dwelling with a thatched or tin roof. Poverty is a serious problem for many in Guatemala, and land ownership is not available to most. In poorer families, children must work as soon as they are able to help support the family. Many rural families have no running water or electricity, although the cities are well equipped with these.

Dating and Marriage

Urban youth begin socializing in groups around age 15. They enjoy going to movies, eating out, or just being together at home or elsewhere. Rural youth take walks, meet after school, visit at church or community events, or meet in town (at the market or water well). A girl's honor is important; a proper couple is "chaperoned" by younger siblings or cousins.

Among *ladinos*, social status is important in choosing a spouse. Traditionally the boy's parents asked for the girl's hand in marriage; now the boy asks the girl's father. Women often marry by age 20, earlier in rural areas, and men by 24. Common-law marriages are accepted and often necessary, especially if the groom cannot afford his responsibility to pay for the wedding, new clothes for the bride, and any celebrations.

Diet

Corn *tortillas* are eaten with every meal. Other foods include black beans, rice, *tamales* (cornmeal or rice dough stuffed with meat and tomato sauce), and fried *plátanos* (bananas) with honey, cream, or black beans. Meats (beef, pork, and chicken) are often stewed, and sauces are important. Often a particular dish is unique to a certain village and the ingredients (such as spices) for the dish are only found in that village. Papaya and breadfruit are among the many fruits eaten in Guatemala. The poorest rural families eat only *tortillas*, whatever food they can grow, and foods gathered in the forest.

Recreation

The most popular sports are soccer, basketball, and volleyball. Recreation is most often enjoyed on holidays and during festivals. Guatemala is noted for the *marimba*, a musical instrument made of wood and played with sticks padded with rubber. The *marimba* can be heard at many of the yearly festivals. *Cofradias* (religious fraternities dedicated to a particular saint) offer a variety of recreational and leisure activities. Urban people enjoy watching television, but visiting is the most common leisure activity for all Guatemalans.

Holidays

In Guatemala, a popular saying claims there are more celebrations than days in the year. This describes the events that occur in villages and towns all year long. Each town has an annual *feria* (fair) to honor the local patron saint. This is often the most important holiday (especially in rural areas).

Major celebrations are divided into two periods: Christmas and Easter. Christmas celebrations begin 7 December, when the people clean their homes and burn the garbage in front of their houses. This cleanses their homes in preparation to receive Christ. On Christmas Day, firecrackers are set off and special foods are eaten. Actually, firecrackers accompany most celebrations, especially New Year's. Easter is celebrated with Holy Week, during which numerous large processions fill the streets. In the processions, figures representing Christ are carried through the streets on special platforms by men wearing purple robes (black robes on Good Friday). On Saturday, effigies of Judas Iscariot are burned.

Important national holidays include Labor Day (1 May), Army Day (30 June), Independence Day (15 September), *Día de la Raza* (Day of the Race or Columbus Day, 12 October), Revolution Day (20 October), and All Saints Day (1 November).

Commerce

Business hours vary from town to town, but they generally range from 8:00 A.M. to 6:00 P.M. in the cities, with an hour-or-two break around noon. Work hours also vary because so many are involved in agriculture. Urban residents purchase food and other basics from small shops and large supermarkets. Fresh produce is available at open-air markets. In rural areas, farmers produce some of their food and buy basics and other produce at open-air markets or small shops. Villages might have a market just twice a week, with one day offering only basic goods. Neighborhood stores are often run from a home; the stock is about the same in all such stores, so one buys from family and friends first. Farmers may also have another job to earn a wage. Other family members may sell handicrafts or livestock to make money. Landless people might work on farms for a wage.

SOCIETY

Government

Guatemala's president is head of state and head of government. His term expires in 1995. The Congress of the Republic has 116 seats. The voting age is 18.

Economy

Guatemala is a relatively poor country. Its Human Development Index (0.489) ranks it 113 out of 173 countries. Real gross domestic product per capita is $2,576, but the average person earns far less than this. Wealth is concentrated among the upper class; three-fourths of the rural population lives in poverty. Even in urban areas, where economic conditions are better, poverty affects two-thirds of the people. Thirty years of rebel sabotage, the existence of large commercial farms that produce for export but keep many rural farmers landless and poor, and the lack of a diverse manufacturing sector hinder progress. About 60 percent of the people are employed in the agricultural sector. Coffee accounts for 25 percent of all export earnings. Other leading agricultural products include cotton, cacao, corn, beans, sugarcane, bananas, and livestock. Nickel, oil, fish, and chicle (used in chewing gum) are important natural resources. Tourism and manufacturing are also important to the economy. The currency is the *quetzal* (Q).

Transportation and Communication

Buses are relatively inexpensive and are the main form of public transportation, especially for long distances. Paved roads connect the capital to major cities and neighboring countries, but most other roads are unimproved. Commuter airlines fly domestically. For short distances, the average person will walk, ride a bicycle or motorcycle, or take the bus. The wealthy have private cars. The communications system is fairly modern and efficient. Telephones are widely used in cities but not in rural areas. Urban newspapers are available, but rural people rely on radio for news and entertainment. Television is popular where there is electricity.

Education

Although there are several thousand primary schools, more than half of the primary-age children do not attend. The adult literacy rate is 55 percent. It is higher for males than females. Girls, however, now tend to stay in school longer than boys. Children often leave school because of family needs or because of inadequacies in the system. In rural areas, many primary school students do not speak Spanish, the language of the teachers. Also, facilities are often crowded, books in short supply, and teachers underpaid. The school day runs for about five hours. Primary school lasts five years. After that, three years of middle school and then three years of secondary schooling are possible. The final three years consists of vocational training. Those desiring to go on to one of Guatemala's five universities must have college preparation, which is usually only available to the wealthy.

Health

Guatemala faces serious health problems, including malnutrition, a lack of potable water in many areas, and disease. Medical resources are concentrated in urban areas, although a national system is structured to provide health posts to outlying areas. Care is generally free or costs a small fee, but medicines must be purchased. Public funding is often inadequate and rural posts are not properly serviced. The infant mortality rate is 56 per 1,000; life expectancy is between 61 and 66 years.

FOR THE TRAVELER

U.S. visitors need a passport and visa or tourist card to enter Guatemala. Malaria suppressants are recommended if traveling to rural and lowland areas. A yellow fever vaccination is necessary if traveling to other countries after Guatemala; they will require proof of vaccination. Other vaccinations may be advisable. Cholera is active in Guatemala. Do not eat raw or undercooked fish or meat. Make sure food is served hot, and drink only boiled or bottled water. Electrical outlets are similar to those in the United States and adaptor plugs are generally not necessary. Because of potential violence against Americans, travelers should call the U.S. State Department at (202) 647–5225 before departure. They should also contact the U.S. embassy upon arrival (7–01 Avenida de la Reforma, Zone 10, Guatemala). For information on travel opportunities, contact the Guatemala Tourist Commission (299 Alhambra Circle, Suite 510, Coral Gables, FL 33134) or the Embassy of Guatemala (2220 R Street NW, Washington, DC 20008).

A *Culturgram* is a product of native commentary and original, expert analysis. Statistics are estimates and information is presented as a matter of opinion. While the editors strive for accuracy and detail, this document should not be considered strictly factual. It is a general introduction to culture, an initial step in building bridges of understanding between peoples. It may not apply to all peoples of the nation. You should therefore consult other sources for more information.

Republic of
Honduras

Boundary representations not necessarily authoritative.

BACKGROUND

Land and Climate

Covering 43,278 square miles (112,090 square kilometers), Honduras is just larger than Tennessee. Located east of El Salvador and Guatemala in Central America, Honduras shares its southern border with Nicaragua and has Pacific and Atlantic Ocean coasts. La Mosquitia, an area of wetlands, mountains, and tropical forests, covers the lower eastern coast. The largest pine forest in Latin America, the Olancho Forest Reserve, is about the size of Connecticut. The climate varies according to elevation: subtropical in the lowlands and temperate at higher levels. The capital, Tegucigalpa, enjoys a relatively mild climate year-round. The rainy season extends from May to November, although rains sometimes may not begin to fall until as late as October. March through May are the hottest months.

While Honduras is mountainous, it is the only Central American country without volcanoes, which is a factor in its low food production. Soil in volcanic regions is usually rich and good for agriculture. Due to the poor soil, many people have practiced migratory agriculture, moving every few years to clear new land and plant crops. This and timber operations have caused Honduras to lose 30 percent of its forest over the past 25 years. Wildlife has also been affected. Many efforts are now underway to reverse this trend and preserve the forests for wildlife, indigenous peoples, and the environment.

Precious woods, gold, silver, copper, lead, zinc, and other such minerals are found in Honduras.

History

The great Mayan Empire flourished in present-day Honduras until about 800 A.D., when the Mayan population decreased. Smaller empires held the area until the arrival of Spanish *conquistadores*. Columbus landed in 1502 and called the area *Honduras* (depths) because of the deep waters off the north coast. The Indians battled against Spanish occupation until 1539, when the last of their chiefs (Lempira) was killed and the Spanish established a provincial capital at Comayagua. Honduras was incorporated into Spain's Captaincy General (colony) of Guatemala. Immigration increased when silver was discovered in the 1570s.

At the request of the Misquito Indians of the Mosquitia region, a British invasion was able to occupy only that area of the country. (The British withdrew in 1859.) In September 1821, Honduras and four other provinces declared independence from Spain and briefly joined the Mexican Empire. Complete independence for Honduras came in 1838, when a republic was established. By the end of the 1800s, the government had become unstable and the country came under Nicaraguan influence. Instability continued until Tiburcio Carías Andino took power in 1932. His military rule ended in 1949, but military leaders continued to exercise control until 1981 when elections restored civilian rule. The

Copyright © 1994. Brigham Young University. Printed in the USA. All rights reserved. It is against the law to copy, reprint, store in a retrieval system, or transmit any part of this publication in any form by any means for any purpose without written permission from the Publications Division of the David M. Kennedy Center for International Studies, Brigham Young University, PO Box 24538, Provo, UT 84602–4538. *Culturgrams* are available for more than 125 areas of the world. To place an order, to receive a free catalog, or to obtain information on traveling abroad, call toll free (800) 528–6279.

elections of 1989 marked the third free election in a decade, as well as the first peaceful transfer of power to an opposition political party in half a century. Rafael Leonardo Callejas took office in 1990, but the military continued to exercise a great deal of power and influence in the country. Callejas was not allowed by constitution to run for a second consecutive term, so two new candidates vied for the presidency in 1993. Carlos Roberto Reina was elected and took office in 1994. He promised to attack corruption and attempt to reduce the military's budget.

THE PEOPLE

Population

There are about 5.1 million people in Honduras, a population that is growing annually at 2.8 percent. Ninety percent of the population is *mestizo* (a mixture of Indian and Spanish), while only 7 percent is native Indian. Two percent is black and 1 percent is white (of European descent). The Indians live mostly in isolated regions such as La Mosquitia (in the east). The principal Indian ethnic groups include Misquito, Payas, and Xicaques. The blacks are primarily Garinagu. There is also a group known as the Sambos—a mixture of black and Indian inhabitants.

Language

Spanish is the official and dominant language. However, some Garinagu speak Garífuna, and the Indians speak a number of different indigenous languages. Creole English is spoken by about 10,000 people, mostly on the Bay Islands. English is a required course in secondary schools, but few people are fluent. Major hotels have bilingual employees.

Religion

About 88 percent of the population is Roman Catholic, but various other Christian groups are active and freedom of religion is guaranteed by law. Protestantism is growing rapidly with a variety of churches present in even the smallest towns. The Catholic church has had a great deal of influence on the people and culture. Many public holidays center on religious themes. Each town and city has a patron saint for whom it celebrates an annual festival.

General Attitudes

In Honduras, as in much of Latin America, social philosophies such as fatalism, *machismo*, and *hora latina*, are evident. Fatalism exists partly due to the difficulties of life in poverty; people are aware of limited social mobility and try to accept their position in life as something they cannot control. This attitude may seem counterproductive, but it can actually relieve frustration and allow people to enjoy what is good in life rather than focus on what is unpleasant. *Machismo* is indicative of a male dominated society in which women are expected to remain submissive. Women only make up about 18 percent of the formal labor force, and most rural women do not work outside the home. *Hora latina* refers to the concept of time and schedules. Since individual needs are more important than schedules, being late for appointments or social events is a way of life. For example, a person would not hesitate to stop and talk to a friend on the way to an appointment, even if it means being late. This can be important even in urban settings, where punctuality is a bit more important, because personal contacts and relationships are often necessary to get things accomplished in business and government. Social events may have an indicated starting time, but hosts and guests understand this is very flexible; being several minutes or an hour late is not uncommon.

Christian beliefs hold great value for the people, as do their ties to the land and to agriculture. Environmental issues are important to Hondurans.

Personal Appearance

Western-style clothing is generally worn. Shorts are rarely worn in public except in the coastal areas where it is hot and humid. Men often wear a *guayabera* (a decorative shirt of light fabric that hangs to just below the waist) instead of a formal shirt and tie. Urban women are especially stylish with respect to clothing, hair, and makeup. In rural areas, where the majority are poor, many people wear second-hand clothing imported from the United States; men wear leather or rubber sandals and women wear thongs. Throughout Honduras, T-shirts with English slogans are popular, even though the wearer probably does not speak English. The wealthy wear the latest Western fashions.

CUSTOMS AND COURTESIES

Greetings

A handshake is an appropriate greeting for men and urban women. Middle and upper class women kiss male and female friends on the cheek. Rural women greet one another by placing one hand on the upper arm of the other woman. The *abrazo* is a warm embrace shared by close friends and relatives. When meeting someone for the first time, a person's official title or *Señor, Señora,* or *Señorita* (Mr., Mrs., or Miss) is used. People also use *Usted* (the formal version of "you") in Spanish when meeting someone for the first time. When entering a room, it is customary to give a general greeting. When meeting a smaller group of people, one should greet each person individually and also say good-bye to each. While passing someone in the street, one says *Adíos.* Literally, that means "Good-bye," but it is meant as a general greeting in this case. One always says *Buen provecho* (Enjoy your meal) at the table before a meal. A person approaching or passing a table in a restaurant also says *Buen provecho* to the people at the table.

Gestures

Hand and body language are important to communication. Waving the index finger is often used to say, "No." Clasping both hands indicates strong approval. Touching the finger below the eye warns caution. And a hand placed under an elbow usually means someone is thought to be stingy. People often point with their lips. Also, to express enthusiasm, they place their middle finger and thumb together and shake their hand, producing a snapping noise. Beckoning is done by waving the hand with the palm facing down. To beckon with the index finger would be rude.

Visiting

Visiting is a common pastime Saturday afternoons and Sundays, and it is often done unannounced. Hondurans are courteous and generous to guests in their homes. Guests are often offered juice, soda, or coffee and maybe some sweets. Unexpected visitors arriving at mealtime are often extended an invitation to eat with the family. Even people of humble circumstance will share whatever they have to make a guest feel welcome. If a guest does not feel like eating, the host may wrap up a little food to send home with the visitor. When leaving a home, guests are especially respectful to the head of the household and should say good-bye to each person.

Eating

Breakfast is served between 6:00 and 8:30 A.M. The main meal begins around noon. A lighter evening meal is eaten sometime between 6:00 and 8:00 P.M. Meals are eaten in a leisurely manner. Both hands (but not elbows) are kept above the table. People customarily use the fork in the right hand and knife in the left, although rural people might also use pieces of corn *tortillas* instead of utensils. Families don't necessarily eat together due to lack of plates or table space, or simply as a matter of convenience. At finer restaurants, a 10 to 15 percent tip is appropriate, while tips are not necessarily expected at less formal restaurants.

LIFESTYLE

Family

Family ties are strong in Honduras. Members of the extended family, including grandparents and other relatives, often occupy the same household. While the father is respected as the head of the household, the mother often has the greatest responsibility and influence in everyday family life. Unfortunately, a large number of families live in poverty. Most Honduran homes do not enjoy modern conveniences. Small adobe houses with dirt floors are common in rural areas. The cities have both modern, luxurious housing, as well as poor slums. People in remote areas lack electricity and other modern conveniences.

Dating and Marriage

Girls have their formal initiation (*La Fiesta Rosa*) into social life at age 15, when elaborate parties are held to recognize their coming of age. Dating usually begins as a group activity or with the girl being accompanied by one or more other girls. Later on, couples date without accompaniment. Activities are simple and usually just involve socializing.

In rural areas, most poor people start their families without marriage, often as young as age 14. Common-law marriages are generally accepted, so many people never officially marry. Single mothers are common in all social classes, and many siblings in these families have only the one parent in common. Young, single mothers often return to live with their parents until they are older or find another spouse.

Diet

Beans, corn, *tortillas*, and rice are the staple foods. Bananas, pineapples, mangos, citrus fruits, coconuts, melons, avocados, potatoes, and yams are the most common fruits and vegetables. Special dishes include *tapado* (a stew of beef, vegetables, and coconut milk), *mondongo* (tripe and beef knuckles), *nacatamales* (pork tamales), and *torrejas* (similar to french toast and served at Christmas). *Topogios* or *charramuscas* (frozen fruit juice in a plastic bag) are popular during the summer months. Soda is also enjoyed. Coffee and coffee with milk are traditional and are usually served with the main meal of the day. Some restaurants in major cities serve pizza, hamburgers, and other North American dishes.

Recreation

Fútbol (soccer) is the national sport. Young boys play the game almost anytime, anywhere, and there is professional competition as well. In recent years, more girls have become involved in *fútbol*, but they are more likely to play basketball. Wealthy Hondurans enjoy cycle races, baseball, golf, tennis, and swimming. In villages on the north coast, men like to play dominoes after they return home from a day's work of fishing.

Holidays

Public holidays include New Year's; Day of the Americas (14 April); Labor Day (1 May); Independence Day (15 September); Birth of Morazán, the national hero (3 October); Columbus Day (12 October); Armed Forces Day (21 October); and Christmas. Independence Day is the most popular national holiday. School children practice for months in preparation for parades and programs. A popular Christmas tradition, especially in rural areas, is constructing nativity scenes. Since money is scarce, the scenes are made from scratch each year with natural resources and clay figures.

Holy Week (*Semana Santa*), which celebrates Easter, is important. During Holy Week, businesses close from Wednesday through the end of the week and people go to the beaches. Popular in Honduras, but not an official holiday, is the Day of the Child (10 September). Children receive sweets and gifts at school and adults congratulate the children when passing them on the street. Private home celebrations may also take place among the wealthy. In addition to these holidays, Honduras has community celebrations honoring patron saints and regional fiestas such as *Carnival* in La Ceiba.

Commerce

Government office hours are from 8:00 A.M. to 4:00 P.M. or 7:30 A.M. to 3:30 P.M., Monday through Friday. Private businesses operate from 8:00 A.M. to noon and 1:00 P.M. to 5:00 P.M., although some do not close at noon for the *siesta* (midday break). Banks usually close by 3:00 P.M., while post offices may remain open as late as 9:00 P.M., depending on the city. On Saturdays, most businesses close between noon and 2:00 P.M. In marketplaces and shops where prices are not posted, barter is common; otherwise prices are fixed.

SOCIETY

Government

The president is chief of state and head of government. He governs with a cabinet and serves a four-year term. The unicameral National Congress has 128 seats. Legislative elections were held in 1993 and will be held again in November 1997. All citizens are required to vote beginning at age 18. The judicial branch of government is independent. Honduras is divided into 18 departments (provinces).

Economy

The economy in Honduras is based largely on agriculture, which employs more than 60 percent of the population. Honduras is one of the poorest countries in the Western Hemisphere, and income and productivitiy are declining. While the economy generally grows at 3 percent a year, it has suffered stagnation in recent years. The most important exports are bananas, coffee, seafood, timber, cotton, sugar, and metals. Manufactured items are slowly becoming more important to the economy. Unemployment is above 15 percent. Underemployment, a condition where people do not have full-time or steady work, is above 30 percent. The currency is the *lempira* (L), but it is sometimes referred to as a *peso*.

Honduras's Human Development Index (0.472) ranks it 116 out of 173 countries. Real gross domestic product per capita is estimated at $1,470, which has increased by about 50 percent in the last generation. These figures reflect the fact that about half of all people live in poverty. Most do not earn an income sufficient for their needs, and economic prosperity is only enjoyed by the wealthiest Hondurans.

Transportation and Communication

Highways connect Tegucigalpa with some other principal cities. The people rely on buses for public transport because few own cars. Rural areas are isolated from the cities due to poor transportation and communication. Tegucigalpa, San Pedro Sula, La Ceiba, the Bay Islands, Puerto Lempira, and some villages in La Mosquitia are accessible by airplane. Private telephones are found only in major cities. Most large towns have one public telephone and a telegraph service. Many people communicate by placing messages on the radio. Mail service is slow but fairly reliable.

Education

Schooling is compulsory for six years beginning at age seven. However, while nearly all children begin their schooling, many drop out before the end—especially among the rural poor. Less than half of all children actually complete the full six years, and less than one-third advance to the secondary level. Children are often needed at home to help with farming or household chores, and having them gone all day at school can be too great a sacrifice for many families. The literacy rate is 73 percent. The National University of Honduras and some trade schools provide higher levels of learning, but only 9 percent of the population advances to those levels of study. Honduras has some of Central America's best agricultural and forestry schools.

Health

Various health challenges face Honduras, which is in the yellow fever endemic zone. Malaria is prevalent below 3,000 feet (about 900 meters), and rabies, typhoid, hepatitis, parasites, and dysentery, as well as intestinal disease, present problems for the population. A serious cholera epidemic struck the country in 1991. The infant mortality rate is 62 per 1,000, and life expectancy ranges from 65 to 68 years. Vaccinations are provided free of charge, and most people have access to them. But, while most (83 percent) Honduran children are immunized, up to half suffer from malnutrition. There are health centers in rural areas, but many villagers must walk hours to reach one. Many facilities are not equipped with medicine. Urban medical care is more adequate but still lacking by modern standards. Basic health care is subsidized throughout the country, but small fees must be paid for each visit. Poorer citizens cannot often afford prescription medicine.

FOR THE TRAVELER

A valid passport is necessary for travel to Honduras, but U.S. citizens staying for a short time do not need a visa to enter the country. Yellow fever and typhoid vaccinations are recommended, as is a shot of gamma globulin. If you plan to travel to areas with malaria, take appropriate anti-malaria medication. Water is not safe for drinking. The electrical outlets use plugs like those in the United States. Honduras offers many vacation opportunities. The Bay Islands off the north coast are popular for their excellent scuba diving and snorkeling. Honduras is also home to the famous Mayan ruins called Copán, located near the Guatemalan border. For more information, contact the Honduras Travel Information Center, Murray Hill Station, PO Box 673, New York, NY 10156. You may also wish to contact the Embassy of Honduras, 3007 Tilden Street, POD 4M NW, Washington, DC 20008. Consulates, which offer the same services as an embassy, are located in several major U.S. cities.

A *Culturgram* is a product of native commentary and original, expert analysis. Statistics are estimates and information is presented as a matter of opinion. While the editors strive for accuracy and detail, this document should not be considered strictly factual. It is a general introduction to culture, an initial step in building bridges of understanding between peoples. It may not apply to all peoples of the nation. You should therefore consult other sources for more information.

Republic of
Hungary

Boundary representations not necessarily authoritative.

BACKGROUND

Land and Climate

Hungary is a landlocked nation in central Europe. Covering 35,919 square miles (93,030 square kilometers), it is slightly smaller than Indiana. Most of the eastern part of the country is flat, but the northwestern area has rolling hills and low mountains. Almost 55 percent of the land is suitable for cultivation, allowing Hungary to be nearly self-sufficient in food. The capital, Budapest, is actually the union of two cities (Buda and Pest) lying on opposite sides of the Danube River. They united in 1872 as Budapest, once called the "Paris of the East." Today, one-fifth of Hungary's population lives in Budapest. The climate is continental, with cold winters and warm, pleasant summers. The average temperature in winter is 32°F (0°C) and in summer, 70°F to 75°F (21–24°C). There are four distinct seasons.

History

Present-day Hungary became part of the Roman empire in 14 B.C. as the province of Pannonia, but the east remained in the hands of Germanic and other tribes. In the fifth century, Magyars began migrating from the east. By the end of the ninth century, the Magyars had conquered the resident Moravians and begun permanent settlement. They were led by Árpád. Christianity was introduced by his grandson Géza, in the late 10th century. Géza's son, Stephen, became Hungary's first king in 1000 A.D., and Stephen converted the people to Christianity. The dynasty lasted until the 14th century, after which time nonnative powers controlled the area. During the Renaissance era of the 15th century, the country reached a high level of culture and political power but was conquered by the Ottoman Turks. Later, Hungary was united under the crown of the Austrian Habsburgs during their rise to world prominence between the 16th and 18th centuries. Hungarians rose in rebellion in 1848, but were defeated after two years of fighting.

In 1867, the Dual Monarchy, a sharing of power between Austrians and Hungarians in Central Europe, was established. The Austro-Hungarian Empire was shattered by heightened national awareness and desire for self-rule among the Slavic minorities. This division within the empire contributed to the beginning of World War I in 1914. In the treaty settlements following the war, Hungary became an independent republic but lost much of its former territory to its neighbors. In 1944, following Germany's invasion, Hungary fought as a German ally. After Soviet occupation and an armistice, free elections in 1945 again established a republic. But the Communist party, under heavy influence from the Soviet Union, seized power within two years and by 1949 had declared Hungary a socialist state called the People's Republic of Hungary.

Communist reformer Imre Nagy tried to change the system that emerged. He even withdrew Hungary from the Warsaw Pact and declared the country neutral in 1956. In response, the Soviet Union attacked Hungary, repressed the movement, executed Nagy, and buried him in disgrace. Until 1988, when he was forced to resign under pressure for reform, Janos Kadar was the leader of the Communist government. By October 1989, Hungary had renamed the country the Republic of Hungary and abolished the Communist monopoly on

Copyright © 1994. Brigham Young University. Printed in the USA. All rights reserved. It is against the law to copy, reprint, store in a retrieval system, or transmit any part of this publication in any form by any means for any purpose without written permission from the Publications Division of the David M. Kennedy Center for International Studies, Brigham Young University, PO Box 24538, Provo, UT 84602–4538. *Culturgrams* are available for more than 125 areas of the world. To place an order, to receive a free catalog, or to obtain information on traveling abroad, call toll free (800) 528–6279.

EUROPE

power. Imre Nagy was reburied as a national hero. In 1990, free elections were held, and Jozsef Antall became the new prime minister. During 1990, six elections completed Hungary's political transformation. Antall died in 1993, and was replaced briefly by Peter Boross. Their party, the Hungarian Democratic Forum, that had swept the Communists from power in 1990, was defeated in May 1994 elections. The Socialists, who gained the parliamentary majority in that vote, are former Communists. Gyula Horn became prime minister. He had been Foreign Minister before 1990. Horn's party received their surprising majority largely because of the people's general disillusionment with the course of economic reform. Horn promises to continue market reforms but also to meet people's basic needs.

THE PEOPLE

Population

The population of Hungary is about 10.3 million, smaller than a few years ago. In fact, rather than growing, the population is shrinking slightly. Magyars (Hungarians) are the largest ethnic group with 90 percent of the population. The Romany ("Gypsies") comprise 4 percent of the population, and also usually account for the poorest of the poor. Germans (2.6 percent), Serbs (2), Slovaks (0.8), and Romanians (0.7) comprise significant minorities. There are two million people in Budapest. When discussing foreign and domestic policy, Hungarians often mention their concerns about many native Hungarians living in surrounding countries (on territory lost after World War I). Hungarians comprize 11 percent of Slovakia's population and 9 percent of Romania's.

Language

The official language is Magyar, or Hungarian, as it is referred to in other countries. Nearly everyone (98 percent) speaks Hungarian. Magyar is part of the Finno-Ugrian group of the Uralic family of languages, which includes Estonian and Finnish. Magyar is a "vowel harmony" language. The sounds of vowels are marked by various accents and change to better agree with other vowels in a word. A word may have a completely different meaning with (or without) accents. Most minority groups also speak their own languages in addition to Hungarian.

Religion

Roughly two-thirds of the population is Roman Catholic. Various other Christian groups make up the other third, including about 20 percent Calvinists and 5 percent Lutherans. During Communist rule, religious groups were carefully regulated through a government agency. In 1990, religious freedom was granted to all. While religion does not affect daily life much, many people consider themselves devout Christians.

General Attitudes

As a nation that experienced a form of democracy before most other European nations, the new democratic Hungary is proud of its heritage. Even during the Communist regime, Hungary was considered one of the most prosperous and open countries in Eastern Europe. It was one of the first to announce sweeping reforms, and was able to accomplish them without violence or serious upheaval. The people earnestly wish to become part of an integrating Europe. Hungarians also look at past achievements and their artists and composers with pride. Franz Liszt and Bela Bartok are just two names that are well-known throughout the world. Hungarian folk music and food are also renowned.

Accompanying pride, however, is also an historical tendency for pessimism. Even if one's neighbors are worse off, a Hungarian will express doubt about his or her own future or condition. Hungarian humor incorporates pessimism, which then becomes a whimsical, light-hearted cynicism. Some say pessimism is only natural for Hungarians, who, as traditional farmers, found it bad luck to predict good harvests. Individually, Hungarians value independence, a strong and stable family, education (including good performance in school, as well as having an advanced degree), security (be it a job, home, or social benefits), property (a home, a garden, and a car), access to or ownership of summer cottages, and travel outside of Hungary. People admire professionals, but do not generally admire the wealthy.

Personal Appearance

Clothing styles in urban areas generally follow those in Western Europe, with blue jeans being the most popular among the youth. Conservative suits are worn by businessmen. Women pay particular attention to style and their appearance.

Traditional costumes are seen only in rural areas and during special celebrations. They may include intricately embroidered blouses and skirts for women, who also wear colorful hats or scarves. Each region has its specialty. The men often wear vests over loose-fitting shirts. Pants may be pleated, baggy, and less than full-length—or tight, black and tucked inside boots. Men wear a variety of hats.

CUSTOMS AND COURTESIES

Greetings

Adults commonly greet each other with a firm handshake. A man usually waits for a woman to first extend her hand. If one's hand is dirty, a wrist or elbow may be offered. Close women friends may hug and kiss each other lightly on the cheek. Polite greetings used between people include *Jó napot kivánok* (Good day), *Jó reggelt kivánok* (Good morning), and *Jó estét kivánok* (Good evening). The *kivánok* is often left off in more casual circumstances or is replaced by a person's name. Children greet older women with *Kezét Csókolom* (I kiss your hand). Men might also use this with older women to show special respect.

Popular informal greetings include *Szervusz* or *Szia*, which mean "hello." These terms are taken from the Latin *servus*, which once meant "I am here to serve you." One might follow a greeting with *Hogy vagy?* (How are you?) or another question. When addressing someone, it is polite to use the person's title (Doctor, Professor, Director) with his or her surname. People often introduce themselves by their surname first, sometimes followed by the given name. Greetings on a first-name basis are usually limited to close friends and relatives. However, adults address young people by their first names and youth address each other with first names. Urban Hungarians do not usually greet strangers on the street, but rural people will. When parting, Hungarians say *Viszontlátásra* (See you again) or simply *Viszlát* or *Szia*.

Visiting

While close friends, relatives, and sometimes neighbors may make short unannounced visits, most are arranged in advance when possible. Relatives visit one another often. First-time visits by new acquaintances are short, ending just after coffee is finished. And most weekday visits end by 11:00 P.M. because of early working hours. Rural visits end even earlier in most cases. Hungarians accompany departing guests outside.

Hungarians enjoy socializing in the home, but also frequently meet at restaurants, coffee houses and tea rooms. Guests in the home are usually offered some refreshments such as coffee, tea, fruit juice, brandy, or one of many popular regional wines. When invited to dinner, it is polite to bring a small gift of flowers, boxed chocolates, or wine. Flowers are presented in odd numbers; they remain in cellophane wrapping until the hostess puts them in the vase. The hosts will usually display the flowers in a room where the guests will be after dinner, or sometimes on the table. Hosts often remove coats for arriving guests. An informal atmosphere prevails.

Eating

Breakfast may be a light meal with only rolls and a drink, or they may be heartier and include eggs, salami, cheese, yogurt, and even hot peppers. Lunch is often the main meal in rural areas, including soup, often salad, a main dish of meat and potatoes, and dessert with coffee. In urban areas, lunch is a light meal. Dinner is the main meal for urban people, but rural people eat a light meal of cold cuts, fruit, bread or rolls, and a drink.

Hands are kept above the table, but elbows do not rest on it It is impolite to leave food on the plate. Although tap water is safe to drink, many people prefer mineral water or some other beverage. As throughout Europe, the continental style of eating is used, with the fork in the left hand and the knife remaining in the right. Tips are customary in restaurants at the same levels as the rest of Europe (10 to 15 percent).

LIFESTYLE

Family

The average Hungarian family has three people. Urban families tend to be smaller than rural ones. The cost of living is high in cities and housing is often limited. The father maintains a dominant role in the family. Both parents usually work. In fact, nearly 80 percent of all women work. Men share some household responsibilities, but traditionally take the "outside" chores (yard work, gardening, etc.). Adult children often live with their parents until married. Aging parents are generally cared for by their children, who may live in the same house or nearby. Urban families live either in small apartments or small single-family homes, while rural families have single-family homes. Most have access to modern appliances and conveniences.

Dating and Marriage

Young people like to go to movies, concerts, and theaters. They enjoy dancing, watching television, and just talking together on park benches. Many go skiing and hiking together. Most Hungarians expect to marry and raise a family. Urban newlyweds tend to be older than rural couples. Most people wait until after they have finished schooling or are working before they marry. Traditional weddings were very big three-day affairs, but these are rare today. Still, the ceremony at city hall is often followed by a lavish dinner. With housing in short supply, young couples must often live with parents for their first few years of marriage.

Diet

Hungary's location in central Europe makes it a prime gathering point for many ethnic culinary specialties. One of the most famous Hungarian specialties is *goulash*, a stew of meat, potatoes, onions, and paprika. Paprika is a familiar spice in many dishes. Pork is the most common meat in the Hungarian diet, but chicken is also popular. Side dishes include noodles, potatoes, and dumplings. A cabbage and vinegar salad is popular with main meals. Except for certain seasonal varieties, vegetables and fruits are in ample supply year-round. Bread and pastries are available in a wide variety. Fish soup *(halászlé)*, stuffed paprika, stuffed chicken, and various kinds of strudel and pancakes are all part of the diet. Hungary is also proud of its many wines.

Recreation

Hungary's most popular sport is soccer. Other important sports include swimming, tennis, fencing, and sailing. Hunting and fishing are popular activities as well. In their leisure time, many Hungarians like to take walks, visit parks or local museums, attend concerts, watch television, or work outside in the garden. They meet in town for afternoon tea or an ice cream treat. For vacations, many like to go to resort spas and baths. For the longer vacation, families often go to Lake Balaton. Many also travel to neighboring countries.

Hungary was once known as a nation of horsemen, especially for the time when the Hussars (15th century light cavalry) were famous for their horsemanship. Today, horses are used mostly in the tourist industry, but some Hungarians enjoying riding them for recreation.

Hungarians consider their performing arts companies, art galleries, and other cultural institutions to be national treasures, and they attend when possible. Hungarian folk music and dancing are still very popular. The youth also enjoy modern music.

Holidays

Public holidays include New Year's Day, War of Freedom Day (15 March, a day marking the 1848 rebellion and war), Easter (Sunday and Monday), Labor Day (1 May), Pentacost, St. Stephan's Day (20 August), National Holiday (23 October, in honor of the 1956 uprising), and Christmas (25–26 December). In addition, local festivals commemorate various folk or religious events throughout the year. At Easter, it is customary in some places for boys to "sprinkle" girls with water or cologne as a sign that the girl is a flower that should not fade. Also popular at this time are elaborately painted Easter eggs. St. Stephan's Day celebrates the harvest and honors the first king of Hungary.

Commerce

Businesses open around 8:00 A.M. and remain open until 6:00 P.M. Some close for an hour at lunch. Many, but not all, businesses are open on Saturday until 2:00 P.M. Produce stands often operate on sidewalks, and open air markets are found in most towns. Produce, fresh bread, and other items are available at these markets. People shop often for fresh produce and dairy products, which are easily obtained at neighborhood stores. Supermarkets are located in large cities. Formalities are important in business dealings. People tend to use formal names, discuss business politely, and treat people with respect. Refreshments are usually served. Important business discussions may be followed by an invitation to dinner, regardless of the progress made in the meeting.

SOCIETY

Government

Hungary has an elected president (Arpad Goncz) as chief of state, and a prime minister (Gyula Horn) as head of government. Parliament has one house, which is called the *Országgyulés* (national assembly); it has 386 seats. The voting age is 18. Hungary has 38 counties.

Economy

Because of its fertile soil, Hungary was mostly an agricultural country before World War II. After the Communist party came to power, a detailed plan for industrialization was implemented and industry now accounts for 40 percent of the gross national product. Important natural resources include bauxite, coal, and natural gas. While Hungary's industrial sector still uses old technology, it is seen as a key to reviving the economy under a free market approach. Hungary welcomes foreign investment and trade in order to build its economy and increase its hard currency reserves. A stock market was established in 1990. The currency is the *forint* (Ft).

The switch from a centralized and government-subsidized economy has been difficult for Hungary's citizens, who now face higher prices and taxes. Despite economic advances that encourage private enterprise, the economy is having some trouble with the transition to a free market. Unemployment is about 11 percent and inflation is 30 percent. Although the government is selling all state-owned small businesses, it continues to subsidize larger ventures. This has contributed to a budget deficit and a 23 percent drop in gross domestic product (GDP) since 1989. The standard of living has also fallen.

Nevertheless, Hungary is performing better than some other former Communist countries and there is hope for a bright future. Strong foreign investment, stable government institutions, a booming small business sector, and a hard-working labor force are key elements that stand in Hungary's favor. The country's Human Development Index (0.887) ranks it 28 out of 173 countries. Real gross domestic product per capita is $6,116. Most people can meet basic needs, and many are able to afford the flood of consumer items now available on the market.

Transportation and Communication

Public transportation in Hungary is well developed. There is a subway in Budapest. Taxis are also available. More and more people own private cars, but public transport is still the principal mode of travel. An extensive train network serves most of the country. Some travel (mostly for tourists) is done on the Danube River. The communications system is modern, although most families do not have telephones. Most homes have a television and radio; cable television is available but expensive. There are several local broadcast channels. Radio Budapest is popular. There are two daily national newspapers and several regional papers. Magazines and other publications abound. The free press is active and striving to be competitive with foreign media companies who are investing in Hungary.

Education

Schooling is free and compulsory for all children ages six to fourteen. Most then go on to secondary schools for technical training or preparation for higher education. Teachers are well trained and students receive a solid education. Foreign languages are offered beginning in elementary school. Those who successfully complete secondary school may go on to any of the five academic, four medical, and nine technical universities in Hungary, provided they pass entrance exams. University education is free and students receive a small stipend to cover living expenses. Several other institutions of higher learning are also available. The literacy rate is 99 percent.

Health

Hungary's health care system is well organized and modern. Standards in hospitals and clinics are high. All citizens receive free care in public institutions and most medicine is paid for. Persons may also see private doctors, but must pay for this care. Health care professionals are well trained, but not necessarily well-paid. Major health hazards include pollution and, for older people, the hardships of the past 40 years. Hungary's infant mortality rate is 13 per 1,000 and life expectancy ranges between 67 and 75 years.

FOR THE TRAVELER

U.S. visitors need a valid passport to enter Hungary, but a visa is only necessary for business travelers or for persons staying longer than 90 days. Hungary has a fairly well-developed tourist industry, offering tours on horseback, on the Danube River, or by train, or stays at traditional country inns. Hotels in Budapest have good standards and English is understood in tourist areas. The country offers interesting architecture in many cities and towns, high-quality and inexpensive performing arts, sailing on Lake Balaton, mountain resorts, fine pastries, and much more. Contact the *Ibusz* Hungarian Travel Bureau (One Parker Plaza, Suite 1104, Fort Lee, NJ 07024) for the latest information and for details on travel opportunities inside Hungary. You may also wish to contact the Embassy of Hungary, 3910 Shoemaker Street NW, Washington, DC 20008.

A *Culturgram* is a product of native commentary and original, expert analysis. Statistics are estimates and information is presented as a matter of opinion. While the editors strive for accuracy and detail, this document should not be considered strictly factual. It is a general introduction to culture, an initial step in building bridges of understanding between peoples. It may not apply to all peoples of the nation. You should therefore consult other sources for more information.

Republic of
Iceland

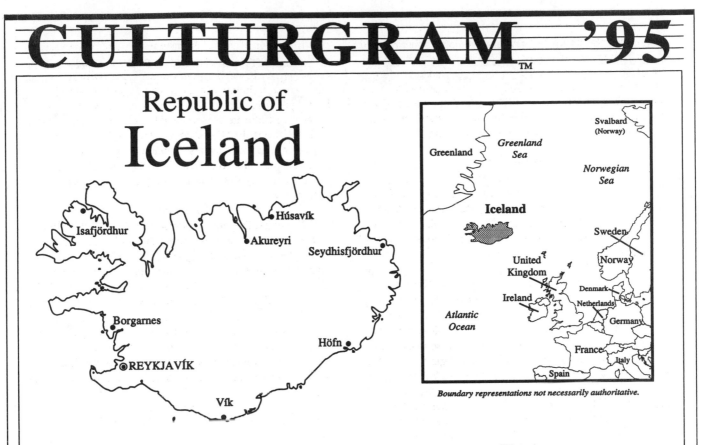

Boundary representations not necessarily authoritative.

BACKGROUND

Land and Climate

Slightly smaller in area than Kentucky, Iceland (39,768 square miles—103,000 square kilometers) is the second largest island in Europe and is surrounded by many smaller islands. The land is rugged with varied scenery. About 80 percent uninhabited, this "land of fire and ice" is one of the most active volcanic countries in the world. It is, in fact, a volcanic island, and averages one eruption every five years. Earthquakes are also frequent, but they are rarely strong enough to cause damage. Iceland has more hot springs than any other country in the world; in fact, the English word "geyser" comes from Icelandic. The uninhabited interior is a popular place for horse riding and camping. Accessible except during winter, it has many beautiful features, including glaciers, mountains, lakes, volcanoes, and even deserts.

Despite the country's northerly location, the climate is much milder than one would expect. The warm Gulf Stream nearly encircles the island. The average annual temperature in Reykjavík is 41°F (5°C). It does, however, often become bitterly cold in both summer and winter when the polar winds blow. There are two or three months of continuous daylight in the summer, while during the winter (from mid-November to January) there may only be four or five hours of daylight (10:00 A.M. to 3:00 P.M.).

History

The first permanent settlers in Iceland were Norwegian and Celtic peoples. Iceland claims the Norwegian Ingólfur Arnarson as the first settler in 874; he founded Reykjavík, the current capital. In 930, the Icelanders created the *Althing*, their national assembly, but there was no central government or monarchy. The *Althing* established laws and also served as a court. Christianity was adopted by the *Althing* in the year 1000, the same year that Leifur Eiríksson is said to have discovered America, landing at Newfoundland.

In 1262, Iceland became subject to the Norwegian crown, partly to end civil war between various local chieftains. Despite the new ruler, Iceland remained fairly autonomous. In 1380, both Iceland and Norway united with the Danish crown. Denmark introduced Lutheranism to Iceland in the 1530s, but met with stiff opposition to the Reformation. The last Catholic Bishop, Jón Arason, was beheaded in 1550 and the Lutheran Church was established. Even though today's Iceland is Lutheran, Arason is a national hero because he resisted the Danes.

By the 1600s, Denmark had established a trade monopoly with Iceland, and Iceland became little more than a Danish colony. Accordingly, the 17th and 18th centuries are now considered a dark period in Iceland's history, a time when it lost its self-government and free trade. This period had a profound influence on later political developments and is one

Copyright © 1994. Brigham Young University. Printed in the USA. All rights reserved. It is against the law to copy, reprint, store in a retrieval system, or transmit any part of this publication in any form by any means for any purpose without written permission from the Publications Division of the David M. Kennedy Center for International Studies, Brigham Young University, PO Box 24538, Provo, UT 84602–4538. *Culturgrams* are available for more than 125 areas of the world. To place an order, to receive a free catalog, or to obtain information on traveling abroad, call toll free (800) 528–6279.

EUROPE

reason why Icelanders are very nationalistic. It is also why Iceland is usually among the first nations to recognize new countries. Iceland was first to recognize the independence of Latvia, Lithuania, and Estonia in 1991.

The 18th century brought famine and economic troubles, but an independence movement did not really begin until the 1800s, when the people experienced a revival of national literature and history. When Denmark's monarchy became subject to a constitutional democracy, Iceland was given an opportunity to regain home rule. A constitution was granted in 1874, but Iceland remained responsible to Denmark.

It wasn't until 1918 that Iceland became an independent sovereign state under a common Danish king. During World War II, the United States and Great Britain helped defend Iceland, and Iceland's ties were essentially broken with Denmark. The Republic of Iceland was formally declared in June 1944 and a new constitution was adopted. Iceland developed a progressive economy and stable political system. Cooperation between political parties has always been high, because nearly all governments have been coalitions—with no one party dominating the *Althing*. Elections in 1991 brought David Oddsson of the Conservative Independence party to power as prime minister.

THE PEOPLE

Population

In terms of population, Iceland is a small country. It has about 261,000 people. The population is growing at 0.9 percent a year. Very few people emigrate to other countries. About half of the population lives in the capital, and the central part of the country is uninhabited. Icelanders are descendents of the Norwegian and Celtic peoples who settled in the ninth and tenth centuries. They are considered a homogeneous people.

Language

The official language is Icelandic. Icelanders are taught Danish and English in the primary and secondary schools, and nearly everyone can speak both of these languages. During the Viking era (8th through 10th centuries), all Nordic peoples shared a common language. After that, separate tongues evolved in the areas of present-day Norway, Sweden, and Denmark. Iceland retained the old language. In fact, modern Icelandic is more similar to ancient Norwegian than modern Norwegian is. Icelandic remained essentially unchanged through the centuries. As a result, Icelanders can read medieval Icelandic *sagas* (stories) from the "Age of Sagas" (1200–1400) with little difficulty. Because of this heritage, Icelanders enjoy tracing their ancestral roots. The *sagas* cover centuries of the history of Scandinavia and the British Isles. Through them, the lives and exploits of the Vikings and peoples that came after them are known to the world today.

Religion

The bulk of the population (over 90 percent) belongs to the state church, the Evangelical Lutheran Church. Despite the existence of a state-sponsored church, religious freedom is fully guaranteed, and other Christian churches (Roman Catholic and Protestant) have members in Iceland. Two percent of the population has no religious affiliation. Attendance at the state church is generally sparse; people usually go to church only twice a year. But while religion is not a public matter, Icelanders are privately very religious. There is a strong belief in spiritual and supernatural things, and people are quite devout.

General Attitudes

Icelanders are proud of their society, which is very egalitarian and highly literate. A person's abilities are more important than their station in life. In general, the people are known to be individualistic and independent. There is little crime and very little pollution in the country. Most areas of the country are heated almost entirely by geothermal energy produced naturally by hot springs. A source of pride for Icelanders, geothermal springs provide the country with renewable, clean energy.

Literature and language are extremely important in Iceland. Whereas many languages will adopt or adapt foreign words (often English) into their language to describe a new item or habit, Icelanders want to keep their language as pure as possible. In fact, an official committee exists for the sole purpose of creating new Icelandic words (such as for "telephone" or "computer") when necessary.

Personal Appearance

Icelanders dress well, especially when attending theaters and fine restaurants. Because the climate is generally cool, warm clothing is necessary during much of the year. Iceland is known for its woolens, especially sweaters. It is very important to dress neatly in public, and most people spend a lot of money on clothing. European fashions are most common.

CUSTOMS AND COURTESIES

Greetings

A handshake is the normal way to greet someone, along with saying *Saell* (to a man) or *Sael* (to a woman). The phrase roughly means "Blessed." A more casual greeting, especially among children, is *Halló* (Hello). All Icelanders are properly and officially called by their first name, even though they also have a last name. This applies to titles also. A woman does not change her name with marriage. A woman's last name is formed by the possessive form of her father's first name, followed by *dóttir*, meaning daughter. A man's last name is the possessive of his father's first name, followed by *son*. Names in a phone book are alphabetized by the first given name, but it is necessary to know the last name as well.

Gestures

Body language has not traditionally been important to communication in Iceland. Consequently, very few hand expressions are used during conversation. People don't normally eat on the street, with the exception of foods like ice cream and hot dogs. Smoking is prohibited in public buildings.

Visiting

It is fairly common to drop in on people unannounced or to telephone just before visiting. Truly formal invitations are rare and people are usually casual about visiting. Visitors may be offered a cup of coffee. Because society is home centered, people entertain more often in the home than going out. Due to the cold weather, a lot of time is spent indoors, and Icelanders devote plenty of time, effort, and money on making their homes pleasant. Indeed, the beautification of the home is a lifetime pursuit and there is a lot of prestige involved in creating a nice atmosphere. Icelandic homes are usually larger and better furnished than the average Scandinavian or European homes and are therefore natural places for entertaining guests.

Guests invited to dinner usually bring a gift (flowers or candy) to the hosts. At the end of a meal, or even refreshments, it is customary for the guests to shake hands with their hosts and thank them. It is not enough to simply make a comment or say thank you at the table; guests actually approach the hosts, offer the hand, and express their appreciation for the hospitality.

Eating

Breakfast is usually a light meal and includes cereal or toast with tea or coffee. Icelanders typically eat lunch around noon, and dinner between 7:00 and 8:00 P.M. The continental style of eating is followed, with the fork in the left hand and the knife remaining in the right.

At restaurants, service charges and tax are included in the bill. Before the mid-1970s, going out to eat was not popular and being a waiter or waitress was a demeaning job. Offering a tip was an insult and emphasized the waiter's position as a servant. Consequently, there is no tradition of tipping in Iceland. Since the 1970s, restaurants have increased dramatically in number and waiting tables is fully respectable. Icelanders still do not tip, but the practice would no longer be considered an insult. The increase in restaurants has also led to a wider variety of foods available in the country. Most European and Scandinavian dishes can be found in Reykjavík.

LIFESTYLE

Family

Family ties are strong and families tend to be larger than other Scandinavian families. Even though people are individualistic, family members rely heavily on each other. Because the country is small, personal ties are important and family relations play a key role. This is evidenced by the tradition of, upon meeting someone for the first time, asking, "Who are your people?" This is an attempt to place a person in a family or professional level. The initial response is to name one's parents. If they aren't known, the parents' professions might be named or the grandparents are named. Today's youth do not practice this, but their parents' generation still does.

More than 80 percent of Icelandic families own their own homes. Family patterns are changing as more women are becoming part of the work force. Though relatively young, the feminist movement is gaining power. For example, in 1983 an all-woman political party won several seats in parliament. They hold fewer seats today, but women's issues are more readily addressed than before.

Dating and Marriage

Dating begins around age 15 or 16. Going to parties and dances are among the most popular activities. The government recognizes common-law marriage, so many couples choose to live together without formal marriage. Some choose to marry at a later date.

Diet

The basics of the Icelandic diet include fish, lamb, and dairy products. Fresh fish is plentiful and includes such varieties as cod, haddock, halibut, plaice (a type of flounder), herring, salmon, and trout. Popular dishes are *hangikjöt* (smoked mutton) and *skyr* (similar to yogurt). Potatoes (usually boiled) are served with most meals. *Hangikjöt* is the traditional meal on Christmas day. In recent years, progress with greenhouse construction has made it possible for Iceland to service its need for vegetables such as tomatoes, peppers, and cucumbers. Water is safe to drink and clean throughout the country.

Recreation

Traveling and camping are favorite pastimes in Iceland. Hiking, trout and salmon fishing, swimming in pools heated by natural hot springs, soccer, skiing, and golf are other common forms of recreation. Many enjoy riding the small horses unique to Iceland. Chess is popular. Iceland is known as a bird-watcher's paradise. Merchants Holiday provides a three-day weekend that is popular for camping. Cities practically empty, as everyone heads to the countryside, especially the interior, to camp. There are many large, established campgrounds where people gather. Some also camp in more private areas.

Holidays

Public holidays include New Year's Day, Easter (Thursday through Monday), First Day of Summer (usually third Thursday in April), Labor Day (1 May), Ascension Day, Whitsunday and Whitmonday, National Day (17 June), Merchants Holiday (first Monday in August), and Christmas

(25–26 December). Christmas Eve is the most sacred and important day of Christmas. It is the evening for exchanging gifts and celebrating the birth of Christ. The 25th is a day for the big family meal and visiting, while the 26th is spent relaxing or enjoying some form of recreation.

New Year's Eve is extremely popular. There are a lot of parties, fireworks, and bonfires. These light up the dark winter night and create excitement throughout the country.

Commerce

Business hours are generally from 9:00 A.M. to 6:00 P.M., Monday through Friday. Some businesses close for one hour at midday and many stay open until 7:00 P.M. on Fridays. Workers often stay much later into the evening, working overtime to earn more money. Saturday's hours depend on the business and season. Stores usually close an hour earlier in the summer. Kiosks or small vending-type shops remain open until 11:30 P.M. All workers receive a mandatory five-week vacation each year, which they definitely take advantage of. In fact, one reason for all of the overtime is so people can afford to take a nice vacation. July is the most popular month for vacationing because it is warm. Many people also vacation abroad, especially favoring southern Europe.

SOCIETY

Government

In June 1980, Iceland selected the world's first freely elected female head of state, Vigdís Finnbogadóttir, who remains very popular. Her position is largely ceremonial and the prime minister runs the government. President Vigdís faced reelection in June 1992, but was unopposed. The *Althing* has 63 seats, shared by five parties, of which the Independence and Progressive parties are the largest. The voting age is 20. The next national elections are in April 1995.

Economy

Fish, the country's most abundant natural resource, is the most important export industry. Even manufacturing efforts tend to focus on the fishing industry; Iceland produces machinery exported for use in fish processing. Thirteen percent of the population is employed in fishing or fish processing, which accounts for about 75 percent of all export earnings. Only 1 percent of the land is suitable for cultivation; agriculture (including raising livestock) employs 6 percent of the population. There are many pastures and meadows used for livestock grazing. Sheep are the most important animals and wool is therefore a primary product.

Industrially, Iceland has a great potential for geothermal and hydroelectric power, and Iceland is developing ways to exploit these renewable resources. Aluminum and aluminum smelting have become profitable industries for the country. Other industries include publishing, cement, and diatomite. Some factories are able to use geothermal energy for power. Iceland is one of the most affluent countries in the world, known for low unemployment rates and strong economic performance. The country's Human Development Index (0.960) ranks it 11 out of 173 countries. Real gross domestic product per capita is $16,496, which has tripled in the last generation. These figures indicate that the majority of Icelanders earn a decent income and have access to economic prosperity. The currency is the *króna* (IKr—*krónur* is the plural).

Transportation and Communication

Most Icelandic families have at least one car for private transportation. In and around Reykjavík, the capital, there is also an excellent bus system. Iceland has no railroad. Some roads outside the capital are not paved, but most are passable year-round. One cannot travel inland or in certain remote areas in the winter. The communications system is modern and efficient.

Education

School attendance is compulsory for ages six to sixteen. Every child must also know how to swim to graduate from elementary school. Education has always been important to Iceland and 100 percent of the population is literate; they have the highest percentage of children enrolled in school in the world. Students learn Danish and English in school. A large percentage of youth continue their education through specialized training schools or college preparation schools, which lead to a university education. The University of Iceland is the only full university and many go abroad for advanced degrees. A small university in Akureyri offers some programs.

Health

Icelanders have one of the world's highest life expectancy rates in the world, living between 76 and 81 years. The infant mortality rate is extremely low at 4 per 1,000. All citizens have compulsory health coverage through a national system. Dental care is partially paid for by the government, although school children receive free care. There are no major health problems in the country.

FOR THE TRAVELER

While passports are required, U.S. citizens do not need visas for visits of up to three months total time in Scandinavia—Denmark, Iceland, Finland, Norway, and Sweden. No vaccinations are required. Iceland offers some unique vacation ideas. For information about travel opportunities, contact the Iceland Tourist Board (655 Third Avenue, New York, NY 10017). You may also wish to contact the Icelandic Embassy, 2022 Connecticut Avenue NW, Washington, DC 20008.

A *Culturgram* is a product of native commentary and original, expert analysis. Statistics are estimates and information is presented as a matter of opinion. While the editors strive for accuracy and detail, this document should not be considered strictly factual. It is a general introduction to culture, an initial step in building bridges of understanding between peoples. It may not apply to all peoples of the nation. You should therefore consult other sources for more information.

Republic of
Ireland
(Éire)

Boundary representations not necessarily authoritative.

E
U
R
O
P
E

BACKGROUND

Land and Climate

Covering 27,135 square miles (70,280 square kilometers), the Republic of Ireland is somewhat larger than the state of West Virginia. The Republic of Ireland covers five-sixths of the island of Ireland, which is off the northwest coast of Europe. It shares the island with Northern Ireland, which is part of the United Kingdom. The island consists of fertile, central plains surrounded by rugged coastal hills and low mountains. Some say Ireland is like a badly baked pie—crusty around the edges and soggy in the middle. No part of the country is more than 70 miles (112 kilometers) from the coast. The Shannon is the longest river. Snow falls only on a few days in winter and quickly melts because of the moderating effect of the North Atlantic Current; winters are therefore wet and mild. The coldest temperatures average 30°F to 40°F (-1–4°C). Summers are cool; the warmest month of July has an average temperature below 65°F (18°C). Ireland's dampness, fog, and rain account for the country's lush greenery.

History

Although the Irish can trace the history of their island back several thousand years, the period of the Celts offers the most famous historical record and marks the beginning of Ireland's modern history. The Celts conquered the island in the fourth century B.C. Legend has it that Saint Patrick came to Ireland in 432 A.D., bringing Christianity and converting the people. Norse Vikings invaded in 795 and established seaports in Ireland. The Norse were eventually defeated in 1014, but then the English began invading in the 12th century. In 1171, King Henry II of England forced Irish nobles to recognize his supreme rule. Over time, though, the English invaders adopted local culture and allowed the Irish some autonomy. In 1603, England established rule over all of Ireland after defeating the last major Gaelic leaders. Irish Anglicans, supported by England, excluded Catholics from controlling land and politics. In 1801, the United Kingdom of Great Britain and Ireland was established with the Act of Union, but it was not popular with Irish Catholics.

The country was devastated in the 1840s by the great potato famine; at least one million people died in five years and another two million emigrated to other countries, particularly the United States. Political conflict intensified after the famine, bringing rebellions and agitation for independence. The movement climaxed in 1921 with the signing of the Anglo-Irish Treaty. This treaty established the Irish Free State as a British dominion and allowed six northern counties (with a Protestant majority) to remain in the United Kingdom as Northern Ireland.

In 1937, a new constitution changed the country's name to *Éire* (Ireland). The country began to decrease its association with the British Commonwealth. In 1949, Ireland formally withdrew from the Commonwealth and declared itself completely independent. The Republic of Ireland has often held talks with British authorities over the question of returning

Copyright © 1994. Brigham Young University. Printed in the USA. All rights reserved. It is against the law to copy, reprint, store in a retrieval system, or transmit any part of this publication in any form by any means for any purpose without written permission from the Publications Division of the David M. Kennedy Center for International Studies, Brigham Young University, PO Box 24538, Provo, UT 84602–4538. *Culturgrams* are available for more than 125 areas of the world. To place an order, to receive a free catalog, or to obtain information on traveling abroad, call toll free (800) 528–6279.

Northern Ireland to Irish sovereignty. Except for a 1985 agreement that allows the republic a consultative role in the affairs of Northern Ireland, these talks have produced little progress. Various negotiations were held in 1991 to determine if home rule would be returned to Northern Ireland, but the talks also dealt with the issue of reunion with Ireland. No significant agreements were reached. The talks, which broke down, were revived but failed again in 1992. They continued on in relative secrecy, focusing primarily on first ending violence in Northern Ireland and terrorism by the Irish Republican Army, an outlawed group in Great Britain. Progress seemed evident in 1994 when a cease-fire was honored, but violence erupted again. Still, the various sides are continuing some discussion, if mostly out of the public eye. Outside of the issue of violence, which most people agree must stop, the question of sovereignty is sensitive. Most Protestants in Northern Ireland wish to remain part of the United Kingdom.

Due to a poor economy and various political issues, Ireland's coalition government collapsed in 1992 after a parliamentary no-confidence vote. Parliament was therefore dissolved and elections were held in November 1992. The prime minister, Albert Reynolds, retained his post but had to form a new coalition. The coalition between Reynolds's Fianna Fail (Warriors of Destiny) and the Labor Party has proven stable since then.

THE PEOPLE

Population

The population of Ireland is slightly more than 3.5 million and is growing at 0.2 percent. In the past, emigration was high, greatly reducing the population. This trend stabilized and the population grew for a time. However, as unemployment rises, so does emigration. Many young people emigrate to the United States or the United Kingdom, but a number also simply move to Dublin from rural areas. Nearly one in four people live in the metropolitan Dublin area. Several thousand people left Ireland in 1990 and 1991, although many soon returned because of the global recession. Ethnically, the people of Ireland are Celtic. There is also a strong Norman influence and a small English (Anglo-Irish) minority.

Language

Although Irish (called Gaelic) is the first officially recognized language, it is only spoken on a daily basis in the small Gaeltacht areas of the western seaboard. English, recognized as Ireland's second language, is spoken by everyone. Government documents and road signs are in both languages, and Gaelic is taught in schools. The government is trying to increase fluency in the primary language.

Religion

About 93 percent of the population is Roman Catholic. Three percent belongs to the Anglican church. The remaining 4 percent holds various other beliefs—both Christian and non-Christian—or has no religious affiliation. The Catholic church has played an important role in Ireland's cultural and political history. Freedom of religion is guaranteed.

General Attitudes

The Irish are easygoing, lighthearted, good-humored, and cheerful. They are quick-witted and have the ability to laugh at themselves. A general attitude that things will work out in the end affects their daily lives. The Catholic faith has a great influence on the values of the people and laws of the land. Traditions are important and material goods do not have the same priority as in the United States. Recent political trends have led some to call for greater liberalization in society, including greater tolerance for nontraditional lifestyles.

Some people wonder what the differences are between the people of the Republic of Ireland and those in Northern Ireland. Because both nations have similar cultural roots, many things are similar. The greatest differences have to do with religion—the majority in the Republic of Ireland are Catholic and the majority in Northern Ireland are Anglican. Political allegiances are also an important difference—the majority of the people in Northern Ireland consider themselves part of Great Britain, not Ireland.

Personal Appearance

European fashions are most common, although traditional Irish styles influence those fashions. For example, colors are more conservative than elsewhere in Europe. Earth tones and warm colors are more popular. Sweaters and other woolen items are common because of the cooler climate. Fine-quality tweeds and linens are produced in Ireland. Casual dress is acceptable in most situations, but attire worn in public is generally conservative. Light rainwear is necessary for anyone living or traveling in Ireland.

CUSTOMS AND COURTESIES

Greetings

The traditional Irish greeting *Céad míle fáilte* literally means "One hundred thousand welcomes." Visitors arriving in the country are greeted with this phrase. However, the Irish greet one another with common English phrases such as "Hello" and "How are you?" Greetings are generally accompanied by a handshake. The Irish are somewhat more reserved in their manner of greeting than U.S. citizens, but this in no way reduces the greeting's meaning or the warmth of the people.

Gestures

Most gestures used in Ireland are similar to those in the United States, although gestures that use the fingers specifically are not as common and should be avoided. Politeness is valued. Hands are not used excessively during conversation. Personal space is valued.

Visiting

The Irish are warm and hospitable, but it is not especially common to invite people to one's home for dinner. People like to have conversation in *pubs* (public houses) and on special occasions. Some say conversation is the national pastime. Many *pubs* feature folk music as entertainment. Visiting in the home takes place during holidays, especially between Christmas and New Year's Day. Parties are also popular during holidays. Because visiting is not frequent outside of holidays, it isn't customary to take a gift when invited to someone's home.

Eating

The Irish eat in the continental style, with the fork in the left hand and the knife remaining in the right. Traditional Irish dishes are hearty, simple, and delicious. In addition to Irish cuisine, European dishes are also popular in Ireland. Many types of restaurants, including U.S. fast food, are found in Ireland. "Farmhouse" restaurants feature traditional recipes. Tea kitchens serve hot drinks and homemade cakes and pastries in the afternoon. Evening meals are often served later in the evening. In restaurants, a service charge is often included in the bill. If not, a 10 to 15 percent tip is customary

LIFESTYLE

Family

Family life in Ireland is very important and families are usually strong. Extended families often live near one another. When work or study takes family members to distant parts of Ireland or to other countries, great efforts are made (such as booking flights several months in advance) to return home for family celebrations—especially Christmas.

Women working outside the home is a fairly recent trend and most women continue to stay at home. About 27 percent of the work force is comprised of women. Competitive salaries and support services for women lag behind those for men. But Ireland's president presses her agenda for greater women's equality.

Although many young families rent an apartment (*flat*) or house, most eventually own a home. In fact, home ownership is very high in Ireland. Houses are usually constructed of brick or concrete. Traditional thatched cottages can still be seen in some western areas, but these are no longer built today. Many families also have resort homes or chalets for summer vacations.

Dating and Marriage

While couples commonly married in their late 20s or later during the 1960s and 1970s, many are now marrying in their early 20s. This may be due to the fact that young people begin dating at an earlier age. Teenagers enjoy going to movies and dancing. The tradition of taking a special date to the graduation ball (similar to the "prom" in the United States) has developed in the last decade. The graduation ball calls for formal suits and dresses, a large meal, and a dance at a local hotel. Going to *pubs* is a very popular social activity for people of all ages. *Pubs*, which serve more than alcohol, are open to those under drinking age and are prized for their food and atmosphere.

Divorce is currently illegal in Ireland. An attempt in 1986 to legalize it failed. However, the government has promised to review the ban and is generally expected to put the issue to a national vote once again. The long-standing ban on divorce, like many laws in Ireland, comes from the Catholic influence. Some feel it is time to open society to a greater variety of values. But many remain committed to traditional values, evident in the fact that voters rejected a proposal in 1992 to legalize abortion. That issue will probably return to the ballots again soon.

Diet

As an agricultural country, Ireland produces many fresh vegetables. Fresh dairy products, breads, and seafood are also widely available. Potatoes are a staple food. Smoked salmon is considered an Irish specialty. Tea is the most common drink. Breakfasts are usually large, such as bacon and eggs. The main meats eaten for dinner include chicken, pork, beef, and mutton.

Recreation

The Irish are sports oriented, and most weekends include some sporting activities for the family or individual. Popular sports include the two national pastimes: Gaelic football and hurling (the women's version of hurling is called *camogie*). Hurling is played on a soccer-type field with wooden sticks and a small leather ball. Gaelic football is played with a round ball and seems like a cross between soccer and basketball. Players can touch the ball with their hands, but they cannot pick it up from the ground. The ball is punched, not thrown, and it can be kicked. Scoring is done in a soccer-type net, but points can also be made for going over the top of the goal. Soccer, rugby, sailing, cycling, golf, and horse racing are also favorite activities. Ireland's national soccer team competed in the 1994 World Cup. Fishing ("angling") is also a common recreational activity, featuring mainly trout and salmon fishing.

Holidays

The main public holidays in Ireland are New Year's Day, St. Patrick's Day (17 March), Easter (Friday through Monday), the bank holidays (the first Monday in both June and August, and the last Monday in October), Christmas, and St. Stephen's Day (26 December). St. Patrick's Day features street parades in every city, but the largest is in Dublin. In honor of Saint Patrick, Ireland's patron saint, the Irish wear a shamrock and have banquets. Some Americans, however, celebrate the day more fervently than the Irish. Christmas is the main family and social celebration. Everyone comes home from wherever they are to share a traditional meal of turkey and ham. It is a popular time for the wealthy to take a "sun" holiday in a warmer climate.

Commerce

Generally, business hours are from 9:00 A.M. to 5:00 P.M., with an hour break for lunch in all but the major cities. Banks close by 3:00 P.M. Shopping centers remain open until 9:00 P.M. on Thursday and Friday evenings.

SOCIETY

Government

The Irish Republic is headed by a popularly elected president who serves a seven-year term. The current president, Mary Robinson, was elected in 1991. Robinson is the first woman to hold the position. The president has no executive power but can use influence to affect politics in the country. A prime minister serves as head of government and holds executive power. The cabinet is drawn from members of parliament. The bicameral legislature is structured to provide both vocational and proportional representation. Only the lower house *(Dail)* is elected; elections are held every five years. All citizens older than age 18 are eligible to vote. Ireland has 26 counties.

Economy

Ireland has a small, open economy that relies heavily on trade, especially with nations of the European Community. In fact, nearly 73 percent of Ireland's gross domestic product is exported. Real gross domestic product per capita is $10,589. That figure has more than tripled in the last generation. Ireland's Human Development Index (0.925) ranks it 21 out of 173 nations. A serious unemployment problem affects 20 percent of the labor force. Still, the government has been able to drastically reduce inflation and is encouraging more exports.

While agriculture was once the main sector of the economy, only 15 percent of the population is now employed in it, and it is less able to generate export earnings. Instead, a diversified economy now relies more heavily on industry, including textiles, chemicals, and machinery. In agriculture, animal husbandry and dairy farming are important. Key crops include potatoes, sugar beets, turnips, barley, and wheat. Ireland is generally self-sufficient in foodstuffs, although fruits and some other items must be imported. The currency is the *punt* (£Ir).

Transportation and Communication

Buses are the most common form of public transportation. They are efficient within and between cities. On double-decker buses, the upper deck is usually used by smokers, although people can sit anywhere they please. Taxis are expensive and not regulated by the government. Irish rail systems provide links to major cities. Nearly all roads are paved and in good condition. Vehicles travel on the left side of the road. Although the communications system is small, it is modern and efficient. There are several radio and television stations in Ireland. A variety of daily newspapers are published throughout the country.

Education

The Irish constitution recognizes that parents have the freedom to provide for the education of their children, either in their own homes, in private schools, or in schools established by the state. The government provides free education in primary and secondary schools and gives substantial aid to universities and other institutions of post-secondary education. Schooling is compulsory between ages four and fifteen, and about two-thirds of all children are still in school full-time at age sixteen.

Primary schools are managed by local boards composed of parent representatives, teaching staff, and relevant religious authorities. To be accepted as a pupil in secondary school, a child must be at least 12 years old and have completed primary education. Following secondary school, one may attend vocational or technical colleges, or a university if the proper examinations are passed. Ireland's literacy rate is about 99 percent.

Health

Well-equipped medical facilities are located throughout Ireland. The state provides free comprehensive health service to those unable to meet the costs of their medical needs. Medical services are free to persons with infectious diseases and to children suffering from certain long-term conditions. The population is generally very healthy. The infant mortality rate is 8 per 1,000. Life expectancy averages between 72 and 78 years.

FOR THE TRAVELER

For U.S. citizens, a visa is not necessary for trips of up to three months, but a valid passport is required. Citizens of some nations must obtain a visa upon arrival, while others must apply in advance. In Ireland, accommodations for tourists vary from bed and breakfast establishments to castle hotels. There are also a number of special travel packages offered by the Irish Tourist Board *(Bord Fáilte)*. Dual-voltage appliances and a plug adaptor kit will be necessary to use electrical outlets. For more detailed information on travel opportunities to Ireland, contact the Irish Tourist Board (345 Park Avenue, New York, NY 10154–0180). You may also wish to contact the Embassy of Ireland, 2234 Massachusetts Avenue NW, Washington, DC 20008. Consulates, which offer the same services as the embassy, are located in Boston, Chicago, New York, and San Francisco.

A *Culturgram* is a product of native commentary and original, expert analysis. Statistics are estimates and information is presented as a matter of opinion. While the editors strive for accuracy and detail, this document should not be considered strictly factual. It is a general introduction to culture, an initial step in building bridges of understanding between peoples. It may not apply to all peoples of the nation. You should therefore consult other sources for more information.

Italy

(Italian Republic)

Boundary representations not necessarily authoritative.

BACKGROUND

Land and Climate

Covering 116,305 square miles (301,230 square kilometers), Italy, including the islands of Sardinia and Sicily, is slightly larger than Arizona. Italy surrounds two independent nations, San Marino and Vatican City. San Marino has been independent since the fourth century. Vatican City was the Papal States, protected by France, in the 19th century. It was occupied by Italy in 1870, but recognized as the sovereign State of Vatican City in 1922.

Italy is shaped like a boot. The "heel" and some coastal areas are fairly low in elevation, but the country is generally mountainous. The Italian Alps and the Dolomite mountains lie along the northern border, and the Apennines form a spine down the peninsula. Sicily and Sardinia are also rocky or mountainous. The Po River basin to the north holds some of Italy's richest farmland and most of its heavy industry. Agricultural areas in the south are subject to droughts. The climate is temperate. Summers are moderately hot (cooler in the north). Winter is cold in the north, cool around Rome, and mild and rainy in the south. Summers in the south can be very hot (up to 100°F or 38°C).

History

Italy's early history is also the early history of Western civilization in that much of the West's culture comes from the Italian peninsula. Although the area's history dates back several thousand years, one of the first civilizations to flourish was that of the Etruscans between the eighth and second centuries B.C. They influenced mostly central Italy and later the Roman Empire. Before the Romans became prominent, Greek civilization dominated the south. Rome adopted much of the Greek culture after it conquered the Greek empire. Rome became a major power after 400 B.C. and expanded throughout the Mediterranean region. The Roman Empire's impact on modern legal, social, political, and military structures can be seen throughout Western nations. By the fifth century A.D., the western Roman Empire had fallen to a number of invasions. The peninsula was then divided into several separate political regions. In addition to local rulers, parts of Italy were ruled by the French, Spanish, and Austrians at various times. The Italian peninsula marked the center of many artistic, cultural, and architectural revolutions, including the great Renaissance of the 15th and 16th centuries.

Risorgimento, the Italian unification movement, began in the 1800s. National unification was declared in 1861 by the first Italian parliament in Turin. A king (Victor Emmanuel) was named and unification was completed in 1870 when Rome was unified with the rest of the area.

Italy had a fascist dictatorship under Benito Mussolini from 1922 to 1943 and initially aided Hitler in World War II. In 1943, the fascists were overthrown and Italy supported the Allies. A republic was established through elections in 1946. The monarchy was officially abolished, King Victor Emmanuel III having abdicated ahead of a national referendum. The 1970s were marked by political violence and terrorism. During the 1980s, conflicts within the coalition governments led

EUROPE

Copyright © 1994. Brigham Young University. Printed in the USA. All rights reserved. It is against the law to copy, reprint, store in a retrieval system, or transmit any part of this publication in any form by any means for any purpose without written permission from the Publications Division of the David M. Kennedy Center for International Studies, Brigham Young University, PO Box 24538, Provo, UT 84602–4538. *Culturgrams* are available for more than 125 areas of the world. To place an order, to receive a free catalog, or to obtain information on traveling abroad, call toll free (800) 528–6279.

to frequent collapses of the government. Political changes in Eastern Europe led Italy's powerful Communist party to consider changing its name and structure to maintain voter loyalty. This came at a time when voting patterns (1990) were shifting to favor such parties as the Social Democrats.

Elections in April 1992 hurt the ruling coalition but failed to bring a strong government to power. The proportional system of voting, originally designed to prevent totalitarianism, was blamed for consistently bringing weak coalitions to power. On its 16th vote in May 1992, parliament finally chose Oscar Luigi Scalfaro, a Christian Democrat, as president. Political stability could still not be achieved, as the country was soon rocked by dozens of political scandals. Numerous top officials resigned, including the prime minister, and charges of past corruption became even more widespread. By 1994, 6,000 individuals were under investigation for corruption. At the same time as this serious crisis, voters were asked to determine whether the proportional system of voting for the Senate should be replaced by a majority system. Turnout was high for the April 1993 referendum and over 80 percent of voters supported the change, among other proposed revisions to Italy's political structure.

In May 1993, a new prime minister (Carlo Azeglio Ciampi) committed the government to political reform and promised to honor voter wishes. As the corruption scandals spread, Ciampi resigned in January 1994. Parliament was dissolved and early elections under the new system were called. On promises of running a clean government and stimulating the economy, Silvio Berlusconi's Forza Italia party won the elections in March. With his party's ties to neo-Fascists and the separatist Northern League, it was difficult for Berlusconi to form a government. In May 1994, the last obstacles were cleared, and Berlusconi formally became prime minister. He disavowed any neo-Fascist views and promised to honor Italy's desire for true democracy.

THE PEOPLE
Population
The population of Italy is 58 million and is growing at 0.2 percent annually. Most people are ethnic Italians, although there are small groups of ethnic Germans and French, as well as Slovene-Italians and Albanian-Italians.

Language
Italian is the official language, although there are different dialects from city to city. The Florentine and Roman dialects had a major influence on modern Italian. There are significant French and German-speaking minorities, and Slovene is spoken by some. Ladin is spoken by an ethnic minority in southern Tyrol. Many Italians are bilingual.

Religion
Nearly all Italians are Roman Catholic, although religious devotion is often neglected. Attendance at services is not high and secularism is more appealing to many segments of society. At the same time, many Catholics are finding alternate ways to worship (through pilgrimages, informal gatherings, praying at shrines, and so forth). The Catholic church does,

however, wield significant social and even political influence in Italy. Vatican City, home of the Roman Catholic pope and headquarters for the Roman Catholic church, is located within Rome.

General Attitudes
Italians in the warm south enjoy a leisurely life and take their time to accomplish business. In contrast, those of industrialized northern Italy feel more pressure and view time as something not to be wasted. There are some tensions between the people of the north and south. Many in the more prosperous north feel they are too heavily taxed to subsidize special projects in the south. Those in the south often resent the higher incomes and better employment rates of the north. These tensions have led to political movements calling for a more federated system, where regions have more autonomy and are less dependent on the central government.

Even as many people favor greater political separation, Italy's culture is becoming less diverse. Regions are losing their cultural identity such that people are becoming less Milanese, Roman, Sicilian, and so forth, but more Italian. Television and other media unite regions so their identities—dialects and traditions—are melting into one. Also, as standards of living rise and traditions disappear, social relations suffer and people find less time for one another. Rural areas are less affected than the cities, but life is slowly changing in the countryside as well.

Personal Appearance
Italians believe it is important to dress well at all times, regardless of where one goes. Worn, dirty, or sloppy clothing is seldom seen. Dark glasses are not worn inside buildings. Older women generally wear dresses, but the youth follow European fashion trends. In fact, Italy is a major center of the European fashion industry.

CUSTOMS AND COURTESIES
Greetings
In Italy, guests are always introduced first. The handshake is the most common greeting. If one's hand is dirty, he may offer a forearm or finger instead, or simply apologize for not shaking hands. Friends say *Ciao* (Hi or Good-bye) as an informal greeting. Other terms include *Buon giorno* (Good day) and *Buona sera* (Good evening). Persons of the same gender often walk arm in arm in public. Good friends may appear to greet each other with a kiss on both cheeks. Actually, friends touch cheeks and "kiss the air."

Gestures
The mouth should be covered when a person yawns or sneezes. Men remove their hats when entering buildings. It is impolite to remove one's shoes in the presence of others. Italians are known for their use of hand gestures during conversation, especially in the south. Hands are often used in communication instead of words. A common gesture is rubbing the thumb rapidly against the fingers to indicate money. A finger placed under the eye and pushed down slightly on the skin says someone is smart or clever. In some areas of the south, "no" might be indicated by nodding the head up. There

are so many gestures that there is actually a dictionary of Italian gestures.

Visiting

Italians enjoy visiting one another, especially on holidays and Sundays. Because schedules are becoming busier, visits are usually planned in urban areas. In villages, where life is less hectic, people are also used to unannounced visits among friends and neighbors. Guests might be offered coffee, cake, ice cream, or drinks. Guests invited to dinner often take a bottle of good wine, a box of chocolates, or flowers to the host. It is customary to give an odd, not even, number of flowers. Chrysanthemums, used to decorate graves, are not given. Unless they are told otherwise, guests wait for the hosts to sit before they are seated, and they also wait for the hosts to begin eating before they eat.

Persons visiting before supper are generally expected to stay for the meal. Not staying may be considered impolite, especially in the south. In the evening before supper or on holidays, Italians enjoy taking a walk in town.

Eating

When eating with guests, Italians do not usually hurry; a meal may last one to four hours. Regular family meals are much shorter. Common discussion topics during meals include soccer, politics, family matters, business, and local events. Compliments on the home and meal are appreciated by the hosts. It is appropriate for guests to give some attention to children in the family.

The continental style of eating is used, with the fork in the left hand and the knife remaining in the right. During the meal, a person's hands are kept above the table; to have hands in the lap is improper. At the table, it is impolite to stretch, even if the meal is over. Utensils are placed parallel to each other on the plate when a person is finished eating. A person does not leave the table before everyone is finished eating. Guests do not volunteer to help clean up. When eating at restaurants, a service charge is often included in the bill, but it is appropriate to also leave a small tip for the waiter.

Italian families have traditionally eaten lunch together. Stores would close so employees could go home. However, with more two-income families and fewer businesses closing for lunch, this tradition is disappearing—especially in large cities. But where possible, families try to get together for lunch. Workers who don't go home may take advantage of cafeterias provided by their companies. Families try to at least sit down together for supper.

LIFESTYLE

Family

Strong, traditional ties bind the Italian family together. Family association is of great importance. Parents try to help their children, even as adults, when necessary. For example, they might help them buy a home or pay for an apartment—even if it means a sacrifice for the parents. In the north, most families live as nuclear units and the average family has one or two children. In the south, families are larger and many generations often live in the same town or house. Urban dwellers generally reside in apartments, while houses are common in suburbs and rural areas. A faster pace of life is affecting the extended family. With more family members working, fewer families can care for their elderly members. Extended families don't get together as often, and fewer are living near each other. Of course, when it is possible to be together or to help each other, Italians enjoy strong ties and honor their family obligations.

Dating and Marriage

Dating is much the same as in other Western countries and is done either in groups or as couples. Dancing and going to movies are frequent activities. A man will rarely marry before he has finished his education and found employment. Therefore, engagements can last several years. Marriage ceremonies follow general Catholic traditions. Divorce is now only granted after at least three years of legal separation.

Diet

An Italian breakfast is very light, consisting of a cup of coffee (warm milk for children), cookies *(biscotti),* and a roll. Lunch, the main meal, is around 1:00 P.M. It usually includes three courses: pasta, fish or meat, and vegetables. In the north, pasta or rice is part of every main meal. Pasta is dominant in the south. A simple salad (lettuce and tomatoes) is served with the second course (meat dish). Salad dressing is simply oil and vinegar, without spices. A light dinner is eaten in the evening. Wine is a common drink at meals and is also widely used in cooking. Meat and tomato sauces are popular with various types of pasta. Veal is a favorite meat. Italian pizza is not the same as American pizza and differs from region to region. Contrary to popular belief in North America, spaghetti and meatballs is not a typical Italian meal. Pasta is a course by itself and meat is served afterwards. Cheese is important in the diet, and there are literally hundreds of different cheeses, including the popular mozzarella and Parmesan.

Recreation

For recreation, Italians go to the beach, the country, the movies, a dance, or to a sports event. Soccer is by far the most popular sport. The World Cup competition is followed by avid fans. Italy has won the World Cup three times; its national soccer team competed in the 1994 World Cup. Bicycling, horse racing, skiing, tennis, boxing, fencing, swimming, and track and field are also popular. Recently, basketball and American football have attracted an Italian following. Italians also enjoy many cultural events. Their country has been a birthplace and center of the arts for centuries, shaping art movements throughout Europe and the world. To socialize any time of day, many Italians go to a bar. A bar is more like a coffee shop; it has a light, open atmosphere. People can get coffee or drinks, both of which are taken standing at a counter, not sitting at a table.

Holidays

Italians celebrate most major Catholic holidays, as well as some national holidays. These include New Year's Day; Epiphany (6 January); Easter (including Easter Monday); Liberation Day (25 April), which commemorates Italy's liberation in World War II; Labor Day (1 May); the Anniversary of the Republic (2 June); the Assumption of the Virgin Mary (15 August); All Saints Day (1 November); Immaculate Conception (8 December); Christmas; and St. Stephen's Day (26 December). Celebrations honoring local patron saints vary according to region, and various festivals are also held throughout the year.

Commerce

The Italian work schedule is from 8:00 or 9:00 A.M. to 1:00 P.M. and from 3:00 to 6:00 or 7:00 P.M., Monday through Friday. Government offices close by 2:00 P.M. Many Italians work six days a week. Grocery stores close one afternoon of the week and barber shops close on Mondays. Businesses are generally closed on Sunday.

SOCIETY

Government

Italy's government has a president, a prime minister, a bicameral parliament, and a Council of Ministers. The prime minister (the leader of the largest party in parliament or leader of a coalition of parties) and the Council of Ministers govern the nation. Parliament's lower house, the Chamber of Deputies, has 630 seats. The upper house, the Senate, has 326 (11 of which are filled by Senators for Life). The country is divided into 20 regions, some of which would like to have greater autonomy from the central government in Rome. Except in senatorial races, where the voting age is 25, all citizens older than 18 may vote. Because so many small parties have seats in parliament, it has traditionally been difficult for one party to have a majority. Most governments have necessarily been coalitions, often of opposing parties. Cooperation often broke down, along with the government. With Italy's new system, Forza Italia was able to capture a majority in the Chamber of Deputies and a substantial voting block in the Senate. Communists (now called the Democratic Party of the Left) have considerable power in the Senate. As the country's 53rd government since World War II, it hopes to last longer than most of its predecessors.

Economy

The national economy is based on agriculture in the south and industry in the north. Before World War II, agriculture was the backbone of the economy; it now employs less than 10 percent of the labor force. Still, agricultural products are important and help Italy to be nearly self-sufficient in food production. Italy is one of the world's largest wine producers and a major producer of cheese and wool. Other important crops include wheat, potatoes, corn, rice, fruits, and olive oil. Italy is a major steel and iron producer; industry accounts for over one-third of the gross national product (GNP). Tourism is also a vital source of revenue. Numerous museums, art galleries, historical sites, beautiful beaches, mountains, and lakes attract many tourists each year.

The economy enjoyed steady annual growth (2–3 percent) before the recession in 1991–92. Growth since then has been low, compounded by the social crisis and Italy's need to make policy changes in order to come in line with European Union treaty requirements. The country's Human Development Index (0.924) ranks it 22 out of 173 countries. Real gross domestic product per capita is $15,890, which has more than tripled in the last generation. Most people earn a decent income and enjoy a standard of life consistent with Italy's standing as one of the world's seven major industrialized countries. The currency is the Italian *lira* (L).

Transportation and Communication

The principal means of public transportation are buses and trains, which are both punctual and inexpensive. Most households have at least one car. Rome has a subway, and taxis are available in all cities. There is also a domestic air system. The surrounding seas are also used for transportation of goods and people. The communications system is modern and extensive, but is not always well maintained. Mail delivery is also at times not reliable. There are numerous radio and television stations as well as newspapers.

Education

School attendance is compulsory from ages six to fourteen. Classes are held Monday through Saturday. Education is a serious matter, and most young people spend a great deal of time doing homework. The literacy rate, which is defined as the percent of people older than age 15 who can read and write, is 97 percent. The oldest university in Europe was founded in Bologna in the 12th century. Italy has more than 30 universities and institutes of higher learning.

Health

Health care services are coordinated through government agencies. Individuals can freely choose their family physician; the government pays for most services. Private care is also available, but the patient must pay for it. Italians enjoy a high life expectancy rate that averages between 74 and 81 years. The infant mortality rate is 8 per 1,000.

FOR THE TRAVELER

A visa is not necessary for stays of up to three months, but a valid passport is required. No immunizations are required. Dual-voltage small appliances or voltage converters and plug adaptors are necessary to use electrical outlets. Italy has long been a favorite travel destination and there are many different things to see and do. From Turin to Venice and from Rome to Sicily, one can experience cultural events, historical sites, and enjoyable resorts. Care should be taken in some larger cities against car thieves and pickpockets. For detailed information about travel opportunities, contact the Italian Government Travel Office (630 Fifth Avenue, New York, NY 10111). You may also wish to contact the Embassy of Italy, 1601 Fuller Street NW, Washington, DC 20009.

A *Culturgram* is a product of native commentary and original, expert analysis. Statistics are estimates and information is presented as a matter of opinion. While the editors strive for accuracy and detail, this document should not be considered strictly factual. It is a general introduction to culture, an initial step in building bridges of understanding between peoples. It may not apply to all peoples of the nation. You should therefore consult other sources for more information.

Jamaica

Boundary representations not necessarily authoritative.

BACKGROUND

Land and Climate

Jamaica is part of the Greater Antilles, a chain of islands that forms the northern boundary of the Caribbean Sea. Its nearest neighbor is Cuba (about 90 miles or 144 kilometers to the north). Jamaica is only 51 miles (81.6 kilometers) across at its widest point. Covering 4,243 square miles (10,990 square kilometers), it is just smaller than Connecticut. Eighty percent of the island is mountainous. Less than 20 percent is suitable for continuous cultivation. Jamaica has a tropical maritime climate, but rainfall varies depending on the region. The average annual rainfall is 32 inches (813 millimeters). The rainy seasons occur in May and October. Hurricanes are possible from June to November. Hurricane Gilbert destroyed or damaged 20 percent of all Jamaican homes in 1988. The tropical island climate prevents extreme temperature variations, and it is generally 80°F to 90°F (26–32°C) on the northern coast. Jamaica's capital, Kingston, is a large port city in the south.

History

Jamaica's original inhabitants were the Arawak Indians, who called the island Xaymaca, meaning "land of wood and water." Columbus landed on the island in 1494. Because of the harsh life imposed on them by settlers, the Arawaks were virtually wiped out within a few decades of Spanish colonization. The Spanish occupied the island until 1655, when it was captured and colonized by the English. By the late 17th century, the English had established sugarcane plantations and were importing large numbers of slaves from Africa. Slavery was abolished in 1838. Some Spaniards stayed in Jamaica, having fled to the hills to fight the British. Over time the Spanish mixed with the African peoples. Today this small group is called the Maroons, a people that has some political autonomy within Jamaica.

From the 1860s, Jamaica was a British crown colony rather than just a colonial possession. During the 1930s, people began to call for self-determination. In 1938, serious social unrest was fomented by long-standing injustices and labor problems. Alexander Bustamante, aided by Norman Manley, championed the cause of the workers and sparked important social change. The two also formed today's key political parties. In 1944, a new constitution was written, ending rule by the British crown colony government and granting adult suffrage. Jamaica remained under nominal British rule, however, until it gained full independence in 1962. A socialist government ruled in the 1970s before being replaced by a conservative government in the 1980s under Edward Seaga. In 1989, socialists again took control through national elections and promised to tackle the country's foreign debt. Seaga challenged the incumbent prime minister, P. J. Patterson, in 1993 elections, but Patterson won in a landslide. He heads the People's National Party.

THE PEOPLE

Population

The current population of Jamaica is just over 2.5 million. It is growing at 0.9 percent annually. The majority of people are Black African (76 percent). Afro-Europeans (15 percent) and Afro-East Indians plus East Indians (3 percent) make up significant minorities. There are whites of European descent (3 percent), some Chinese, and other groups as well. More than 50 percent of the people live in urban areas. Kingston is the largest city and Montego Bay is the second largest. Because of heavy emigration, nearly as many Jamaicans live

Copyright © 1994. Brigham Young University. Printed in the USA. All rights reserved. It is against the law to copy, reprint, store in a retrieval system, or transmit any part of this publication in any form by any means for any purpose without written permission from the Publications Division of the David M. Kennedy Center for International Studies, Brigham Young University, PO Box 24538, Provo, UT 84602–4538. Culturgrams are available for more than 125 areas of the world. To place an order, to receive a free catalog, or to obtain information on traveling abroad, call toll free (800) 528–6279.

outside of Jamaica as on the island. Most of these expatriates live in England and the eastern United States.

Language

English is the official language of Jamaica. However, *Patois* (Creole), a combination of English and some African languages, is spoken in rural areas and is gaining popularity in urban areas. Most Jamaicans can speak or understand *Patois*, but it is not a written language. Jamaican speech, even in English, has a distinctive rhythmic/melodic quality.

Religion

Most Jamaicans are Christians, and all major denominations are represented on the island. The Anglican church is the official national church, but there are also many Roman Catholics (5 percent) and various Protestant churches. Anglicans and other Protestants together represent about 55 percent of the population. Small groups practice, to varying degrees of authenticity, ceremonies and rituals from Africa, India, and China. All have been Jamaicanized, and ecumenism (unity among all churches) comes naturally to Jamaicans. Religion plays an important role in society, not only for its spiritual values, but also for the social opportunities it provides. Church gatherings are particularly valuable to rural women.

Hindu ceremonies have support from Jamaicans of every ethnic origin and religious persuasion. Similarly, Muslim celebrations are shared with Hindus and other Jamaicans. There is a long-standing Jewish community, the first of whom came with Columbus as ship hands to escape the Spanish Inquisition. Although the Jews usually attend services as families, the vast majority of churchgoers in other religions are women and children. Religious education is commonly included in the curricula of schools.

General Attitudes

Jamaicans like to be with people and are generally outgoing. They enjoy lively conversation and often hold strong views. People are warm and hospitable, but they may hold back with strangers until they get to know them. Jamaicans have a fairly flexible approach to life. A common good-natured answer to life's challenges is "No problem, man," even if there is no solution at hand. Flexibility is also evident in the attitude toward time and schedules. A common phrase is "Soon come," which can mean anything from five minutes to next week. Events and meetings do not necessarily begin on time, although people are more punctual in urban areas.

Rural Jamaicans particularly appreciate honesty and hard work. Urban Jamaicans are increasingly building a strong professional and cooperative atmosphere for business and work. Throughout the country, having wealth or connections with someone who is wealthy or powerful is important. Financial security, prestige, a home and property, and a motor vehicle are valued possessions. Jamaicans are generally aware of others' opinions of them. Men are often judged by sexual prowess, while women are often judged by physical appearance.

Personal Appearance

Jamaicans are conscious of clothing fashions and like to wear jewelry. Women are generally mindful of appropriate dress for themselves and their children, though many reserve the right to dress according to their own tastes. Women usually wear skirts or dresses; professional women are very well dressed in colorful clothing. These are often made by local seamstresses rather than purchased in a store. Many institutions (banks, insurance companies) often provide their employees, particularly women, with uniforms. Women often have headdresses to match or complement their dresses. Men tend to dress more casually than women. They wear Western-style clothing for most occasions. Sunday is the day for women and children to wear their best clothes to church. Rural children often have shoes only for church or school. The youth wear very colorful clothing, following trends set in the music industry. For example, "dance hall" (a popular form of music) outfits are commonly worn on weekends. They include tight dresses for young women and baggy pants or long shorts for young men.

CUSTOMS AND COURTESIES

Greetings

In Jamaica, greetings range from a nod or bow, to a handshake or a slap on the back, to a kiss—all depending on the persons involved and the occasion. When people are first introduced, a handshake is usually used, followed by "Good morning," "Good afternoon," or "Good evening." Jamaicans are formal in their introductions: Mr., Mrs., Miss, or professional titles are used with the surname unless people are well acquainted. Children usually refer to adults other than family (parents, aunts, uncles, or grandparents) as "Sir," "Mr.," "Mrs.," or "Miss." Elderly people in rural areas occasionally curtsy when greeting. People passing on the road often call out greetings to friends and acquaintances and receive a warm response. It is considered rude to not properly greet someone before beginning a conversation or asking a question. Greetings among friends are casual. A common phrase is "Wha-apun?" (What's happening?) or "Alright, alright" (as if to bypass asking and responding to "How are you?"). Common phrases for saying good-bye include "Later," "Tomorrow then," and "Next time."

When addressing others in formal situations, titles and surnames are used. But in casual situations, it is common to use nicknames. A Jamaican might have many nicknames (also called "pet" or "yard" names) that are given to him (usually men) by various friends or groups. The nickname usually has to do with a physical trait or station in life. Some examples include *Fatty* (for a fat person; it is a compliment because it indicates the person must be wealthy and does not have to work hard); *Whitey* (white person; also not an insult, but one would never call a Black Jamaican "Blacky"); or *Juicy* (man who sells juice on the street). In addition, people often shorten their names ("Nicky" for Nicholas) or slightly alter their given names to create a nickname by which they want to be called.

Gestures

Jamaicans can be very animated when speaking and tend to use many hand gestures to help make a point (especially if men are talking about cricket or politics). They also like to emphasize greetings by holding onto an initial handshake for a while, or by touching the person's arm or shoulder during the greeting or later in the conversation. People show respect for or approval of shared ideas by touching fists. To hail a taxi, the hand is kept down and waved, not held above the head. To get someone's attention, one might say, "pssssst," clap hands, or tap on a grill or gate of a home. Jamaicans, particularly women, make a sound by sucking air through their teeth to express "give me a break."

Social gestures generally follow traditional lines in Jamaica. Men offer older women, women with young children, or pregnant women seats on a bus. Seated passengers often offer to hold packages or children for standing passengers. Men open doors for women in urban areas. Kissing, chewing gum, or combing one's hair are not common in public. Women rarely smoke in public.

Visiting

Informal visits are accepted at the house gate. People usually don't approach the door until greeted and invited past the gate. A visitor simply knocks, rings a buzzer, or otherwise calls attention to himself, and the person at home will greet him. Conversations held on the street are referred to as "meet-and-greet" activities. Visitors inside homes are usually offered a drink and sometimes a meal. Guests often take a small gift for the host or hostess. A gift, even in urban settings, might be fresh produce, flowers from the guest's garden, or a bottle of wine. Families and friends find time to get together often and always enjoy a good laugh. Because Jamaica has traditionally not had telephones and many rural homes still lack them, it is common to visit someone's home unannounced. There is no need to call ahead; surprise guests are nearly always welcome. Urban visitors will often keep the visit brief if they have not called ahead.

Eating

Rural families tend to eat dinner together each day after 4:00 P.M., while urban families might not have opportunity to eat together except on weekends. Meals are casual and specific table manners are less important than enjoying the food.

When guests are invited for a meal, the occasion is usually relaxed and sociable. Buffet meals are popular. Invitations are sometimes extended for breakfast or brunch, in addition to the usual lunch and dinner. Dress and table settings vary according to degree of formality. Eating outdoors is popular, especially in gardens and on patios. The continental style of eating is followed, with the fork in the left hand and the knife remaining in the right. Restaurants range from informal diners that serve simple Jamaican dishes to sophisticated gourmet establishments.

Take-out (*take-away*) meals served in boxes are common. These may be purchased from caterers, restaurants, or street vendors. Different foods sold by street vendors are plentiful and relatively inexpensive. They are sometimes eaten on the spot. Pineapples, melons, and water coconuts are often sold from roadside stalls or carts as quick snacks or thirst quenchers. It is inappropriate to eat while walking in public. In restaurants a service charge is usually included in the bill, but if not, a 10 to 15 percent tip is given. Good table manners are considered an important social refinement. Many Jamaicans say grace before or after meals.

LIFESTYLE

Family

The family structure varies in Jamaica according to several factors, one of which is social standing. For example, families in lower socioeconomic groups are usually larger than those in the middle or upper classes. In addition, women of the lower groups commonly have several children by different men, known as "baby fathers." The men refer to these women as their "baby mothers" (as opposed to wives or girlfriends). Those engaged in having more than one child out of wedlock believe men prove their virility by fathering a child and that women must give birth to prove their femininity. Women assume the primary responsibility for child care, but the children often live with grandparents, other relatives, or godparents when the mother works outside the home. In these circles, therefore, the extended family plays a crucial role.

Most families live in houses or town houses. Apartments are not common. Homes are generally built of concrete or, in rural areas, wood.

Diet

Jamaican food is generally very spicy. *Ackee* and salt fish, the national dish, is usually eaten for breakfast. Other favorites include rice and peas or beans, stews, and various types of fish. Fish may be eaten at least twice a week. Curries are popular. Curried goat is a common meal. Most meals are served with rice and peas (red beans) and may also include boiled green bananas or fried dumplings. A typical salad includes cabbage and carrots. Vegetables (yams, tomatoes, green peppers, etc.) and fruits (mangoes, bananas, papaya, pineapple, oranges, grapefruit) play an important role in the diet. Fruit is plentiful and there is usually one or more types in season. *Jerk* is a favorite of Jamaicans and visitors alike. It is a spicy hot piece of barbecued pork or chicken, roasted in open pits or on makeshift grills. *Jerk* is often served with a bland, hard-dough bread. *Bammy* (cassava/manioc bread) is a standard food; it is still prepared in the style of the Arawak Indians. *Bammy* with fried fish is a frequent combination, as is *festival* (fried dough) with fish. Indian and Chinese dishes are widely enjoyed. Drinks made from boiled roots, herbal teas, fruit juices, and a variety of alcoholic beverages are common. Coffee and tea are popular, and it is customary for all hot drinks to be called "tea" (coffee, cocoa, green tea, etc.). Beer and white rum are especially popular. Women do not usually drink alcohol in public.

Recreation

Cricket and soccer (*football*) are the most popular sports in Jamaica. Dominoes is the favorite indoor game. Many also enjoy table tennis, field hockey, tennis, and track and field (*athletics*). Girls play netball in school. Music of all types, theater, and dancing are popular activities. Comedies written and performed in *Patois* are popular. Young Jamaicans enjoy reggae, Social Calypso (SOCA), and "dance hall" music. The latter incorporates elements of reggae, disco, and rap. SOCA is very popular during *Carnival*, a grand springtime festival involving parades, costumes, and parties. Listening to prerecorded music from stereo systems outside of rum bars is a frequent pastime.

People attend discos, community centers, and clubs. Other leisure activities include going to movies and enjoying spectator sports, such as boxing or team competitions. Various festivals, community events, and church activities provide entertainment and recreation. Jamaicans also take advantage of the many outdoor activities their island offers.

Holidays

Official Jamaican holidays include New Year's Day, Ash Wednesday, Easter (Friday–Monday), Labor Day (23 May, a day for community improvement projects), Independence Day (first Monday in August), National Heroes Day (third

Monday in October), Christmas, and Boxing Day (26 December). Boxing Day is a day to visit family and friends. The Maroons celebrate 6 January as their independence day.

Commerce

Business hours generally extend from 9:00 P.M. to 5:00 P.M., Monday through Thursday, and until 4:00 P.M. on Friday. Banks close weekdays around 2:00 P.M. except on Friday, when they stay open for a few more hours. Grocery stores and other shops might open earlier and stay open later, depending on the town and type of shop. Street vendors sell goods and food from early in the morning until late at night. Open air markets sell fresh produce. Prices in these markets are fixed. Rural people shop more often than urban residents, as few have access to refrigeration.

SOCIETY

Government

Jamaica has a two-party Westminster (British) model parliamentary system. Elections must be held at least every five years, but the prime minister can call them earlier. The voting age is 18. Members of Parliament are elected, but members of the Senate are appointed. The cabinet, led by the prime minister, holds executive power. Although Jamaica is independent from Great Britain, it is part of the Commonwealth of Nations and recognizes Queen Elizabeth II as head of state. She is represented in Jamaica by a governor general, whom she appoints on the advice of the Jamaican prime minister.

Economy

Jamaica's foreign debt and the global recession challenge economic growth. Still, gains in the bauxite and aluminum industries in recent years have allowed the economy to grow moderately. Sugar, bauxite, bananas, and coffee are important exports. Agriculture employs over 20 percent of the population. Tourism is becoming more important as ties with the United States are strengthened. Jamaica is part of the Caribbean Basin Initiative (CBI), a program designed to improve economic relations between the United States and nations of the Caribbean. The government is moving to reduce the foreign debt and stimulate further economic growth. Unemployment is 15 percent and inflation is above 50 percent. The currency is the Jamaican dollar (J$). Jamaica's Human Development Index (0.736) ranks it 69 out of 173 countries. Real gross national product per capita is $2,979, which has improved steadily during the last generation. These figures indicate that a growing portion of the population earns a decent income and has access to improving economic conditions. Rural poverty and slow economic growth, however, inhibit greater prosperity.

Transportation and Communication

Buses serve all parts of the island. Cars and buses are the most common form of transportation. Most roads are paved. Following the British tradition, traffic moves on the left side of the road. Buses are often crowded; they are numbered but their schedules are not always evident. "Route cabs" are taxis that follow certain local routes. Regular taxis are plentiful; fares are negotiated. Jamaica's communication system is modern and adequate, although rural people seldom have phones in their homes. Public phone booths, usually found near police stations or post offices, require phone cards (not coins) that are purchased at post offices and some stores. There are several radio and television stations and various daily newspapers.

Education

Schools are organized into preprimary, infant, and basic schools (ages three to six), primary schools (six to twelve), and secondary schools (12 to 17). Secondary schools include technical, comprehensive, vocational and high schools. Enrollment in these is limited and admission is determined by competitive examinations each year. Education up to age 12 is free. A lack of money for fees, uniforms, lunch, or transportation makes attendance difficult for some rural poor. The government tries to help those who cannot pay for these things themselves. With rare exception, children must wear uniforms to school. Most children (93 percent) who enter school finish the primary level. About 60 percent of all eligible children are enrolled in secondary schools. Most Jamaican adults have completed at least five years of education.

The literacy rate (98 percent) is defined as ever having attended school, which is not necessarily accurate. The actual rate is closer to 75 percent. Girls are often more serious about education than young men, as boys do not necessarily see education as a means to earning a living. Young women are increasingly influenced by Jamaicans living in other countries and by their desire for economic autonomy; they recognize the value of education in providing for a better future. There are more girls in secondary school than boys, and the number of women in post-secondary institutions is coming closer to that of men.

Higher education is provided at six teacher-training colleges; a college of art, science, and technology; a college of agriculture; schools of music, art, dance, and drama; and the University of the West Indies.

Health

Most large towns or cities have a hospital. Medical clinics are community based and are available across Jamaica. The public health care system covers basic care for all citizens at no or low cost. Fees might be required in some cases, or for more complicated care. Private facilities are available. Kingston and resort areas have doctors available 24 hours a day. Facilities and care are generally of high quality. Piped water is safe to drink. The infant mortality rate is 18 per 1,000. Life expectancy has risen in recent years to between 72 and 76 years.

FOR THE TRAVELER

Visas are not required of U.S. tourists. However, proof of citizenship (such as a passport) and onward passage are necessary to travel to Jamaica. No immunizations are required. The tourist industry is well developed. For information on travel opportunities contact the Jamaica Tourist Board 801 Second Avenue, 20th Floor, New York, NY 10017. You may also wish to contact the Embassy of Jamaica, 1520 New Hampshire Avenue NW, Washington, DC 20036.

A *Culturgram* is a product of native commentary and original, expert analysis. Statistics are estimates and information is presented as a matter of opinion. While the editors strive for accuracy and detail, this document should not be considered strictly factual. It is a general introduction to culture, an initial step in building bridges of understanding between peoples. It may not apply to all peoples of the nation. You should therefore consult other sources for more information.

CULTURGRAM '95

Principality of
Liechtenstein

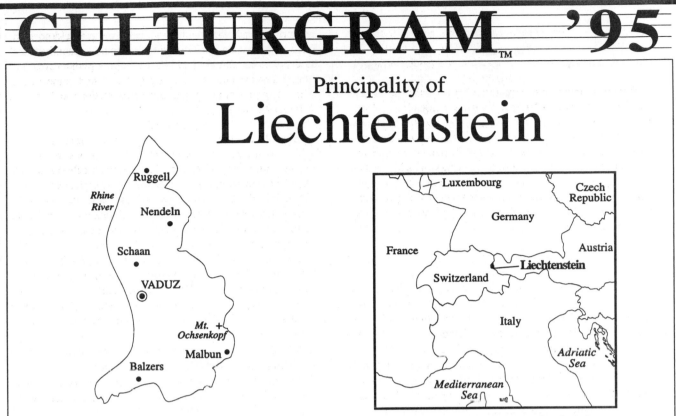

Boundary representations not necessarily authoritative.

BACKGROUND

Land and Climate

Covering 60.6 square miles (160 square kilometers), Liechtenstein (LIK-ten-shtine) is the fourth smallest state in Europe, situated between Austria and Switzerland. The principality enjoys a beautiful Alpine landscape that is dominated by the valley of the Rhine river and the *Rhaetikon* massif. The highest point is *Grauspitz* at 8,525 feet (2,599 meters). Small vineyards are found in the foothills. The climate is temperate and strongly influenced by the *Föhn*, a warm southerly wind. The *Föhn* was one of the three "national plagues" that once endangered the country. It sometimes kindled extensive fires, jeopardizing the then mostly wooden houses. Today, building materials are mainly brick and concrete and each village maintains a well-equipped voluntary fire brigade. Like the *Föhn*, the other two sources of natural disaster have also been brought under control. High embankments contain the formerly wild Rhine river; the last big flooding (*Rheinnot*) of the river took place in 1927. The debris slides (*Rüfen*) coming down from the mountains have been enclosed and rendered harmless.

History

The area of Liechtenstein has been permanently inhabited since 3,000 B.C. It was colonized by Celts and Rhaetians. In 15 B.C., the Romans conquered the territory. In the fifth century, the Alemanni settled it and, in the 12th century, the German language established an exclusive foothold. Historically Liechtenstein is composed of two areas, the Lordship of Schellenberg and the County of Vaduz. The two domains had been owned by various dynasties of counts before Prince Johann Adam of Liechtenstein purchased them in 1699 and 1712, respectively. As territories under the direct suzerainty of the German Empire, they provided the prince with a seat in the Diet of the Princes.

In 1719, the two domains were united and elevated to the Imperial Principality of Liechtenstein. It is the only country that still carries the name of its dynasty. Napoleon made Liechtenstein and 15 other regions part of the Rhine Confederation in 1806, granting each independence in exchange for loyalty. At the Vienna Congress of 1815 (after Napoleon's defeat), Liechtenstein became part of the German Confederation. It remained a member until the Confederation was dissolved in 1866. Since then Liechtenstein has remained fully sovereign. It has had no army since 1868 and is a neutral country. From 1852 to 1919 it formed a customs union with Austria-Hungary. Since 1924 Liechtenstein has benefited from a customs union with Switzerland and the use of the Swiss *franc* as its currency.

The constitution of 1921, which is still in force today, established "a constitutional hereditary monarchy upon a democratic and parliamentary basis." Prince Franz Josef II became the first prince to reside in Liechtenstein rather than in Vienna, Austria. He ruled from 1938 until his death in 1989. He was succeeded by his son, Prince Hans Adam II, who rules today. Liechtenstein joined the United Nations in 1990. It has always enjoyed political stability. A rare interruption was a vote of no confidence in 1993 for a newly appointed prime minister. Parliament was dissolved and new elections were held to seat the current government.

Copyright © 1994. Brigham Young University. Printed in the USA. All rights reserved. It is against the law to copy, reprint, store in a retrieval system, or transmit any part of this publication in any form by any means for any purpose without written permission from the Publications Division of the David M. Kennedy Center for International Studies, Brigham Young University, PO Box 24538, Provo, UT 84602–4538. Culturgrams are available for more than 125 areas of the world. To place an order, to receive a free catalog, or to obtain information on traveling abroad, call toll free (800) 528–6279.

EUROPE

THE PEOPLE
Population

The population of Liechtenstein is about 30,000 and is growing at 1 percent annually. It expanded rapidly after World War II due to an increased demand for imported labor. Approximately 37 percent of the inhabitants today do not possess Liechtenstein citizenship. The high number of foreign nationals, who come mainly from German-speaking countries, has led the government to pursue a restrictive immigration policy. As a result, the nation's growth has stabilized, but the numbers of daily commuters from the Swiss and Austrian border regions have increased. Only 40 percent of the workforce is native to Liechtenstein.

Language

The language spoken in Liechtenstein is German. Whereas High German is taught at school and is used as a written language, people speak an Alemannic dialect. This dialect is similar to Swiss German (*Schwiizertütsch*) and is difficult to understand for people from other German-speaking countries. Its nuances vary from village to village. The mountain commune of *Triesenberg* was founded in the 13th century by people from southwestern Switzerland. Their descendants still speak a *Walser* dialect. The primary foreign languages taught at school are French and English.

Religion

The constitution guarantees religious freedom. The people of Liechtenstein are mostly (88 percent) Roman Catholics. The Catholic church is the state church. The priests are employed by the communes. Twelve percent of the people belong to a variety of other Christian churches or to no church at all. Religion still has some impact on daily life, but society has become more secularized in recent years.

General Attitudes

Liechtensteiners are proud of their high standard of living and modern achievements, but they cherish tradition as well. They value hard work and a good sense of humor. Conservative, deliberate, and pragmatic, they are also sincere and warmhearted. Many view Liechtenstein as one of the most beautiful spots on earth and consider it good luck to be so small and unimportant. Despite the lack of an army, for instance, it has escaped war since the end of the 18th century. Moreover, people tend to know each other well. This creates a sense of personal responsibility but also encourages gossiping and envy. The small society depends on the commitment of its citizens to participate, and civic duties are taken seriously. Liechtensteiners like to talk politics and many of them are somehow involved in it.

The national identity of Liechtensteiners is closely linked to their respective communes and to the princely house. The prince plays an important role in public life and enjoys far-reaching constitutional rights. In contrast to other European monarchs, his tasks are not just representational. Liechtensteiners have always held the princely house in high esteem. It is only recently that attitudes towards the monarchy have become more critical. In addition to a current debate on constitutional reform, Liechtenstein faces the challenge of defining its place in international society. A more active foreign policy has recently opened Liechtenstein to the outside world. This has heightened the awareness of being a distinct nation but also of the limits of independence. Political efforts to participate in European integration are likely to have a profound impact on the way Liechtensteiners view themselves.

Personal Appearance

People in Liechtenstein generally dress well and neatly. They prefer modern European fashions that tend to be more colorful than in the United States. Overly casual or sloppy attire in public is frowned upon. *Trachten* (traditional costumes) are only worn on special occasions, especially by women. The typical woman's *Tracht* consists of a dress with gathered waist, full skirt, an apron, and a headdress. A man's traditional attire includes knee breeches, a straight loden jacket, and a flat black hat.

CUSTOMS AND COURTESIES
Greetings

A handshake is usually the appropriate form of greeting. To waive or nod to somebody across the street is acceptable. It is also common to greet people verbally on the street or when entering a store. The traditional terms to address strangers are either the Swiss German *Grüezi!*, or the *Grüss Gott!* used in Austria and southern Germany. Both terms mean "Greetings." It is appropriate to add the other person's name, if known. Among friends, young and old greet each other with a short *Hoi!* Most people living in Liechtenstein address each other with the familiar "du" form and young people generally use first names. This is, however, only common among locals and not towards foreigners. The prince is addressed as *Durchlaucht* (Your Serene Highness). Greetings in languages other than German are also acceptable; keeping silent might be considered impolite. English, French, and Italian are the foreign languages most likely to be understood.

Gestures

Hands are not used much during conversation, but it is impolite to talk with hands in the pockets. Gloves are removed before shaking hands. Pointing the index finger to one's head is an insult. Any acts of personal hygiene, such as cleaning one's fingernails, are not appropriate in public. If a yawn cannot be suppressed, a hand covers the open mouth. Both men and women may sit with legs crossed with one knee over the other.

Toasting with alcoholic beverages is common. Whether in the home or at a restaurant, a toast usually precedes any drinking. It is extremely impolite to begin sipping or drinking from one's glass before the host proposes the first toast. The host will not do this until all persons have a full glass. Once the first toast is made, all guests are free to take a drink and propose additional toasts. In a group, the glasses are lightly tapped simultaneously in pairs, but not crosswise, and this is always done with eye contact.

Visiting

For business meetings, punctuality is important. Dinner guests are expected to arrive no more than a quarter of an hour late. They often bring flowers, candy, or a bottle of wine. Flowers are unwrapped before being given to the hostess, but other small gifts are not. Red roses are reserved for romantic occasions. In formal situations, guests wait to sit down until they are invited to do so. Even for short visits guests are usually offered refreshments such as coffee, beer, wine, or mineral water. It is appropriate to give notice of a visit in advance. Dropping by is only common between neighbors or close friends and relatives. While dinner invitations may last well into the night, daytime visits are usually short.

Eating

Lunch is typically eaten at noon, and dinner around 6:00 or 7:00 P.M. When going out for dinner, people meet around 8:00 P.M. The continental style of eating is used, with the fork in the left hand and the knife remaining in the right. Wrists may rest on the table edge. Soft food such as potatoes, dumplings, and fish are cut with the fork. Fish may also be cut with a special knife. Lettuce and spaghetti are not cut at all. It is considered polite to not leave any food on the plate. Second helpings are interpreted as a compliment to the cook. When finished, the utensils are placed side by side on the plate. In restaurants, leftovers are not taken home. Most people drink bottled mineral water, wine, or beer with meals. Soft drinks are served without ice. The bill is paid at the table. The waiter usually asks whether each person prefers to pay separately. Service charges are included, but customers usually round the total up to the next *franc* or more as a *Trinkgeld* (an extra tip).

LIFESTYLE

Family

The nuclear family is the most important social unit in Liechtenstein's society. Family bonds play an important role. The father is generally the head of the household. Both men and women train for careers and an increasing number of married women work outside the home. The size of the average family has decreased to about two children. While singles and couples often live in apartments, families tend to prefer houses. The majority lives in single-family homes, but more and more young families are becoming tenants because real estate is expensive. Many people prefer to settle in the village where they grew up. Adult unmarried children usually move out of their parents' homes by the time they finish their professional training.

Dating and Marriage

Young people socialize on a casual basis in school and in numerous recreation clubs. There are close to 300 clubs and *Vereine* (associations). Dating practices are different from those in the United States and there is no German word that precisely means "dating." Either sex can suggest an activity and it is assumed that they each pay for their own entertainment. People usually marry in their late twenties. It is considered important to first complete one's education and enjoy some financial security and independence. Some couples live together before or instead of marriage. Legal marriages are performed at the national Registry Office. To have a church wedding is optional but common. It usually takes place the day after the civil marriage. Some old wedding customs are still practiced, such as decorating the door frames of the couple's home with garlands or organizing a mock kidnapping of the bride.

Diet

Zmorga (breakfast) usually consists of bread with jam and coffee. There are many different kinds of bread. *Zmittag* (the main meal) is served at midday and includes a soup or salad, a main dish, and dessert. *Znacht* (dinner) is typically light and often consists of open-faced sandwiches with cheese and meat. Full meals are served for dinner invitations and in restaurants. The national dish, *Riebel*, is made of cornmeal stirred in a frying pan with milk, water, and salt. It is often eaten with elderberry purée. Other traditional dishes are *Käsknöpfle*, a sort of pasta with sharp cheese, and *Rösti*, grated and fried potatoes.

Recreation

People in Liechtenstein love nature and outdoor activities such as hiking, cycling, and skiing. They enjoy a diversity of leisure-time clubs. Among the most popular team activities are soccer, gymnastics, music bands, and choirs. Many clubs organize public festivals and other social events. People also enjoy traveling abroad. A great cultural attraction is the prince's art collection, which includes world-famous paintings. A small part of this extensive private collection is exhibited in connection with the State Art Collection in Vaduz. A new, larger art museum has been planned but is not yet built.

Holidays

Liechtenstein recognizes many Catholic holidays as public holidays: Epiphany (6 January), Candlemas (2 February), Feast of St. Joseph (19 March), Easter (Good Friday through Easter Monday), Ascension, Whit Monday, Corpus Christi, Nativity of our Lady (8 September), All Saints' Day (1 November), Immaculate Conception (8 December), and Christmas (24–26 December). Christmas is the biggest celebration of the year. Gifts are exchanged on Christmas Eve when the family gathers around the Christmas tree. Most people relax on Christmas Day and visit relatives and friends on 26 December. In addition to these religious holidays, New Year's Day (1 January) and Labor Day (1 May) are public holidays. The national holiday is celebrated on 15 August with speeches and fireworks. Mother's Day is celebrated the second Sunday in May. Many old customs, partly pagan in origin, are still continued as folklore, such as *Funkasunntig* (Bonfire Sunday) or *Fasnacht* (Carnival).

Commerce

Business hours may vary. In general, they are from 8:00 A.M. to noon, when everything closes for lunch, and from 1:30 to 6:30 P.M., Monday through Friday. On Saturdays, stores close at 4:00 P.M., and some shops are closed Monday morning. There are no supermarkets in Liechtenstein, so people buy their food and other consumer goods in a variety of small shops.

SOCIETY

Government

Liechtenstein is divided into 11 communes that uphold their traditional autonomy. They enjoy extensive rights, are organized as cooperatives with a strong sense of community, and have their individual coats of arms. The capital is Vaduz. It has about 5,000 inhabitants. The communes form two regions that correspond to the two historical domains. They are called the *Oberland* (Upper Country) and the *Unterland* (Lower Country). The principality of Liechtenstein combines democracy and monarchy, as people and prince govern together. The *Fürst* (ruling prince) is the head of state. He sanctions all laws, and he can issue pardons and emergency decrees.

Landtag (parliament) has 25 members elected for four years. The traditional two parties are both conservative people's parties. In 1993, a more liberal third party joined parliament for the first time. The government has traditionally been a two-party coalition, governed by a *Regierungschef* (prime minister). In the courts there are not only Liechtenstein judges, but also Swiss and Austrian; this is due to the country's size and the fact that its legal system is a combination of Austrian, Swiss, and Liechtenstein law. The right to vote was extended to women only in 1984. The people enjoy direct democratic rights, such as the rights of political initiative and referendum.

Liechtenstein is currently facing some crucial political questions. On the domestic level a debate on constitutional reform aims to clearly define the authority of the prince, government, and parliament. Internationally, negotiations are underway to modify the customs treaty with Switzerland. This became necessary after Swiss voters rejected, but Liechtenstein voters approved, the Agreement on the European Economic Area (EEA), a free trade agreement between the European Free Trade Association, of which Switzerland and Liechtenstein are both members, and the European Union. Liechtenstein aims to participate in the EEA while maintaining its open border with Switzerland.

Economy

Despite a lack of natural resources, Liechtenstein has a strong, modern economy. It enjoys one of the highest standards of living in the world. The Human Development Index rating is 0.978, meaning most people have access to a decent income, a useful education, and adequate health care. There are no budget deficits, and inflation and unemployment rates are low.

After World War II, Liechtenstein experienced an economic boom as many companies invested heavily in the country. They took advantage of low taxes and other favorable conditions to build firms and factories, rapidly transforming the agrarian economy into an industrial state. Today, only about 2 percent of the gainfully employed are still working in agriculture. Industry is highly technical, manufacturing capital and research-intensive products. The largest branch is engaged in metal finishing, mainly machines and machine parts. Textiles, ceramics, and chemicals/pharmaceuticals all have long traditions in Liechtenstein. While industry produces mainly for export, a large number of small enterprises produce goods for domestic consumption. Industry and trade used to be the most important employers, but the service sector has recently caught up and today provides about 48 percent of all jobs. Liechtenstein's high level of economic prosperity is due mainly to the economic and monetary union with Switzerland, the favorable tax situation, and political stability. The currency is the Swiss *franc* (SFr).

Transportation and Communication

Liechtenstein's road network is well developed. Private cars are the most important means of transport. Public transportation is provided by postal buses at low cost. Only one railway line crosses the country; it is operated by the Austrian Federal Railways. Good international connections are available through the nearby Swiss train stations and *Autobahn* (expressways). The closest international airport is in Zürich, Switzerland.

Communication facilities are good. The telephone and postal services are managed by Switzerland, but Liechtenstein issues its own postal stamps. They are renowned for their beautiful design and collected throughout the world. With regard to media, Liechtenstein is rather underdeveloped. There are two daily newspapers that function as the mouthpieces of the two political parties. The first radio station is scheduled to begin broadcasting in 1994. Television broadcasts come from other countries.

Education

School education is free and mandatory between the ages of seven and sixteen. Pupils may thereafter continue studying in preparation for attending a university or entering vocational training. The system of apprenticeships is quite popular and successful. Up to the level of the university entrance qualification, the *Matura*, Liechtenstein has a well-developed educational system. For further training, agreements with Switzerland and Austria ensure that Liechtensteiners have places in educational institutions abroad. There is no illiteracy, and adult education is actively promoted.

Health

Medical care is provided by a relatively high density of private doctors. There is one small public hospital in Liechtenstein. In addition, the country has concluded agreements with its Swiss and Austrian neighboring regions that ensure the availability of beds in hospitals there. The government provides for age and disability insurance, unemployment benefits, and social welfare. It requires people to purchase private health insurance. The infant mortality rate is very low at 5 per 1,000; life expectancy averages 78 years.

FOR THE TRAVELER

U.S. visitors do not need a visa for stays of up to three months, but a valid passport is required. No vaccinations are necessary. There are no customs formalities on the Liechtenstein-Swiss border, but normal practices apply on the Austrian border. Tourism is well developed. The country offers beautiful scenery, historical sites, and recreational activities. For further information, you may wish to contact the Liechtenstein National Tourist Office, PO Box 139, 9490 Vaduz, Liechtenstein. The Swiss National Tourist Office (608 Fifth Avenue, New York, NY 10020) can also provide information about travel to Liechtenstein. It also has offices in Chicago and El Segundo, California. You may also wish to contact the Embassy of Switzerland (2900 Cathedral Avenue NW, Washington, DC 20008), which represents Liechtenstein's diplomatic interests in the United States.

A *Culturgram* is a product of native commentary and original, expert analysis. Statistics are estimates and information is presented as a matter of opinion. While the editors strive for accuracy and detail, this document should not be considered strictly factual. It is a general introduction to culture, an initial step in building bridges of understanding between peoples. It may not apply to all peoples of the nation. You should therefore consult other sources for more information.

Republic of
Lithuania

Boundary representations not necessarily authoritative.

BACKGROUND

Land and Climate

Lithuania is about the same size as Washington state (25,174 square miles or 65,200 square kilometers). It lies on the western fringe of the East European plain. It is a very green country with more than 750 rivers and 2,800 lakes. Summers are short and winters are cold and foggy. The general climate is comparable to that of southeastern Canada. Forests cover about 30 percent of the country and are rich in wild animals, mushrooms, and berries. These forests are favorite destinations for recreation. Rain falls throughout the year but less so in the summer. A westerly breeze is common. The average January temperature is 23°F (–5°C) and in July it is 63°F (17°C).

History

Although the Lithuanian people had existed for centuries, it was not until 1236 that Duke Mindaugas united the lands inhabited by them with those of the Yatwingians and Couronians to form the Grand Duchy of Lithuania. The new state grew in prominence, especially during the 14th century when it annexed neighboring lands and was ruled by strong monarchs. Vilnius became the capital in 1323. In 1386, reacting to a serious threat from Germanic invaders, the Grand Duke Jogaila married the Polish crown princess and became king. This alliance brought Lithuania into a dynastic union with Poland, which eventually allowed the two nations to defeat the German (Teutonic) invaders in 1410. Because of the union, the Lithuanians adopted Roman Catholicism in 1387 and began to adopt Western culture. Poland and Lithuania tightened their association in 1569 when they united under the Lublin Union.

After the Polish-Lithuanian state was partitioned by its neighbors (in 1772, 1793, and 1795), the Grand Duchy of Lithuania was left largely a part of the Russian empire. Many attempts were made to regain independence, but all were unsuccessful. In World War I, Lithuania was occupied by the Germans. Then, after the Russian Revolution in 1917, the Germans permitted Lithuania to elect its own officials. In February 1918, those officials declared Lithuania an independent state. But in December of that year, Communists in Lithuania established a government and the Bolsheviks invaded from Russia.

Later, in 1919, the Soviet army was driven from most of Lithuania, whose people were determined to regain sovereignty. At about the same time, Poland fought the Soviets, seeking to restore the territory it had claimed before 1795. Lithuania resisted Polish plans and signed a peace treaty with the Soviets that recognized Vilnius as belonging to Lithuania; the same treaty was later signed with Poland, which was to give up its claims to the city and region. Unfortunately, the Polish army ignored the treaty and seized Vilnius. Kaunas then became the capital of Lithuania.

In the interwar period (1920–40), Lithuania was independent and had a free market economy, trading agricultural products with European and Scandinavian countries. After the joint German-Soviet attack on Poland in 1939, Lithuania was forced to accept Soviet military bases on its territory. As compensation, the Soviets took Vilnius from Poland and

Copyright © 1994. Brigham Young University. Printed in the USA. All rights reserved. It is against the law to copy, reprint, store in a retrieval system, or transmit any part of this publication in any form by any means for any purpose without written permission from the Publications Division of the David M. Kennedy Center for International Studies, Brigham Young University, PO Box 24538, Provo, UT 84602–4538. *Culturgrams* are available for more than 125 areas of the world. To place an order, to receive a free catalog, or to obtain information on traveling abroad, call toll free (800) 528–6279.

EUROPE

returned it to Lithuanian sovereignty. Unfortunately, Soviet activity on Lithuanian soil increased; the Soviets soon dismissed the government and officially occupied the entire nation in 1940.

Lithuania was therefore incorporated into the Soviet empire early in World War II. Thousands of armed partisan fighters, known as "Forest Brothers," fought unsuccessfully for independence between 1940 and 1954. As a result of the resistance and Stalin's policies toward the Baltics, Lithuania suffered mass deportations and other difficulties. Relations were less confrontational after the 1950s, but Lithuanians never gave up their goal for independence. Their desires were realized in 1990 when the freely elected legislature of Lithuania re-declared independence (first declared in 1918). Since the Soviet government had been weakened by various international and domestic factors, it could not force Lithuania to cancel its declaration.

After the entire Soviet Union collapsed in 1991, Russia recognized Lithuania's independence, which had already been recognized by many countries. The government, led by members of the political movement called *Sajudis*, embarked on an aggressive campaign to reform the economy and other social structures. Hampered by a poor global economy and soaring energy prices, among other variables, progress was slow and painful. For that reason, in national elections held in 1992, voters rejected the *Sajudis* leadership in favor of former Communists, who had formed a new political party advocating slower reform and more balanced ties with neighboring countries, especially Russia. The new government pledged to remain committed to democracy, but slowed privatization and other reform measures to soften the impact of political and social change. In late 1993, through more cooperative relations with Russia, Lithania's leaders were able to effect a full withdrawal of Russian troops. For now, they are concentrating on strengthening and stabilizing fledgling democratic institutions, as well as improving economic performance.

THE PEOPLE

Population

The population of Lithuania is 3.8 million, with nearly 70 percent living in urban areas. Most people (80 percent) are ethnic Lithuanian, but the country is also home to Russians (8.6 percent), Poles (7.7), Belarussians (1.5), and Ukrainians (1.2), among a few other small groups. The term "Lithuania" was first used by Tacitus in the first century A.D. in reference to one of many peoples emerging from the Balts, who inhabited the Baltic region between the first and fourth centuries. Lithuanians began to form their distinct society in the early 100s. In Lithuania, all national minorities have full citizenship rights and are treated as equals. Minority peoples generally maintain their own customs and have not adopted Lithuanian culture.

Language

Lithuanian, the country's official language, is known as one of the oldest Indo-European languages still in everyday use. It belongs to the Baltic language group along with Latvian and some extinct tongues like Yatvangian and Old Prussian. Grammatically, Lithuanian is similar to Sanskrit and Homeric Greek. The formation of standard Lithuanian was not completed until the 19th century because Polish (and sometimes other languages) had been used as the state language after the 13th century. By the 17th century, Lithuanian survived only among rural peasants because urban dwellers spoke Polish. After 1795, when Lithuania and Poland ceased to exist, Russian was introduced and encouraged among Lithuanians. When Lithuanian was later revived, a number of dialects began to assimilate into four main dialects. Russian was reintroduced by the Soviets and today about 80 percent of Lithuanians can speak Russian. English is becoming popular.

Religion

Most Lithuanians belong to the Roman Catholic church, which is regaining influence in the country. Under Soviet occupation, many churches closed, clergymen were repressed, and teachers were not allowed to teach religion. Religion was therefore practiced mainly in the home. In 1990, the Act of Restitution of the Catholic Church restored it to its prominence and allowed religious freedom. Many different Christian churches now operate in the country. Muslims and Jews also have active congregations.

General Attitudes

Lithuanians are generally reserved, although they are sincere and full of emotion. They simply mask their feelings to maintain privacy. They appreciate punctuality, skill, and intelligence. They are often critical of their own personal faults and are openly critical of public institutions. Nevertheless, Lithuanians are generally optimistic, patient, and industrious. They value moderate thrift but look at strong thrift as stingy. Lithuanians are proud of their heritage, but not of the Soviet period. For the future, they wish to be politically neutral and peaceful; however, they are willing to defend themselves to maintain Lithuania's independence. Many people are frustrated with the current period of transition and are uncertain of the future. Lithuanians value education, the family, and loyalty to one's nationality.

Personal Appearance

It is important to be cleanly dressed. Styles are taken mainly from Europe and increasingly from the United States. Lithuania's national dress is used only on special occasions. Because clothing is expensive and the market does not always meet demand, handmade clothing is often worn, especially in rural areas or by persons wishing to create their own style. As Lithuania's economy continues to integrate with the world, the use of handmade clothing is expected to decline. Older rural women wear scarves on their heads. Hats are common in winter; Lithuanians wear European-style hats and Russians often wear a *ushanki*, the traditional Russian fur hat. Men remove their hats in a building. Wool and fur are commonly used for clothing when it is cold. Cosmetics are worn sparingly.

CUSTOMS AND COURTESIES

Greetings

It is customary to shake hands with men and, less often, women when greeting. A handshake is nearly always used in professional contacts. When introducing a man, one uses *ponas* (Mr.) before the last name; for a woman, the term is *ponia* (Mrs.) or *panele* (Miss). A person's professional title is also used before the last name when applicable. Men sometimes kiss the extended hand of women in greeting, and good friends may kiss cheeks. First names are not used among adults until one is invited to do so, but young people are called by their first names. Men raise their hats or nod to greet people at a distance. The most common terms for greeting are *Laba diena* (Good day), *Labas rytas* (Good morning), *Labas vakaras* (Good evening), *Labas* (Hello), and *Sveikas* or *Sveiki* (both mean "How do you do?" but *Sveiki* is more casual).

Gestures

It is impolite to talk with one's hands in one's pockets. Eye contact is appreciated during conversation. The thumb is sometimes extended up to express approval, but verbal communication is preferred. Using the hands during or instead of conversation is generally not polite. Chewing gum in public is not appropriate for adults.

Visiting

Visiting in the home is popular because outside social opportunities are somewhat limited. Punctuality is expected. It is customary to bring an odd number of fresh flowers for even a brief visit. Dinner guests often bring flowers and wine. The flowers should be unwrapped before being given to the hostess. White flowers are usually reserved for brides, and carnations for times of mourning or certain special occasions. Spontaneous visits, even between friends and neighbors, are not very common. Before any visit it is polite to call, but unannounced guests will be welcome. In formal situations, guests wait to sit down until they are invited to or until the host sits. For informal gatherings, guests may act more at home. Guests are always offered refreshments, which may include coffee (or tea) and cake or cookies. The length of an evening visit depends on the occasion. If the hour is late, a host may accompany a guest outside when he leaves.

Eating

The continental style of eating is used, with the fork in the left hand and the knife remaining in the right. People usually eat three meals each day. Breakfast is between 7:00 and 9:00 A.M., dinner 1:00 and 3:00 P.M., and supper 6:00 and 8:00 P.M. In rural areas, meals are eaten as much as two hours earlier. The midday meal is the main meal of the day, and most businesses close for it. People either go home or eat at worksite canteens. It is impolite to leave food on the plate, as that suggests to the hostess that the meal was not good. In restaurants, the bill must be requested from the waiter and is paid at the table. Toasting is common for dinner and supper, whether guests are present or not. Tipping is not customary but is becoming more common.

LIFESTYLE

Family

The average family has one or two children. Larger families are not common. The father is generally the head of the family, but both parents share in raising children and working outside the home. In cities, most people live in apartments, but single-family homes are more common in rural areas. Small gardens on the outskirts of a city are very popular for urban people to own or rent. The gardens are a source of fresh food, relaxation, and contact with the land.

Dating and Marriage

Young people enjoy dancing, going to club activities, and traveling together. They usually marry while in their twenties, but some wait until they have some financial security. Most young families are not able to live separately from their parents because of a housing shortage. In fact, young couples often rely on financial support from their parents for a time. It is becoming more popular to live together before, or instead of, getting married. Legal marriages are performed at a city hall; many now also have a religious ceremony in a church.

Rural weddings may be quite lavish, and it is becoming popular to practice older traditions. For example, after the wedding ceremony, the wedding party's way home is blocked by "ropes" of flowers. The groom's friends and the matchmaker have to "buy" their way out with candy and whiskey. Sweets are also given to children along the way. The last rope is usually stretched across the gate of the couple's home. Parents meet the newlyweds at the door with bread, salt, and wine glasses filled with water. Many customs surround the two-day wedding celebration, including the mock punishment of the matchmaker for convincing the bride to marry the groom.

Diet

Lithuanian cuisine has been influenced by many cultures, but traditional specialties include smoked sausage, various cheeses, *cepelinai* (meat cooked inside a ball of potato dough, served with a special sauce), and *vedarai* (cooked potatoes and sausage stuffed into pig intestines). Soup is commonly served with dinner. Local fruits (apples, pears, plums, strawberries, etc.) and vegetables (carrots, cabbage, peas, beets, etc.) are popular. Rye bread and dairy products are regularly eaten. Tea, milk, and coffee are the most common drinks.

Recreation

The favorite sports of Lithuanians include basketball, soccer, boating (rowing), volleyball, cycling, tennis, skiing, and others. Lithuanians are proud of their 1992 Olympic basketball team, which won the bronze medal. Camping is popular for family outings, as is going to the beach on the Baltic Sea. Watching television or visiting are common leisure activities. People also relax by gardening and visiting at their garden plots outside of town. Many enjoy going to cultural events, especially ones involving national dance and song.

Holidays

The official public holidays of Lithuania include New Year's Day, the Restoration of the Lithuanian State (16 February),

Mother's Day (first Sunday in May), the Anniversary of the Coronation of Grand Duke Mindaugas of Lithuania (6 July), the National Day of Hope and Mourning (1 November), and Christmas (25–26 December). The Day of Hope and Mourning, also known as All Soul's Day, is a day to remember the dead. Various local festivals are held throughout the year. Easter is celebrated throughout the country.

Commerce

Businesses are open weekdays 9:00 A.M. to 6:00 P.M., with an hour break for dinner at 1:00 P.M. Food shops are open 8:00 A.M. to 7:00 P.M., Monday through Saturday, with a break at 2:00 P.M. Some shops are open 10:00 A.M. to 10:00 P.M., with a break around 2:00 P.M. Factories run weekdays from 7:00 A.M. to 4:00 P.M., with an hour break for dinner. Banks are open weekdays 9:00 A.M. to noon. Kiosks and small shops have more flexible hours. Business is generally kept separate from socializing. Lithuania's business sector basically operates along free market lines with state coordination in key areas.

SOCIETY

Government

A new constitution went into effect in 1992. It provides for a president as head of state to serve a five-year term. Algirdas Brazauskas was elected president in 1993. The prime minister, currently Adolfas Slezevicius, is head of government and a member of parliament. The parliament (*Seimas*) is the highest body of state power; its members are directly elected in national elections.

Economy

Lithuania is an industrial state, concentrating on the production of precision machinery and spare parts, processed foods, and light industrial products. Lithuania has very few natural resources, so the country depends heavily on imported raw materials. The main exports include machinery and parts, meat and dairy products, and consumer goods. Imports include oil and gas, chemicals, metals, and equipment. Production declined with independence, as traditional supply arrangements were interrupted, but ties are being sought with Western governments and neighboring countries to improve revenue, foreign investment, and productivity.

The radical economic reform program of the *Sajudis* government began the vital process of privatization and price liberalization, but it was unable to quickly improve living standards. High inflation has increased poverty as salaries and pensions have not kept up. Lithuania's Human Development Index (0.881) ranks it 29 out of 173 countries. Real gross domestic product per capita is $4,913. These figures indicate that basic social institutions exist to provide access to economic prosperity. Most people earn a decent income. However, due to the difficulties Lithuania faces in the transition from one social system to another, these figures will likely be somewhat lower for the near future. The national currency is the *Litas*.

Transportation and Communication

Public transportation is efficient and important because many families do not have private vehicles. Local buses and trolleys operate in cities, and a country-wide bus service radiates from the main towns. Lithuanian Aviation flies to and from various European destinations. Sea ferries connect Lithuania with Germany, and trains connect to Warsaw, Poland, and Berlin, Germany. There are three state-owned government newspapers, one each written in Lithuanian, Russian, and Polish. A number of private papers appear and disappear as the free press continues to form.

Education

Children are required to attend elementary school for nine years. They may continue with secondary school for three years. The literacy rate is above 95 percent. Education is provided free at all levels. There are 16 institutions of higher education, including Vilnius University, the University of Vytautas Magnus, and the Vilnius Technical University. Entrance is by exam only and is difficult to obtain. General education schools offer an optional course in religion. Sunday schools are open for Jews, Karaites (a group descended from the Tatars of the 14th century), and other religious minorities. Ethnic minorities have the right to be taught in schools that use their language; Russian and Polish are the basic languages of instruction in more than 300 schools.

Health

Lithuania has a national health care system, but some parts of it are scheduled to be privatized and some private clinics already exist. The system generally provides for the needs of the people, although modern equipment is lacking. The infant mortality rate is 16 per 1,000. Life expectancy averages between 66 and 76 years.

FOR THE TRAVELER

U.S. travelers need a valid passport and visa to enter Lithuania. Credit card and traveler's check acceptance is not yet widespread. Dual-voltage small appliances or a voltage converter and adapter are necessary to use electrical outlets. Lithuania does not have a tourist office in the United States, but some private companies offer tours to the country. For more information, contact the Embassy of the Republic of Lithuania, 2622 16th Street, Washington, DC 20009.

A *Culturgram* is a product of native commentary and original, expert analysis. Statistics are estimates and information is presented as a matter of opinion. While the editors strive for accuracy and detail, this document should not be considered strictly factual. It is a general introduction to culture, an initial step in building bridges of understanding between peoples. It may not apply to all peoples of the nation. You should therefore consult other sources for more information.

CULTURGRAM '95

Grand Duchy of
Luxembourg

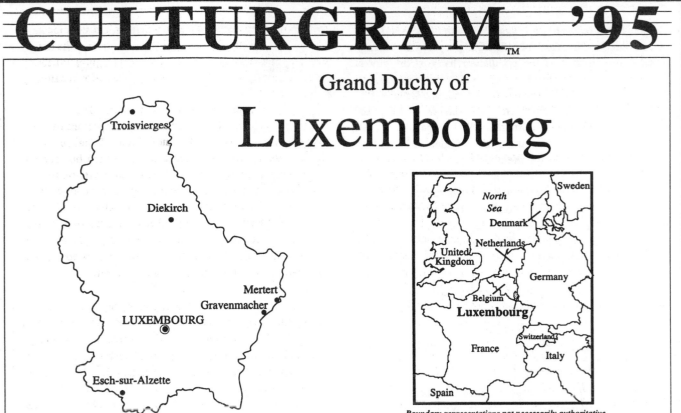

Boundary representations not necessarily authoritative.

EUROPE

BACKGROUND

Land and Climate

Luxembourg is a small, landlocked country bordered by France to the south, Belgium to the north, and Germany to the east. Covering 998 square miles (2,586 square kilometers), it is about the same size as Rhode Island. Nearly 25 percent of the land is suitable for cultivation. Luxembourg has gently rolling hills with shallow valleys and many forests, including those in the Ardennes uplands of the north. The south (the "Good Land") is dominated by farmland and woods. The landscape is dotted by castles and the ruins of castles and fortresses. The Moselle River forms the southern border. The climate is mild. Winter temperatures are generally above freezing and summer temperatures average 75°F (24°C). The sunniest summer months are May and June.

History

Luxembourg is one of Europe's oldest and smallest independent countries. But before it became independent, the area was ruled by many kingdoms, including that of the Romans and much later, Charlemagne's. In 963, Count Siegfried of the Ardennes built a castle in present-day Luxembourg and founded the Luxembourg dynasty. Charles of Luxembourg became the king of Bohemia in the 14th century and strove to make Prague (now in the Czech Republic) as beautiful as Paris. Indeed, Luxembourg gave more than one monarch to other countries during the medieval period.

Luxembourg was ruled by the Austrian Habsburgs in the 17th and 18th centuries, and then by the Netherlands. In 1815 it became a Grand Duchy in the Dutch kingdom. The Luxembourgers revolted in 1830 after the Belgians also revolted against Dutch control. After the revolt, Luxembourg was divided between Belgium and the Netherlands. The Netherlands' portion is what eventually gained independence as today's Luxembourg. The 1867 Treaty of London declared Luxembourg an independent neutral state, although it remained closely tied to the Netherlands. Personal union between the monarchs of the Netherlands and Luxembourg ended in 1890 when both died without leaving heirs to their thrones. In Luxembourg, the crown passed to the House of Nassau, which holds it today.

Although neutral, Luxembourg was invaded by Germany in World War I and World War II. After its liberation, Luxembourg ended its neutrality (in 1949) and joined the Western European alliances, including NATO. In 1964, the Grand Duchess Charlotte abdicated, allowing her son, Grand Duke Jean to become the country's ruler. Since that time, Luxembourg has enjoyed peace, economic growth, and beneficial relations with other European nations.

THE PEOPLE

Population

The population of Luxembourg was steady for several years, experiencing almost zero growth for many years until

Copyright © 1994. Brigham Young University. Printed in the USA. All rights reserved. It is against the law to copy, reprint, store in a retrieval system, or transmit any part of this publication in any form by any means for any purpose without written permission from the Publications Division of the David M. Kennedy Center for International Studies, Brigham Young University, PO Box 24538, Provo, UT 84602–4538. *Culturgrams* are available for more than 125 areas of the world. To place an order, to receive a free catalog, or to obtain information on traveling abroad, call toll free (800) 528–6279.

1990 when it began to grow again. Growth in 1992 and 1993 was 1 percent. There are about 398,000 people in the country. Nearly one-quarter of the population lives in the city of Luxembourg. The Luxembourgers, which are an ethnic mixture of French and German origins, account for about 75 percent of the population. The rest consists of guest and worker residents from Portugal, Italy, France, and other European countries. The immigrant population is growing faster than that of native Luxembourgers.

Language

Luxembourgish is the mother tongue of the Luxembourgers. It comes from a Franco-Moselle dialect, mixed with many German and French words. It was declared the national language in 1984, although it had always been used as the daily language of the people. Luxembourgish is used more as a spoken language than a written one. French and German also have official status. German is often used for newspapers, while French is the official language of the civil service, law, and parliament. Children begin learning German in school at the age of six and French at seven. English is also taught in the schools and is widely understood.

Religion

The Roman Catholic church claims membership among more than 90 percent of the population. While most adhere to Catholic traditions, society is basically secular. The remaining population belongs to various Protestant groups, is Jewish, or claims no religious affiliation. Most Christians do not attend church services on a regular basis, but many show their devotion through actions or attitudes (such as tolerance, charity, etc.).

General Attitudes

Although the people of Luxembourg are descendants of different nationalities and speak several different languages, they maintain a strong feeling of national pride. Their independence and separate identity in Europe are important. This character is reflected in the national motto: *Mir wëlle bleiwe wat mer sin!* (We want to remain what we are). By both conquest and peaceful exchange, Luxembourg has been influenced by the neighboring countries of Belgium, Germany, and France. Many traditions of each of these countries are evident in the customs of the Luxembourgers. There are differences, however. For example, the pace of everyday life in Luxembourg is not as hurried as in other European countries. Luxembourgers value education, privacy, friendship, and humor. Loud behavior is not appreciated in polite company or in public.

Personal Appearance

Luxembourgers follow European fashion trends, chiefly those from France, Germany, and Italy. Men wear suits to work. Many men wear hats. Women wear dresses somewhat more often than pants. The youth follow the latest fashion trends. People are always well dressed in public. Cleanliness and neatness are important. Very casual clothing is reserved for the home or recreational activities. Tattered clothing is not worn in public.

CUSTOMS AND COURTESIES

Greetings

A gentle handshake is most common and most appropriate in greeting acquaintances and when meeting someone for the first time. Close female friends may hug three times. Other close friends who have not seen each other for a long time may kiss each others cheeks three times. Polite inquiries about a friend's health or colleague's work might accompany a greeting. The most common verbal greetings in Luxembourgish include *Moien* (Morning), *Gudden Owend* (Good evening), and *Wéi geet et?* (How are you?). Also common is *Bonjour*, French for "Good day." Upon parting, one might say *Äddi*, a casual "good-bye" or the more formal *Au revoir*. Young people like to use *Salut* or *Ciao* as a quick good-bye. Friends and acquaintances also use longer phrases, such as *Bis eng aner Kéier* or *Bis härno*, both of which roughly mean "See you later." *Äddi, bis mar* (Until tomorrow) is used when appropriate. Like most Europeans, Luxembourgers are reserved when first meeting strangers. They are friendly, however, and they remember those who befriend them. Friends and relatives address each other by given names or nicknames, while acquaintances use titles and surnames. High-ranking persons may be addressed by more than one title, such as *Här Minister* (Mr. Minister), with or without the surname.

Gestures

Although Luxembourgers might use hands to emphasize their speech during conversation, specific gestures are rarely used to complement or replace verbal communication. Proper behavior in public is expected, such that one refrains from yawning, shouting, or using offensive language. Handkerchiefs are used inconspicuously. Chewing gum while speaking is impolite.

Visiting

The people of Luxembourg enjoy visiting friends and relatives at home, but they rarely drop by unannounced. Most visits are prearranged, usually by invitation. Hosts take care to make their guests feel welcome. Refreshments are nearly always offered, usually in the form of something to drink. Before a meal, a cocktail is common.

Good friends visiting a couple that has just moved into a new home bring bread, salt, and a bottle of wine to wish them well. Guests invited for dinner normally take flowers, chocolates, a small gift, or a bottle of wine to their hosts. Among younger people, the guests might bring dessert. Good friends and relatives might bring gifts on holidays or for special occasions (first communion, final exams at secondary school, obtaining a college degree, birthday, and so forth).

When guests depart, they thank the hosts and are accompanied outside of the home. Guests are seldom invited to the home to discuss business. Such matters are taken care of in public places, such as restaurants, cafés, or offices.

Eating

Breakfast is usually eaten between 7:00 and 9:00 A.M., lunch at noon, and dinner around 7:00 P.M. Some people have coffee around 4:00 P.M. The main meal of the day was traditionally at midday, but this is not possible for people who work all day or are too far from home each day to eat at that time. For these families, lunch is light and dinner is the main meal. For the family meal, dishes are placed on the table for each person to choose a portion. When guests are present, each person's plate is usually prepared in advance. Hosts expect their guests to ask for second helpings. Some cooks will feel their food is not liked if guests do not eat seconds. The continental style of eating is used, with the fork in the left hand and the knife remaining in the right. Both hands, but not the elbows, are kept above the table at all times. It is not proper to have one's hands resting in the lap during a meal. Burping at the table is not appropriate.

In a restaurant, the waiter is usually paid at the table. A service fee is often included in the bill. If it is not included, a tip of 10 to 15 percent is appropriate. If the service fee is included, an extra tip is not necessary but appreciated.

LIFESTYLE

Family

The importance of the family is well established in Luxembourg. Parents still exert influence on the social and professional choices of their children. Parents are required by law to pay for their children's education, and adult children are required to meet certain financial obligations of their parents if in need. Over the past decade, traditional family ties have been somewhat weakened as more and more young people travel abroad for study or employment. Bonds are still maintained, however, through family gatherings and celebrations. Families are usually small, having on average fewer than two children. Many women work outside the home, comprising one-third of the labor force. If they have young children, grandparents may be called upon to care for them during the day. Day care facilities and other options are also available. More than 60 percent of all families own the homes or apartments in which they live.

Dating and Marriage

Dating usually begins at age 15, after compulsory education requirements have been met. Parental approval, although less important that in the past, is still a factor in a young person's dating choices. The youth enjoy going to movies and theaters, eating at cafés and restaurants, having parties or dinners, and dancing. Couples may postpone marriage until they are financially established or complete their educational goals. Some couples choose to live together before marriage, but this is not an official union, and most Luxembourgers expect to eventually get married.

Only civil marriages are recognized by law. To be married in a church, a couple must present a certificate that they have been legally married by a civil authority. A reception for acquaintances and friends may follow a civil wedding, while a dinner for close friends and relatives traditionally follows a church ceremony.

Diet

Food in Luxembourg is influenced by French and German traditions, but it has its own unique flavor. People appreciate fine foods and have many national favorites. Popular dishes include *Judd mat Gaardebounen* (smoked collar of pork with broad beans), *Bouneschlupp* (bean soup), *Kachkéis* (a soft cheese known as *cancoillotte* in French), *Quetschentaart* (plum tart), *Fritten, Ham an Zalot* (french fries, ham and salad), *Träipen* (black pudding commonly eaten on Christmas Eve), and freshwater fish (usually trout). Sausages, potatoes, and sauerkraut are common elements of the diet. Fresh fruits and vegetables are eaten in season. A variety of cheeses and other dairy products are important. Coffee, wine, juice, and beer are popular drinks. Luxembourg also exports some domestic wines and beer to other countries in Europe.

Recreation

Cycling and hiking are favorite activities in Luxembourg, mostly because of the beautiful scenery. Part of the famous *Tour de France* bicycle race passes through Luxembourg. Soccer, jogging, and volleyball are also enjoyed. There are facilities for golf, tennis, squash, and water sports. Hunting and fishing are popular seasonal activities. Numerous parks, theaters, movie theaters, and museums are available. Gardening and watching television are popular leisure activities. The cultural arts are important. Besides attending performances or museums, Luxembourgers like to paint, play musical instruments, or perform in village playhouses.

Holidays

In addition to some national holidays, several religious holidays are celebrated in Luxembourg. The national holidays include New Year's Day, Labor Day (1 May), the Grand Duke's Birthday—also called National Day (23 June), and Fair Day (early September). Fair Day occurs during fair season in the capital city. An ancient shepherd's market serves as the fairgrounds and many traditions focus on shepherding.

The religious holidays include Shrove Tuesday (February), Easter (including Monday), Ascension, Whit Monday, Assumption (15 August), All Saints Day (1 November), All Souls Day (2 November), and Christmas (24–26 December). Christmas and Easter are the most important holidays.

At Easter, young children take part in a tradition called *klibbere goen*. According to legend, all church bells go to Rome three days before Easter for confessional. So the boys use rattles to announce church services—since the bells can't ring. When the bells return on the Saturday before Easter, the children collect money and colorful Easter eggs from each home in the neighborhood as their reward. Every family colors Easter eggs during this season, and on Easter Sunday, children receive the eggs and other gifts hidden in the garden.

Christmas celebrations begin weeks before the actual holiday. Some time before 6 December, small children place a shoe outside their bedroom before bedtime and expect to receive a piece of chocolate from St. Nicholas (*Kleeschen*) if they have been good. Otherwise they might receive a birch twig from his helper, *Housecker*. Then, on 6 December, *Kleeschen* visits good children and brings them gifts. Small parades are often held in various cities to celebrate the event. On Christmas Eve, families have a big meal and Catholics go to mass. Nearly all families have a tree in the home, many a nativity scene. Christmas Day is a family day.

Carnival is celebrated in the spring in many cities. There are also wine fairs, art festivals, and festivities to mark historical events.

Commerce

Business hours are generally from 8:30 A.M. to 5:30 P.M., Monday through Friday. Some shopping and recreational facilities are open longer. Some small shops may close for an hour at lunchtime. Most people shop in large supermarkets for their groceries, but a fresh produce open air market operates on Wednesday and Saturday. Luxembourg has a favorable business climate and there are few labor disputes. All workers receive 25 vacation days each year. Women receive from four to six months maternity leave.

SOCIETY

Government

The Grand Duchy is a constitutional monarchy, led by the Grand Duke Jean. However, the constitution vests sovereignty in the people. The unicameral legislature (Council of Deputies) is directly elected and is led by a prime minister. There is also a Council of State that advises the legislature. Most governments are coalitions. All citizens over age 18 are required to vote in national elections. Parliamentary elections were held in 1994.

Economy

Luxembourg enjoys a high standard of living. The country's Human Development Index (0.943) ranks it 18 out of 173 countries. Real gross domestic product per capita is $19,244, the third highest in the world. More important is the constant stability enjoyed by the economy. Despite its lack of natural resources and its policy to no longer exploit its iron ore reserves, the economy has been able to develop, diversify, and remain strong. The agriculture sector is modern and employs less than 5 percent of the labor force. About one-third of all workers in Luxembourg are foreign laborers from Portugal, Italy, France, Belgium, and Germany. As the manufacturing sector of the economy, based on the steel industry, has become less important, the service sector of the economy has grown substantially. Today, services (especially financial) employ almost half of the work force. Nevertheless, steel, chemicals, rubber, and other products are still important exports.

Luxembourg has benefited from European economic integration and cooperates closely with Belgium and the Netherlands in the BENELUX economic union. Luxembourg is also a member of the European Union (EU). Inflation and unemployment have generally been low in Luxembourg. The government actively encourages foreign investment. Both the Belgian *franc* and the Luxembourg *franc* are accepted in the country and have equal value.

Transportation and Communication

Luxembourg is a hub of travel in Europe. Roads and railways are in excellent condition. Most families own cars. Taxis are plentiful in the cities. The urban bus system is efficient. Trains connect to most major European cities and are well maintained. The communications system is modern and efficient. The government administrates telephone, telegraph, and postal systems. Television, radio, and newspapers are privately owned.

Education

Luxembourg's education system is well developed; literacy is 100 percent. Children attend primary school for six years and secondary school for seven years. Upon successfully passing exams at the end of the secondary level, students may go on to university studies. This might include a two-year banking course at Luxembourg's university, *Cours Universitaire*, or teacher training for primary level teachers at the *Institut Supérieur d'Etudes et de Recherches Pédagogiques*, or the first year of college studies at the *Cours Universitaire*. That first year in humanities, law, economics, secondary education, science, or medicine is recognized by many foreign universities to which Luxembourgers must transfer to complete their studies. Various technical and vocational schools exist to train those who seek careers outside of these professions.

Health

Public health standards are high, facilities are modern and advanced, and the cost to patients is low because of a compulsory social insurance system. Private insurance may also be carried to cover certain expenses. Clinics serve local needs, and hospitals are located in large towns. The infant mortality rate is 8 per 1,000. Life expectancy ranges from 73 to 80 years.

FOR THE TRAVELER

No visa is required for U.S. visitors staying up to three months, but a valid passport is necessary. No vaccinations are required. Dual-voltage small appliances or an adaptor and a plug adaptor are necessary to use electrical outlets. Interesting attractions include the old fortress of Luxembourg, the Battle of the Bulge museum at Diekirch, the Moselle Valley, and the newly restored exhibition "The Family of Man" by Edward Steichen in the castle of Clervaux, among others. For more detailed information on travel opportunities in Luxembourg, contact the Luxembourg National Tourist Office, 17 Beckman Place, New York, NY 10022. You may also wish to contact the Embassy of Luxembourg, 2200 Massachusetts Avenue NW, Washington, DC 20008.

A *Culturgram* is a product of native commentary and original, expert analysis. Statistics are estimates and information is presented as a matter of opinion. While the editors strive for accuracy and detail, this document should not be considered strictly factual. It is a general introduction to culture, an initial step in building bridges of understanding between peoples. It may not apply to all peoples of the nation. You should therefore consult other sources for more information.

CULTURGRAM ™ '95

Mexico
(United Mexican States)

Boundary representations not necessarily authoritative.

BACKGROUND

Land and Climate

Covering 761,602 square miles (1,972,550 square kilometers), Mexico is about three times the size of Texas, or about one-fifth the size of the United States. It shares its northern border with the United States and its southern border with Guatemala and Belize. Much of the north is dry and hot, while tropical jungles are found in the south. Mexico is rich in natural resources, including oil, natural gas, silver, iron ore, coal, copper, gold, lead, and zinc. The central plateau, where Mexico City is located, is bounded by two mountain ranges, the Sierra Madre Oriental on the east and the Sierra Madre Occidental on the west. In all, two-thirds of the country is covered by mountains, many of which are extinct volcanos. Temperature and rainfall vary with elevation and region. In the mountains, alpine conditions prevail. In Mexico City, the climate is more temperate. Rain falls mainly between November and May on the plateau. In the south, humidity and temperatures are higher.

History

The history of Mexico boasts a long line of advanced Indian civilizations whose accomplishments rival those of the Egyptians and early Europeans. They had accurate calendars, understood astronomy, were skilled artisans, and built huge empires. The Olmecs are considered to have been among the first inhabitants of the area around 2000 B.C. The Mayan Empire built incredible cities throughout North and Central America but fell in the 12th century. The Aztecs were the last great empire and were conquered by the Spanish in 1519. The Spanish virtually destroyed the Aztec culture. They also brought Christianity to the land and ruled until the 19th century.

A drive for independence began in September 1810, led by Miguel Hidalgo, a Mexican priest. Independence was gained in 1821. Mexico was one of the first countries to revolt against Spain. A constitution was adopted in 1824 and a republic was established. However, Antonio López de Santa Ana took power in 1833 and ruled as a dictator. During his regime, Texas seceded (1836) and joined the United States. Also, Mexico fought a war (1846–48) with the United States and lost more territory (much of the current western United States). Santa Ana resigned in 1855 and Benito Juárez became president. In 1861, French troops invaded Mexico City and named Austrian Archduke Maximilian the emperor of Mexico. Forces under Juárez overthrew Maximilian in 1867. Another dictator, Porfirio Díaz, came to power in 1877 and was overthrown in 1910, when Mexico entered a period of internal political unrest and violence.

That period, ending in the 1920s, became Mexico's social revolution. The Institutional Revolutionary Party (PRI) emerged as the leader of the nation in 1929. Political unrest continued in the 1930s, but Mexico has been basically stable since 1940. However, the PRI ruled the country as a single party and restricted political dissent for many years. In 1988, when Carlos Salinas de Gortari was elected president, promises

Copyright © 1994. Brigham Young University. Printed in the USA. All rights reserved. It is against the law to copy, reprint, store in a retrieval system, or transmit any part of this publication in any form by any means for any purpose without written permission from the Publications Division of the David M. Kennedy Center for International Studies, Brigham Young University, PO Box 24538, Provo, UT 84602–4538. *Culturgrams* are available for more than 125 areas of the world. To place an order, to receive a free catalog, or to obtain information on traveling abroad, call toll free (800) 528–6279.

were made to bring greater democracy to Mexico through political and economic reform. Many changes did take place, but none that would seem to challenge the PRI's position. Two 1994 events, however, seemed to weaken the ruling party's future. The first was the January Zapatista rebellion in the state of Chiapas (bordering Guatemala). Rebel Indians were protesting poverty conditions and the centralization of power; they demanded the resignation of the government and democratic change. While the actual rebellion was put down, the violent event raised serious issues in the minds of all Mexicans about the realities of conditions in certain areas. The other incident was the assassination of a leading presidential candidate, Luis Donaldo Colosio, who was expected to replace outgoing President Salinas in the August 1994 vote. The two events have led to concerns about political stability, but have also sparked a movement for greater democracy that reaches to all areas of Mexico.

THE PEOPLE
Population
There are 90.4 million people in Mexico, a population that is growing at 1.9 percent annually. Mexico City, the capital, has a population of over 19 million—one of the largest cities in the world. About 60 percent of the population is *mestizo* (mixed Spanish and Indian). Thirty percent of the people belong to various Amerindian groups. Most of these are descendants of the Mayan and Aztec empires. About 9 percent is of European ancestry. Most Mexicans tend to identify with their Amerindian and Spanish heritages.

Language
Spanish is the official language of Mexico. Written Spanish in Mexico is the same as written Spanish in Spain or Latin America. Differences occur in the pronunciation of some words and in the use of idioms. There are perhaps as many as 100 Amerindian languages still spoken in parts of Mexico, such as Tzotzil, Nahuatl (Aztec), Maya, Otomi, Zapotec, Mixtec, or Tzeltal. Generally, those who speak an Amerindian language also speak Spanish. Only a small minority does not. English is understood by many in large urban areas.

Religion
The majority of Mexicans (89 percent) are Roman Catholic. The Catholic church is very much a part of the culture, attitudes, and history of all Mexicans, but it does not have very much political influence. Other Christian churches are very active in Mexico. Some are growing quite rapidly. The constitution guarantees freedom of worship. Until recently, however, public displays of worship were banned and churches did not have the right to own property or exist as legal entities. The Mexican constitution, drafted after the revolution in an attempt to take power from the Catholic church and give it to the people, banned all churches from teaching religion in public schools.

In 1992, however, the law was changed so any church can become legal, can own property and buildings (although existing buildings remain property of the government), can open schools, and can worship openly. Members of the clergy are allowed to vote and foreign clergy are now allowed to be in Mexico. The law also gives religious groups access to radio and television. While the previous restrictions were often ignored, even by many government officials, the new law relieves a great deal of tension between the state and various religions—without forcing the government to endorse a specific church.

General Attitudes
The concept of time is less precise in Mexico than in the United States, although this is changing in urban areas. Generally, Mexicans feel individuals are more important than schedules. If a visitor or business associate drops in unexpectedly, most Mexicans will stop to talk, regardless of how long it takes and even if it makes them late for something else. Business contacts are often made during the two or three-hour lunch break. Actually, these are social meetings, for the most part, and business is conducted in the last few minutes. The Mexican people are generally proud of their country, despite the difficult challenges it continues to face. Mexicans call citizens of the United States *americanos*. However, they also like to remind U.S. citizens they are not the only Americans. Mexico is part of North America, so Mexicans are also North Americans.

Personal Appearance
Most Mexicans wear clothing that is also common in the United States, especially in the urban areas. But there are also many types of traditional clothing worn in rural areas—either daily or for festivals. In some areas, a man wears a wool *poncho* (*sarape*) over his shirt and pants when it is cold. He also may wear a wide-brimmed hat made of straw. A woman may wear a long, full skirt. In cooler weather, a shawl (*rebozo*) may cover her blouse. The designs and colors are often markers of a specific region. The Maya sometimes wear traditional clothing. People from various regions of Mexico wear many different kinds of clothing, but color and beauty are two common features for all of them.

CUSTOMS AND COURTESIES
Greetings
The usual greeting is a handshake or a nod of the head, although a full embrace between friends is common. Women often greet each other with a kiss on the cheek. Mexicans typically stand close to each other while talking, sometimes touching their friend's clothing. Mexicans are generally very friendly and polite in their greetings. Verbal greetings vary, but some common ones are: *¡Buenos días!* (Good morning), *¡Buenas tardes!* (Good afternoon), *¡Buenas noches!* (Good evening or Good night), and *¿Cómo esta?* (How are you?). A casual greeting is *¡Hola!* (Hello). Men are referred to as *Señor* (Mr.), women as *Señorita* (Miss). Only when one is sure a woman is married is the title *Señora* (Mrs.) used.

Gestures
"No" can be indicated by shaking the hand from side to side with the index finger extended and palm outward. The "thumbs up" gesture is used for approval. Items are handed, not tossed, to another person. Tossing an item shows a lack of manners

and is offensive. If someone sneezes, a person may say *¡Salud!* (Good health). Hand and arm gestures are often used in conversation.

Visiting

Mexicans are very hospitable. Unannounced visitors are usually welcomed and served refreshments. It is impolite to refuse refreshments. Unannounced visits are fairly common, but as more people get telephones, more are calling ahead first. Mexicans enjoy conversation and socializing with relatives or friends. If they invite people over for dinner, the meal might not be served until after 8:00 P.M., partly because many people work late and because they socialize for a while before eating. On special occasions such as birthdays or Mother's Day, gifts are important and serenading is still popular (usually in rural areas). First-time visitors usually receive a tour of the host's home.

Eating

When eating, both hands are kept above the table. Guests do not leave directly after the meal, but stay for conversation. On weeknights, guests might leave a bit earlier than on weekends, when conversation could last until very late. Lunch is usually the main meal of the day. A light meal, called a *merienda*, may be eaten between lunch and dinner. Dinner might be light or heavy, depending on the family. Food purchased on the street is usually eaten at the stand. It is inappropriate for adults to eat while walking on the street. Bland foods such as bread or rice are eaten with spicy foods to relieve the burning sensation. Many also use a pinch of salt for relief. Hot, spicy food is called *picante*, while hot (temperature) food is called *caliente*. Some foods are eaten with utensils, others with the hand. *Tortillas* are often used as scoops for sauces.

LIFESTYLE

Family

Except in urban areas, where the trend is to have smaller families, Mexican families are generally large (more than three children). Family unity is very important. Indeed, family responsibilities often come before all other responsibilities. Divorce is relatively low, due in part to the dominance of the Catholic faith. The father is the leader of the family, but the mother runs the household. A household, especially in rural areas, may include members of the extended family.

Dating and Marriage

When dating, a boy often meets the girl at a prearranged place, rather than picking her up at her home. Parental approval of the boyfriend, however, is important. In some rural areas, it is considered a mark of poor character for a girl to go out alone after dark, so she may be called on at home. It is common for Mexican males to make *piropos* (flattering personal comments) in passing to females, to which the females generally do not respond. Marriage customs follow Catholic traditions. Common-law marriage is also practiced and recognized.

Diet

Staple foods include corn, beans, rice, and chiles. They are combined with spices, vegetables, and meats or fish in the daily meals. Of course, different foods are eaten in different parts of the country, but some are common throughout the nation. For example, *tortillas* (made from cornmeal) are eaten everywhere, either alone as bread or as part of a meal. Some common foods include *frijoles refritos* (refried beans), *torta* (hollow roll stuffed with meat or cheese), *quesadilla* (tortilla baked with cheese), *mole* (spicy sauce), *taco* (folded *tortilla* filled with meat, cheese, and onions), and many others. Two popular soups are *pozole* (vegetable soup with pork) and *birria* (goat soup). *Enchiladas* are *tortillas* with chicken inside, covered with a hot sauce. *Enfrijoladas* are chicken-filled *tortillas* covered with a bean sauce and cheese. Many names of Mexican food are common in the United States because of the popularity of Mexican restaurants, but many Mexicans doubt the authenticity of U.S.-produced Mexican food.

Recreation

Fútbol (soccer) is the most popular sport in Mexico. Mexico's national soccer team competed in the 1994 World Cup. The sport that draws the next highest number of spectators is the bullfight. *Jai alai*, a fast-moving type of handball, is both a spectator and participation sport. Other participation sports include baseball, basketball, tennis, golf, and volleyball. Mexicans enjoy their own form of the rodeo called *charreada*, which is often accompanied by a fair-like atmosphere. The people's love for music and dancing is evident in the many recreational activities that involve both. Day-long *fiestas* and week-long festivals nearly always include a *mariachi* band or other type of musical group playing for dancing or just listening. Fireworks, feasts, and bullfights are also common festival activities. Watching television is a favorite leisure activity, especially in urban areas.

Holidays

As a predominantly Catholic nation, Mexico celebrates many Catholic holidays. Every village, town, and city has a patron saint, for which there is an annual celebration. Some of the main religious holidays include St. Anthony's Day (17 January), when children take their pets to church to be blessed by St. Anthony, the patron saint of animals; Carnival Week, the week of parties and parades before Lent; Easter (Thursday through Sunday); Corpus Christi (May or June); Assumption (15 August); All Saints Day (1 November); and All Souls Day (2 November). The period from 31 October to 2 November is also called *Día de los Muertos* or Day of the Dead. Graves are swept, special altars are built to honor the newly dead, food or other items are placed on graves to accompany spirits on their journey to heaven, and families gather to celebrate life while they honor the dead. Festivities in some areas are quite lavish and include parades, markets, and concerts. Christmas celebrations begin as early as 16 December with nightly parties (*posadas*). The poinsettia flower originated in Mexico and is associated with the legend of a poor boy's gift to the Christ child. Many Mexicans attend a midnight mass on Christmas Eve.

National public holidays include New Year's Day, the birthday of Benito Juárez (21 March), Labor Day (1 May), *Cinco de Mayo* (5 May, which celebrates an 1867 victory over the French), Independence Day (16 September), Columbus

Day (12 October), Revolution Day (20 November), and the Day of the Virgin Guadalupe (12 December). This last holiday is not technically a public holiday because of its religious connections. But it is so popular that most offices and businesses honor it as a holiday. Guadalupe is the Catholic patron saint of Mexico.

Commerce

Businesses are generally open from 9:00 A.M. to 6:00 P.M., although many shops in smaller towns close between 2:00 and 4:00 P.M. for the midday meal. Street vendors and open-air markets are common. Bargaining is common in these instances. Purchased items are customarily wrapped or placed in a bag before being carried in public. Government offices usually close by 2:30 P.M. In rural areas, weekly market days provide foods and other goods to the people.

SOCIETY

Government

Mexico has a federal government led by a president. There is no vice president. The president is elected directly by the people. Voting is compulsory (but not enforced) for all adults 18 and older. A president may only serve one term, and a legislator is not allowed to serve two consecutive terms. The legislature is composed of a Senate and Chamber of Deputies. While the states are autonomous, the federal government has strong powers and controls things such as education and certain industries.

Economy

In the 1980s, low world oil prices, high debt, high inflation, and unemployment, as well as a destructive earthquake in Mexico City, all severely hindered Mexico's economic growth. However, the economy is currently making a strong comeback, with growth at about 3 percent and inflation below 10 percent. To stimulate the economy, the government sold some state-owned companies, attracted foreign investment, and liberalized trading regulations. The currency is the New Mexican *peso*, which replaced the old *peso* in 1993.

Mexico's Human Development Index (0.805) ranks it 53 out of 173 countries. Real gross domestic product per capita is $5,918, which has about doubled in the last generation. Economic opportunities are improving for a greater number of people; however, regional poverty continues to hinder economic progress.

Agricultural pursuits employ about 26 percent of the labor force. Major crops include corn, cotton, wheat, coffee, sugarcane, sorghum, oilseed, and vegetables. The agriculture sector also produces rubber, cocoa, and chicle (used in making chewing gum). Unfortunately, Mexico is also a major supplier of marijuana. Government efforts to stem the drug trade have been significant, but they have also cost a great deal of money. Mexico cooperates with the United States in fighting drug traffickers.

Mining and petroleum are the two most important industries, but they employ less than 2 percent of the labor force.

Tourism is important for earning foreign exchange and it provides employment for many people. In addition to oil and coffee, Mexico exports agricultural products, shrimp, cotton, and engines. The United States is Mexico's principal trading partner. The two countries and Canada signed the North American Free Trade Agreement (NAFTA) in 1993, which will eventually provide for the freer movement of capital and goods between the countries. In anticipation, border industries (*maquiladoras*), where U.S. investment employs Mexican labor, are thriving.

Transportation and Communication

Personal cars are common in urban areas, but most people use public transportation. Buses are plentiful and inexpensive. Mexico City has a fine subway system. There are numerous taxis, but many operate illegally. Mexico has an extensive system of roads, but many remain unpaved or semi-paved. There is a national railway system and a domestic airline. Buses also provide service between cities. Communications are well developed and modern, although many rural families do not have telephones in their homes. Numerous radio and television stations serve the public and several daily newspapers are available.

Education

Education is compulsory and free between ages six and fourteen. After the first six years of primary education, students enter either three years of secondary school, five years of college preparatory education, or a six-year teacher-training school. There are also numerous vocational schools to choose from. After secondary school, a student may enter one of the above tracks or may enroll in a professional school. A university education lasts from three to seven years. The National University of Mexico is prestigious, and only one-third of the applicants are able to pass the entrance exams. University enrollment has increased rapidly in the last decade. The literacy rate is 87 percent.

Health

Water is potable in most cities, but in some smaller towns or rural areas, bottled water is recommended. Medical facilities are good in urban areas. The infant mortality rate is 28 per 1,000 and life expectancy ranges from 69 to 76 years.

FOR THE TRAVELER

No visa is necessary for U.S. citizens staying up to three months, although proof of citizenship is required. Children traveling without their parents or with one parent must either have a passport or a notarized consent letter from the absent parent(s) to enter Mexico. No vaccinations are needed. For some locations, malaria suppressants may be advisable. Mexico's tourist industry is well developed and offers beaches, archaeological sites, grand colonial cities, and many other attractions. Contact the Mexican Government Tourist Office, 405 Park Avenue, Suite 1401, New York, NY 10022, for information. You may also wish to contact the Embassy of Mexico, 1911 Pennslyvania Avenue NW, Washington, DC 20006.

A *Culturgram* is a product of native commentary and original, expert analysis. Statistics are estimates and information is presented as a matter of opinion. While the editors strive for accuracy and detail, this document should not be considered strictly factual. It is a general introduction to culture, an initial step in building bridges of understanding between peoples. It may not apply to all peoples of the nation. You should therefore consult other sources for more information.

Printed on recycled paper

Montserrat

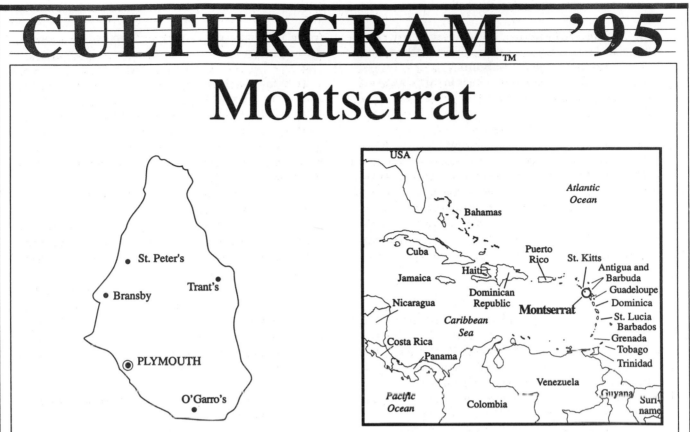

Boundary representations not necessarily authoritative.

BACKGROUND

Land and Climate

Montserrat is located in the Caribbean sea about 250 miles (400 kilometers) southeast of Puerto Rico. Part of the British West Indies, it is considered one of the Leeward Islands of the Lesser Antilles. Montserrat is known as the Emerald Isle and has a land area of only 39 square miles (101 square kilometers), or about half the size of Washington, D.C. The island is volcanic in origin and several fumaroles still emit sulfur fumes, steam, and boiling water. Chances Peak is the highest mountain at 3,000 feet (914 meters). Natural vegetation is confined mostly to the summits of the Soufriere Hills (in the south) and the Centre Hills. Sheltered bays are few and all beaches but one have black volcanic sand.

The climate is tropical, with temperatures ranging from 76°F to 86°F (24–30°C) year-round. Abundant rainfall keeps the island green and the sea breeze is constant. The wettest months are September, October, and November, with the dry season lasting between March and June. The hurricane season usually occurs between June and November. In 1989, Hurricane Hugo devastated the island, but the international community helped rebuild it.

History

The pre-Columbian name of Montserrat was *Alliouagana* (Land of the prickly bush), named by the Carib Indians who overtook the Arawaks long before the coming of Europeans. Christopher Columbus named Montserrat in 1493 after a monastery near Seville, Spain. The Spanish, however, did not settle the island. In 1632, Thomas Warner from neighboring St. Kitts came to settle Montserrat with English and Irish Catholics. These colonists were uncomfortable in Protestant St. Kitts and soon Montserrat was established as an Irish-Catholic colony. Montserrat developed into a sugar and slave colony in the 17th century. With sugar and slavery firmly established, overbearing rich planters emerged. As the slave population grew, so did fear, repression, and rebellion, which culminated in the slave uprising on St. Patrick's Day in 1768. All of the leaders of the uprising were executed, and the rebellion failed.

In the 17th and 18th centuries, France and Britain fought for dominance over the sugar islands of the Caribbean. Montserrat changed hands several times, being occupied briefly by France in 1667 and 1782 before finally coming into permanent English possession after British Admiral Rodney's victory at Les Saints, near the French island of Guadeloupe. The Treaty of Versailles in 1783 made Montserrat permanently British. It remains a dependent territory of the United Kingdom.

The sugar industry peaked in about 1791. In 1834, Britain's parliament abolished slavery in the Caribbean and the slaves were freed. Many properties became burdened with debt and were sold. Former estates were cultivated by sharecroppers and black laborers. When the sugar industry collapsed, the cultivation of limes and cotton replaced it. Montserrat lime

Copyright © 1994. Brigham Young University. Printed in the USA. All rights reserved. It is against the law to copy, reprint, store in a retrieval system, or transmit any part of this publication in any form by any means for any purpose without written permission from the Publications Division of the David M. Kennedy Center for International Studies, Brigham Young University, PO Box 24538, Provo, UT 84602–4538. *Culturgrams* are available for more than 125 areas of the world. To place an order, to receive a free catalog, or to obtain information on traveling abroad, call toll free (800) 528–6279.

juice was particularly in demand by the British Navy for combating scurvy, and the juice is said to have been the source of the nickname *Limey* used for the British.

After the decline of cotton and limes in the 20th century, many Montserratians emigrated. Some went to work on the Panama Canal, others went to Cuba, the Dominican Republic, the United States, and the United Kingdom in search of work. Those employed sent money home to relatives. When these remittances declined, the island turned to real estate and construction. Many American, Canadian, and British citizens now own plush villas and homes for their winter residences.

THE PEOPLE

Population

Montserrat has an estimated population of 11,000. The figure was as high as 14,000, but emigration and smaller families have led to the decline. Between 1959 and 1962, nearly one-third of the population emigrated to England; since then, another one-fifth has gone to North America. The greatest concentration of people live in the capital of Plymouth. The majority of Montserratians are of African descent, with an infusion of North American, European, and East Indian residents in recent years.

Language

The official language is English, but a West Indian dialect is widely spoken by most people. The dialect is really a form of English mixed with elements of French and various African tongues. Idiomatic expressions are commonly employed using this dialect. This is referred to as *speaking Montserratian*, or *speaking dialect*. Some people consider using the dialect as improper, but most enjoy how it makes speech more colorful and even poetic.

Religion

Montserratians are religious, with Anglican, Methodist, and Roman Catholic being the main Christian denominations. Seventh-Day Adventists, Pentecostals, and other Christian churches are assuming an increasing importance.

Religion affects many aspects of daily life. Public schools have prayer and gospel singing every day before classes begin. Most public functions are opened and sometimes closed with prayer. Adults participate in many gospel choirs and concerts. People are genuine about their religious devotion. This is manifest by the dignity and respect with which Montserratians treat each other and strangers.

General Attitudes

Montserratians take great pride in their country and (recently) in their African roots. Friendliness, forthrightness, and honesty are viewed as proud assets of the island. Interactions are easy and amiable and most people display politeness, courtesy, and respect to all. The general attitude is one of tolerance and live-and-let-live. People take time to talk to each other and the concept of time is not as literal as in industrialized countries. When a given time is stated for an event or function, it will sometimes go on much later than advertised. Likewise, people are more important than schedules and being late is not a problem. Montserratians are observant of people and things; very little goes unnoticed when one is watching a group, passersby, a scene, or an activity.

Personal Appearance

Montserratians dress up in their finest clothes for church or any other important social function. Women wear dresses or dressy skirts and blouses to work, along with sandals. Men wear sport shirts or a shirt-jacket (cotton shirt, cut square, that is worn like a jacket), slacks, and shoes. Most men do not wear ties due to the climate. Jeans and tight-fitting clothing are also too hot for most people. Loose-fitting clothes made of lightweight fabric are most comfortable and popular. Older, rural women rarely wear pants, but younger and urban women do. All public schools require students to wear uniforms; each school has its own color for boys and girls. Teachers stress neatness and cleanliness for all.

CUSTOMS AND COURTESIES

Greetings

Montserratian greetings include the more polite "Good morning," "Good day," "Good evening," and "Good night" (after dark), as well as the casual *You alright?*, which means "How are you?" The response is "Okay." When parting, people might say "Good-bye" or "All the best."

People often shake hands or touch when greeting. The youth sometimes touch clenched fists after a traditional handshake to show solidarity. When addressing friends and relatives, Montserratians use colorful nicknames that were usually acquired in childhood. Some nicknames may also be acquired in adulthood as a result of one's occupation or something else, but these do not stick to the person throughout life as the childhood name does. One's nickname might also be used instead of the given name by acquaintances, but formal situations call for the use of given names and titles. An older person or superior at work might be called *Mas* (for men) or *Miss* (for women), but most people use the more complete Mr., Mrs., or Miss.

Gestures

Montserratians are affectionate and loving. They commonly touch each other's hands, arms, or shoulders while talking. Hand gestures might be used to complement verbal expressions, especially between friends. A quick "pssst" or hissing sound is often used to get one's attention while walking by or when in a crowd.

Visiting

Montserratians are friendly with their neighbors and often stop by to see how they are doing or to *talk up* the latest island news. When neighbors visit, they might bring such homemade gifts as banana bread or some guava juice. People often have house parties for special occasions such as birthdays, anniversaries, or graduations.

When Montserratians get together, the atmosphere is amiable, courteous, and relaxed. Invited guests are usually offered at least something to drink (soft drinks, juice, etc.).

The most popular form of socializing for men takes place at the local rum shop, a small neighborhood tavern. Friends and neighbors socialize, watch television, listen to music, or eat chicken or bread. Women more commonly socialize in the home or in connection with their children's activities.

Eating

Lunch and dinner are the main meals, as breakfast is usually light. Many Montserratians in Plymouth eat lunch at restaurants. They might have fried chicken and chips, a hamburger, or *peleau* (rice, beans, and chicken). Bread and cheese are eaten for a quick meal. Families usually eat dinner together at home. For community or family gatherings, a barbecue is popular.

LIFESTYLE

Family

The extended family is the primary social unit in Montserrat. Grandparents often live with their children's families and help to raise the grandchildren. Siblings usually have the same mother, but they may have different fathers. Women generally hold the family together. They care for the household and also usually work outside the home (in schools, stores, hotels, and restaurants). Men support their families and help raise children with a firm but loving hand. Discipline is stressed and children are well behaved.

Dating and Marriage

Dating begins in secondary school and is centered around social or school functions. Young couples enjoy going to basketball games, cricket matches, or concerts. When churches have *fetes*, young people enjoy getting together for the games, music, food, and fun. The few nightclubs and discos are popular on weekends.

Couples marry in their twenties or thirties and begin to raise a family. Formal marriage is stressed by churches, but common-law unions are not unusual. There are many single mothers, but they generally receive support from the fathers of their children.

Weddings are traditionally held in a church, and a reception follows the ceremony. At the reception, the bride and groom and their parents will give testimonials in tribute to each other's families while toasting with champagne. Musical entertainment follows, and there is plenty of food for guests.

Diet

Local and imported chicken, rice, white potatoes, and breadfruit are the main staples of the diet. Meats and fish are popular, but chicken is by far the most consumed protein food. Bread is also important, and many small bakeries operate on the island.

Foods imported from Miami via Puerto Rico are expensive, and the island is trying to become more self-sufficient. The production of meats and vegetables to replace imports is actively encouraged. Locally grown produce includes potatoes, tomatoes, mangos, papayas, and yams. Popular dishes include *goat water* (stewed mutton), *mountain chicken* (actually frog), *saltfish* (usually dried cod), and dumplings. Soft drinks, homemade fruit juices, and beer are drunk with meals. Coffee, tea, lemonade, and iced tea are also popular drinks for mealtime and at other times.

Recreation

Cultural activities such as school arts festivals, folklore and gospel choir concerts, and productions of local plays and shows all have community support and participation. Calypso, soca, reggae, gospel, folk, steel pan, and *dub* (disc jockeys rapping street poems) are the favorite types of music. They are often part of social activities. *Jumpups* (block parties that involve street dancing) are the most popular form of getting together to enjoy music with friends on a Friday or Saturday night.

The national sport of Montserrat and the West Indies is cricket. During a "test match," schools and businesses often close for a half day so people can go to Sturge Park (the main stadium) to watch Montserratian athletes compete. Basketball, *netball* (for girls), football (soccer), tennis, swimming, biking, boating, jogging, and hiking are increasingly popular.

Some Montserratians travel in July and August when school is out. The festival season in December is anticipated and planned in detail months in advance. This is generally the happiest and most popular time of year for people.

Holidays

Christmas and Easter are the most important holidays on Montserrat. Traditional Christmas practices of gift giving, carol singing, and attending church are combined with other celebrations. On Christmas Eve, many people celebrate in Plymouth with a large block party. The Montserrat Festival, a Caribbean carnival, is held every December during the Christmas season. Cultural shows, calypso competitions, dancing, and parades are all part of the celebrations. Many Montserratians who live overseas return every year for the festival, which culminates in the Festival Day Parade on New Year's Day. Easter is also a time for family gatherings and church services.

St. Patrick's Day (17 March) is celebrated as a national holiday in memory of the 1768 slave uprising. The holiday is used to raise awareness of Montserrat's turbulent history. Other important holidays include Emancipation Day (1 August, but celebrated on the first Monday in August), Whit Monday, Labor Day (1 May, but celebrated on the first Monday in May), and Queen Elizabeth II's Birthday (second Saturday in June).

Commerce

Normal business hours are from 8:00 A.M. to 4:00 P.M., with an hour taken for lunch. Businesses close at noon on Wednesdays and Saturdays. With the exception of convenience stores and gas stations, most places are closed on Sunday. An open-air market in Plymouth is open every day, but the variety and quantity of food is largest on Friday and Saturday. Fresh produce and meats are the main features of the market.

SOCIETY

Government

Montserrat, as a territory of the United Kingdom, recognizes Queen Elizabeth II as the head of state. According to the 1960 constitution, the island has a crown-appointed governor who maintains responsibility for defense, external affairs, internal security, administration of public services, and the judicial system. The governor has an Executive Council that includes a chief minister and five other members. Reuben T. Meade was elected chief minister in 1991 for a five-year term. A Legislative Council has eleven members, seven of whom are elected. It is presided over by a speaker (currently Howard Fergus), who is elected by the council outside of its membership. The next general elections for the Legislative Council are in 1996; the voting age is 18. Montserrat has three parishes (Saint Anthony, Saint Georges, and Saint Peter). The legal system is based on English common law, and the highest judicial authority is the East Caribbean Supreme Court.

Economy

Montserrat's economy is based on agriculture, real estate, construction, tourism, and some light industry (mostly assembly). Incentives, promotions, radio shows, and an agricultural fair are being used to encourage agricultural self-sufficiency. The island can support a variety of animals and crops. Cattle, chicken, local fruits and vegetables, and sea-island cotton are a few of the products being produced.

Tourism and construction of holiday villas and condominiums provide jobs and bring visitors and revenue to the island. A newly completed deep-water port in Plymouth will bring the added tourist business of cruise ships. Small factories assemble electronic components and manufacture plastic bags. A number of off-shore banks are in business, but they are regulated by the government to ensure they remain reputable.

Montserratians generally enjoy a decent standard of living. The country has low unemployment, steady economic growth, and a gross domestic product per capita of about US$5,800. Montserrat is a member of CARICOM (Caribbean Community) and other regional bodies that are important to the economy. The stable East Caribbean dollar (EC$) is the currency.

Transportation and Communication

There is no ferry boat service between islands in this part of the Caribbean, so many Montserratians travel off island by air. All regional business, government, and pleasure travel is by small plane. The government also plans to realign the airport runway to accommodate small jets.

Villages are linked to each other and to Plymouth by paved roads on the western side of the island. Private cars and trucks account for a large portion of traffic. Public minivans travel between villages and Plymouth. Taxis are available in Plymouth. Children walk to schools located near their village or town, and a few older men ride donkeys for their transport.

Telephone and telecommunication services are available island-wide. Radio Montserrat is government-owned, and GEM Radio Caribbean broadcasts from Plymouth. Cable television was introduced during the rebuilding of Montserrat after Hurricane Hugo. All major channels are available and most homes have televisions. There are two newspapers.

Education

The education system reflects a strong British influence. Free primary and secondary education is provided for all school-aged children. There are a number of private pre-primary schools and children can attend these beginning at age three. Pupils usually attend school for 13 years and most complete secondary school. School-leaving (graduation) exams are set by London and Cambridge syndicates, and the Caribbean Examinations Council is the examining board.

When students graduate, some go on to Montserrat's Technical College, the University of the West Indies, or to overseas colleges. Others begin to work; a small number of pupils drop out before graduation to begin working. An offshore medical school (American University of the Caribbean) is located in Montserrat, but it caters to students from abroad and does not supply doctors to Montserrat.

Health

Montserrat is a healthy island with an abundance of clean drinking water. Glendon Hospital in Plymouth provides surgical, medical, obstetric, and dental services. For special treatments or certain emergencies, patients are flown to Barbados or Jamaica. There are 12 district health centers that provide care and health education. Free care is provided to children and the elderly. Working adults have health insurance to cover their medical costs. A number of private doctors are in practice, and ear and eye specialists from other countries visit at times to provide care. The infant mortality rate is 12 per 1,000; life expectancy ranges from 74 to 78 years.

FOR THE TRAVELER

U.S. citizens require proof of identification (a passport is the best form, but a birth certificate or driver's license is acceptable) and a return ticket to enter Montserrat. Vaccinations are not required. A departure tax of $12 is charged at Blackburne Airport. Montserrat has a number of small hotels and other accommodations for the traveler. Visitors will enjoy a museum in a restored sugar mill, Galway's Plantation ruins, Trant's Estate (sight of an Amerindian village), and other ruins. Beaches, bays, fumaroles, and Galway's Soufriere (a volcano) are also interesting. For more information, contact the Montserrat Tourist Board, PO Box 7, Plymouth, Montserrat, British West Indies, or the Chamber of Commerce, PO Box 384, Plymouth, Montserrat, British West Indies.

A *Culturgram* is a product of native commentary and original, expert analysis. Statistics are estimates and information is presented as a matter of opinion. While the editors strive for accuracy and detail, this document should not be considered strictly factual. It is a general introduction to culture, an initial step in building bridges of understanding between peoples. It may not apply to all peoples of the nation. You should therefore consult other sources for more information.

Printed on recycled paper

CULTURGRAM™ '95

Kingdom of the
Netherlands

Boundary representations not necessarily authoritative.

BACKGROUND

Land and Climate

The Netherlands is about the size of Massachusetts and Connecticut combined. It covers 14,413 square miles (37,330 square kilometers). In the west, areas that have been reclaimed from the sea are called *polders*. In the past, water was pumped from the land by windmills, and dikes held back the ocean. Today, modern machines do the pumping, but about 930 windmills (out of an original 10,000) still dot the landscape. Close to 300 continue to function, mostly for tourists, but others mill grains or perform other work. In the east, the land is above sea level and even has a few hills. Grasslands used for grazing are common in the north, while the south has a more varied landscape. The climate is temperate. Rain is common throughout the year. Winters can be cold, but some are quite mild. Likewise, summers can be warm and sometimes cool.

History

Although its official name is the Kingdom of the Netherlands, Holland is the name by which most Americans know the country. However, its use is not really appreciated by the Dutch who do not live in either North or South Holland provinces. In medieval times, the area was a group of autonomous duchies and counties. They were known as the Low Countries in the 1500s, along with Belgium and Luxembourg. During this time, the countries were ruled by a Spanish monarch. In 1568, Prince William of Orange rebelled against the Spanish crown and began an 80-year war for independence. In 1648, with the Peace of Westphalia, the Netherlands became independent. In the years following, it built a vast overseas empire, becoming for a time the world's leading maritime and commercial power. In 1795, French forces made the Netherlands a vassal state and Napoleon completely annexed the territory in 1810. The Congress of Vienna ended French occupation, and the United Kingdom of the Netherlands was created in 1815. It originally included Belgium, which seceded in 1830.

The Netherlands remained neutral during World War I but was invaded by Germany in World War II. After World War II, the Netherlands played an important role in European economic development. Most overseas holdings were granted independence after World War II, including Indonesia and Surinam. In 1980, Queen Juliana abdicated in favor of her daughter, Queen Beatrix, who is the head of state today. The heir to the throne is her son, the Crown Prince Willem Alexander. If he ascends to the throne, he will be the first male monarch since 1890. The United States and the Netherlands have enjoyed unbroken diplomatic relations since 1782.

THE PEOPLE

Population

The Netherlands has a population of approximately 15.2 million, which is growing annually at 0.6 percent. More than 40 percent of the population lives in the two western provinces of *Noord* (North) Holland and *Zuid* (South) Holland. These two provinces, from which the Netherlands received its nickname, "Holland," contain the three largest cities of the country: Amsterdam, Rotterdam, and The Hague. The population is 95 percent ethnic Dutch, although there are some Indonesians (50,000) and Surinamese (210,000). Turkish and Moroccan guest workers and their families or descendents number more than 250,000.

Copyright © 1994. Brigham Young University. Printed in the USA. All rights reserved. It is against the law to copy, reprint, store in a retrieval system, or transmit any part of this publication in any form by any means for any purpose without written permission from the Publications Division of the David M. Kennedy Center for International Studies, Brigham Young University, PO Box 24538, Provo, UT 84602–4538. *Culturgrams* are available for more than 125 areas of the world. To place an order, to receive a free catalog, or to obtain information on traveling abroad, call toll free (800) 528–6279.

EUROPE

Also included in the Kingdom of the Netherlands are the Caribbean islands of Aruba (population 62,500) and the Netherlands Antilles (population 183,000). These islands have unique cultural aspects and are therefore not discussed in this *Culturgram*.

Language

The official language is Dutch, a Germanic language. Frisian is also spoken in the northeastern province of Friesland. English, German, and French are commonly understood and spoken and are taught in the secondary schools. Flemish, a form of Dutch, is spoken in a region of Belgium called Flanders.

Religion

About 36 percent of the people are Roman Catholic. Most Catholics live in the southern provinces of Brabant and Limburg. Another 27 percent are Protestant (mostly Dutch Reformed), 6 percent belong to other churches, and the rest are not officially affiliated with any religion. The royal family belongs to the Dutch Reformed Church. The Netherlands, like many European countries, is a secular society, in which the role of religion has been diminishing steadily for some time. There is a strong tradition of maintaining church and state separate.

General Attitudes

There is a noticeable difference in attitudes among those who live north of the Rhine delta, in what is traditionally the Protestant (Calvinist) part of the country, and those who live in the traditionally Catholic south. By reputation, people in the south are more gregarious than those in the north. As a small, trade-dependent nation, the Netherlands has recognized the importance throughout history of being internationally minded. They have a strong tradition of involvement in international (primarily European since World War II) affairs. They are active in the United Nations. Dutch attitudes about society helped them create one of the most extensive welfare systems in the world, which still has a high priority in the country despite the increasing difficulty of supporting it.

Dutch openness to the world has made them no less proud of their own culture and heritage, whether it be in the arts, politics, technology, or a strong tradition of liberalism. Through hard work and engineering skill, the Dutch took much of their territory from the sea by pumping water from land that is below sea level and building dikes to keep the water back. Because of this feat and their pioneering spirit, the Dutch have a saying: "God made the earth, but the Dutch made Holland." However, these diligent efforts eventually led to sinking land, water pollution, and problems with the water table. So, the government is buying up thousands of acres of agricultural land (which is what the reclaimed territory consists of) and returning it to nature. Some dikes are being destroyed, and marshes and wetlands are gradually being allowed to return to their original state.

Personal Appearance

European fashions are popular. The Dutch enjoy stylish casual attire, as long as it is neat and clean. Traditional attire is rarely worn. The Dutch are famous for the wooden shoes or clogs *(klompen)* they produce. There are different *klompen* for different purposes, such as working in the fields, for leisure time, and even for getting married. Today, most *klompen* are exported. In the Netherlands, *klompen* are no longer worn in everyday situations, except for on the farm, where they might still be worn by field workers.

CUSTOMS AND COURTESIES

Greetings

A warm and hearty handshake is an appropriate greeting for both men and women. It is also popular among friends to kiss on alternating cheeks three times when greeting. A common phrase is *Hoe gaat het* (How are you?). While people may wave if greeting from a distance, it is impolite to shout. The use of given names is generally reserved for close friends and relatives, except among the youth. Otherwise, titles and family names are used when addressing people. When answering the telephone, both the caller and the receiver always identify themselves before starting a conversation. It is rude not to do so.

Gestures

Eye contact and facial expressions are important. The mouth is covered when a person yawns. When someone sneezes, a person nearby will say *proost* or *gezondheid*, the equivalent of saying "bless you." It is impolite to chew gum while speaking. Pointing the index finger to the forehead to imply someone is crazy is an insult. Wagging the index finger emphasizes a point.

Visiting

The Dutch are hospitable and enjoy having visitors. Unannounced visiting is not common, except between very close friends or relatives. If a time to visit is stated, it is important to be punctual. If no time is stated for an evening visit to new acquaintances, it is usual to arrive not before 8:30 P.M. and to leave between 11:00 P.M. and midnight. When visiting, it is customary to shake hands with everyone present, including children. Refreshments are nearly always offered to guests. In most cases, hosts serve their guests, who do not help themselves or go into the kitchen to get something. On a first visit to someone's home, a guest does not expect a meal (unless specifically invited to dinner). Rather, coffee or tea is served with sweet biscuits, and then drinks are served later in the evening. Dinner guests usually bring flowers or another small gift to their hosts. The Netherlands is known for its flowers, which are purchased regularly to adorn window boxes, other parts of the home, restaurants, and businesses. Green house plants are also extremely popular.

Eating

The Dutch generally eat three meals a day. Dinner (around 6:00 P.M.) is the main meal for most people, but rural families and older people sometimes retain the tradition of eating the main meal at midday. For them, the evening meal is light and often consists of bread, cold cuts, cheese, and some sort of salad.

It is impolite to begin eating before others at the table. A parent or host often indicates when to eat, usually by saying *Eet smakelijk* (pronounced ATE smahk-AY-lick), which literally means "eat deliciously" but is used in the same was as *bon appetit* (good appetite). It is proper to keep hands above the table, not in the lap, but to not rest elbows on the table. The continental style of eating is used, with the fork in the left hand and the knife remaining in the right. Forks are not used to eat dessert; small spoons are provided. One does not leave the table until all have finished eating.

LIFESTYLE

Family

The Dutch have strong families, which are moderate in size. Most have only one or two children but southern (Catholic) families tend to be a bit larger. People generally live close to extended family, and mobility is not a high as in the United States. Many holidays emphasize family gatherings. As is the case throughout Europe, both parents often work outside the home. However, Dutch women are somewhat less likely to work outside the home than most other women in Europe. Thirty-five percent of the labor force is female. However, more and more younger women are entering the job market, partly due to a better access to education. One fifth of all legislative seats are held by women. Young people often leave home at age 18 in order to continue their education or to work.

Dating and Marriage

Dating habits are similar to those throughout Europe. Teenagers begin with group activities. Dancing, watching movies, and going to cafés are popular. It is common for couples to live together before, or instead of, getting married.

Diet

Bread or toast with jelly, Dutch cheese or meats, and coffee or tea are the most common foods for a Dutch breakfast. The most popular varieties of bread include multigrain or other dark grains. Most people, especially children, eat something sweet on their bread for breakfast or lunch. Typical is chocolate sprinkles (*Hagelslag*) or chocolate spread. Children often eat hot cereal with breakfast. *Krentebollen* (raisin rolls) are a favorite as well. Open-faced sandwiches are common for lunch, as is *kroket* (a deep-fried sausage). The main meal usually consists of potatoes and gravy with seasonal vegetables and meat or fish. Some typical dishes include herring, smoked eel, *poffertjes* (small puffed pancakes served on special occasions), pea soup, and *hutspot* (mashed potatoes with carrots and onions).

Dutch pastries are world famous. Favorite snacks include fries (eaten with mayonnaise, not ketchup), *stroopwafels* (syrup waffles), and Dutch licorice (many varieties). A wide variety of cuisine is offered by restaurants in larger towns, and Indonesian food has become an established part of the Dutch diet. Eating out is a special affair and is not as common as in the United States. Most families continue to eat a majority of their meals in the home.

Recreation

The most popular sport is soccer. The Netherlands' national soccer team competed in the 1994 World Cup. Tennis, field hockey, swimming, sailing, ice skating, wind surfing, basketball, badminton, and many other sports are also enjoyed. Many Dutch participate in cycling—nearly every person old enough to ride a bicycle has one. Bike paths *(Fietspaden)* are available throughout the country. A few Dutch ride in competition, but most ride for their health and for transportation. People ride to work, to go shopping, for fun, or just to get around town. A visitor could easily tour the entire country on a bicycle. People participate in sports through clubs. Games are organized locally, regionally, or nationally depending on the level of the players. Each sport has a national association that oversees its organization.

Some people enjoy *korfbal*, a sport played on a grass field (or indoors) that seems to combine principles of soccer and basketball. A ball must pass through a basket high over the heads of the players for points to be scored. Men and women play together in teams of twelve or eight. Some people in Friesland play *Kaatsen*, a team sport similar to baseball (a small, soft ball is hit with the hand). Poles were traditionally used for jumping over ditches, and pole vaulting (for distance, not height) is popular in the north. It is called *Fiereljeppen*. Also in Friesland, in years when the ice is hard enough, a day-long ice skating race takes place on a route that encompasses all of the province's 11 main towns and involves going across some parts of the sea. As many as 80,000 people may participate.

The Dutch and tourists alike take advantage of sandy beaches on the North Sea, although it is windy and the water is often cold. Discos are popular gathering places for young people. Most people also enjoy drama, music, and art. There are over 600 museums in the Netherlands, and with good reason. Some of the world's most famous artists are Dutch, including Rembrandt, Vermeer, and Van Gogh.

Holidays

Official public holidays include New Year's Day, Easter (Friday through Monday), the Queen's Birthday (30 April), Ascension, Liberation Day (5 May), Whit Monday, and two days for Christmas (25 and 26 December).

Christmas festivities actually begin well before Christmas day. The Dutch do not usually exchange gifts on Christmas day; it is a day for families and feasts. Some families do exchange gifts on Christmas eve, but gift-giving is traditionally associated with St. Nicholas Day (6 December). St. Nicholas is the Santa Claus (*Sinterklaas*) for the Dutch. *Sinterklaas* is dressed like a Catholic Bishop, rides a white horse, and leaves gifts in shoes. Children place hay or a carrot in their shoes for the horse and it is replaced with candy or a small present. *Sinterklaas* also rides in parades and visits children wherever they may be. His servant throws small pieces of gingerbread candy (*pepernoten*) for children to gather and eat. Family members and friends who exchange gifts at this time (evening of 5 December) must disguise or hide the presents. They are all anonymous (said to have come from *Sinterklaas*) and are accompanied by an amusing poem about the receiver. Good-natured kidding and embarrassing others comes along with this festivity.

Each region is also known for local festivals throughout the year, often in celebration of the harvest. *Vlaggetjesdag* (Little Flag Day) is celebrated in coastal areas. Held in May, it marks the beginning of the herring season. Ships leave harbor decorated with little flags. In the south, Carnival celebrations are popular. They begin on the Sunday before Lent and end at midnight Tuesday. Businesses may close or cut back work, and many people enjoy festivities in Den Bosch, Breda, and Maastricht.

The Dutch receive a month of paid vacation each year. Many people take a week at Christmas, a week at Easter, and two weeks in the summer.

Commerce

Business hours are usually between 8:30 or 9:00 A.M. and 5:00 or 5:30 P.M., Monday through Friday. Summer hours might begin and end earlier. Shops often close one morning each week, usually on Monday. Some are also closed at lunch, although not in large urban areas. Except in large cities, all shops close by 6:00 P.M. Amsterdam's so-called "night stores" are open later, but charge higher prices. No businesses are open on Sunday and there is no Sunday newspaper.

SOCIETY

Government

The Kingdom is a constitutional monarchy. The queen is the head of state, but the prime minister is the head of government. Elections that would determine a new prime minister were held in 1994. A Council of State, of which the queen is president, serves as an advisory body that must be consulted before legislation is passed. Legislation can be introduced by the crown or the lower house of parliament. The prime minister and other ministers are responsible to the bicameral parliament (States General). The members of the lower house (First Chamber) are directly elected by the people, while those in the upper house (Second Chamber) are elected by provincial councils. Although the capital is Amsterdam, the government is headquartered at The Hague. First Chamber elections were held in 1991, and Second Chamber elections were conducted in 1994. The voting age is 18.

Economy

The Netherlands has a strong economy. Based on private enterprise, it is highly industrialized and efficient. The country's Human Development Index (0.970) ranks it ninth out of 173 countries. Real gross domestic product (GDP) per capita is $15,695, which has tripled since 1960. The distribution of income is among the most equitable in Europe. The Netherlands responded to the global recession of the early 1990s by enacting austerity measures and trimming welfare programs. It is now structurally more sound and able to compete. Trade is important, accounting for half of the country's GDP.

Although agriculture and horticulture employ less than 6 percent of the labor force, the Netherlands produces food for export, as well as large numbers of cut flowers and bulbs for Europe and other parts of the world. The Netherlands accounts for over half of the world's flower exports. Animal husbandry is a chief agricultural activity, producing meats, cheeses, and other dairy items. Leading industries include petroleum refining, machinery, chemicals, and construction. Banking and tourism are also key sectors of the economy. The currency is the *guilder* (G), also known as the *gulden* (G) or *florin* (Fl). The currency is marked with raised dots to help the blind distinguish denominations.

Transportation and Communication

The public transportation system in the Netherlands is one of Europe's best. An efficient network of trains connects major and minor cities. Most people also own cars. In fact, with the high cost of public transportation, many people prefer to use their cars for daily travel. Buses and streetcars are common in urban areas, and Amsterdam and Rotterdam have subways. The country is divided into zones for public transportation. A universal ticket called a *Strippenkaart* is purchased at stations or from drivers or machines. When entering a bus, streetcar, or most trains, a passenger pushes the ticket into the slot of a machine that stamps it. The number of zones being traveled is thereby subtracted from the ticket. Rotterdam is one of Europe's most important ports, handling 30 percent of Europe's sea transit; it is the world's largest port.

The communications system is efficient and well maintained. Television and radio stations are privately owned and there are dozens of newspapers and periodicals. The national radio and television associations affiliated with each station have certain backgrounds, such as liberal, socialist, Protestant, Catholic, or neutral.

Education

Schooling is free and compulsory between the ages of five and sixteen. An optional year may be taken at age four. Primary education ends at age twelve. Students may go to a Catholic, Protestant, or "non-religious" school, but the basic curriculum is the same. Secondary school begins with three years of "basic education," in which all students study the same 15 subjects that emphasize the practical application of knowledge. After that, students can choose between different types of education, ranging from pre-vocational to pre-university high schools. The number of years varies with the program. Vocational schools train students in such professions as accounting, nursing, or teaching. Graduates of vocational programs and general high schools often enter apprenticeships. Higher education is subsidized by the government. There are 13 universities, the oldest of which is Leiden. It was founded by William of Orange in 1575. The literacy rate is 99 percent.

Health

Medical facilities are excellent and subsidized by the government. For persons earning less than a specified amount, the government coordinates insurance and health care. Those making over the specified amount are required to have private insurance. The government also provides unemployment and disability benefits. The average life expectancy for the Dutch ranges from 75 to 81 years. The infant mortality rate is 7 per 1,000.

FOR THE TRAVELER

U.S. travelers do not need a visa for visits of up to three months, but a valid passport is required. Tourism is very important in the Netherlands, and facilities are well developed. There are no vaccinations required. A plug adaptor and dual-voltage appliances are necessary to use electrical outlets. The Netherlands Board of Tourism (225 North Michigan Avenue, Chicago, IL 60601) has carefully prepared information brochures for the traveler and has information regarding travel opportunities in the country. They also have an office in San Francisco. You may wish to contact the Royal Netherlands Embassy, 4200 Linnean Avenue NW, Washington, DC 20008.

A *Culturgram* is a product of native commentary and original, expert analysis. Statistics are estimates and information is presented as a matter of opinion. While the editors strive for accuracy and detail, this document should not be considered strictly factual. It is a general introduction to culture, an initial step in building bridges of understanding between peoples. It may not apply to all peoples of the nation. You should therefore consult other sources for more information.

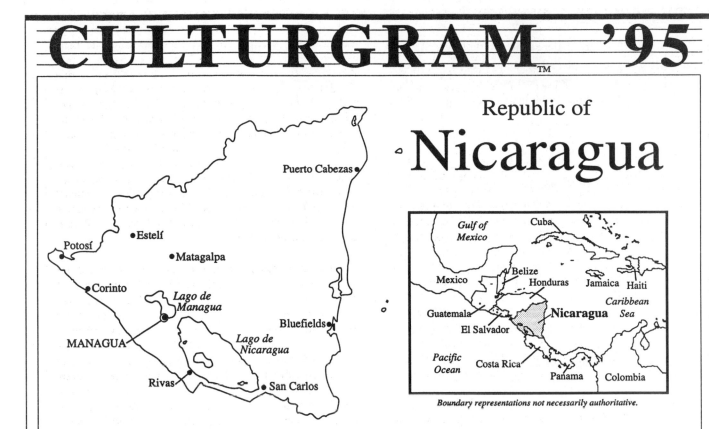

Republic of

Nicaragua

Boundary representations not necessarily authoritative.

BACKGROUND

Land and Climate

Covering 49,998 square miles (129,494 square kilometers), Nicaragua is about the size of Iowa. Although it is the largest country in Central America only about 9 percent of the land is suitable for cultivation. *Lago de Nicaragua* (Lake Nicaragua), a large freshwater lake, borders the Pacific Ocean. It is the only freshwater lake in the world to have sharks and sawfish. Low mountains and hills covered with pine forests run the length of the country near the center, separating the populated west from the east. The east is covered with wetlands (along the coast) and tropical rain forests. In fact, one-third of the country is forested. Natural resources include gold, silver, copper, lead, zinc, and timber. Nicaragua's climate is tropical, although it is cooler in the highlands. Humidity is generally high and the average temperature is 80°F (27°C). There are many volcanoes in the country and earthquakes are not uncommon. Occasional hurricanes, such as one in 1988 that left 300,000 people homeless, can be very destructive along the coasts. A tidal wave struck Nicaragua in 1992, causing extensive damage.

History

Columbus was the first European to visit Nicaragua (1502), which was later explored by Spanish *conquistadores*. Spanish settlements date from the 1520s. Indigenous groups resisted the Spanish until they were finally conquered in 1552. British settlements were established along the Mosquito Coast (the Caribbean Coast) in the 17th century, leading Britain to claim sovereignty over the coast in 1740. By and large, however, Nicaragua was ruled by Spain until 1821, when it declared independence. With independence it became a member of the United Provinces of Central America, but it chose to become an independent republic in 1838. Political power alternated between the Liberals and Conservatives over the next few decades. The competition sometimes led to violence.

Internal chaos and U.S. economic interests led to the intervention of U.S. Marines at various intervals, beginning in 1909. During the 1920s and 1930s, guerrillas led by Augusto Cesar Sandino fought the U.S. occupation. Sandino was assassinated in 1934. In 1936, General Anastasio Somoza García seized the presidency. He ruled as dictator until his assassination in 1956. After his death, the Somoza family continued to rule the country, beginning with Somoza's son, Luis Somoza Debayle, who died in 1967. He was followed in that year by his brother, General Anastasio Samoza Debayle.

In 1962, a revolutionary group called the Sandinistas (named after the martyr Sandino) was formed, with the goal of overthrowing the Somozas. For the next 15 years the Sandinistas carried out various unsuccessful terrorist attacks on Somoza's National Guard, which was armed by the United

Copyright © 1994. Brigham Young University. Printed in the USA. All rights reserved. It is against the law to copy, reprint, store in a retrieval system, or transmit any part of this publication in any form by any means for any purpose without written permission from the Publications Division of the David M. Kennedy Center for International Studies, Brigham Young University, PO Box 24538, Provo, UT 84602–4538. *Culturgrams* are available for more than 125 areas of the world. To place an order, to receive a free catalog, or to obtain information on traveling abroad, call toll free (800) 528–6279.

States. In 1972, when a major earthquake destroyed Managua and killed 10,000 people, relief funds were sent from other countries. Much of the money sent was believed to have been diverted into the Somoza family's private fortune, deepening resentment of Somoza.

After the assassination of a prominent anti-Somoza newspaper editor (Pedro Joaquín Chamorro) in 1978, riots broke out, the Sandinistas stormed the national palace in Managua, and civil war followed. Somoza was forced to flee the country in July 1979, when the Sandinistas took control. Fifty thousand people were killed in the civil war.

The new Marxist-oriented government seized the Somoza fortune, redistributed their lands to the peasants, suspended the constitution, and began tightening controls. Anti-Sandinista activity on the part of the so-called *Contras* began as early as 1980. The Sandinistas suspended elections until 1984. Concerned that the Sandinistas were aiding Marxist rebels in El Salvador, the U.S. government suspended economic aid to Nicaragua in 1981, beginning a decade of strained relations between the two nations.

During the 1980s, the *Contras* were aided in their opposition to Sandinista rule by U.S. funds. General elections in 1984 brought Sandinista leader Daniel Ortega Saaverda to power in 1985. The United States imposed a trade embargo on the country, severely handicapping the economy, and continued funding the *Contra* forces, even though some of the funding was illegally obtained. A peace plan proposed by Costa Rican President Oscar Arias Sánchez in 1987 led to negotiations between the Sandinistas and *Contras*. Although talks often broke down and fighting continued, the Sandinista government agreed to ensure free elections in 1990 if the *Contras* would agree to disarm.

Difficulties continued to plague the peace process, but elections were held in February 1990. Ortega was defeated by Violeta Barrios de Chamorro, the widow of the newspaper editor who was assassinated in 1978 and the candidate endorsed by a national coalition (UNO) of several political parties. The United States backed her candidacy and pledged to end trade restrictions and send aid to rebuild the economy. The *Contras* began to disband in 1990. The new government was faced with violent strikes and a weak economy, but it was able to make some progress in its first year.

Unfortunately, strikes, hyperinflation, and the slow progress of land distribution contributed to severe economic difficulties in 1991. The currency became nearly worthless and had to be replaced, violence erupted in many areas, and many former Sandinista soldiers and *Contras* began to rearm. In 1992, former soldiers held an entire town hostage until they received money for their weapons and promises of land. While some fear the two sides will resume fighting, others support efforts to negotiate peaceful solutions. By 1993, with support for the government dwindling and Sandinistas still controlling the army, questions were raised as to Nicaragua's ability to maintain a lasting democracy.

THE PEOPLE

Population

The population of Nicaragua is 3.87 million. It is growing at 2.8 percent annually. The majority of the people (69 percent) are *mestizo*, a mixture of indigenous Indian and ethnic Spanish. Seventeen percent are of European descent. About 9 percent are black and 5 percent native Indian. Most people live on the plains of the Pacific side of the country. The capital, Managua, has a population of nearly 800,000. The Caribbean side is sparsely populated—mostly by smaller ethnic groups. Nicaragua's population is young; about 45 percent of the people are under age 15.

Language

Spanish is the official and predominant language. Along the Caribbean coast, small groups speak English or other ethnic languages. Garífuna is common among the Black population, while some Indian groups speak Misquito, Sumo, and Rama. English is understood by some in the capital city.

Religion

Approximately 95 percent of the population is Roman Catholic. Most of the rest are members of Protestant or other Christian organizations. Freedom of religion is guaranteed.

General Attitudes

Nicaraguans enjoy being with other people and are sociable. Honor is important and defended vigorously, sometimes even physically. Personal criticism is taken seriously and should be avoided. The family is important and is the foundation of society. However, youth clubs and social groups are increasing in importance. Because individuals are considered far more important than schedules, punctuality at meetings may be admired but not strictly observed. People living in urban areas are more exposed to cosmopolitan values. They tend to be less traditional and more modern. Those living in rural areas, on the other hand, still value tradition. For example, *machismo*, a traditional concept that men are superior to women, is prevalent in rural areas. Also, persons holding power are traditionally considered to be the only ones whose opinions count and who should enjoy wealth. Power is therefore highly valued and often sought.

Personal Appearance

Men wear clothes made from washable cotton cord or other lightweight material. Women wear cool, cotton dresses. Businessmen seldom wear suit coats during the hottest months of the year. There are also various traditional costumes worn for special occasions and festivals.

CUSTOMS AND COURTESIES

Greetings

When meeting another person for the first time, Nicaraguans smile, shake hands, and say either *Mucho gusto de conocerle* (Glad to meet you) or *¿Cómo está usted?* (How are you?). Inquiring about the health of family members demonstrates friendliness between acquaintances. Complete attention is given to the person being greeted. Common terms for greeting include *¡Buenos días!* (Good morning), *¡Buenas tardes!* (Good afternoon), and *¡Buenas noches!* (Good evening). A casual greeting, especially among the youth, is *¡Hola!* (Hi). Men greet each other with a hearty handshake, and close friends hug and pat each other on the back. Between female friends, the usual greeting is a kiss on the cheek and a gentle hug. Those of higher social standing are greeted with titles, such as *Señor, Señora,* or *Señorita* (Mr., Mrs., or Miss) to show respect. The titles *Don* and *Doña* are used with men's and women's first names, respectively, to indicate special respect and familiarity or affection. For example, most Nicaraguans refer to President Chamorro as Doña Violeta.

Gestures

Most gestures common in the United States are also acceptable in Nicaragua. However, a fist with the thumb positioned between the index and middle fingers is vulgar.

Visiting

Visitors are always welcome, as the Nicaraguans are very hospitable people. They love to meet strangers. Expressing admiration for material objects is not as important in Nicaragua as complimenting others on their good personality traits. Dinner guests may take small gifts, such as flowers or candy, to the hosts. Gifts are also given on special occasions, such as anniversaries, birthdays, and Catholic ceremonies (baptism, confirmation).

Eating

Eating is complemented with pleasant conversation. Meals generally last longer than they do in the United States. Table manners vary from family to family, but both hands (not elbows) should remain on or above the table at all times. The main meal is eaten at midday. A *siesta*, or afternoon rest, is normally taken after the meal. A person can relax or even sleep during this time. A *siesta* usually coincides with the hottest time of the day, when work is difficult.

LIFESTYLE

Family

The extended family is the basis of society and exerts a major influence on an individual's life and decisions. It is not uncommon to have parents, children, aunts, uncles, and cousins all living together. During the Sandinista rule, women were given a greater role in society. A new constitution promised them the right to more actively participate in family matters. Service in the military was common for women under the Sandinista regime and many became involved in civic affairs. About one-fourth of the labor force is female. As in many Latin American nations, a person has two family names. The last name is the mother's family name and the second-to-last name is the father's family name, which functions as the surname. Therefore, a person named José Muñoz Gómez would be called Señor Muñoz.

Dating and Marriage

A girl formally enters social life at age 15. At that time, a big *fiesta* (party) is held in her honor. Thereafter, she is allowed to attend dances, enjoy other entertainment, and have a boyfriend. Group dating is common among the youth. Although marriage is a valued institution, some infidelity among men is tolerated. This is part of *machismo*. Some women have spoken out against this in recent years.

Diet

Obtaining a well-balanced meal is difficult for many of the people. Beans and rice are eaten with most meals. Corn is an important ingredient in many foods. Typical dishes include *tortillas, enchiladas, nacatamales* (meat and vegetables, with spices), *mondongo* (tripe and beef knuckles), and *baho* (meat, vegetables, and plantain). Tropical fruits are usually plentiful. Fried bananas *(plátanos)* are popular. A typical vegetable dish is called *vigorón*.

Recreation

Club activities are popular, and dancing is a favorite social pastime. Celebrations honoring local patron saints are the main annual events in their respective towns and regions. Baseball is the national sport and the people love it. Soccer, boxing, softball, basketball, and volleyball are also enjoyed. Bullfights and cockfights are held in rural regions, usually on weekends and holidays or *fiesta* days.

Holidays

Public holidays include New Year's Day, Easter (Thursday to Sunday), Labor Day (1 May), Battle of San Jacinto (14 September), Independence Day (15 September), Feast of the Immaculate Conception (8 December), and Christmas. Workers also receive a half-day vacation on Christmas Eve. Numerous local holidays are held during the year.

Commerce

Most merchants' shops are open from 8:00 A.M. to noon and from 2:00 to 6:00 P.M., Monday through Friday, and on Saturdays from 8:00 A.M. to noon. Government offices are generally open from 7:00 A.M. to 5:00 P.M., Monday through Friday. In rural areas business hours vary; work schedules depend on the crops cultivated.

SOCIETY

Government

The Republic of Nicaragua has a president, vice president, and cabinet that form the executive branch. The National Assembly has 92 members. Legislators are directly elected to serve six-year terms. The voting age is 16. Nicaragua has 17 departments (provinces).

Economy

The 1972 earthquake, the 1988 hurricane, the decade of central planning under the Sandinistas coupled with the U.S. trade embargo, and the difficult transition to a free market all combined to devastate the Nicaraguan economy. During the 1980s, living standards dropped to 1940s' levels. Banks and major industries were nationalized. Rationing restricted domestic buying. In the early 1990s, economic growth was negligible and unemployment rose to 40 percent.

The economy relies on foreign aid and the export of agricultural commodities such as coffee, cotton, sugar, bananas, seafood, and meat. About 44 percent of the labor force is employed in agriculture. The currency is currently the *gold córdoba* (C$), introduced in 1991.

The economy remains the country's greatest challenge, as expectations for change have greatly exceeded the government's ability to provide it. However, more than half of all state enterprises have been sold to the private sector. While economic output fell in 1990 and 1991, it remained stable for 1992 and 1993. Inflation has dropped significantly since 1991, and unemployment is also dropping. Underemployment remains a problem yet to be adequately addressed. Nicaragua has the potential for a much stronger economy, and current trends are encouraging. For now, the country's Human Development Index (0.500) ranks it 111 out of 173 countries. Real gross domestic product per capita is $1,497, lower than it was in 1960. About one-fifth of the population lives in poverty. These figures suggest that while absolute poverty does not abound, the country as a whole is poor. Most people do not earn a decent income, and economic opportunities are limited (especially in rural areas).

Transportation and Communication

Years of fighting and the poor economy damaged both the transportation and communications systems. The national railroad is largely inoperative. There are only about 1,500 miles of paved road in the country, and much of it is in disrepair. Most roads are not paved and many areas cannot be reached by car. In some cases, ox cart trails are used to access rural regions. Postal, telegraph, and telephone services do not generally serve rural areas. The press is free and there are many newspapers.

Education

Education improved under the Sandinistas, who filled teacher shortages by hiring Cuban instructors. The literacy rate rose to about 80 percent. Schooling is mandatory and free between the ages of six and thirteen. Most primary-age children begin primary school, but only 36 percent complete it. Those that do complete primary training, however, generally proceed to the secondary level. There are two universities: the National University of Nicaragua and the Central American University.

Health

Health care facilities are not available in many areas of Nicaragua. The government is seeking ways to improve the system, but many people do not have access to adequate care. Still, three-fourths of all infants are immunized and about the same number of women receive some prenatal care. The infant mortality rate is 55 per 1,000 and life expectancy averages 64 years. Water is not safe in rural areas.

FOR THE TRAVELER

Although the Chamorro government and the United States have good relations, troubles still exist in Nicaragua and it might be wise for U.S. citizens to contact the State Department for advisories before traveling there. For recorded messages on travel conditions, call (202) 647–5225. Nicaragua is a beautiful country of large lakes, lovely mountains, and interesting people. A visa is not required for stays of less than 30 days. For longer visits, a visa is necessary and can be acquired from the embassy. No vaccinations are required, however, some may be advisable depending on the nature and length of the trip. Electrical outlets use a voltage and plugs comparable with those in the United States; no adaptors are necessary. For more information on travel opportunities, contact the Office of Tourism (Plaza España, Managua, Nicaragua). You may also wish to contact the Embassy of Nicaragua, 1627 New Hampshire Avenue NW, Washington, DC 20009.

A *Culturgram* is a product of native commentary and original, expert analysis. Statistics are estimates and information is presented as a matter of opinion. While the editors strive for accuracy and detail, this document should not be considered strictly factual. It is a general introduction to culture, an initial step in building bridges of understanding between peoples. It may not apply to all peoples of the nation. You should therefore consult other sources for more information.

Northern Ireland

(United Kingdom)

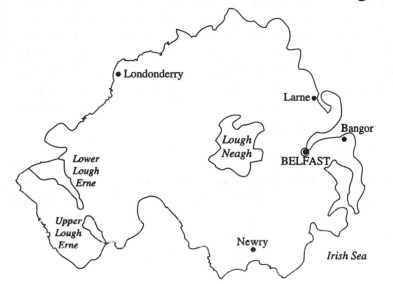

Boundary representations not necessarily authoritative.

BACKGROUND

Land and Climate

Northern Ireland is the smallest of the four nations that make up the United Kingdom. Covering 5,482 square miles (14,199 square kilometers), it is about the same size as Connecticut. Summers are mild (average 55°F or 13°C) and wet; winters are cold (average 32°F or 0°C) and windy. The climate makes for a lush green countryside. Northern Ireland consists of the six northern counties on the island it shares with the Republic of Ireland. The six counties, together with three in the Republic of Ireland, make up what is called *Ulster.* Northern Ireland itself is often just referred to as *Ulster.* A large lake (*Lough Neagh*) dominates the terrain near Belfast. Rolling hills, a few low mountains, a rugged coastline, and forests are all part of the Northern Ireland landscape.

History

Celtic tribes invaded the island during the fourth century B.C. In the fifth century A.D., legend holds that Saint Patrick converted the island to Christianity. The English began invading in the 12th century. In 1603, Irish revolts caused England's King James I to force Irish Roman Catholics in Northern Ireland to give up their land to English and Scottish Protestants. In 1801,

the United Kingdom of Great Britain and Ireland was formed by the British parliament.

In southern Ireland, the Easter Rebellion against British rule took place in 1916. This led to the Irish Free State, established in 1921 under British dominion. However, the south was largely Catholic. Meanwhile, the mainly Protestant northern counties of *Ulster* chose to remain in the United Kingdom as Northern Ireland. In 1949, the Irish Free State (not including Northern Ireland) became the Republic of Ireland and formally withdrew from the Commonwealth.

Seeking to unite all of Ireland, the Irish Republican Army (IRA), which is made up primarily of Catholics, has carried out a campaign of assassinations and bombings against the Northern Ireland Protestants and British soldiers stationed in the country since 1969. The soldiers had been sent to maintain order after rioting broke out in Londonderry over issues of religious discrimination. Protestant extremists have often retaliated in similarly violent ways, thus leading to the present political problems of Northern Ireland. The British government instituted direct rule in 1972. That means Northern Ireland, except regarding limited local matters, is governed by central government officials based in London, rather than local authorities.

EUROPE

Copyright © 1994. Brigham Young University. Printed in the USA. All rights reserved. It is against the law to copy, reprint, store in a retrieval system, or transmit any part of this publication in any form by any means for any purpose without written permission from the Publications Division of the David M. Kennedy Center for International Studies, Brigham Young University, PO Box 24538, Provo, UT 84602–4538. *Culturgrams* are available for more than 125 areas of the world. To place an order, to receive a free catalog, or to obtain information on traveling abroad, call toll free (800) 528–6279.

In 1975, Protestant and Catholic voters elected a 78-member convention with the responsibility of drafting a constitution and organizing a government for home rule acceptable to both sides. Unable to come to an agreement the convention disbanded 10 months later. The widely publicized struggles during the last two decades have been initiated by extremists on both sides and are not generally supported by either Catholics or Protestants. Although the English still rule, the strife has severely damaged government structures.

In 1985, after talks with the United Kingdom, the Republic of Ireland was awarded a consultative role in the affairs of Northern Ireland. The majority of those in Northern Ireland continue to favor inclusion in the United Kingdom, but the political situation also continues to be unstable. In 1991, talks opened again on the issue of home rule, relations with the Irish Republic, and power sharing between Catholics and Protestants. Many hoped that compromises would be reached between nationalists (those who seek union with Ireland) and unionists (those who support the current union with the United Kingdom). The talks collapsed after only a few months. They resumed again in 1992, but ended after four months with little hope for future talks. Inflexibility on the part of leaders from both sides, as well as continued violence made it difficult for talks to proceed. They did take place, however, in secret for several months in 1993.

Near the end of the year, a framework for peace was jointly announced by Ireland and Britain. The announcement represented a possible breakthrough because the IRA indicated it might accept the plan and end its violent struggle. The IRA even abided by a short cease-fire as a show of good will. The leader of Sinn Fein (the IRA's political arm), Gerry Adams, came out in favor of the plan. Essentially, the new peace process aims to end the violence, incorporate Sinn Fein into the peace talks (previously held only between governments), and hold a referendum in Northern Ireland as to who should govern. The government of Ireland favors a united Ireland, but has agreed to accept the vote of Northern Ireland's people. Ireland's prime minister, Albert Reynolds, strongly supports the peace process, as do many key British officials. No exact timetable has been given for when such a vote would take place, but all sides seem more optimistic than in the past about the possibility of ending the centuries-old conflict.

THE PEOPLE

Population

The population of Northern Ireland is about 1.7 million and is growing at only 0.2 percent per year. Northern Ireland is basically homogeneous; nearly all inhabitants are Irish, while some have Scottish roots. Belfast is the capital and largest city with about 360,000 people.

Language

English is the official language. Irish English is different from American English. It is, however, basically the same as British English, with only some idiomatic variations. Gaelic was the ancient language of Ireland but is no longer spoken in Northern Ireland.

Religion

In contrast to the Republic of Ireland (*Éire*), which has a Catholic majority, Northern Ireland (*Ulster*) has a Protestant majority. There are 950,000 Protestants, compared to some 650,000 Catholics. The largest Protestant churches include Presbyterian, the Church of Ireland, and Methodist. This division between Catholics and Protestants has been a major source of conflict throughout Irish history and not just since the twentieth century.

General Attitudes

The Irish believe in hard work, but on the whole the pace of life is more relaxed than in the United States. Religion and politics have long been sources of conflict in this politically troubled nation and are generally avoided as topics of conversation. The Irish are friendly, sincere, and keenly sensitive to the beauties of nature. They appreciate honorable people and those who keep their word. Those loyal to the British Crown are proud of the Queen of England. Although Northern Ireland is part of the United Kingdom, the people are not English, but Irish. The majority support Northern Ireland's position as part of the United Kingdom, and many therefore think of themselves as British in addition to Irish.

The Irish consider their land as one of ancient tales and rich history. They believe this endows their nation with a certain "magic" that is hard to express but easy to feel. Folklore plays an important role in creating that magic.

Personal Appearance

European styles are most common in clothing. Sweaters are often worn in the summer because of the cool climate. Wool clothing is popular. The people tend to dress more conservatively than in the United States.

CUSTOMS AND COURTESIES

Greetings

A handshake is the common greeting in Northern Ireland. Initial conversations and greetings are similar to those in the United States. "Hello," "Hi," and "How are you?" are all common greetings. People wave at others who are too distant for a verbal greeting. Strangers may offer a brief greeting or wave on uncrowded streets. First names are generally used only with close friends and family, although this practice is changing among the youth, who are more informal.

Gestures

Most gestures used in Northern Ireland are similar to those of the United States. Excessive hand gestures are not used in conversation. Personal space is important.

Visiting

Women are seated first when visiting for a meal. While formal rules of etiquette have been important in the past, less formal practices are now more common. For example, formal behavior dictates that women should not cross their legs at the knees, but crossing one's legs is now widely accepted. The degree to which one would want to follow etiquette when visiting another depends largely on the event and the preferences of the hosts. Among good friends, people often drop by unannounced and are always warmly welcomed. If the host is in the middle of something, the guests will probably be told to make themselves at home—or asked to join in. While it is not necessary to take gifts to hosts, it is appreciated. When gifts are received, they are opened immediately in the presence of the giver. Refreshments are nearly always served, but guests are not required to eat them. Socializing not only takes place in the home, but also in the *pubs* (public houses).

Eating

The Irish use the continental style of eating, with the fork in the left hand and the knife remaining in the right. Hands are kept above the table. In restaurants, the waiter brings the bill to the table. A 15 percent service charge is usually included; if not, the money should be left as a tip. Also included is a 15 percent value-added tax. The most important meal of the week for families is on Sunday. A large, formal meal is served and the family enjoys spending time together. The evening meal is called *tea*. The term *high tea* refers to a light evening meal such as fish and chips.

LIFESTYLE

Family

Although the father dominates in the home, the mother enjoys considerable influence in family affairs. And while women have traditionally played conservative roles by staying at home, this is changing. Many now work outside the home. Men generally do not participate in household chores, and some continue to maintain a separate social life with their male friends after marriage. Still, there is a very low divorce rate in Northern Ireland. Commitment to family ties is important.

Dating and Marriage

Teenagers begin associating with groups of friends, and start dating not long thereafter. Dancing and going to movies are popular activities. Engagements are usually long and may last two or more years. Women marry at about age 23; men at about 25.

Diet

Mealtime has traditionally been important to the people in Northern Ireland. In the past, this called for large meals and a great deal of preparation. However, as women spend more time working, this is no longer possible and meals are becoming less formal. Popular in the Irish diet are fried foods, but this is also changing as health issues become more important. Fresh produce, especially vegetables, are often homegrown and are readily available. Two types of potatoes are common and are an important staple in the Irish diet. Fresh seafood, fish, lamb, pork, and beef are all frequently eaten. There are many different bread varieties to choose from, as well as scones and pastries. The people also enjoy *dulse* (dried, edible seaweed). Irish stew, homemade tarts, and *pasties* (meat pies in the shape of burgers) are popular dishes.

Recreation

Soccer, hurling, Gaelic football, lawn bowling, golf, fishing, cricket, bicycling, sailing, hiking, and rugby are all popular sports in Northern Ireland. Hurling is played on a soccer-type field with wooden sticks and a small leather ball. Gaelic football is played with a round ball and seems like a cross between soccer and basketball. Players can touch the ball with their hands, but they cannot pick it up from the ground. The ball is punched, not thrown, and it can be kicked. Scoring is done in a soccer-type net, but points can also be made for going over the top of the goal.

Horse, dog, and car racing are also common. The people are also avid movie fans. Amateur clubs and societies (such as bingo clubs) are enjoyed by some.

Holidays

Official holidays include New Year's Day; St. Patrick's Day (17 March); Easter (Thursday to Monday); Labor Day (1 May); Battle of the Boyne (12 July), a part of Orange Day festivities that can last a full week and that consist of parades, speeches, and other celebrations; Halloween (31 October); Christmas; and Boxing Day (26 December). Boxing Day comes from the British tradition of giving small boxed gifts to service workers. It is now a day for visiting friends and relaxing. Fairs that celebrate the harvest, historical figures, or folk traditions are also common throughout the area.

Commerce

Generally, business hours extend from 9:00 A.M. to 5:00 P.M., Monday through Friday. Government offices are often closed for an hour at lunchtime and remain open until 5:30 P.M.

SOCIETY

Government

Northern Ireland has 17 seats in the United Kingdom's House of Commons. The majority of those seats are held by Protestants who support the nation's union with Great Britain.

Before direct rule from London began in 1972, Northern Ireland also had a regional assembly that governed local affairs. As part of the United Kingdom, Northern Ireland accepts Queen Elizabeth II as head of state and John Major as prime minister. The voting age is 18.

Economy

Farming, fishing, tobacco, shipbuilding, and aircraft manufacturing are the major economic enterprises. Farmers commonly raise cattle, hogs, and sheep, and produce dairy products, poultry, and potatoes, among other things. Northern Ireland's standard of living is comparable to England's. The United Kingdom's Human Development Index (0.964) ranks it 10 out of 173 nations. Real gross domestic product per capita is $15,804, a figure that is generally lower than in other European nations. Still, most people earn a decent income. The currency of the United Kingdom is the British pound sterling (£).

Transportation and Communication

Transportation is excellent, with buses being the most common and best means of travel within a city. On two-level omnibuses, nonsmokers use the lower level and smokers go to the upper level. On one-level buses, smokers must use the back of the bus. Taxis are also available. In areas of recent or frequent violence, bus service is limited and caution must be exercised. These areas are called "control zones." Private cars provide long-distance transportation. Traffic moves on the left side of the road. Communication systems are completely modern. All phone calls, including local ones, are billed by the length of the call. Therefore, a person borrowing someone's phone offers to pay for the call.

Education

Children attend either Catholic or Protestant schools. Primary school is required for children between ages four and eleven. At age 11, all students take a difficult government-sponsored exam. If they do well, they go to grammar school, which prepares them for a university education. If they fail to score high marks, they go either to a secondary (or intermediate) school or a technical college to prepare for a profession or trade. They can still choose to go to grammar school if the family is able to pay tuition and fees. After this first exam, there are two more government-sponsored exams that must be taken for admission to a university. Programs of study are much stricter than those in the United States. A bachelor's degree can be obtained in three years, but the exams taken before one is admitted to a university are recognized as being equal to a first-year university exam. Public education at the university level is paid for by the government. Literacy in the United Kingdom is 99 percent.

Health

As throughout the United Kingdom, the residents of Northern Ireland enjoy relatively good health. Hospital facilities are readily available. Northern Ireland is served by the National Health Service, which provides free or low-cost medical care to all citizens of the United Kingdom. Prescriptions and some dental costs are paid for by the individual. The infant mortality rate is 8 per 1,000; the average life expectancy is between 73 and 79 years.

FOR THE TRAVELER

U.S. travelers do not need a visa to visit Northern Ireland, but a valid passport is required. Visitors should be careful to fully cooperate with police officers. Carefully obey all regulations regarding the control zones. Violence is generally limited to small areas, and you will probably never see any evidence of it. A green and beautiful countryside is inviting to tourists and tourist facilities are well developed. For information regarding travel opportunities in Northern Ireland, contact the Northern Ireland Tourist Board (551 Fifth Avenue, Suite 701, New York, NY 10176). You may also wish to contact the representative for Northern Ireland at the Embassy of the United Kingdom, 3100 Massachusetts Avenue NW, Washington, DC 20008.

A *Culturgram* is a product of native commentary and original, expert analysis. Statistics are estimates and information is presented as a matter of opinion. While the editors strive for accuracy and detail, this document should not be considered strictly factual. It is a general introduction to culture, an initial step in building bridges of understanding between peoples. It may not apply to all peoples of the nation. You should therefore consult other sources for more information.

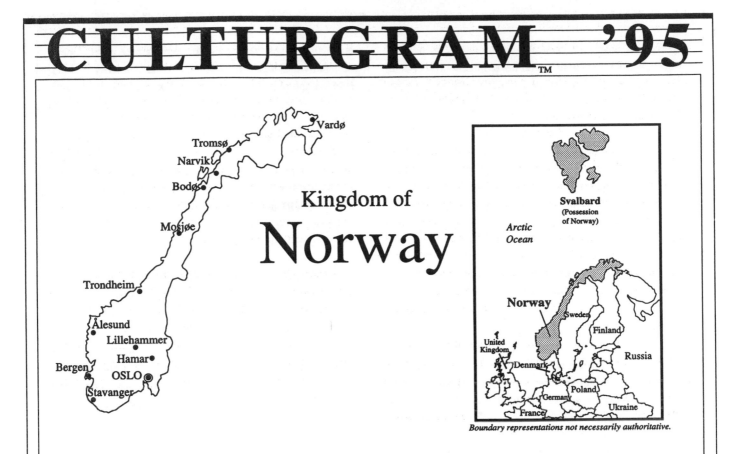

Kingdom of Norway

Boundary representations not necessarily authoritative.

EUROPE

BACKGROUND

Land and Climate

Norway, one of the "three fingers" of Scandinavia, is just larger than New Mexico. It covers 125,181 square miles (324,220 square kilometers). Its coastline, indented with beautiful fjords, stretches over 1,000 miles from the North Sea to the Arctic Ocean. Norway means "the northern way." In fact, the Arctic Circle crosses the country almost in its middle. Along the fjords on the western coast are numerous small islands. Norway is generally mountainous, and it has several glaciers. The mountains and high plateaus are interrupted by fertile valleys and small plains, but only about 3 percent of the total land area is suitable for cultivation.

There are many natural resources, including crude oil (in the North Sea), copper, nickel, zinc, lead, and timber. More than one-fourth of the land is forested. The North Atlantic Drift moderates the otherwise cold climate and allows for ice-free harbors and mildly warm summers. Rain is abundant on the west coast. In the interior, winters are colder and summers warmer than on the coast. Snow lasts for several months of the year. Above the Arctic Circle the sun shines day and night for part of the summer and does not rise above the horizon for part of the winter. In the absence of the sun the northern lights *(aurora borealis)* are visible for a period of time.

History

During the Age of the Vikings (800–1050), Vikings conquered many areas in Scandinavia and Europe and even settled briefly in parts of North America. For example, Leifur Eiríksson landed in present-day Canada. In Norway, Viking leader Harald the Fairhead became the first supreme ruler of a unified kingdom around 872. Christianity had spread throughout the area by 1030. The country came under Danish domination from 1381 to 1814 before it was given to Sweden as a peace treaty provision to punish Denmark's alliance with Napoleon during the Napoleonic Wars. In reaction to being given to Sweden, Norway declared its independence and drafted a constitution. Still, the Swedish king was accepted as monarch and the two nations were unified. The union was dissolved by referendum in 1905 and a Danish prince (Carl) was chosen to be the constitutional monarch of an independent Kingdom of Norway. He took the name Haakon VII.

Norway was neutral in World War I, but Germany attacked in World War II (April 1940) and held Norway until its liberation in May 1945. During that time the monarchy was out of the country supporting the Allied effort against the Germans. The son of Haakon VII, Olav V, was king of Norway from 1957 to 1991. Upon his death, his son, Harald V, took the throne and is king today.

Copyright © 1994. Brigham Young University. Printed in the USA. All rights reserved. It is against the law to copy, reprint, store in a retrieval system, or transmit any part of this publication in any form by any means for any purpose without written permission from the Publications Division of the David M. Kennedy Center for International Studies, Brigham Young University, PO Box 24538, Provo, UT 84602–4538. *Culturgrams* are available for more than 125 areas of the world. To place an order, to receive a free catalog, or to obtain information on traveling abroad, call toll free (800) 528–6279.

Norway's post-war period has been marked by political stability, economic progress, and development. The country has good relations with the United States. Norway is a member of the North Atlantic Treaty Organization (NATO) and the European Free Trade Area. It has applied for membership in the European Union (EU) and is working to be part of the European Economic Area (EEA). The issue of joining the EU is fairly sensitive in Norway; it led to the resignation in 1990 of Prime Minister Jan Syse. The opposition leader, Gro Harlem Brundtland, replaced him and served until elections in September 1993. She was then reelected prime minister for a four-year term.

THE PEOPLE

Population

The population of Norway is 4.29 million and is growing annually at only 0.4 percent, a rate similar to much of Europe and Scandinavia. Norway is one of the most sparsely populated countries in the world. The population is predominantly of Nordic (Scandinavian) descent. There is also a small minority (20,000) of native Sámis (Laplanders), who live mostly in the north. Their ancestors were the original inhabitants of northern Norway. Although Norway limits immigration, immigrant workers from other countries have become more common since the discovery of oil in the North Sea.

Language

Norwegian, the official language, has two forms. *Bokmål*, or "book language" is used in most written works and is spoken by more than 80 percent of the people, especially those living in urban areas. It is also the main language of instruction and broadcasting, although laws require that the other form, *Nynorsk*, be used in a certain percentage of schools and broadcasting media. *Nynorsk* was actually created in the 1800s as a combination of the many rural dialects then in existence. *Bokmål* is heavily influenced by Danish due to 400 years of Danish rule. The Sámis speak Sámi (Lappish) but learn Norwegian in the schools as a second language. English is taught in the schools beginning at age 11, and it is widely spoken as a second language.

Religion

More than 85 percent of the population belongs to the state church, the Church of Norway, which is Evangelical Lutheran. Still, freedom of religion is guaranteed, and there are many other Christian churches active in the country. Among them are the Pentecostals, Roman Catholics, and various Protestant groups. Most people only attend church services on special occasions or holidays.

General Attitudes

Tolerance, human kindness, and independence are important Norwegian ideals. Criticism of other peoples or systems is considered inappropriate. Norwegians take great pride in their individual and national independence. Sincerity in friendship is important, but reserve should be shown in the expression of personal feelings. Neighbors, even in large cities, get along very well and usually consider each other close friends. Punctuality is important. Norwegians generally do not appreciate seemingly unfavorable comparisons, such as, "In the United States, we do it this way." Social equality and a good standard of living are important values that have shaped post-World War II politics. Norwegians love the outdoors and work to protect their environment. Peace and progress are common themes in Norway, the country that sponsors the Nobel Peace prize.

Personal Appearance

Dress generally follows conservative, European fashions and is influenced by the necessity to keep warm. Traditional costumes (*bunad*), which vary according to region, are worn on special occasions such as weddings and national and local holidays. They are often hand sewn and have elaborate embroidery. For women, these costumes usually consist of a white blouse (often embroidered), a jumper-type skirt, an apron, and a headdress. Men wear knee pants, shirts, and vests.

CUSTOMS AND COURTESIES

Greetings

Norwegians often take the initiative by introducing themselves to strangers. Natural courtesy is important in good relations. Shaking hands is the normal custom. Everyday acquaintances greet each other with a casual *Morn* (literally "Morning"), regardless of the time of day. The term is roughly equivalent to "Hi." *Hei* also means "Hi" and is as common as *Morn*. A slightly more formal greeting is *God dag* (Good day). Traditionally, only close friends addressed each other by first name, but the youth are increasingly using first names once introduced. Older individuals continue to follow the custom of using titles with a family name. When being introduced for the first time, a person addresses the other by both the first and last names.

Gestures

It is impolite to yawn without covering the mouth. It is common to offer a seat on public transportation to a woman or elderly person. Courtesy and good behavior are important in all cases.

Visiting

When visiting a home for the first time, it is customary to bring a gift of flowers, sweets, or other small token of appreciation to the hosts. Guests wait to be invited in by the host, who traditionally helps them remove their coats as a gesture of hospitality. Guests also wait until they are invited to sit down. Not everyone, of course, adheres to these rules of formal etiquette. It is considered poor taste to leave directly after dinner. Personal privacy is important; topics such as income and social status are avoided in casual conversation. If a guest has been invited, it is considered rude to refuse any refreshments the hosts offer. In the past, people visited unannounced, but now a call in advance is appreciated.

Eating

Guests do not start eating until everyone is seated and the host invites them to begin. The continental style of eating is followed, with the fork in the left hand and knife remaining in the right. It is impolite to leave food on the plate. At the end of a meal, whether in casual or formal situations, the person who prepared or is responsible for the meal should be thanked. Indeed, children are taught to say *Takk for maten* ("Thank you for the food") before leaving the table. Hands are kept above the table during the meal. In a restaurant, the waiter is summoned by a raised hand. A service fee is usually included in the bill, but a small tip (perhaps 5 to 10 percent) is also customary.

LIFESTYLE

Family

The family unit is important in Norway. Husbands and wives usually consider each other equal in authority. In fact, general equality for women is rather advanced. Women have a strong presence in politics (comprising one-third of parliament) and make up 40 percent of the labor force. Their influence has helped Norway develop strong child-care, educational, and family programs. Families are usually small. Many own their homes or condominiums. More than one-third also own or share a cabin in the mountains or by the sea. Spending time in these cottages is a favorite family activity. Although divorce was once uncommon, a dramatic increase has occurred over the last decade. Still, about half of all adults are married.

Dating and Marriage

Serious dating is discouraged among the youth, but group dating usually starts between the ages of 14 and 18. Dancing, participating in outdoor activities, and going to movies are favorite activities. It is not uncommon for couples to live together before marriage or instead of getting married. Men usually marry around age 25 and women slightly younger.

Diet

Breakfast usually consists of open-faced sandwiches and milk or coffee; lunch is often the same. Meat or fish, potatoes, vegetables, and a soup or dessert are generally prepared for the main meal (5:00 P.M.). A common meal is meatballs with potatoes and brown gravy, served with vegetables. Norwegians may also have a light evening snack. Norwegian specialities include fish balls in a sauce, smoked salmon, *lutefisk* (cod or coalfish, soaked in potash lye), *fårikål* (cabbage and mutton), *smalahode* (sheep's head), and a variety of other dishes. Ready-made or frozen foods are popular. Delis usually have ready-made fried fish, fish cakes, fish pudding, and meatballs.

Recreation

Most Norwegians are physically active. Nearly every Norwegian can ski and children learn at a very young age. A saying claims that Norwegians are born with skis on their feet. Norway is one of the world's centers for skiing, both Alpine (downhill) and Nordic (cross-country), and ice skating. The small city of Lillehammer was in the world spotlight in 1994 as the site of the Winter Olympics. Fishing is excellent and popular; trout, pike, and salmon abound in Norwegian waters. Soccer, swimming, and hiking are enjoyed during the summer months. Norway's national soccer team competed in the 1994 World Cup. Boating is popular when the frozen lakes and fjords thaw.

Sports are not connected to school activities, but each area and community has its own sports clubs for individual and team competition. Winning is not emphasized as much as participation. Most families are actively involved in these clubs. A lot of families also participate in cultural arts, either by performing themselves or by attending the theater, concerts, and other cultural events. Reading is a popular leisure activity.

Holidays

Official holidays include New Year's Day, Easter (Thursday through Monday), Labor Day (1 May), Constitution Day (17 May), and Christmas (24–26 December). The Norwegian flag is prominent for all holidays; it is even used to decorate Christmas trees. Constitution Day is celebrated much like the Fourth of July in the United States, with parades, flags, family gatherings, and the like. Families often take ski vacations during the Easter holiday. Christmas is the biggest celebration of the year. As in other countries, preparations begin well in advance. At 5:00 P.M. on Christmas Eve, bells ring and the holiday officially begins. Families gather for a big meal and to exchange gifts. Parties are common on Christmas Day and thereafter until the new year begins.

Commerce

The average workweek in Norway is about 37.5 hours, one of the shortest in the world. Office hours are usually from 8:00 A.M. to 4:00 P.M., Monday through Friday. Stores open from 9:00 or 10:00 A.M. to 4:00 or 5:00 P.M. In large towns, stores often stay open as late as 7:00 P.M. each Thursday. Shops close by 2:00 P.M. on Saturdays and are closed on Sunday.

SOCIETY

Government

Norway is a constitutional monarchy. The king has limited authority, except as head of the military and as a symbol of continuity and stability. Executive power is vested in the prime minister, who presides over the dominant party in the country's parliament (*Storting*). The 165 members of parliament are elected every four years. The *Storting* has an Upper Chamber (*Lagting*) and an Lower Chamber (*Odelsting*). The Labor and the Conservative parties dominate in parliament. Prime Minister Gro Harlem Brundtland is the leader of the Labor Party. The voting age is 18. Norway has 19 provinces (*fylker*).

Economy

Norway, which enjoys a strong economy, has one of the highest standards of living in the world. However, higher unemployment (about 10 percent) and slower growth in the early 1990s has led to some economic difficulties. The government is attempting to diversify the economy to reduce its dependency on the oil sector.

Norway's Human Development Index (0.979) ranks it third out of 173 countries. Real gross domestic product per capita is estimated at $16,028, which has tripled in the last generation. These data indicate most people have access to a decent income, and that highly developed social institutions are able to provide for general economic prosperity. The poorest 40 percent of households earn 20 percent of the nation's income.

The most important exports are petroleum products, natural gas, ships, and fish. Aluminum and some manufactured items, such as furniture, are also exported. Norway is a major producer of aluminum. Important to the domestic economy is agriculture, employing 7 percent of the labor force in livestock raising, fishing, and crop cultivation. Oil drilling, textiles, chemicals, and food processing are among the key industries in Norway. The currency is the Norwegian *krone* (Kr).

Transportation and Communication

The transportation system is excellent. Trains, buses, and airplanes connect cities and towns. Most people own cars. Boats are used in some areas for transportation. Likewise, the communications system is highly developed and fully modern. Telephone and postal services are reliable.

Education

Schooling is free and compulsory for all children between the ages of seven and sixteen. The first six years constitute primary school, while the latter three are lower secondary school. Upper secondary school is open to anyone, although students are usually between the ages of 16 and 18. It includes both general education (preparation for higher education) and vocational training.

After secondary school, many people begin working. Others are admitted to a university or college, and a small number attend the folk high school, a boarding school for teaching liberal arts (after the Danish tradition). The literacy rate is nearly 100 percent. Four universities are located in Oslo, Bergen, Tromsø, and Trondheim. There are a number of specialized colleges and institutes. Instruction is readily available to most citizens and basically free at all levels, including higher education. Space is limited at universities, however, and many students travel to other countries for their college education.

Health

In keeping with its commitment to social welfare, the government has an extensive system that provides not only health and hospital services to all, but housing and work for needy Norwegians. There are very few private hospitals in Norway. Socialized medicine pays for all hospital charges, although small fees are charged for medicine and some procedures. Costs are shared between the central and local governments. The infant mortality rate is 6 per 1,000. Life expectancy ranges from 74 to 81 years.

FOR THE TRAVELER

While passports are required, U.S. citizens do not need visas for visits of up to three months total time in Scandinavia—Denmark, Iceland, Finland, Norway, and Sweden. No vaccinations are required. Dual-voltage small appliances or a voltage adaptor and a plug adaptor are necessary to use electrical outlets. Cruises along the fjords, hiking, skiing, and a variety of other vacation options are available in Norway. For more information, contact the Norwegian Information Service (825 Third Avenue, 38th Floor, New York, NY 10022) or the Norwegian Tourist Board (655 Third Avenue, New York, NY 10017). You may also wish to contact the Royal Norwegian Embassy, 2720 34th Street NW, Washington, DC 20008.

A *Culturgram* is a product of native commentary and original, expert analysis. Statistics are estimates and information is presented as a matter of opinion. While the editors strive for accuracy and detail, this document should not be considered strictly factual. It is a general introduction to culture, an initial step in building bridges of understanding between peoples. It may not apply to all peoples of the nation. You should therefore consult other sources for more information.

Republic of
Panama

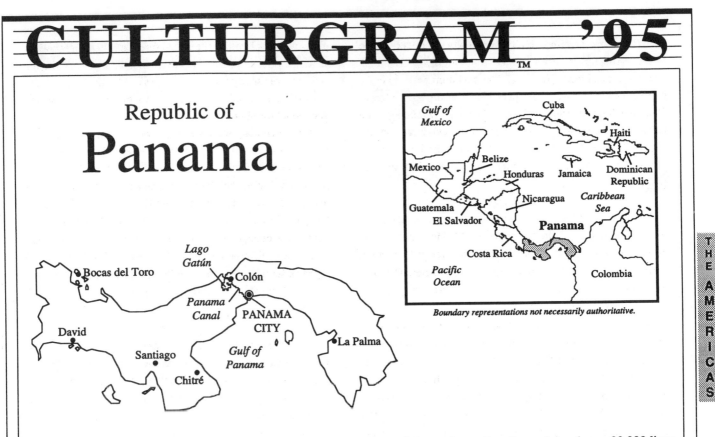

Boundary representations not necessarily authoritative.

THE AMERICAS

BACKGROUND

Land and Climate

Panama is a fairly rugged, mountainous country connecting Central and South America. It is bordered by Costa Rica to the northwest and Colombia to the southeast. Covering 30,193 square miles (78,200 square kilometers), Panama's total land area is just smaller than South Carolina. Volcanic activity has made the soil very fertile in some areas. About half the country is forested and 6 percent is suitable for cultivation. The Panama Canal, a man-made structure, runs through one of the narrowest points of the country, from Panama City to Colón. It runs through *Lago Gatún* (Lake Gatún). Colón and Panama City are the country's two largest cities. They are home to most of the country's urban population. Areas outside the Canal Zone, which stretches between and includes the two cities, are collectively called *los interioranos* (the interior). The Tabasara Mountains form a spine down the center of the western interior; there are also mountains in the eastern interior. Except for the higher elevations, the tropical climate is hot and humid. The average annual temperature is 80°F (27°C). In the mountains, the average is about 55°F (13°C).

History

The history of Panama has been greatly affected by its strategic location between the Atlantic and Pacific Oceans. Rodrigo de Bastidas, a Spanish explorer, visited Panama in 1501. Columbus claimed the area for Spain the next year. In the 16th and 17th centuries, Panama served as the route for shipping Incan treasures to Spain. In 1821, Spanish rule was overthrown, and Panama became a province of Colombia. During the 1880s, France attempted to build a canal across the narrow isthmus, but yellow fever claimed over 20,000 lives and the canal rights were sold to the United States.

On 3 November 1903, Panama declared its independence from Colombia and the United States sent troops to support the new Panamanian government. Construction of the Panama canal began in 1907 under U.S. supervision. The canal was completed seven years later. It became an important passage for ships traveling from the Atlantic to the Pacific and vice versa. The United States controlled the canal and U.S. citizens worked in most managerial positions. In 1978, the U.S. Senate ratified a treaty signed by President Jimmy Carter concerning the permanent neutrality and operation of the canal after the year 1999. According to the treaty, Panama will assume control of canal operations and the United States will continue to guarantee its neutrality.

Omar Torrijos Herrera, commander of the national guard, seized control of Panama in 1968. He is credited with negotiating the Canal Treaty with the United States. Although he ruled as a dictator, most Panamanians now revere him as a national hero. He turned daily government powers over to a civilian administration in 1978, and allowed free, multiparty legislative elections in 1980. When he died in 1983, his defense minister, Manuel Antonio Noriega, became the strongest military leader in the country. Noriega soon consolidated power as head of the Panama Defense Forces.

Arturo Delvalle Henríquez, who became president in 1985, was ousted in 1988 for trying to fire Noriega, who had effectively suspended the constitution and civil rights in 1987. Noriega ruled under a state of emergency and controlled the national assembly. Although he allowed regularly scheduled

Copyright © 1994. Brigham Young University. Printed in the USA. All rights reserved. It is against the law to copy, reprint, store in a retrieval system, or transmit any part of this publication in any form by any means for any purpose without written permission from the Publications Division of the David M. Kennedy Center for International Studies, Brigham Young University, PO Box 24538, Provo, UT 84602–4538. *Culturgrams* are available for more than 125 areas of the world. To place an order, to receive a free catalog, or to obtain information on traveling abroad, call toll free (800) 528–6279.

elections to take place in May 1989, he refused to allow the newly elected president (who opposed Noriega) to take office. Noriega's rule became increasingly repressive in Panama and relations with the United States worsened. When a 1989 coup attempt against Noriega failed, the United States responded to growing concerns regarding corruption, violence, and Noriega's threats against U.S. interests by sending troops to Panama in December 1989.

Panamanian troops loyal to Noriega were defeated and Noriega was eventually taken prisoner. When the elected government was installed, Noriega was extradited to the United States to stand trial for various drug trafficking charges. He was convicted in 1992 and is serving a 40-year prison sentence.

The new government, under President Guillermo Endara, began the task of rebuilding the nation that had severe economic and social problems. Endara was unsuccessful in addressing many issues and he was not able to effect his desired constitutional changes. Strikes, crime, social unrest, poverty, and corruption continued to hinder progress. Still, democracy has prevailed under Endara and free elections were held in May 1994. Promising to end corruption and attack poverty, Ernesto Peréz Balladares was elected president.

THE PEOPLE
Population

The population of Panama is about 2.58 million, growing annually at 2 percent. Next to Belize, Panama has the smallest population in Central America. *Mestizos*, people of mixed European and Indian heritage, comprise about 70 percent of Panama's citizens. Fourteen percent of the population is black, descendants of laborers from the Caribbean (mostly the West Indies) who came to work on the canal in the early 1900s. Ten percent of the people are white, having European ancestry, and the remaining people are members of various indigenous groups. These groups have their own rich cultural heritage and they have often chosen to not integrate into Panamanian society. The capital, Panama City, has about 700,000 residents.

Language

Spanish is the official language of Panama. About 14 percent of the people speak English as a native tongue, and many others speak English as a second language. Many blacks speak Creole English. The indigenous Indians speak various languages, according to their ethnic background. Most prevalent are Cuna and Guaymí, both of which are spoken by more than 40,000 people. Many Panamanians are bilingual.

Religion

About 85 percent of the population is Roman Catholic. Another 6 percent belongs to various other Christian organizations. There is also a small minority of Muslims in the country. Even though the Catholic church has great influence on the lives of the people, Panama has complete freedom of worship and separation of church and state. Many Catholics are critical of local ecclesiastical authorities but remain loyal to the pope.

General Attitudes

Although society is stratified in traditional social classes, Panamanians consider all people to be of worth. One should be treated with dignity and respect regardless of their class.

This value for the individual is also evident in Panamanians' respect for personal strength and charisma. Tradition, family loyalty, stability, and wealth are all important values in Panamanian society. Panamanians generally characterize males as being very masculine; the ideal man is a man of action, who is forceful, daring, and virile. But he is also polite. The ideal woman is well-bred, understanding, and feminine. People in the large urban areas are more cosmopolitan in their approach to these traditions.

Nationalism is strong in Panama. The motto of Panama is, "For the benefit of the world." It is a reflection of the country's strategic position in the world and the service it provides to all nations. Most citizens, even interior *campesinos* (farmers), are well-informed on topics relating to national and international politics. Panamanians are also aware of their country's association with the United States. Many resent the relationship as unequal, but others appreciate its benefits. Panamanians also appreciate their Spanish heritage and, to a lesser extent, their indigenous roots.

Personal Appearance

Most male urban workers wear open-necked, shirts called *camisillas*. Bankers and other executives wear dark suits and ties. Women dress in styles similar to those in the United States. Dress habits are informal, and sandals are common footwear. Women tend to pay more attention to their appearance, and urban women rarely wear sloppy clothing. They admire a polished appearance. Traditional costumes are worn on special occasions. For women, this includes a *pollera*, a full-length dress with embroidery. For men, it is baggy shorts and matching embroidered top, leather sandals, and palm fiber hats. Indigenous groups have their own styles of dress.

CUSTOMS AND COURTESIES
Greetings

When greeting, many women (and sometimes between men and women) *abrazo* (hug). That is, they clasp hands as in a handshake, lean forward and press cheeks. Men shake hands with one another, often patting the other on the shoulder at the same time. *Campesinos* usually only shake hands when greeting. The most common verbal greetings include *¿Cómo está?* (How are you?), *¡Buenos!* (Good day!), *¿Qué tal?* (What's up?), *¿Qué hay de bueno?* (What's good?), *¿Cómo le ha ido?* (How's it been?), *¿Cómo le va?* (How's it going?), and *Hola* (Hi). It is polite to inquire about the welfare of one's family members after an initial greeting. Common terms for saying good-bye include *¡Hasta luego!* (See you later), *¡Que le vaya bien!* (May things go well for you), and in the cities, *Ciao* (Good-bye). *Adiós* is rarely used because it is considered fairly permanent.

In formal situations among the educated, it is very important to address people by their educational title, such as *Maestro/a* (teacher), *Profesor/a* (professor), *Ingeniero/a* (person with a bachelor of science degree), or *Doctor/a* (doctor). The person's given name, not surname, is usually used with these titles. In written correspondence, the entire name is used. Other titles include *Señor* (Mr.), *Señora* (Mrs.), and *Señorita* (Miss). *Don* and *Doña* are used for respected or elderly men and women, respectively. In informal situations, nicknames are common, and people often say one's given name or nickname as a greeting. It is not polite to use the nickname unless one is close friends with the person. People often address each other by terms of relationship: *hermano/a* (brother/sister), *amigo/a* (friend), *tio/a* (uncle/aunt), and so forth.

Gestures

People in the interior use nonverbal communication more than in urban settings. For example, people pucker their lips to point, to indicate "over there" or "time to go," or for many other uses. One might ask, "What's up?" by shrugging and facing palms up. "No" can be expressed by wagging the index finger from side to side. Drawing a circle with the finger in the air means one is coming right back.

Politeness is important, and chivalry is common. Men commonly offer their seats on public transportation to women or the elderly. Deference to elders in any situation is important. Personal space is generally small, and people sit or stand close when they converse. Eye contact is important. It is polite to cover the mouth when yawning.

Visiting

Panamanians are proud of their tradition of hospitality, and they enjoy hosting others in their homes. They are open, generous, and informal with their guests. Hosts customarily do not establish an ending time to a visit, as that might indicate to the guests that they are not as important as the hosts' schedule. It is polite for guests to allow themselves to be taken care of by the hosts. That is, they do not help with dishes, they take any offers of the best seat or food, and they graciously accept any good-bye gifts. Gifts are usually not taken by guests to a host when invited to dinner; this would imply the host is not expected to be thorough in providing hospitality. Rather than giving a gift, guests generally expect to return the favor of a dinner invitation.

Relatives and friends visit one another often. A visit is a compliment; it is expected of friends. Unannounced visitors are always welcome. In the interior, relatives see each other almost daily, depending on their relationship and how far they live from one another. Urban dwellers enjoy Sunday visits. All visitors are offered refreshments, such as a fruit drink and some crackers.

Sending (exchanging) gifts is common among friends in the interior, but only items such as food or seedlings are sent, not expensive items. The custom is a way of sharing one's good fortune with friends. It is not commonly practiced in the cities.

Eating

Panamanians generally eat three meals a day. In urban areas, the mealtimes are about the same as in the United States. In the interior, people often have a big breakfast early, a main meal at midday, and a small dinner around 5:00 P.M. Urban families try to eat together, but *campesino* families often do not have the opportunity because of their work schedules. Hands are generally kept above the table during a meal. The spoon is used most often in the interior.

When guests are present, they are served first, followed by the men, children, and the women and/or cooks. The cook or hostess usually prepares a plate for each person. Extra food might be put out for second helpings. Guests often compliment the cook on the meal. Urbanites eat out often, but campesinos rarely do. Tips of between 5 and 10 percent are usually given to the server.

LIFESTYLE

Family

In Panamanian families, the mother generally takes responsibility for the home. This traditional role is still quite admired and respected. Less than 30 percent of the labor force is composed of women. The father's responsibilities are usually outside the home, but he is still considered the undisputed leader of the family. As in other Latin American countries, the family is the basic unit of society. Due to the changing tempo of modern life, nuclear families are gaining prominence over the extended family. However, adult children expect to care for their aging parents, even if they do not live with them. In such cases they are sure to send money or food, visit them, and arrange for their basic needs to be met. A large number of births take place out of wedlock, but many of these are within stable common-law marriages. Families in urban areas often live in rented apartments, while rural families may own a small home.

Dating and Marriage

Most girls begin group dating around age 14. Compared with girls of other Latin American countries, urban Panamanian girls experience a great degree of freedom. However, girls in the interior are often not allowed to date until much later and are subject to parental restrictions. Urban women usually marry in their early 20s; in the interior, women often marry by age 20. In most areas, rural and urban, boys have nearly complete freedom. Although rural boys have farm responsibilities, they have little supervision outside of school and have no domestic duties. When dating, couples enjoy going for walks, dancing, and watching movies. In the interior, common-law marriages are usual and are generally as well accepted and stable as legal marriages performed by the state. Couples desiring a church marriage must obtain a license; a registered religious official can then perform the marriage. Church weddings are common in urban areas.

Diet

In Panama, it is commonly said that one hasn't eaten if one hasn't had rice. Rice is served with nearly every meal, along with a source of protein (eggs, chicken, sardines, meat, fish, or beans). Corn and plantain are also staples. Fish is inexpensive and often made into a soup. Vegetables are usually eaten as part of the main dish or in a salad. Fruit is often eaten as a snack. *Chicha*, a popular drink, is made from fresh fruit, water, and sugar. Coffee is usually part of breakfast. Common dishes in the interior include *sancocho* (chicken soup), *guacho* (rice soup), *bollo* (corn mush that has been boiled in the husk), corn tortillas, and *guisado* (stewed meat with tomatoes and spices). *Arroz con pollo* (rice with chicken) is eaten on special occasions. Urban people eat traditional foods as well as a wider variety of international foods.

Recreation

In urban areas, many participate in team sports. Baseball is the most popular sport, while soccer, boxing, and basketball, are also favorites. Panamanians enjoy horse races, cockfights, and going to the movies. The national lottery is popular. Socializing on the porch or visiting friends is an important leisure activity. Leisure time for rural women often revolves around domestic events; they may get together to socialize and make *bollo* when the new corn comes in or to make crafts. Dramatic poetry readings are popular. Traditional Panamanian music, called *Tipico,* is played by a band consisting of a singer and players with an accordion, a guitar, some percussion, and sometimes a violin. Lyrics usually pertain to love and life. *Tipico* is more common in rural areas, and is joined in cities by samba, jazz, and reggae. On the Caribbean coast, drumming and singing to an African beat are popular.

Holidays

Official holidays include New Year's Day (celebrated 1–2 January), Day of the Martyrs (9 January), Easter (Friday through Sunday), Independence from Colombia Day (3 November), the Uprising of Los Santos (11 November), Independence from Spain Day (28 November), Mother's Day (second Sunday in December), and Christmas. Each village or city has its own celebrations to honor the local patron saint. *Carnival* celebrations are held during the few days before Ash Wednesday (usually in February or March).

Commerce

The business day begins as early as 7:00 A.M. and ends somewhere between 3:30 and 4:00 P.M. Many stores stay open until 6:00 P.M. During holidays, they may remain open until 9:00 or 10:00 P.M. Most businesses are open Saturday until 6:00 P.M., with the exception of government offices and banks, which are closed on Saturday and Sunday. Urbanites shop at large grocery stores and open air markets for most basics. Interior people may shop daily for small amounts of items they need; they also collect from their own harvests and exchange produce with friends and relatives. When necessary, they travel to larger towns to shop at open air markets or shops for goods that are not available in the village.

SOCIETY

Government

Panama is a multiparty democracy. The president has two vice presidents, and the three of them lead the executive branch. The National Assembly has 67 elected members. Panama has nine provinces. The voting age is 18, and all eligible citizens are required by law to vote.

Economy

Panama's potentially strong economy has been weakened first by the years of political instability and authoritarian rule and second by U.S. economic sanctions between 1988 and 1990. Although vital trade relations have been restored with the United States and growth has been above 7 percent since 1991, it will take time before economic prosperity can be realized. Despite a booming construction industry and increased investment, unemployment remains one of the greatest problems. Panama's Human Development Index (0.738) ranks it 68 out of 173 countries. Real gross domestic product per capita is $3,317, which has doubled in the last generation. One-fourth of Panamanians live in absolute poverty. These figures indicate economic opportunities are available, but many people do not yet earn a decent income.

The United States is Panama's largest trading partner. Key exports include bananas, shrimp, coffee, sugar, and clothing.

The operation of the Panama Canal is also vital to the domestic economy because it provides foreign exchange earnings. The canal is a major international trade route. Tourism is another important sector. Panama has a shortage of skilled labor and an oversupply of unskilled labor. About 27 percent of the labor force is employed in agriculture-related industries. The official currency is the *balboa* (B), which consists mostly of coins. Bills are usually U.S. dollars, which are legal tender.

Transportation and Communication

The highway system is the hub of transportation in Panama. Roads are generally in good condition, especially in and around urban areas. There is a domestic airline, a railroad, and some travel on shallow waterways. The Inter-American Highway runs through Panama City. The capital is linked to Colón by the Trans-Isthmian Highway. Revenues from the national lottery help build and maintain roads. In cities, buses and *chivas* (minibuses) are used for public transportation. In the interior, people walk, use *chivas* or buses, or ride horses. Taxis are readily available. The majority of the people do not own cars. Most telephones are owned by people living in urban areas. In the interior, centrally located public telephones are available. Communication facilities are well developed. A free press flourishes and there are many newspapers.

Education

Primary education is compulsory and free between the ages of seven and fifteen. Most (72 percent) school-aged children complete primary schooling and go on to secondary education. Rural families have a more difficult time sending children to secondary schools because they are usually located in larger towns. Poor families cannot afford to pay for daily transportation or room and board in the city. After completion of the secondary level, a student may go on to one of several vocational schools or prepare to enter a university. There is a national university that was established in 1935 as well as a Catholic university and other church-owned schools. The literacy rate in Panama is 88 percent.

Health

Panama's public health program is part of the national security system. It provides such services as free examinations, care for the needy, and intensified health education and sanitation programs. Most people have access to modern medical care of some kind, although the best facilities and personnel are located in Panama City and Colón. Malaria and yellow fever are active in the eastern areas near Colombia. The infant mortality rate is 17 per 1,000. Life expectancy ranges from 72 to 77 years.

FOR THE TRAVELER

U.S. travelers need a passport or tourist card to enter Panama. A 30-day tourist card is issued through travel agencies or airlines. Vaccinations are recommended for some tropical diseases if one plans on leaving the main urban areas. Water is not always safe to drink, especially in the interior. No plug adaptors are necessary to use electrical outlets. For more information, contact the Embassy of Panama, 2862 McGill Terrace NW, Washington, DC 20008.

A *Culturgram* is a product of native commentary and original, expert analysis. Statistics are estimates and information is presented as a matter of opinion. While the editors strive for accuracy and detail, this document should not be considered strictly factual. It is a general introduction to culture, an initial step in building bridges of understanding between peoples. It may not apply to all peoples of the nation. You should therefore consult other sources for more information.

Republic of
Paraguay

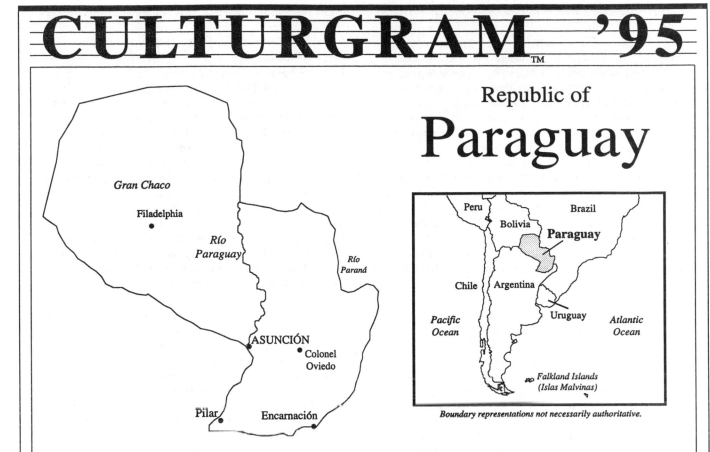

Gran Chaco

Filadelphia

Río Paraguay

Río Paraná

ASUNCIÓN

Colonel Oviedo

Pilar

Encarnación

Peru

Brazil

Bolivia

Paraguay

Chile

Argentina

Uruguay

Pacific Ocean

Atlantic Ocean

Falkland Islands (Islas Malvinas)

Boundary representations not necessarily authoritative.

BACKGROUND

Land and Climate

Paraguay is a landlocked country in central South America. Covering 157,046 square miles (406,570 square kilometers), it is slightly smaller than California. Over one-third of the country is forest or woodlands, although deforestation is a significant problem. About 20 percent of all territory is suitable for cultivation. There are no high elevations in the country and no real mountains. Paraguay is divided into two different regions by the Paraguay River (*Río Paraguay*). To the northwest lies the arid, sparsely settled region known as the *Gran Chaco* or simply *Chaco*. Near the river, the *Chaco* is mostly wetlands. Southeast of the river is the fertile *Paraná* plateau, where the population and agricultural centers are located. The plateau is subtropical and has a hot, humid, and rainy climate. Paraguay is south of the equator; seasonal changes are opposite those in the northern hemisphere. Summer is from September to June. The cooler rainy season is from June to September.

History

Spanish explorers came to Paraguay in 1524 and established Asunción in 1537. Colonial rule lasted until the 19th century. Paraguay peacefully gained independence in 1811, and José Gaspar Rodríguez Francia established the first in a long line of dictatorships. He closed the country to the outside world and ruled until 1840. In 1865, Francisco Solano López took Paraguay into the War of the Triple Alliance against Brazil, Argentina, and Uruguay. Ultimately (1870), the war

was lost, along with 55,000 square miles (142,450 square kilometers) of territory and 500,000 lives. Foreign troops stayed until 1876, and Paraguay remained politically unstable for another generation.

In 1932, Paraguay successfully waged a three-year Chaco War with Bolivia in a territorial dispute, but the victory cost the country a good portion of its male population and did not stabilize the nation. Various dictators and one elected president ruled until 1954, when General Alfredo Stroessner, commander of the army, took control of the Paraguayan government and established a long-term dictatorship. Although his tenure brought some economic development (mainly in the form of three hydroelectric dams), his government was responsible for human rights violations, corruption, and oppression.

A coup in 1989 ousted Stroessner, who now lives in Brazil. A new government came to power promising democratic reform. General Andrés Rodríguez Pedotti, who led the coup, was elected that same year as the country's president. He restored civil rights, legalized political parties, and promised not to serve past 1993. Rodríguez was the first leader to successfully implement many democratic reforms. He authorized elections that established a constitutional convention. A new constitution was ratified in June 1992. Because of Rodríguez's administration, Paraguay has emerged from its isolation under decades of dictatorship to join in regional and international organizations. National elections were held in May 1993; Juan Carlos Wasmosy was elected president.

Copyright © 1994. Brigham Young University. Printed in the USA. All rights reserved. It is against the law to copy, reprint, store in a retrieval system, or transmit any part of this publication in any form by any means for any purpose without written permission from the Publications Division of the David M. Kennedy Center for International Studies, Brigham Young University, PO Box 24538, Provo, UT 84602–4538. *Culturgrams* are available for more than 125 areas of the world. To place an order, to receive a free catalog, or to obtain information on traveling abroad, call toll free (800) 528–6279.

THE AMERICAS

PEOPLE

Population

Paraguay's population of about five million people is growing annually at 2.8 percent. Paraguay is the most ethnically homogeneous country in South America, partially due to its many years in virtual isolation. Up to 95 percent of the population is *mestizo* (a mixture of descendants of Spanish and native Guaraní). Pure native Guaraní are few in number today; most live around Asunción or in northern Paraguay. Some Koreans, who are generally merchants, other Asians, and Italians and Arabs also reside in Paraguay, but they are not assimilated into Paraguayan culture. There is also a small number of Mennonites, mostly around Filadelphia, whose distinct lifestyle is based on their European agricultural heritage. About half of all Paraguayans live in urban areas. Asunción has about 800,000 inhabitants. More than 40 percent of the population is under age 15.

Language

Paraguay has two official languages, Spanish and Guaraní. Spanish is the language of government, urban commerce, and schooling, but Guaraní is the common language. In rural areas, some people speak only Guaraní, although most also speak or understand Spanish. Portuguese is spoken along the Brazilian border. Paraguay's Spanish is called *Castellano* (Castillian), not *Español*. Many Guaraní words are mixed with Spanish, and Paraguayans do not generally use the *tú* form of address (more often it is the *vos* form). Many vocabulary words are different than in other Spanish-speaking countries.

Religion

About 90 percent of all Paraguayans are Roman Catholic. Catholic holidays play an important role in society. Women tend to be more religious than men. Various other Christian churches, both Protestant and other, also have members in Paraguay. The Mennonites practice their own religion. Many rural people also include a belief of mythical or mystical powers in their worship.

General Attitudes

Paraguayans are proud of being Paraguayan. They often define themselves by three aspects of their culture: speaking Guaraní, drinking yerba tea, and eating *mandioca* (cassava). Paraguayans say that Spanish is the language of the head, but Guaraní is the language of the heart. *Mandioca* is a staple food and is served at nearly every meal. Yerba leaves are made into a mildly stimulating tea. Served cold, it is called *tereré*. Served hot, it is *maté*. These teas have been part of the culture for hundreds of years.

Paraguay is a traditional society. Large families, property, beauty, virility, money, and status are valued. Paraguayans are generally concerned with not having problems; that is, an ultimate desire is *tranquilo* (tranquillity). Deviations from traditional mores and loud, disruptive behavior are not appreciated. Due to generations of isolation, wars with neighboring countries, and other factors, the *mestizo* population tends to look down upon people with darker skin tones, including some foreigners, resident Asians, and dark-skinned or Black South Americans.

Paraguayans do not appreciate stereotypes about poverty and inferiority in developing countries; they are proud of their particular heritage. At the same time they feel other countries take advantage of their nation. They do not appreciate people from the United States referring to themselves as "Americans." Paraguayans are South Americans. The preferred reference to residents of the United States is *norteamericano* or *norteamericana* (North American).

Personal Appearance

Western-style clothing is worn throughout Paraguay. Cleanliness is emphasized; even the poorest people have clean clothing and clean shoes. Adults do not wear shorts in public. Men generally do not wear sandals. Men wear slacks and a shirt for working, but suits and ties are less common because of the hot climate. Clothing is often lightweight; cotton is a popular fabric. Men often wear hats.

Women pay particular attention to their appearance, regardless of economic conditions. Styled hair, manicured nails, jewelry, and makeup are all important. Rural women nearly always wear dresses. Women in Asunción are especially fashionable. Society generally considers it important for women to be beautiful. The youth enjoy North American fashions.

CUSTOMS AND COURTESIES

Greetings

Spanish greetings, such as *¡Mucho gusto!* (Pleased to meet you), are often used with strangers or for formal situations. Acquaintances might use less formal Spanish, such as *¡Hola! ¿Cómo estás?* (Hi. How are you?), but friends and relatives more often use Guaraní greetings. The most common phrase is *Mba'eixapa* (pronounced, m-buy-ay-SHA-pah), which means "How are you?" The reply is almost always *¡Iporã!* (Just fine). Often the thumbs up gesture accompanies *¡Iporã!* In the countryside, it is friendly and polite to call out a greeting (*Adió*, holding the "o" out) to a friend passing one's house.

Except in the work place, men and women always shake hands when greeting, even if for the second or third time in a day. When friends greet for the first time in a day, if at least one is a woman, they will kiss each other on each cheek, as well as shake hands. Rural women are more likely to just pat the other's arm rather than kiss. When departing, most people repeat whatever gesture was used in greeting.

Urban men are respectfully addressed by the last name, often accompanied by *Don*. For women, it is customary to use *Doña* with the first name. Professional titles are also used to show respect. Young people refer to each other by their first names. In rural areas, *campesinos* (farmers) often address one another by first name, preceded with *Ña* or *Kai* for women and men, respectively. Paraguayans often greet respected elders by holding their hands in prayer position and waiting to be blessed by the elder.

Gestures

Perhaps the most common hand gesture is "thumbs up," which expresses anything positive or encouraging. A person uses the gesture when saying *Iporã!* or answering a question. Wagging a vertical index finger means "no" or "I don't think so." The North American "OK" sign (tip of thumb and tip of index finger touching to form a circle) is offensive in Paraguay. Winking has romantic, even sexual, connotations; it is not used as a casual gesture.

Paraguayans are soft-spoken; they do not shout to get someone's attention. If making a "tssst tssst" sound does not work, a Paraguayan might whistle or run after the person. Paraguayan men usually give up their bus seats to older or pregnant women or women with babies. Seated bus passengers usually offer to hold packages or children for standing passengers. When making one's presence known at a home, one claps at the gate. It is impolite to enter the yard until invited.

Visiting

Paraguayans visit one another often. Unannounced visits are common and welcome. Paraguayans enjoy hosting friends and new acquaintances. Guests are offered refreshments for most visits. If the hosts are currently eating a meal or drinking *tereré*, visitors will be invited to join in. Otherwise, guests might be offered a soft drink (in the city), coffee, juice, or water. *Tereré* is offered to unannounced visitors only if the host wants them to stay a while. The tea is often drunk from a common *guampa* (container, usually made of wood, cattle horns, or gourds) through a *bombilla* (metal straw). Powdered yerba is mixed with cold water to produce *tereré* (hot water for *maté*, which is drunk less often). The host passes it to one person, who drinks and returns the container to the host, who makes another portion for the next person. This important social custom is enjoyed along with conversation and relaxation.

Urban residents like to invite friends to their homes for a meal, while rural people generally extend invitations only for special occasions. Punctuality is not expected of guests; being late is accepted and more comfortable for all involved. Invited dinner guests might take a gift of wine, beer, or a dessert. These guests are usually expected to stay after a meal for conversation and tea.

Eating

Mealtimes and eating habits vary according to region and family. Rural people often eat when they can; they don't necessarily sit down to a daily family meal. Farmers might eat lunch, for example, in their fields rather than go home. Urban families usually eat their main meal together.

When guests (not relatives) are invited, children might eat before the guests arrive or before they are served. Guests usually receive their plates of food fully served. Additional portions can be taken from serving dishes on the table. Not finishing one's food is considered an insult to the cook. Hosts usually insist their guests take second helpings. Proper etiquette is important in very formal situations, including not placing hands in the lap (they rest on the table edge) or waiting for the hosts to begin eating.

Few people, especially in rural areas, drink during the meal. They wait until they are done eating. At rural parties or celebrations, women eat after men do, or they eat at separate tables. The *asado* (barbecue) is a popular family gathering in many areas.

Street vendors sell a great deal of food on urban streets, and eating or drinking in public is common. A common custom in Paraguay is that food or drink is shared. In restaurants, one rarely buys a drink for oneself; a larger pitcher is ordered for all at the table. Additional rounds are ordered by other diners. Whenever one has a snack or small meal, the food is offered to whomever is around. It is not impolite to decline the offer. In restaurants, service is included in the bill and tips are not expected.

LIFESTYLE
Family

Society is centered around the extended family. Three or four generations might live in one home or on one farm. Children are well behaved and polite. They generally show respect to their elders and they expect to care for their aging parents when they are themselves adults. The father heads the family, with the wife taking care of the household. Most rural women, like the men, are involved in agriculture. Up to 40 percent of the urban labor force is female.

Rural families have few modern conveniences. They live in wooden homes with dirt floors and grass or tin roofs. Urban homes are made of concrete with tile roofs. Nearly all homes in Asunción have running water and electricity.

Dating and Marriage

Most Paraguayan girls have a party at age 15 to celebrate becoming a *señorita*. They are then allowed to go to dances. In traditional homes they are still not allowed to date for another year or two. Young people get to know each other at community fiestas, large family gatherings, dances, and so forth. Customarily, a boy must have a girl's parents' permission to date her. Then he can only visit her on traditional visiting days (Tuesday, Thursday, Saturday, and Sunday). Later in a relationship, dating couples might be accompanied by a relative of the girl. Parents generally expect to approve of any marriage partners. For a marriage to be legal, the wedding must be performed civilly. In addition, couples may have a church wedding. Many couples enter into common-law relationships. Others have children together but do not live together.

Diet

Breakfast usually consists of *cocido* (yerba, cooked sugar, milk) or coffee, bread and butter, and rolls or pastries. Lunch (the main meal) is eaten around midday, and dinner is often served after dark when work is finished. The most important staple foods include *mandioca*, *sopa Paraguaya* (cornbread baked with cheese, onions, sometimes meat), *chipa* (hard cheese bread), *tortillas*, and *empanadas* (deep-fried meat or vegetable pockets). Small rural gardens provide *campesino* families with tomatoes, onions, carrots, garlic, squash, watermelon, cabbage, and other produce. Fruit is obtained from surrounding trees and bushes. Beef is very important to the adult diet. Paraguayans also eat chicken and pork dishes.

Recreation

Soccer is the most popular spectator sport, but volleyball is the most common participation sport. Urban men often play volleyball in the evenings. Women generally do not play sports. Urban people might attend theater, go to movies, or enjoy other cultural events. The Paraguayan harp is world famous. Rural people relax by drinking *tereré* and *maté* and visiting each other, as do urban residents. Latino polka music is quite popular in many areas. The youth enjoy music with a distinct beat (disco, rap, etc.).

Holidays

Paraguayans celebrate New Year's Day, Epiphany (6 January), *Carnaval* (a week of parades and parties in February),

Heroes Day (1 March), *Semana Santa* (Holy Week before Easter), Labor Day (1 May), Independence Day (14–15 May), Mother's Day (15 May), the Chaco Armistice (12 June), *Dia del Amistad* (Friendship Day, 30 July), Founding of Asunción City (celebrated with large parades, 15 August), Constitution Day (25 August), the Victory of Boqueron (29 September), Columbus Day (12 October), All Saints Day (1 November), Virgin of Cacupe (8 December), and Christmas. *Semana Santa* is most important holiday period and is a week for family gatherings.

Commerce

Urban business hours extend from 7:00 A.M. to noon and from 3:00 to 6:00 P.M. People in both urban and rural areas take a *siesta* during the three-hour break and eat their main meal of the day. Rural Paraguayans grow much of their own food; they purchase staples and other goods at small neighborhood stores, which are located in homes. Shopping must often be done on a daily basis due to the lack of refrigeration. Urban people purchase their food from markets or small stores.

SOCIETY

Government

An elected president heads the executive branch of the government. The legislature has two chambers, the Chamber of Senators and the Chamber of Deputies. There is an independent judiciary. The voting age is 18; all adults to age 60 are required by law to vote, although this is not generally enforced. The country is divided into 19 departments (provinces).

Economy

Paraguay's economy is based on agriculture, with cotton being grown by most rural families as their primary cash crop. Soy beans are grown by the Mennonites. Other crops include sugarcane, corn, cassava, yerba, and tobacco. Beef is an important export; cattle are raised on expansive ranches usually owned by nonresident foreigners. As the price of Paraguayan cotton has been falling, the government is seeking ways to decrease dependence on the crop. Little progress has been realized, and the economy is a major challenge for the new democratic system. Many families, especially in rural areas, send one or more members to Argentina to work. Many farmers must keep their children out of school to help with crop production.

About one-fifth of all workers are employed by industry (meat packing, textiles, light consumer goods, etc.). Contraband trade is a problem in Ciudad del Este. Inflation, foreign debt, and high unemployment are serious problems inhibiting economic progress. Deforestation has effectively ruined the potential for a sustainable timber industry. Land redistribution, foreign investment, and economic diversification are all necessary to improve conditions. Paraguay's Human Development Index (0.641) ranks it 90 out of 173 countries. Real gross domestic product per capita averages $2,790, which has doubled in the last generation. Forty percent of the population lives in poverty. Together these figures indicate that what the country does earn is held by a small wealthy class, and that economic opportunities are limited to urban residents. The currency is the *guaraní* (G).

Transportation and Communication

While construction of paved highways has taken place in Paraguay, most roads are not paved. Many are impassable during heavy rains. Buses serve as the main form of public transportation in Asunción and throughout the country. Otherwise, rural people walk. Wealthier urban residents have cars. Taxis are available in Asunción. There are two television channels, one government owned and the other private. A private cable company services Asunción. Both AM and FM radio stations broadcast throughout the country. Most people do not have telephones, but public phones are available.

Education

Public education is provided free of charge, but students must buy uniforms and are asked to contribute to the school fund to help buy supplies. Facilities tend to be crowded. Instruction is in Spanish, which is a hardship on rural children. Most children begin school, but fewer than 60 percent complete all six years of primary school. Less than one-third of eligible children attend secondary school. The school year runs from March to November. Opportunities for those who finish school are limited, and many either work in the fields or go to Argentina or other countries to find work. There are some vocational schools and other institutions of higher learning. The official literacy rate is 90 percent, but this does not reflect reality in rural areas.

Health

The health care system includes hospitals and clinics in major towns. The smaller the town, the smaller the clinic. Rural health posts are staffed a few days a week by a nurse. Rural people use traditional herbs and cures to treat minor ailments. While Paraguayans value cleanliness, many unsanitary conditions (dirt floors, unprotected water sources, poor sewage systems, etc.) contribute to poor health. Malnutrition affects children. Severe dental problems afflict a majority of the population (especially in rural areas). The bite of the *vinchuga* bug is often deadly to rural dwellers who do not sleep under mosquito netting. The bug bites one's face at night, injecting a parasite that can kill the person several years later. Paraguay's infant mortality rate is 48 per 1,000; life expectancy averages 67 years.

FOR THE TRAVELER

U.S. travelers need a valid passport to enter Paraguay, but a visa is not necessary for stays of up to three months. Some vaccinations may be necessary; check with your health care provider. Water is not safe to drink outside of Asunción. For information on travel opportunities, send a self-addressed envelope with two stamps to Paraguay's Consulate at 2121 Avenue of the Stars, Suite 1560, Century City, CA 90067. Paraguay's embassy is located at 2400 Massachusetts Avenue NW, Washington, DC 20008.

A *Culturgram* is a product of native commentary and original, expert analysis. Statistics are estimates and information is presented as a matter of opinion. While the editors strive for accuracy and detail, this document should not be considered strictly factual. It is a general introduction to culture, an initial step in building bridges of understanding between peoples. It may not apply to all peoples of the nation. You should therefore consult other sources for more information.

Republic of
Peru

Boundary representations not necessarily authoritative.

BACKGROUND

Land and Climate

Almost the same size as Alaska, Peru is the third largest country in South America. It covers 496,223 square miles (1,285,220 square kilometers). Peru is divided into three distinct geographical regions: the narrow, dry coastal plain (*costa*) in the west; the high Andes mountains (*sierra*), roughly in the center; and the tropical lowlands of the Amazon Basin (*selva*) to the east. The population is concentrated in the west. Because of the Andes and the Amazon Basin, more than half of the country is covered with forests. Only about 3 percent is suitable for farming. Earthquakes are common but usually mild, although they are potentially dangerous, such as those that struck in 1990 and killed several hundred people. Peru shares the famous Lake Titicaca, the highest navigable body of water in the world, with Bolivia. There is little rainfall along the coast, although the winter is foggy, humid, and cool. In Lima, the temperature is moderate year-round. Temperatures vary significantly between the rugged Andes (up to 22,000 feet or 6,700 meters above sea level) and the eastern jungles.

History

Several of South America's most advanced cultures lived in pre-Columbian Peru. The great Incan Empire, which was unsurpassed in the art of stonecutting and which also achieved a high degree of economic and political development, was the last of these groups. Incan and earlier Chimu ruins, notably at Cuzco, Chan Chan, and Machu Picchu, make Peru a favorite destination for archaeologists and tourists. In 1532, the Spanish invaded Peru under the leadership of Francisco Pizarro. They conquered the Incas the next year. The area soon became the richest and most powerful Spanish colony in South America because of its location and many mineral treasures.

Under the leadership of South American liberator José de San Martín, Peru declared independence from Spain in July 1821. With the help of Simón Bolívar, the Venezuelan general who liberated several other countries, the victory was complete by 1826.

The 1933 constitution provided Peru with a president and legislature to be elected for six-year terms, but military leaders and dictators dominated Peru's history from that time. A free, multiparty election was held in 1963 and Fernando Belaúnde Terry was elected president. He was deposed in 1968 by a military junta that ruled for 12 years (a period called the *dictadura*). Belaúnde was reelected in 1980 when the military agreed to return control of the government to civilians. Troubles with the economy, which began during the *dictadura,* worsened under Belaúnde and were only temporarily resolved in the beginning years of Alán García's presidency (1985–90).

In 1980, the *Sendero Luminoso*, or Shining Path, began a decade of violent guerrilla warfare against the government.

Copyright © 1994. Brigham Young University. Printed in the USA. All rights reserved. It is against the law to copy, reprint, store in a retrieval system, or transmit any part of this publication in any form by any means for any purpose without written permission from the Publications Division of the David M. Kennedy Center for International Studies, Brigham Young University, PO Box 24538, Provo, UT 84602–4538. *Culturgrams* are available for more than 125 areas of the world. To place an order, to receive a free catalog, or to obtain information on traveling abroad, call toll free (800) 528–6279.

THE AMERICAS

The Shining Path, a Maoist group that has vowed to overthrow the government, and other terrorist organizations were responsible for some 18,000 deaths during the 1980s. They consolidated power in the Upper Huallaga Valley (several hours north of Lima), where they are paid by drug traffickers for protection and the right to operate in the region. The drug traffickers encourage farmers to grow coca leaf (from which cocaine is made), which is made into paste and sold to Colombian drug cartels for eventual export. The farmers, now tired of facing Shining Path intimidation, control by drug traffickers, and government drug eradication efforts, have begun to ask for help in switching crops to coffee or cacao, both legal products.

During García's administration, key industries and institutions were nationalized, the foreign debt crisis deepened, and relations with the United States were not very strong. In 1990, however, plans for major military cooperation between the two countries to fight drug trafficking were implemented.

Despite many problems, including terrorist attacks against the government, the country maintained democratic institutions and free elections. In June 1990, Alberto Fujimori, a son of Japanese immigrants, was elected as García's successor. He promised justice and ethics in government and he vowed to overcome Peru's economic problems. In 1991, Shining Path guerrillas moved their attacks closer to Lima and important government installations. At the same time, the country was trying to deal with the president's economic austerity program designed to solve (in the long-term) Peru's economic problems.

Citing Shining Path insurgency, government corruption, and legislative inefficiency, Fujimori suspended the constitution in April 1992 and dissolved congress. He took emergency powers and restricted civil liberties. His goal was to defeat the Shining Path and reform the government while proceeding with economic reforms. A majority of people seemed to support the move, but domestic and international pressure soon mounted. Fujimori promised a quick return to democracy, but elections were delayed. He sponsored a constitutional assembly in 1992 that drafted a new constitution. The new document was approved in a national referendum in October 1993. It enshrines principles of a free market economy and a democratic system following elections to be held in 1995. Fujimori plans to run for president in those elections. His popularity is generally high, but charges of human rights abuses have hurt his image at home and abroad.

While still in power, Fujimori turned his attention to two main problems: the Shining Path and the economy. He successfully lowered inflation and took the economy to a 7 percent growth rate for 1993. And, in 1992, his forces captured Shining Path leader Abimael Guzmán Reynoso. Guzmán was tried and sentenced to life in prison. Shining Path violence continued, but desertions from the organization were high in 1993. Most experts agree that the organization's power is now limited. Within a year of his imprisonment, the initially belligerent Guzmán began encouraging his former followers to end the war and talk peace with the government.

THE PEOPLE

Population

The population of Peru is approximately 23.2 million, and it is growing at 2 percent annually. Population density is generally low, however, because of Peru's large land area. Peru's population is ethnically diverse. About 45 percent is Indian, descendants of the great Incan Empire. There are many ethnic and linguistic divisions among the Indians, some of whom are still fairly isolated in the Amazon jungle. Another 37 percent of the people are *mestizos* (mixed European and Indian heritage). Fifteen percent are of European descent (mostly Spanish) and the remaining 3 percent are composed of blacks (descendants of West African slaves), Japanese, Chinese, and other smaller groups. About half of the population is younger than age 20. Lima is the largest city, with more than six million residents. Seventy percent of all people live in urban areas.

Language

Spanish and the Indian language, Quechua, are both officially recognized languages. Another Indian language, Aymara, is also spoken widely. Many Peruvians speak both Spanish and one Indian language. About 30 percent of the people speak no Spanish at all; they speak either Quechua, Aymara, or another native language. Some Peruvians, mostly among the wealthy and educated elite, speak English.

Religion

Until 1979, the Roman Catholic church was the state church in Peru. Today, even though there is freedom of religion and all churches enjoy the same political status as the Catholic church, most people are Roman Catholic and the church plays a significant role in the people's lives. Many Protestant and Evangelical churches also operate in the country. Many of the Indians who are Roman Catholic mix their traditional Indian beliefs with their Christian values, sometimes calling their gods by Christian names.

General Attitudes

Peruvians are strong willed and nationalistic. They have been through many trials, politically and economically, but they maintain a strong desire to endure and succeed. The people have a good sense of humor and are accommodating and eager to please. Still, they are also very sensitive about some things. Jokes about their lifestyle, especially those coming from foreigners, are offensive. Personal criticism, if necessary, is expected to be expressed in a positive manner. The Peruvian concept of time is more relaxed than in industrialized nations. Appointments and other meetings may not begin on time and Peruvians generally consider people to be more important than schedules. However, international visitors, to whom punctuality is more important, are expected to be on time for appointments.

Many native Indians, especially those who belong to the Shining Path, feel they are discriminated against by Peru's *mestizo* and European populations. Indians are usually rural people, but even those who move to the city are not accepted. This has fueled great resentment among Indians and is one source of the country's social problems. As the Shining Path loses power, rural people are looking to promises of increased investment coming from international organizations and the government. Urban residents, particularly in Lima, are turning their attention to economic progress. People are generally optimistic about the country's future, especially about a hopeful end to the guerrilla war and establishment of a more equitable democracy.

Personal Appearance

Although Western-style clothing is worn regularly in Lima, the capital, and other urban areas, rural *campesinos* (farmers) often wear traditional clothing related to their ethnic background. Handwoven fabrics are commonly used to make their clothes.

CUSTOMS AND COURTESIES

Greetings

Both men and women shake hands when meeting and parting. Close friends often greet each other with a kiss on one cheek. Men may greet close friends with an *abrazo* (hug). An arm around the shoulder or a pat on the back is a polite way to greet youth. First names are used among friends, but elderly people and officials are referred to by their title and last names.

Gestures

To beckon a person, all of the fingers are waved with the palm facing down. People stand close to each other during conversation and constant eye contact is important. When seated, placing the ankle of one leg on the knee of the other is inappropriate for women, but okay for men. On the other hand, women can cross their legs at the knee, but this is not done by men. Hand gestures are used a great deal during conversation.

Visiting

Peruvians enjoy visiting one another. Between friends and relatives, most visits are unannounced. In other cases, it is polite to make advance arrangements. Visitors are expected to feel at home and to be comfortable. The traditional greeting, *Está en su casa* (You are in your house), reflects Peruvian hospitality. Drinks are always offered, but it is not impolite for one to decline them. Other refreshments may also be offered. In many areas, if the visit occurs after 5:30 P.M., the guest is invited to stay for *lonche*, which is a light breakfast-type meal around 6:00 P.M. Special acknowledgment of children in the home is appreciated by the hosts. It is polite to show concern for the health of the host's family and relatives. Gifts are not expected when one visits the home, but small gifts such as fruit or wine are welcome on any occasion. These would commonly be given by those invited to dinner.

Eating

A polite guest eats all the food that is offered. Excuses for not eating something should be very tactful. Proper table manners are important. The continental style of eating is followed; the fork is held in the left hand, while the knife remains in the right. Both hands (but not elbows) are kept above the table at all times. Families enjoy having visitors eat with them. Casual conversation freely accompanies the meal.

Reading at the table is rude. In a restaurant, the waiter is summoned by waving. If service is included in the bill, a small tip is still given, and if service is not included, a tip is expected.

LIFESTYLE

Family

The family unit is important in Peru. Nuclear families have, on average, three children. The father is the undisputed head of the family, while the mother spends most of her time directing and performing household duties. Women occasionally work outside the home, a trend that is more evident in urban areas. About one-fourth of the labor force is female. Most families live in humble circumstances without many of the modern conveniences common in more industrialized nations.

Dating and Marriage

Some group dating occurs in the late teen years, but dating in couples is almost strictly reserved for courtship. The youth in urban areas enjoy dancing and other activities. Men usually marry in their late twenties, while women generally marry in their early twenties. In rural areas, the age is often somewhat lower. Common-law marriages are prevalent and widely accepted, except among the upper classes.

Diet

The main staples in the diet include rice, beans, fish, and a variety of tropical fruits. Soups are common. Corn, native to Peru, is the main staple among the Indians. *Cebiche* (raw fish seasoned with lemon and vinegar) is popular on the coast. Potatoes, onions, and garlic are frequent ingredients for dishes in the highlands. Fresh vegetables are eaten in season. Most food is purchased on a daily basis, either in small corner stores (in cities) or large open-air markets. Bargaining is common in the markets.

Recreation

The most popular sport in Peru is soccer. World Cup competition is carefully followed, especially when Peru has a team participating. Basketball, volleyball, and gymnastics are also favorites. Families enjoy picnics, and movies provide entertainment. Sunday is a favorite day for outings.

Holidays

Many local holidays honor patron saints, celebrate the harvest, or provide recreation. National holidays include New Year's Day, Easter (Thursday through Sunday), Countryman's Day (24 June), St. Peter and St. Paul's Day (29 June), Independence Day (28 July), National Day (29 July), St. Rose of Lima Day (30 August), Navy Day (8 October), All Saints Day (1 November), Immaculate Conception (8 December), and Christmas.

Commece

The average workweek in Peru is slightly more than 48 hours, one of the longest in the world. Businesses are open at least six days a week. Some small businesses close between 1:00 P.M. to 3:00 P.M. each day for a *siesta* (break), but this is not as common today as it once was. Many shops are open late into the evening. Business hours vary slightly according to the season, but generally they are between 8:00 A.M. and 5:00 P.M. Some government offices may close as early as 1:00 P.M.

SOCIETY

Government

The president holds executive power and serves a five-year term. The legislature consists of a Senate and a Chamber of Deputies, but is currently dissolved. The country has 24 departments, which are like states, and one province. Some government structures are expected to change in 1995. All citizens older than age 18 may vote.

Economy

In 1990, the Peruvian economy faced severe strains. Revenues from illegal exports exceeded those from legal exports, inflation peaked at more than 7,600 percent, the economy declined by 12 percent, and real wages continued to fall. Since 1992, inflation has fallen to less than 40 percent and continues to drop. Wages are rising, and foreign investment is flowing in to create jobs, tap resources, and improve conditions in the poorest regions. Although the country remains poor, its potential for progress is high and people expect living conditions to improve substantially in the next few years.

The country's Human Development Index (0.592) ranks it 95 out of 173 countries. Real gross domestic product per capita is $2,622, a figure that has not improved since the 1970s but is expected to rise. Peru has many advantages that point to a bright future. Some factors include a commitment to a free market economy, vast untapped resources, an educated work force, and a fairly equal distribution of income. The greatest hindrance, beyond the insurgency and rural poverty, is the drug trade. Peru is the world's largest producer of coca leaf, which is exported to other countries before it is made into cocaine.

Peru's natural resources include copper, silver, gold, oil, timber, fish, and iron ore. It has a relatively wide economic base, with a variety of industries it can depend on for growth. Wheat, potatoes, beans, rice, and coffee are important agricultural products. Agriculture accounts for 37 percent of all employment. Peru's fish catch is one of the largest in the world. The currency is the *inti*.

Transportation and Communication

Most people travel by bus in the cities, but travel in rural areas is accomplished on foot or with the help of animals. More and more Peruvians in urban areas have cars. Most roads are not paved. Train and air travel are available, but on a limited basis. However, some train routes are very scenic. The telecommunications system is fairly adequate for domestic and international use. Pay phones accept tokens that are purchased at newsstands. There are several daily newspapers.

Education

Public education is free and compulsory between ages seven and sixteen. Basic materials are lacking and facilities are inadequate. In the 1980s, Peru increased efforts to extend primary schools into remote areas. In some areas, the Shining Path controls school facilities. Secondary education is also free in Peru. More than two-thirds of eligible children are enrolled in secondary schools. The average adult has completed at least six years of school, and more young people are staying in school. Peru has more than 30 universities, including the University of San Marcos in Lima, one of the oldest in South America. The literacy rate is about 85 percent and it is higher among teenagers.

Health

Medical care is inadequate. Quality care is only available through expensive private clinics. Hospitals are often short on medicine and food, among other things. Many Peruvians are superstitious about health care and are reluctant to use medical facilities. They prefer to use home remedies made of herbs and roots before going to a doctor. Care in small towns is not reliable and not always available. As with education, the Shining Path guerrillas sometimes coordinate health services in rural areas. In 1991, Peru was overwhelmed by a cholera epidemic that killed more than 1,200 people and caused about 200,000 to become ill. Peru's infant mortality rate is 56 per 1,000. Life expectancy averages from 63 to 67 years.

FOR THE TRAVELER

Visas are not required of U.S. travelers for stays of as long as 90 days, but a valid passport and proof of onward passage are required. Yellow fever vaccinations are recommended and even required in some cases. Dual-voltage small appliances or a voltage converter are necessary to use electrical outlets. Water is usually not potable and should be boiled or treated before drinking. Avoid eating uncooked vegetables, and carefully peel and wash all fruits before eating. If visiting rural areas, consider vaccinations against cholera, typhoid, hepatitis, and perhaps other diseases. In the highlands, it may take some time to adjust to the altitude.

Because of violence related to the Shining Path and drug traffickers, the U.S. Department of State advises all tourists to be cautious. Even in large tourist areas, violence and crime are possible. For recorded travel advisories, call (202) 647–5225. There are many attractions in Peru, including the archaeological sites mentioned earlier. For details on travel opportunities, contact the South American Explorers' Club at (800) 277–0488 or write to 126 Indian Creek Road, Ithaca, NY 14850. You may also wish to contact the Embassy of Peru, 1700 Massachusetts Avenue NW, Washington, DC 20036.

A *Culturgram* is a product of native commentary and original, expert analysis. Statistics are estimates and information is presented as a matter of opinion. While the editors strive for accuracy and detail, this document should not be considered strictly factual. It is a general introduction to culture, an initial step in building bridges of understanding between peoples. It may not apply to all peoples of the nation. You should therefore consult other sources for more information.

CULTURGRAM '95

Republic of
Poland

Boundary representations not necessarily authoritative.

EUROPE

BACKGROUND

Land and Climate

The name *Polska* (Poland) comes from the word *Polane*, which means "plain" or "field." From the sky, Poland appears to be a vast, prairie-like expanse, flat except for the impressive Tatra and Sudety mountains in the southeast, which host the country's skiing and resort areas. Because of the plains, 48 percent of the total land area is suitable for cultivation. Poland's flat terrain has also made it vulnerable to territory-seeking European armies throughout history, and its borders have changed several times. Covering 120,726 square miles (312,680 square kilometers), the total land area today is about the size of New Mexico. The climate is temperate, with mild summers. It is, however, susceptible to extreme temperature variations within short periods of time. Winters are generally cold and precipitation is common throughout the year. The Poles say one must always carry an umbrella because the weather can change instantly. Poland has important natural resources, including coal, sulfur, silver, natural gas, copper, lead, and salt.

History

The Poles are descendants of a Slavic people that settled between the Oder and Vistula Rivers before the time of Christ. King Mieszko I adopted the Roman Catholic faith for his family and the monarchy in 966 A.D. In the late 14th century, Polish life and culture flourished during the reign of King Kasimir the Great. Poland combined with Lithuania in the late Middle Ages, creating a mighty empire that was a major power in Europe. An enlightened constitution in 1791 was patterned after the American Constitution and gave freedom to the serfs. Due to political infighting among the ruling nobles, as well as other factors, the monarchy declined to the point in 1795 that is was invaded and partitioned by Prussia, Austria, and Russia. For the next 125 years, Polish identity and culture were preserved by the Roman Catholic church in Poland.

Poland became a nation again in 1918, at the end of World War I. Unfortunately, political life was neither stable nor strong. The country did not have much of a chance to stabilize, as the German army invaded in 1939. Within days of the German invasion to the west, the Soviets invaded from the east and Poland was again partitioned. More than six million Poles died during World War II, including three million Polish Jews who died in the Holocaust. The Soviets were given administrative control over the regions liberated from German occupation when Germany was defeated. Elections were held, but by 1948 a Soviet-backed Communist government was in firm control and the country's political system came to be patterned after that in the Soviet Union, with some exceptions (such as land ownership and matters of religion).

In 1981, following a series of crippling strikes and the formation and activity of the Solidarity Labor Union, General Wojciech Jaruzelski declared martial law. The *Sejm* (parliament) outlawed Solidarity and its leaders were jailed. Martial law was lifted in 1983, and Lech Walesa, the leader of the still-outlawed Solidarity union, received the Nobel Peace Prize in recognition of his efforts to win freedom and a better standard of living for the Polish people. Solidarity maintained pressure on the Jaruzelski government, winning international support and admiration.

In 1989, the Polish government legalized Solidarity (which won many parliamentary seats in national elections) and

Copyright © 1994. Brigham Young University. Printed in the USA. All rights reserved. It is against the law to copy, reprint, store in a retrieval system, or transmit any part of this publication in any form by any means for any purpose without written permission from the Publications Division of the David M. Kennedy Center for International Studies, Brigham Young University, PO Box 24538, Provo, UT 84602–4538. *Culturgrams* are available for more than 125 areas of the world. To place an order, to receive a free catalog, or to obtain information on traveling abroad, call toll free (800) 528–6279.

implemented changes in the government, including the creation of the office of president. Jaruzelski was elected president in July and stepped down from his leadership of the Communist party. After pressure for reform, the *Sejm* named a top Solidarity official, Tadeusz Mazowiecki, as prime minister. This opened the way for Solidarity-led reforms. The government soon began a transition to a market economy to accompany its new democratic government. A bold economic program, referred to as "shock therapy," was instituted in 1990. It caused prices to rise sharply and led immediately to at least 10 percent unemployment.

Jaruzelski resigned to speed political reform and Lech Walesa was elected president in late 1990. After nearly a year in power, Walesa came under increasing criticism for rising unemployment and economic recession. Parliamentary elections in 1991 reduced his power base and prompted a reassessment of the government's economic program. In 1992 and 1993, parliament rejected every major reform package, and four different prime ministers failed to retain office. In 1993, former Communists made a strong showing in parliamentary elections with the victory of the Democratic Left Alliance and the Polish Peasant Party. The two formed a coalition government, and the leader of the Polish Peasant Party, Waldemar Pawlak, was named prime minister. His party represents mainly rural farmers, who have considerable power and who were among those most hurt by economic reforms. The new government made plans to slow the course of economic reform, but to continue the transition to a market economy.

THE PEOPLE

Population

The population of Poland is 38.5 million and is growing at 0.3 percent annually. Urbanization is relatively high; about 60 percent of the population lives in cities. The country is also very homogeneous, with 98 percent of the people being of Polish origin. There are some Ukrainians (0.6 percent) and Belarusians (0.5 percent) in the country, as well as Germans (1.3 percent) in Silesia, an area bordering Germany.

Language

Polish is the official language. Smaller ethnic groups speak their own languages in addition to Polish. Polish is a Slavic language, belonging to the Indo-European family of languages. Polish uses a Latin alphabet, modified with a few unique letters (these look like normal Latin letters with accent markings, but are distinct letters). Written Polish emerged in the 12th century but did not flourish until the 16th century when it began to overtake Latin, which was used by the ruling class. Under communism, Russian was a required course in school, but this is no longer the case. English is the most popular second language.

Religion

The overwhelming majority of Poles belong to the Roman Catholic church, which has had great influence in the country since Poland was catholicized in the 10th century. Approximately 75 percent of the people are practicing Catholics, and another 15 percent belong to the church. Because the Catholic church is a strong and unified entity, it has played an important political role in the past. The church has historically been nationalistic in Poland and very patriotic, championing the cause of the people while under the Communist regime. The Catholic pope, John Paul II, is a native Pole.

There are also other churches represented in Poland as well, including Russian Orthodox, various Protestant faiths, the Uniate faith (a combination of Russian Orthodox practices and loyalty to papal authority), and others. The issue of Catholicism's influence in Poland is currently being debated. Some people prefer that laws and social customs remain secular, while others would like them to more fully reflect Catholic values.

General Attitudes

Polish people value self-reliance and individualism. The Poles are generally outgoing and outspoken. They value generosity and do not highly regard those who are not willing to share their time, resources, or power. People are generally strait-forward and unaccustomed to cynicism. They place great emphasis on the family and on education. Poles are proud of their cultural heritage and their ability to survive war, losses of territory, and subordination to other governments. During periods of foreign domination, the Poles looked to their past heritage as a great power in order to retain a belief they were not a conquered or subordinate people. Prior to World War II, the Polish noble class considered itself better than occupying forces, which gave Poles the desire to maintain their culture and language.

Poland's new democracy and transition to a free market has tarnished some hopes. Many people express concern that they did not expect freedom to be so painful. Yet, despite the fact that the poor were better off economically under communism, few people express a desire to return to the old system. They recognize the future has greater potential.

Personal Appearance

Because clothing is expensive, people's wardrobes remain small. Many Poles wear handmade clothing as well. Fashions are generally conservative, although the youth favor current European trends. Business people wear conservative suits or dresses. Women do not generally wear pants. Older rural women continue to wear a scarf around their heads, full skirts, and thick stockings. Denim jeans are especially popular among the youth and in academic and artistic circles. Teenagers like sweatshirts with English slogans or emblems. Children are expected to be clean and well-groomed in school.

CUSTOMS AND COURTESIES

Greetings

Adults generally shake hands upon meeting. When introducing a man, one uses *pan* (pronounced "pahn") before the last name; for a woman, the term is *pani*. A professional person's title is used before his or her last name. Only the person's title is used in formal conversation or in business. Teenagers and children are called by their first names, but between adults first names are used only by mutual consent. People on a first name basis greet each other with *Cze*, a way of saying "hi." A young man may kiss the extended hand of an older woman in greeting, or an older man may kiss the hand of a younger woman. But a younger man will not generally kiss the hand of a woman who is about the same age. Women greet close female friends by kissing both cheeks. Some common Polish greetings include *Dzien dobry* (JEAN du-BREE), which means "Hello" or "Good morning"; *Dobry wieczór* (du-BREE vyeh-CHOOR), "Good evening"; and *Do widzenia* (DUH veed-TZAYN-ya), "Good-bye." When Poles sign their name, they sign their family name first and then the given name.

Visiting

Unannounced visits among friends and relatives are common. This is especially true in rural areas where people are less likely to have telephones. Unarranged visits do not generally last more than a few hours. More formal, longer visits are arranged in advance. Poles often invite friends over for dinner or just for cake and tea, and they like to have formal parties on special occasions. It is customary to give hosts an odd number of flowers for even a brief arranged visit. The flowers are unwrapped before being given to the hostess. Red roses express romantic feelings. A guest is nearly always offered tea or coffee, but it is not impolite to refuse refreshments. Guests may be entertained at a *kawiarna* (café), which offers a variety of French pastries in addition to its own specialties. Such visits often last several hours. Entertaining is more commonly done in the home, however, because going out is expensive. Because Poles generally go to work early in the morning, weekday evening visits do not usually extend beyond 11:00 P.M. Weekend visits may, however, last until 6:00 A.M. the next morning in areas where buses do not run between 11:00 P.M. and 6:00 A.M.

Eating

Poles generally eat breakfast between 6:30 and 8:00 A.M. Some people eat a second breakfast around 10:00 A.M. The main meal is at 3:00 P.M. and is the meal the family expects to gather for. The lighter evening meal is eaten between 6:00 and 8:30 P.M. Tea or cocoa is commonly drunk at breakfast, while fruit compote is typical for the main meal. The compote, usually homemade, is a combination of fruit juice, fruit, and water. The liquid is drunk during the meal, and the remaining fruit is eaten at the end of the meal. Tea is commonly drunk in the evening. Coffee is usually reserved for breaks. The continental style of eating is used, with the fork in the left hand and the knife remaining in the right. Both hands (not the elbows) are kept above the table during the meal. Eating should not begin until everyone has been served and the host or head of the family has begun. Conversation during the meal is minimal, but it is polite to sit around the table just after eating to talk. When eating as a guest, it is impolite not to finish one's first helping. Taking seconds is appreciated, and not finishing that portion is acceptable. In restaurants, the bill must be requested from the waiter and is paid at the table. Tips are generally expected. Toasting is often a part of both formal and informal dinners. Vodka or wine, served between courses, may be used by the host to toast the guest. It is appropriate for the guest to return the gesture later in the meal.

LIFESTYLE

Family

The average family has one or two children. Rural families often have three or four. The father, traditionally a dominant authority figure, demands obedience yet wants his children ultimately to be independent and have self-discipline. In all households, children are given considerable responsibility from an early age. Because both parents usually work outside the home, the children often get their own breakfasts (school starts after work does) and go to school by themselves. Older children clean, sometimes cook, and often care for younger siblings. The economic situation of most families demands the equal involvement of both parents in raising the family and working outside the home, although women still bear most responsibility for homemaking. Women comprise nearly half the labor force. The elderly are often cared for by their adult children.

Dating and Marriage

Young people who start work after the minimum required schooling marry earlier than those who continue their education. Women marry between ages 18 and 20; men begin marrying at age 21. Those who go to technical schools and universities usually marry after age 25. Parents of the couple often give financial assistance and allow the couple to live in their home for the first few years. This is necessary because housing is in short supply and is very expensive. Living together before being married is discouraged.

Diet

Because workdays begin early, Poles often have only a light breakfast, taking a sandwich along to eat at 10:00 A.M. Many rural people, however, eat hot or cold cereal for breakfast. The main meal consists of soup, meat or fish, salad, and potatoes. Pastries or ice cream are eaten for a late-afternoon snack. Bread, dairy products, and canned fish are plentiful. Most foods are readily available. Some common dishes include *pierogi* (dumplings with cream cheese and potatoes), *uszka* (a kind of ravioli), *bigos* (sausage, mushrooms, cabbage), braised pork and cabbage, poppy seed desserts, and cheese cake. Bread is purchased several times a week, sometimes even daily. Only people who live far from a store eat bread that is more than two days old. Pork is more popular than beef. With the switch to a market economy, more food in greater variety is available, but prices are much higher and many families spend much of their income on food.

Recreation

Soccer is popular in Poland. Poles also participate in track and field events, cycling, table tennis, skiing, basketball, volleyball, and various individual sports. Bridge is a favorite card game. Attending cultural events and visiting friends are common recreational activities. Poland has a rich heritage in music, art and literature. Frederic Chopin (1810–48) is the best known musician. His most popular pieces include the "Mazurek" and the "Polonaise." Many internationally acclaimed artists, composers, authors, and filmmakers come from Poland. Nobel Prizes for poetry and literature have been earned by a number of famous Poles. Fame also extends to other areas, such as science (Copernicus and Marie Curie were Poles) and politics (Jan III Sobieski was the king who broke the Ottoman siege of Vienna in 1683).

Holidays

Official holidays in Poland include New Year's Day, Easter (two days), Labor Day (1 May), Constitution Day (3 May), Corpus Christi (in May or June), All Saints Day (1 November), Independence Day (11 November), and Christmas. Family graves are decorated on All Saints Day. People celebrate not only their birthdays but also their name days (the day assigned to the Catholic saint after whom a person is named). Christmas is the most important holiday. On 6 December, children receive small gifts from Saint Nicholas. On Christmas Eve, the family gathers for a large meatless meal that usually includes fresh fish, dishes featuring poppy seeds or mushrooms, a special compote, and other traditional foods. On the 26th, Poles visit and relax. Nativity scenes and caroling are popular throughout the season. Easter is also a time of many traditions: Easter eggs, feasts, and pageants. Throughout the year there are also local festivals, such as the Folk Art Fair in Kraków, and other celebrations.

Commerce

Banks are generally open from 8:00 A.M. until 3:00 P.M., Monday through Friday. Most close at 10:30 A.M. on Saturday. Stores are generally open from 7:00 A.M. to 7:00 P.M., Monday through Saturday, although hours vary according to location and function. *Kiosks*, small shops that offer a variety of goods, are common in Poland's cities. Large cities have supermarkets, but these do not usually carry fresh meat or produce. Meat is acquired from a butcher and produce in the open-air market. Basic foods are purchased from the supermarkets, or, in smaller towns, from neighborhood stores. Bread is sold in grocery stores because it is considered a basic food. Bakeries are for pastries and other sweet things.

SOCIETY

Government

The president is the head of state and the prime minister is the head of government. The president is elected by the people, but he appoints the prime minister, who is usually the leader of the majority party in parliament. Prime Minister Pawlak's party does not have the most seats in parliament, but in order to form a government, its coalition partner, the Democratic Left Alliance, accepted the Polish Peasant Party's demand that Pawlak be given the top government post. A new constitution was ratified in 1992, confirming Poland's status as a democratic country. The country's parliament, or National Assembly, has an upper house (Senate) and a lower house (Diet or *Sejm*). Poland's voting age is 18.

Economy

The 1980s brought an economic crisis to the country that led to strikes and unrest that eventually brought down the government. The 1990 economic "shock therapy" that was designed to rapidly create a market economy caused the standard of living to fall even further. The people faced many hardships under the plan, but understood the need for radical reform in order to successfully join other prosperous European countries as a free market economy. With enough outside investment and tight control of the budget, Poland will be able to capitalize on its natural resources and skilled labor. This may take some time, however, because in 1993, inflation was 20 percent and unemployment was above 15 percent.

Still, the private sector is booming, and the economy grew by a strong 4 percent in 1993. Poland's Human Development Index (0.831) ranks it 48 out of 173 nations. Real gross domestic product per capita is $4,237. Most people earn enough for basic needs, but the gap between rich and poor is expanding quickly. This is a social problem contributing to political instability and general distrust of the government among the Polish people. In the past, wealth was associated with corruption, because only corrupt Communist officials had wealth. So today's wealthy, no matter how honest, are viewed with some suspicion.

About 25 percent of the labor force is engaged in agriculture, which has always remained in private hands despite Communist-era attempts at collectivization. Important products include grains, sugar beets, oilseed, potatoes, and pork, as well as dairy products. Poland has a strong industrial sector. Nearly half of all exports consist of machinery and equipment. Another 10 percent are manufactured items. Poland is a major producer of minerals and steel. The currency is the *zloty* (Zl).

Transportation and Communication

Public transportation is generally efficient and inexpensive. Most families do not have a car, but car ownership is on the rise. Most cities have streetcars and bus systems. On all trams there are a few seats clearly marked and reserved for the handicapped, the elderly, and women with small children. Travelers purchase tickets from *kiosks* and, on boarding, punch the tickets in machines mounted near the door. Large cities are connected by railroads and airlines. Most people have televisions and many have telephones. There are several daily newspapers.

Education

Education is free and mandatory for 10 years, beginning with kindergarten. Education has traditionally been very important to the Polish people and the literacy rate is 98 percent. Entrance to a university is determined by competitive examination; only about 5 percent of all applicants are accepted into the best schools. A university education takes five to six years to complete. There are also four and five-year technical and professional high schools, as well as three-year vocational training schools. Two-thirds of dental and medical students are women.

Health

The government provides health care to all citizens. Facilities are generally accessible, but they are not up to Western standards. The poor economy has forced hospitals and other clinics to cut some services, to ask patients for donations, and to solicit help from family members in caring for patients. Private care in doctors' offices is better, but one must pay for it. The infant mortality rate is 14 per 1,000. Life expectancy ranges from 68 to 77 years.

FOR THE TRAVELER

U.S. travelers do not need a visa for stays as long as 90 days, but a valid passport is required. Poland is actively encouraging tourism and has a good network of tourist offices to assist travelers. Be prepared to pay for some services in hard currency (such as dollars or German marks). Avoid converting large sums of money into *zloty*; frequent, smaller transactions are better. For more information, contact the Embassy of Poland, 2640 16th Street NW, Washington, DC 20009.

A *Culturgram* is a product of native commentary and original, expert analysis. Statistics are estimates and information is presented as a matter of opinion. While the editors strive for accuracy and detail, this document should not be considered strictly factual. It is a general introduction to culture, an initial step in building bridges of understanding between peoples. It may not apply to all peoples of the nation. You should therefore consult other sources for more information.

(Portuguese Republic)
Portugal

Boundary representations not necessarily authoritative.

BACKGROUND

Land and Climate

Portugal is situated on the west coast of the Iberian Peninsula, which it shares with Spain. The Portuguese Republic includes the mainland, the Azores and Madeira Islands (over 600 miles or 950 kilometers off the Atlantic coast), and Macao (a small colony near Hong Kong). Covering 35,552 square miles (92,080 square kilometers), the total land area (not including Macao) is about the size of Indiana. Portugal is divided into two zones by the Tagus River, whose mouth is at Lisbon. In the north, the land is fairly mountainous (including the Estrela mountain range) and the climate is cool and rainy. The northwest experiences temperate winters and short summers while the northeast has long, cold winters with snow. South of the Tagus River, the terrain is less rugged, formed by hills and valleys, and the climate is warmer and more moderate. About one-third of the land is suitable for agriculture. Forty percent is forested.

History

Ancient Phoenicians, Carthaginians, and Greeks all built colonies on Portugal's coast. In 27 B.C., the Romans took control of the area and made it a province. After the Romans, the Visigoths ruled until they were defeated by the Moors. The Moors governed from the eighth century to the twelfth century. By 1140, Portugal was an independent nation under King Afonso Henriques. In the 14th and 15th centuries, Portuguese explorers gave Portugal a huge overseas empire. Phillip II of Spain ruled Portugal as Phillip I for a short time (1580–98) because Portugal's previous king had left no heirs and Phillip defeated other hopefuls. Phillip's sons also reigned in Portugal, but control was lost to the native nobility while Spain was at war with France. Portugal's monarchy was eventually overthrown (1910), and a republic was established.

However, political rivalries resulted in an unstable regime and a military coup overthrew the democracy in 1926. From 1928 to 1968, António de Oliveira Salazar led an authoritarian dictatorship, denying the people basic civil rights. When he fell ill, Marcello Caetano succeeded him. Caetano tried to effect some reforms while maintaining the basic authoritarian government. In April 1974, a socialist military group, led by General Antonio de Spinola, took control of the government and vowed to restore democracy. In 1975, the junta held elections that led to the Third Republic. As politics shifted to the left, some industry was nationalized and some farmland collectivized.

Until 1985, the political situation remained somewhat unstable. In the 1985 elections, however, voting patterns were more concrete and Mário Soares (a center-right candidate) was chosen to lead Portugal. Under his leadership, and that of

EUROPE

Copyright © 1994. Brigham Young University. Printed in the USA. All rights reserved. It is against the law to copy, reprint, store in a retrieval system, or transmit any part of this publication in any form by any means for any purpose without written permission from the Publications Division of the David M. Kennedy Center for International Studies, Brigham Young University, PO Box 24538, Provo, UT 84602–4538. *Culturgrams* are available for more than 125 areas of the world. To place an order, to receive a free catalog, or to obtain information on traveling abroad, call toll free (800) 528–6279.

Prime Minister Aníbal Cavaco Silva, the government began privatization efforts, joined Portugal to the European Union (EU), and started a series of other reforms. Cavaco's leadership proved popular and he was reelected in 1991.

THE PEOPLE

Population

Portugal has a population of approximately 10.4 million, which is growing at 0.3 percent annually. In the 1960s and 1970s, Portugal's population declined somewhat because many people emigrated. Today, migration takes place more within the country than from Portugal to other countries. Most Portuguese are of ethnic Mediterranean stock; there is not much ethnic diversity. During decolonization, Black Africans began migrating to Portugal, but they comprise less than 1 percent of the population. Unlike many industrialized countries, Portugal has a relatively low urban population. Nearly two-thirds of the people live in rural areas or small towns. Lisbon, the capital, is the largest city, with 950,000 people. Several smaller cities are located near Lisbon.

Language

The official language is Portuguese. English, French, and German are taught in the schools, and are therefore often understood by the Portuguese.

Religion

More than 95 percent of the population is Roman Catholic and Catholic traditions have a strong influence on the lives of the people. Approximately 1 percent belongs to other Christian denominations, and some non-Christian religions are also practiced in Portugal. Freedom of religion is guaranteed. Portugal is much less secularized than other European countries.

General Attitudes

The Portuguese are generally traditional and conservative. They usually accept change and innovation only after careful consideration, but then quietly. People and relationships are more important than time, so punctuality is not always stressed. Being on time is considered impressive, but not crucial, although more urban dwellers are finding it important. Portugal is an open, liberal society, but there is a greater emphasis on religious faith and moral values than in other European nations. Political issues (not parties) are avidly discussed. The Portuguese are proud of their cultural heritage, sense of nation, and economic progress. They are very open and friendly to people of other nations. The Portuguese believe that friendships should be strong and should last a lifetime.

Personal Appearance

The Portuguese are generally conservative in dress. Men wear suits to work, although sport jackets are also popular among some. Tattered clothing is improper. Leather dress shoes are worn for most occasions; tennis shoes are for recreation, not everyday wear. Clothing is usually ironed well; wrinkles are considered sloppy. People are careful to be well dressed in public. Each region of Portugal has a distinct national costume that is worn for festivals and special occasions. They are often elaborate and very colorful. For women, most costumes include scarves for the head and/or shoulders and skirts with aprons. Men's costumes usually include hats, vests, and a scarf. Older women, especially in rural areas, often wear black clothing all the time after their husbands die.

CUSTOMS AND COURTESIES

Greetings

A warm, firm handshake is an appropriate greeting for anyone, although some Portuguese prefer lighter handshakes. Friends often hug. Relatives or close female friends often appear to kiss each cheek, beginning with the right. Actually, they "kiss the air" while brushing cheeks. Children are expected to kiss adults in the extended family when greeting them. Touching is a common part of greeting because it shows friendship. First names are used for friends, youth, and children. Otherwise, a title is used with a surname to address an adult. Sometimes the title is combined with the first name, rather than the last; it depends on personal preference and the relationship between the speakers. Some common terms used for greeting are *Bom dia* (Good day) and *Boa noite* (Good evening).

Gestures

Although the Portuguese are rather reserved, they use a lot of physical gestures in conversation. It is impolite to point directly at a person with the index finger. To beckon, all fingers are waved with the palm facing up. Pinching the earlobe and shaking it gently while raising the eyebrows means something (a meal, for instance) is really good. Pulling down on the skin just below the eye with the index finger can mean, "You are perceptive," or "You're kidding me." Spreading the fingers with palm down and rocking the hand means "more or less." Rubbing the thumb against the first two fingers with the palm facing up is a sign for money. Touching the tips of all fingers to the tip of the thumb with the palm facing up signifies fear or cowardice. It is a serious insult to make a "V" sign or "rabbit ears" behind someone's head, because it connotes a lack of morals.

Visiting

When visiting a family, guests wait outside the door until invited inside the home; likewise, guests do not let themselves out when leaving, but they let the hosts open the door. In urban areas, guests are more or less on time, but rural people are not as concerned with schedules. Because homemakers keep their homes very clean, guests are expected to wipe their feet before entering. Dirty shoes are removed entirely. It is polite to converse about a guest's family, positive aspects of Portugal, and personal interests. Guests usually avoid inquisitive personal questions. Guests often take small gifts to their hosts or send a thank-you note after a dinner engagement. Sincere compliments about the home and its decor are welcome. Refreshments are usually served and it is impolite for guests to refuse them.

Most socializing is done in the home, but it is common for business associates to go to a restaurant. People enjoy getting together at a café for casual conversation, sweets, and tea or coffee. Visiting relatives, especially those living in one's rural "homeland," is very popular. Urban people have strong roots to their hometowns or regions and try to visit as often as possible.

Eating

Time for conversation is taken during the meal. To avoid seeming in a hurry, diners try not to finish before anyone else. They try to finish at the same time as others at the table. The continental style of eating is followed, with the fork in the left hand and the knife remaining in the right. A special knife and fork are used when eating fish; a regular meat knife should never be used. It is important to keep the hands above the table at all times, and it is impolite to stretch at the table. Stretching implies one is tired or bored with the company. The mouth is covered when using a toothpick. Except for ice cream cones, it is considered improper for adults to eat while walking in public.

A small breakfast is eaten around 8:00 A.M., a large lunch at about 1:00 P.M., and dinner is generally served between 8:00 and 9:00 P.M. The main meal of the day might consist of two main dishes (meat and fish), a soup, vegetables, and more than one dessert. *Bica*, a strong espresso-type coffee, is often served after the meal. In some areas of the north, *bica* is called *cimbalino*. If rabbit, pig, or fish is eaten, the father or guest of honor receives the head.

In restaurants, the waiter is summoned with a raised hand. A service charge is usually not included in the bill, so a 15 percent tip is customary. Tips are also given to people for most personal services, from ushering to carrying luggage to driving a taxi.

LIFESTYLE

Family

The family is the core of Portuguese life. Families are strengthened by a clan spirit that extends to aunts, uncles, cousins, and beyond. Nuclear families tend to be small, averaging two children. Although families in urban areas enjoy most modern conveniences and have a faster-paced lifestyle, people living in rural areas still lead fairly simple lives. Their homes are small and many luxury items are too expensive to buy. Women often work outside the home in urban areas. More than one-third of the labor force is female.

Dating and Marriage

Dating habits in Portugal are similar to those currently prevailing in the rest of Europe, although they are more conservative in the rural areas. Young people associate in groups first and later pair off in couples. Actually, going on a date signifies a serious relationship. Engagements are usually lengthy while the couple saves money for an apartment. Marriage ceremonies generally follow the Catholic tradition. It is not uncommon for young people to live together before getting married.

Diet

The staple foods in Portugal include fish, vegetables, and fruits. One of the national dishes is *bacalhau* (dried cod), which is usually served with potatoes and green vegetables, and sometimes beans. *Bacalhau* is eaten often and can be prepared in a variety of ways, such as deep-fried with potatoes (called *pasteis*). The traditional Portuguese salad includes dark green lettuce, tomatoes, onions, vinegar, olive oil, and salt. Chicken is eaten throughout the country in many forms, such as *frango na pucara* (chicken in a pot) or *cabidela* (chicken with rice). Pork, partridge, quail, and rabbit are also typical meats in Portugal. All parts of the pig are eaten in Portugal. A popular dish is *cozido à Portuguesa*, which contains potatoes, many vegetables, rice, and various meats. Olive oil is the favorite cooking oil, and garlic is a commonly used seasoning. Sweets are very popular, and Portugal has many pastry shops. Wine is inexpensive and consumed by all members of the family with their meals.

Recreation

For recreation, families take walks, go to the park, have picnics, or go to the beach. Portugal's coast is very beautiful, so its beaches are popular destinations. People often take short trips or visit relatives. Sitting outdoors or at a sidewalk café is popular. Going to movies is also common, as is going to night clubs or discos for dancing. A popular type of theater is the *revista*, which satirizes the government, international topics, or social issues. Soccer is by far the most popular sport. Roller skating, hockey, and sailing are also enjoyed. Portugal is known for its tradition with horses, and Portuguese bullfights incorporate the graceful movements of the horse and rider with the charges of the bull. At bullfights in Portugal, the bull is not killed as in other countries. A *forcado* must tackle the bull with his bare hands, but he is assisted by several others in the ring who distract the bull, hold on to its tail, and perform other functions. The bullfight is a favorite spectator sport; participants are amateurs, not professionals.

Holidays

National holidays in Portugal include New Year's Day, Easter (including Good Friday), Anniversary of the Revolution (25 April), Labor Day (1 May), Corpus Christi (in June), National Day of Portugal (10 June), Assumption (15 August), Proclamation of the Republic (5 October), All Saints Day (1 November), Independence Day (1 December), Day of the Immaculate Conception (8 December), and Christmas. On National Day, the poet Luis de Camões is honored and the Portuguese communities scattered abroad are remembered. Throughout the year, local festivals honor patron saints or celebrate such things as the harvest.

Commerce

Business hours vary from place to place, but the traditional workday is from 9:00 A.M. to 1:00 P.M. and 3:00 to 7:00 P.M. Shopping centers are open later and do not close for lunch. Banks and government offices close early.

SOCIETY

Government

The executive branch is formed by the president (Soares) and the prime minister. The unicameral legislature, called the Assembly of the Republic, has 230 members, all of which are directly elected. All citizens over age 18 have the right to vote. The next legislative elections are in October 1995.

Economy

Since joining the European Union in 1986, Portugal has enjoyed strong growth and rapid economic development. Foreign investment has greatly expanded, some state-owned industries have been privatized, and the standard of living has increased.

Portugal's Human Development Index (0.853) ranks it 41 out of 173 countries. Real gross domestic product per capita is estimated at $8,870, which has more than tripled in the last generation. These figures indicate that, while Portugal lags behind its neighbors, economic prosperity is available to a growing number of people. Social institutions exist that can expand economic opportunities and improve conditions for the rising generation. Most people earn enough to meet their basic needs.

So far, development has favored urban areas over rural ones, but the entire country has benefited from a more stable government and brighter prospects for the future. Although inflation is high (12 percent), unemployment is below 6 percent, and the economy is expected to continue growing. Twenty percent of the labor force is engaged in agriculture, but Portugal must still import much of its food. Its most important crops include grains, potatoes, olives, and grapes.

Portugal exports cotton textiles, cork (from cork trees) and cork products, canned fish, wine, timber, and machinery. Tourism is an increasingly important source of income. The currency is the Portuguese *escudo* (Esc).

Transportation and Communication

Portugal has a good network of paved roads, but few roads are as modern as those in other European Union countries. Driving is hazardous. Portuguese drivers have a reputation for driving too fast in wet conditions, passing cars around blind corners, and driving drunk. Traffic accidents are a leading cause of death and injury in Portugal. Buses and trains connect most areas. Lisbon has an efficient subway, and taxis are available in most urban areas. In cities, passengers on buses must have exact change to buy a ticket from the driver. Train tickets must be purchased in advance, not from the conductor. The communications system is good. Portugal has over 30 daily newspapers.

Education

Primary education is compulsory for ages seven through twelve. There are private schools and free public schools. After elementary school, students may attend three years of high school and two years of college preparation, or three to four years of vocational schooling that also incorporates some college preparatory courses. There are 18 universities in Portugal. The University of Coimbra, founded in the 13th century, is one of the oldest in Europe. The literacy rate is 85 percent. It has improved through the 1980s, but remains lower than most of Western Europe because of a low average literacy rate in rural areas (50 percent).

Health

Health care is subsidized by the government. Facilities are generally good and are improving. The infant mortality rate is 10 per 1,000. Life expectancy ranges from 71 to 78 years.

FOR THE TRAVELER

A valid passport is necessary to visit Portugal, but a visa is not necessary for those staying less than 60 days. No vaccinations are required unless one is traveling to the islands or is coming from a yellow fever endemic zone. Water is safe for drinking. In rural areas, however, one should exercise caution about the drinking water during the dry season. Dual-voltage small appliances or a voltage converter and a plug adaptor are necessary to use electrical outlets. Portugal is increasingly becoming a favorite tourist destination. For information on travel opportunities, contact the Portuguese National Tourist Office (590 Fifth Avenue, New York, NY 10036). You may also wish to contact the Embassy of Portugal, 2125 Kalorama Road NW, Washington, DC 20008.

A *Culturgram* is a product of native commentary and original, expert analysis. Statistics are estimates and information is presented as a matter of opinion. While the editors strive for accuracy and detail, this document should not be considered strictly factual. It is a general introduction to culture, an initial step in building bridges of understanding between peoples. It may not apply to all peoples of the nation. You should therefore consult other sources for more information.

The Commonwealth of
Puerto Rico

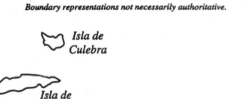

Boundary representations not necessarily authoritative.

BACKGROUND

Land and Climate

Puerto Rico is an island in the Caribbean, just east of Haiti and the Dominican Republic. At 3,515 square miles (9,104 square kilometers), it is about the same size as Rhode Island and Delaware combined. Puerto Rico also includes the smaller Culebra Island and Vieques Island. The land consists of a variety of mountains, deserts, rain forests, coastal plains, and beaches. Three-fourths of the main island is mountainous, leaving little land (8 percent) for cultivation. The coastal plains are densely populated. The island's climate is mildly tropical. The weather is warm and sunny with regular rainfall, especially from May to December. Rainfall is moderate in the coastal regions and heavier in the interior mountains. Temperatures average 70°F to 80°F (21–27°C) year-round. The island is often hit by destructive hurricanes. Hurricane Hugo (1989) did a great deal of damage to the island.

History

Columbus claimed the island for Spain in 1493, calling it San Juan Bautista. Spanish settlers colonized the island beginning in 1508 and began importing African slaves in 1513. Male members of the indigenous Taino Indian tribe were annihilated in the 16th century, but the women remained. Slavery was abolished in 1873. In 1897, Spain granted self-government to Puerto Rico. The government was led by Luis Muñoz Rivera.

In 1898, as part of the Spanish-American War, the United States invaded the island and conquered the Spanish defenders. Spain ceded the island to the United States that same year. In 1917, Puerto Rico became a U.S. territory and its people were granted citizenship. The depression of the 1930s caused widespread suffering and 60 percent unemployment on the island. In 1946, the first island-born governor, Jesus Toribio Pinero, was appointed by President Harry S. Truman. Two years later, Puerto Ricans elected a governor, Luis Muñoz Marin.

Puerto Rico became a commonwealth of the United States with its own constitution in July 1952. A resident high Commissioner represents Puerto Rico in the U.S. House of Representatives. The high commissioner can introduce legislation but cannot vote. As citizens of a commonwealth, Puerto Ricans do not vote in national elections and do not pay federal income tax, but they do elect their own local officials. They are also subject to the draft and only receive partial welfare benefits. They have no voting representation in the federal government and are restricted by federal controls in

Copyright © 1994. Brigham Young University. Printed in the USA. All rights reserved. It is against the law to copy, reprint, store in a retrieval system, or transmit any part of this publication in any form by any means for any purpose without written permission from the Publications Division of the David M. Kennedy Center for International Studies, Brigham Young University, PO Box 24538, Provo, UT 84602–4538. *Culturgrams* are available for more than 125 areas of the world. To place an order, to receive a free catalog, or to obtain information on traveling abroad, call toll free (800) 528–6279.

managing their territory. In the past, resistance against commonwealth status has erupted into violence. In 1954, militants from Puerto Rico shot several congressmen in Washington during a session of the House of Representatives.

Currently, the people are divided by the issue of whether to request statehood or remain a commonwealth. A smaller group advocates full independence. A national referendum in November 1993 did not seem to fully settle the issue, as the decision to remain a commonwealth passed by only a slim margin. The governor favors statehood. Referendums in 1967 and 1981 passed the commonwealth status by a greater margin, so attitudes are changing over time. It will probably be a number of years before another such referendum is held.

THE PEOPLE

Population

Puerto Rico's population is approximately 3.7 million, growing annually at 0.1 percent. This growth rate was higher for 1992–1993 because more Puerto Ricans were not migrating to states on the mainland when the U.S. economy was weak. As the economy strengthens, migration will increase and Puerto Rico's population growth will drop. More than 95 percent of the people are native Puerto Ricans of Hispanic descent. The capital of Puerto Rico is San Juan, which has a population of about 450,000. However, the largest Puerto Rican community, consisting of about one million people, is in New York City, the destination of most emigrants.

Language

Spanish and English both share official status in Puerto Rico. For a short time in the early 1990s, Spanish was declared the only official language, but English has since regained equal status. Spanish is the language of instruction in school and the language of daily life. English is required as a second language in school and is used in business. Most people can speak English. The official status of either language often depends on the political climate regarding Puerto Rico's relationship with the United States.

Religion

Roman Catholicism is the major Christian religion in Puerto Rico and claims about 85 percent of the population as members. Approximately 15 percent of the people belong to various Protestant and other Christian churches, and their numbers are growing. Although there is a separation of church and state, Catholic traditions and customs prevail among the people. Spiritualistic practices are also common.

General Attitudes

The Puerto Rican concept of time is more relaxed than in industrialized countries. People are considered more important than schedules. If a friend, relative, or business associate drops in unexpectedly, the person he wishes to see will stop everything to visit with him, even if doing so makes the person late for other appointments. Business contacts are not made during lunchtime. Puerto Ricans consider open criticism, aggressiveness, and greed offensive. Many believe a person's destiny is God's will, although individuals must also watch for opportunities.

Progress and education are important. National and regional pride is strong, and political power is coveted. People are sensitive, quick to express sympathy, and equally quick to resent a slight. They are gregarious and fond of *fiestas*. Cleanliness is emphasized, and even though a family is poor, the home will be clean. Political and religious topics are often sensitive and therefore avoided in casual conversation.

Personal Appearance

Lightweight, casual clothing is generally worn, but too much informality in dress may be offensive. Formal clothing is expected at parties and social gatherings.

CUSTOMS AND COURTESIES

Greetings

People usually shake hands when greeting, although close friends may embrace after a long absence. Women often greet each other by grasping shoulders and kissing each other on the cheek. People stand very close when talking, and those of the same sex often touch each other with their hands. Moving away, even slightly, may be considered an insult. Although Spanish is most common, both Spanish and English greetings are used. So, one might hear "Good morning" or *¡Buenas días!*, "Good afternoon" or *¡Buenas tardes!*, "Good evening" or *¡Buenas noches!*, and "Hi" or *¡Hola!*

Gestures

Beckoning is done by waving all fingers with the palm down; it is improper to beckon people with the palm facing up. Wiggling the nose can mean, "What's going on?" People often point with pursed or puckered lips. Small items are not tossed or thrown to another person, only handed. During conversation, Puerto Ricans might interrupt each other; this is generally not considered rude. Although peers will tease each other in informal situations, such joking is not appropriate in formal settings. Men often smile and stare at women, but it is considered improper for a woman to smile indiscriminately at strangers. It is appropriate for a man to offer his seat to a woman on public transportation. On longer trips, people often share food, and it is impolite to refuse such an offer.

Visiting

Visits are relaxed and the entire family participates. Visitors may compliment the host's home or family, but they should be careful not to compliment objects or possessions too much; otherwise the host may feel obligated to offer the item to the guest. Gifts are freely given and unwrapped immediately. Before guests accept a gift or an invitation to dinner, they will often politely decline the offer a few times.

Eating

At mealtime, the atmosphere is relaxed and cordial. Still, there are rules of etiquette. Both hands should remain above the table. Bread is often used to push food onto a fork. Guests do not leave directly after the meal; they stay to relax and enjoy conversation with the hosts. Food purchased at a stand along the street is eaten at the stand. It is not appropriate for adults to eat while walking in public. At a restaurant it is customary to leave a 15 percent tip when service is not included in the bill. Waiters in Spanish-speaking restaurants may be summoned with a "pssst" sound.

LIFESTYLE

Family

Husbands and wives take their roles and responsibilities seriously, although many women now hold positions outside the home. The family is the basic unit of society. It is closely knit and aids its members, including distant relatives. Children show respect for their parents by taking care of them in their old age.

Dating and Marriage

Although Puerto Rican youths generally begin dating in groups, they move quickly to boyfriend-girlfriend relationships. Having a boyfriend or a girlfriend is important, and dating begins at a fairly young age (12 to 13 years old). In rural areas the relationship usually does not become serious until the boy has met the girl's parents. Dates may include going to the movies or on a picnic, dancing, or spending time at the beach. This early dating leads some Puerto Ricans to marry, either formally or in a common-law partnership, at an early age (16–17). Civil weddings are the general rule, but whether the marriage is performed by a judge or in a church (generally in the Catholic tradition), a wedding is a time of great celebration. Families gather and large amounts of money are spent on decorations, food, and music, both traditional and modern.

Diet

Foods in Puerto Rico come from a variety of ethnic backgrounds, including Spanish, Indian, and African. Popular dishes include *arroz con pollo* (rice and chicken), *paella* (a spicy stew of rice, chicken, seafood, and vegetables), *arroz con gandules y pernil* (rice with idler and roasted pig), and foods made with plantain. Plantain is a starchy banana-like fruit that must be cooked to be eaten. Seafood and tropical fruits are also common in the diet.

Recreation

The favorite sport is baseball. Cockfighting is popular among men. The arts enjoy a widespread following. Long before the United States took possession of Puerto Rico, a strong tradition of literature and music, as well as scholarship, had been established. Indeed, art and music are fostered in the home; nearly everyone can play a musical instrument, and a display of musical talent is usually expected at parties. Puerto Rican films and other cultural arts are known throughout the world.

Holidays

Puerto Ricans celebrate New Year's Day as part of the Christmas holiday season. The Day of the Three Kings (6 January) marks the end of the Christmas season and each child receives a gift. Puerto Rico celebrates both locally important holidays and U.S. national holidays. Holidays include the birth of Eugenio Maria de Hostos (11 January), Martin Luther King, Jr.'s birthday (second Monday in January), Presidents' Day (third Monday in February), the Abolition of Slavery (22 March), Easter (including Good Friday), José de Diego's birthday (third Monday in April), Memorial Day (25 May), American Independence Day (4 July), Luis Muñoz Rivera's Day (17 July), Constitution Day (25 July), José Celso Barbosa's birthday (28 July), Labor Day (first Monday in September), All Souls Day (2 November), Discovery of Puerto Rico Day (19 November), Thanksgiving, and Christmas. One important part of the Christmas season is the *Parrandas*, a caroling tradition where groups of friends go to homes of people they might know or don't know and sing Christmas songs. They expect food and drinks in return.

One of the most popular events is the Pablo Casal's Festival in late May and early June. Also, every town honors its patron saint annually with several days of activities that include going to amusement parks, gambling, singing, dancing, and religious ceremonies. A beauty queen is selected for almost every activity. During February or March, *Carnival* celebrations held before Lent (in the Catholic tradition) are most visible in Ponce, where "monsters" (called *vejigantes*) wearing papier-mâché masks with multiple horns roam the streets hitting people on the heads with a dried pig's bladder. The masks are handmade and can be elaborate. The monsters are just one part of the lively celebrations in Ponce.

Commerce

Business hours generally run between 9:00 A.M. and 5:00 P.M., although there are variations. American companies doing business in Puerto Rico enjoy a tax-exempt status because Puerto Rico is a commonwealth, where federal taxes do not apply.

SOCIETY

Government

The Puerto Rican legislature is divided into a senate and a house of representatives. A governor, currently Pedro J. Rosselló, is directly elected for a four-year term. All citizens age 18 and older may vote. Gubernatorial elections, the last of which was in 1992, are held every four years.

Economy

Since World War II, industrialization on the island has transformed the once-poor area into the nation with the highest per capita income in Latin America (US$6,100). Industrial production has become more important than agriculture, and duty-free trade with the United States has stimulated growth. Annual economic growth is usually around 4 percent.

Only 4 percent of the population is engaged in agriculture; 18 percent works in the manufacturing sector. Puerto Rico exports sugar, coffee, petroleum products, chemicals, textiles, and electronic equipment. Some people question industrialization, however, because the replacement of agriculture with industry has led to the importation of food, which is more expensive. Tourism is also important to the economy. Inflation and unemployment have been relatively high in the past few years, leading many to emigrate. Still, Puerto Rico has important natural resources and a generally healthy economy when compared with other Latin American nations. The United States dollar ($) is the official currency.

Transportation and Communication

Roads are generally in good condition and many people own cars. Buses and taxis are available in the large urban areas. *Públicos* (nonscheduled, five-passenger cars) serve most of the island. There is also air service. Puerto Rico has dozens of radio and television stations, as well as newspapers. Most people have telephones and the communications network is good.

Education

Education is highly valued and the school system is continually improving. The requirements for primary and secondary schooling are similar to those in the United States. Higher education is provided by several universities and colleges, including the University of Puerto Rico, which has nine campuses and over 45,000 students. Other institutions include the Inter American University, Catholic University, Central University, World University, and the Puerto Rico Junior College. The literacy rate is 89 percent.

Health

A network of urban and rural health care centers and two medical schools (one public and one private) serve Puerto Rico's medical needs. The system of health care is similar to that in the United States, although the people are not always eligible for the same amount of federal funds for certain needs. The infant mortality rate is 14 per 1,000; life expectancy ranges from 70 to 78 years.

FOR THE TRAVELER

U.S. citizens do not need a visa or passport when traveling to Puerto Rico. However, because a passport is a good form of identification, those who have one may want to consider carrying it in Puerto Rico. Tap water is safe for drinking and no vaccinations are necessary. Puerto Rico is a favorite vacation destination because of the pleasant climate, good beach resorts, and an English-speaking population. For more information about travel opportunities, contact the Puerto Rico Government Tourism Company, 575 Fifth Avenue, 23d Floor, New York, NY 10017. There are also offices in Los Angeles, Miami, and Chicago.

A *Culturgram* is a product of native commentary and original, expert analysis. Statistics are estimates and information is presented as a matter of opinion. While the editors strive for accuracy and detail, this document should not be considered strictly factual. It is a general introduction to culture, an initial step in building bridges of understanding between peoples. It may not apply to all peoples of the nation. You should therefore consult other sources for more information.

Republic of

Romania

Boundary representations not necessarily authoritative.

BACKGROUND

Land and Climate

Romania is located at the edge of Eastern Europe, sharing borders with several nations and the Black Sea. Covering 91,699 square miles (237,500 square kilometers), it is about the size of Oregon. The capital of Romania is Bucharest. Two mountain ranges dominate the central and northern regions. The Carpathians in the north run roughly north to southeast and the Transylvanian Alps run east to west in the center of the country. The famous Danube River, which begins in Germany and flows through several European countries, forms much of Romania's southern border. It runs north through a small portion of Romania's eastern territory and empties into the Black Sea. There are low plains along the southern and eastern borders.

Romanian summers are warm and sunny; winters are cold and cloudy. The average temperature in July is 70°F (21°C); the average for January is 30°F (–1°C). Romania's natural resources include crude oil, natural gas, coal, iron, and timber. More than 40 percent of the land is arable and 28 percent is forested. Romania faces severe pollution problems due to excessive industrialization in past decades and old technology. Many rivers, towns, and forests are contaminated and the people suffer from respiratory diseases in some areas. The current government is seeking ways to address the problems, but it lacks the necessary funds, experience, and technology to make significant progress.

History

The ancestors of today's Romanians were Geto-Dacians, an Indo-European people. Between the sixth and fourth centuries B.C., the Dacians assimilated surrounding influences to form their own unique civilization. Around 100 A.D., the Romans conquered most of Dacia and made the area a province to supply grain, gold, and cattle to the empire. The province's natives soon adopted the Roman language and culture. The name "Romania" means "Land of the Romans." Between 200 and 1100, various barbarian tribes invaded the region. In the 14th century, Moldavia (to the east) and Wallachia (in the south) became independent principalities. In 1500, the principalities fell under Turkish control, but they were never an integral part of the Ottoman (Turkish) empire. Several European wars led to exchanges of Romanian territory among various countries. Complete freedom from Turkish rule did not come until 1877, after Romania joined again with Moldavia and Wallachia.

Because of its part in the Allied alliance with France and England in World War I, Romania acquired Bessarabia from Russia and three provinces from the defeated Austro-Hungarian Empire. These acquisitions doubled the size of Romania but alienated it from its neighbors. Romania was occupied by Nazi Germany in 1940 and joined the German army in attacking Soviet Russia in 1941. In 1944, however, Romania switched to the Allied side and Russian troops occupied the country. Romania came under Soviet influence, the

Copyright © 1994. Brigham Young University. Printed in the USA. All rights reserved. It is against the law to copy, reprint, store in a retrieval system, or transmit any part of this publication in any form by any means for any purpose without written permission from the Publications Division of the David M. Kennedy Center for International Studies, Brigham Young University, PO Box 24538, Provo, UT 84602–4538. *Culturgrams* are available for more than 125 areas of the world. To place an order, to receive a free catalog, or to obtain information on traveling abroad, call toll free (800) 528–6279.

monarchy was abolished, and a Communist regime was established.

After 1965, when Nicolae Ceausescu came to power in Romania, the country broke with the Soviet Union and pursued an independent policy. The 1965 constitution recognized the primacy of the Communist party in the country. Relations with the Soviets remained poor and Romania was fairly isolated from other Communist countries. Ceausescu ruled with complete control and the Communist party governed all aspects of local life. The extensive internal security system, *Securitate*, stifled dissent. Corruption and human rights violations were common.

When democratic movements swept Europe in 1989, Ceausescu vowed nothing would change in Romania. However, large groups of demonstrators soon protested his regime. When security forces turned on the crowds, rioting broke out and the people occupied some government facilities. With the army supporting the people's revolution, the regime fell after several days of fighting. Ceausescu and his wife were executed, and the National Salvation Front took control. It removed certain restrictions and organized elections. National Salvation Front leader, Ion Iliescu, won the election (May 1990), despite his close ties to the former regime. While Iliescu's government restricted civil rights, some democratic reforms were carried out, including a declaration of freedom of speech. A bicameral parliament was elected. It produced a new constitution that was ratified in December 1991. National elections were scheduled and plans for economic reform moved forward.

Civil unrest, including violent riots by miners, eventually led the president to form an interim government in 1991 that governed until elections in September 1992. Iliescu was reelected president and began to try and improve Romania's international image.

THE PEOPLE

Population

The population of Romania is about 23.2 million and is currently not growing. Ethnic Romanians comprise most of the population (84 percent). There is a significant minority of Hungarians (7 percent) that lives mostly in Transylvania. The Roma (Gypsies) comprise over 8 percent of the population. An exact count has never been made. This group tends to live separately from the Romanians, and is generally not accepted by other ethnic groups. Romas are poor, undereducated, and underemployed; they do not integrate into mainstream society and are often subject to discrimination.

Other minority groups include Germans and Ukrainians. There are also small numbers of Serbs, Croats, Russians, and Turks. The German population has declined because many have emigrated to Germany. Large numbers of other ethnic groups are also trying to leave Romania, but they are meeting increasing resistance in other countries. Over half of Romania's population lives in cities, largely because of forced urbanization under Ceausescu. Forty percent of the population is under age 25.

Language

The official language is Romanian. Romanian is a Latin-based language in the same family as Spanish, French, Italian, and Portuguese. The Germans and Hungarians speak their native ethnic tongues. The Roma speak Romany.

Religion

Nearly all Romanians are Christian. About 70 percent belong to the Romanian Orthodox church. Six percent of the people (mostly Hungarians) are Roman Catholic and 3 percent are Uniate (Greek Catholic). Islam, Judaism, and other Christian religions are also practiced. During the Ceausescu regime, religious organizations were carefully regulated, but freedom of religion has again been established. Devotion to religion is especially strong in the rural areas. About 15 percent of the population claims no religious affiliation.

General Attitudes

The Romanian people seem confused and divided about their future. Having emerged from the authoritarian regime of the Nicolae Ceausescu era (1965–89), but still not possessing the economic and political freedoms they thought would be theirs, they worry that the future is no longer bright. Many people, especially in large urban areas, continue to distrust the government and would like to see greater democracy. These people favor a country where many opinions (political, religious, and social) can be expressed and appreciated. They seek to change traditional Romanian society to make it more similar to other European societies. Other people would like to see economic reform, but not necessarily a change in government or traditional society; they would be more prone to accept a single political party and a single approach to social order. These conflicting attitudes about the future of the nation have led to violence, instability, and the rise of dangerous tensions between ethnic groups. Economic troubles have led to greater poverty, crime, and disillusionment. Resolving their differences is one of the greatest tasks facing the people in the 1990s. Unfortunately, most people have to deal with the more urgent concern of feeding and housing their families.

Personal Appearance

Romanians attach importance to their appearance, but few have the means to buy fashionable clothing. The youth prize denim jeans, T-shirts, and Western-style clothing. People generally dress conservatively in public. Family members mourning the death of a loved one may remain in black from six weeks to a year. In general, the elderly wear dark, conservative colors. Conservative business suits are appropriate for men. Female office workers usually wear a skirt and a blouse with a scarf. Hats are common for men and some women wear scarves on their heads. Colorful folk costumes are worn at festivals and on special occasions. Some of Romania's ethnic minorities in the rural areas also continue to wear traditional clothing.

CUSTOMS AND COURTESIES

Greetings

Greetings on a first-name basis are usually made only between close friends and relatives. However, adults normally address young people by their first names. Where applicable, it is most polite to use a person's title (Doctor, Professor) before the surname. Adults commonly greet each other with a handshake, but a man usually waits for a woman to extend her hand first. In cities, some men might greet a woman by kissing her hand. In rural areas, everyone is greeted individually; people also greet strangers and expect their greeting to be returned.

Gestures

It is impolite to yawn without covering the mouth. When one sneezes, one is wished *Noroc* (Bless you) or *Sanatate* (Good health). *Noroc* is also used at parties to mean "Cheers." On public transportation, men will generally offer their seat to a woman. Hats are removed by gentlemen before they enter buildings, except stores.

Visiting

Romanians like to receive and pay visits. In the home, guests are usually offered a drink—coffee, tea, brandy, or a popular regional wine. Other refreshments may also be offered. When invited to dinner, it is considered polite for the guest to bring an odd number of flowers (three or more) or a small gift for the hostess. Red roses are avoided for such an occasion, however, because they are a sign of romantic affection. Evening visits usually end before 11:00 P.M. because work begins early in the morning.

Eating

The continental style of eating is used, with the fork in the left hand and the knife remaining in the right. Both hands (not elbows) are kept above the table during a meal. The hostess indicates when the meal will begin and when it will end. Toasting is usually a part of formal and informal lunches and dinners. Romanians generally consider it a great honor to entertain guests, and visitors will usually be invited out as much as possible.

LIFESTYLE

Family

The family has always been important to Romanians and the father maintains a dominant role. Urban families tend to be smaller than rural families because of a shortage of housing and the high cost of living. Most women work outside the home, but they are also responsible for the upkeep of the home and the children. Men are generally not involved in household chores. Grandparents often live with the family.

A private farm includes a two or three-bedroom home, a garden and orchard, and small farm buildings. Ceausescu attempted to destroy these farmsteads—and, with them, rural individualism—by tearing down homes and forcing people to move into large housing blocks. The apartments had no running water, bathrooms, or heat, and strictly enforced regulations limited the amount of electricity each apartment could use. These buildings are bitterly resented in rural areas, and some have called for their destruction. A housing shortage prevents that from happening at this time. While forced urbanization and the limits on electricity use are no longer practiced, improvements in living standards have not yet occurred because of a poor economy. Many families, urban and rural, lack proper housing and most go without modern conveniences.

Dating and Marriage

People in rural areas marry at a fairly early age and follow local and ethnic customs regarding courtship and marriage. In the past, most students in the cities waited until completion of university or other graduate training before getting married. More recently, however, students have begun to marry in their last year of school because it has been easier to get housing and a job in a city if a person is married.

Diet

Romanian food is characterized by distinctive ethnic specialties including *mititei* (grilled meatballs), *patricieni* (grilled sausage), and *mamaliga* (cornmeal mush served like mashed potatoes). Breakfast usually consists of eggs, cheese, rolls or other breads, and coffee. Lunch is the main meal of the day and generally consists of soup, meat, potatoes, bread, and a vegetable. Wine or beer is usually served as the drink. A special plum brandy called *tzuica* is also popular. Supper is similar to lunch, but the servings are somewhat smaller. Pastries are popular for dessert. In the past, food shortages were common. Although food is now generally available, people cannot easily afford the much higher prices.

Recreation

Romanians enjoy sports, particularly soccer. Romania's national soccer team competed in the 1994 World Cup. *Oina*, a kind of baseball, is a traditional sport. Romanian athletes have done well in international competitions, especially in gymnastics, weightlifting, and tennis. Leisure activities include meeting with friends or family, watching television, taking walks, reading, or going to the theater. Folk shows, with music and dancing, are enjoyed by many.

Holidays

Under the Ceausescu regime, there were only three national holidays. They included the New Year (1–2 January), Labor Day (1–2 May), and National Liberation Day (23–24 August). No religious holidays were officially recognized or celebrated. Christmas and Easter and other such events were commemorated privately. With the fall of Ceausescu, people now celebrate religious events openly. Romanians are free to honor any religious holiday. More national holidays are expected in the future. Romania's national day is now 1 December, which marks the day in 1918 when the kingdom of Romania was united with three smaller territories. Much of the territory was subsequently lost in 1940. Many would like to see it become part of Romania again in the future.

Commerce

The usual workday begins at 7:00 A.M. for factory workers, but at 8:00 or 9:00 A.M. for office workers. The day ends somewhere between 3:00 and 5:00 P.M., depending on the institution. Most factories are closed on Saturdays and Sundays, with Fridays being a shortened workday. Stores may be closed a few hours around lunchtime, but then remain open later in the evening. General department stores are open all day. Except restaurants, coffee stops, and some private shops, everything is closed on Sunday. Vacations of two to four weeks are provided, depending on one's seniority.

SOCIETY

Government

Romania's new constitution established it as a republic. The president is head of state, but also has broader powers. Romania's prime minister (Teodor Stolojan) is head of government. The parliament has a Senate and an Assembly of Deputies. The voting age is 18.

Economy

Before World War II, Romania was an agricultural nation. However, postwar policy led to rapid industrialization and a transformation of the economy. Industry came to account for over 60 percent of the gross national product (GNP), while agriculture fell to less than 10 percent. During the 1980s, in an attempt to reduce the foreign debt, Ceausescu diverted large portions of the domestic agricultural crop to exports. While the plan succeeded in decreasing the debt substantially, it also caused food rationing and lowered the standard of living. In 1989, the plan was halted; food is now more plentiful on the domestic market.

The most important exports have traditionally been machinery and equipment, natural gas and oil products, consumer goods, and foods. During the 1980s, Romania increased its trade with Western European nations—part of the effort to increase export earnings. Trade with European nations continues and the government has begun to sell land and businesses to private interests. A law established in 1991 provides for the return of farmland to the families who owned it before communism. The law is designed to encourage private ownership and enterprise in the agricultural sector. Unfortunately, land transfer has been very slow. Even if it were quicker, most farmers lack credit or capital and could therefore not buy equipment, seeds, or fertilizers. Thus, the collective-farm system remains.

High inflation, unemployment, and political instability have hampered economic progress and kept foreign investment away. If the country became more stable its extensive industrial complex, in addition to its well-trained workers, would constitute a positive environment for investment. Romania's Human Development Index (0.709) ranks it 77 out of 173 countries. Real gross domestic product per capita is estimated at $2,800. These figures indicate that most people do not have an income sufficient for their needs. Although the country is industrialized, it ranks below many developing nations in its ability to create economic opportunities for the people. Romania's currency is the *leu* (L).

Transportation and Communication

Public transportation in the cities is reasonably efficient and inexpensive. Boarding passes for buses are obtained from ticket booths and magazine stands. The train network links major cities, but many trains are poorly maintained and lack heat in the winter. In rural areas, travel by bicycle and horse- or donkey-drawn carts (called *leiterwagons*) is still common. Few people own cars. In urban areas, many people have telephones; communications systems are limited in some rural areas. The press is free to print what it wishes.

Education

Education is compulsory and free between the ages of six and sixteen. Students then seek employment, enter vocational training, or prepare for a university education. Most students complete some education beyond the required 10 years. University entrance was determined in the past by loyalty to the Communist party and good performance in school. Loyalty to the party is no longer required, and university students are among the most vocal supporters of political change. The literacy rate is 95 percent.

Health

There are many important health problems facing the people of Romania. Due to a practice of giving newborn babies blood transfusions if they appeared anemic, many children contracted AIDS from contaminated needles and blood. Romania has large concentrations of AIDS-infected children. Likewise, many women also have the disease (whereas it affects mostly men in other countries). Hepatitis B is also a danger to many people. Illnesses associated with heavy pollution are common. Health facilities are often poorly equipped and understaffed. Large groups of orphaned children do not receive necessary attention or care. With the help of Western nations, the government is now moving to address these problems. The infant mortality rate is 22 per 1,000. Life expectancy averages 68 to 74 years.

FOR THE TRAVELER

U.S. travelers must have a visa and a valid passport to enter Romania. Visas can be obtained at the border or can be applied for at the embassy. No vaccinations are required, but some may be advisable depending on the itinerary. Credit card use is somewhat limited, but increasing. There are many interesting places to visit in Romania; the people are genuine and friendly. Rural areas and areas isolated by mountains offer a look at a culture that has not changed for decades. For the most current information on travel opportunities, contact Carpati International, 152 Madison Avenue, Suite 1103, New York, NY 10016. You may also wish to contact the Embassy of Romania, 1607 23d Street NW, Washington, DC 20008.

A *Culturgram* is a product of native commentary and original, expert analysis. Statistics are estimates and information is presented as a matter of opinion. While the editors strive for accuracy and detail, this document should not be considered strictly factual. It is a general introduction to culture, an initial step in building bridges of understanding between peoples. It may not apply to all peoples of the nation. You should therefore consult other sources for more information.

CULTURGRAM ™ '95

Russia
(Russian Federation)

Franz Joseph Land
Novaya Zemlya
Kara Sea
Laptev Sea
Barents Sea
East Siberian Sea
Murmansk
Siberia
Lena River
Nizhniy Novgorod
Ob River
Yenisey River
Kasan • Yekaterinburg
Angara River
Magadan
St. Petersburg
Volga River
Sea of Okhotsk
MOSCOW • Samara
Lake Baikal
Amur River
Voronezh
Vladivostok

Boundary representations not necessarily authoritative.

BACKGROUND

Land and Climate

Russia is the largest country in the world. At 6,592,734 square miles (17,075,200 square kilometers), it is nearly twice the size of the United States. Russia is bounded by the Arctic Ocean in the north, by the Pacific Ocean in the east, and in the south and west by many countries. Four of the world's largest rivers (Lena, Ob, Volga, and Yenisey) and the world's deepest freshwater lake (Baikal) are in Russia. Most of the country's territory consists of great plains, but there is a large tundra in the extreme north and much of western Russia is covered by forests. Parts of eastern Russia are desert. The low Ural mountains divide Russia in two parts: the smaller European and the larger Asian regions. The climate is generally dry and continental, with long, subzero winters and short, temperate summers.

History

Slavic peoples settled in eastern Europe during the early Christian era. In 988, they were converted to Christianity by Prince Vladimir. At the beginning of the 13th century, the area was conquered by the Mongols, who dominated the Slavs for 240 years. In 1480, the Slavs defeated the Mongols and regained their sovereignty. Ivan the Terrible (1533–84) was the first Russian ruler actually crowned Czar of Russia in 1547. He expanded Russia's territory, as did Peter the Great (1682–1724) and Catherine the Great (1762–96). The empire reached from Warsaw in the west to Vladivostok in the east. In 1812, Russian troops defeated France's Napoleon, and Russia took its place as one of the most powerful states on earth.

When Czar Nicholas II abdicated because of popular unrest during World War I, Vladimir Lenin, head of the Bolshevik party, led the 1917 revolt that brought down the provisional government and put the Communists in power. Lenin disbanded the legislature and banned all other political parties. A civil war between Lenin's Red Army and the White Army lasted until 1921, with Lenin victorious.

In 1922, the Bolsheviks formed the Union of Soviet Socialist Republics (USSR) and forcibly incorporated Armenia, Azerbaijan, Georgia, Ukraine, and Belarus into the union. During Lenin's rule, which ended with his death in 1924, many died as a result of his radical restructuring of society. Lenin was followed by Joseph Stalin, a dictator who forced industrialization and collective agriculture on the people. Millions died in labor camps and from starvation. At the start of World War II, Stalin signed a nonaggression pact with Hitler, but Hitler soon invaded the Soviet Union in 1941, and the war eventually took more than 25 million Soviet lives.

Nikita Khrushchev, who took over after Stalin's death in 1953, declared he would build real communism within 20 years, but his reforms and policy of *détente* with the West were opposed by hard-liners and he was replaced by Leonid Brezhnev in 1964. Brezhnev orchestrated the expansion of Soviet influence in the developing world and ordered the invasion of Afghanistan. Brezhnev died in 1982 and was followed by two short-lived leaders, Chernenko and Andropov.

After emerging as the new leader of the Soviet Union, Gorbachev started *perestroika* in 1986. He attempted to

EURASIA

Copyright © 1994. Brigham Young University. Printed in the USA. All rights reserved. It is against the law to copy, reprint, store in a retrieval system, or transmit any part of this publication in any form by any means for any purpose without written permission from the Publications Division of the David M. Kennedy Center for International Studies, Brigham Young University, PO Box 24538, Provo, UT 84602–4538. *Culturgrams* are available for more than 125 areas of the world. To place an order, to receive a free catalog, or to obtain information on traveling abroad, call toll free (800) 528–6279.

reform the system by introducing *glasnost* (openness) and new freedoms, such as freedom of speech. He promised to allow privatization and free enterprise, but many reforms failed. An unsuccessful coup in August 1991 exposed inherent weaknesses in the Soviet system, and the country quickly unraveled. Russia, led by its elected president, Boris Yeltsin, became an independent country and moved to introduce democratic and free-market reforms.

Often challenged by hard-liners, Yeltsin found it difficult to pass reform legislation. In 1993, after months of political battles between Yeltsin and legislators, Yeltsin dissolved Parliament (in September) and called for elections in December. Parliament voted to impeach Yeltsin and his opponents seized the White House (parliament building) in an effort to overthrow the government. Following street riots, the showdown turned violent and militants were forced from the building by tank fire and the military. Even with that crisis over, Russians were not sure of the government's general course. In parliamentary elections (December 1993), an anti-Yeltsin ultranationalist party emerged far stronger than expected. On the other hand, voters approved a new constitution supported by Yeltsin. In 1994, Yeltsin continued to face challenges from the ultranationalist leader Vladimir Zhirinovsky and others and Russia continued to face an unsettled political future.

THE PEOPLE

Population

The population of Russia is about 149.3 million. With more deaths than births in 1993, the country's population is now shrinking. There are some 120 different ethnic groups, but most are small. Ethnic Russians form 82 percent of the entire population. Other groups include Tartars (4 percent), Ukrainians (3 percent), Belarusians (less than 1 percent), Udmurts, Kazakhs, and others. The capital and largest city is Moscow, with a population of more than 10 million. Other large cities (one to three million residents each) include St. Petersburg, Novosibirsk, Nizhniy Novgorod, Yekaterinburg, and Samara. Most Russians still live in rural areas, but there is a clear trend for young people to move to the cities.

Language

Russian is the official language in the country, and it was also the main language of the Soviet Union. Russian uses the Cyrillic alphabet, which consists of 33 letters, many of them unlike any letter in the Roman (Latin) alphabet. Non-Russians also speak their own languages. For example, Tartars speak Tartar, Chuvashes speak Chuvash, and Udmurts speak Udmurt. These individual languages are only taught at schools in the republic (state) of Russia where the ethnic group is prominent. Non-Russians speak Russian in addition to their native language. They often consider Russian a second language and do not speak it on a daily basis. For their part, ethnic Russians are not required to study other local languages. Foreign language courses are growing in popularity, with English, French, German, and Spanish being most common.

Religion

The Russian Orthodox church is the dominant religion. After the October Revolution (1917), the Communists separated the church from the state (which were previously tightly bonded) and began to discourage all religious worship. Many churches were forced to close under Lenin and Stalin. Mikhail Gorbachev was the first Soviet leader to change official policy and tolerate—even support—religion. Yeltsin has also embraced the church, which is regaining its political influence. There are almost only Russian Orthodox churches in rural areas, but nearly every major religion and many Christian churches have members in large cities. Islam is practiced in many southern regions.

General Attitudes

Russia's long history of totalitarianism has made fatalism a vital tool for survival. The inhabitants of Russia have had few opportunities to make their own decisions, whether ruled by a Czar or the Communist party. Personal initiative, responsibility for oneself, and the desire to work independently were suppressed by the state, and one was expected to conform to official opinion and behavior.

Now that communism has been dismantled, Russians are searching for new social values. The resulting confusion and chaos have led some to wonder whether the old ways weren't better. Many Russians are not happy with their rapidly changing society, which is characterized by high prices, increasingly violent and rampant crime, unemployment, and a reduced quality of life. Some are not certain they are prepared to pay such a high price for economic freedom or wait so long for the benefits of a free market to become apparent. Others are eagerly taking advantage of the open environment.

Although proud of "Mother Russia" and its achievements, Russians are basically pessimistic and usually do not express much hope for a better life in the future (except among the youth). Even a generally happy and optimistic Russian might not show his true feelings in public, but rather express frustration with everyday life. A general feeling in Russia is that the "soul" of Russia is different from that of other countries, that development cannot take the same course as Europe, for example. Russians often believe they must find a different path that takes into account their unique historical heritage and social structure.

Friendship is extremely important in Russia. Russians are open with and trusting of their friends, and they rely on their network of friends when times are hard. Russians are learning the value of discussion and compromise, of personal creativity, and of taking risks. This long-term process may only bear fruit with the younger generation. The transition carries such hard lessons as financial loss, political polarization, economic instability, and social disruption. When *perestroika* (restructuring) began in the late 1980s, urban society became politically active. By 1992, however, people became frustrated with the pace of reforms and felt they could not impact the decision-making process. Most people ended their political participation and concentrated on making ends meet.

Personal Appearance

Russian clothing styles are the same as in Europe, but not as sophisticated. Jeans are popular among most age groups. In winter, people wear *ushanki* (fur hats). Shorts are becoming popular among the younger generation. The older generation dresses conservatively.

CUSTOMS AND COURTESIES
Greetings

When meeting, Russians shake hands firmly and might say *Zdravstvuyte* (pronounced sdrav-STVUH-teh, it means "Hello"), *Dobry dien* (Good day), or *Privet* (Hello). Some women prefer not to shake hands, but it is impolite for a man not to offer his hand. Friends and family may kiss on the cheek. The question, *Kak dela?* (How are you?) is taken literally; Russians answer in detail and at length. Asking the question without waiting for a full response is rude. *Kak dela?* is not used as a formal greeting. Titles such as *Gospodin* (Mr.) and *Gospozha* (Mrs.) were not used under the Communists, but they are being revived. In addressing an older or respected person, one uses the given name and a patronymic (possessive of father's first name), but surnames are preferred in formal greetings.

Gestures

Pointing with the index finger is improper but commonly practiced. It is impolite to talk (especially to an older person) with one's hands in the pockets or arms folded across the chest.

Visiting

Russians like to visit and have guests. Sitting around the kitchen table and talking for hours is a favorite pastime. Shoes are sometimes removed upon entering a home. Refreshments are usually offered, but guests may decline them. Friends and family may visit anytime without prior arrangement. They make themselves at home and can usually expect to be welcomed for any length of time. Visits with new acquaintances are more formal.

Giving gifts is a strong tradition in Russia, and almost every event (birthdays, weddings, holidays, etc.) is accompanied by presents. For casual visits, it is common (but not required) for guests to bring a simple gift (flowers, food, vodka) to their hosts. What is given is less important than the friendship expressed by the act. Flowers are given in odd numbers; even number are for funerals. If a bottle of vodka (which means "little water") is opened, custom dictates it be emptied by those present.

Eating

Eating with the fork in the left hand and the knife in the right is standard, but many people use only a fork. Hands are kept above the table and not in the lap. Most Russians like to eat a large breakfast whenever possible. Soup is common for lunch or dinner. Traditionally, a popular feature of any meal is *zakuski* (appetizers). There are many different kinds of *zakuski*; eating too many may spoil an appetite. Russians put more food than they can eat on the table and leave some on the plate to indicate there is abundance (whether true or not) in the house. Guests who leave food on the plate indicate they have eaten well.

Russians generally don't go to lunch in cafes or restaurants because the few that exist are fairly expensive. Instead, people eat at cafeterias where they work or bring food from home.

LIFESTYLE
Family

The family is the basic social unit in Russia and most people expect to marry and have children. The average urban couple has one child, but rural families are larger. Because housing is difficult to obtain, young couples often live with their parents for some time. It is the normal practice to financially support children until they reach adulthood. The father is considered head of the family. Both husband and wife usually work, but women are also responsible for housekeeping. Men rarely share in household duties. Child care is available, but few families can afford it. When the elderly live with their children, they often provide child care and do the shopping.

Urban apartments are small and it is common for a family of three or more to live in one room. A typical apartment has one room, a kitchen, and a bathroom. Rural homes are small, but larger than apartments. While they have more room, they often lack running water.

Dating and Marriage

When young people date, they usually go to movies or for a walk in a city park. Sometimes they go to bars or cafés, but this is presently too expensive for many people. Instead, the youth like to have parties in their apartments when their parents are not home. Many couples live together before or instead of marriage. There is a new trend to be married in a church first and then to have an official civil ceremony in a "wedding palace," the only place people could get married before 1991.

Diet

Although food is plentiful, many products are very expensive or can only be found in hard currency markets. For the common person, this means fruits and vegetables are hard to come by. Hence, their menu consists mainly of bread, meat, and potatoes. Those on fixed and limited incomes (mainly the elderly) eat more bread than anything else. Common Russian foods include *borsch* (cabbage soup with beets), *pirozhki* (a stuffed roll), and *blini* (pancakes) with black caviar. *Borsch* is still one of the most popular foods in the country. Its ingredients (potatoes, cabbages, carrots, beets, and onions) almost complete the list of vegetables used in everyday life. Pork, sausage, chicken, and cheeses are popular, but they are often very expensive. Russians prefer tea to coffee. Mineral water, juice, and soda are readily available at high prices. Russians drink far more vodka than wine.

Recreation

Russians have little leisure time because of the hours they must devote to getting food, working extra jobs, or taking care of their households. Urban Russians spend their spare time at their *dachas* (country cottages), if they have them, relaxing and growing fruits and vegetables for the winter. There are no nightclubs and entertainment usually ends by 11:00 P.M. Even Moscow is essentially dark and quiet after that.

The country's favorite sport is soccer. Russia's national soccer team competed in the 1994 World Cup. Sports in general, particularly winter sports such as ice skating, hockey, and cross-country skiing, are popular in Russia. Watching television is the most common way to spend extra time. Gathering mushrooms is a favorite summer activity. Theaters and movies are highly appreciated, but they are only available in big cities. Rural people can watch movies at *dvorets kultury* (palaces of culture), which serve as community recreation centers.

Holidays

New Year's Day is the most popular holiday in Russia. Almost everyone decorates fir trees and has parties to celebrate the new year. Grandfather Frost leaves presents for children to find on New Year's Day. Christmas is on 7 January, according to the Julian calendar used by the Russian Orthodox Church. Women's Day is 8 March. Solidarity Day (1 May, also known as May Day) is a day for parades. Before 1991, people were required to attend; now they do it voluntarily and the nature of the celebrations has changed dramatically. Victory Day (9 May) commemorates the end of World War II and is especially important to the older generation. Easter and Christmas observances, long interrupted by communism, regained their prominence in 1990.

Commerce

The business week is 40 hours, with Saturdays and Sundays off. Offices are generally open from 9:00 A.M. to 6:00 P.M. They close at lunchtime (1:00 P.M.). Prices in state stores are not negotiable, but prices on the streets, where an increasing number of items are being sold, are flexible. Capitalism is booming in Russia and a new generation of entrepreneurs is beginning to thrive. Numerous small businesses and joint ventures with foreign firms are finding success and employees are buying state-run factories and working to make them profitable.

Under communism, there were no incentives for bureaucrats to perform well or even be nice to clients, so the usual answer to any question was "no." This practice is still found in society, but "no" is no longer final. One must simply bargain and be persistent to get what one wants. Russians prefer to have social interaction before discussing business. Trying to do business on the phone without seeing the prospective business partner is ineffective. One spends a lot of time in meetings before even a small deal can succeed.

SOCIETY

Government

The constitution approved in 1993 provides for a president as head of state and a prime minister as head of government. Viktor S. Chernomyrdin became prime minister with the 1993 elections. The president is strong and has power to dissolve parliament and set foreign policy, as well as appoint the prime minister. Yeltsin's term ends in 1996. The Federal Assembly has two houses, a Federation Council and the State *Duma*. The upper Council has 89 members, and the lower *Duma* has 450. The Constitutional Court is the highest in the land. Russia's voting age is 18.

Economy

Russia's natural resources give it great potential for economic growth and development. Natural gas, coal, gold, oil, diamonds, copper, silver, and lead are all abundant. Heavy industry dominates the economy, although the agricultural sector is potentially strong. Russia's economy is weak because of past Communist policies and the current disruption of production and distribution. In 1992, Yeltsin launched radical reforms designed to liberalize prices, attract foreign

investment, and privatize the economy. Prices skyrocketed even as privatization began to see some success. When the government brought inflation under control, unemployment began to soar. At 7 percent, it is climbing higher as inefficient factories are forced to let thousands of workers go. A society accustomed to a social safety net and guaranteed employment is now faced with the realities of a market economy. While extraordinary change has occurred and many bright economic spots can be found, there is as much that is not promising. The country's Human Development Index (0.862) ranks it 37 out of 173 countries. Real gross domestic product per capita is $7,968, but this figure could fall before it rises, given a climate in which poverty is increasing as fast as wealth. The currency is the *ruble* (R).

Transportation and Communication

Most people use public transportation. Major cities have subways, trolleys, and buses. Taxis are expensive and hard to find, but unofficial taxis are increasingly common. *Aeroflot*, the national airline, provides domestic and international air travel, but it is unreliable. Railroads are extensive, but the system's service is poor. The telephone system is old and inadequate. The press is free, active, and constantly changing.

Education

Education is free and compulsory between ages six and seventeen. In 1994, new curriculum guidelines were introduced to encourage choice and innovation over previous approaches to teaching, but many public schools are unable or unwilling to implement reform due to lack of money and clear local leadership. According to the program, students attend primary, middle, and high school. They specialize in their last two years, and several electives are available. Private schools now exist and provide high quality education to the wealthy and influential. The literacy rate is 99 percent. There are more than 500 universities, medical schools, and technical academies.

Health

Medical care is free, but the quality of service is poor. Doctors are highly trained and qualified but lack modern equipment and medicine to adequately treat their patients. The infant mortality rate is 27 per 1,000. Life expectancy ranges from 60 to 74 years. Common major diseases are alcoholism, cancer, diabetes, and heart ailments.

FOR THE TRAVELER

U.S. travelers are required to have a valid visa and passport to enter Russia. Visas are also necessary to visit individual cities. Vaccinations are not required, but some may be recommended. Drinking water is generally safe, but bottled water is recommended. There are many opportunities to experience the Russian culture through travel; contact your travel agent for more information. You may also wish to contact the Consular Section of the Russian Embassy, 1825 Phelps Place NW, Washington, DC 20008.

A *Culturgram* is a product of native commentary and original, expert analysis. Statistics are estimates and information is presented as a matter of opinion. While the editors strive for accuracy and detail, this document should not be considered strictly factual. It is a general introduction to culture, an initial step in building bridges of understanding between peoples. It may not apply to all peoples of the nation. You should therefore consult other sources for more information.

Orkney Islands

Hebrides

Inverness

Aberdeen •

Perth •

Edinbourgh •

Glasgow •

Scotland
(United Kingdom)

Boundary representations not necessarily authoritative.

BACKGROUND

Land and Climate

Covering 29,909 square miles (77,464 square kilometers), Scotland is about the same size as South Carolina. It lies north of England on the same island. Both northern and southern Scotland are essentially uplands, while the mineral wealth of the central region makes it the wealthiest and most populated part of Scotland. In the far north are the famous granite highlands. The country's rugged mountains, green valleys (*glens*), deep blue lakes (*lochs*), and offshore islands provide beautiful scenery. The most fertile agricultural land lies mainly to the east and in the southern border regions. Scotland has roughly two climate zones between the east and west. The west experiences heavier rains and stronger winds than the east. Throughout the country, however, the climate is generally temperate and wet. Average temperatures vary little between seasons, with the largest average difference between summer and winter being less than 20°F (6°C). Summer temperatures generally range from 60°F to 70°F (15–21°C), while winter temperatures usually remain above freezing.

History

The Scots are descendants of Celtic peoples. Scotland's name comes from a colony of Scots (a Celtic people) who came from Ireland in the sixth century and united with the original inhabitants (Picts) in the ninth century. The Scots fought for many years against Vikings from the north and English from the south. Finally, King James I, son of Mary, Queen of Scots (Mary Stuart), came to the English throne and united Scotland and England under one monarchy in 1603.

Since that time, Scotland's history has been closely intermingled with England's. In 1707, the Scottish and English parliaments were united by the Act of Union, which founded the constitutional monarchy of the Kingdom of Great Britain. The kingdom became known as the United Kingdom in 1801 when Ireland was joined to the union. Scotland shared England's industrial revolution, the great British Empire that spanned the globe, and the trials of the world wars. Despite its close ties with England and its function in the kingdom, Scotland has remained a distinct political and cultural entity. Actually, local histories of the individual cities and towns tell far more about the people of Scotland than the political history of the United Kingdom.

Since 1990, a budding nationalist movement has been gaining momentum in Scotland. A minority believes Scotland should declare independence, but a far greater number thinks Scotland should at least have more control of its own economy and politics. Opinion polls show that most people (75 percent) want change. To avert actual independence, some politicians

Copyright © 1994. Brigham Young University. Printed in the USA. All rights reserved. It is against the law to copy, reprint, store in a retrieval system, or transmit any part of this publication in any form by any means for any purpose without written permission from the Publications Division of the David M. Kennedy Center for International Studies, Brigham Young University, PO Box 24538, Provo, UT 84602–4538. *Culturgrams* are available for more than 125 areas of the world. To place an order, to receive a free catalog, or to obtain information on traveling abroad, call toll free (800) 528–6279.

EUROPE

have proposed a separate tax system and general assembly (legislature) for a Scotland that would remain part of the United Kingdom.

THE PEOPLE

Population

Scotland's population of 5.7 million is found mostly in the crowded industrial cities and towns of central Scotland. Few people live in the rugged highlands of the north. Most of the people are Scots, but there are some Indians, Pakistanis, and Chinese (from Hong Kong) in the larger cities like Glasgow and Edinburgh. Scotland's population accounts for about 10 percent of the total population of the United Kingdom, which also includes England, Wales, and Northern Ireland.

Language

English is the official language of Scotland. The Scots speak English with a soft, melodic accent. They also use many terms derived from Gaelic (a Celtic language and Scotland's original tongue) with English to create a rather unique language. For example, the word for dull is *dreich*. A *brae* is a hill; a *bairn* is a baby. As in all English-speaking cultures, the Scots also use certain English idioms and pronunciations unique to their culture. For example, rather than saying "How's he doing?" a Scot says, "How's he keeping?" Further, some Gaelic words have been incorporated into standard English, such as *slogan* or *galore*, which are used in other English-speaking countries. The words *fanny*, *bugger*, *bloody*, and *suspenders* (call them *braces*), should never be used when speaking to a Scot. Foreign visitors should note that a *fag* is a cigarette, an *ass* is a donkey, and a *rubber* is an eraser.

Many (about 60,000) of the people that do live in the highlands still speak Gaelic, as do some people on Scotland's offshore islands. In these areas, people are encouraged to study Gaelic. Of course, they also speak English, although Gaelic is their primary language. In those areas, shop and street signs are in Gaelic.

Religion

The Church of Scotland (or Presbyterian church) is the official church, but people may worship as they choose. The world headquarters for the Presbyterian church is located in Scotland's capital, Edinburgh. While the Church of Scotland has the most members (up to two million), there are also Roman Catholics, Baptists, Congregationalists, Episcopalians, Free Presbyterians, Methodists, and a number of others. Younger Scots, especially in the east, are sometimes more secular and therefore less interested in religion or less influenced by religious traditions.

General Attitudes

Scots are proud of their heritage. Indeed, Scotland has produced many of Britain's most talented people, such as the poet Robert Burns. The people are called Scots, not Scotch, and their ways are Scottish. Scotch is a drink. Scots are offended by those who refer to Scotland as a part of England; England and Scotland are distinctly separate parts of the United Kingdom. Indeed, many Scots are considering independence from—or at least greater autonomy within—the United Kingdom.

Scots are known for their courtesy and their reserve with acquaintances until they get to know them better. Often critical and very independent, the Scottish character has been described as a "combination of realism and reckless sentiment," including rashness, moodiness, and the ability to relentlessly persevere. Attitudes differ somewhat between the various regional and class groupings throughout Scotland. The people take pride in their high standard of education and are well-informed about international affairs. Therefore, they have little patience with foreigners who demonstrate ignorance of their own country's basic customs and attitudes.

Personal Appearance

Popular European fashions are worn in Scotland. However, climate also influences the choice of clothing. Tweed suits and woolen sweaters are popular during the cooler months. Lighter fabrics are more common in the summer. The traditional kilt (not to be called a "skirt") is often worn by men for formal occasions and occasionally in other situations. Many women also still wear kilts. The term for underclothing in Scotland is "pants." Men and women wear "trousers" over "pants."

CUSTOMS AND COURTESIES

Greetings

A handshake is a common introductory greeting for the people, but it is used less often than in other European countries. Handshakes are generally light and not aggressive. Standard English greetings such as "Hello" and "How do you do?" are common. The Scots are generally more reserved and a bit more formal in their greetings than U.S. citizens, but they are nevertheless friendly. A common greeting among friends is "Alright?" to which the response is "Alright." Among friends in the north, "Fit like?" replaces "How are you?" Hugging is not common, even between close friends.

Gestures

It is rude to shout in public. Forming a "V" with the index and middle fingers and the palm facing inward is vulgar and should be avoided. It is polite for a man to give his seat to a woman on public transportation. Politeness is valued.

Visiting

In Scotland, visits to the home are usually prearranged. Only close friends and family drop by unannounced. Outside of the home, most social interaction takes place in *pubs* (public houses).

People go to *pubs* not only for drinks but also for meals and socializing. It is quite common for entire families to go to a *pub*. When hosting visitors, the Scots go out of their way to make guests feel welcome and comfortable. Refreshments are usually offered, and it is polite to accept them after a couple of weak refusals. When visitors arrive, the television and radio are usually turned off so as not to distract the conversation. Scots are open and candid in conversation and have a keen but subtle sense of humor. Religion, salary, and (less often) politics are topics to be avoided. It is customary to take a small gift to the hostess when invited to a home. Flowers or chocolates are the most common gifts. Foreign guests should give a souvenir from their country.

Eating

Proper table etiquette is important and admired. The continental style of eating is followed, with the fork in the left hand and the knife remaining in the right. Breakfast is generally light, consisting of some kind of cereal and tea. Lunch is a light meal often consisting of sandwiches, soup, and a drink. Called *tea* (sometimes "dinner"), the evening meal is the main meal of the day. Dessert (either pudding or cake) is often served with a cup of tea in the afternoon. Biscuits (cookies) and pastries are also popular. In restaurants, it is common to tip about 15 percent. It is not common to give tips in *pubs*.

LIFESTYLE

Family

Early highland families were loyal to their clan, but contemporary clans have relatively little importance in the life of individual family members today. Each clan is still headed by a chieftain, but he is mainly symbolic and has no real authority over the members of the clan. In urban areas, families are small and generally close-knit. Although relatives visit each other often, families are independent from each other. The elderly prefer to stay in their own homes and remain independent as long as possible rather than live with their married children. About half of all families live in rented homes or apartments (*flats*).

Dating and Marriage

Dating in Scotland is different than in the United States. Relationships are formed and maintained within a social circle, not as separate couples. Then, rather than dating many different people, Scots date one person at a time. Marriage becomes legal at age 16, but usually occurs in the mid to late 20s. Marriage customs are much the same as in the United States.

Diet

While daily meals are not usually elaborate in Scotland, many Scottish dishes can be complex and exquisite. The normal diet consists of *mince* and *tatties* (ground meat and potatoes),

fish suppers (fish and chips seasoned with salt and vinegar), stews, beef, lamb, *neeps* (turnips) and simple vegetables. *Haggis* are made from ground sheep entrails that are mixed with oats and spices, tied in a sheep's stomach, and cooked. They are the national dish. *Stovies* (corned beef, onions, and potatoes) are also popular. Scots enjoy very sweet desserts such as chocolates and cakes. Whiskey, an important part of the economy, is a common drink, as is beer.

Recreation

The most popular organized sport is *football* (soccer), followed by rugby. Basketball, volleyball, and badminton are played in the high schools. The Scots invented golf in the 1500s and it is still one of their favorite games. Scotland's golf courses are some of the world's best and are spread over the rolling, green countryside. The Highland Games, which resemble track meets, are held in the highlands in the late summer. Popular winter sports include curling and skiing. Curling involves two teams of four players that slide iron "stones" over ice to reach a target. Television and movies are also favorite leisure activities. Social drinking is common, and there are many lounges and *pubs*.

Holidays

Scotland celebrates many of the United Kingdom's holidays, including New Year's Day, Good Friday, May Day (1 May), Easter, the Queen's Birthday (second Saturday in June), Remembrance Day (closest Sunday to 11 November), Christmas, and Boxing Day (26 December). Virtually everything closes down for Christmas, including restaurants and subway shops. Boxing Day comes from a British tradition in which service workers were given small boxed gifts the day after Christmas. It is now a day for visiting and relaxing. New Year's Eve is called *Hogmanay*. It is the biggest holiday of the year. In January, banquets called Burns Suppers are held in honor of the Scottish poet, Robert Burns. *Haggis* are one of the most common dishes served at these suppers. On varying dates from town to town, Scots also enjoy a Monday spring holiday and autumn holiday.

Commerce

Businesses are open generally from 9:00 A.M. to 5:30 or 6:00 P.M., Monday through Friday. Government offices close between 1:00 and 2:00 P.M. and stay open until 5:30 P.M. One day a week, many shops close by 1:00 P.M. Glasgow and Edinburgh are the main centers of business, and major stores often remain open until 8:00 P.M. at least one night a week.

SOCIETY

Government

The United Kingdom's constitutional monarchy, with Queen Elizabeth II as head of state, is a parliamentary system. The House of Lords (with noblemen, life appointees, and Church of England bishops) has little legislative power, although it is the highest judicial body in the land. The House of Commons is elected by the people. The leader of the majority party, appointed by the Queen as prime minister, selects a cabinet and runs the government. The current prime minister is John Major. Elections are held at least every five years, but they may be held sooner if called by the prime minister. The last parliamentary elections were in April 1992. Scotland maintains its own legal system, related to but different from that of England. It also has its own police force and other departments that are not directly controlled from London.

Economy

Agriculture has traditionally been the mainstay of the economy, and now modern machinery makes the land even more productive with less labor. The most important agricultural products include potatoes, vegetables, and grains. Many Scots are employed in fishing, mining, manufacturing, textiles, and shipbuilding. Whiskey is an important industry. Several newer industries have also taken hold in Scotland, such as chemicals. The discovery of oil in the North Sea has brought economic growth to the area. Scotland has many fine ports from which the United Kingdom conducts trade. The currency is the pound sterling (£).

The United Kingdom's Human Development Index (0.964) ranks it 10 out of 173 countries. Real gross domestic product per capita is $15,804, which has more than doubled in the last generation. These figures indicate most people have access to a decent income, although there is a larger gap between the wealthy and the poor than in some other European countries. Likewise, the United Kingdom's middle class is not as prosperous as its counterpart in other developed nations.

Transportation and Communication

Scotland is linked by international and domestic air services. Railroads also connect most parts of the country, except in the northwest. Most roads are paved, and most people own cars. Following the British tradition, traffic moves on the left side of the road. Buses and taxis are common in the cities. The public transportation system is excellent. Telecommunications are well advanced, with international fiber-optic cable links and satellite systems. There are a number of daily newspapers and nearly every home has a television.

Education

Education is free and compulsory from ages five to sixteen. Scotland's school system differs from that of other parts of the United Kingdom. The examinations given at the completion of secondary schools are not the same as in England. Both public (called state) schools and private (called public) schools are available in Scotland. Private schools receive some state funding and are subject to some control. There are various vocational schools, as well as eight universities and a number of colleges. University education is free. The universities of St. Andrews, Aberdeen, and Glasgow were founded in the 1400s. The literacy rate is 99 percent.

Health

The United Kingdom's National Health Service provides, on the basis of taxation, free medical treatment and many other social services to the people. Only prescriptions and some dental services must be paid for by the individual. Medical facilities are advanced and life expectancy (73 to 79 years) is similar to that in the United States. Scotland has a high rate of lung cancer and heart disease. Infant mortality is 7 per 1,000.

FOR THE TRAVELER

While a valid passport is necessary, no visa is required of U.S. citizens. No vaccinations are required. Water is safe to drink. Victorian architecture, cultural events, castles, beautiful countryside, the fabled Loch Ness, and much more await visitors. For more information, contact the Scottish Tourist Board (23 Ravelston Terrace, Edinburgh EH4 3EU, United Kingdom). Also, a number of travel agencies throughout the United States have been specially trained (through the S.C.O.T.S. program) in travel to Scotland. Ask your travel agent. The British Tourist Authority (551 Fifth Avenue, 7th Floor, New York, NY 10176) may also have additional information. The BTA also has offices in Chicago, Dallas, and Los Angeles. You may also wish to contact the Embassy of the United Kingdom, 3100 Massachusetts Avenue NW, Washington, DC 20008. Also write to the British Information Service, 845 Third Avenue, New York, NY 10022.

A *Culturgram* is a product of native commentary and original, expert analysis. Statistics are estimates and information is presented as a matter of opinion. While the editors strive for accuracy and detail, this document should not be considered strictly factual. It is a general introduction to culture, an initial step in building bridges of understanding between peoples. It may not apply to all peoples of the nation. You should therefore consult other sources for more information.

Slovakia

Boundary representations not necessarily authoritative.

BACKGROUND

Land and Climate

Slovakia is a landlocked country situated in the heart of central Europe. Covering 18,859 square miles (48,845 square kilometers), it is about the size of West Virginia. Slovakia is mountainous, with the Carpathian and Tatra ranges being most prominent. The highest peak is Gerlach at 8,707 feet (2,857 meters). Mountain ridges historically inhibited travel and contributed to Slovakia's variety of dialects and customs. The country's fertile south is part of the Great Hungarian Plain. Slovakia is rich in natural resources such as timber, copper, zinc, mercury, limestone, and iron ore. With a continental climate, summers are hot (especially in southern lowlands) and winters are cold and snowy (especially in northern highlands). Corn, oats, wheat, and potatoes are the most abundant crops. Much of the east is covered with forests. Bratislava is the capital.

History

Slavic peoples first settled in the area during the fifth century. In 863, they founded a loose confederation that became the Great Moravian Empire. Its brief history ended in 907 with the invasion of nomadic Magyars (today called Hungarians) and the area came under Hungarian rule. In 1526, Hungary became subject to Austrian Habsburg rule. Upon its defeat in World War I (1918), the Austro-Hungarian Empire disintegrated. Slovaks joined with Czechs under the leadership of Thomas Masaryk and Milan Rastislav Štefánik in founding the First Czecho-Slovak Republic (the hyphen was dropped in 1920).

Czechoslovakia became the most democratic of the Habsburg successor states, although some Slovaks wished for more autonomy within the union. In 1938, the country was not able to withstand Hitler's foreign policy machinations. Even as Germany was annexing Czech lands, Slovakia declared independence in March 1939 and allied with Germany throughout World War II. The move still stirs controversy today. Central and eastern Slovaks staged a revolt in 1944 that was quickly crushed. Upon Germany's defeat, the Soviet Union's Red Army helped install a new unitary Czechoslovak government.

After 1948, Communists seized control of the government, all major institutions, and significant property. Slovaks suffered under forced Stalinization and persecution in the 1950s. During the 1960s, the reform-minded Slovak Communist, Alexander Dubček, led a movement to create "socialism with a human face." Censorship was relaxed and a spirit of revival and hope swept the country. The experiment met with an abrupt end when Soviet-led Warsaw Pact troops crushed the movement in August 1968. Within two years nearly all reforms were abolished except that Slovakia was granted the status of a republic and allowed more regional government offices.

During the 1970s Gustav Husák's regime attempted to satisfy citizens by making consumer goods more available, but ruthless repression of political dissent continued. Economic stagnation and Mikhail Gorbachev's changes in the Soviet Union laid the foundations for the fall of communism in 1989. Censorship and travel restrictions were lifted, and the iron curtain collapsed. All of this happened without one person being killed, so the events have been called the "Velvet" or "Gentle" Revolution.

The burst of emotions that came with the revolution soon gave way to the sobering reality of the need to rebuild democracy. Nationalism reemerged as a major issue. In 1990,

EUROPE

Copyright © 1994. Brigham Young University. Printed in the USA. All rights reserved. It is against the law to copy, reprint, store in a retrieval system, or transmit any part of this publication in any form by any means for any purpose without written permission from the Publications Division of the David M. Kennedy Center for International Studies, Brigham Young University, PO Box 24538, Provo, UT 84602–4538. *Culturgrams* are available for more than 125 areas of the world. To place an order, to receive a free catalog, or to obtain information on traveling abroad, call toll free (800) 528–6279.

Slovaks began pressing for a greater voice in their own affairs. Disagreements over the amount of autonomy for Slovakia and regarding the pace of economic reform led to victory for Slovak nationalists in 1992 elections. When the newly elected Czech and Slovak national governments could not agree about the division of federal powers, Czech Prime Minister Vaćlav Klaus and Slovak Prime Minister Vladimír Mečiar decided to split the state peacefully and fairly.

After Slovakia became independent on 1 January 1993, Mečiar continued market reforms but slowed the pace of privatization of large enterprises in order to alleviate rising unemployment. However, economic stagnation and Mečiar's confrontational leadership led parliament to remove him from office on a vote of no confidence in March 1994. Jozef Moravčik became the new prime minister to serve until special elections in September 1994.

THE PEOPLE
Population
About 5.3 million people live in Slovakia, and more than 80 percent of them are Slovaks. Hungarians (Magyars) constitute the largest minority (10.8 percent) and most of them live in southern Slovakia. The Romany (Gypsy) ethnic group officially accounts for a documented 1.5 percent of the population, but this figure may actually be as high as 9 or 10 percent. The Romany are nomadic and difficult to count, and many listed themselves as Slovaks in the 1992 census. The Romany are not well integrated into mainstream society, especially in rural areas, and they have been struggling against discrimination in many countries.

Smaller ethnic groups that are more integrated in society include Czechs (1 percent), Carpatho-Rusyns (Ruthenians), Ukrainians, Germans, Poles, Moravians, and others. About half of all people live in towns with more than 10,000 inhabitants.

Language
Slovaks speak Slovak, a tongue in the Slavic language group that also includes Czech, Polish, Russian, and other languages. Slovak uses a Latin script. Literary Slovak is used in official capacities, but numerous dialects exist in various regions. Hungarian is the second most commonly spoken language, especially in the south. Hungarians desire their language to have official status, but this is generally opposed by Slovaks. Still, Hungarian cultural institutions and media receive some public funding. The Romany speak Romany, an unwritten tongue with Indo-Aryan roots. They also speak Slovak.

German is widely understood, while English is the language of choice to study in school. Russian was required before 1989. Other languages are also offered.

Religion
Freedom of worship is guaranteed in Slovakia and many people have deep religious convictions. About 60.4 percent of the population belongs to the Roman Catholic church, followed by the Evangelical Lutherans (6.2), and the Greek Catholics (3.4). Smaller groups include the Calvinist Reformed (1.6 percent), Eastern Orthodox (0.7), Baptist, and others. Nearly 10 percent are atheists, while the rest of the population either belongs to various smaller groups or has no religious affiliation.

General Attitudes
Slovakia is going through a difficult transition that is a natural part of newly acquired statehood. Some people are extremely sensitive about topics related to independence. People are particularly interested in the way foreigners view them, and they are anxious to foster a positive image abroad.

Although Slovakia has industrialized, particularly since 1948, a romantic attachment to peasant ideals and the countryside remains in the hearts of many Slovaks. Poetry, literature, song, and dance glamorize those rural roots. Slovaks are proud of their rich cultural heritage, as well as famous Americans with Slovak roots: pop artist Andy Warhol, whose parents are from Miková; astronaut Eugene Černan; radio inventor Joseph Murgáš; and parachute inventor, Štefan Banič.

Slovaks are usually outgoing and value good humor and hard work. They are also generous, especially in the countryside, and will go out of their way to help a stranger. Education, modesty, and honesty are admired. Those who are self-confident or aggressive are often interpreted as being "too" self-confident or "too" aggressive. Entrepreneurs are considered to be "price gougers" and greedy, especially in rural areas. This attitude is changing in urban areas as economic change progresses.

Personal Appearance
Clothing in urban areas is fashionable, while older, rural people remain more conservative. Businessmen wear suits; women and girls wear dresses and skirts. Professional women dress up for work and most Slovaks are very concerned with their appearance. Jeans and T-shirts are quite popular and short pants are increasingly common in the summer. Traditional folk costumes might still be worn by villagers for special occasions.

CUSTOMS AND COURTESIES
Greetings
Shaking hands is the most common form of greeting, but one does not cross over another handshake to shake hands in a group. A man usually waits for a woman to extend her hand. Upon parting, it is often thought proper for men to hug women or kiss them on both cheeks (sometimes not really touching) and to firmly shake hands with men.

Formal titles carry a particular significance. People are addressed as *Pán* (Mr.) or *Pani* (Mrs.), followed by any professional title (doctor, engineer, professor), and then the surname. First names are used upon mutual consent, among friends, or among the youth. More formal greetings include *Dobrý deň* (Good day) or *Velmi ma teši* (Pleased to meet you). Good-bye is *Dovidenia*. More casual terms are *Ahoj* (Hi), *Čiao*, and *Servus* (both mean "Hello" or "Good-bye"). Some older villagers still use the traditional *S Bohom* (God be with you). Thank you is expressed with *Ďakujem*. The use of *Prosím* (Please) is considered polite before making any requests and for saying "You're welcome."

Gestures
Hand gestures are frequently used to emphasize speech. To wish luck, instead of crossing fingers, Slovaks "hold thumbs." That is, they fold the thumb in and close the fingers on it. Yawning in public is considered improper, and

chewing gum is not acceptable during polite social interaction. Smiling is courteous.

Visiting

Impromptu visits are common, but only between close friends and family members. Invited guests, especially those coming from a distance, receive warm welcomes. An invitation to dinner is usually in a home rather than a restaurant. Guests remove hats and shoes in a home; hosts often provide slippers. Visitors wait for hosts to invite them to be seated. Invited guests often present the hosts with a gift of flowers, wine, liquor, or something else. Flowers are fresh, unwrapped, and given in odd numbers (three, five, or seven). Even numbers and dried flowers are for funerals; red roses imply romantic intentions. Visitors should not overly admire anything in the home, as the item will be given to them, even if it is a prized heirloom.

Refreshments are usually offered to guests. Rural Slovaks might serve friends or relatives *slanina* (home-smoked bacon) and bread, as well as a drink. Typical is homemade *slivovica* (plum liquor), but beer, coffee, tea, and other drinks may also be offered. Urban guests tend to serve chips, nuts, and wine rather than homemade refreshments. On special occasions, a tray of ham, cheese, eggs, vegetables, and sweets may be offered. Out of courtesy, guests often politely decline offers before eventually accepting them. It is impolite to refuse refreshments all together, but one may decline liquor or another specific item without offending. An empty cup or glass will be refilled, so guests leave a little bit of drink when they are finished.

If guests wish to wash up before a meal, they knock on the bathroom door before entering. All doors in a home are typically closed, even if no one is in the room. Homes often have water closets (toilets) separate from the bathroom.

Since the workday starts early, most visits conclude before 11:00 P.M. Slovaks typically accompany their departing guests outside and then wave to them until they are out of sight. Guests may turn often and return the wave.

Eating

Slovaks eat in the continental style, holding the fork in the left hand and the knife in the right. Three meals are eaten each day. Breakfast consists of bread and rolls, sliced meat or sausage, and cheese. Soup is commonly served with the main meal at midday, when meat, dumplings or potatoes, and a vegetable are eaten. A lighter meal of cold cuts, cheese, and bread is eaten in the evening. Mid-morning and mid-afternoon snacks are common. Families usually eat together on weekends, but not as often on weekdays. Before eating, the head of the home says *Dobrú chut* (equivalent of *Bon appetit*), and others at the table respond with the same. Both hands are kept above the table, but elbows do not rest on the table. Napkins are used on the table, not in the lap. A plate of baked goods is often served before the meal.

When guests are present, women typically serve the meal but do not eat at the table. Often, only the guests are fed. Slovak guests wait to be offered second helpings, but it is greatly appreciated if a foreigner asks for seconds. Conversation usually occurs after the meal. Toasting with *Na zdravie* (To your health) is common on both formal and informal occasions.

Restaurants do not provide water unless requested. Beer, wine, soft drinks, and mineral water are commonly ordered. Slovaks consider milk a drink for children. Meals are frequently completed with a small cup of Turkish coffee. Tipping is accepted at most sit-down restaurants; it is added to the bill, not left on the table.

LIFESTYLE

Family

Typical Slovak families have two or three children. The state used to provide families with free medical care, schooling, and social security, but budget cuts have resulted in charges for some services. Paid maternity leave for mothers, a cash allowance for each birth, and child-care facilities are still provided. While most women hold jobs outside the home and comprise 47 percent of the labor force, they are also usually responsible for the home and children. However, some men are beginning to share in household duties. Most urban families live in small, modest apartments built during the Communist era. Rural inhabitants continue to reside in single-family homes that provide a more pleasant environment.

Dating and Marriage

Popular dating activities include dancing and going to the movies or theater. Festivals are also popular. Men marry between the ages of 23 and 26, and women marry about three years earlier. Most Slovak weddings involve church ceremonies, and brides are often paraded around the village in a traditional procession. The reception afterward lasts until morning and it may go on for days. The groom carries his bride over the threshold of their new home. Due to a housing shortage, new couples must often live with parents until an apartment is available.

Diet

Among the most popular Slovak foods are *rezeň* (breaded steak) and potatoes, as well as other kinds of meat served with potatoes, rice, dumplings, or pasta and sauce. Slovakia also has a variety of sweet dishes served as a main course (such as prune dumplings). The national dish is *bryndzové halušky* (small dumplings with processed sheep cheese), but it is not eaten often in the home. Fresh-baked bread and soup are considered staples at the dinner table. Dairy products such as milk, cheese, and butter are widely available. Fresh fruits (apples, plums, grapes) are abundant and eaten in season. Bananas and oranges are popular for holidays. Potatoes, cabbage, and carrots are the most frequently eaten vegetables. Popular desserts include *koláč* (nut or poppy seed rolls) and *torte* (cake).

Recreation

Soccer, ice hockey, skiing, and tennis are the most popular sports in Slovakia. Other forms of recreation include movie-going, hiking, camping, swimming, and attending local festivals, cultural events, or art exhibits.

Slovaks take special pride in their folk music. They sing with marked enthusiasm at gatherings, and knowing folk songs is considered part of being Slovak. Slovaks have a saying: *Kde Slovák, tam spev* (Wherever there is a Slovak, there is a song). Folk art is also appreciated and is often given to foreign visitors as a gift. It is mostly available in special stores, as few people carry on the old traditions of embroidery and woodcarving.

Many Slovaks spend weekends or vacations in the beautiful Tatra Mountains, at health spas, or in the countryside. More Slovaks are beginning to tour other parts of Europe.

Holidays

Holidays include St. Sylvester's Day (New Year's Eve), New Year's Day (also Independence Day), Easter, and Cyril and Methodius Day (5 July), which honors the two saints who introduced Christianity to the region and who developed the Cyrillic alphabet used with many Slavic languages. Slovak National Uprising Day (29 August) commemorates the 1944 rebellion against the Nazis. Constitution Day is 1 September. Christmas is the most celebrated holiday. Children receive gifts of candy, fruit, and nuts on St. Nicholas Day (6 December). A Christmas Eve supper, called *vilija*, includes mushroom soup, fish, peas, prunes, and pastries. Following the meal, the tree is decorated and gifts are exchanged. Christmas Day is celebrated with family gatherings featuring ham, baked goods, and drinking. Church attendance is also traditional.

Birthdays are celebrated more as family events, whereas name days are occasions for parties among friends or colleagues. The name day is usually more important, involving gifts and flowers; it is celebrated on the saint's day whose name one has.

Commerce

Some grocers open before 8:00 A.M. and most other businesses and government offices open at 8:00 A.M. and close by 3:00 or 4:00 P.M. Shops are open until 6:00 P.M. weekdays and 2:00 P.M. Saturdays. Except for a few restaurants and stores, nearly all businesses close on Sunday. Small urban shops and most rural businesses close for lunch. Many people grow their own fruits and vegetables in addition to buying them from markets. Even urban residents often have gardens in the countryside.

Most employees have four weeks of vacation each year. Retirement occurs between ages 53 and 60. Friendly social relationships are important between business associates. Foreign business representatives should also have an interest in Slovak culture and accept any offered hospitality.

SOCIETY

Government

Slovakia's president, Michal Kováč, is head of state. The prime minister is head of government. The Slovak National Council has 150 elected members. The voting age is 18. Slovakia has four departments (regions) and several smaller districts. Court judges are chosen by the National Council.

Economy

Although agriculture dominated the economy before World War II, rapid industrialization occurred under Communist rule and many factories are found throughout the country. In addition to many military-related industries, there are also steel, chemical, textile, cement, and glass factories. Many products are semifinished rather than fully manufactured.

Slovakia has proceeded at a slower pace than the Czech Republic with market reforms and privatization. Under Vladimír Mečiar, who was not only prime minister but also in charge of privatization, many large firms remained in state control. This inhibited foreign investment and contributed to a decline in productivity. The current government is addressing the economy's main problems of unemployment (nearly 15 percent) and inflation (23 percent), while quickening the pace of privatization. The economy is handicapped by inefficient and environmentally unsound industries, but foreign investment will help them modernize. Military industries have the capacity, but not yet the capital, to switch to civilian products. Many industries have goods that will be competitive on the world market once the political climate fully stabilizes.

The country's Human Development Index (0.892) and rank (26 out of 173 nations) were figured before independence, as was real gross domestic product per capita ($7,300). Although the figures may have slipped as real wages have fallen, Slovaks generally enjoy a good standard of living. The currency is the Slovak crown (*koruna*).

Transportation and Communication

Although Slovak families usually have a car, extremely high fuel prices discourage regular use. Instead, public transportation by bus, streetcar, and train is common. Main roads are paved, but there are only a few good superhighways. More are being planned. Railroads link major cities.

Slovakia's press expanded rapidly with the freedom introduced in 1989. More than 120 newspapers are published, as well as numerous magazines. There are several television and radio stations. People with satellite dishes can access international programming.

Education

Education, which is free at public institutions, begins at age six and is compulsory for ten years. Education and research have a high priority, and literacy is 99 percent. Although public universities charge no tuition, admission is limited and highly competitive. The oldest of Slovakia's 13 universities is Comenius University in Bratislava. Those who do not attend college can obtain work skills through vocational schools.

Health

Slovakia's national health-care system, anchored by state-run hospitals, is undergoing change. Nearly all people have access to physicians, and medical advances have lowered the infant mortality rate to 11 per 1,000. Life expectancy averages 71 years. Health spas service patients from around the world. Pollution poses serious health hazards in both rural and urban environments. Funds are lacking to clean water and air, and to restore decimated forests.

FOR THE TRAVELER

If staying fewer than 30 days, U.S. travelers only need a passport to visit Slovakia. For additional information, consult the Embassy of the Slovak Republic, 2201 Wisconsin Avenue NW, Suite 380, Washington, DC 20007.

A *Culturgram* is a product of native commentary and original, expert analysis. Statistics are estimates and information is presented as a matter of opinion. While the editors strive for accuracy and detail, this document should not be considered strictly factual. It is a general introduction to culture, an initial step in building bridges of understanding between peoples. It may not apply to all peoples of the nation. You should therefore consult other sources for more information.

Spain

(Spanish State)

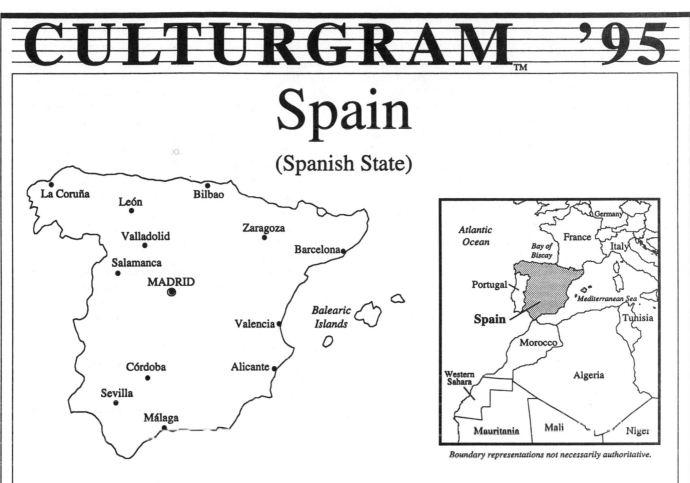

Boundary representations not necessarily authoritative.

EUROPE

BACKGROUND

Land and Climate

Spain occupies the majority of the Iberian peninsula in Europe. Covering 194,884 square miles (504,750 square kilometers), it is nearly as large as Nevada and Utah combined. Much of central Spain is a high plateau, surrounded with low coastal plains. The famous Pyrénées mountains are in the north. Other important mountain ranges include the Iberians in the central part of the country and the Sierra Nevadas in the south. The northern coasts enjoy a moderate climate with some rainfall year-round. The southern and eastern coasts have a more Mediterranean climate, with long, dry summers and mild winters. Spain has many natural resources, including coal, iron ore, uranium, mercury, gypsum, zinc, copper, potash, and others. About 30 percent of the land is forested. The Spanish State also contains various islands. The Canary Islands, in the Atlantic off the Moroccan coast, are a popular tourist retreat. Also included in Spain's territory are the Balaeric Islands, Ceuta, and Melilla (both on the northern coast of Morocco).

History

Civilization on the Iberian peninsula has been recorded as far back as 2000 B.C. Various people migrated over the centuries to populate the area. Rome began to exercise its influence around 218 B.C. and controlled the entire peninsula by the time of Christ. In the centuries after the Roman Empire fell, Spain was first ruled by the Visigoths, Germanic tribes who invaded in the fifth century, and then by the Muslim Moors, who invaded from North Africa in 711. Christians began to fight the Muslim empire and finally defeated the Moorish king. Two kingdoms emerged in 1479; they united by 1492.

During the 16th century, Spain was one of the largest and most powerful empires in the world. Its territories in the Americas were extensive and wealthy. Spain was a monarchy during its colonial period. One of its most famous rulers was Philip II (1556–98). He was a staunch supporter of the Roman Catholic Church and fought many wars in the name of destroying Protestantism. Several Spanish territories in Europe were lost during the War of the Spanish Succession (1701–14). Spain was involved in the Napoleonic wars that ended in 1814. By 1850, Spain had lost most of its overseas possessions. Spain then lost a war (and the Philippines, plus other territory) to the United States in 1898.

King Alfonso XIII abdicated his throne in 1931 when the people called for a republic. Unfortunately, civil war erupted in 1936 between the Nationalists (led by Francisco Franco)

Copyright © 1994. Brigham Young University. Printed in the USA. All rights reserved. It is against the law to copy, reprint, store in a retrieval system, or transmit any part of this publication in any form by any means for any purpose without written permission from the Publications Division of the David M. Kennedy Center for International Studies, Brigham Young University, PO Box 24538, Provo, UT 84602–4538. *Culturgrams* are available for more than 125 areas of the world. To place an order, to receive a free catalog, or to obtain information on traveling abroad, call toll free (800) 528–6279.

and the Republicans. After a brutal war, Franco's forces were victorious in 1939. Franco assumed complete control of the government and ruled as a dictator until 1975. In 1969, Franco named Juan Carlos de Borbón y Borbón as his eventual successor. When Franco died in 1975, Juan Carlos restored the monarchy and became King Juan Carlos I. He restored democracy and instituted a constitutional monarchy; he remains popular today for those actions. Elections were held in 1977, and the political system was reformed to protect human rights.

The Socialist Democrats, who took power in 1977, continued in office through the 1980s but had to form a coalition government when they lost their parliamentary majority in 1990. Spain, although a member of the North Atlantic Treaty Alliance (NATO), threatened at one time to withdraw from the alliance. Relations with Europe and the United States improved in the latter 1980s. Difficulties with Basque Separatists (ETA) have caused problems for the government, but Spain is cooperating with France on addressing the issue.

Domestic political and economic problems in 1992 did not dampen Spanish enthusiasm for what the people called the "Year of Spain" because of the summer Olympics, the World's Fair, and the 500th anniversary of Columbus's voyage to the Americas. The troubles did lead Prime Minister Felipe González to call for elections a few months ahead of schedule. In June 1993 voters chose to return him to office for another term by a narrow margin. By 1994, a political crisis was evident and threatened to bring down the government. Many sources called for the prime minister's resignation for not cracking down on high level corruption. Several government ministers and officials resigned; some were arrested. González vowed to stay in office until the end of his term in 1997.

THE PEOPLE

Population

The population of Spain is 39.2 million and is growing annually at 0.2 percent. This includes the people on several islands that are part of Spain. The Spanish are a composite of Mediterranean and Nordic ancestry and are considered a homogeneous ethnic group. A small portion of the population is composed of immigrants from Latin American nations, other European countries, Africa, and Asia. More than three-fourths of the population lives in urban areas. Madrid, the capital, has the largest population with 3.6 million people. Barcelona is the next largest with 1.8 million (3 million including suburbs).

Language

There are four official languages in Spain. The first, Castilian Spanish, is the main language of business and government. The other languages include Catalan (17 percent), Galician (7 percent), and Basque (2 percent). In areas where Catalan is spoken (mostly in the northeast corner, down the coast to Valencia, and on the Balearic Islands) nearly everyone speaks Catalan and many may not speak Castilian. The same goes for the other official languages. Galician is spoken in the northwest and Basque is spoken in the north. English can be heard in tourist centers, and many Spaniards know some French. Catalan was an official language (with Spanish, English, and French) of the 1992 Summer Olympics because Barcelona is in Catalonia.

Religion

Spain has historically been a Roman Catholic nation and 99 percent of the people are baptized members. All aspects of Spanish life are influenced by deep-rooted Catholic traditions. Freedom of religion was granted in the 1970s, opening the way for many Spaniards to begin joining other churches. One percent of the population is involved with other (mostly Christian) religious groups. Participation (such as attendance at worship services) in these smaller groups is much higher per person than it is in the Catholic Church. Some Muslims and Jews also reside in Spain.

General Attitudes

The Spanish are generally friendly, helpful, and individualistic. They enjoy conversation and giving advice. The Spanish often consider it their duty to correct "errors" as they see them in others. Along with the spirit of individualism comes a strong sense of personal pride. Spanish people feel it is very important to project an impression of affluence and social position. Appearance is extremely important. Regional pride and devotion are strong and increasingly expressed.

Personal Appearance

The Spanish are concerned with dress. Style and quality of clothing are important indicators of a person's status and respectability. Men usually dress conservatively, avoiding flashy or bright colors. Women try to be stylish and children are dressed as nicely as possible. Many colorful regional costumes are sometimes worn for festivities.

CUSTOMS AND COURTESIES

Greetings

The usual greeting by Spanish males is a handshake. Good friends often add a pat on the back and, if they have not seen each other for some time, an *abrazo* (hug). Women also shake hands when greeting others, but close female friends also kiss each other on the cheek. A slight embrace and kiss on the cheek are also used among women when parting. Family names and titles, such as *Señor* (Mr.), *Señora* (Mrs.), and *Señorita* (Miss) may be used to address older people or professionals. In some areas the titles *Don* and *Doña* are used with the first name to show special respect. First names are used among close friends and by young people.

Visiting

When invited to someone's home, a person may decline at first, because the invitation may be only a polite courtesy. If the hosts insist on a visit, then it may be accepted. Guests invited to a home usually expect to stay from one to two hours. It is polite for a guest to take or send flowers, especially if the visit is a dinner invitation or if someone is ill. On special occasions, hosts might give gifts to guests, which are opened immediately in the presence of the host. Refreshments are usually served.

Eating

In a formal dinner, the host or hostess indicates the seating arrangements. Ladies and older people are seated first. Compliments on the meal are welcome. The continental style of eating is followed, with the fork in the left hand and the knife remaining in the right. The knife is used to push food onto the fork; fingers or other food are never used to push food onto the fork. Upon finishing the meal, the knife and fork are laid side by side on the plate. Leaving them crossed or on opposite sides of the plate indicates that a person wishes to eat more.

Hands (not elbows) are kept above the table at all times and are not placed in the lap during the meal. If a person enters a home or room where others are eating, an invitation will be extended to join in eating. The invitation is usually out of courtesy, and the person generally refuses politely, saying *Que aproveche* ("Enjoy your meal"). It is considered bad manners for adults to eat while walking down the street. In restaurants, the waiter is summoned by a raised hand. The bill is paid to the waiter. Usually, a service charge is included in the bill, but it is customary to leave a small tip. Compliments or friendly remarks to waiters or other service people are generally appreciated.

LIFESTYLE

Family

The family is very important in Spain. Divorce rates are low. The average family has two children. The father is traditionally the undisputed head of the home. Generally the wife is responsible for caring for the house and children, although many living in urban areas also work outside the home. About one-third of the labor force is female. It is common for grandparents, aunts, uncles, and cousins to have close relations with the nuclear family. Men are expected to be strong and masculine, while women are expected to be understanding and feminine. These attitudes are changing in urban areas, but they still play a key role among rural peoples. In such cases, men enjoy more social freedom than do women.

Dating and Marriage

Dating usually begins around age 14 with group activities. Couples begin dating at about age 18, although in some areas couples only date if they plan to marry. Otherwise, group activities prevail. Rather than call on a girl at her home, a boy often meets a girl at a prearranged site. Couples are normally engaged for a long time while they work and save money to pay for an apartment. Potential spouses must usually be approved by parents. The average marriage age for men is 27, while women marry between 20 and 24.

Diet

Typical Spanish food includes fresh vegetables, meat, eggs, chicken, and fish. Most fried foods are cooked in olive oil. Breakfast is generally a light meal of coffee or hot chocolate, bread and jam, or sometimes *churros* (a batter made of flour and butter, deep-fried and sprinkled with sugar). A substantial meal is eaten at about 2:00 P.M., usually including soup, a salad, a dish consisting of some kind of fish, a main dish, and fresh fruit. Adults usually drink wine with their meals and children drink mineral water or soft drinks. There is always plenty of bread (French style). At 5:00 or 6:00 P.M., Spaniards eat a snack *(merienda)*, usually a sandwich *(bocadillo)*, or sweet bread or crackers with tea or hot milk. Dinner is usually at 9:00 or 10:00 P.M. and is not as large as the midday meal. Common dinner foods include soup and a *tortilla española* (omelet with potatoes and onions). Each region also has it own specialities, including seafoods, ham and pork sausages, lamb stew, roasted meats, *gazpacho* (cold vegetable soup), *paella* (rice with fish, seafood and/or meat), *Arros negre* (rice with calamar ink), *Cocido* (Castillian soup), and a wide variety of other foods.

Recreation

The main spectator sport is soccer. When important teams play, local bars are crowded with fans watching the matches on television. Many also watch from their homes. During the World Cup competition, the entire country is involved. Spain participated in the 1990 and 1994 World Cup. Bullfighting, a popular attraction, is considered more an art than a sport. Spaniards interested in participating in sports (tennis, basketball, swimming, and others) join private clubs. Team sports are not part of school programs. Hunting, skiing, and fishing are popular activities in certain areas of Spain. Many Spaniards enjoy going to movies, watching television, or going for walks. *Tertulias* are popular intimate social groups that meet together regularly in cafés to discuss ideas, events, and politics. Men play dominoes, cards, or other games in bars.

Holidays

Festivals play a major role in Spanish life. They are eagerly awaited and planned well in advance. Each city and region has its own special *fiesta*, often in honor of a patron saint. Activities associated with *fiestas* include processions, fireworks, dancing, bullfights, amusement attractions, and wearing regional costumes. The official national holidays include New Year's Day, Feast of San José (19 March), Holy Week and Easter, Labor Day (1 May), Corpus Christi, The King's Birthday (24 June), Santiago Day (25 June), National Day (12 October), All Saints Day (1 November), Constitution Day (6 December), Immaculate Conception (8 December), and Christmas. Christmas gifts are not opened until the Day of the Three Kings or Wise Men on 6 January.

Commerce

Businesses are traditionally open six days a week from about 9:00 A.M. to 1:30 P.M. and from 5:00 to 8:00 P.M. Banks are open from 9:00 A.M. to 2:00 P.M. The midday break traditionally gave families time to be together for the main meal and a *siesta* (a time for relaxing). This practice is disappearing, however, and families might not eat the midday meal together. Children often eat at school. Businesses are increasingly staying open all day or having a shorter meal break. *Siesta* is no longer common in urban areas. Because of the high cost of living, many men have two jobs. Boys over 14 years old and girls over 16 sometimes work during the day and go to high school at night. Their wages are often used to supplement the family income. Vacations are usually taken for three to four weeks in July or August. Those living in central Spain go to the beaches or mountains to escape the heat. Business is usually not conducted during these months because so many people are away.

SOCIETY

Government

Although King Juan Carlos I is the head of state, the prime minister is president of the government. There is a bicameral legislature *(Cortes Generales),* consisting of a Senate and a Congress of Deputies, the latter having the greater power. The voting age is 18.

Spain is divided into 17 autonomous communities (regions). Each region has its own rights, elected officials, and justice system. Catalan, Galician, and Basque nationalities are recognized by the constitution as having distinct historic and cultural heritages.

Economy

Although Spain was traditionally one of the poorest countries in Western Europe, conditions improved substantially after it joined the European Union in 1986. Spain's Human Development Index (0.923) ranks it 23 out of 173 nations. Real gross national product per capita is $15,890, which has more than tripled in the last generation. These figures indicate that economic opportunities are now available to the bulk of the population. Most people earn a decent income. Unemployment (19 percent), however, represents a major problem for the economy. Still, inflation is low and growth is stable. Spain's modern economic institutions are well suited to European integration.

Although industry is vital to the economy and employs 35 percent of the labor force, the services sector (including tourism) employs 55 percent. Agriculture is less important to the economy than it was a generation ago, but still employs 10 percent of the labor force. Agricultural products include grains, citrus and other fruits, vegetables, and wine grapes. The country exports some food as well as live animals. Spain is a world leader in the production of wine. Tourism is increasingly important to economic development, especially in the coastal regions. Tourists enjoy visiting Spain for its climate, and it is a popular destination for many other Europeans. The currency in Spain is the *peseta* (Pta).

Transportation and Communication

Efficient air and rail service is available throughout the country. Trains connect most cities. Many private bus companies serve rural areas. Madrid and Barcelona have subway systems. Buses are also common in the large cities. Taxis are normally available. The telecommunications system is generally modern and good for domestic and international use. Dozens of radio and television stations serve the country.

Education

School is compulsory between the ages of six and fourteen. Many schools are operated by the Roman Catholic Church or by private organizations. Middle- and higher-income families spend a good share of their incomes on private education. Spain's literacy rate is 95 percent. While many young people quit school and begin work at age 14, an increasing number are finishing high school and continuing their education in vocational schools. Others prepare for a university education.

Health

The Spanish enjoy a good system of medical care that is coordinated by the government. The infant mortality rate is 7 per 1,000. Life expectancy ranges from 74 to 81 years.

FOR THE TRAVELER

Although a passport is necessary for travel to Spain, a visa is not required of U.S. visitors for stays of up to six months. No vaccinations are necessary. Dual-voltage small appliances or a voltage convertor and a plug adaptor are usually needed to use electrical outlets. Spain has a well-developed tourist industry. For more information on travel opportunities, contact the Tourist Office of Spain, 665 Fifth Avenue, New York, NY 10022. You may also wish to contact the Embassy of Spain, 2375 Pennsylvania Avenue NW, Washington, DC 20037.

A *Culturgram* is a product of native commentary and original, expert analysis. Statistics are estimates and information is presented as a matter of opinion. While the editors strive for accuracy and detail, this document should not be considered strictly factual. It is a general introduction to culture, an initial step in building bridges of understanding between peoples. It may not apply to all peoples of the nation. You should therefore consult other sources for more information.

CULTURGRAM '95

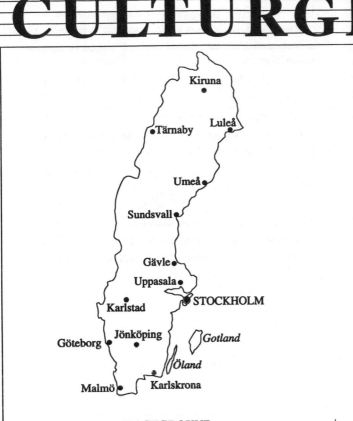

Kingdom of
Sweden

Boundary representations not necessarily authoritative.

BACKGROUND

Land and Climate

Sweden, one of the "three fingers" of Scandinavia, is just larger than the state of California. It covers 173,731 square miles (449,964 square kilometers). From the northern tip to the southern, one travels about 1,000 miles (1,610 kilometers). Thousands of tiny islands line the coast. Mountains form much of the northwest, but most of Sweden is relatively flat with some rolling hills. Many rivers flow from the mountains through the forests and into the Baltic Sea. Sweden is dotted with lakes, which, with the rivers, provide ample water for the country. Over half of Sweden is forested. North of the Arctic Circle, winters are long and relatively cold while summers are short and pleasant. But summer's "midnight sun" makes the days long. Most of Sweden, although located far to the north, has a temperate climate, moderated by the warm Gulf Stream. Sweden has many natural resources, including its hydroelectric power potential from the many waterways. Timber, silver, zinc, lead, iron ore, and copper are also important.

History

Sweden has been inhabited for nearly 5,000 years and is the home of the Gothic peoples who battled the Roman empire. In the ninth century, Rurik, a semilegendary chief of the Swedes, is said to have founded Russia. Christianity was introduced in the 11th century and adopted by the monarchy. Queen Margrethe I of Denmark united Denmark, Norway, and Sweden in the Union of Kalmar in 1397. Sweden remained fairly autonomous and even had its own parliament in 1435. It became an independent kingdom in 1523, with Gustaf I Vasa

as ruler. Wars were fought with Denmark and Russia in the 16th and 17th centuries, and by the 17th century Sweden was one of the Great Powers of Europe. It acquired Norway in 1814 through the Napoleonic Wars. Swedish power declined in the 19th century. Finland was an integral part of Sweden until 1809, when it briefly became an archdukedom of Russia. Norway became independent in 1905. The Frenchman Jean Baptiste Bernadotte was elected Sweden's crown prince in 1810 and became king in 1818 as Karl XIV Johan. His dynasty continues today.

During the 20th century, neutrality and nonalignment have been the cornerstone of Sweden's foreign policy, keeping it out of both World Wars and allowing it to transform its rather poor society into a prosperous social welfare state. The Social Democratic party dominated politics and led every government until 1976, when its rule was interrupted until 1982.

Sweden prides itself on being a peaceful, egalitarian society in which crime has been relatively low. That image was shaken in 1986 when Prime Minister Olof Palme was assassinated on the streets of Stockholm after attending a movie. And, unfortunately, crime has recently been on the rise. Palme was succeeded by Ingvar Carlsson. Faced with a declining economy, Carlsson introduced an austerity package in 1990. When it was rejected, he resigned and formed a new minority government, which he led until elections in 1991. After the elections, Carl Bildt of the Moderate Party formed a coalition government. His administration concentrated on economic challenges and Sweden's relations with Europe. Elections were set for September 1994, and Bildt was not expected to remain in power.

Copyright © 1994. Brigham Young University. Printed in the USA. All rights reserved. It is against the law to copy, reprint, store in a retrieval system, or transmit any part of this publication in any form by any means for any purpose without written permission from the Publications Division of the David M. Kennedy Center for International Studies, Brigham Young University, PO Box 24538, Provo, UT 84602–4538. *Culturgrams* are available for more than 125 areas of the world. To place an order, to receive a free catalog, or to obtain information on traveling abroad, call toll free (800) 528–6279.

THE PEOPLE

Population

Sweden has a population of 8.7 million and an annual growth rate of 0.4 percent. At least 85 percent of the people are ethnic Swedes. Finns compose about 5 percent of the population; most of them are immigrants from Finland, but some are native to northern Sweden. A small indigenous minority (up to 20,000 people), the Sámis, live in the north. Traditionally, they herded reindeer for a living. While some continue that occupation, most are involved in other fields. The Sámis are known to some as "Lapps," but this is a derogatory term and therefore not used in Sweden. Since the 1960s, many immigrants have added to Sweden's population. Today there are many foreign-born or first-generation immigrants from Yugoslavia, Greece, Turkey, and some Latin American countries, among others. Immigrants from other Scandinavian nations, such as Denmark, Finland, and Norway, also live in Sweden. Today, non-Swedes account for about 12 percent of the population.

Language

The Swedes speak Swedish, a Germanic language related to Danish, Norwegian, and Icelandic. Swedish emerged as a distinct language around the 10th century. The Sámis speak their own language and the Finnish minority speaks Finnish. Most new immigrants continue to speak their native tongue in the home. Many people speak English, which is also taught in the schools.

Religion

Sweden, like most of Europe, is a highly secular society. Freedom of religion is guaranteed by the constitution. Most Swedes (more than 90 percent) are members of the Evangelical Lutheran Church, which is supported by the state. But most of these members rarely attend church services. Membership is growing in other religious organizations. Most of these are various other Christian churches, such as the Roman Catholic faith, which has a following of about 1 percent of the population. But other groups, such as Muslims and Jews, are expanding, primarily due to the immigrant population.

General Attitudes

Swedes are somewhat more reserved than people in the United States, although that does not make them less friendly. They are very proud of their nation and its accomplishments. Local patriotism is often important. People are proud of their towns and regions. Visitors who recognize this pride are careful not to praise another area over the one being visited. Swedes value modesty and material security.

Roughly since World War II, Sweden has built one of the most egalitarian societies in the world and has managed to develop a strong capitalist economy. Swedes can rely on a generous social welfare system to provide health, education, and retirement benefits. While public sentiment in the early 1990s led to some cuts in the system, most people oppose deep changes in what is called cradle-to-grave benefits.

With the exception of the Nobel Peace Prize, which Norway sponsors, Sweden awards the Nobel prizes each year. These prizes are given to significant contributors in the areas of chemistry, literature, medicine, and physics. Alfred Bernhard Nobel (1833–96), the inventor of dynamite and a wealthy businessman, was born in Sweden.

Personal Appearance

General European fashions are common in Sweden. A cool climate prevails longer than in other European countries, so warm clothing is worn more often. The Swedes generally dress conservatively; it is important to be neat and clean in public. Swedes may not "dress up" as much as people in other countries when they go out. They prefer to avoid glamorous clothing, but they are still very fashionable. As in other Scandinavian countries, Sweden also has traditional costumes that are worn on special occasions.

CUSTOMS AND COURTESIES

Greetings

Swedes commonly shake hands upon meeting. From a distance, one may nod the head or raise the hand to greet another person. People usually address each other by their first names; titles are only used in very formal situations. More formal greetings include *God dag* (Good day) or *God morgon* (Good morning). Most people, however, are more casual and say *Hej* (pronounced "hey," meaning Hi). *Hallå* (Hello) is used when answering the phone, along with clearly identifying oneself. Good-bye is *Adjö* or, more casually, *Hej då*.

Gestures

Eye contact is important during conversation. Excessive hand gestures are avoided when speaking. It is generally considered impolite to chew gum, yawn, or have one's hands in the pockets when speaking to another person. Although it was once uncommon to see people embrace in public or put their arm around another's shoulder, the population in general is becoming more casual and such displays of friendship are increasing.

Visiting

Swedes enjoy visiting one another, but they do not often visit without prior arrangement. Guests are usually offered coffee or something else to drink. It is popular to invite friends over for an evening meal. Entertaining is most often done in the home, although going out is becoming more popular. Still, one does not usually invite someone to a restaurant instead of the home. Guests invited to dinner should arrive on time because the meal is usually served first. If the weather is bad, guests are expected to change shoes (they bring an "indoor" pair) when entering the home. An odd number of flowers or a box of chocolates is taken as a gift to the hosts. Sweets for the children are appropriate if the parents approve. Flowers are unwrapped before being presented to the hostess. If a gift is not given, guests usually send a thank-you card later in the mail. It is also customary to thank the host or hostess for their hospitality the next time the guest sees them.

During the visit, it is impolite to eat and run. Swedes expect to stay for coffee and conversation, even until as late as 11:00 P.M. Conversation, ranging over a wide variety of topics, is a popular pastime. When leaving, guests say good-bye before they put on their coats.

Eating

Swedes eat a light breakfast around 7:00 A.M. and might have a coffee or tea break at midmorning. The main meal (*middag*) was traditionally eaten at midday. This is still the case in most rural areas, but urban residents have only a light lunch at noon and then their main meal in the evening around 6:00 P.M. The continental style of eating is followed, with the fork in the left hand and the knife remaining in the right. A dinner knife is not used as a butter knife, since separate butter knives are usually provided. Hands, not elbows, are kept above the table during the meal. When a person is finished eating, the utensils are placed side by side on the plate. It is impolite to leave any food on the plate. When guests are present, they usually wait for the hosts to offer second helpings. It is not impolite to decline, but one may take more if desired. Food is placed in serving dishes on the table, so if they are empty there is usually no more food and it would be impolite to ask for more.

For some occasions, the host makes a welcome speech at the beginning of the meal. The host then makes a toast (*skål*) and all dinner guests taste the wine. The guest of honor makes a speech during the dessert, elaborating on the meal and the charm of the hostess. Each guest personally thanks the host directly after the meal.

LIFESTYLE
Family

As in many countries, the structure of the family in Sweden has changed over the years. Extended family relationships are maintained through gatherings and holiday visits. The nuclear family is the basic social unit, but it is usually strong and close knit. Most families have only one or two children. Many women work outside the home, comprising nearly half of the labor force. Young children are cared for during working hours at day care centers. Adult children are expected to be independent. Elderly individuals generally rely on the social system or themselves for their care and support.

Many urban families live in apartments, but most people in smaller towns and rural areas have single-family dwellings. Sweden is known for its red wooden houses built in the 18th and 19th centuries that still dot the countryside.

Dating and Marriage

Although serious dating is reserved for older teens, Swedes start to date very early. They enjoy going to movies, eating out, having parties, and dancing. Many people choose to live together rather than get married, or they live together for several years before getting married. Often, the couple marries when they have a child. Divorce and single parent homes are on the rise. Unmarried couples who live together have nearly the same rights and obligations as married couples. That is, cohabitation is nearly the same as marriage under the law.

Diet

The Swedish diet, as with other parts of society, has changed over the years. Health concerns have affected eating patterns in much the same way they have in other industrialized countries. Once heavy in meat, fish, and cheese, the diet now includes many fresh vegetables and fruits. Common foods include potatoes (eaten a few times a week), cheeses of many types, seafoods, and other fresh foods. For breakfast, one might eat *fil* (a kind of yogurt), *knäckebröd* (crisp bread) with margarine, and coffee. Open sandwiches (*smörgåsar*) are also popular. Some favorite main meal dishes include *Köttbullar med kokt potatis, brun sås och*

lingonsylt (meatballs with brown sauce, boiled potatoes and lingonberry jam); *Stekt falukorv med senap och potatis* (fried slices of thick German sausage with mustard and boiled or fried potatoes); and *grillad lax med spenat, citron och potatis eller ris* (grilled slices of salmon with spinach, slices of lemon, and potatoes or rice).

The *smörgåsbord* is a lavish buffet eaten on special occasions or at parties. It is not an everyday meal. A *smörgåsbord* includes warm and cold dishes, meat, fish, and desserts. Many families have a special type of *smörgåsbord* on Christmas Eve.

Recreation

Swedes are sports enthusiasts. Soccer, skiing, tennis, golf, swimming, ice hockey, and bandy are all popular. Sweden's national soccer team competed in the 1994 World Cup. Bandy is a game related to hockey and believed to be its prototype. Skating and other winter sports are common. Even more popular than sports are activities such as hiking, fishing, bird watching, and orienteering (using a map and compass to cross an area). The Swedes love nature and spend as much time as possible involved in it. For many, the ideal is owning a summer cottage for weekends and vacations. Sweden's mountains and fells are popular destinations. Favorite leisure activities also include reading, attending cultural events such as the theater or concerts, and watching movies and television. Most people have a great interest in music, whether modern or traditional. Singing in choirs is by far Sweden's most popular hobby, with 1.5 million participants.

Holidays

Sweden's national holidays include New Year's Day, May Day (1 May), and National Day (6 June). There are, of course, many other holidays, often associated with the season or a religious event. In late June, usually around the 24th, when the summer days are much longer than the nights, *Midsommar* (Midsummer) celebrations are held, including dancing around the maypole and having picnics. At *Påsk* (Easter), children dress up like old witches with brooms and go door to door (among friends and neighbors only) to collect candy. Colored Easter eggs are also common at this time.

In contrast to the *Midsommar* celebrations, *Lucia* coincides with the longest night of the year. On the morning of 13 December, a girl in the family assumes the role of St. Lucia (the "light queen") and dresses in white with a crown of candles in her hair. She sings the family a special song and serves them coffee and *lussekatter* (Lucia cats), a type of roll. This often marks the beginning of *Jul* (Christmas) celebrations. The climax is Christmas Eve, when a family *smörgåsbord* is accompanied by gift giving. The *Jultomte* (the Swedish Santa Claus, but once the Christmas gnome that lived under the house) brings gifts to the door for the children. A Christmas tree is only placed in the house a couple of days before Christmas Eve. Christmas Day is spent relaxing, while 26 December is for visiting family and friends.

Commerce

Business hours generally run from 9:00 A.M. to 5:00 P.M., with some variations. For example, many businesses (but not shops) close by 4:00 P.M. in the summer. Banks usually close at 3:00 P.M. People buy their food and other goods from supermarkets and department stores, as well as smaller neighborhood shops. Open air markets are open in some places; they usually only sell fresh produce.

Swedish workers enjoy one of the shortest workweeks in the industrialized world. They also enjoy at least five weeks of vacation each year, as well as other benefits. Some benefits were recently cut to reverse a trend toward lower productivity and absenteeism.

SOCIETY
Government

Sweden is a constitutional monarchy. King Carl XVI Gustaf, a descendant of the Bernadotte dynasty, has ruled since 1973. His duties are mostly ceremonial. The head of government is the prime minister. Members of parliament (*Riksdag*) are elected for three-year terms. Municipal councils handle local affairs. The voting age is 18. Immigrants must reside in the country three years before they can vote in local elections. Citizenship is required to vote in national elections.

Economy

Sweden has one of the most prosperous economies in the world. It is highly industrialized, has a modern distribution system, and boasts a skilled and educated labor force. About 5 percent of the work force is engaged in agriculture, while 22 percent labors in mining and manufacturing. Sweden is a major producer of automobiles (such as Volvo and Saab) and also exports machinery and steel products. Timber exports (mostly pulp for paper products) are also important.

The economy usually grows by about 2 percent per year, but growth in 1992 was minimal. Like many countries, Sweden suffered from the global recession of the early 1990s. The economy is recovering and unemployment (6 percent in 1992) is declining. About half of all unemployed participate in government retraining programs. The country's Human Development Index (0.977) ranks it fifth out of 173 countries. Real gross domestic product per capita is $17,014. Sweden's ranking is based less on gross domestic product than on its social welfare system that provides for nearly everyone's needs. It has, however, been under pressure because of the high cost of living. Income tax is used to fund the system. When the rate peaked at 70 percent in 1989, society began calling for private alternatives and other changes. Taxes were lowered in 1991 to 51 percent, and several cuts were made to encourage greater productivity and reduce overall cost. The challenge for the future is for the government to stimulate growth, be globally competitive, and preserve the key elements of the social welfare system.

Sweden's political leaders favor joining the European Union, but voter sentiment may not agree. A referendum in the fall of 1994 will decide the issue. Membership would require further changes in Sweden's system, but would also provide greater opportunities for trade. Sweden's currency is the Swedish *krona* (SKr).

Transportation and Communication

In Sweden, only one in four households does not own a car. Although private cars provide important transportation, public transport is well developed and frequently used. Trains, buses, subways, and streetcars are common. There are three international airports. Most roads are paved and in good condition. The telecommunications system is excellent and highly developed. Numerous newspapers and radio stations serve the country. The Swedish Broadcasting Corporation, which used to have a legal monopoly on television broadcasting, is now facing competition from other broadcasters. Cable and satellite television are available.

Education

Illiteracy is virtually unknown in Sweden. The Swedish government spends more money per pupil than most other countries. The public school system is a comprehensive nine-year program that children begin at age seven. All education is free and one free hot meal is provided each day. Immigrant children have the right to some instruction in their native language. When compulsory education ends at age 16, students have several choices. About one-fifth start working. The others choose between a three-year high school, with either a social science or theoretical natural focus, and a three-year vocational school.

There are more than 30 institutions of higher learning. Tuition is free and loans are available for living costs. There is also an extensive adult education program.

Health

All Swedes are covered by a national health insurance. Nearly all fees incurred for medical care are paid by the government. Day care costs are covered to at least 85 percent. Dental fees are shared by the individual. While basic health care is covered, elective surgery must often wait several months before being approved. In response to public demand, private health care options are now more widely available, as are private child care facilities. The government pays an ill person's wages for an extended period. Parents share a total of 12 months leave when a child is born. The infant mortality rate is one of the lowest in the world at 6 per 1,000. Swedes can expect to live between 75 and 81 years.

FOR THE TRAVELER

While passports are required, U.S. citizens do not need visas for visits of up to three months total time in Scandinavia—Denmark, Iceland, Finland, Norway, and Sweden. No vaccinations are needed. Warm clothing is advised for winter months. Sweden offers a number of vacation opportunities, from outdoor recreation to resorts and beautiful scenery. The tourist industry is well developed and plenty of printed material is available to assist the traveler. For more information, contact the Swedish Tourist Board (655 Third Avenue, New York, NY 10017). You may also wish to contact the Embassy of Sweden, 1501 M Street NW, Washington, DC 20005. Also, the Swedish Institute publishes a variety of information brochures. Contact the Swedish Information Service (One Dag Hammarskjold Plaza, 45th Floor, New York, NY 10017–2201) or the Swedish Institute (Box 7434, S–10391 Stockholm, Sweden).

A *Culturgram* is a product of native commentary and original, expert analysis. Statistics are estimates and information is presented as a matter of opinion. While the editors strive for accuracy and detail, this document should not be considered strictly factual. It is a general introduction to culture, an initial step in building bridges of understanding between peoples. It may not apply to all peoples of the nation. You should therefore consult other sources for more information.

CULTURGRAM '95™

Switzerland

(Swiss Confederation)

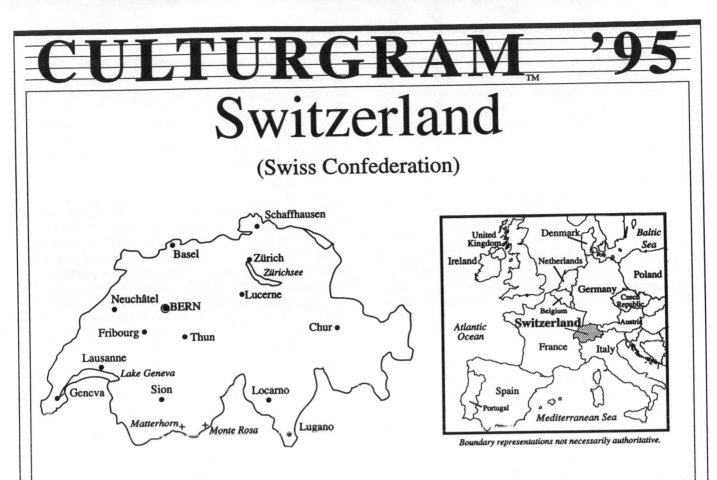

Boundary representations not necessarily authoritative.

BACKGROUND

Land and Climate

Covering 15,942 square miles (41,290 square kilometers), Switzerland is just smaller than Denmark or a bit more than twice as large as New Jersey. The country is landlocked and shares borders with France, Germany, Austria, and Italy. Switzerland is sometimes called the "roof of Europe" because of its towering Alps. When people from other countries wish to describe scenic beauty, they often use Switzerland as a standard. It is truly one of the most beautiful places on earth. The Alps cover over half of the country, running east to west. The Jura mountains (running north to south in the west near Geneva) cover another 10 percent of the territory. Green valleys are interspersed throughout the mountains. Swiss waters drain into five key European rivers: the Rhine, Rhône, Po, Adige, and Danube. The highest mountain peaks include Monte Rosa (15,209 feet or 4,635 meters) and the Matterhorn (14,691 feet or 4,478 meters). While the climate varies according to elevation and region, it is generally temperate. Winters can be long and snowy, while summers are mild.

History

The Celtic tribes that occupied the area of present-day Switzerland were part of the Roman Empire for five centuries. Later, Burgundian tribes settled in the west and Alemannians in the east; both were Germanic tribes, but they developed along different lines. During most of the Middle Ages, Switzerland was part of the Holy Roman Empire.

The founding of the Swiss Confederation took place on 1 August 1291, when the three mountain cantons of Uri, Schwyz, and Unterwalden began a revolt against Austrian Habsburg control by signing the Perpetual Covenant of 1291. Through a series of military victories, Swiss soldiers gained a reputation for their fighting prowess. Later, by adding other cantons (Luzern, Zürich, Bern), the confederation grew more powerful. After withstanding the turmoil and war of the 16th and early 17th centuries, Switzerland received official recognition as an independent nation in the 1648 Treaty of Westphalia.

In 1815, because of a brief invasion by Napoleon, Switzerland became permanently neutral. Early in the 19th century, the Swiss proclaimed the Helvetic Republic—*Helvetia*—and Switzerland became a centralized nation-state. In 1848, it adopted a constitution, making it a federal state. In 1874, direct democracy by the people became an integral part of the constitution. During the 19th century, Switzerland became industrialized and urbanized. While other neutral European nations fell to attacking armies during World Wars I and II, Switzerland, aided by natural geography, remained neutral and was not invaded.

EUROPE

Copyright © 1994. Brigham Young University. Printed in the USA. All rights reserved. It is against the law to copy, reprint, store in a retrieval system, or transmit any part of this publication in any form by any means for any purpose without written permission from the Publications Division of the David M. Kennedy Center for International Studies, Brigham Young University, PO Box 24538, Provo, UT 84602–4538. *Culturgrams* are available for more than 125 areas of the world. To place an order, to receive a free catalog, or to obtain information on traveling abroad, call toll free (800) 528–6279.

As part of its neutrality, the Swiss Federation is not presently a member of the United Nations (it has observer status), the North Atlantic Treaty Organization (NATO), or the European Union (EU). Still, it has solid relations with many nations. In August 1991, the Swiss celebrated their 700th anniversary as a confederation. The anniversary gave the Swiss cause to honor their nation as one of the world's oldest democracies.

THE PEOPLE

Population

The population of Switzerland is about 6.9 million and is growing at 0.8 percent annually. Switzerland is made up of a variety of ethnic groups. In the east and central cantons, Germans dominate and account for 65 percent of the total population. The French are located mostly in the west and comprise 18 percent of the population. In parts of the south, most people are of Italian descent and make up 10 percent of the total. One percent of the population has Romansch ancestry. Currently living in Switzerland are many peoples (6 percent of the population) from different lands: the former Yugoslavia, Spain, Greece, Italy, some Middle Eastern nations, and a variety of others. Most of them are guest workers and do not have Swiss citizenship.

Language

Four official languages are spoken in Switzerland: German, French, Italian, and Romansch. Each canton has the right to declare which language it will use. All street signs are in that language only. In the schools, all the languages are available for study, but the language of instruction is that of the canton. Most Swiss can understand at least one of the other official languages of the confederation, and many speak English, which is also offered in the schools. Although French and Italian are basically spoken as written, there is a difference between written German (standard German) and what is spoken every day by the German Swiss. Their dialect (*Schweizerdeutsch*) is rather unique and difficult for other German-speaking peoples to understand. Protection of minority languages and relations between the different language groups continue to be important political issues the confederation must address.

Religion

Close to half of the people are Roman Catholic and the other half belong to various other Christian churches, mostly Protestant. There is a small Jewish minority (0.3 percent of the population). Switzerland is a secular society and participation in religion is often reserved for special events and holidays. Switzerland was the center of the Zwingli and Calvin Protestant Reformations of the 16th century and has produced important modern theologians. Swiss Protestant churches are locally controlled and democratic. Both Catholic and Protestant churches have generally worked toward greater harmony. As elsewhere in Europe, religion has greater influence in rural areas than in the cities.

General Attitudes

The Swiss have a high regard for nature and beauty, and they are proud of their efforts to protect the environment. Their attitudes have been influenced by the majestic mountains and beautiful lakes found throughout Switzerland. The Swiss also value hard work, sobriety, thrift, and independence. They prize tolerance, punctuality, and a sense of responsibility. A favorite saying claims that if people are late, they are either not wearing Swiss watches or are not riding Swiss trains. The Swiss are proud of their unique system. For example, every physically fit male serves in the Swiss Army. They train on occasion and keep their gun and uniform at home—always ready to form a militia to defend the country. There are only a few professional officers; most are part-time. While this structure has been recently challenged, it remains intact. The Swiss are politically neutral and sponsor the International Red Cross. Another key to Switzerland's strength is the federal system that unites different groups into one country. The motto is "Unity, yes; uniformity, no."

Switzerland's self-confidence has been affected by changes in Europe, social problems, and a debate over immigration. When certain elements of society supported joining the EU's European Economic Area, the voters rejected the proposal through a national referendum. Many feel this will isolate Switzerland from the future course of Europe's economy. In another referendum, voters also banned heavy truck traffic from its roads, effectively causing large transportation problems for other European nations. For the future, the Swiss may have to redefine their role in Europe and determine how best to adapt their grass-roots form of democracy to the 21st century. This is a challenging task to face because of intense national pride in the Swiss way of life.

Personal Appearance

The Swiss place a high value on cleanliness, neatness, and orderliness. People dress conservatively and well. Overly casual or grubby attire in public is frowned upon. The Swiss wear modern European fashions but also have traditional costumes that are worn on special occasions.

CUSTOMS AND COURTESIES

Greetings

A handshake is appropriate for men and women. Waving to someone across the street is also acceptable. When entering an elevator or a store, most Swiss exchange simple greetings, even among strangers. Because the Swiss Confederation is a multilingual society, actual verbal greetings vary. They also vary according to the time of day and the situation. It is most polite to address another person by their title and surname. Although the youth use first names, adults generally reserve first names for close friends and family members. While the Swiss appreciate foreign visitors who speak (or try to speak) the language of the area they are in, most also understand English greetings.

Gestures

Chewing gum or cleaning one's fingernails in public is not appropriate. Talking to an older person with one's hands in the pockets is disrespectful. Legs are crossed with one knee over the other and are not placed on a desk, chair, or table. Pointing the index finger to one's own head to indicate a person is crazy may be considered a serious insult by some.

Visiting

The Swiss are hospitable to guests, and expect courtesy in return. Visits are generally arranged in advance. It is polite for guests to wipe their feet before entering the home. Visitors often bring candy or flowers to the hosts, especially if visiting for the first time. Flowers are generally presented in odd numbers and are unwrapped before being given to the hosts. Red roses are only given to signify romantic love. When leaving a home, it is customary to shake hands with all members of the family or group.

Eating

In the home, a family waits to begin eating until one of the parents begins. The continental style of eating is followed, with the fork in the left hand and the knife remaining in the right. Soft foods, such as potatoes, are cut with a fork, not a knife. Cutting such foods with a knife implies they are improperly cooked. The best compliment one can give is to take additional helpings. It is often considered an insult if someone asks for salt or pepper because it implies the food is improperly spiced. When a person is finished eating, the utensils are placed side by side on the plate. If they are placed another way, it may mean the person wants to eat more. During a meal, hands (not elbows) are always kept above the table. In restaurants, service charges are usually included in the bill, which is paid at the table.

LIFESTYLE

Family

The nuclear family is the most important social unit in Swiss society. Families are generally small, with only one or two children. The man is traditionally the head of the household. Family privacy is very important. Women often work outside the home, although to a lesser extent than in many other European countries. About 37 percent of the workforce is female. Parliamentary representation among women is also lower than elsewhere in Europe. Only in 1971 did women receive the right to vote in national elections and in most cantons. By 1990, only the Appenzell canton of Inner-Rhoden continued to deny women the right to vote on local issues.

Dating and Marriage

Young people often socialize in groups as early as age 14; they begin dating a few years later. The legal age for marriage is 18 for women and 20 for men. Most adults marry in their mid- to late twenties. Many couples prefer to live together for several years before getting married or instead of marriage. It is often important to finish one's education or to become financially established before getting married.

Diet

With so many ethnic backgrounds in the country, the Swiss diet is diverse. There are numerous regional specialties, including various sausages, leek soup, rich cheeses, fish, special wines, and pork. Breakfast is usually light and might include various types of fresh breads, cheeses, and coffee. The main meal of the day is traditionally at midday and usually consists of a main dish with meat and some form of potatoes or pasta and salad. A light dinner is served between 6:00 and 7:00 P.M.; it often consists of open-faced sandwiches. In major urban areas, the trend is to have the main meal in the evening.

Recreation

The Swiss enjoy vacationing, either within their own country or abroad. They love nature and the outdoors and enjoy hiking, skiing, and other such activities. Mountain climbing is a favorite for some. Soccer and cycling are the most popular sports. Switzerland competed in the 1994 World Cup. A small number of Swiss also enjoy traditional games unique to Switzerland. For example, a type of wrestling (*Schwinger*) is found in some areas. It is similar to Graeco-Roman wrestling but does not have weight classifications. The Swiss enjoy taking walks, watching movies, and attending cultural events.

Holidays

The most important holidays in Switzerland include New Year's Day, Easter (Friday through Monday), Labor Day (1 May), Ascension, Whit Sunday and Whit Monday, National Day (1 August), Federal Day of Prayers (a thanksgiving holiday in mid-September), and Christmas. Christmas is the biggest celebration of the year. Gifts are exchanged on Christmas Eve, when the family gathers for a large meal. The family relaxes on Christmas Day and visits friends on 26 December. New Year's Eve is a time for parties and fireworks.

Commerce

In general, business hours are from 8:00 A.M. to noon and from 2:00 to 6:00 P.M., Monday through Friday, although large stores do not close at midday. Some stores remain open later in the evening on certain nights, and hours vary between the different cantons.

SOCIETY

Government

Switzerland is a highly decentralized federal state with most political power residing in the 26 cantons, as well as local communities. Constitutional amendments can be initiated by a "popular initiative," and virtually all important legislation is subject to popular referendums. Each community has its own constitution and laws but is under the supervision of the canton. Each canton also has its own constitution and has control over such things as school systems, police, welfare, and local issues. At these two levels, decisions are made by the people.

At the federal level, democracy becomes representative. The Federal Assembly has two houses, one with representatives of the people (National Council) and one with representatives of the cantons (Council of States). The members are directly elected. Elections for the National Council were last held in October 1991. The next are in 1995. A Federal Council constitutes the executive branch; it has seven members elected to a four-year term by the Federal Assembly. Each year, the council selects one council member to serves as its president. That person is then technically the president of Switzerland for a calendar year because that is the highest office in the land. A vice president is also chosen for a year. The federal government is responsible for foreign policy and matters affecting all cantons.

Economy

Despite a lack of natural resources, Switzerland has one of the strongest economies in the world. It has the highest gross national product (GNP) per capita in the world (US$32,250), although not in terms of actual purchasing power. With the high cost of living, the real GNP per capita is $20,874. That is, however, second only to the United States. Switzerland's Human Development Index (0.978) ranks it fourth out of 173 nations. These figures reflect an economy with low unemployment, low inflation, high standards of performance, and a strong middle class. Poverty is nearly nonexistent.

Switzerland is known as the banking and finance capital of the world. Its finance industry has fueled economic success. Tourism is an important part of the economy, as is industrial production. The Swiss not only produce fine watches and cheeses, but also machinery, chemicals, textiles, and various precision instruments. They are known for their excellent quality and craftsmanship. Switzerland donates money to various development projects around the world. The currency is the Swiss *franc* (SFr).

Education

Education is the responsibility of the individual cantons. Although there are differences between the systems, similarities can be found. Education is free and compulsory for eight or nine years, usually ending at age sixteen. There are three basic levels: primary, secondary, and high school *(gymnasia)*. The high schools provide preparation for a university education. Many students choose to enter a vocational school after their secondary education. The literacy rate is 99 percent. There are a number of private schools, in addition to the state schools. Seven cantonal universities, two federal institutes of technology, a college of education, and a university for economic and social sciences serve more than 70,000 students. Many students also travel abroad for advanced training.

Transportation and Communication

Due to Switzerland's small land area and high population density, the country has a very well-developed public transportation system. Buses, streetcars, and trains form the backbone of the transportation network. Still, most families have cars and private transport is common. Like the transportation network, communication facilities are excellent and completely modern.

Health

Both private and public hospitals exist. Medical facilities and personnel are well trained and offer efficient care. While the government provides for such things as old-age benefits and social welfare, it does not have a uniform system of health insurance. Each canton has different laws regarding insurance, but most people must purchase private insurance. The infant mortality rate is 6 per 1,000. Life expectancy ranges from 76 to 83 years.

FOR THE TRAVELER

U.S. travelers do not need visas for stays of up to three months, but a valid passport is required. No vaccinations are necessary. Switzerland is a popular tourist destination and offers a wide variety of attractions and activities. The Swiss National Tourist Office produces a number of brochures for tourists, provides discount tickets for public transportation, and has ideas for travel itineraries. They have three offices in the United States: 222 North Sepulveda Boulevard, Suite 1570, El Segundo, CA 90245; 150 North Michigan Avenue, Suite 2930, Chicago, IL 60601; and 608 Fifth Avenue, New York, NY 10020. You may also wish to contact the Embassy of Switzerland, 2900 Cathedral Avenue NW, Washington, DC 20008, or one of several consulates.

A *Culturgram* is a product of native commentary and original, expert analysis. Statistics are estimates and information is presented as a matter of opinion. While the editors strive for accuracy and detail, this document should not be considered strictly factual. It is a general introduction to culture, an initial step in building bridges of understanding between peoples. It may not apply to all peoples of the nation. You should therefore consult other sources for more information.

CULTURGRAM™ '95

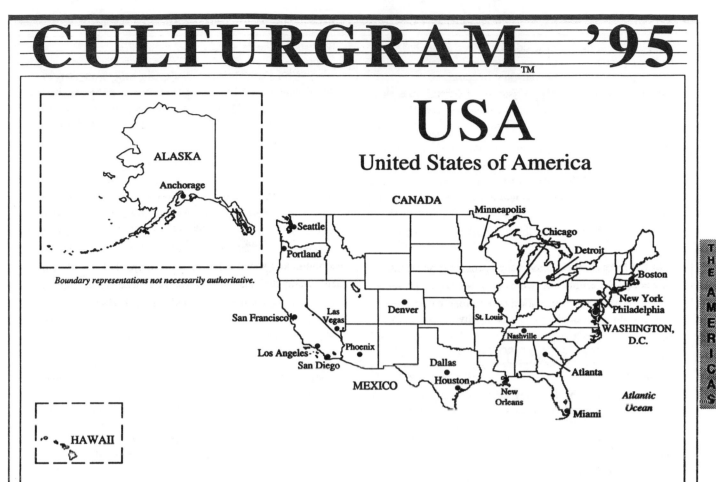

USA
United States of America

ALASKA
Anchorage

Boundary representations not necessarily authoritative.

HAWAII

CANADA

Seattle
Portland
San Francisco
Los Angeles
San Diego
Las Vegas
Phoenix
Denver
Minneapolis
Chicago
Detroit
Boston
New York
Philadelphia
WASHINGTON, D.C.
St. Louis
Nashville
Dallas
Houston
New Orleans
Atlanta
Miami
MEXICO
Atlantic Ocean

THE AMERICAS

BACKGROUND

Land and Climate

The United States covers the central portion of North America and includes Alaska and Hawaii. Covering 3,618,765 square miles (9,372,610 square kilometers), it is the fourth largest country in the world. Because of its size and location, the United States experiences many different climates and has a variety of geographical features. Large mountains, vast deserts, wide canyons, extensive coasts, subtropical forests, wetlands, rolling hills, prairies, frozen tundra, and more features can be found. Beyond the beaches and mountains of California, the Rocky Mountains in the west give way to a vast central plain, which merges with the rolling hills and low mountains of the east. Hawaii's rugged, volcanic topography is lush and green year round. Alaska has towering mountains, broad valleys, glaciers, and a varied landscape. Climates throughout the country are as varied as the terrain. Natural resources include coal, copper, lead, uranium, bauxite, gold, phosphate, iron, mercury, nickel, silver, petroleum, natural gas, timber and much more. Natural disasters such as floods, hurricanes, tornadoes, earthquakes, and severe winter storms impact various regions.

History

North America's history before Europeans arrived is incomplete, but the original inhabitants had advanced civilizations. From the 17th century on, Native Americans were displaced by European settlers who had come for riches, territory, and a new world. British colonies (the Thirteen Colonies) were established on the east coast of North America. The American Revolution of 1776 led to independence from Britain and a loose confederation of states. The Constitution of 1787 established the basic form of government as it exists today. Explorers and pioneers headed west and settled large areas of land. The United States acquired territory from France, Mexico, and Spain throughout the 19th century, expanding its borders from the Atlantic Ocean to the Pacific.

In 1861, civil war broke out between Union states in the north and Confederate states in the south over issues of slavery, secession, and economic differences. Union forces, under President Abraham Lincoln, defeated the Confederates in 1865 and reunited the country.

Although American troops were only involved in the last year of World War I, the United States was a major combatant in World War II, from which it emerged as the strongest economic and military power in the world. It became a major donor of financial aid and technological assistance to developing countries and spread American values and ideals throughout the world (which were not always welcome). In the 1970s, after the U.S. defeat in Vietnam, American prominence declined. This trend seemed to reverse toward the beginning of the 1990s, and, in 1991, the United States led a coalition of nations against Iraq in the Gulf War. Since 1991, the United States has been a key sponsor of the Middle East Peace Conference. It is an active member of the United Nations and

Copyright © 1994. Brigham Young University. Printed in the USA. All rights reserved. It is against the law to copy, reprint, store in a retrieval system, or transmit any part of this publication in any form by any means for any purpose without written permission from the Publications Division of the David M. Kennedy Center for International Studies, Brigham Young University, PO Box 24538, Provo, UT 84602–4538. *Culturgrams* are available for more than 125 areas of the world. To place an order, to receive a free catalog, or to obtain information on traveling abroad, call toll free (800) 528–6279.

a key donor of international aid. The United States has always had free elections to determine its leadership, and it considers itself a guardian of democracy and freedom.

THE PEOPLE

Population

The population of the United States (about 258 million) is the third largest in the world, following China and India. Eighty percent of America's population is white, which includes people of European, Middle Eastern, and Hispanic origins. Other racial groups include African Americans (12 percent), Asians (3 percent), and Native Americans (1 percent). As a minority, Hispanics, which can be of any race, comprise 9 percent of the total population. "Hispanic" is an artificial government term not always accepted by members of that diverse group. Most Hispanics (or Latinos) prefer to be called by their country of origin (e.g., Mexican-American). The term Hispanic is only used here to identify a group that consists of many peoples otherwise too diverse to list. Indeed, all designated minority groups are represented by many smaller groups with origins in nearly every country around the world. Primarily because of immigration, Asians are the fastest-growing minority.

Although members of any ethnic group can be found anywhere in the country, the mixture is not the same in every region. For example, California's population is only 57 percent white, while New Hampshire's is 98 percent. Hispanics reside mostly in the west and southwest, while African Americans are found mostly in the east and southeast. More than 60 percent of the people in Hawaii are Asians. Whites commonly live in rural and suburban areas, while minorities tend to live in large urban areas. Nearly 80 percent of all Americans live in metropolitan areas. "American" is the term most often used to describe a citizen or product of the United States, even outside of the country.

Language

English is the predominant language of the United States and is spoken by most citizens. The English spoken in the United States is referred to in other English-speaking nations as "American English." It is characterized by spelling and pronunciation variations from "British English," as well as unique idioms. Spoken English is very flexible, while written communication is more formal and standardized. Many first, second, or even third-generation immigrants also speak their native tongue. In fact, one in seven Americans speaks a language other than English in the home. Spanish is spoken in many Hispanic communities. Native Americans speak a variety of Amerindian languages.

Religion

Although the United States has never had an official state church, about 90 percent of the population has some religious affiliation. Most of these people (86 percent) are Christians. As the early European settlers were mostly Christian, the Constitution and the Bill of Rights are based, in part, on Christian values and principles. The Constitution, however, dictates that church and state remain separate. There are dozens of different Christian churches throughout the country. About 26 percent of the population is Roman Catholic.

Baptists, Methodists, and Lutherans are the largest Protestant groups. Between 40 and 55 percent of Christians attend services on a weekly basis. Jews, Muslims, Buddhists, and other non-Christians also have substantial memberships in the United States. Religion is generally a personal matter for Americans, but those with an active interest in religion often discuss their beliefs with others.

General Attitudes

Americans are frank and outspoken. They openly voice their opinions and share their views on a variety of subjects. In general, they appreciate people who are candid. There are few subjects that an American will not discuss. Of course, there are variations, and religious values may keep some from discussing certain issues. Extremely personal questions are avoided by those who are not close friends. Americans value innovation, industry, and integrity. They enjoy a good sense of humor, including sarcasm. Americans have the ability to laugh at themselves as well as at others. They are proud of their country. Even though they may criticize the government, most are patriotic and believe the United States is one of the greatest countries in the world. Americans strongly value their freedom and independence, both as a nation and as individuals. Individualism, as opposed to conformity, is often cited as an American characteristic. Even when working as a team, Americans usually think in terms of several distinct individuals blending their efforts rather than a group working as one unit.

Personal Appearance

Clothing habits are a matter of personal preference in the United States. Although fashion trends affect general clothing patterns, a person usually feels free to wear whatever he or she pleases. Americans emphasize cleanliness, but they may purposely wear tattered clothing or casual attire in public. Clothing is often used to make a social or personal statement. Nevertheless, formal clothing is popular and is worn for certain social occasions. Appearance, in general, is important to the individual American.

CUSTOMS AND COURTESIES

Greetings

Both men and women usually smile and shake hands when greeting. The American handshake is often firm. Good friends and family members may embrace when they meet, especially after a long absence. In casual situations, a wave may be used instead of a handshake. Friends also often wave to each other at a distance, and Americans may greet strangers on the street saying *Hello* or *Good morning*, although they may pass by without any greeting. Among the youth, verbal greetings or various hand-slapping gestures (such as the "high five") are common. Except in formal situations, people address one another by their given names once acquainted. Combining a title (Mrs., Dr., Miss, for example) with a family name shows respect. When greeting someone for the first time, Americans commonly say *Pleased to meet you* or *How do you do?* A simple *Hello* or *Hi* is also common. There are regional variations such as *Aloha* in Hawaii or *Howdy* in parts of the West. Friends often greet each other with *How are you?* and respond *Fine, thanks*. Americans do not really expect any further answer to the question.

Gestures

Americans do not stand close when conversing; there are generally about two feet between individuals. However, they may spontaneously touch one another on the arm or shoulder during conversation. It is common for members of the opposite sex to hold hands or show affection in public. To point, a person extends the index finger. Beckoning is done by waving all fingers (or the index finger) with the palm facing up. Direct eye contact is not necessary for the duration of a conversation, but moments of eye contact are essential to ensure one's sincerity. When sitting, Americans are casual, and may prop their feet up on chairs or place the ankle of one leg on the knee of the other. Crossing legs at the knee is just as common as sitting with legs spread apart. Poor posture is not appropriate, but is not uncommon.

Visiting

Although Americans are informal, they are generally conscious of time. Appointments are expected to begin promptly. Guests invited to a home for dinner should arrive on time because the meal is often served first. Hospitality takes on many forms: a formal dinner served on fine dishes, an outdoor barbecue with paper plates, or a leisurely visit with no refreshments. Most events are casual. Guests are expected to feel comfortable, to sit where they like, and to enjoy themselves. Gifts are not expected when visiting, but a small token such as wine, flowers, or a handicraft might be appreciated. Among close friends, dinner guests may be asked to bring a food item to serve with the meal. Americans enjoy socializing; they gather in small and large groups for nearly any occasion, and they enjoy talking, watching television or a movie, eating, and relaxing together.

Eating

Eating styles and habits vary between people of different backgrounds, but Americans generally eat with the fork in the hand with which they write. A knife is used for cutting and spreading. Otherwise it is laid on the plate or table. When a knife is used, the fork is switched to the other hand. Bread is often used to push food onto the fork. Some foods, such as french fries, fried chicken, hamburgers, pizza, and tacos are eaten with the hands. Napkins are generally placed in the lap. It is usually considered impolite to rest elbows on the table. Dessert, coffee, or other after-dinner refreshments are frequently served away from the dining table. Guests are expected to stay for a while after the meal to visit with the hosts. In restaurants, a service charge is usually not included in the bill, and it is customary to leave at least a 15 percent tip.

LIFESTYLE

Family

The American family is the basic unit of society, but it has been changing. A generation ago, the average family consisted of a mother, father, and two or more children. The nuclear family often maintained important ties to members of the extended family. Today, the *traditional* American family consists of a mother, father, and one or two children, but this only accounts for about one-fourth of all households. *Nontraditional* family structures are more common, including families with a single parent, or unmarried couples with or without children. One out of every four children is born out of wedlock. Children may live with or be cared for by grandparents, especially if the parent is young and not married. More than half of all households have no children.

Nearly half of all working Americans are women. In homes where both the husband and wife work, men are expected to share household duties. Men also play a greater role in raising children. With both parents working, the use of and need for day-care facilities is increasing. This is especially true for single-parent families. Elderly individuals who cannot care for themselves live in retirement communities or other institutions; many live with their adult children. Otherwise, the elderly live in their own homes and comprise a rapidly expanding segment of the population. Over half of all young, unmarried adults (aged 18 to 24) live with their parents. The American family is mobile. It is common to move from one region of the country to another for education, employment, or a change in living conditions.

Dating and Marriage

Dating is a social pastime in the United States. Youth may begin to date as couples as early as age 13, although group activities are more common at that age. More serious dating begins around age 15. Going to movies, dancing, having picnics, participating in sports, or eating out are all popular activities. Casual sexual relationships are common. Many couples choose to live together before or instead of marriage. Still, marriage is the most preferred living arrangement. Weddings can be either lavish or simple, depending on the region and one's religious affiliation. The age for marriage averages 26 for men and 24 for women.

Diet

The abundance of fast-food restaurants in the United States seems to indicate that the national foods are hamburgers, french fries, pizza, and chicken. While these foods are popular among most segments of the population, they reflect a busy life-style as much as preference, and it would be difficult to name a national dish. Americans eat beef, pork, chicken, and other fowl in fairly large quantities, although eating habits have changed with health concerns. Fresh vegetables and fruits are available year-round. Americans consume large amounts of candy, ice cream, and other sweets. Most Americans will readily try any food, and the culture easily adapts to new tastes.

Recreation

Baseball, basketball, and American football are the most popular spectator and participation sports. Public schools provide team sports for the youth. Professional sports are an important part of the culture. Americans also enjoy soccer, cycling, racquetball, handball, tennis, swimming, golf, bowling, jogging, and aerobic exercising. Leisure activities include watching television, going to movies, picnicking, attending music concerts, and traveling.

Holidays

Each state has its own public holidays and each city may have celebrations. National public holidays include New Year's Day, Martin Luther King, Jr.'s Birthday (third Monday in January), President's Day (third Monday in February), Memorial Day (last Monday in May), Independence Day

(4 July), Labor Day (first Monday in September), Columbus Day (second Monday in October), Veterans Day (11 November), Thanksgiving (fourth Thursday in November), and Christmas. Although they are not holidays, other observances include: Ground Hog Day (2 February), Valentine's Day (14 February), St. Patrick's Day (17 March), Easter, Mother's Day (second Sunday in May), Father's Day (third Sunday in June), Flag Day (14 June), Halloween (31 October), and others.

Commerce

Business office hours usually extend from 8:00 or 9:00 A.M. to 5:00 or 6:00 P.M. Retail and grocery stores, however, often remain open until 9:00 P.M. and many are open twenty-four hours a day, seven days a week. Suburban Americans shop for groceries and other goods in supermarkets, large enclosed malls with department and specialty stores, smaller open-air "strip" malls that feature specialty shops, and chain discount stores. Urban residents shop in many of the same stores, but might also buy goods at small neighborhood grocery stores or shops that are part of large office or apartment buildings.

SOCIETY

Government

The government is a federal system. Individual states hold sovereignty over their territory and have rights that are not reserved by the federal government. Each state has its own legislature for enacting local laws. The federal government has a president (Bill Clinton), elected by an electoral college of delegates chosen to represent the vote of the people in each state. The bicameral legislature has two houses: the House of Representatives, whose members serve two-year terms; and the Senate, whose members serve six-year terms. There is a separate judicial branch. The voting age is 18.

Economy

The United States has the largest economy in the world, although it does not have the strongest growth rate or the highest Human Development Index (0.976), which ranks it sixth out of 173 countries. Real gross domestic product per capita is $21,449, which is the highest in the world. These figures indicate that the average American has greater buying power than people in other countries, but that certain social benefits (health care and employment) are not as accessible. Hence, while American society as a whole is prosperous, there is a widening gap between the wealthy and the poor, and even between those who earn a comfortable income and those who strive to meet basic needs.

The country's economic strength is based on diversified industrial and services sectors, investments abroad, the dollar as a major world currency, a demand-driven consumer society, and exports. The services sector employs more people than manufacturing, but industry is still the most vital part of the economy. The United States exports capital goods, cars, consumer goods, food, and machinery. It also exports pop culture (movies, music, television programming, fashion trends, and more), which can fuel demand for American goods. The United States is a key world financial center, and its economic fortunes affect global markets and international economic growth. The currency is the U.S. dollar ($).

Transportation and Communication

The United States has an extensive network of paved highways and the private car is the chief form of transportation. In large cities, urban mass-transit systems are common. In many areas, however, public transportation systems are not well developed. Many people travel by air, and the United States has the largest number of private airline companies in the world. Train travel is limited to short commuter distances and relatively few cross-country routes. Goods are, however, frequently transported by train. The communications network is extensive and modern. Most people have a telephone. There are literally thousands of radio and television stations in operation throughout the country, mostly privately owned. Freedom of the press is guaranteed. Although newspapers are available everywhere, only about half of the people read one every day. Others watch television for news.

Education

Education is free and compulsory for ages five through sixteen. Each state has responsibility for its own educational system. As most students are in high school at age 16, most finish their education with grade 12 at age 17 or 18. Many enter the labor force at that age or seek vocational and technical training. Others enter a university or junior college to pursue higher education degrees. The literacy rate is 98 percent, although functional illiteracy is a problem for many adults.

Health

The health problems facing Americans are different than those in some other countries in that a sedentary life-style and risky physical behavior are the two greatest causes of adult health problems. Most people must be covered by private insurance to receive medical care without paying very high prices. The health network is extensive and modern, except in some rural areas. The United States is the only industrialized country in the world without a national (public) health care system. Each state has its own regulations regarding health care, and there are some national standards as well. Public and private reform movements are changing how health care is provided and paid for. The United States is a world leader in medical research and training. The infant mortality rate is 8 per 1,000. Life expectancy ranges from 72 to 80 years.

FOR THE TRAVELER

While many Americans enjoy traveling to other countries, most vacation in the United States. Each state usually has an agency that promotes travel because tourism is important to many state economies. While people often prefer to explore the country on their own, information available from travel agencies and state travel bureaus may be valuable.

A *Culturgram* is a product of native commentary and original, expert analysis. Statistics are estimates and information is presented as a matter of opinion. While the editors strive for accuracy and detail, this document should not be considered strictly factual. It is a general introduction to culture, an initial step in building bridges of understanding between peoples. It may not apply to all peoples of the nation. You should therefore consult other sources for more information.

CULTURGRAM '95

Oriental Republic of
Uruguay

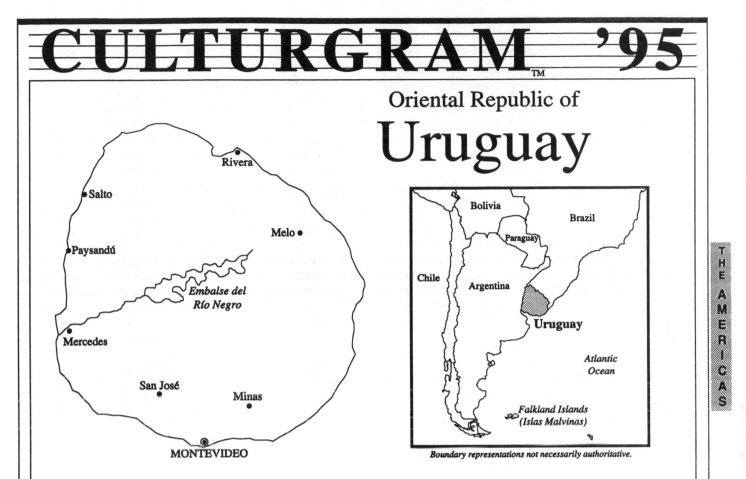

Rivera
Salto
Melo
Paysandú
Embalse del Río Negro
Mercedes
San José
Minas
MONTEVIDEO

Bolivia
Brazil
Paraguay
Chile
Argentina
Uruguay
Atlantic Ocean
Falkland Islands (Islas Malvinas)

Boundary representations not necessarily authoritative.

THE AMERICAS

BACKGROUND

Land and Climate

Uruguay is located in South America just south of Brazil and east of Argentina. Covering 68,039 square miles (176,220 square kilometers), Uruguay is about the same size as Washington state. The country is mostly rolling, lowland plains covered with prairie grass (78 percent of the territory). The pasturage provided by these plains is excellent for stock raising and agriculture. The climate is temperate and the seasons are opposite those in North America. June is the coolest month, with temperatures averaging above freezing; January is the warmest month, with temperatures up to the 80s. Uruguay's coastline has several fine beaches.

History

Originally, Uruguay was home to a group of small native Indian tribes called the Charúas. Spanish explorers first came to the area in 1516. Their first settlement was in 1624 at Soriano. The Portuguese had a presence in the area from 1680 to about 1726, when the Spanish drove them out and pursued colonization. Nearly all of the indigenous Indians were conquered, killed, or driven out.

A war of independence began in 1811 in conjunction with a general uprising throughout South America. After five years of fighting, Uruguay was unsuccessful in breaking from Spanish rule, despite the efforts of José Gervasio Artigas, leader of the revolt. Although he failed, he is considered the "Father of Uruguay." His efforts inspired another uprising in 1825, when a group of patriots known as the "Thirty-Three Immortals" declared Uruguay an independent republic.

At the time, Uruguay was dominated by the Portuguese from Brazil. Spanish rule had effectively ended in 1820 when the Portuguese invaded. The country gained freedom from Brazil in 1828, when full independence was granted. Civil war (1839–51) and war with Paraguay (1865–70) were followed by dictatorship. The first president (José Batlle y Ordóñez) was finally elected in 1903. Ordóñez served two terms, then changed the constitution to allow himself to govern until 1929.

Uruguay was the first South American country to give women the right to vote and among the first to legalize divorce (1905). It was also the first to recognize the rights of trade unions. Through the first part of the 20th century, liberal governments applied socialist principles to the political and economic systems.

In 1970, terrorist violence and unrest due to severe economic problems led President Juan M. Bordaberry to ban all

Copyright © 1994. Brigham Young University. Printed in the USA. All rights reserved. It is against the law to copy, reprint, store in a retrieval system, or transmit any part of this publication in any form by any means for any purpose without written permission from the Publications Division of the David M. Kennedy Center for International Studies, Brigham Young University, PO Box 24538, Provo, UT 84602–4538. *Culturgrams* are available for more than 125 areas of the world. To place an order, to receive a free catalog, or to obtain information on traveling abroad, call toll free (800) 528–6279.

political activities in an attempt to restore control. A military coup in 1973 ousted him from power. Fourteen years of brutal military rule followed, during which thousands were detained and tortured. Elections were held in 1980 to decide whether the military should retain control of the government. When the vote went against the military, the military nullified the results and appointed General Gregorio Alvarez president in 1981.

Reforms during Alvarez's tenure, such as the re-legalization of trade unions, paved the way for general elections in 1984. The military stepped down when the elected president, Julio Maria Sanguinetti, took office in 1985. Basic human rights were restored. To avoid clashes with the military, amnesty was given to personnel suspected of human rights violations. Elections in 1989 marked the first democratic transfer of power from one elected government to another since 1971. Luis Alberto Lacalle Herrera was elected president. Lacalle encouraged market-oriented solutions to Uruguay's economic troubles.

THE PEOPLE

Population

Uruguay has a population of 3.17 million. Unlike most other nations in South America, it has a low annual growth rate: 0.75 percent. More than 85 percent of the people live in urban areas. People of European descent, mostly Spanish and Italian, account for 88 percent of the total population, a figure also dissimilar to other South American countries, where *mestizos*, a mixture of native Indian and Spanish backgrounds, are usually the majority ethnic group. In Uruguay, *mestizos* comprise only 8 percent of the population. Four percent of the people are black (descendants of slaves who were imported by the Spanish). Montevideo (MOAN-tay-vee-DAY-oh) is the capital and largest city, with about 1.5 million people. It is the country's financial, political, and cultural center.

Language

Spanish is the official language of Uruguay and is spoken by nearly the entire population. Italian and other languages are spoken by small minorities.

Religion

Uruguay is perhaps the most secular of Latin American countries. Although 65 percent of the population belong to the Roman Catholic church, less than half regularly attend services. There is no official religion, and church and state are strictly separated. Religious freedom is guaranteed. About 2 percent of the population is Protestant and roughly the same amount is Jewish. The rest, about 30 percent, belongs to various other faiths (Christian and others) or professes no religion at all.

General Attitudes

In Uruguay, punctuality is not as important as it is in some other countries. Arriving later than a scheduled time is not improper. However, the more formal a meeting, the more important it is to be on time. Uruguayans are generally pessimistic, opinionated, and individualistic, but they do not like aggressiveness. The immediate family is very tight and devoted to each other, but community involvement is limited. Education is highly valued and parents will often go to great lengths to make sure their children have good schooling. The elderly are respected and adult children often take care of aging parents. Uruguayans are extremely proud of their country, but they are also aware of its problems. They do not appreciate individuals who praise other countries over Uruguay—not because they do not appreciate other countries but because they do not want others to treat them as inferior.

Personal Appearance

Conservative, well-tailored clothing is the general rule. Fashion generally indicates a person's social status. Women wear fewer cosmetics and less jewelry than women in the United States, and they wear dresses more often. European fashions are common. Businessmen wear conservative suits.

CUSTOMS AND COURTESIES

Greetings

The most common way to greet someone is with a warm, firm handshake. Women appear to kiss one cheek when greeting each other. Actually, they brush cheeks and "kiss the air." Men might use an *abrazo* (hearty hug) in greeting other men if they are good friends or wish to demonstrate how well they know each other. Verbal greetings depend on the time of day or situation. *¡Hola!* (Hi) is common for a casual greeting. Especially popular in the morning is *¡Buen día!* (Good day). People do not generally greet strangers when passing on the street, particularly in cities. It might be misunderstood by the other person if one were to extend a greeting or even a smile. Rural people are more open and more likely to greet strangers. This is partly because of a less hectic lifestyle and because of a feeling that everyone knows everyone else in a village. All individuals in a small group are greeted when one arrives at a social function. Group greetings and farewells are considered impolite. In general, people address each other by an appropriate title and surname. For example, *Señor* (Mr.), *Señora* (Mrs.), or *Señorita* (Miss) are used with the family name. Only close friends and family members address each other by their given names.

Gestures

To beckon, it is common to snap the fingers or make a *ch-ch* sound. The *ch-ch* sound is used for many things, such as to get someone's attention or to have a bus stop. Hand gestures are used a great deal in conversation. One avoids hiding the hands or fidgeting with them when conversing because such actions can convey unintended messages. Forming a zero with the index finger and thumb is extremely rude. Brushing the back of the hand under the chin means "I don't know." Raising one's shoulders quickly can mean "What's up?"

It is improper to rest the feet on a table or other object in a room. People sit on a chair, not on a table or ledge. Yawning in public usually indicates that one is sleepy, bored, or not enjoying the company. In order to avoid insulting a host or guest, yawns are avoided as much as possible. On public transportation, a man should offer his seat to a woman.

Visiting

Visiting between friends and relatives is important, but the facts of urban life and variable schedules are making this increasingly difficult to do. Uruguayans are sensitive to each other's actions, and they strive to appear in the best light in any situation. Therefore, when visiting a home, guests are on their best behavior. Courtesy is expected and appreciated. Invited guests are not expected to take gifts to their hosts, but flowers or chocolates are considered a nice gesture. Guests are always offered refreshments. The type of refreshment depends on whether the visit was planned or not. People usually keep something in reserve in case an unexpected visitor shows up. Because appearance is so important, a Uruguayan does not like to entertain guests if the home is not clean. Thus, people prefer that visits be arranged in advance, but they keep their homes as clean as possible in the likely event a friend or relative drops by. It is impolite to visit unannounced during regular mealtimes.

Eating

Uruguayans use the continental style of eating, with the fork in the left hand and the knife remaining in the right. Hands (not elbows) are kept above the table, not in the lap, during the meal. When finished eating, a person places the utensils side by side on the plate. It is common for a person to wipe the plate clean with bread when finishing. Taking second helpings is a way of showing how much one likes the food. It is impolite to use a toothpick in public or to read a newspaper at the family table. Dinner guests remain at the table until all are finished eating.

Although habits are changing in urban areas to accommodate cosmopolitan schedules, Uruguayans traditionally eat a small breakfast and then have their main meal at midday. When possible, workers go home for this meal. Dinner is lighter and later in the evening. Children usually have a snack when they get home from school.

LIFESTYLE

Family

Strong ties traditionally unite the Uruguayan family. The father presides in the home and plays an important role as patriarch. Although this patriarchal order is still predominant, the role of women is increasing in significance. A great deal of family responsibility is given to the mother, but a large percentage of women also work or study outside the home. In fact, there are more professional women than men. But men rarely share in household duties. The average family has two children and nuclear families are the norm. There is a small number of wealthy families who generally control politics and the economy. Many more families live in humble circumstances. Most families rent their home or apartment because of the difficulty and cost involved in financing a home purchase.

Dating and Marriage

Dating customs are similar to those in the United States, although some families have retained some traditional European customs. In many cases, a boy is required to ask the parents' permission to date a girl for the first time. He must also request her hand before getting engaged. Both families play a large role in preparing for the wedding. The two families often associate closely after their children are married. Although extended families do not live together, they play an important role in the social lives of Uruguayans. The marriage reception usually includes a formal, catered party, from which the couple generally leaves early.

Diet

Wide varieties of meats, fish, vegetables, and fruits are available. Roasts, stews, and meat pies are popular menu items. The normal eating schedule consists of a light breakfast of coffee and bread, a large midday meal at home, a snack at 5:00 P.M., and a late supper at 9:00 or 10:00 P.M.

Recreation

Fútbol (soccer) is the national sport. Uruguay has an excellent national team that represented the country in the 1990 World Cup. Basketball, volleyball, swimming, and other water sports are also popular. Uruguayans also enjoy watching movies or television and attending cultural events. Going to the beach is very popular, especially during summer vacations.

Holidays

The most important holidays in Uruguay are New Year's Day; Carnival; Easter (including Holy Thursday and Good Friday); the Landing of the 33 Patriots (19 April), honoring those who fought for independence in 1825; Labor Day (1 May); Constitution Day (18 July); Independence Day (25 August); Christmas Eve; and Christmas. Most Catholics have celebrations to honor local patron saints, and some celebrate name days. Christmas Eve and New Year's Eve are celebrated with large family parties and midnight fireworks.

Commerce

Business hours are from 9:00 A.M. to 7:00 P.M., Monday through Friday. Government hours vary between the seasons, running primarily in the morning during the summer and in the afternoon and evening during the winter.

SOCIETY

Government

The executive branch is headed by the president and vice president. The legislature is called the General Assembly and it has two houses: a Chamber of Senators and a Chamber of Representatives. All citizens are required to vote at age 18. The next national elections are set for November 1994.

Economy

Uruguay's greatest natural resource is its fertile land. Over 80 percent of the land is used for agriculture and livestock production. Agriculture employs about 20 percent of the labor force. Uruguay is a world leader in the production of cattle and wool. Other products include wheat, rice, corn, and sorghum. The industrial sector is tied to agriculture as well, with the chief industries being meat processing, wool and hides, footwear, leather apparel, and fish processing.

The economy suffered several setbacks in the 1980s due to depressed world prices and uncertain political conditions. During the early 1990s, Uruguay's economy has improved with the annual economic growth rate above 7 percent in 1992. However, inflation remains high and poor labor relations result in long and frequent strikes. The country's currency is the new Uruguayan *peso* (N$Ur).

Uruguay's Human Development Index (0.881) ranks it 30 out of 173 countries. Real gross domestic product per capita is $5,916, which has improved substantially in the last generation. These figures indicate incomes are generally low for most people, but they are sufficient to meet basic needs. In addition, the rising generation can expect better economic conditions because existing social institutions are able to empower them to take advantage of employment opportunities.

Transportation and Communication

Buses are the primary form of public transportation. Many Uruguayans also travel in private automobiles. Taxis are readily available in the cities. Roads are generally good around the major urban areas, but less developed in the rural areas. While key highways are paved, most other roads are not paved. There is no passenger railroad. Uruguay has international airway links. The communications system is being updated; the best facilities are in Montevideo, and the country has a national radio relay system. Newspapers enjoy wide circulation. A number of radio and television stations serve the country.

Education

Uruguay has one of the highest literacy rates in South America at 96 percent. Primary schooling is compulsory for nine years. Afterwards, those who do well on the state examinations are eligible to enter a government-subsidized *liceo* (secondary school). Others may choose to receive technical training at a vocational school. The government provides all education free of charge. Uruguay has a rich national tradition in the arts and literature. The University of Montevideo, founded in 1849, and the Catholic University have fine reputations throughout South America.

Health

Uruguay has good health standards, and modern facilities are available in Montevideo. Health and other social programs are highly valued by Uruguay's citizens. Sanitation is good. The infant mortality rate is 18 per 1,000. Life expectancy is between 70 and 77 years.

FOR THE TRAVELER

U.S. travelers need a valid passport, but do not need a visa for stays lasting less than three months. No vaccinations are required. Dual-voltage small appliances or a voltage converter and a plug adaptor are needed to use electrical outlets. Uruguay is known for its fine beach resorts and pleasant climate. For more information, contact a travel agent or write to the Consulate of Uruguay, Tourism Office, 1077 Ponce De Leon Boulevard, Coral Gables, FL 33134. You may also wish to contact the Embassy of Uruguay, 1918 F Street NW, Washington, DC 20006.

A *Culturgram* is a product of native commentary and original, expert analysis. Statistics are estimates and information is presented as a matter of opinion. While the editors strive for accuracy and detail, this document should not be considered strictly factual. It is a general introduction to culture, an initial step in building bridges of understanding between peoples. It may not apply to all peoples of the nation. You should therefore consult other sources for more information.

Republic of
Venezuela

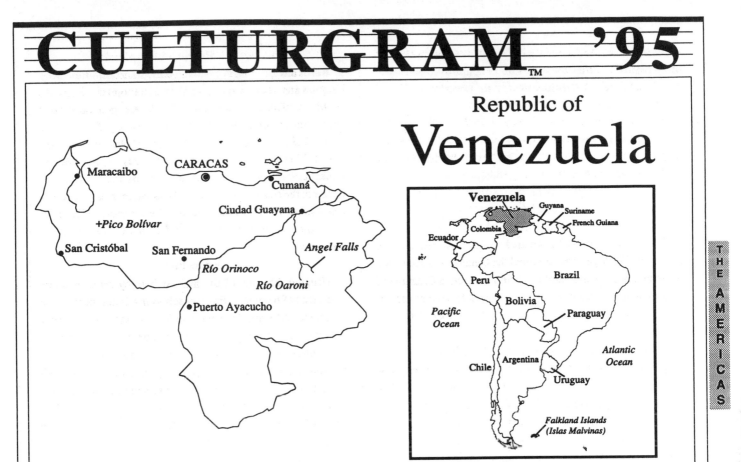

THE AMERICAS

Boundary representations not necessarily authoritative.

BACKGROUND

Land and Climate

Venezuela is a tropical land located in the northern part of South America. It shares borders with Guyana, Brazil, and Colombia. Covering 352,143 square miles (912,050 square kilometers), it is slightly larger than Texas and Oklahoma combined. The country is roughly divided into four geographical zones: west, central, east, and south. The Andes mountains dominate the west, where Pico Bolívar rises 16,427 feet (5,007 meters) above sea level. The central zone includes the northern coast and Venezuela's largest cities. To the east of the Orinoco River is a large plain (llano). The south is dominated by high plateaus and jungle. Angel Falls, the highest waterfall in the world at 3,300 feet (1,005 meters), displays its beauty in the southeast. Venezuela's tropical climate is moderated at higher altitudes. The rainy season is from May to November. Temperatures average between 70°F and 85°F (21–25°C), but the mountains can experience cool temperatures and some Andean peaks are snowcapped year-round.

In 1991, the government created a reserve for the country's 14,000 Yanomami Indians in the far south. Covering 32,000 square miles (almost 83,000 square kilometers), the area is off-limits to farmers, miners, and all non-Yanomami settlers.

History

Before the arrival of Columbus, Venezuela was inhabited by a number of indigenous groups, including the Caracas, Arawaks, and Cumanagatos, among others. Columbus discovered the area in 1498. The Spanish soon began conquering offshore islands and coastal regions. They named the area Venezuela ("little Venice") because the coastal homes were built on stilts, reminding them of Venice. Caracas, the capital, was founded in 1527. The Spanish Crown, which claimed the territory, controlled Venezuela through the 18th century. In 1811, after various failed revolts, a congress that declared independence was formed. This began a 10-year struggle to achieve the desired freedoms. Finally, in 1821, the forces of Simón Bolívar were victorious at the Battle of Carabobo, and a republic was declared. The republic (Greater Colombia) contained Venezuela, Ecuador, and Colombia. It dissolved in 1830 and Venezuela became independent.

Venezuela experienced instability and dictatorships for several years. In fact, the 20th century began under a dictator (Cipriano Castro). He was deposed by his vice president, Juan

Copyright © 1994. Brigham Young University. Printed in the USA. All rights reserved. It is against the law to copy, reprint, store in a retrieval system, or transmit any part of this publication in any form by any means for any purpose without written permission from the Publications Division of the David M. Kennedy Center for International Studies, Brigham Young University, PO Box 24538, Provo, UT 84602–4538. Culturgrams are available for more than 125 areas of the world. To place an order, to receive a free catalog, or to obtain information on traveling abroad, call toll free (800) 528–6279.

Vicente Gómez, who ruled as a brutal dictator until 1935. More political instability and military coups followed.

A freely elected president came to power in 1958, and democratic elections have been held since. For a time, Venezuela was the most stable country in South America and it was one of the wealthiest. Its oil reserves are the largest in the world outside of the Persian Gulf region, and it benefited from high oil prices in the 1970s and 1980s. Carlos Andrés Pérez, who took office as president in 1989, introduced a controversial economic austerity plan to address the plummeting price of oil and rising foreign debt. Riots were put down by the military and Pérez continued to introduce economic reforms. The reforms boosted gross domestic product and produced growth, but the wealth was concentrated in the hands of the few. Poverty increased, inflation and unemployment rose, and violent opposition soon rose to challenge Pérez. He was nearly overthrown by two coups in 1992. In 1993, he was forced from office in the wake of a corruption scandal. An interim president took office until a new president could be elected.

December 1993 elections brought a former president, Rafael Caldera, to office. He promised to slow privatization that had begun under Peréz, to end corruption, and to stabilize the economy. His task is daunting, as inflation and unemployment remain high. The country is still politically unstable, as Caldera's government does not have a majority in congress.

THE PEOPLE

Population

Venezuela has a population of 20.1 million, which is growing at 2.4 percent annually. More than 90 percent of the people live in urban areas. Caracas has 3.3 million inhabitants. The majority (67 percent) of the population is *mestizo* (mixed Indian and Spanish heritage). In coastal regions, many people (21 percent) are either of European descent (mostly Italian or Spanish) or *mulattos* (mixed European and black). About 10 percent of the population is black and 2 percent is Indian.

Language

Spanish is the official language, but English is a required second language in the schools. There is a great deal of Portuguese influence in Venezuela, so it is not uncommon to hear Portuguese spoken along with Spanish, especially in Caracas. The indigenous groups speak a variety of native languages. The Spanish spoken in Venezuela differs from that in other Latin American countries. For example, a papaya is called a *lechosa*. The word *papaya* is vulgar in Venezuela. In addition, while a banana may be called a *plátano*, it is also called a *cambur*.

Religion

Religious freedom is guaranteed by the constitution. Most people (90 percent) are Roman Catholic. Protestant and other Christian faiths are becoming more prevalent.

General Attitudes

Venezuela is the most urban country in South America and also the richest. As a cosmopolitan nation, changes and improvements occur often in all phases of life. It is not uncommon to see the old and new side by side, whether it be transportation, housing, or entertainment. The people are somewhat less religious compared to those of other Latin American countries. They tend to be spontaneous in their expressions. Venezuelans feel that the joy of an event or the needs of an individual are more important than the demands of a time schedule. Therefore, they may be late for appointments and scheduled events may last longer than expected. Venezuelans have a good sense of humor.

Venezuelans also feel great pride in their country. The South American liberator, Simón Bolívar, was Venezuelan. While he is honored in many other nations, he is a national treasure to Venezuela. Most cities have a *Plaza Bolívar* that occupies a block near the city center. It is rude to behave disrespectfully in that plaza and it is an insult to refer negatively to Bolívar.

Personal Appearance

Venezuelans are quite fashion conscious; the latest European styles are worn in the cities. High society movie theaters and restaurants require jackets for men and dresses for women. In the summer, cotton clothing is the most common and comfortable. Shorts and swim wear are only worn in urban recreation areas and at the beach.

CUSTOMS AND COURTESIES

Greetings

Men greet close friends with an *abrazo* (a full embrace, while patting each other on the back), while women greet with an *abrazo* and a kiss on the cheek. Usually *abrazos* are given between men and women only if they are close friends or relatives. A handshake is common among acquaintances and strangers. During conversation, people stand much closer than in the United States. It is improper to back away. Some common greetings include ¡Buenos días! (Good morning), ¡Buenas tardes! (Good afternoon), and ¡Buenas noches! (Good evening). The youth generally use the more casual ¡Hola! (Hi). In addition, greetings often include polite inquiries about a person's health.

Gestures

It is courteous to maintain continual eye contact during conversation. When sitting, a slouched posture is inappropriate and a person does not prop the feet up on any object.

Pointing with the index finger can be considered rude; motioning with the entire hand is more polite.

Visiting

When visitors arrive at a home, a business, or the office of a government official, they are often served *un cafecito* (a black, thick coffee) in a very small cup. This is a symbol of hospitality and a way of extending friendship. Polite discussion usually precedes any business matters. Venezuelans generally only invite close friends to their homes, but they will often invite business contacts and other visitors to dine at a restaurant. Venezuelans are hospitable and are careful to provide for their guests.

While gifts are not expected by hosts, they are appropriate gestures of friendship. A woman appreciates flowers, especially an orchid, the national flower. Men enjoy useful items for the home or office. It is also customary for service personnel, such as garbage collectors or postal carriers, to present a calling card requesting a *regalo* (gift) in the form of money at Christmastime. Failure to respond to this request may result in the discontinuance of service. The expediting of needed services or supplies sometimes requires a tip in advance.

Eating

Out of respect for parents, the head and foot of the dinner table are usually reserved for the mother and father of a family. Invited guests take seats at the table's sides. Varying styles of eating are used. Some people follow the continental style of eating, with the fork in the left hand and the knife in the right. Others use the style more common in the United States, with the fork in the right hand, unless the knife is picked up to cut something. In this case, the tips of utensils not in current use are rested on the edge of the plate; the handle rests on the table. When a person is finished, the utensils are placed together at the center of the plate. It is not appropriate for adults to eat on the street. In restaurants, a service charge is usually added to the bill, but a small additional tip is also expected.

LIFESTYLE

Family

Family ties are strong and most families are close-knit, especially among the upper and middle classes. Lower-class families are less dependent on each other. As many as half of all births in Venezuela are out of wedlock or in common-law marriages. In Venezuelan homes, the father dominates. The responsibility for raising the children and managing the household rests with the mother. An increasing number of women also work outside the home, especially in Caracas. In all, women comprise about one-fifth of the labor force. If members of a family enjoy good fortune, they customarily share their affluence with less fortunate relatives.

Diet

Much of the Venezuelan diet consists of hot foods, casseroles, meat pies, stews, and pasta dishes. One favorite is the *arepa*, a deep-fried thick pancake made from white corn flour and sometimes filled with butter, meat, and cheese. Corn is the basis of many dishes. *Punta-trasera* is a favorite tender steak. Rice is common. *Pabellón criollo* is made of black beans, rice, shredded meat, and plantain. In most cities, open markets provide a large variety of tropical fruits and fresh vegetables. Hot chocolate is almost as popular as coffee.

Recreation

The most popular spectator sport in Venezuela is baseball. Horse racing, bullfighting, and soccer are also enjoyed. Venezuelans participate in fishing, hunting, swimming, tennis, basketball, and golf. Private recreational clubs are expensive and are generally available only to the wealthy. For entertainment, Venezuelans like to go dancing, to movies, or to cultural events. In rural areas, local festivals provide recreation.

Holidays

Official public holidays include New Year's Day, *Carnival* (two days before Ash Wednesday), Ash Wednesday, Easter (including Holy Thursday and Good Friday), Declaration of Independence Day (19 April), May Day (1 May), Battle of Carabobo (24 June), Independence Day (5 July), Simón Bolívar's Birthday (24 July), Public Officials' Day (first Monday in September), Columbus Day (12 October), Christmas Eve and Christmas, and New Year's Eve. During *Carnival*, water fights, parades, dancing in the streets, amusements, and other activities are popular. Flowers are important in Venezuelan celebrations. During each holiday, statues of Simón Bolívar, the father of Venezuela, are decorated with colorful wreaths.

Commerce

Business hours generally extend from 8:00 A.M. to 6:00 P.M. (with a one or two-hour break), Monday through Friday. Government offices maintain similar hours, with regional variations.

SOCIETY

Government

Venezuela's president serves a five-year term. He is the chief of state and head of government. The Congress of the Republic has two houses, a Senate and a Chamber of Deputies. The voting age is 18. Venezuela is divided into 21 states, one federal dependency, one federal district, and one territory.

Economy

Venezuela's most important natural resource, petroleum, is the cornerstone of the economy. It accounts for 82 percent of all export earnings. Oil revenues have allowed the country to develop a modern infrastructure. However, oil has also made

Venezuela subject to market fluctuations. When the price of oil drops, the entire economy suffers. Therefore, the government stresses economic diversification. The country also exports some minerals and other raw materials. Agriculture employs 6 percent of the population and produces grains, sugar, fruits, coffee, and rice. Inflation is above 30 percent, and unemployment is rising above 11 percent. The economy grew by almost 9 percent in 1992, but the increased wealth did not benefit the bulk of the people. Growth in 1993 was only 3 percent. Several major banks faltered in 1994, adding to concerns about economic stability. Venezuela's currency is the *bolívar* ($B).

Venezuela's Human Development Index (0.824) ranks it 50 out of 173 countries. Real gross domestic product per capita is $6,605, which has nearly doubled in a generation. These figures reflect Venezuela's oil wealth; they indicate economic prosperity is available to more people than 30 years ago, but it still eludes a significant proportion of the population. However, if political stability can be achieved, social institutions exist to help people realize better economic conditions in the future.

Transportation and Communication

Domestic transportation is handled by private cars, buses, taxis, or the domestic airline. *Por puesto* is a popular system of taxi-like automobiles that travel a regular route throughout the city, picking up and letting off passengers at any point. The cost is less than a taxi but more than a bus. Highways are excellent in Venezuela, but driving is often hazardous. Because Venezuela assembles U.S. and other foreign vehicles, many people are able to buy cars. Railroads are generally not used for passenger travel. The communications system is modern and expanding. Private phones are expensive, but public phones are readily available. Several radio and television stations broadcast in Venezuela.

Education

Elementary education is compulsory from ages seven to fourteen. All education, including university level, is free in government-financed institutions. The government has taken great strides to eliminate illiteracy in the country and has made steady improvements in the literacy rate; it is currently 88 percent. About three-fourths of all students complete primary school, and most of those children go on to secondary school. But about two-thirds of the overall school-aged population does not attend a secondary school. After secondary school, students may choose from a variety of vocational schools or prepare to enter institutions of higher learning.

Health

Good medical facilities can be found, but rural facilities are inadequate. Malaria is active in some rural areas. Only about two-thirds of all infants are immunized against childhood diseases. The infant mortality rate is 29 per 1,000. Life expectancy ranges from 71 to 78 years.

FOR THE TRAVELER

A visa and a valid passport are necessary for U.S. travelers for stays of more than 60 days. A tourist card issued by an airline is adequate for stays of up to 60 days. All travelers pay a departure tax at the airport. No vaccinations are required, but malaria suppressants are recommended for travel to certain areas. Bottled water is safest to drink. Plug, but not voltage, adaptors may be necessary to use electrical outlets. There are some beautiful sights in Venezuela, as well as numerous cosmopolitan resorts. For information on travel packages and opportunities, contact the nation's airline, Avensa (645 Olympic Tower, Fifth Avenue; Fifth Floor, East Wing; New York, NY 10022). You may also wish to contact the Embassy of Venezuela, 1099 Thirtieth Street NW, Washington, DC 20007.

A *Culturgram* is a product of native commentary and original, expert analysis. Statistics are estimates and information is presented as a matter of opinion. While the editors strive for accuracy and detail, this document should not be considered strictly factual. It is a general introduction to culture, an initial step in building bridges of understanding between peoples. It may not apply to all peoples of the nation. You should therefore consult other sources for more information.

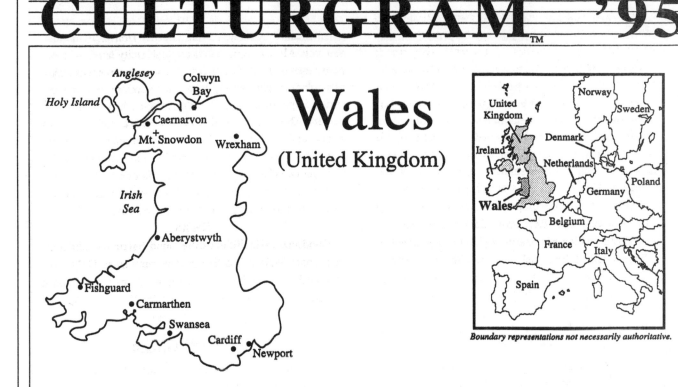

Wales

(United Kingdom)

Boundary representations not necessarily authoritative.

EUROPE

BACKGROUND

Land and Climate

Wales, situated in the west of Britain, has an area of 8,019 square miles (20,769 square kilometers); it is slightly larger than New Jersey. It is a mostly mountainous nation, bordering England to the east. The Irish (or Celtic) Sea is to the west; Wales is bounded on three sides by water. The climate is mild and wet, and the landscape is generally green. This makes the land, especially in the countryside, very picturesque. The highest mountain is Snowdon (3,560 feet or 1,085 meters). Valleys just north of Cardiff tend to be densely populated. Wales has three national parks.

History

The Welsh are descendants of the Britons, who were already on the island of Britain when the Romans first arrived in the first century B.C. After the Roman withdrawal in the fifth century A.D., Britain was invaded by Saxons who remained in the southeast. The Saxons gradually absorbed the British population and then extended their dominion over what later became England. The Welsh, under their native princes, preserved their independence in the western part of the island until long after the Norman Conquest of England in 1066, even though William the Conqueror proclaimed himself Lord of Wales in 1071. The Welsh were eventually defeated in the 13th century when Llywelyn ap Gruffydd, known to the Welsh as the "Last Prince," was killed by the English under King Edward I in 1282. In 1301, King Edward named his heir the Prince of Wales, and that title has, since then, been given to the oldest son of the British monarch (England's Prince Charles is the Prince of Wales).

The national hero of the Welsh, Owain Glyndwr, rose against the English in 1400, but without success. Wales was formally incorporated with England by the Act of Union in 1536; this gave Welshmen the same rights as Englishmen, but it outlawed the Welsh language (which survived anyway). The Welsh were early converts to Protestantism, but they broke away from England's established church, leading to the development of separate religious traditions for the Welsh. Scotland joined the Union in 1707 and Ireland in 1801, after which the union was called the United Kingdom of Great Britain and Ireland. Only Northern Ireland is included today; most of Ireland became independent in 1921.

With the creation of the University of Wales toward the end of the 19th century, by which time Wales had become an industrial nation, there was a renaissance in Welsh culture that has continued to the present. Indeed, since 1950 there has been a growth in Welsh nationalism and in calls for greater Welsh autonomy. Still, when a 1979 referendum gave the Welsh the chance to have limited self-government, the people chose to maintain their existing ties with England. The Welsh are well represented in British politics; in the

Copyright © 1994. Brigham Young University. Printed in the USA. All rights reserved. It is against the law to copy, reprint, store in a retrieval system, or transmit any part of this publication in any form by any means for any purpose without written permission from the Publications Division of the David M. Kennedy Center for International Studies, Brigham Young University, PO Box 24538, Provo, UT 84602–4538. *Culturgrams* are available for more than 125 areas of the world. To place an order, to receive a free catalog, or to obtain information on traveling abroad, call toll free (800) 528–6279.

1992 parliamentary elections, Welshman Neil Kinnock (then, leader of the Labor party) was a candidate for prime minister.

THE PEOPLE

Population

The population of Wales is about 2.9 million. About half live in the industrial urban areas of the south—mainly in Cardiff, the capital city, and its hinterland, including the valleys to the north. The rest of Wales is sparsely populated, the inhabitants living mostly in small towns and villages. The majority are ethnic Welsh, but many English people have recently settled in the country, especially along the northern coast. There are also people of Irish descent, mainly in the industrial valleys, as well as other ethnic groups. Immigrants from former British colonies are found mostly in Cardiff and the large towns such as Newport and Swansea. Wales has suffered badly from emigration, many of its people having left in search of work. It is not known exactly how many Welsh people live in England.

Language

English is spoken nearly everywhere in Wales and has official status. Welsh, a Celtic language related to Breton, Irish, and Scottish Gaelic, is also spoken by about 20 percent of the population. The heartlands of the Welsh language are in the north (Gwynedd) and west (Dyfed). There are also many Welsh-speakers in Cardiff and other areas. Welsh has a degree of official status throughout Wales and can be seen, for example, on road signs and public buildings. The language is extensively used in cultural affairs. Several organizations encourage its use, and there are a number of magazines and books published in Welsh. A movement of young people, *Cymdeithas yr Iaith Gymraeg* (Welsh Language Society), campaigns for official status for the language in such areas as law, education, and local government. The Welsh name for Wales is *Cymru* (the land of compatriots), *Wales* being the English name for "the land of the foreigners."

Religion

Wales is basically a secular society. The sister organization to the Church of England (Anglican church) is the Church in Wales; it has its own archbishop. Most Welsh people are of Christian Protestant (nonconformist) stock, which means they are affiliated through faith or family tradition to the Presbyterian Church of Wales (Calvanistic Methodists), the Welsh Baptist Union, the Methodist Church (Wesleyans), the Union of Welsh Independents (Congregationalists), or the Church in Wales. Other Christian denominations are also represented in Wales.

General Attitudes

The Welsh regard themselves as a nation and a people who are different from the English, although many still think of themselves as British as well. They are, after all, descendants of the original Britons who first inhabited the island of Britain.

They have a reputation for being warmhearted, gregarious, articulate, and democratic. They are also emotional, inquisitive, quick-tempered, and individualistic. Local pride is well developed; every Welsh person feels a strong attachment to a particular place. Some differences can be observed between northerners and southerners, but they have much more in common. Most Welsh belong to the working class or have working-class origins, but there is also a middle class. Few belong to an upper class. Traditionally the Welsh have a keen interest in genealogy and a respect for education. Famous Welsh people include: David Lloyd George (former prime minister of Great Britain), Dylan Thomas (poet), Richard Burton and Anthony Hopkins (actors), and Tom Jones (singer).

Personal Appearance

There is not much difference between fashions in Wales and those in the rest of Britain, although some clothes are made from Welsh materials. The national costume is seen only on ceremonial occasions. On Sundays, people tend to dress in their best clothes—suits for men and more expensive dresses for women. It is usually possible to distinguish, say, a farmer from an office worker by the style of their clothes. High fashion is seen only in the larger towns. Dinner jackets are worn only on very formal occasions; the expectation of formal dress is usually indicated on invitation cards.

CUSTOMS AND COURTESIES

Greetings

The Welsh are known for their friendliness and hospitality. With strangers, they shake hands on first being introduced but not thereafter unless they have not seen them for some time. A firm handshake is better than a limp one. The Welsh use first names soon after meeting. When meeting for the first time, they say, *How d'you do?* or *Pleased to meet you,* or even *How are you?*, but not *Hi!* Good friends, especially the youth, use *Hello* and *Hi* to greet each other. Women who are close friends may embrace, kissing each other once lightly on the cheek; men may also kiss women this way. Women remain seated when being introduced and shaking hands, while men stand up. Introductions usually begin with, *This is . . .* or *I'd like you to meet . . .* or *Have you met . . .* or, more formally, *May I introduce. . . .* It is polite, if practical, to introduce each person in the company and to shake hands with them. Children and teenagers are introduced and will usually shake hands. Gentlemen stand when a lady or unknown man enters the room, and sit down only after the other person is seated.

Gestures

It is impolite to keep one's hands in the pockets during conversation, and money should not be rattled in pockets. It is okay to cross one's arms during conversation. Legs may be crossed at the knees, but the ankle of one leg should not be placed on the knee of the other. Feet must be kept off all furniture. Eye contact should be maintained during conversation. Yawns, coughs, burps, and sneezes are covered with the hand. A gentleman gives up his seat on a train or bus to a lady. Women should not put on makeup in public. Pointing at people is avoided, as is touching other people (on the arm, knee, or shoulder) unless one is well acquainted. Whispering is considered impolite. Chewing gum is generally thought unsophisticated, as are public nose picking, nail cutting, and head scratching.

Visiting

The Welsh enjoy good company. They like visiting friends and neighbors in their homes, often without an invitation, for a chat and a cup of tea. It is customary to always offer guests refreshments. Friends who have traveled a long distance are offered a meal. Otherwise, lunch or dinner is usually by invitation. At more formal meals, old friends often bring a bottle of wine and sometimes a delicacy. Strangers on their first visit are not expected to bring a gift, although the hostess will appreciate flowers. It is considered impolite to arrive for a meal more than a half-hour late. Sherry is usually served before lunch or dinner; wine is served with the meal, unless the hosts abstain from alcohol. After the meal, guests are invited to sit in a comfortable place, perhaps to have a cup of coffee. Only friends offer to help with clearing the table or washing the dishes. Guests invited to lunch usually stay for the afternoon. Dinner guests often stay until about 11:00 P.M., except on weekends when they may stay later. It is considered good manners to call the hosts within a day or two after the meal to thank them for their hospitality, or more formally, to write, especially after visits of a few days.

Eating

Breakfast (toast, marmalade, cereal, bacon and eggs, sausages, coffee) is eaten between 7:00 and 9:00 A.M., and a bit later on weekends. Many people eat a lighter breakfast of cereal, toast, and tea or coffee. Lunch (meat or fish, vegetables) is at about 1:00 P.M. Tea (a cup of tea and cakes, or bread and butter with jam) is between 4:00 and 5:00 P.M. Dinner (meat, vegetables, and dessert) is at 7:00 or 8:00 P.M. In Wales, lunch is often called dinner and dinner is known as supper; tea can be a substantial meal. Guests are sometimes invited for coffee at about 11:00 A.M. Lunch on Sunday tends to be an important meal.

At meals, the food is placed in dishes on the table and guests are asked to help themselves, or else the hostess serves it. The knife is held in the right hand and the fork in the left; the fork is never used as a scoop, and the knife is never put in the mouth. Fingers are not used to pick up food, except among friends. The napkin is placed on the lap; elbows are not placed on the table. Guests are expected to talk at the table and to share the conversation with the persons sitting next to them. The hostess likes to be complimented on the meal and second helpings show an appreciation for the food. In restaurants, at the end of a meal, the waiter is asked for the bill and it is paid by the host, either to the waiter or to the cashier. Tips of between 5 and 10 percent are given to the waiter.

LIFESTYLE

Family

The Welsh usually live in houses rather than flats (apartments), which are common only in the cities. Houses may be detached or semidetached, as in suburban areas, or in terraces, as in the industrial valleys. Families are usually closely knit. The nominal head of the household is the father, but the mother plays an equally important role in all family affairs. Many women work outside the home after their children have grown up. Elderly grandparents sometimes live with the family. Unmarried children live at home or move into their own apartment. Single-parent families are becoming more common. The average number of children in a family is two or three.

The main family celebrations occur at Christmas and Easter, or for birthdays and weddings. There are special celebrations for a person's 18th birthday, when he or she comes of age, is eligible to vote, and gains other legal rights.

Dating and Marriage

Dating usually begins by the age of 15 or 16. Young people enjoy discos, clubs, movies, and parties. They also spend a lot of time in each other's homes. Marriage is legal at 16, but most marry in their mid-20s. Many young people live together before or instead of getting married. While most couples remain married for life, divorce is on the rise.

Diet

There are some traditional Welsh dishes such as *cawl* (a soup), *bara lawr* (laver bread), *bara brith* (currant cake), and Welsh pancakes, but the Welsh eat a variety of foods common throughout Europe. The Welsh enjoy all kinds of food, from fish and chips to Chinese and Indian cooking to the cuisine of France and Italy. Beer, wine, and other alcoholic drinks are sold in pubs. Snacks, tea, coffee, and sandwiches are available in cafés. At home, the Welsh drink water, lemonade, fruit juice, or beer with meals. They drink wine on special occasions or when entertaining guests. After the main course, there is a dessert, sometimes called a *sweet* or *pudding*. It is customary to serve bread and butter with canned fruit.

Recreation

The national sport in Wales is rugby, also known as rugby football. The national stadium is the Cardiff Arms Park. Soccer (or football) and cricket are also popular, among other sports. Most people also enjoy watching television or listening to the radio. There are movie theaters and arts centers in most large towns. The National *Eisteddfod* (an arts festival and social gathering) is held every year during the first week of August, alternately in the north and south of Wales. The festival is conducted in Welsh. There is also an annual week-long *Eisteddfod* for youth. The Welsh like to sing in choirs and enjoy singing in public places (sporting events, pubs, etc.). Pubs are popular places for socializing.

Holidays

Wales has the same national holidays as England, including New Year's Day, Good Friday (before Easter Sunday), May Day (1 May), the spring and summer bank holidays, Christmas, and Boxing Day. Boxing Day comes from the tradition of giving small, boxed gifts to service people. It is now a day for relaxing and visiting friends. St. David's Day (1 March), named for the nation's patron saint, is not an official holiday but is celebrated with dinners, concerts, and special programs. On St. David's Day, people wear a leek or daffodil (the national emblem) on their clothing.

Commerce

Factory hours are from 8:00 A.M. to 4:30 P.M. and office hours are from 9:00 A.M. to 5:00 P.M. Some people work on Saturday morning. Some shops close for a half day during the week. Offices and smaller shops close for an hour at lunchtime. Supermarkets are open until 8:00 or even 10:00 P.M. Banks are open between 9:30 A.M. and 3:30 P.M. Stores are closed on Sunday because of a law (in England and Wales) banning Sunday trade, but many businesses are trying to have the law changed. Small towns have market days for vendors to sell items from outdoor booths.

SOCIETY

Government

Eight counties, governed by their own councils, make up what is officially known as the Principality of Wales. The Welsh tend to elect Labor party parliamentary representatives because of Labor's traditional support for greater self-rule in Wales. Britain's constitutional monarchy, with Queen Elizabeth II as head of state, has two houses in parliament. The House of Lords (with noblemen, life appointees, and Church of England bishops) has little legislative power. The House of Commons, whose members are elected by the people, is where laws are passed. Wales has 38 seats in the House of Commons. The leader of the majority party (currently the Conservative party) is appointed by the Queen as prime minister (currently John Major). Elections are held at least every five years, but can be called sooner. Major was reelected in 1992.

Economy

The heavy industries of Wales (steel and coal) are increasingly being replaced by light industries, agriculture, business, and service industries. Unemployment in Wales is usually higher than in England. Income is usually a bit lower. The United Kingdom's Human Development Index (0.964) ranks it 10 out of 173 countries. Real gross domestic product per capita is $15,804, which has more than doubled in a generation.

These figures indicate that most people have access to a decent income, although there is a larger gap between the wealthy and the poor than in other European countries. Likewise, the middle class is not as prosperous as its counterpart in other European nations. The currency is the pound sterling (£).

Transportation and Communication

While all parts of Wales are accessible by road, some roads are difficult to travel because of mountainous terrain. Because Wales has many small towns that generally lack extensive public transportation, private cars are the main form of transport. Ferries regularly go from Wales to Ireland, and an international airport is located near Cardiff. Cardiff is two hours away (by rail) from London. Many homes have telephones. Television and radio are controlled by BBC Wales and one independent company. Channel S4C operates in Welsh. Postal service is reliable.

Education

The education system is connected to that of England's. Welsh is taught as a subject, and English is the official language of instruction. Some schools are, however, teaching classes in Welsh. Schooling is free and compulsory between ages five and sixteen. At age 16, students take the General Certificate of Secondary Education exam. Some spend two more years in school and then take the Advanced Level exams, which are basically used as entrance exams by universities. The University of Wales has campuses in five cities. There is also an Open University, which offers correspondence and broadcast courses. There are several colleges of education. The Polytechnic of Wales is changing its name to the University of Glamorgan. Many Welsh students attend universities in England. The literacy rate is 99 percent.

Health

Standards of health are comparable to those in England, although industrial illnesses still exist. Wales participates in Britain's National Health Service, under which free medical care is provided on the basis of taxation. There is a small charge for prescriptions and dental treatment. Infant mortality is 7 per 1,000. Life expectancy ranges from 73 to 79 years.

FOR THE TRAVELER

The U.S. visitor to Wales needs a passport, but not a visa. No vaccinations are required. Tap water is safe to drink. Many parts of Wales are worth visiting. For suggestions and lodging information, contact the British Tourist Authority (551 Fifth Avenue, Seventh Floor, New York, NY 10176) or the Wales Tourist Board (Brunel House, 2 Fitzalan Road, Cardiff CF2 1UY, United Kingdom). You may also wish to contact the Embassy of the United Kingdom, 3100 Massachusetts Avenue NW Washington, DC 20008, or the British Information Service, 845 Third Avenue, New York, NY 10022.

A *Culturgram* is a product of native commentary and original, expert analysis. Statistics are estimates and information is presented as a matter of opinion. While the editors strive for accuracy and detail, this document should not be considered strictly factual. It is a general introduction to culture, an initial step in building bridges of understanding between peoples. It may not apply to all peoples of the nation. You should therefore consult other sources for more information.

ERNORS STATE UNIVERSITY
VERSITY PARK
60466

STATE UNIVERSITY
......

GOV
UN